Contributions to the Economics of International Labor Standards

World Scientific Studies in International Economics
(ISSN: 1793-3641)

Vol. 48 The New International Financial System: Analyzing the Cumulative Impact of Regulatory Reform
edited by Douglas Evanoff (Federal Reserve Bank of Chicago, USA), Andrew G. Haldane (Bank of England, UK) & George Kaufman (Loyola University Chicago, USA)

Vol. 49 The Economics of International Migration
by Giovanni Peri (UC Davis)

Vol. 50 The Legal and Economic Analysis of the WTO/FTA System
by Dukgeun Ahn (Seoul National University, Korea)

Vol. 51 The Political Economy of Trade Policy: Theory, Evidence and Applications
by Devashish Mitra (Syracuse University, USA)

Vol. 52 Microeconometrics of International Trade
by Joachim Wagner (Leuphana University Lueneburg, Germany)

Vol. 53 Multinational Enterprises and Host Country Development
by Holger Görg (Kiel Institute for the World Economy, Germany)

Vol. 54 Globalization: The Macroeconomic Implications of Microeconomic Heterogeneity
by Andrei A. Levchenko (University of Michigan, USA)

Vol. 55 The Future of Large, Internationally Active Banks
edited by Asli Demirgüç-Kunt (World Bank, USA), Douglas D. Evanoff (Federal Reserve Bank of Chicago, USA) & George G. Kaufman (Loyola University Chicago, USA)

Vol. 56 Nontariff Measures and International Trade
edited by John Christopher Beghin (Iowa State University, USA)

Vol. 57 Trade Policies for Development and Transition
by David G. Tarr (The World Bank, USA)

Vol. 58 International Economic Integration and Domestic Performance
edited by Mary E. Lovely (Syracuse University, USA)

Vol. 59 Contributions to the Economics of International Labor Standards
edited by Arnab K. Basu (Cornell) & Nancy H. Chau (Cornell)

The complete list of the published volumes in the series can be found at
http://www.worldscientific.com/series/wssie

59 World Scientific Studies in International Economics

Contributions to the Economics of International Labor Standards

Editors

Arnab K. Basu
Nancy H. Chau
Cornell

World Scientific

NEW JERSEY • LONDON • SINGAPORE • BEIJING • SHANGHAI • HONG KONG • TAIPEI • CHENNAI • TOKYO

Published by

World Scientific Publishing Co. Pte. Ltd.
5 Toh Tuck Link, Singapore 596224
USA office: 27 Warren Street, Suite 401-402, Hackensack, NJ 07601
UK office: 57 Shelton Street, Covent Garden, London WC2H 9HE

British Library Cataloguing-in-Publication Data
A catalogue record for this book is available from the British Library.

World Scientific Studies in International Economics — Vol. 59
CONTRIBUTIONS TO THE ECONOMICS OF INTERNATIONAL LABOR STANDARDS

ISBN 978-981-3142-74-9

Desk Editor: Philly Lim

Typeset by Stallion Press
Email: enquiries@stallionpress.com

Printed in Singapore

Dedication

To our parents.

Contents

About the Authors

Arnab K. Basu is Professor at the Dyson School of Applied Economics and Management at Cornell University, a Senior Fellow at the Center for Development Research (ZEF), University of Bonn, a Research Fellow at the Institute of Labor Economics (IZA) in Bonn, Germany and a Fellow of the Global Labor Organization (GLO). He received his PhD in Economics from the Johns Hopkins University, Baltimore and his Master's and undergraduate degrees respectively from the Delhi School of Economics, University of Delhi and St. Xavier's College, University of Calcutta (both in India). Basu was awarded a Research Fellowship from the Alexander von Humboldt Foundation in Germany and is a recipient of the Theodore W Schultz Young Economist Prize awarded by the International Association of Agricultural Economists (IAAE).

Nancy H. Chau is Professor at the Charles H. Dyson School of Applied Economics and Management at the S. C. Johnson College of Business at Cornell University. She is a Research Fellow at the Institute for the Study of Labor, a Senior Research Fellow at the Center for Development Research at the University of Bonn, a Fellow at Centro Studi Luca d'Agliano at the University of Milan, and a Fellow at the Global Labor Organization. She was awarded the Alexander von Humboldt Research Fellowship, and served on the editorial boards of Agricultural Economics, American Journal of Agricultural Economics, and the IZA Journal of Labor and Development. Her recent research focuses on labor in the global economy with particular emphasis on labor market institutions. She has published widely, in journals such as the *Economic Journal*, *International Economic Review*, *Journal of Development Economics*, *Journal of Economic Growth*, *Journal of Economic Theory*, *Journal of Labor Economics*, *Journal of Law and Economics*, *Journal of Public Economics*, and the *World Bank Economic Review*.

Acknowledgements

We wish to acknowledge with sincere appreciation the contributions of many individuals who have made a real impact on this body of work. We owe a debt of gratitude to Joachim von Braun for jump starting our work in the area of child labor almost two decades ago, and for his hospitality and support while we were visiting research fellows at the Center for Development Research (ZEF) in Bonn. Thanks are also due to Klaus Zimmermann for his tremendous hospitality and generosity in funding a six-month visit at the Institute for the Study of Labor (IZA) during which we completed several papers and laid the groundwork of a number of other manuscripts that appear in this book. We thank the Alexander von Humboldt Foundation for generous financial support during our year-long stay in Germany as Humboldt Research Fellows, as well as for awarding our project on transnational trafficking the Transcoop Research Grant. Over the years, we have collaborated with a number of individuals, to whom we owe intellectual debt: Randy Akee, Arjun Bedi, Gary Fields, Hideaki Goto, Ravi Kanbur, Ulrike Grote, and Zahra Siddique. Our work has also benefitted from many stimulating conversations with and comments from colleagues we met at ZEF, IZA, College of William and Mary, Cornell, and at conferences and workshops: Berhanu Abegaz, Kaushik Basu, Jim Berry, Francois Bourguignon, Drusilla Brown, Judith Dean, Gil Epstein, Rolf Fare, David Feldman, Gary Fields, Guido Friebel, Ira Gang, Rob Hicks, Melanie Khamis, Sajal Lahiri, Wolfgang Mayer, Carol Ann Rogers, Hilmar Schneider, Ken Swinnerton, Eric Thorbecke, Henry Wan, Eden Yu and Xiaobo Zhang. Nathan Lauderback provided excellent research assistance.

The authors of this book would also like to thank the publishers, and journals for providing the permissions to reproduce the articles here in this volume. In the order of the chapter numbers, these are the full citations of the papers featured:

Basu, Arnab K. and Nancy H. Chau. 2004. "Exploitation of Child Labor and the Dynamics of Debt Bondage," *Journal of Economic Growth* 9: 209–238.

Randall Akee, Arnab K. Basu, Arjun Bedi, and Nancy H. Chau. 2014. "Transnational Trafficking, Law Enforcement, and Victim Protection: A Middleman Trackers Perspective," *Journal of Law and Economics* 57(2): 349–386.

Nancy H. Chau. 2016. "On Sweatshop Jobs and Decent Work," *Journal of Development Economics* 121: 120–134.

Basu, Arnab K., Nancy H. Chau, and Ravi Kanbur. 2015. "Contractual Dualism, Market Power and Informality," *Economic Journal* 125: 1534–1573.

Nancy H. Chau and Ravi Kanbur. 2013. "On Footloose Industries and Labor Disputes with Endogenous Information Asymmetry," *Review of Development Economics* 17(2): 319–341.

Basu, Arnab K., Nancy H. Chau, and Ulrike Grote. 2006. "Guaranteed Manufactured without Child Labor: The Economics of Consumer Boycotts, Social Labeling and Trade Sanctions," *Review of Development Economics* 10(3): 466–491.

Chau, Nancy H., Hideaki Goto, and Ravi Kanbur. 2016. "Middlemen, Fair Traders and Poverty," *Journal of Economic Inequality* 14(1): 81–108.

Basu, Arnab K. 2013. "Impact of Rural Employment Guarantee Schemes on Seasonal Labor Markets: Optimum Compensation and Workers' Welfare," *Journal of Economic Inequality* 11(1): 1–34.

Chau, Nancy H. and Ravi Kanbur. 2006. "A Race to the Bottom, From the Bottom," *Economica* 73(290): 193–228.

Chau, Nancy H. and Ravi Kanbur. 2002. The Adoption of International Labor Standard Conventions: Who, When and Why? *Brookings Trade Forum* 2001: 113–156.

Basu, Arnab K., Nancy H. Chau, and Ravi Kanbur. 2010. "Turning a Blind Eye: Costly Enforcement, Credible Commitment and Minimum Wage Laws," *Economic Journal* 120: 244–269.

Basu, Arnab K., Nancy H. Chau, and Ravi Kanbur. 2009. "A Theory of Employment Guarantees: Contestability, Credibility and Distributional Concerns," *Journal of Public Economics* 93(3–4): 482–497.

Basu, Arnab K., Nancy H. Chau, and Zahra Siddique. 2012. "Tax Evasion, Minimum Wage Non-Compliance and Informality," *Research in Labor Economics* 34: 1–53.

Chapter 1

Introduction

In both advanced industrial economies and emerging markets, labor standards as market determined realities often deviate greatly from labor standards aspirations. Market determined labor standards embody a collection of *de facto* labor market outcomes, including wages and employment, workplace safety and overtime, labor market institutions governing employer-worker relations such as freedom of association and the right to form unions, as well as contractual processes such as whether middlemen are involved. Meanwhile, labor standards aspirations are grounded in moral and ethical motivations about how employment relations ought to be conducted. Some examples include an individual's right to a living wage; to be free from forced labor and slavery; to receive wage and/or employment independent of gender, religion, class or caste; and to have indiscriminate access to legal protection in case of workplace abuse. The history of international labor standards is replete with examples where the gap between labor market realities and aspirations constitute two extremes of a full spectrum of labor market conditions. Serving as negotiated minimum requirements, *de jure* labor standards spell out relevant policy standards somewhere along the spectrum.

Debates concerning this gap between labor standard realities and aspirations naturally bring together interests from both the demand and the supply sides of the labor market, often transcending national borders and stakeholder groups. The upshot is that labor standards negotiations are contentious as multiple constituencies confront a collection of interlinked collective action problems. In recent decades, calls for international coordination in labor standards have intensified. These are evident in proposals for a social clause in the World Trade Organization, and the various labor side agreements in regional trade agreements, for example. In this introductory chapter, we lay out in broad strokes a number of global campaigns and trends that have motivated proposals to safeguard labor standards, with an emphasis on the implications of these trends for labor standards research. These include: (i) the global fight against poverty, (ii) the global exchange in goods, people and capital, and (iii) the call for credible and well enforced labor standards.

Poverty and Labor Standards

The apparent failure of market-based solutions to deliver the fruits of economic growth to lift most of the world's poor out of poverty has been a singularly important global trend justifying labor standards. The evidence is plain. 12.8% of the global population or 896 million individuals continue to live in extreme poverty, or at less than US$1.90 a day. At less than US$3.1 a day, the poverty headcount increases to 2.1 billion individuals, or close to 30% of the global population. Amid remarkable progress in many parts of the world, such as East Asia and the Pacific which saw extreme poverty rate falling from 50.8% as recently as 1990 to the 2012 level at 7.2%, poverty continues to be pervasive both in low- as well as in low-middle-income countries (World Bank 2015).

Further to these international differences in poverty incidence, studies have shown that there are select labor market institutions in which workers are particularly vulnerable to poverty. For instance, children make up more than half of the global population living under $1.9 a day. According to the latest statistics, 150 million children aged 5–14 are engaged in child labor (UNICEF 2016). In the context of poverty eradication, child labor is arguably a double-edged sword, for participation in the labor force brings economic resources to poor households at the cost of skill and human capital accumulation through education. Another class of employment options frequently linked to poverty is informal employment, where as high as 60 percent of the work force find job opportunities in some developing countries (Bacchetta, Ernst and Bustamante 2009). While the precise definition of informal employment has varied, some unifying features of informal employment include low pay, poor security, subpar work conditions and inadequate access to welfare and education programs.

Labor market institutions such as child labor and informal employment puts into sharp relief the irony of lofty *de jure* labor standards aspirations and their potential adverse *de facto* labor standards consequences. For example, when formal employment is protected by costly employment regulations, employers are incentivized to turn to child labor, or informal workers instead. Likewise, international calls to boycott products made by child labor, or workers who toil without legal protection can ultimately render these very workers worse off as demand for their services diminishes. Many studies on labor standards starting from some of the earliest come under this category,[1] where the fundamental issue is whether regulation is at all called for in markets where all decisions are voluntary, and where labor standard regulations stand to ensure decent labor standards for some at the risk of persistent poverty for others.

Globalization and Labor Standards

Globalization and labor standards have always been inextricably linked. While globalization per se is not new, the most recent wave in the last four decades is particularly notable in the context of labor standards (Robertson 2008), marking the first time when developing countries participated more openly and actively in the world trading system. Some argue that more stringent regulations regarding labor standards stand in the way of free and fair competition, and prevent countries from realizing the full gains from trade particularly when evidence is amounting that "globalizers" fare better than "non-globalizers" (for example, Collier and Dollar 2002). Others contend that the causality goes in reverse, wherein globalization unleashes a race to the bottom in labor standards driven by the need to cut costs to remain competitive in a globalized world. Important nuances nonetheless apply depending on what is being traded: in workers through migration, in capital through foreign direct investment, and in goods and services.

Beginning with migration, the most recent estimates suggest that there are 232 million international migrants globally (OECD 2013). If one includes involuntary migration through international and regional trafficking, the figure rises by 9.1 million based on the latest estimates of the number of trafficked persons world wide (ILO 2012). While migration is often a strategy in response to poverty and joblessness, migrants as a group can become a particularly vulnerable segment of the working population in the

[1]For example, Robinson (1964) famously states that "The only thing worse than being exploited by a capitalist is not being exploited by a capitalist".

face of macro-economics shocks.[2] The vulnerability of migrants is magnified manyfold when migrants are deceived or coerced. Particularly in the case of involuntary migration through trafficking, for example, appropriately framed labor standards can assist in the discovery of trafficked victims cum illegal migrants, and offer legal protection to safeguard the safety and rights of these individuals. Examples of this class of labor standards includes the Trafficking Victims Protection Act of the United States. Critics argue, however, that such safeguards do not address the source of the problem, and will only result in even more trafficking as long as demand remains unabated.

Foreign direct investment has increased significantly in the past few decades to reach US$1.7 trillion (UNCTAD 2016). Over 50% of this global flow of capital finds destinations in the developed countries of the world. This observation has prompted investigations concerning why capital fail to flow to developing countries (Banerjee and Duflo 2005, Alfaro, Kalemni-Ozcan and Volosovych 2005). Even when capital does flow, investigations have shed light on the employment generating capabilities of FDI and the role of labor standards in the process (Nocke and Yeaple 2008). Findings on whether foreign firms pay higher wages have also been mixed (Heyman Sjöholm and Tingvall 2007, Almeida 2007), and the causal effects of FDI ownership on total factor productivity have tended to be highly country and context-specific (Aitken and Harrison 1999, Haskel, Pereira and Slaughter 2007, Javorcik, Keller and Tybout 2007). But the very fact that capital is footloose can present a challenge to workers as well (Rodrik 1996), by eroding their ability to bargain for high wages even in the presence of unions.

The local labor market consequences of trade liberalization, through the relaxation of policies protecting workers in import competing sectors for example, has received a great deal of attention. The orthodox prediction à la Stolper-Samuelson in the context of the Heckscher-Ohlin theory of international trade holds that workers in poor countries where the supply of labor is abundant will gain in both nominal and real terms by trading with countries with an abundant supply of capital. A second theoretical

[2]For example, 15.2% of the foreign born population in EU-28 countries are unemployed compared to the native figure at 9.9% in 2014 (OECD 2014). The pattern is interestingly reversed in the United States where the unemployment rate of foreign-born is lower than that of natives (OECD 2014), and where second-generation individuals fare better still in the U.S. labor market.

argument stems from growth theory, based on a two-part argument which holds that openness is good for growth through R&D and productivity gains (Grossman and Helpman 1989, Romer 1990, Frankel and Romer 1999), and that growth benefits the poor (Dollar and Kraay 2001, Besley and Burgess 2003).[3] Recent studies have increasing questioned the validity of the Stolper-Samuelson prediction. For example, new insights have emerged as the standard Heckcshcer Ohlin framework is extended to (i) enrich the specification of product space to allow more flexibility in terms of number of varieties of goods exchanged, and the substitutability of domestic and foreign goods (Feenstra and Hanson 1996, Xu 2003) (ii) incorporate learning-by-doing thus making the dynamic link between trade and growth more evident (Matsuyama 1991, Young 1988), and (iii) introduce riskiness in production (Newbery and Stiglitz 1984, Hoff 1994 and Chau 1998), to name a few. The robustness of the openness and growth link have also been under scrutiny (Rodriguez and Rodrik 2000), with studies showing no significant relationship, or even a negative relationship. (Ravallion 2004, Agénor 2004).

Thus, an extremely active research agenda on how *de facto* labor standards have been impacted by globalization has given rise to a series of very nuanced conclusions depending in particular on whether the trade is in humans (e.g. rights of migrants), capital (e.g. collective bargaining), or goods (e.g. wages and employment). In parallel, research on how globalization also impacts *de jure* labor standards setting has also emerged. A notable example is Olney (2013), which documents evidence of a race to the bottom in labor standards to compete for mobile capital in the form of a convergence in employment protection laws among recipient countries of foreign direct investment. An important takeaway here is that labor standards in both *de facto* and *de jure* terms are subject to the forces of globalization. This has important implications on how researchers evaluate the effectiveness of labor regulations on labor standard realities. For example,

[3]For example, for the case of the U.S., Autor et al. (2013) and Schott (2012) both find results consistent with manufacturing employment and wage decline upon exposure to Chinese imports. In developing countries, Topalova (2005) finds that trade liberalization decreases poverty reduction in rural India, but had no impact on poverty in urban India. McCaig (2009) came to similar conclusions for the case of Vietnam, where trade liberalization through higher tariff reductions tend to delay improvements in poverty, but access to foreign markets causes greater decreases in poverty. By contrast, Verhoogen (2008) articulates a quality upgrading and firm selection channel which is consistent with the increase in wages and employment experienced in the Mexican export sector subsequent to the Peso crisis.

recognizing the endogeneity of labor standards, researchers interested in the labor market consequences of labor regulations have increasingly turned to country studies in search of more plausibly exogenous variations in labor standards, so far with mixed results.[4]

Credible Labor Standards

Beginning as early as the English Factory Act of 1802, virtually every nation has put in place provisions for labor protection via the legislation of a set of minimally acceptable labor standards. These *de jure* labor standards tend to vary greatly across countries, and across sectors and workers within countries. With the establishment of the International Labor Organization in 1919, a formal arena has thus been created in which countries can engage in dialogue and negotiations about what a set of internationally acceptable minimum labor standards should encompass. In 1998, the ILO announced the declaration of the Fundamental Principles and Rights at Work. The 186 member states of the ILO are committed to follow and promote four categories of principles and rights at work. Importantly, this commitment is independent of whether or individual countries have ratified the relevant labor standards conventions. These principles and rights include: freedom of association and the effective recognition of the right to collective bargaining, the elimination of forced or compulsory labour, the abolition of child labour and the elimination of discrimination in employment.

The drive to raise labor standards extends well beyond national and international legislative bodies. With ethical consumerism on the rise, firms — both for- and non-profits — have responded with products that bear particular social and/or environmental sustainability claims. For example in the United Kingdom, ethical spending was valued at £32.2 billion in 2014, and sales of Fairtrade products alone was valued at £1.74 billion. Notably, consumers also engage in personal boycott against particular products. In 2014, boycotts in the United Kingdom was valued at £2.64 billion. 17% of consumers surveyed cite labor standards as the topic of concern in their decision to boycott products (Ethical Consumer 2014).

[4] For example, Besley and Burgess (2004) shows that Indian states that adopted pro-worker labor legislations experience a reduction in output, employment, investment and productivity in formal sector manufacturing. Harrison and Scorse (2010) finds that anti-sweatshop activisim in Indonesia has raised wages, but at the cost of reduced investment, profits, and heightened probability of closure particularly for smaller establishments. These mixed findings corroborate other cross countries studies.

Despite all the actions on setting standards, a fully spelled out strategy on labor standards is not complete without monitoring and enforcement (Elliott and Freeman 2003). Already, however, what we know suggest that non-compliance is a key issue. In one of the earliest studies, Ashenfelter and Smith (1979) finds that overall compliance to the U.S. federal minimum wage stood at 65% in 1973 and compliance fell by another 10% after the minimum wage revision in 1975. Later, a United States General Accounting Office (USGAO) report (USGAO 1988) interviewed 53 federal enforcement officials, of which 40 indicated sweatshop conditions in violation of the Fair Labor Standards Act are pervasive particularly in the apparel industry, meat packing and restaurant establishments. At the firm level, the Fair Labor Association routinely audits factories under contract with companies with voluntary codes of conduct. Violations are very common even in this select group of companies with voluntary codes of conduct. Violations are particularly pervasive in the area of health and safety conditions, followed by hours of work; wages, benefits and overtime, and freedom of association (Fair Labor Association 2013).[5]

In summary, growing out of the three global campaigns and trends discussed here, research on labor standards has always emphasized the important distinction between *de jure* and *de facto* standards: research on the global campaigns against poverty sheds light on the effectiveness of labor standard regulations on actual labor market outcome, while the globalization and labor standards debate cautions against casual inference about a causal link between labor regulations and labor market outcomes, for both are in fact subject to the forces of globalization. Finally, research on the credibility of labor standards utilizes the sharp distinction between *de facto* and *de jure* as the research program, and questions why governments turn a blind eye to the legislations they have themselves set.

We take a cue from this discussion of the literature, and organize the rest of this volume into three sections. The first section contains five essay on the determinants of *de facto* labor standards. The second section contains five essays on the issue of *de jure* labor standards. And the final

[5]Concerns over enforcement has led to proposals that the WTO, instead of the ILO, should take over the authority of enforcing labor standards. For example, Rodrik (1996), Bhakshi and Kerr (2010) and Flanagan (2003) in their cross-country estimations use proxies of labor rights such as the number of ILO conventions and do not find empirical support for the notion that adoption of international labor standards harms exports. OECD (1996) considers the role of violations of union and collective bargaining rights on exports and comes to similar conclusions.

section contains three essays on credible enforcement and compliance of standards.

De facto Labor Standards

While enormous strides have been made in the area of the determinants of *de facto* labor standards, as our survey above shows, the devil is in the details, and main research challenge is to identify the specifics of the labor market institutions that perpetuate the labor standards deficit. In this section, we present five essays in which we take an in depth look at a number of labor market institutions that intersect with one or more of the following issues: lack of agency of workers, the substitutability of compensations and work conditions, and the credible enforcement of labor standards.

With respect to the the lack of agency among workers, some of the most egregious violations of labor standard takes place when the agency of individual workers is compromised. For example, the ILO defines forced labor as

> *all work or service which is exacted from any person under the menace of any penalty and for which the said person has not offered himself voluntarily*

while child labor of the worst form is defined by the ILO as

> *all forms of slavery or practices similar to slavery, such as the sale and trafficking of children, debt bondage and serfdom and forced or compulsory labour, including forced or compulsory recruitment of children for use in armed conflict.*

In these circumstances canonical models of labor demand and supply no longer apply since deceits and/or coercion rob workers of their ability to make independent decisions. Research in this area is just emerging:[6] What specific forms can the lack of agency take? What are some facilitating factors? What forms should policy interventions take?

Next, we examine the interplay between compensation and work conditions. While *de facto* labor standards is concerned chiefly with the conditions of work, to date, we know very little about how firms make these decisions and how workers respond to the tradeoffs between work conditions and pay. Standard arguments would dictate that unless workers are explicitly coerced, any difference in work conditions should surely be

[6]A notable exception is Rogers and Swinnerton (2008), which presents a model of exploitative labor when workers are lured into employment without full information.

accounted for via a compensating differential in wages (Smith 1776, Rosen 1986). However, one of the key irony of sweatshops, for example, is the co-incidence of low wage, long over time, and poor conditions (Powell and Skarbek 2006). How do we reconcile the apparent failure on the part of workers to claim compensation commensurate with their labor?

Another topic concerns the endogeneity of employer market power. The basic economic model that drives many of the economic intuitions regarding the economics of labor standards is based on a world of competitive firms (e.g. Krueger 1997, Bagwell and Staiger 1999, Brown, Deardoff and Stern 1996). Recent studies have shown that many salient features of developing country labor markets are difficult to reconcile together if a competitive setting is assumed.[7] Nonetheless, the policy implications of such an assumption is non-trivial, and the economic efficiency implications of a broad class of labor standards, including guaranteeing wage bargaining rights, for example, hinge critically on whether labor markets are competitive.

Chapters 2–6 present five essays that address these issues. In Chapter 2, we investigate the institution of debt bondage and child labor employment as a first example that showcases how the agency of a worker to refrain from labor contracts can be compromised even without employer coercion. We explore the contract between moneylending landlords and tenants, and examine the conditions under which the interlinkage between credit and labor contracts can give rise to a vicious cycle of debt, bonded child labor, and poverty from which indebted households cannot escape. We show that this "market" for child labor generates intertemporal spillover effects that can perpetuate the institution of debt bondage over generation. We furthermore argue that this spillover effect justifies direct policy interventions that breaks the cycle of perpetual indebtedness.

Chapter 3 proposes a theory of international trafficking where employment decisions are made by middlemen traffickers. For this reason the familiar link between compensation and work condition is severed. The chapter entertains a setting where internationally mobile middlemen traffickers engage in two-way bargaining between potential buyers of the services of trafficked victims both in the origin and the destination country. Their

[7]The labor market implications of a minimum wage hike is one such example. While employment is expected to fall with a minimum wage hike in a competitive setting, empirical findings using minimum hike episodes from around the world have been mixed. See also Soundararajan (2014) for an in depth discussion and a study of the non-monotonic employment impact of minimum wage hikes in India.

ability to extract surplus from these bargaining relationships depend on the cross-border ease of mobility of traffickers, and the elasticity of buyers' demand. Importantly, we show that the nature of origin-destination coordination in anti-trafficking policies depends critically on the size of these two parameters, about which we know very little. The paper then employs a novel dataset of transnational trafficking and estimate a gravity equation of trafficking flows. Based on implications of the theoretical model we propose, we arrive at the conclusion that traffickers enjoy considerable ease of mobility and are faced with inelastic buyer's demand.

In Chapter 4, we canvassed reports by international organizations, academics, civil society groups and non-profit organizations to come up with as set of work conditions prevalent in so-called sweatshop jobs. Emerging from this evidence is a picture of sweatshop jobs that clearly reflects sweatshop conditions as both harmful to the capacity of a worker to be productive at work, and to the capability of the worker to be vertically mobile. The paper makes the point that the harm done to a workers' capability both in terms of productivity and vertical mobility can explain the paradox of the lack of a compensating differential for sweatshop work even in the absence of coercion. Furthermore, the paper shows that a ban on sweatshop jobs can lead to overall efficiency gains even in spite of an increase in unemployment.

The next two essays address the issue of endogenous employer market power. In Chapter 5, we revisit the issue of informal sector employment. Contrary to popular assumption, we argue that employers in the informal sector enjoy more market power in equilibrium, for their inability to sign credible wage contracts prevents wages from rising too far in equilibrium. In this context, an enforced minimum wage in the formal sector provides employers with a commitment technology enforced by third party. The paper contends that the realized levels of market power of employers in the formal and informal sectors are functions of the extent to which employment contracts credible, as well as the level of the minimal wage enforced in the formal sector of the economy. We then show how the optimal (unemployment minimizing) minimal wage can be adjusted in view of the contractual dualism between the formal and informal sector.

Chapter 6 examines the issue of employer market power in the presence of footloose capital. We consider an explicit bargaining setting where an employer and a union have asymmetric information about the productivity of the firm. We are interested in the employer market power implicit in this form of information asymmetry, and how this market power changes as owners of capital becomes footloose. Depending on how the information structure of the dispute changes endogenously with capital mobility, we show that the outcome of the wage bargain may well be tilted in favor or against workers. Interestingly, the main thrust of the argument hinges on whether international investment incentives selectively favor the outflow of capital from the most or the least productive firms.

De jure Labor Standards

In this section, we exam the determinants of *de jure* labor standards at the level of profit-seeking firms, non-profits, national governments and international organizations. The first two essays respectively consider decisions on the part of profit-seeking and nonprofit firms to engage in the production and sales of products made to satisfy ethical consumerism. These products may come in the form of goods made without child labor, or goods that by-pass the middlemen so that a higher share of the revenue is passed on to the farm-gate level.

In Chapter 7, we question whether labeling products "Child-Labor Free" can provide a market-based solution to the child labor problem. In a model of North-South trade where consumers share an inherent preference to boycott goods made with child labor, we show that a labeling guarantee that no child labor is used in the production process is far from a guarantee to eradicate child labor in the economy. If adopted voluntarily in equilibrium by Southern producers, these labeling programs necessarily benefit producers, and make children worse off as a result of labor market discrimination. Furthermore, unless policies are in place to address the underlying cause of the child labor problem, trade sanctions against Southern unlabeled products have no impact on child labor employment.

Chapter 8 introduces the non-profits as fair-traders. Specifically, we consider a model of labor standards setting in which consumer preferences reward producers with particular non-profit goals — such as serving as traders for farmers in geographically remote locations while they do away with the traditional middlemen traders. We show that such rewards can improve farmers welfare in a number of ways, including farmers' access to export market, the revenue they receive conditional on access, and the extent of price international pass-through to the farmgate level. With geography playing an important role in this setting, we show that ethical consumerism through fair-traders can furthermore decrease intra-/inter-regional poverty incidence. In this setup where fairtraders partner with poorer farmers and in more geographically distant locations, we show that for governments who wish to minimize the poverty gap, resources should be directed to subsidize fair trade organizations, and/or to producers with no access to markets, rather than to local middlemen intermediaries.

In the next two essays, we examine labeling standards decision-making from the vantage point of national governments. A key point we emphasize in these works is that national governments frequently contend with multiple goals and objectives, and the resulting labor standards should be understood as optimal tradeoffs between these objectives.

Chapter 9 considers a rural employment setting in which employment conditions are seasonal, and labor protection particularly in the lean season can directly improve income distribution. Employment protection can induce additional aggregate welfare gains as well when workers are risk averse. In this paper, the labor standards under consideration is an employment guarantee program, following national intiatives to provide safety nets for the rural poor for example in India through the National Rural Employment Guarantee Act. We solve the problem of a government faced with two objectives: a utilitarian objective to maximize productive efficiency in agriculture, and a Rawlsian objective to welfare maximization of the laborers. We show that the optimal wage offer to workers in the employment guarantee program depends critically on the tradeoffs between employment generation and wages, as well as efficiency tradeoffs in the allocation of workers between private sector employment and public sector employment guarantee.

In the next chapter, we model government attempts to improve labor standards, while it engages in North-South trade. We are interested in a setting where competition for market share and better terms of trade takes place between Northern countries with already high labor standards, between Southern countries who can strategically choose labor standards, and between Northern and Southern countries. We examine the question of a Southern race to the bottom in labor standards, and show that trade concerns can influence labor standards decisions. Interestingly, in this simple model where costly labor standards can allow a Southern country to reap terms of trade gains through a reduction in output, we find that a number of factors external to the Southern country now plays a significant role in determining labor standards. These include the nature of the demand elasticity of the Nothern country, the relative size of the large exporters in the North and in the South, and the competitive fringe of other exporters who do not experience terms of trade effects because of their size.

Chapter 11 presents an empirical analysis of the adoption of ILO international labor standard conventions, in which we contend that if the ILO is indeed a toothless tiger as popularly claimed, then country-level ratification patterns of ILO labor standards should not exhibit any systemic pattern. Interestingly, we find that the opposite is true. While economic variables such as real per capita income do not explain ratification, legal systems do. Furthermore, for some Conventions, we find that peer effects are in play, thus providing empirical support for the hypothesis of strategic complementarity in labor standards.

Enforcement and Credibility of Labor Standards

Naturally, labor standards that are set without explicit or implicit monitoring and enforcement are destined to be of little relevance. In this section we explore the issue of enforcement credibility in three specific contexts.

In Chapter 12, we study the issue of the credibility of a minimum wage guarantee, and explore the question of why governments turn a blind eye to the minimum wage law they have themselves passed. We show that the enforcement of minimum wage laws has an inherent credibility problem, in that once contracts are struck, the actual enforcement of the minimum wage represents a costly (enforcement induced) transfer of income from employers to workers with no other efficiency gains. Thus, ex post, governments have a tendency to under-invest in enforcement. We then consider the problem of a government in choosing a minimum wage in a fully rational setting accounting for the possibility of imperfect enforcement, and accordingly firms comply imperfectly in rational expectation of the enforcement deficit. Interestingly, we find that a distributionally sensitive government is more able to credibly commit to a minimum wage policy backed by enforcement, even if less than imperfect.

The next chapter considers the credibility of an employment guarantee, consisting of a wage guarantee to contracted workers, and the ease with which workers can access the program — an implicit rationing device. We show that this combination of wage and access can deliver both efficiency improvement and distributional gains in a labor market where private employers have market power. Even more intriguing, we find that the credibility of a government to refrain from rationing employment protection ex post depends critically on whether the social welfare function gives weight to poverty. In particular, a government with a concern for poverty is more able to implement credible *efficiency enhancing* labor standard reforms.

In the final chaper, we present a setting where a government has at its disposal multiple policy instruments in addition to labor standards. Consequently, the need for full enforcement of the minimum wage is no longer clear. In particular, we examine the impact of corporate tax and minimum wage reforms and their collective impact on the size of the informal economy, where workers can no longer avail themselves to minimum wage protection, and where tax evasion is pervasive. We are interested in the possible complementarity between tax and minimum wage, wage enforcement, and whether minimum wage and tax compliance depends on the size of the minimum wage and the tax rate, conditional on enforcement. The answer to these questions turns out to be quite nuanced. To pick a particular case in point, we find that for minimum wages that are sufficiently higher than worker productivity, employers evade profit taxes by overstating the wage they pay to workers. Here, keeping tax enforcement constant, we find that wage payment can exhibit a spike at the minimum wage even without minimum wage enforcement.

In summary of the key takeaways from this research program, the overarching observation to note is that the overall merits and distributional consequences of a fully enforced labor standard depends critically on the institutional conditions of the market including market competitiveness, enforceability of contracts, the presence of footloose industries, and the interactions, if any, between non-profits and for-profits in the market place, to name a few. These observations have strong implications for data collection related to *de jure* labor standard regulation. In particular, in addition to oft-used labor regulation indicators covering relevant laws and minimal standards, our findings point towards the need to assemble corresponding indicators on "labor standards facilitating institutions", to order to better reflect circumstances that contribute to the usefulness of *de jure* labor standards that improve the well-being of workers.

Second, our findings suggest that labor standards should embody a collection of attributes, inclusive of wages, the conditions of work, and importantly, the agency of the worker to make independent decisions, as our analyses on sweatshop laborers, debt bondage, and international trafficking have shown. Thus, in developing measures of *de facto* labor standards, standard labor market performance indicators such as wages and employment should be complemented by measures that indicate the agency of employed and unemployed workers, including their ability to resign, to choose overtime, to be productive, and to have access to information relevant to the labor market, for example.

Finally, while we have touched upon the issue of the credibility of labor standard enforcement in a national government regulation setting, there is now a host of labor standard setting institutions, including private firms and non-profit enterprises at the establishment level, and partners in a trade agreement or members in the International Labor Organization, for example. Our knowledge gap is significant in these contexts, in which issues related to the determinants of the level of *de jure* standards imposed by these organizations, and the corresponding determinants of the incentives to enforce such standards are open questions that await future research.

References

Agénor, Pierre-Richard. 2004. "Does Globalization Hurt the Poor?" *International Economics and Economic Policy* 1(1): 21–51.

Aitken, Brian and Ann Harrison. 1999. "Do Domestic Firms Benefit from Direct Foreign Investment? Evidence from Venezuela," *American Economic Review* 89(3): 605–618.

Alfaro, Laura, Sebnem Kalemli-Ozcan, and Vadym Volosovych. 2005."Why Doesn't Capital Flow from Rich to Poor Countries: An Empirical Investigation," *Review of Economics and Statistics* 90(2): 347–368.

Almeida, Rita. 2007. "The Labor Market Effects of Foreign Owned Firms," *Journal of International Economics* 72: 75–96.

Ashenfelter, Orley and Robert S. Smith. 1979. "Compliance with the Minimum Wage Law," *Journal of Political Economy* 87(2): 333–350.

Bacchetta, Marc, Ekkehard Ernst and Juanna P. Bustamante. 2009. *Globalization and Informal Jobs in Developing Country.* Switzerland, WTO Secretariat.

Bagwell, Kyle and Robert Staiger. 1999. "The Simple Economics of Labor Standards and the GATT," In Alan V. Deardorff and Robert M. Stern (eds.). *Social Dimensions of the U.S. Trade Policies.* Ann Arbor: University of Michigan Press pp. 195–244.

Bakshi, Samira, and William A. Kerr. 2010. "Labour Standards as a Justification for Trade Barriers: Consumer Concerns, Protectionism, and the Evidence." *The Estey Centre Journal of International Law and Trade Policy* 11(1): 153–181.

Banerjee, Abhijit V., and Esther Duflo. 2005. "Growth Theory through the Lens of Development Economics." In: *Handbook of Economic Growth.* Philippe Aghion and Steven N. Durlauf (eds.), Volume 1 (A). Holland: Elsevier, pp. 473–552.

Besley, Timothy and Robin Burgess. 2003. "Having Global Poverty," *Journal of Economic Perspectives* 17(3): 3–22.

Besley, Timothy and Robin Burgess. 2004. "Can Labor Regulation Hinder Economic Performance? Evidence from India," *Quarterly Journal of Economics* 119(1): 91–134.

Brown, Drusilla K., Alan V. Deardorff and Robert M. Stern. 1996. "International Labor Standards and Trade: A Theoretical Analysis." In: Jagdish Bhagwati and Robert Hudec (eds.), *Fair Trade and Harmonization: Prerequisites for Free Trade?*, Volume 1. Cambridge, MA: Cambridge University Press.

Chau, Nancy H. 1998. "Dynamic Stability and International Trade under Uncertainty," *Economica* 65: 381–399.

Collier, Paul and David Dollar. 2002. *Globalization, Growth and Poverty.* Oxford University Press. New York.

Dollar, David and Aart Kraay. 2002. "Growth Is Good for the Poor," *Journal of Economic Growth* 7(3): 195–225.

Ebert, Franz Christian and Anne Posthuma. 2010. "Labour Provisions in Trade Arrangements: Current Trends and Perspectives," *International Institute for Labor Studies Discussion Paper Series.* Web/pdf: 978-92-9014-993-4.

Elliott, Kimberly Ann and Richard D. Freeman. 2003. *Can Labor Standards Improve under Globalization.* Peterson Institute of International Economics: Washington DC.

Ethical Consumer. 2014. *Ethical Consumers Marketing Report 2014.* Consumer Data Research Center.

Fair Labor Association. 2013. *Fair Labor Association 2012 Annual Report.* Fair Labor Association: Washington DC.

Feenstra, Robert C., and Gordon H. Hanson. 1996. "Foreign Investment, Outsourcing and Relative Wages." In *The Political Economy of Trade Policy: Papers in Honor of Jagdish Bhagwati,* Robert C. Feenstra, Gene M. Grossman and Douglas A. Irwin (eds.). Cambridge, MA: MIT Press. pp. 89–127.

Flanagan, Robert J. 2003. "Labor Standards and International Competitive Advantage." In *International Labor Standards: Globalization, Trade, and Public Policy,* Robert J. Flanagan and William B. Gould (eds.). Stanford, CA.: Stanford University Press. pp. 15–59.

Frankel, Jeffrey. A., and David Romer. 1999. "Does Trade Cause Growth?" *American Economic Review* 89(3): 379–399.

Grossman, Gene M., and Elhanan Helpman. 1989. "Product Development and International Trade," *Journal of Political Economy* 97(6): 1261–1283.

Harrison, Ann and Jason Scorse. 2010. "Multinationals and Anti-sweatshop Activism," *American Economic Review* 100(1): 247–273.

Haskel, Jonathan E., Sonia C. Pereira, and Matthew J. Slaughter. 2007. "Does Inward Foreign Direct Investment Boost the Productivity of Domestic Firms?" *Review of Economics and Statistics* 89(2): 482–496.

Javorcik, Beata S., Wolfgang Keller and James Tybout. 2008. "Openness and Industrial Response in a Wal-Mart World: A Case Study of Mexican Soaps, Detergents and Surfactant Producers," *World Economy* 31(12): 1558–1580.

Krueger, Alan. 1997. "Observations on International Labor Standards and Trade," In *Annual World Bank Conference on Development Economics, 1996.* Bruno, Michael and Boris Pleskovic (eds.). Washington, DC: The World Bank. pp. 281–302.

Heyman, Fredrik, Fredrik Sjöholm, and Patrik Tingvall. 2007. "Multinationals, Cross-border Acquisitions and Wage Dispersion." *Canadian Journal of Economics* 44(2): 627–650.

Hoff, Karla. 1994. "A Reexamination of the Neoclassical Trade Model under Uncertainty," *Journal of International Economics* 36(1–2): 1–27.

McCaig, Brian. 2011. "Exporting out of poverty: Provincial Poverty in Vietnam and U.S. Market Access," *Journal of International Economics* 85(1): 102–113.

Nocke, Volker and Stephen Yeaple. 2008. "An Assignment Theory of Foreign Direct Investment," *Review of Economic Studies* 75(2): 529–557.

OECD. 1996. *Trade, Employment and Labor Standards: A Study of Core Workers' Rights and International Trade*. Paris: OECD.

OECD. 2014. *OECD Factbook: Economic, Environmental and Social Statistics*. OECD Publishing, Paris.

Olney, William W. 2013. "A Race to the Bottom? Employment Protection and Foreign Direct Investment." *Journal of International Economics* 91(2): 191–203.

Powell, Benjamin and David Skarbek. 2006. "Sweatshops and Third World Living Standards: Are the Jobs Worth the Sweat?" *Journal of Labor Research* 27(2): 263–274.

Ravallion, Martin. 2004. "Looking Beyond Averages in the Trade and Poverty Debate," *World Bank Policy Research Working Paper* No. 3461. Washington DC: World Bank, November.

Robertson, Robbie. 2008. *The Three Waves of Globalization*. Chicago: University of Chicago Press.

Robinson, Joan. 1964. *Economic Philosophy*. Garden City NY: Doubleday.

Rodríguez, Francisco and Dani Rodrik. 2000. "Trade Policy and Economic Growth: A Skeptic's Guide to the Cross-national Evidence." In *NBER Macroeconomics Annual 2000* Volume 15, Ben Bernanke and Kenneth Rogoff (eds.) MIT Press. pp. 261–338.

Rodrik, Dani. 1996. "Labor Standards in International Trade: Do They Matter and What Do We Do About Them?" In *Emerging Agenda for Global Trade: High Stakesfor Developing Countries*, Robert Z. Lawrence, Dani Rodrik, and John Walley (eds.). Washington, DC: Johns Hopkins University Press for the Overseas Development Council. pp. 35–79.

Rogers, Carol Ann and Kenneth A. Swinnerton. 2008. "A Theory of Exploitative Child Labor." *Oxford Economic Papers* 60(1): 20–41.

Rosen, Sherwin. 1986. "The Theory of Equalizing Differences." In *Handbook of Labor Economics*. Orley Ashenfelter and Richard Layard (eds.). Volume I. Amsterdam: North Holland.

Smith, Adam. 1776. *An Inquiry into the Nature and Causes of the Wealth of Nations*. London: Methuen and Co., Ltd. (Fifth edition).

Soundararajan, Vidhya. 2014. "Minimum Wage Effects at Different Enforcement levels: Evidence from Employment Surveys in India," *Charles H. Dyson School of Applied Economics and Management Working Paper 2014-12*.

Topalova, Petia. 2007. "Trade Liberalization, Poverty and Inequality: Evidence from Indian Districts," in *Globalization and Poverty* Ann Harrison (ed.). NBER Books, National Bureau of Economic Research. pp. 297–336.

UNICEF. 2016. *State of the Worlds' Children Report.* New York: UNICEF.

UNCTAD. 2016. *Global Investment Monitor* No. 22. January. UNCTAD.

US General Accounting Office (USGA0). 1988. " 'Sweatshops' in the U.S. Opinions on their Extent and Possible Enforcement Options." GAP/HRD-88-130BR.

Verhoogen, Eric A. 2008. "Trade, Quality Upgrading, and Wage Inequality in the Mexican Manufacturing Sector," *Quarterly Journal of Economics* 123(2): 489–530.

World Bank. 2015. World Bank Policy Research Note No.3: Ending Extreme Poverty and Sharing Prosperity: Progress and Policies.

Xu, Bin. 2003. "Trade Liberalization, Wage Inequality and Endogenously Determined Non-traded Goods," *Journal of International Economics* 60(2): 417–431.

Journal of Economic Growth, 9, 209–238, 2004

Exploitation of Child Labor and the Dynamics of Debt Bondage

ARNAB K. BASU akbasu@wm.edu

Department of Economics, College of William and Mary, Williamsburg VA 23187, USA

NANCY H. CHAU hyc3@cornell.edu

Department of Applied Economics and Management, Cornell University, Ithaca NY 14853, USA

This paper is concerned with the institution of debt bondage and child labor employment in the context of an agrarian economy with overlapping generations. The model explores the principal-agent interaction between landlords and tenants, and identifies a set of reasons why households put children to work in response to the need to service outstanding debts, only to realize that child labor work is " exploited", and households are made strictly worse off in general equilibrium. Debt bondage in one generation is further shown to leave spillover effects, and contribute to the cycle of debt, bonded child labor and poverty across generations. In this context, the effectiveness of trade sanctions as a policy response to bonded child labor is evaluated. Contrary to expectations, a trade ban can set off a sequence of increasing indebtedness among agrarian households that offset the intended (static) disincentives to employ child labor.

Keywords: credit–labor interlinked markets, bonded child labor, co-ordination failures, trade sanctions

JEL classification: F16, J43, O12, O16

1. Introduction

Adopted unanimously by the 174 member states of the International Labor Organization (ILO) in June 1999, the "Worst Forms of Child Labor" Convention calls for an immediate end to the engagement of children in slave labor, debt bondage,[1] and other forms of abusive child labor.[2] The 1999 Convention underscores an array of existing multinational commitments to eradicate bonded child labor. Of these, some provided direct intervention

1 The United Nations' 1956 Supplementary Convention on the Abolition of Slavery, the Slave Trade and Institutions and Practices Similar to Slavery. The 1956 Convention defines debt bondage as "the status or condition arising from a pledge by a debtor of his personal services or of those of a person under his control as security for a debt, if the value of those services as reasonably assessed is not applied towards the liquidation of the debt or the length and nature of those services are not respectively limited and defined."

2 As of November 2001, 112 countries have ratified Convention 182 since it was adopted in June 1999. In contrast, the ILO adopted the Minimum Age Convention in 1974. Over 70 of a total of 116 ratifications took place after 1995.

through monetary transfers or access to credit for indebted households.[3] Others took a carrot or stick approach, respectively via the granting or withdrawal of international trade privileges. For example, the United States partially suspended general system of preference (GSP) benefits to Pakistan in October 1996 specifically due to reported child and bonded labor problems.[4] Meanwhile, alleged violations of labor rights in countries such as Myanmar, Guatemala, Liberia, Maldives have also led to partial or total suspension of GSP privileges. In 1998, the European Union began offering additional GSP benefits to countries that apply laws consistent with ILO Conventions, and further allows for the suspension of GSP privileges in countries where any form of slavery is practiced or where slave labor is utilized, as defined by the ILO and Geneva Conventions (Brenton, 2000).

Notwithstanding these campaigns and policy interventions aimed at confronting the problem of bonded child labor, formal economic analysis of the problem is as yet lacking. The purpose of this paper is therefore to analyze the institutional arrangements that lead to the emergence and persistence of the phenomenon of bonded child labor, and to explore the static and dynamic consequences of policy interventions. In consonance with existing economic analyses concerning child labor, where poverty is explicitly recognized as but one of its root causes (Rosenzweig, 1981; Grootaert and Kanbur, 1995; Basu and Van, 1998), the phenonmenon of bonded child labor also calls into attention the lack of reliable and legal channels through which the poor can secure loans, and safeguard against hunger or unexpected consumption needs. In an environment where money lenders also control local wealth in the form of land and capital, bonded child labor grows out of an institutional arrangement wherein labor and credit contracts are interlinked,[5] and outstanding household debts are paid at least in part via labor services provided by children.

In the context of the campaign to eliminate debt bondage as one of the worst forms of child labor, a number of questions naturally arise: Is there a causal link between the prevalence of interlinked credit-labor transactions and the incidence of child labor? Should these child labor–credit transactions be viewed as exploitative, even when participation is voluntary rather than coerced? Without external intervention, can child labor become endemic across generations due solely to the institution of debt bondage? Finally, and in terms of searching for an effective intervention, can international pressure, such as the termination of GSP status, be justified as a viable tool to lower the incidence of bonded child labor?

---

3 For example, in November 2000, a US$3.5 million program was launched by the ILO to achieve the sustainable liberation of an estimated 75,000 men, women and children in Nepal from bonded labor (IPEC, 1992).

4 See Office of the United States Trade Representative (1997) for a list of GSP suspensions, partial suspensions and reviews.

5 In the agrarian economies of South Asia and Latin America, interlinked credit-labor arrangement is pervasive and has been studied extensively. These studies focus on the virtues of interlinkage based on incentive and efficiency grounds, particularly when the problem of moral hazard in laborer's effort allocation is a concern. See Braverman and Stiglitz (1982), Bardhan (1983), Basu (1987), Braverman and Srinivasan (1984) and Sadoulet (1992). In none of these studies, however, is the possibility of bonded child labor accounted for as another outcome of interlinkage.

This paper scrutinizes each of these questions, with particular emphasis on the principal-agent problem confronting landlords-cum-moneylenders and agrarian households that has not been made transparent either in theories concerning child labor, or theories concerning interlinked transactions. To begin with, participation in debt bondage is shown to tip the balance between the household's (i) disutility of sending the child to work and (ii) income benefits derived from child labor in favor of the latter. Thus, households' response to the need to service outstanding debts take the form of an increase in the supply of contracted child labor. This enables landlords to rationally anticipate a decline in the residual demand for wage laborers, and in particular, the demand for labor services from families who opt not to engage in interlinkage. In a principal-agent setup, such a failure on the part of individual households to coordinate child labor supply decisions can be used against the interests of households that are engaged in interlinked transactions, since the reservation utility of every household declines with a rising supply of bonded child labor.

In response to our second line of inquiry, we have, therefore, a case of exploitative child labor—agrarian households respond to the need to service outstanding debts by putting children work, only to realize that they are worse off in general equilibrium, relative to the case where no consumption smoothing device through interlinked transactions exist. The prevalence of bonded child labor can thus be looked upon as both a symptom, and a contributing factor in the cycle of poverty.

A third observation we make is the effect of debt bondage across generations.[6] In particular, individual generations in the agrarian economy are taken to be linked via intergenerational transfers (Becker, 1981; Galor and Zeira, 1993). For altruistic parents, these transfers serve to smooth consumption and raise the welfare of the next generation. In the context of debt bondage, however, these transfers become the channel through which participation in interlinked transactions by one generation can set off a sequence of increasing indebtedness which affects the welfare, and the ability to break free from debt bondage for all subsequent generations. We show that if the degree of credit market imperfection (as measured by the difference between the interest rate that landlords have access to and the subjective time rate of discount of agrarian households) is sufficiently acute, the size of outstanding debt will eventually become large enough to justify putting children to work. Thereafter, intergenerational externalities due to interlinkage work both through a direct effect on the savings for future generations, as well as through the downward pressure on the market wage as child labor supply increases. Child labor in this context is thus endemic across generations, and prevails as a steady state phenomenon.[7]

Taken together, these observations highlight the features of the "second best" world in

---

6 In the context of credit market imperfection for the purpose of human capital accumulation, Hazan and Berdugo (2002) also demonstrate that child labor can prevail as a steady state outcome.

7 Grote et al. (1999) and Baland and Robinson (2000) study the welfare consequences of child labor in a context of credit market imperfection which puts limits on education undertakings. The appeal of removing child labor away from the work force thus lies in overcoming the undersupply of educated laborers. While we also take credit market imperfection as a starting point, we find that rational anticipation on the part of landlords that child labor supply will rise with interlinkage turns out to be sufficient for debt bondage to have perverse welfare implications for households.

which debt bondage is shown to have adverse welfare consequences. These include the lack of access to credit markets that facilitates consumption smoothing, the inability to collectively bargain and finally, household decision-making that fail to internalize the intergenerational implications of debt bondage. In particular, even though debt bondage fills the gap left open by the lack of formal credit markets for consumption smoothing, agrarian households can in fact be made worse off, so long as the remaining failures (collective bargaining and intergenerational externalities) remain unaccounted for.[8]

Once the link between debt bondage and child labor is established, we find that the effectiveness of trade sanction as a policy response to eradicate child labor is no longer clear-cut. Specifically, policies that artificially deteriorate the terms of trade facing agrarian economies have two opposing effects. First, trade sanctions have an expected impact or demand-side effect, which directly depresses the the derived demand for labor. In addition, there is a dynamic or supply-side effect running contrary to the intended static disincentives of a trade ban, as low wages render households increasingly less capable of providing transfers to future generations. With lower wages and smaller transfers, subsequent generations are at once more susceptible to debt bondage, while the same amount of adult labor can command only a smaller amount of wage income. Thus, children are put back to work in subsequent generations. Indeed, we find that this dynamic supply-side effect can completely offset the impact effect, leaving the steady state incidence of child labor strictly unaltered, but the steady state welfare of households strictly lower.

The rest of this paper is organized as follows: A number of common themes in three relatively well-documented cases of debt bondage are summarized in the following section. Section 3 develops a benchmark regime without interlinkage in order to evaluate the conditions that give rise to child labor. Sections 4 and 5 present a model that extends Bardhan (1989) by incorporating both endogenous child labor supply and the intergenerational externalities implied by interlinkage. In Section 6, the impact and dynamic effects of trade sanctions on the incidence of bonded child labor is examined. The penultimate section discusses extensions and Section 8 concludes.

2. Some Stylized Facts

Table 1 presents the economic, credit market and labor right indicators of 98 developing countries for which the existence (45 countries)/non-existence (53 countries) of child labor in debt bondage is reported in Bureau of Democracy, Human Rights and Labor (1999).[9] As shown, developing countries with reported incidence of bonded child labor have on average a much lower GDP per capita, a substantially larger share of the labor force

8 We thank an anonymous referee for pointing out the second-best interpretation of our results here to us.

9 With very few exceptions, estimates of the size of the bonded child labor population on a national basis do not exist. See Basu and Chau (2003) for an empirical analysis based on a similarly constructed 0-1 indicator variable of bonded child labor in developed and developing countries as reported in Bureau of Democracy, Human Rights and Labor (1999).

Table 1. Economic, labor and credit market characteristics of developing countries with debt bondage.

	I. No Reported Incidence of Child Labor in Debt Bondage			II. Positive Incidence of Child Labor in Debt Bondage			I and II		
Variable	Mean	Std. Dev.	Obs	Mean	Std. Dev.	Obs	Mean	Std. Dev.	Obs
GDP per capita, 1995 (PPP$)	5,207.920	3,300.508	50	2,892.744	4,712.905	43	4,137.462	4,157.982	93
Labor Force in Agriculture, 1990 (%)	25.936	13.287	43	62.703	21.914	43	44.319	25.816	86
Child Labor, 1998 (% 10–14 years of age)	1.054	3.299	45	23.674	13.703	45	12.364	15.085	90
Private credit, 1990–1995 average (% GDP)	0.404	0.220	9	0.217	0.162	19	0.277	0.200	28
Freedom of Assoc. and Rights to Organize Score (1–4)	2.769	0.927	13	2.133	0.640	15	2.429	0.836	28
Exporters of non-fuel primary products (0, 1)	0.094	0.295	53	0.422	0.499	45	0.245	0.432	98

Sources: US Dept. of State 1999; UNDP 1998; World Bank 2001; OECD 2000; Beck Demirguc-Kunt and Levine 2000.

engaged in agriculture, and a much higher percentage of economically active children (10–14 years of age). In addition, based on the average shares of private credit by deposit money banks and other financial institutions to GDP (Beck et al., 2000), credit markets are better developed in countries free from child labor in debt bondage.[10] In terms of basic worker rights, and based on the four-point score reported in OECD (2000),[11] the enforcement of freedom of association and rights to organize is relatively more adequate in countries free from debt bondage. Finally, in terms of trade links, more than 42 percent of the developing countries with positive reported incidence of children in debt bondage derive more than 50 percent of their export revenue from the export of non-fuel primary products.

This preliminary cross-national evidence notwithstanding, features such as the degree of reliance on agrarian production, access to credits, and the enforcement of workers' rights can similarly be singled out from a number of well-documented cases of bonded child labor. Since these features motivate the analytical framework developed in the sequel, we briefly discuss here child labor arising out of debt bondage in India, Nepal and Pakistan.

The Bonded Labor System (Abolition) Act of 1976 prohibits all bonded labor, by adults and children in India. Bonded child labor is nevertheless prevalent in rural India,

---

10 Basu and Chau (2003) makes use of three other alternative credit market indicators and arrives at similar conclusions.

11 A score of 4 indicates that enforcement is adequate, while a score of 1 indicates severe violation of freedom of association and rights to organize.

particularly in the states of Bihar, Orissa, and Andhra Pradesh where agrarian production is the mainstay of economic activity (US Department of Labor, 1995). Official estimates put the number of bonded workers, children and adult combined, at 353,000, and NGO estimates range from 2.6 to 15 million workers. A specific form of bonded labor, referred to as the ''Kuthias'', are bonded laborers ranging in age from 10 to 14, and pledged to employers by parents in exchange for a loan (US Department of Labor, 1995). These bonded child laborers perform agricultural tasks, and otherwise assist bonded adults in other agricultural chores for the creditor as payment. In a 1979 survey conducted in ten states of India, about 30 percent of families under debt bondage put one or more children into bondage mostly to cover debt repayment.

In terms of the ability of the agricultural work force to negotiate wages, the Indian Constitution provides for the right of association and the right to bargain collectively. In addition, discrimination against union members and organizers is prohibited. In practice, however, legal protections of worker rights are effective only for the 28 million workers in the organized industrial sector, out of a total work force of more than 397.2 million (Bureau of Democracy, Human Rights and Labor, 1999).

Like India, Nepal has ratified the UN Slavery Convention and Supplementary Convention on Slavery. The Nepal Labor Act specifically prohibits forced or bonded child labor (Bureau of Democracy, Human Rights and Labor, 1999). Bonded labor is a continuing problem, however, especially in agriculture. An estimated 100,000 people work under the ''Kamaiya'' or bonded labor system in the southern Terai region. These ''Kamaiyas'' are agricultural workers who may have worked for the same landlords for many generations. According to an NGO survey of bonded labor in three districts of Western Nepal, the ''Kamaiya'' family typically enters into a 1-year binding verbal contract with an employer or a landowner, and borrows in cash or kind from land owners and perform agricultural tasks in exchange (Informal Sector Service Center, 1992). In many cases, the entire family, including children, are involved in performing the tasks required, and bondage with the landlord is expected to terminate when the debt is paid off in full.

For these and other agrarian families, the Nepalese Constitution provides for the freedom to establish and to join unions and associations. However, union participation is significant only in the formal sector, and accounts for only a small portion of the labor force. Collective bargaining agreements cover an estimated 20 percent of wage earners in the organized sector (Bureau of Democracy, Human Rights and Labor, 1999).

In Pakistan, the Constitution of 1973 (article 11) bans the use of slaves and forced labor. In addition, the Bonded Labor System (Abolition) Act adopted in 1992 outlawed bonded labor, canceled existing bonded debts, and forbade lawsuits for the recovery of existing debts (Bureau of Democracy, Human Rights and Labor, 1999). Nevertheless, debt-bondage in Pakistan is endemic and widespread (ILO, 1993), and bonded child laborers are extensively used in labor intensive sugar cane and cotton farms. Poor harvests, agricultural input purchase along with the demand for other necessities constitute some of the reasons why households willingly incur debt (US Department of Labor, 1995).

In terms of workers' rights, the Industrial Relations Ordinance of 1969 provides for the right of industrial workers to form trade unions but is subject to major restrictions in some employment areas. The Essential Services Maintenance Act of 1952 covers sectors associated with the state administration (Karim, 1995). However, there is no provision in the law granting the right of association for agricultural workers.

These cases will serve as motivations for three main features of the model. First, agrarian households and landlords have asymmetric access to formal credit markets. For an agrarian household, their only access to credit is through a local landlord who is also the employer of the household's labor services. Second, interlinked transactions of the credit-labor (adult/child labor) variety will be examined. Finally, we take as starting point the inability on the part agrarian households to organize and to collectively negotiate contract terns with employers, either due to coordination failure, standard free rider concerns or explicit legal restrictions on union activities. In the following section, we show that the emergence and persistence of the institution of bonded child labor can be understood with these features in place.

3. The Basic Model

3.1. Employers

Consider an agrarian economy in which a typical time period $t = 1, 2, \ldots, \infty$ is characterized by two seasons, lean and harvest.[12] During the lean season, a spot labor market does not exist. During the harvest season, N identical landlords compete in employing labor, $L_{it}, i = 1, \ldots, N$. Let T denote the endowment of land of the representative landlord. Output per landlord $F(L_{it}, T) = L_{it}^{1-\eta} T^{\eta}$ is increasing, twice continuously differentiable, and exhibits diminishing marginal products in the two inputs. Also, let p denote an exogenously given world price of the agricultural output.

We take adult and child labor as substitutes in harvest work, with each unit of child labor work equivalent to $0 < a < 1$ amount of adult labor work. The spot returns respectively to a unit of adult and child labor are w_t and aw_t during the harvest season of time period t, with $w_t = pF_L(L_{it}, T)$. Let $\bar{w}$ denote the spot wage when there is no child labor employment, $\bar{w} = pF_L(n/N, T)$.

3.2. Peasant Households

The supply side of the agrarian labor market comprises of overlapping generations of n identical peasant households. Each household consists of an adult and a child. Without access to credit market, households rely solely on inheritance from the previous generation to meet consumption needs during the lean season. During the harvest season, each household supplies inelastically one physical unit of adult labor, and has discretion over

12 Seasonality in agricultural production is a common feature in South Asia and is deemed a primary cause behind the emergence and persistence of a variety of labor, land and credit market arrangements (see for instance, Bardhan, 1983; Otsuka et al., 1992; Eswaran and Kotwal, 1985; Mukherjee and Ray, 1995; Basu, 2002).

how much of one physical unit of the child's time is to be devoted to harvest work. Household utility over the two seasons (lt, ht) depends on (i) consumption in the two seasons (c_{lt}, c_{ht}), (ii) disutility of the child's time spent on harvest work (ℓ_t^k),[13] and (iii) transfers passed on to the child (B_t):

$$U(c_{lt}, c_{ht}, \ell_t^k, B_t) = \log c_{lt} + \beta(\alpha \log c_{ht} + (1-\alpha)\log(1-\ell_t^k)) + \beta^2 \log B_t, \qquad (1)$$

where the fractions α and β, respectively parameterize household disutility of putting the child to work and the subjective discount factor.

3.3. *Pure Wage Contracts with No Access to Credit*

Landlords have access to formal credit markets, and face an interest rate $r > 0$ per season. With respect to households, we begin with a benchmark with pure wage contracts, in which households do not have access to credit. Taking inheritance B_{t-1} as given, the household (i) allocates child labor time between leisure and work during the harvest season, and (ii) determines the amount of intergenerational transfers B_t devoted to support the consumption of the next generation during the lean season. We take the range of feasible inheritance to be $[0, \bar{w}/(\beta(\alpha+\beta))]$, which ensures that households do not lend in the lean season. As will become clear in the sequel, this condition is also necessary for the prevalence of debt bondage contracts.[14] Thus, the lean and harvest season budget constraints respectively for each generation t household are:

$$c_{lt} = B_{t-1}, \quad c_{ht} = w_t(1 + a\ell_t^k) - B_t \qquad (2)$$

where $w_t(1 + a\ell_t^k)$ denotes the disposable harvest season income of the household.[15]

Maximizing U with respect ℓ_t^k and B_t subject to the two budget constraints, we have

$$\ell_t^k = \max\left\{0, 1 - \frac{1-\alpha}{1+\beta}\frac{(1+a)}{a}\right\}. \qquad (3)$$

Thus, $\ell_t^k = 0$ if and only if (i) the disutility of child labor work is sufficiently high, and (ii) child labor is relatively inefficient, so that $(1-\alpha)(1+a)/[(1+\beta)a] > 1$, or equivalently, if a is less than $(1-\alpha)/(\alpha+\beta)$. Harvest season consumption thus consists only of wage income from adult labor employment, net of transfers B_t, with

13 The parameter $1-\alpha$ can be interpreted more generally as household disutility when the child spend time away from school, and engage in hazardous or disease-prone work environment.

14 In what follows, it will also be shown that for any starting level of inheritance that falls within the range $[0, \bar{w}/(\beta(\alpha+\beta))]$, inheritance for all subsequent generations will stay within this range.

15 The household maximization problem examined here can be readily extended to a case where each generation makes consumption and child labor supply decisions over multiple years. Specifically, if inheritance is less than $\bar{w}/(\beta(\alpha+\beta))$, the discounted utility maximization problem of the household over T years simplifies to the maximization of equation (1) at the beginning of each year t, harvest season savings B_{t-1} is fully consumed during the lean season of year t, and thus have no impact on the utility of the household thereafter. Details are relegated to Appendix A.

$$c_{ht} = \frac{\alpha}{\alpha+\beta} w_t, \quad B_t = \frac{\beta}{\alpha+\beta} w_t. \tag{4}$$

Total labor supply is equal to the n adult laborers, and the spot harvest wage is just

$$w_t = pF_L\left(\frac{n}{N}, T\right) \equiv \bar{w}.$$

In contrast, if $a > (1-\alpha)/(\alpha+\beta)$, total labor supply is made up of adult and child labor, with

$$c_{ht} = \frac{\alpha}{1+\beta} w_t(1+a), \quad \text{and} \quad B_t = \frac{\beta}{1+\beta} w_t(1+a). \tag{5}$$

In addition, total effective labor supply is equal to the n adult laborers plus child labor $an\ell_t^k = an(1-(1-\alpha)(1+a)/((1+\beta)a))$. This gives the equilibrium spot wage as:

$$w_t = pF_L\left(\frac{n(1+a)(\alpha+\beta)}{N(1+\beta)}, T\right) < \bar{w},$$

where the inequality follows from diminishing marginal product, and the fact that $\ell_t^k > 0$. Note that in both of these cases, transfers made in the harvest season, B_t, are independent of inheritance B_{t-1}, as B_{t-1} is fully consumed in the lean season. The supply of child labor ℓ_t^k is similarly independent of inheritance B_{t-1}. We have thus:

Proposition 1 *When households do not have access to consumption smoothing credit, there is no equilibrium incidence of child labor at every t if and only if*

$$\frac{1-\alpha}{1+\beta}\frac{(1+a)}{a} > 1.$$

In addition, the utility of a typical household is given by:

$$V_0(B_{t-1}, \bar{w}) = \log B_{t-1} + \beta((\alpha+\beta)\log \bar{w} + K) \equiv \bar{V}_o(B_{t-1}),$$

where $K = \alpha\log(\alpha/(\alpha+\beta)) + \beta\log(\beta/(\alpha+\beta))$ *is a constant.*

The profit of the representative landlord is given by:

$$pF\left(\frac{n}{N}, T\right) - \bar{w}\frac{n}{N}.$$

4. Equilibrium with Interlinked Transactions

An interlinked debt bondage contract involves two parties, a household and a landlord. Each one of the n households is matched with a landlord. Let n_{it} denote the number of households that each landlord $i = 1, \ldots, N$ is matched with in generation t, with $\sum_{i=1}^{N} n_{it} = n$. An interlinked credit-labor contract between the two parties at the beginning of the lean season stipulates the following terms:

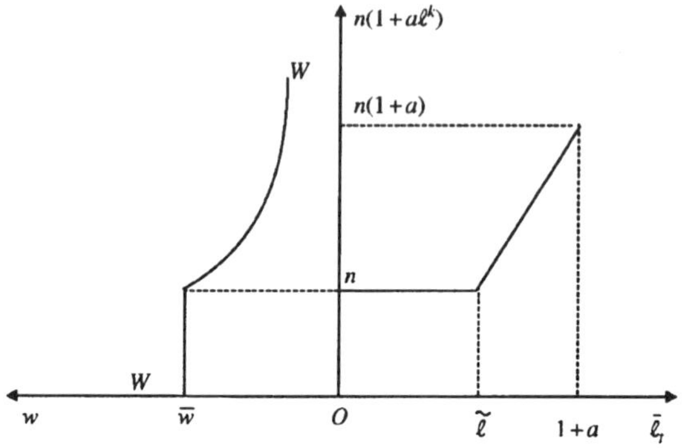

Figure 1. Child labor supply and indebtedness.

- the landlord offers the household a loan of D_t amount to supplement lean period consumption;
- in return, the household repays the landlord $\bar{\ell}_t$ amount of effective labor during the harvest season, regardless of whether or not the household repays via adult labor solely, or a combination of adult and child labor;
- the household may search for harvest season employment elsewhere only after $\bar{\ell}_t$ amount of effective labor services is repaid in full to the landlord.

The terms of the debt bondage contract thus subsidize lean season consumption at the expense of harvest season consumption for participating households in the following way:

$$c_{lt} = B_{t-1} + D_t, \quad c_{ht} = w_t(1 + a\ell_t^k - \bar{\ell}_t) - B_t. \tag{6}$$

Utility maximizing child labor supply is thus:

$$\ell_t^k = \max\left\{0, 1 - \frac{(1-\alpha)(1+a-\bar{\ell}_t)}{(1+\beta)a}\right\}, \tag{7}$$

where $\ell_t^k > 0$ if and only if

$$\frac{(1-\alpha)(1+a-\bar{\ell}_t)}{(1+\beta)a} < 1 \Leftrightarrow \bar{\ell}_t \geq 1 - \frac{a(\alpha+\beta)}{1-\alpha}. \tag{8}$$

Total effective household labor supply participating in debt bondage is increasing and piece-wise continuously differentiable with respect to outstanding debt $\bar{\ell}_t$. This is shown in Figure 1, where child labor supply is strictly positive and strictly increasing with respect to $\bar{\ell}_t$ if and only if the labor cost of the consumption loan $\bar{\ell}_t$ exceeds

$$\tilde{\ell} \equiv 1 - a(\alpha+\beta)/(1-\alpha). \tag{9}$$

In addition, as $\bar{\ell}_t$ tends to the maximal effective labor supply $(1+a)$, the household devotes all of the child's time to work. The left panel of Figure 1 plots the corresponding spot market wage in the agrarian economy given total adult and child labor supply by the n households.

Proposition 2 summarizes these observations, and makes use of the utility maximizing levels of harvest season consumption and transfers as given by:

$$B_t = \begin{cases} \beta w_t(1-\bar{\ell}_t)/(\alpha+\beta), & \text{if } \bar{\ell}_t \le \tilde{\ell}; \\ \beta w_t(1+a-\bar{\ell}_t)/(1+\beta), & \text{otherwise}, \end{cases} \tag{10}$$

$$c_{ht} = \begin{cases} \alpha w_t(1-\bar{\ell}_t)/(\alpha+\beta), & \text{if } \bar{\ell}_t \le \tilde{\ell}; \\ \alpha w_t(1+a-\bar{\ell}_t)/(1+\beta), & \text{otherwise}. \end{cases} \tag{11}$$

Proposition 2 *The incidence of child labor for households participating in debt bondage is strictly positive if and only if $\bar{\ell}_t > \tilde{\ell}$. The utility of such a household in generation t is:*

$$V_I(D_t, \bar{\ell}_t, B_{t-1}, w_t) \equiv \begin{cases} \log(B_{t-1}+D_t) \\ \quad + \beta\big((\alpha+\beta)\log w_t(1-\bar{\ell}_t) + K\big), & \text{if } \bar{\ell}_t \le \tilde{\ell}; \\ \log(B_{t-1}+D_t) \\ \quad + \beta\big((\alpha+\beta)\log w_t + (1+\beta)\log(1+a-\bar{\ell}_t) + K'\big), & \text{otherwise}. \end{cases} \tag{12}$$

where $K' = \alpha\log(\alpha/(1+\beta)) + (1-\alpha)\log((1-\alpha)/((1+\beta)a)) - \beta\log(\beta/(1+\beta))$ *is a constant.*

4.1. Participation in Debt Bondage

Individual household's decision to engage in debt bondage would in general depend on whether the n households are able to collectively bargain with employers. Here, we adopt the final observation discussed in Section 2, and households are henceforth taken to be unable to collectively negotiate contract terms, either due to coordination failure, or explicit legal restrictions on unionization activities.

With rational expectation about the spot wage (w_t), therefore, a household with inheritance B_{t-1} voluntarily participates in debt bondage if and only if

$$V_I(D_t, \bar{\ell}_t, B_{t-1}, w_t) \ge V_0(B_{t-1}, w_t) \tag{13}$$

from Propositions 1 and 2. Since $V_I(\cdot)$ depends on the size of the household debt relative to the critical value $\tilde{\ell}$, inequality (13) along with the definitions of $V_I(\cdot)$ and $V_0(\cdot)$ imply a lean season loan requirement schedule:

$$D(\bar{\ell}_t, B_{t-1}) = \begin{cases} D^1(\bar{\ell}_t, B_{t-1}) \equiv B_{t-1}\left((1-\bar{\ell}_t)^{-\beta(\alpha+\beta)} - 1\right), & \text{if } \bar{\ell}_t \leq \tilde{\ell}; \\ D^2(\bar{\ell}_t, B_{t-1}) \equiv B_{t-1}\left((1-\tilde{\ell})^{-\beta(\alpha+\beta)}\left(\frac{1+a-\bar{\ell}_t}{1+a-\tilde{\ell}}\right)^{-\beta(1+\beta)} - 1\right), & \text{otherwise.} \end{cases} \tag{14}$$

$D(\bar{\ell}_t, B_{t-1})$ traces out the smallest loan required to induce households to voluntarily participate in debt bondage, given $\bar{\ell}_t$ and B_{t-1}. Note that $D(\bar{\ell}_t, B_{t-1})$ is continuous, piecewise twice continuously differentiable and convex in $\bar{\ell}_t$.[16] $D(\cdot)$ is also increasing in $\bar{\ell}_t$, with

$$\frac{\partial D(\bar{\ell}_t, B_{t-1})}{\partial \bar{\ell}_t} = \begin{cases} B_{t-1}\beta(\alpha+\beta)(1-\bar{\ell}_t)^{-1-\beta(\alpha+\beta)}, & \text{if } \bar{\ell}_t \leq \tilde{\ell}; \\ B_{t-1}\beta(\alpha+\beta)(1-\tilde{\ell})^{-1-\beta(\alpha+\beta)}\left(\frac{1+a-\bar{\ell}_t}{1+a-\tilde{\ell}_t}\right)^{-1-\beta(1+\beta)} & \text{otherwise.} \end{cases}$$

$$\geq 0. \tag{15}$$

As such, the scope for landlords to impose strict labor service repayment terms is bounded above, as the marginal (loan) cost $\lim_{\bar{\ell}_t \to 0}(\partial D/\partial \bar{\ell}_t) = B_{t-1}\beta(\alpha+\beta) > 0$ and $\lim_{\bar{\ell}_t \to 1+a}(\partial D/\partial \bar{\ell}_t) = \infty$ for $B_{t-1} > 0$. As may be expected, $D(\bar{\ell}_t, B_{t-1})$ also depends on the desire for households to smooth consumption over the two seasons. In particular, an increase in B_{t-1} and β both increase the loan requirement $D(\cdot)$.

4.2. Terms of the Interlinked Contract

Consider therefore a typical landlord's problem in the lean season, which entails the choice of (i) an amount of lean season consumption loan D_t, and (ii) an amount of effective labor service to be demanded from each borrowing household $\bar{\ell}_t$. The landlord has rational expectations about the spot market wage w_t in the harvest season, and correctly anticipates the minimal loan requirement and child labor supply decisions of the n_{it} households. In the harvest season, the landlord hires any additional workers (ℓ_{ht}) from the spot labor market at wage w_t that may be required to maximize profits given the effective labor input already available, $n_{it}\bar{\ell}_t$. Beginning with the harvest season decision-making problem, and taking $\{D_t, \bar{\ell}_t\}$ as given, we have

$$\max_{\ell_{ht}} pF(n_{it}\bar{\ell}_t + \ell_{ht}, T) - w_t\ell_{ht} - n_{it}(1+r)D_t.$$

We have thus

$$pF_L(L_{it}, T) = w_t \tag{16}$$

16 To see this, note that $D^1(\tilde{\ell}, B_{t-1}) = D^2(\tilde{\ell}, B_{t-1})$. Since $D^1(\cdot)$ and $D^2(\cdot)$ are individually twice continuously differentiable and strictly convex in $\bar{\ell}_t$, convexity of $D(\cdot)$ follows since $(\partial D^1(\bar{\ell}_t, B_{t-1})/\partial \bar{\ell}_t)\big|_{\bar{\ell}_t = \tilde{\ell}} = (\partial D^2(\bar{\ell}_t, B_{t-1})/\partial \bar{\ell}_t)\big|_{\bar{\ell}_t = \tilde{\ell}} = B_{t-1}\beta(\alpha+\beta)(1-\tilde{\ell})^{-1-\beta(\alpha+\beta)}$.

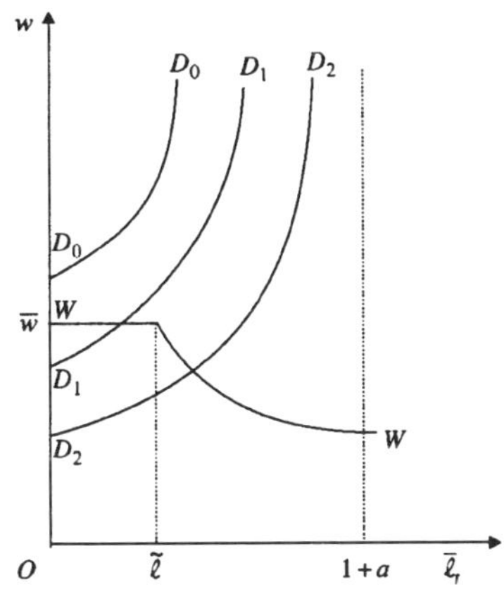

Figure 2. Harvest season spot market wage and interlinkage.

where profit maximizing effective labor service $L_{it}(w_t,p)$ depends only on the spot market wage, with

$$\frac{\partial L_{it}(w_t,p)}{\partial w_t}=\frac{1}{pF_{LL}(L_{it}(w_t,p),T)}<0,\quad \frac{\partial L_{it}(w_t,p)}{\partial p}=-\frac{F_L(L_{it}(w_t,p),T)}{pF_{LL}(L_{it}(w_t,p),T)}>0.$$

The lean season decision problem of the landlord can accordingly be simplified as follows:

$$\Pi_t=\max_{D_t,\bar{\ell}_t} pF(L_{it}(w_t,p),T)-w_t[L_{it}(w_t,p)-n_{it}\bar{\ell}_t]-n_{it}(1+r)D_t$$
$$\text{s.t.}\quad D_t=D(\bar{\ell}_t,B_{t-1}).$$

Equivalently, the landlord maximizes wage savings net of interest plus principal costs of the consumption loan in the lean season, $n_{it}\left(w_t\bar{\ell}_t-(1+r)D(\bar{\ell}_t,B_{t-1})\right)$ by choice of $\bar{\ell}_t$, with

$$\Pi_t=\max_{\bar{\ell}_t}[pF(L_{it}(w_t,p),T)-w_tL_{it}(w_t,p)]+n_{it}\left[w_t\bar{\ell}_t-(1+r)D(\bar{\ell}_t,B_{t-1})\right].\quad (17)$$

The first order conditions are given by

$$w_t\le(1+r)\frac{\partial D}{\partial\bar{\ell}_t},\quad \left(w_t-(1+r)\frac{\partial D}{\partial\bar{\ell}_t}\right)\bar{\ell}_t=0.\quad (18)$$

Equation (18) simply requires that marginal wage savings be equal to the marginal cost of consumption loan for an interior maximum. In addition, since $\partial D(\bar{\ell}_t,B_{t-1})/\partial\bar{\ell}_t$ is monotonically increasing with no discrete jumps (equation (15)), there always exist a unique (corner/interior) solution to the landlord's problem.

Figure 2 illustrates the upward sloping *DD* schedules plot a family of marginal loan requirement schedules $(1+r)\partial D(\cdot)/\partial\bar{\ell}_t$, with successively decreasing values of B_{t-1} from D_oD_o to D_2D_2. The downward sloping schedule *WW* is a translation of the *WW* schedule in Figure 1, and traces out the relationship between the spot market wage and $\bar{\ell}_t$. Note that since the DD schedules asymptotically approaches infinity as $\bar{\ell}_t$ approaches $1+a$ (equation (15)), while the WW schedule is nonincreasing, there is never more than one intersection point.

Starting from one end of the spectrum, where inheritance B_{t-1} is large enough so that the D_oD_o schedule applies, we have a case where the two schedules D_oD_o and WW do not intersect. In other words, landlords refrain from interlinked transaction, as wage savings are insufficient to cover marginal loan costs (equations (15) and (18)):

$$w_t|_{\bar{\ell}_t=0} = \bar{w} < (1+r)\frac{\partial D}{\partial \bar{\ell}_t}|_{\bar{\ell}_t=0} \Leftrightarrow B_{t-1} > \frac{\bar{w}}{\beta(1+r)(\alpha+\beta)} \equiv \hat{B}_0.$$

The D_1D_1 schedule illustrates the intermediate case where B_{t-1} is relatively small, where there is active labor-credit exchange between landlords and households, although the amount of outstanding debt is not high enough to justify putting children to work. From equations (15) and (18), this applies when

$$w_t|_{\bar{\ell}_t=0} = \bar{w} \geq (1+r)\frac{\partial D}{\partial \bar{\ell}_t}|_{\bar{\ell}_t=0}, \quad \text{and} \quad w_t|_{\bar{\ell}_t=\tilde{\ell}} = \bar{w} \leq (1+r)\frac{\partial D}{\partial \bar{\ell}_t}|_{\bar{\ell}_t=\tilde{\ell}}$$

or,

$$\hat{B}_0 \geq B_{t-1} > \frac{\bar{w}}{\beta(1+r)(\alpha+\beta)(1-\tilde{\ell})^{-1-\beta(\alpha+\beta)}} \equiv \hat{B}_k.$$

The parameter $1-\tilde{\ell}$ is thus key to determining the distance between the right and left extremes of this range of inheritance, B_{t-1}, wherein interlinkage need not imply child labor. Since $1-\tilde{\ell} \equiv a(\alpha+\beta)/(1-\alpha)$, strong household preference against child labor $(1-\alpha)$ and relatively inefficient child labor (a) both contribute to widen the range of inheritance wherein children are not put to work in order to service outstanding debts.

The D_2D_2 schedule illustrates a third possibility, where B_{t-1} is small enough for the incidence of child labor to be strictly positive, and the equilibrium spot market wage is strictly less than the no child labor benchmark, $\bar{w}$. Any additional reduction in B_{t-1} shifts the D_2D_2 downwards even further. The equilibrium spot market wage thus decreases with decreasing inheritance B_{t-1}, since from equations (15), (16) and (18),

$$\frac{\partial w_t}{\partial B_{t-1}} = -pF_{LL}(1-\alpha)n \Big/ \left[B_{t-1}\left(\frac{\eta(1-\alpha)}{1+a\ell_t^k} + (1+\beta)\frac{1+\beta(1+\beta)}{1+a-\bar{\ell}_t}\right)\right] > 0,$$

at given land endowment for each employer, and $\eta \equiv -d\log pF_L/d\log L_{it}$ denotes the elasticity of labor demand in the harvest season. We have

Proposition 3 *There exist two critical levels of transfers, respectively* $\hat{B}_0$ *and* $\hat{B}_k$, *with* $\hat{B}_0 > \hat{B}_k$, *such that for all feasible values of*

1. $B_{t-1} \geq \hat{B}_0$, *landlords do not engage in interlinked transaction, and child labor does not exist. The equilibrium harvest season spot market wage is* $\bar{w}$;

2. $B_{t-1} \in (\hat{B}_0, \hat{B}_k]$, *landlords engage in interlinked transactions, but child labor does not exist. The equilibrium harvest season spot market wage is* $\bar{w}$;

3. $B_{t-1} < \hat{B}_k$, *landlords engage in interlinked transactions, and the incidence of child labor is strictly positive. The equilibrium harvest season spot market wage is strictly less than* $\bar{w}$. *Furthermore, the equilibrium spot wage is strictly increasing in* B_{t-1}.

Note that the two critical threshold levels of inheritance, $\hat{B}_0$ and $\hat{B}_k$, are both increasing in p and $1/\beta(1+r)$. Thus, the tighter the labor market, or the larger the size of credit market imperfection, the more likely that any given B_{t-1} is less than the two thresholds.

4.3. Welfare Effects

We now turn to an evaluation of the static and intergenerational welfare effects of debt bondage. Within a generation, and given bequests, the welfare of households depends critically on how aggregate labor supply, and hence the equilibrium spot wage, respond to household participation in debt bondage. In particular, from the participation constraint, debt bondage worsens the welfare of generation t households if and only if $\ell_t^k \geq 0$, or $B_{t-1} \leq \hat{B}_k$, since

$$\begin{aligned} V_I(D_t, \bar{\ell}_t, B_{t-1}, w_t) &= V_0(B_{t-1}, w_t) \\ &\leq V_0(B_{t-1}, \bar{w}) \equiv \bar{V}_0(B_{t-1}) \end{aligned}$$

if and only if $w_t \leq \bar{w}$. To recall, $\bar{V}_0(B_{t-1})$ denotes indirect household utility when households do not participate in debt bondage (Proposition 1). Since the welfare of households is pinned down to its reservation level in general equilibrium, the inequality above holds despite the fact that one of the virtues of interlinked contracts is precisely to smooth consumption over lean and harvest seasons. In comparison, landlords reap the benefits of a lower spot wage, and the additional profits derived from lean season consumption loans (equation (17)).

We have thus a situation where households voluntarily participate in debt bondage, and child labor employment arises specifically to repay outstanding debts when inheritance is sufficiently small $B_{t-1} < \hat{B}_k$. Yet, the same condition also ensures that the contribution of child labor to harvest work necessarily leaves households worse off, compared to when there is no access to credit and no child labor. Two interrelated features of the model are in fact in play here: (i) coordination failure among households, and (ii) rational expectations on the part of landlords. The first problem is associated with the failure to coordinate actions among households to limit bonded child labor supply and thus to raise the harvest wage. The result is therefore a lower reservation utility for all households which choose to opt out of interlinked transactions.

Second, landlords correctly anticipate that any ex-ante commitment by a single household, or groups of households, to refrain from putting children to work will fall through in the peak period due to the coordination failure. The resulting terms of the interlinked contract accordingly embody this rational expectation, so that a low reservation utility shows up in the debt bondage contract as a lower actual utility for bonded households. In sum:

Corollary 1 *The welfare of generation t households engaged in debt bondage* $V_t(D_t, \bar{\ell}_t, B_{t-1}, w_t)$ *is given by* $V_0(B_{t-1}, w_t)$, *with*

1. $V_0(B_{t-1}, w_t) = V_0(B_{t-1}, \bar{w}) = \bar{V}_0(B_{t-1})$ *for* $B_{t-1} \geq \hat{B}_k$,

2. $V_0(B_{t-1}, w_t) < \bar{V}_0(B_{t-1})$ *for* $B_{t-1} < \hat{B}_k$.

Turning now to intergenerational welfare effects, recall from the participation constraint that the welfare of a generation $t+1$ household, whether or not it participates in debt bondage, is given by

$$V_0(B_t, w_{t+1}) = \log B_t + \beta\big((\alpha + \beta)\log w_{t+1} + K\big),$$

where K is defined in Proposition 1. As such, transfers decision of a generation t household can affect the welfare of the next generation via two distinct routes. First, a higher B_t has a direct impact on the minimal level of lean season consumption as $c_{lt+1} = B_t$ for households that do not resort to borrowing from landlords. The second effect never runs contrary to the first, and operates through the indirect impact of an increase in B_t on the spot labor market wage, w_{t+1}. From Proposition 3, $w_{t+1} = \bar{w}$ is invariant to small changes in B_t for all $B_t \geq \hat{B}_k$. Otherwise, for $B_t < \hat{B}_k$, a lower B_t decreases the spot market wage w_{t+1}, as child labor employment rises reflecting an increase in the size of outstanding debt.

Thus, to determine the intergenerational externality generated by debt bondage in generation t, it suffices to confirm that the savings of generation t households for generation $t+1$, B_t, is less than the benchmark $\bar{B}_o$ which would apply if generation t households do not engage in interlinkage. To this end, equations (10), (14), (15) and (18) jointly imply that given any feasible B_{t-1}, $B_t = B(B_{t-1})$ is given by[17]

$$\begin{cases} \beta\bar{w}/(\alpha+\beta) \equiv \bar{B}_o, & \text{if } B_{t-1} \geq \hat{B}_0; \\ \bar{B}_o\left(\frac{B_{t-1}}{\hat{B}_0}\right)^{\frac{1}{1+\beta(\alpha+\beta)}} \equiv B^1(B_{t-1}), & \text{if } \hat{B}_o > B_{t-1} \geq \hat{B}_k; \\ \bar{B}_o(1-\tilde{\ell})\left(\frac{B_{t-1}}{\hat{B}_k}\left(\frac{w_t}{\bar{w}}\right)^{\beta(1+\beta)}\right)^{\frac{1}{1+\beta(1+\beta)}} \equiv B^2(B_{t-1}), & \text{otherwise.} \end{cases} \tag{19}$$

It is straightforward to verify that:[18]

17 The dependence of B_t on the price level, the number of agrarian households, preference and technological parameters are suppressed for notational economy.

18 If $B_{t-1} \geq \hat{B}_0$, $B_t = \bar{B}_o$ from equation (19) since generation t is free from interlinkage. If $\hat{B}_o > B_{t-1} \geq \hat{B}_k$, however, it follows from equation (19) that $B_t = B^1(B_{t-1}) < \bar{B}_o$. Finally, since $w_{t+1} \leq \bar{w}$ holds with strictly inequality whenever $B(B_{t-1}) < \hat{B}_k$, $B^2(B_{t-1}) < \bar{B}_o$ again from equation (19). Consequently, Corollary 2 follows upon observing that V_o is increasing both in B_t and w_{t+1}.

Corollary 2 *The welfare of generation* $t+1$ *households engaged in interlinkage* $V_l(D_{t+1}, \bar{\ell}_{t+1}, B_t, w_{t+1})$ *is given by* $V_0(B(B_{t-1}), w_{t+1})$ *from the participation constraint, and*

1. $V_0(B(B_{t-1}), w_{t+1}) \leq \bar{V}_0(\beta\bar{w}/(\alpha+\beta))$ *for* $B_{t-1} \geq \hat{B}_o$,
2. $V_0(B(B_{t-1}), w_{t+1}) < \bar{V}_0(\beta\bar{w}/(\alpha+\beta))$ *for* $\hat{B}_o > B_{t-1} \geq \hat{B}_k$,
3. $V_0(B(B_{t-1}), w_{t+1}) < \bar{V}_0(\beta\bar{w}/(\alpha+\beta))$ *for* $B_{t-1} < \hat{B}_k$.

5. Dynamics and Steady State

Our findings so far take transfers decision of generation $t-1$ as given. It remains to show how the incidence of child labor and the welfare of households that engage in debt bondage evolve over time, and whether the range of inheritance $B_{t-1} \in [0, \hat{B}_k)$ that entails positive incidence of child labor is purely transitional.

Figures 3(a) and (b) plot B_t as displayed in equation (19) with respect to B_{t-1}. Note that the B_t schedule has two kinks, respectively at $\hat{B}_0$ and $\hat{B}_k$.[19] From equation (19), the transfer schedules $B^1(B_{t-1})$ and $B^2(B_{t-1})$, respectively for inheritance $B_{t-1} \in [\hat{B}_k, \hat{B}_0)$ and $B_{t-1} \in [0, \hat{B}_k)$, are both strictly increasing and concave in B_{t-1}. An interior steady state is given by the intersection of the 45° line and the B_t schedule. It can be readily verified that an interior steady state $B^* = (B|B(B) = B)$ exists, is uniquely determined and dynamically stable,[20] with $(\partial B_t/\partial B_{t-1})|_{B_{t-1}=B^*} < 1$.[21]

To examine the geometry of Figure 3 in greater detail, note that the range of inheritance B_{t-1} is divided into three subsets. For $B_{t-1} \geq \hat{B}_0$, transfers at time t is independent of inheritance at $\beta\bar{w}/(\alpha+\beta)$ and debt bondage does not arise. Indeed, the unique steady state B^* cannot be greater than $\hat{B}_0$ if and only if $B(\hat{B}_0)$ is less than $\hat{B}_0$:

$$B(\hat{B}_0) = \frac{\beta}{\alpha+\beta}\bar{w} < \frac{\bar{w}}{\beta(1+r)(\alpha+\beta)} = \hat{B}_0$$

or equivalently, if and only if credit market imperfection is sufficiently acute:

---

19 This follows from the definitions of $B^1(B_{t-1})$ and $B^2(B_{t-1})$ in equation (19). Routine manipulation yields $(\partial B^1(B_{t-1})/\partial B_{t-1})|_{B_{t-1}=\hat{B}_0} > 0$. In addition, $(\partial B^2(B_{t-1})/\partial B_{t-1})|_{B_{t-1}=\hat{B}_k} < (\partial B^1(B_{t-1})/\partial B_{t-1})|_{B_{t-1}=\hat{B}_k}$.

20 The proof of these claims is relegated to Appendix B

21 To see this, note that

$$\left.\frac{\partial B_t}{\partial B_{t-1}}\right|_{B_t=B_{t-1}} = \begin{cases} 0, & \text{if } B_{t-1} \geq \hat{B}_0; \\ \dfrac{1}{1+\beta(\alpha+\beta)} < 1, & \text{if } \hat{B}_0 > B_{t-1} \geq \hat{B}_k; \\ \left(\dfrac{\eta(1-\alpha)}{1+a\ell^{*k}} + \dfrac{1+\beta}{1+a-\ell^*}\right) \Big/ \left(\dfrac{\eta(1-\alpha)}{1+a\ell^{*k}} + \dfrac{(1+\beta)(1+\beta(1+\beta))}{1+a-\ell^*}\right) < 1, & \text{otherwise} \end{cases}$$

where an asterisk denotes steady-state values.

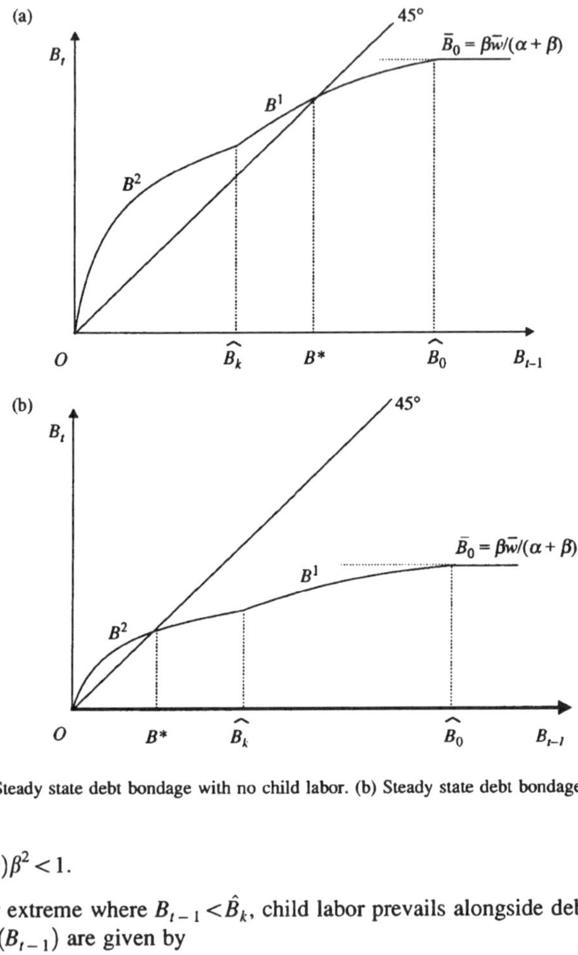

Figure 3. (a) Steady state debt bondage with no child labor. (b) Steady state debt bondage with bonded child labor.

$$(1+r)\beta^2 < 1.$$

At the other extreme where $B_{t-1} < \hat{B}_k$, child labor prevails alongside debt bondage, and transfers $B^2(B_{t-1})$ are given by

$$\bar{B}_0(1-\tilde{\ell})\left(\frac{B_{t-1}}{\hat{B}_k}\left(\frac{w_t}{\bar{w}}\right)^{\beta(1+\beta)}\right)^{1/1+\beta(1+\beta)}$$

from equation (19). It follows, therefore, that child labor arising out of debt bondage exists in a steady state, and B^* falls within the range $[0, \hat{B}_k)$ if $B(\hat{B}_k) < \hat{B}_k$, or

$$(1+r)\beta^2 < \left(\frac{a(\alpha+\beta)}{1-\alpha}\right)^{\beta(\alpha+\beta)} \tag{20}$$

by definition of $\hat{B}_k$ and equation (19). For intermediate values of $B_{t-1} \in [\hat{B}_k, \hat{B}_0)$, wherein debt bondage prevails but with no child labor, equation (19) gives:

$$B_t = \bar{B}_o \left(\frac{B_{t-1}}{\hat{B}_0} \right)^{1/(1+\beta(\alpha+\beta))}.$$

It follows that for child labor to be a transitory phenomenon even in the presence of interlinkage, the extent of credit market imperfection must not be too severe, with

$$\left(\frac{a(\alpha+\beta)}{1-\alpha} \right)^{\beta(\alpha+\beta)} \leq (1+r)\beta^2 < 1. \tag{21}$$

This is shown in Figure 3(a), wherein the inequality in (21) above holds, and child labor is purely transitory even though and debt bondage prevails in a steady state.

In contrast, consider a decrease in β (and hence $(1+r)\beta^2$), or an increase in preference weight attached to consumption α until the inequality in equation (20), requiring that credit market imperfection be sufficiently acute, is satisfied. The steady state level of inheritance is depicted in Figure 3(b), and shows a $B(B_{t-1})$ schedule that is shifted downwards reflecting the change in α, β, or both.[22]

Proposition 4 *In the presence of interlinked transactions, there always exist a unique and dynamically stable steady level of intergenerational transfers, B^*. Incidence of bonded child labor is strictly positive in a steady state if and only if*

$$(1+r)\beta^2 < \left(\frac{a(\alpha+\beta)}{1-\alpha} \right)^{\beta(\alpha+\beta)}.$$

In addition, steady state intergenerational transfers B^* in the presence of bonded child labor is strictly less than $\bar{B}_o$, and is given by

$$B^* = \frac{\beta w^*}{\alpha+\beta}((1+r)\beta^2))^{1/(\beta(1+\beta))} \left(\frac{a(\alpha+\beta)}{1-\alpha} \right)^{(1-\alpha)/(1+\beta)} < \bar{B}_o.$$

where $w^* < \bar{w}$ is the corresponding steady state spot wage. The utility of the typical household in a steady state is strictly less than

$$\bar{V}_0 \left(\frac{\beta \bar{w}}{\alpha+\beta} \right).$$

Profit of the representative landlord is strictly greater than

$$F\left(\frac{n}{N}, T \right) - \bar{w}\frac{n}{N}.$$

---

22 Note that the dynamics and steady state of the model illustrated here applies in the absence of factor accumulation (such as that of human capital and population growth), and factor mobility (such as interregional migration). In Section 7, the basic model is extended to account for each one of these possibilities.

6. Trade Sanctions and Child Labor

We are now in a position to consider the oft-noted policy prescription in the face of child labor in debt bondage—a trade sanction on countries that export products made with child labor. Based on the model, we argue that wholesale implementation of such measures without due considerations of the underlying agrarian institutions that bring out the incidence of bonded child labor, can have impact and dynamic effects that run in opposite directions. Indeed, the results to follow apply whenever countries inflicted with bonded child labor face declining agricultural terms of trade. Thus, agricultural subsidies that encourage production in food importing/exporting countries, or an increase trade preferences given to countries where child labor is not an issue, can both have qualitatively similar welfare and child labor effects as a trade ban.

Figure 4 illustrates the impact effect of a ban or a tax on the export of the agrarian output. The resulting reduction in the terms of trade shifts the *WW* schedule downwards. The trade ban thus have the anticipated impact—the reduction in the demand for agrarian labor reduces landlords' incentives to engage in interlinked transactions, and the equilibrium labor service requirement $\bar{\ell}_t$ for any given level of B_{t-1} decreases.

For any given B_{t-1}, a trade ban issued at the beginning of time period t decreases the spot wage. Thus, intergenerational transfers B_t for every given B_{t-1} falls, and the subsequent generation $(t+1)$ will be willing to sacrifice even more harvest season labor services to service consumption loan incurred in the lean season. This is shown in Figure 4 as a downward shift of the D_2D_2 schedule, which indicates that the cost of extending consumption loans to households fall as inheritance from the previous period continues to decline. In fact, Proposition 4 guarantees that the steady state level of intergenerational transfer is proportional to the prevailing harvest season wage rate. Meanwhile, the steady state level of indebtedness ℓ^* in terms of the number of effective units of labor services

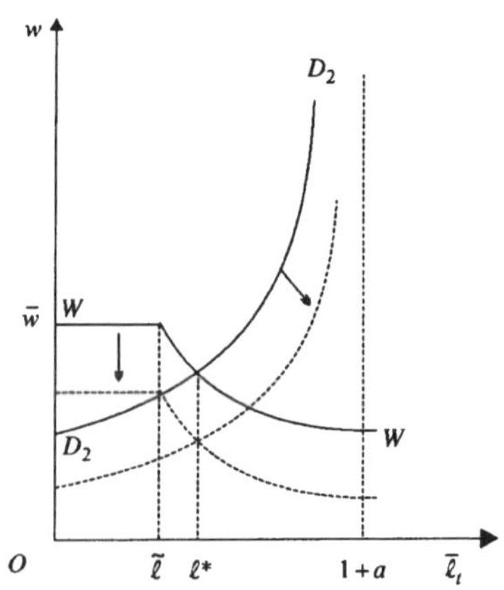

Figure 4. Impact and dynamic effects of trade sanction.

owed to the landlord is in fact independent of p, since equations (15), (18) and (19) jointly imply that

$$\ell^* = \begin{cases} 0, & \text{if } B^* \geq \hat{B}_0 \\ 1 - \left((1+r)\beta^2\right)^{1/\beta(\alpha+\beta)}, & \text{if } B^* \in [\hat{B}_k, \hat{B}_0) \\ 1 + a - \dfrac{1+\beta}{\alpha+\beta}\left((1+r)\beta^2\right)^{1/(\beta(1+\beta))}\left(\dfrac{a(\alpha+\beta)}{1-\alpha}\right)^{(1-\alpha)/(1+\beta)}, & \text{if } B^* < \hat{B}_k. \end{cases}$$

We thus have:

Proposition 5 *A trade barrier that adversely affects the price level p of the agrarian output has*

1. *an impact effect that is effective in temporarily deterring the incidence of bonded child labor so long as $B(\hat{B}_k) < \hat{B}_k$, and*
2. *a dynamic effect that offsets the impact effect, leaving the steady state incidence of bonded child labor strictly unaltered, but the steady state welfare of the household strictly lower than when free trade prevails.*

Proposition 5 highlights the interactions between the short-term labor market implications of policy interventions to combat child labor, and the corresponding long-term consequences that depend on the institution of debt bondage. In addition, it shows that rather than relying on trade-based intervention that impacts the agrarian terms of trade p, measures that decrease the size of credit market imperfection (an increase in $(1+r)\beta^2$) will be effective in reducing size of $\bar{\ell}$ in a steady state, and hence the incidence of bonded child labor.

7. Discussion

Our analysis began with three observations with respect to the vulnerability of agrarian households to debt bondage: the lack of access to credit, the lack of collateral other than the promise of labor services, and the inability to collectively bargain and coordinate child labor supply. Within a generation, bonded child labor arises out of coordination failure, and the associated downward pressure on the spot wage (hence the welfare of households that refrain from bondage) is exploited by landlords via the participation constraint. Across generations, the same child labor induced wage reduction puts checks on intergenerational transfers, and perpetuates the institution of debt bondage.

We are now in a position to relax a number assumptions in the basic setup.[23] The objective here is to develop additional intuitions and insights with respect to the effects of debt bondage in a more general setting.

---

23 We are grateful to an anonymous referee for suggesting these extensions.

7.1. Heterogeneity

One extension that naturally suggests itself is that of heterogeneity amongst households. Specifically, suppose that inheritance from the previous generation differs across households. From the participation constraint, and the decision problem of the landlord, the equilibrium number of households who borrow, along with the incidence of child labor, will depend critically on the left-hand tail of the distribution of inheritance. In addition, since inheritance is itself endogenous, the distribution of inheritance varies both with time, and with the incidence of debt bondage in the generation(s) prior. The question that becomes important, therefore, is whether debt bondage and debt-induced child labor can continue to prevail as a long run equilibrium outcome for all landless households, so long as credit market imperfection is sufficiently acute (Proposition 4).

To see that the answer is in fact in the affirmative, note that at any time t, a household whose predecessor remained free from bondage at time $t-1$ inherits $B_{t-1} = \beta w_{t-1}/(\alpha+\beta)$. For this household to continue to remain free from debt bondage, it must be the case, from equation (18), that

$$B_{t-1} = \frac{\beta w_{t-1}}{\alpha+\beta} > \frac{w_t}{\beta(1+r)(\alpha+\beta)}.$$

In a steady state, where $w_{t-1} = w_t$, the corresponding condition becomes,

$$\beta^2(1+r) > 1,$$

an impossibility given the condition stated in Proposition 4, with $\beta^2(1+r) < (1-\bar{\ell})^{\beta(\alpha+\beta)} < 1$. Thus, while the sequence in which households eventually participate in debt bondage may change, heterogeneity in starting values of inheritance alone is not sufficient to affect the long run equilibrium outcome elaborated in Section 5.

7.2. Endogenous Fertility

Since labor services served as the only available means of debt repayment in our analysis, a natural question arises as to how and whether households may tailor their fertility decisions, and hence the maximal household supply of child labor, based on the anticipation of the need to repay outstanding debts. To fix ideas, let m_t denote the number of children in the household, and e be the amount of parental labor time required to care for each child.[24] Let preferences of a generation t household be represented by the utility function

$$\log c_{lt} + \beta\big(\alpha \log c_{ht} + (1-\alpha)\log(1-\ell_t^k)\big) + \gamma \log m_t + \beta^2 \log B_t, \tag{22}$$

24 See Hazan and Berdugo (2002) for the interplay between fertility, child labor (in the absence of debt bondage), and the transition process of economic growth, with particular attention to the possibility of development traps and the role of a ban on child labor on the transition process. Doepke (2001) also entertains the role of endogenous fertility in the context of child labor in the absence of debt bondage and economic growth, and provides several illustrative country examples of policies targeting child labor.

where $c_{lt} = (B_{t-1} + D_t)/(1 + m_t)$, and $c_{ht} = (w_t(1 - em_t + am_t\ell_t^k - \bar{\ell}_t) - m_tB_t)/(1 + m_t)$ denote respectively per capita consumption level during the lean and the harvest season for a household participating in debt bondage. Assume in addition that $e < 1$, and $\gamma > \beta(1 - \alpha + \beta)$. The former implies that $1/e > 1$ is the maximal number of children that the parent can care for, while the latter ensures that the utility gains from having one more child is sufficiently large for m_t to be positive for a utility maximizing household, with $e \geq 0$.

By inspection of equation (22), the costs of increasing the size of the household involve the direct costs of parental marketable labor time forgone (w_tem_t), along with an reduction in per capita consumption, all else equal. The benefits of increasing the size of the household include household preference for children as parameterized by $\gamma > 0$, and the increase in full income as the number of children increases $(am_t\ell_t^k)$.

Given inherited transfers B_{t-1} and the size of adult population n_{t-1} as given at time period t, it can be readily verified that the utility maximizing fertility and child labor supply in the presence of bondage simultaneously solve:

$$m_t\ell_t^k = m_t\left(1 - \frac{1-\alpha}{1+\beta}\frac{a-e}{a}\right) - \frac{1-\alpha}{1+\beta}\frac{1-\bar{\ell}_t}{a} > 0, \tag{23}$$

$$\frac{1+\beta\alpha}{1+m_t} = \frac{\beta(1+\beta)(a-e)}{1+(a-e)m_t - \bar{\ell}_t} + \frac{\gamma - \beta(1-\alpha+\beta)}{m_t} \tag{24}$$

if $\bar{\ell}_t$ is sufficiently high so that the right-hand side of equation (23) above is strictly positive.[25] Finally,

$$B_t = \frac{\beta}{1+\beta}\frac{w_t(1+(a-e)m_t - \bar{\ell}_t)}{m_t}. \tag{25}$$

With marginal productivity pricing in the harvest season, the spot market wage is given by

$$w_t = pF_L(n_{t-1}(1 + am_t\ell_t^k)/N, T). \tag{26}$$

Routine manipulation of equations (23)–(26) yields a number of additional observations. To begin with, so long as the second order condition is satisfied, bondage has now two mutually reinforcing effects on household welfare within a generation, via the size of the child labor population, and the amount of time each child devotes to harvest work. It can be readily verified that increasing indebtedness (via an increase in $\bar{\ell}_t$) provides incentives for households to increase the full income of the family by increasing the number of children if an additional child increases the full income of the household, or if $a - e > 0$ (equation (24)).[26]

---

25 An in-depth analysis of the intricacies involved in the transition to long run equilibrium when population and bonded child labor are both endogenous warrants a separate full-length paper. The case we identify here applies whenever indebtedness, or $\bar{\ell}_t$ is sufficiently high so that ℓ_t^k is strictly positive.

26 To see this, implicit differentiation of equation (24) yields $\partial m_t/\partial\bar{\ell}_t = \Delta\beta(1+\beta)(a-e)/(1+(a-e)m_t - \bar{\ell}_t)^2$ where $\Delta > 0$ if and only if the second order conditions of utility maximization are satisfied.

This first round effect puts downward pressure on wages. With wages lower, the balance between the disutility of child labor work and household consumption is once again tilted, so that each child will be spending more time doing harvest work. Thus, endogenizing the fertility decision in the context of debt bondage only strengthens our earlier conclusion that coordination failure on the part of households implies that households are worse off within generation.

Across generations, the same increase in $\bar{\ell}_t$, and the subsequent reduction in the spot wage at time t naturally reduces the amount of household income that can be devoted to each member of the household's offspring. In addition, from equation (24), full income of the household per offspring $(1 + (a - e)m_t - \bar{\ell}_t)/m_t$ is strictly decreasing in the number of offsprings. Debt bondage thus perpetuates as B_t strictly decreases with $\bar{\ell}_t$, and the need for consumption smoothing for the next generation $(t + 1)$ rises. A complete analysis of the dynamics of population growth and debt bondage is beyond the scope of this paper, but these preliminary observations suggest that incorporating fertility decisions may in fact reinforce the forces at work that contribute to the prevalence of debt bondage in a steady state.

7.3. *Exit Options*

Yet another way in which the population of landless households may vary in the face of debt bondage is rural–urban migration. Consider therefore the problem of an altruistic household head faced with the decision between providing (costly) education for the child, with the anticipation that this will enhance the urban employment prospects of the child when he migrates upon reaching adulthood. Specifically, let the cost of education be C per season, and the urban wage be given by θw^*, where θ denotes the innate ability of the child. To make the problem as transparent as possible, let education be a full time endeavor, so that the utility of such a household is given by

$$U^e = \log(c_{lt} - C) + \beta(\alpha \log(c_{ht} - C) + \beta \log \theta w^*), \tag{27}$$

where c_{lt} and c_{ht} are defined as in equations (2) and (6) above, depending on whether or not the household is engaged in debt bondage.

Making use of equation (27), the definitions of V_I and V_0 in Propositions 1 and 2, along with the participation constraint,[27] it is now a simple matter to see that a necessary and sufficient condition for households to refrain from putting children to work is[28]

27 Note that there are now four groups of households. V_I and V_0 are the indirect utilities of households in which children do not undertake education, but respectively participate and refrain from debt bondage. Let V_I^e and V_0^e denote the indirect utilities of the two groups of households in which children undertake education, where the subscripts I and 0 again, respectively denote those households that participate in bondage and those that do not. Formally, there are thus two participation constraints, requiring $V_I^e \geq V_0^e$, and $V_I \geq V_0$, depending on the education decision of the household.

28 Equation (28) follows from the observation that landlords set debt bondage contract terms such that the two participation constraints are just satisfied. The equilibrium indirect utilities of households that undertake education is thus just V_0^e, and V_0 otherwise.

$$B_{t-1} - C \geq B_{t-1}\left(\frac{\alpha}{\alpha+\beta}\frac{w_t}{w_t - C}\right)^{\beta\alpha}\left(\frac{\beta}{\alpha+\beta}\frac{w_t}{\theta w^*}\right)^{\beta^2}. \tag{28}$$

In other words, education will be the preferred option if and only if inherited savings B_{t-1} is sufficiently large, and if innate ability is sufficiently high. What is less clear, however, is how the spot wage plays a role in education decision-making. Contrary to what may be expected, subsequent to a reduction in w_t—due either to trade sanctions, or debt bondage itself as child labor supply from other household rises—the right-hand side of equation (28) increases if and only if the following inequality is satisfied:

$$\frac{\beta w_t}{\alpha+\beta} < C. \tag{29}$$

In other words, a reduction in rural wage can, in fact, stifle the incentives on the part of households to allow children to undertake education and migrate to the urban area. The intuition here goes back to our underlying theme of credit market imperfection. Specifically, a reduction in w_t has two opposing effects. First, it reduces B_t, and encourages the household in favor of education and migration as the child's income will be θw^*. However, the same reduction in w_t also decreases the household's ability to pay for education, as the marginal utility of an increase in household earnings rises. The latter effect dominates, naturally, whenever wages w_t are sufficiently low to begin with, as the inequality in equation (29) suggests.

8. Conclusion

By accounting for the principal-agent interactions between landlords-cum-moneylenders and agrarian households, this paper examines the institution child labor in the face of debt bondage. The model takes as building blocks (i) asymmetric access to credit by households and landlords, (ii) interlinked transactions that exchanges consumption credit for labor services and (iii) inability to coordinate actions and negotiate interlinked contract terms among agrarian households. In view of recent campaigns to eradicate bonded child labor, a basic model is formulated to address a number of questions. Can poverty and credit market imperfection induced interlinked credit-labor market transactions be identified as root causes of bonded child labor? Can a reverse causality running from bonded child labor and poverty be identified? Can debt bondage be a steady state phenomenon? Finally, to what extent can international pressure such as a trade ban act as an effective tool in lowering the incidence of bonded child labor?

We find that as long as the degree of asymmetry in credit access is large enough, the answer to the first three questions are in the affirmative, and debt bondage turns out to be an important feature in the cycle of poverty and bonded child labor in agrarian economies. In particular, we show that the inability of agrarian households to coordinate actions play a key role in the analysis. Thus, basic labor rights such as freedom of association, and the rights to organize, complement efforts to eradicate forced and bonded child labor. These observations are consistent with the recent campaign to improve basic labor and human rights worldwide. Indeed, freedom of association, rights to organize, forced labor, and minimum wage constitute four core labor standards of the ILO.

Our analysis also highlights the role of agrarian institutions in determining the effectiveness of policy measures to combat child labor. In particular, while standard disincentives, such as a trade sanction, can be expected to reduce child labor on impact, the dynamic effect dictates that these policy measures have limited impact on the incidence of bonded child labor per se, and an unambiguous negative impact on the welfare of agrarian households. These results echo similar findings in the search of market-based mechanisms to eliminate child labor,[29] in that unless measures are in place to enforce basic labor rights and employers' choice of technique of production, wholesale implementation of policy measures that put downward pressure on labor demand in developing countries can be counter-productive.

Appendix A

We show here that our findings remain robust even in an explicitly multi-period setting for each generation, wherein each generation lasts T years. Specifically, we show that as long as bequests from the previous generation is less than $\bar{w}/(\beta(\alpha+\beta))$, households' savings decision during the harvest season of each year is observationally equivalent to one in which households' planning horizon is cut short to include only the current harvest season, and the lean season of the following year, as displayed in the text.

To this end, let the lifetime utility of a household (as before, made up of an adult and a child) with T-period life be

$$W = \sum_{t=1}^{T} \beta^{2(t-1)}(\log c_{lt} + \beta(\alpha \log c_{ht} + (1-\alpha)\log(1-\ell_t^k))) + \beta^2 T \log B_T,$$

where B_T denotes bequests to the next generation. Also, let (i) B_0 be the amount of bequests available from the previous generation, (ii) S_t be the amount of lean season savings at year $t = 1, \ldots, T$, and (iii) B_t, $t = 1, \ldots, T-1$ be the amount of harvest season savings at year $t = 1, \ldots, T$. The lean and harvest seasons' budget constraint of the household free from debt bondage can thus be written as

$$c_{lt} = B_{t-1} - S_t, \quad c_{h1} = w_1(1 + a\ell_t^k) + S_t - B_t, \quad t = 1, \ldots, T.$$

Maximizing W with respect to S_t, B_t, and ℓ_t^k, $t = 1, \ldots, T$, subject to the budget constraints above, routine manipulations of the first order conditions yields a system of equations that characterize the size of lean and harvest seasons savings at each time t. In particular, it can be readily verified that $\ell_t^k = 0$ if $S_t \geq 0$ and if the inequality in Proposition 1 holds. In addition, suppose that $S_t > 0$ and $B_t > 0$ for all $t = 1, \ldots, T$,

29 See, for instance, Basu et al. (2000) for an examination of social labeling schemes.

$$\frac{\beta_2}{B_T} = \frac{\alpha\beta}{w_T + S_T - B_T}, \quad \frac{1}{B_{t-1} - S_t} = \frac{\alpha\beta}{w_t + S_t - B_t},$$
$$t = 1, \ldots, T, \quad \frac{\beta}{B_{t-1} - S_t} = \frac{\alpha}{w_{t-1} + S_{t-1} - B_{t-1}}.$$

Solving backwards, we obtain

$$S_1 = \frac{\sum_{s=0}^{T-1} (\beta(\alpha + \beta)\beta^{2s} B_0 - w_{T-s})}{1 + \beta(\alpha + \beta) \sum_{s=0}^{T-1} \beta^{2s}}.$$

Since $\beta < 1$, $S_1 < 0$, if $\beta(\alpha + \beta)B_0 < w_{T-s}$. Also, since $\ell_s^k = 0$, $w_{T-s} = \bar{w}$ for all $s = 0, \ldots, T-1$. We have a contradiction as S_1 cannot be less than zero with imperfect credit markets. In addition, since $S_1 = 0$, we have from the budget constraints that $c_{l1} = B_0$ and $c_{h1} = \bar{w} - B_1$. Repeating the arguments above starting from $t = 2, \ldots, T$, and substituting $S_1 = 0$, we have $S_t \leq 0$ for each $t = 2, \ldots, T$. Summarizing these arguments, the lean and harvest seasons budget constraints are simply given by $c_{lt} = B_{t-1}$, and $c_{ht} = w_t(1 + a\ell_t^k) - B_t$ for $t = 1, \ldots, T$ and thus

$$\max_{\{B_t, S_t, \ell_t^k\}_{t=1}^T} U = \log B_0 + \sum_{t=1}^{T} \max_{B_t, \ell_t^k} \beta^{2t-1}(\alpha \log(w_t(1 + a\ell_t^k)) - B_t)$$
$$+ (1 - \alpha)\log(1 - \ell_t^k) + \beta \log B_t).$$

As such, in the complete absence of lean season savings, the household behaves as though the planning horizon starting from any year t is cut short to include only the current harvest season, and the lean season of the next year. As a final note, if $B_0 > \bar{w}/(\beta(\alpha + \beta))$, S_t can be positive for at least some years t. However, we also have $B_0 > \bar{w}/(\beta(1 + r)(\alpha + \beta))$, for any positive interest rate r, and from Proposition 4, interlinkage will not be an equilibrium phenomenon.

Appendix B

Proof of Proposition 4. Note that since $B^1(\cdot)$ and $B^2(\cdot)$ are both continuous in B_{t-1}, $B(B_{t-1})$ is likewise continuous in B_{t-1} since $B^1(\hat{B}_o) = \bar{B}_o$ and $B^1(\hat{B}_k) = B^2(\hat{B}_k)$. Thus, at least one fixed point $B^* = (B|B(B) = B)$ exists for each $p > 0$. Existence of an interior steady state follows upon observing that $\lim_{B_{t-1} \to 0} \partial B(B_{t-1})/\partial B_{t-1} = \infty$ and $\lim_{B_{t-1} > \hat{B}_o} \partial B(B_{t-1})/\partial B_{t-1} = 0$. To demonstrate uniqueness of the interior steady state, we observe that (i) B^1 and B^2 are individually strictly concave in B_{t-1} in the relevant range and (ii) $B^1(B_{t-1}) = B^2(B_{t-1})$ if $B_{t-1} = \hat{B}_k$, or if $B_{t-1} = 0$.

Strict concavity of $B^1(B_{t-1})$ in B_{t-1} is immediate from equation (19). Strict concavity of $B^2(B_{t-1})$ in B_{t-1} follows since

$$\frac{\partial B^2}{\partial B_{t-1}} = \frac{B_t}{B_{t-1}} \left(\frac{\eta(1 - \alpha)}{1 + a\ell_t^k} + \frac{1 + \beta}{1 + a - \bar{\ell}_t} \right) \Big/ \left(\frac{\eta\beta}{1 + a\ell_t^k} + \frac{(1 + \beta)(1 + \beta(1 + \beta))}{1 + a - \bar{\ell}_t} \right) \equiv \frac{B_t}{B_{t-1}} \Omega.$$

Substitute using equations (7) and (10), we have

$$\Omega = \frac{1 + a - (1 - \alpha)(1 - \eta)(1 + a - \bar{\ell}_t)/(1 + \beta)}{(1 + \beta(1 + \beta))(1 + a) - (1 - \alpha)(1 - \eta)(1 + a - \bar{\ell}_t)/(1 + \beta)} < 1.$$

Routine differentiation yields

$$\frac{\partial^2 B^2}{\partial B_{t-1}^2} = \frac{B_t}{B_{t-1}^2}\Omega(\Omega - 1) + \frac{B_t}{B_{t-1}}\frac{\partial \Omega}{\partial \bar{\ell}_t}\frac{\partial \bar{\ell}_t}{\partial B_{t-1}} < 0 \tag{30}$$

where the inequality follows since Ω is strictly increasing in $\bar{\ell}_t$ and $\bar{\ell}_t$ is decreasing in B_{t-1} from equation (18).

The second observation follows by definition of B^1 and B^2 in equation (19). In particular,

$$\frac{B^1(\hat{B}_k)}{B^2(\hat{B}_k)} = \frac{(\hat{B}_k/\hat{B}_o)^{\frac{1}{1+\beta(\alpha+\beta)}}}{(1 - \tilde{\ell})} = 1, \quad B^2(0) = 0 = B^1(0). \tag{31}$$

Suppose therefore that there are two distinct interior steady states, denoted as B^{*1} and B^{*2}. By strict concavity of B^1 and B^2, and equation (31), there are three possibilities. First, $B^{*1} = \{B|B^1(B) = B\}$ and $B^{*2} = \{B|B^2(B) = B\}$, with $B^{*2} < \hat{B}_k < B^{*1}$. By strict concavity and equation (31), we have

$$B^1(\hat{B}^k) > \hat{B}^k, \quad B^2(\hat{B}^k) < \hat{B}^k.$$

This contradicts equation (31). A second possibility is that $B^{*1} = \bar{B}_o$ and $B^{*2} = \{B|B^1(B) = B\}$. We have thus

$$\hat{B}_0 \leq \bar{B}_o. \tag{32}$$

Once again by strict concavity of $B^1(B_{t-1})$ and equation (31), we have

$$B^1(\hat{B}_0) < \hat{B}_0.$$

This contradicts equation (32) since $B^1(\hat{B}_0) = \bar{B}_o$ by definition (equation (19)).

Finally, suppose that the two steady states are $B^{*1} = \bar{B}_o$ and $B^{*2} = \{B|B^2(B) = B\}$. This requires simultaneously that

$$B^1(\hat{B}_0) > \hat{B}_0, \quad B^2(\hat{B}_k) < \hat{B}_k.$$

Or equivalently, that

$$\beta_2(1 + r) > 1, \quad \beta_2(1 + r) < \left(\frac{a(\alpha + \beta)}{1 - \alpha}\right)^{\beta(\alpha+\beta)} = (1 - \tilde{\ell})^{\beta(\alpha+\beta)}$$

an impossibility as $\tilde{\ell} > 0$. The rest of Proposition 4 follows straightforwardly from the definition of B^*, equations (13) and (17). ■

Acknowledgments

We thank seminar participants at the European Society of Population Economics Conference, the Midwest International Trade Conference, the University of Arkansas, and the University of North Carolina at Chapel Hill for discussions and comments. Detailed suggestions and comments from two anonymous referees are also gratefully acknowledged.

Reference

Baland, J.-M., and J. A. Robinson. (2000). "Is Child Labor Inefficient?" *Journal of Political Economy* 108(4), 663–679.

Bardhan, P. K. (1989). "A Note on Interlinked Rural Economic Arrangements." In P. K. Bardhan (ed.), *The Economic Theory of Agrarian Institutions*. Oxford: Oxford University Press, pp. 237–242.

Bardhan, P. K. (1983). "Labor-Tying in a Poor Agrarian Economy: A Theoretical and Empirical Analysis," *Quarterly Journal of Economics* 98, 501–514.

Basu, A. K. (2002). "Oligopsonistic Landlords, Segmented Labor Markets and the Persistence of Tied-Labor Contracts," *American Journal of Agricultural Economics* 84(2), 438–453.

Basu, A. K., and N. H. Chau. (2002). "Targeting Child Labor in Debt Bondage: Evidence and Policy Implications," *World Bank Economic Review* 17(2), 253–281.

Basu, A. K., N. H. Chau, and U. Grote. (2000). "Guaranteed Manufactured without Child Labor," Working paper Series #2000-04, Department of Applied Economics and Management, Cornell University.

Basu, K. (1987). "Disneyland Monopoly, Interlinkage and Usurious Interest Rates," *Journal of Public Economics* 34, 1–17.

Basu, K., and P. H. Van. (1998). "The Economics of Child Labor," *American Economic Review* 88, 412–427.

Beck, T., D.-K. Asli, and R. Levine. (2000). "A New Database on Financial Development and Structure," *World Bank Economic Review* September, 597–605.

Becker, G. S. (1981). *A Treatise on the Family*. Cambridge, MA: Harvard University Press.

Braverman, A., and T. N. Srinivasan. (1984). " Agrarian Reforms in Developing Rural Economies Characterized by Interlinked Credit and Tenancy Markets." In H. P., Binswanger, and R. Rosenzweig (eds), *Contractual Arrangements, Employment, and Wages in Rural Labor Markets in Asia*. New Haven and London: Yale University Press, pp. 63–81.

Braverman, A., and J. Stiglitz. (1982). "Sharecropping and the Interlinking of Agrarian Markets," *American Economic Review* 72, 695–715.

Brenton, P. (2000). Globalisation and Social Exclusion in the EU, Policy Implications. CEPS Working Document No. 159.

Bureau of Democracy, Human Rights and Labor. (1999). *Country Report on Human Rights Practices for 1998*. Washington DC: US Department of State.

Doepke, M. (2001). "Accounting for Fertility Decline during the Transition to Growth." UCLA mimeo.

Eswaran, M., and A. Kotwal. (1985). "A Theory of Two-Tier Labor Markets in Agrarian Economies," *American Economic Review* 75, 162–177.

Eswaran, M. (1996). "Fertility, Literacy and the Institution of Child Labor," Manuscript Vancouver: University of British Columbia, Department of Economics.

Galor, O., and J. Zeira. (1993). "Income Distribution and Macroeconomics," *Review of Economic Studies* 60, 35–52.

Grootaert, C., and R. M. Kanbur. (1995). "Child Labour: An Economic Perspective," *International Labour Review* 134(2), 187–203.

Grote, U., A. K. Basu, and D. Weinhold. (1999). "Child Labor and the International Policy Debate-The Education/Child Labor Trade-Off and the Consequences of Trade Sanctions," *ZEF-Discussion Papers on Development Policy*. No. 1: Center for Development Research, Bonn.

Hazan, M., and B. Berdugo. (2002). ''Child Labor, Fertility, and Economic Growth,'' *The Economic Journal* 112(October), 810–828.

Karim, F. (1995). *Contemporary Forms of Slavery in Pakistan*. New York: Human Rights Watch.

Informal Sector Service Center. (1992). *Bonded Labor in Nepal under the Kamaiya System*. Kathmandu, Informal Sector Service Center.

IPEC (International Programme on the Elimination of Child Labour). (1992). *Children in Bondage: A Call for Action*. Geneva: ILO/UN Centre for Human Rights.

International Labour Office (ILO). (1993). *World Labour Report*. Geneva: International Labor Office.

Mukherjee, A., and D. Ray. (1995). ''Labor-Tying,'' *Journal of Development Economics* 47, 207–239.

Office of the United States Trade Representative. (1997). ''Monitoring and Enforcing Trade Laws and Agreements—Fact Sheet,'' Office of the United States Trade Representative, Executive Office of the President, Washington, DC, September 30.

Organization for Economic Cooperation and Development (2000). ''International Trade and Core Labor Standards''. Paris: Directorate for Employment Labor and Social Affairs, OECD.

Otsuka, K., H. Chuma, and Y. Hayami. (1992). ''Land and Labor Contracts in Agrarian Economics,'' *Journal of Economic Literature* 30, 1965–2018.

Rosenzweig, M. R. (1981). ''Household and Non-household Activities of Youths, Issues of Modelling, Data and Estimation Strategies.'' In G. Rodgers, and G. Standing (eds), *Child Work, Poverty and Underdevelopment*. Geneva: International Labour Office.

Sadoulet, E. (1992). ''Labor-Service Tenancy Contracts in a Latin American Context,'' *American Economic Review* 82, 1031–1042.

Srinivasan, T. N. (1979). ''Bonded Labor Contracts and Incentives to Adopt Yield-Raising Innovation in Semi-feudal Agriculture,'' *Economic Journal* 89, 416–419.

Tucker, L. (1996). *The Small Hands of Slavery, Bonded Child Labor In India*. New York: Human Rights Watch.

US Department of Labor. (1995). *By the Sweat and Toil of Children. Vol II*. Washington DC: Bureau of Labor Affairs, US Department of Labor.

US Department of Labor. (1998). *By the Sweat and Toil of Children. Vol V*. Washington DC: Bureau of Labor Affairs, US Department of Labor.

Transnational Trafficking, Law Enforcement, and Victim Protection: A Middleman Trafficker's Perspective

Randall Akee *University of California, Los Angeles*
Arnab K. Basu *Cornell University*
Arjun Bedi *Erasmus University Rotterdam*
Nancy H. Chau *Cornell University*

Abstract

We explore two hitherto poorly understood characteristics of the human-trafficking market—the cross-border ease of mobility of traffickers and the elasticity of buyers' demand. In a model of two-way bargaining, the exact configuration of these characteristics is shown to determine whether domestic and foreign crackdowns on illicit employment mutually reinforce or counteract one another in efforts to stem the tide of trafficking. Estimation results from a gravity model of trafficking present evidence consistent with the mutual-reinforcement view, indicating considerable ease of mobility and inelastic demand.

1. Introduction

Transnational human trafficking is one of the least studied forms of international movement in persons. But what little is known about it suggests that it is a

Bedi is also a visiting professor at the School of Foreign Service, Georgetown University, Doha. For suggestions and comments on earlier versions of this paper, we thank Amit Batabyal, Guido Friebel, Jyot-sna Jalan, Stephan Klonner, Ben Lawrance, Sugata Marjit, Keith Maskus, Ray Reizman, Enrico Spolaore, Jeffrey Williamson, Xiaobo Zhang, and seminar participants at the 2007 and 2008 Allied Social Science Associations annual meetings; the 2007 Humboldt Network meeting; the Paul H. Nitze School of Advanced International Studies at Johns Hopkins University; the International Food Policy Research Institute; the 2010 International Economics Finance Society annual meeting; the final conference of the Transnationality of Migrants Network (2010); the Institute for the Study of Labor Conference on Illegal and Illicit Migration (2010); the International Institute of Social Studies in the Hague; the Poverty Reduction, Equity, and Growth Network Conference (2009); the Fourth Annual Conference on Development and Institutions (Brunel University); the Centre for

[*Journal of Law and Economics*, vol. 57 (May 2014)]

highly lucrative business. A recent International Labour Organization (ILO) report puts the total illicit profits produced each year by trafficked laborers at U.S.$31.7 billion and the estimated stock of forced labor due to trafficking at U.S.$2.45 million (ILO 2005). Together these figures imply a level of illicit profits per trafficked person per year at close to U.S.$13,000. An overwhelming majority of trafficked persons are women and girls, and sexual exploitation is the most commonly identified form of profiteering on trafficked persons (U.S. Department of State 2009).[1] Research has shown that the perpetrators of trafficking are driven primarily by local criminal networks in source countries (UNODC 2009), with some directing victims domestically to feed domestic illicit demand, while others direct victims internationally to service foreign buyers, often using diaspora populations from the same source country as conduits.

These salient features of the market for illicit trade in humans uncovered to date—buyer-demand-driven exploitative employment that operates underground and footloose middleman traffickers with multiple possible buyer sources reaching across national borders—reveal two critical though hitherto poorly understood sets of issues related to anti-trafficking-policy design. First, with possibly competing demand for trafficked victims coming from both domestic and foreign sources, how effective is a stand-alone crackdown on domestic illicit activities that acts on domestic buyers' willingness to pay but leaves foreign demand untouched? Conversely, what about stricter foreign law enforcement or victim-protection programs, such as an amnesty, that facilitate discovery by law enforcement in destination countries?

These are the questions that guide the tasks set forth in this paper. Our goal is to contribute to the debate on the choice and coordination of international efforts to curb transnational trafficking by means of legislation that directly acts on the demand-side incentives of middlemen to engage in trafficking.

More broadly, the issues addressed here have many parallels with other forms of illicit international trade in goods such as drugs, endangered species, and arms, for example, and many of the lessons learned here for the case of trafficking can be more broadly applied to alternative forms of illicit international trade. Closely related to our work, Becker, Murphy, and Grossman (2006) examines the effectiveness of law enforcement on the volume of illicit-drug activities in a competitive setting in a single country and highlights the importance of the

Studies in Social Sciences (Kolkata); the University of Hannover; the Rochester Institute of Technology; and the College of William and Mary. We are grateful to an anonymous referee and the editor for valuable suggestions that led to substantial improvements in this paper. Financial support from the Alexander von Humboldt Foundation is gratefully acknowledged.

[1] These figures refer specifically to worldwide profits from human trafficking as opposed to more voluntary forms of migration and/or human smuggling. The Protocol to Prevent, Suppress, and Punish Trafficking in Persons, Especially Women and Children (November 15, 2000, 2237 U.N.T.S. 319), defines the crime of trafficking in human beings to mean "the recruitment, transportation, transfer, harbouring or receipt of persons, by means of the threat or use of force or other forms of coercion, of abduction, of fraud, of deception, of the abuse of power or of a position of vulnerability or of the giving or receiving of payments or benefits to achieve the consent of a person having control over another person, for the purpose of exploitation."

elasticity of demand in determining the answer. Our analysis builds on and substantially adds to the theoretical insights developed therein and does so theoretically by proposing a two-way bargaining framework that enables us to better understand the negotiation problem of an internationally mobile trafficker and empirically by putting together a novel data set that enables us to test the implications of the model. The specification of the model showcases two features of the trafficking market: the nature of buyer preferences in domestic and foreign countries and the bargaining problem between middleman traffickers facing both domestic and foreign demand.

Buyers' willingness to pay is taken to be endogenously determined by policies, through victim-protection programs, such as an amnesty granted to trafficked victims, and law enforcement against prostitution. The former raises the likelihood of work stoppage by empowering victims to access host-country police authorities, and the latter achieves similar ends through direct law enforcement. Consistent with Becker, Murphy, and Grossman (2006), if buyer demand is inelastic, for example, an increase in the likelihood of discovery in the destination country will raise buyers' willingness to pay there, which thus encourages the inflow of trafficked victims. But a similar increase in the likelihood of discovery in the source country will raise source-country buyers' willingness to pay, which thus discourages the outflow of trafficked victims. A priori, therefore, source and destination crackdowns on illicit activities should be expected to have opposite impacts on the incidence of transnational trafficking, if the trafficker reaps the full measure of buyers' willingness to pay.

Next, we endogenize the division of buyers' willingness to pay between the trafficker and the buyer. The novelty of this setting is threefold: First, we formally depart from settings requiring free and open competition between buyers for sellers to a setting where the clandestine operations of the trafficking market make searching for buyers justifiably more costly and where payoffs are determined by bargaining within buyer-seller pairs. Departing from canonical Nash bargaining problems, we specify a two-way bilateral Nash bargaining problem in which the threat-point profit of the trafficker in the domestic country is taken to be the foreign equilibrium profit, while the threat point profit of the same trafficker in the foreign country is the domestic equilibrium profit. This allows for the simultaneous endogeneity of the traffickers' threat-point bargaining positions at home and abroad, depending jointly on the configuration of host- and source-country policies on illicit employment and victim protection. Finally, to account for the extent to which a trafficker is mobile between countries and between occupations, we introduce heterogeneity among traffickers' cross-border mobility in terms of a search cost for buyers abroad and heterogeneity among potential traffickers' reservation income.

In this setting where the threat-point profits of traffickers in the two countries are simultaneously determined, we show that crackdowns on illicit activities in the destination and the source countries can in fact reinforce one another, contrary to the implications of Becker, Murphy, and Grossman (2006). The argument comes in two parts. Take the case of inelastic demand, for example. In the destination country, law enforcement against prostitution raises traffickers' profits as the increase in buyer willingness to pay more than compensates for the increased risk of detection. For individuals in the source country deciding between domestic and transnational trafficking, such a change favors transnational trafficking. For individuals deciding between transnational trafficking and receiving reservation income in the source country, such a change also encourages transnational trafficking. For all potential transnational traffickers, therefore, law enforcement in the destination country against prostitution exacerbates the trafficking problem when demand is inelastic.

By contrast, in the source country, law enforcement against prostitution raises buyers' willingness to pay there. For individuals in the source country deciding between domestic and transnational trafficking, we show that such a change does indeed favor domestic trafficking. But for individuals deciding between transnational trafficking and receiving reservation income in the source country, such a change in fact raises transnational traffickers' profit as the threat-point expected profit of traffickers negotiating with buyers in destination countries rises with source-country willingness to pay. We show that the latter effect dominates when the search cost is low for most of the traffickers whose decisions are impacted by this policy change. Thus, destination- and source-country legislative efforts against prostitution can mutually reinforce one another in exacerbating the problem of transnational trafficking.

We conclude our theoretical analysis by displaying four distinctive configurations of market-characteristic combinations wherein the effectiveness of source and host policies on trafficking can potentially increase, decrease, counteract, or mutually reinforce each other depending on the elasticity of buyer demand and the cross-border mobility of traffickers.[2] Our analysis underscores the challenge that policy makers can face in their efforts to coordinate policies internationally in the presence of internationally mobile traffickers. As shown, effective policy making requires detailed information not just on demand elasticity but critically also on the cross-border reach of the traffickers.

The empirical part of the paper accordingly takes these issues to the data and employs a novel 187 × 187 matrix of the incidence of bilateral international trafficking collected for the purpose of this research using the *Trafficking in Persons Report* (*TIP Report*) (U.S. Department of State 2003) and the *Human Rights Report on Trafficking in Persons, Especially Women and Children* (*HR Report*), from The Protection Project (TPP 2002). We estimate a modified gravity model of international trafficking, and in so doing we simultaneously account

[2] In a working paper version of this paper (Akee et al. 2011), we present a number of extensions including a buyer penalty that depends on whether trafficked victims self-report their plight or are discovered by law enforcement, for example. Such extensions can generate an even larger number of variations in possible configurations of the effectiveness of domestic and foreign policies on trafficking. Despite these complications, the qualitative conclusions of this paper concerning the potentially mutually reinforcing role of source and destination country on transnational trafficking remain.

for the push and pull forces of international trafficking in determining the bilateral match between host and destination countries.[3] We augment a standard gravity model of international migration by including a measure of host-country granting of legal amnesty to discovered victims of trafficking. After controlling for potential unobserved heterogeneity and endogeneity using a two-stage least squares regression, we find that countries that grant legal amnesty to immigrants have an increased likelihood of experiencing human trafficking. This empirical finding is robust to the choice of data source (*TIP Report* only, *HR Report* only, or both) and the use of different specifications. We also include prostitution laws in the host and the source countries in our estimation. Based on our theoretical model, these empirical results present evidence supportive of inelastic final buyers' demand and considerable cross-border reach in traffickers' ability to identify buyers.

In the context of the policy debate on antitrafficking measures, the issues addressed here are of vital importance. As set out in the United Nations Protocol to Prevent, Suppress, and Punish Trafficking in Persons, signatory governments agree to adopt legislative measures to discourage the demand that fosters the exploitation of persons that leads to trafficking. But whether stricter enforcement of legislation banning prostitution can in fact achieve this goal and stem the tide of transnational trafficking is a matter of vigorous debate. The *TIP Report* (U.S. Department of State 2007) for example discusses the view in favor of a crackdown on prostitution, while the *Trafficking in Human Beings* report of the Bureau of the Dutch National Rapporteur on Trafficking in Human Beings (2005) notes that regardless of the legislation, prostitution will continue. This literature has clearly recognized the importance of demand elasticity. Bales (2004), for example, emphasizes the role of law enforcement in trafficking, discusses demand elasticity as one important determinant, and provides arguments suggesting that demand for trafficked victims in illicit sectors is likely inelastic. By contrast, Kara (2010) finds that demand for commercial sex is highly elastic. The theoretical and empirical findings in this paper argue strongly that a better-informed debate should account for both the demand elasticity of buyers and the cross-border mobility of traffickers.

Our modified gravity approach introduces a new dimension to a very small but growing literature on the empirics of trafficking in humans. These studies empirically examine the pattern of trafficking, using distinctive measures such as country-level indicators of "out trafficking" and "in-trafficking" (Bales 1999; Danailova-Trainor and Belser 2006), the incidence of forced labor in illicit sectors, of which trafficking in persons is a subset (Busse and Braun 2002), and data from surveys of victims and families (Mahmoud and Trebesch 2010). These studies single out a list of factors that are associated with trafficking: socioeconomic and governance indicators in both host and source countries such as poverty, unemployment, and government corruption; the practice of migration

[3] See Basu and Chau (2008) for a preliminary examination of these issues.

for work in the source country; and trade and foreign-direct-investment linkages. Clearly, much more remains to be uncovered concerning the determinants of a bilateral match between source and destination countries, depending on the combination of source- and destination-country legislation directed toward the illicit sectors where victims are ultimately employed.

A theoretical literature on the more general issue of exploitative labor and intermediary-assisted migration also exists but is substantially thinner. Most closely related to our work dealing with trafficking policy formation, Rogers and Swinnerton (2008) provides theoretical justification for a complete ban on exploitative labor, where employment is made possible only by the deception of firms concerning the true nature of work. Friebel and Guriev (2006) examine the role of deportation policies on debt-financed illegal immigration in an innovative model in which wealth-constrained individuals repay their debt to smugglers by entering into servitude contracts and such servitude contracts are easier to enforce in illicit sectors of employment. They show the intriguing result that stricter border controls can in fact increase debt-financed migration as smugglers respond to policy-induced change in the market value of a migrant by adjusting the volume of smuggling. Dessy and Palage (2003) investigate the interplay between trafficking legislation and the incidence of child labor. Our paper contributes to this growing literature by introducing a two-country setup in which both domestic and transnational trafficking are in the trafficker's choice set, and the impact of legislation is shown to interact in important ways with the market structure in which traffickers operate.

2. The Basic Model

We consider a model featuring the interactions between a buyer of the services of trafficked victims and a middleman trafficker. Potential buyers originate from two sources, the illicit sector in the domestic (source) country (D) and the illicit sector in the foreign (host) country (F), while middleman traffickers serve as intermediaries delivering trafficked victims from source D to buyers in D and/or F.[4]

Let V_i denote the monetary-equivalent buyer valuation of the services per victim in i = D, F. A buyer's willingness to pay depends on two sets of considerations that each individual buyer takes as given: the overall availability of victims in i and the risk of discovery and prosecution. Each of these considerations depends critically on the likelihood of a crackdown on illicit employment in D and F, along with the legal protection offered to transnational victims of trafficking, particularly in F.[5]

[4] Our definition of illicit-sector employment, whether domestic or foreign, is simply any work relationship from which victims of trafficking can derive no benefit.

[5] Other country-specific reasons that govern the valuation of victims are taken to be embodied in the valuation function V_i for each i. Our objective in the model is to specifically assess the role of law enforcement and victim protection. In our empirical analysis, we use a battery of variables to control other sources of heterogeneity of V_i across countries.

In particular, in the domestic country D, enforcement of legislation outlawing illicit-sector employment, such as legislation banning prostitution, gives rise to a probability $p_D \in [0, 1]$ of discovery and of buyer penalty $c_D \geq 0$. From the perspective of the overall availability of victims in i, we specify V_i simply as a function of the likelihood that victims remain undiscovered, $V_D(1 - p_D)$, and assume that $V_i(\cdot)$ is positive and strictly decreasing in the perceived availability of victims in $1 - p_D$, consistent with diminishing marginal utility. Turning to buyer discovery and prosecution, we see that law enforcement gives rise to a probability p_D of work stoppage and buyer penalty. The corresponding maximal willingness to pay per trafficked victim is

$$(1 - p_D)\, V_D(1 - p_D) - p_D c_D.$$

In the foreign country F, the likelihood of discovery and of buyer penalty p_F is made up of two parts: the frequency of active law enforcement ρ_F and victim self-reporting a_F, with $p_F = \rho_F + a_F$. For example, many host countries formally provide protection and other assistance to trafficked victims through the granting of amnesty. We take the victim protection that an amnesty confers—as opposed to a policy of indifference or one that gives discovered trafficked victims the same legal status as an illegal immigrant, for example—to contribute to raising the likelihood of victim discovery from ρ_F to $\rho_F + a_F \in [0, 1]$. The corresponding maximal willingness to pay in F is thus

$$(1 - p_F)\, V_F(1 - p_F) - p_F c_F = (1 - \rho_F - a_F)\, V_F(1 - \rho_F - a_F) - (\rho_F + a_F)\, c_F.$$

Denote $\delta_i \geq 0$ as the cost required to capture and traffic a victim from D to work in i. The net expected value generated per victim trafficked, to be ultimately divided between the buyer and the middleman trafficker, is thus

$$EV_D \equiv (1 - p_D)V_D(1 - p_D) - p_D c_D - \delta_D \tag{1}$$

in D and

$$\begin{aligned} EV_F &\equiv (1 - \rho_F - a_F)V_F(1 - \rho_F - a_F) - (\rho_F + a_F)c_F - \delta_F \\ &= (1 - p_F)V_F(1 - p_F) - p_F c_F - \delta_F \end{aligned} \tag{2}$$

in F.

Henceforth, denote θ_j^i as the marginal impacts of policy j_i on the expected value EV_i in the illicit sector of country i, $\partial EV_i/\partial j_i$. Of the five policy parameters, c_D, c_F, p_D, ρ_F, and a_F, the role of penalty c_i is the most straightforward. Since EV_i decreases strictly with penalty c_i, it follows that θ_c^i must be strictly negative as long as there is a strictly positive likelihood of discovery ($p_i > 0$) in i = D, F from expressions (1) and (2).

Two opposite forces impact the role of discovery frequencies (p_D and $p_F = \rho_F + a_F$) on the net expected value. Working to decrease EV_i, discovery directly leads to work stoppages and fines. But in the opposite direction, discovery also contributes to rising scarcity of workers in i and thus the value per worker there $V_i(\cdot)$. It follows that if the quantity demand for illicit workers is sufficiently inelastic ($|\partial \log V_i / \partial \log(1 - p_i)| \gg 1$), the expected value of a victim rises with p_D in D and $p_F = \rho_F + a_F$ in F, or $\theta_p^D > 0$, $\theta_\rho^F > 0$, and $\theta_a^F > 0$.

2.1. The Two-Way Bargaining Problem

Linking victims in D to buyers in D and/or F, we consider a pool of heterogeneous middleman traffickers in the domestic country, with size normalized to one.[6] All middleman traffickers enjoy direct cost-free contact with one domestic illicit buyer. Heterogeneity among middleman traffickers can be gauged along two dimensions: their costs of foreign-buyer access and their reservation income levels as fallback options in case they choose to refrain from trafficking. We parameterize the cross-border reach of a trafficker by a search cost ($k \geq 0$) required to solicit a final buyer in the foreign country. The reservation income of a trafficker is denoted $\bar{y} \geq 0$, the forgone income of a trafficker. Assume henceforth that the cumulative distribution function characterizing the pool of heterogeneous middlemen on the two-dimensional $(k, \bar{y})$ plane is given by $G(k, \bar{y})$, with density function $g(k, \bar{y}) \geq 0$ for $k \geq 0$ and $\bar{y} \geq 0$.

The problem of a potential middleman trafficker is two staged. In the first, he decides whether to engage in trafficking. If not, he earns his reservation income $\bar{y}$. Otherwise, a second-stage decision needs to be made about the choice between trafficking destinations D and F.

Starting from the second stage, we take the clandestine nature of employment in illicit sectors to naturally hinder open competition for trafficked victims. Transaction between a buyer and a trafficker is accordingly modeled as an outcome of two-way Nash bilateral bargaining. The equilibrium incomes of a trafficker delivering a victim to a buyer in D and F, $y_D(k)$ and $y_F(k) - k$, are the simultaneous solutions to the following Nash bargaining problems:

$$y_D(k) = \arg\max_{y_D} [y_D - (y_F(k) - k)]^{\alpha_D} (EV_D - y_D)^{1-\alpha_D} \tag{3}$$

and

$$y_F(k) - k = \max\{\arg\max_{y_F} [y_F - y_D(k)]^{\alpha_F} (EV_F - y_F)^{1-\alpha_F} - k,\ 0\}, \tag{4}$$

taking as given host and source policies. Equations (3) and (4) jointly highlight a number of notable features of the two-way bargaining problem. First, y_i and $EV_i - y_i$ together divide the victim's expected value (EV_i) completely between the trafficker and the buyer in i = D, F. The relative bargaining strength of the middleman in the exchange is parameterized by $\alpha_i \in (0, 1)$.

Next, equations (3) and (4) show that the domestic and foreign illicit markets are inextricably linked—in equation (3) the threat-point income of a trafficker operating domestically is the expected income that the same trafficker can anticipate in the foreign country $y_F(k) - k$, while in equation (4) the threat-point

[6] The symmetric problem of a middleman trafficker based in the foreign country can be worked out as well. Other than the positioning of the search cost, the analytics are identical to the case considered here.

income of the trafficker in the foreign country is the expected income he can earn domestically $y_D(k)$. In equilibrium, both threat points are endogenous, to be determined as the joint solutions to the two-way bargaining problem in equations (3) and (4). The threat-point income of the buyers in i in case an agreement cannot be struck is normalized at zero. Finally, note that in equations (3) and (4) traffickers are free to quit at any point, and as such $y_F(k) - k$ never falls below zero.

2.1.1. Gains from Transnational Trafficking

The solution $y_F(k) - k$ to equations (3) and (4) gives the expected income from transnational trafficking as

$$y_F(k) - k = \max\{\beta(\alpha_F EV_F - k) + \beta_F \alpha_D EV_D, 0\}, \tag{5}$$

where $\beta = 1/[1 - (1 - \alpha_D)(1 - \alpha_F)]$ and $\beta_F = (1 - \alpha_F)\beta$. As shown, $y_F(k) - k$ depends on the expected value of a victim in both D and F (EV_D and EV_F) in addition to the bargaining strength of middlemen in D and F (α_D and α_F). From expressions (1) and (2), these expected values EV_i are in turn dependent on law enforcement (p_D and ρ_F) and on the degree of victim protection accorded in the form of an amnesty (a_F) in F.

Schedule D_F in Figure 1 illustrates $y_F(k) - k$ as the cross-border reach of traffickers k varies for bargaining strengths of the trafficker $\alpha_i \in (0, 1)$. Naturally, D_F is downward sloping, as a higher search cost k decreases a trafficker's income from transnational trafficking. For trafficker immobility sufficiently acute, or k beyond $\hat{k} \equiv \alpha_F EV_F + (1 - \alpha_F)\alpha_D EV_D$, the search cost is too high to justify transnational trafficking, and $y_F - k$ is thereafter equal to zero.

2.1.2. Gains from Domestic Trafficking

The other solution to equations (3) and (4) gives the expected income from domestic trafficking $y_D(k)$:

$$y_D(k) = \max\{\beta\alpha_D EV_D + \beta_D(\alpha_F EV_F - k), \alpha_D EV_D\}, \tag{6}$$

where $\beta = 1/[1 - (1 - \alpha_D)(1 - \alpha_F)]$ and $\beta_D = (1 - \alpha_D)\beta$. Like $y_F(k) - k$, $y_D(k)$ depends on the expected values of a victim in both D and F in addition to the bargaining strengths α_D and α_F of the middleman trafficker. It follows from expressions (1) and (2) that the extent of law enforcement in the two countries (p_D and ρ_F) and the availability of victim protection (a_F) will also enter into the determination of the equilibrium income of a trafficker engaged in domestic trafficking, $y_D(k)$.

The D_D schedule in Figure 1 illustrates $y_D(k)$, evaluated at bargaining strengths of the middleman trafficker $\alpha_i \in (0, 1)$ and assuming in addition that $EV_F > EV_D$, for otherwise no trafficker will engage in international trafficking.[7] As

[7] The opposite case with $EV_D > EV_F$ can be plotted in symmetric fashion in a figure like Figure 1. It can be easily confirmed that if $EV_D > EV_F$, the D_F schedule lies uniformly below the D_D schedule, and as such no traffickers will engage in international trafficking.

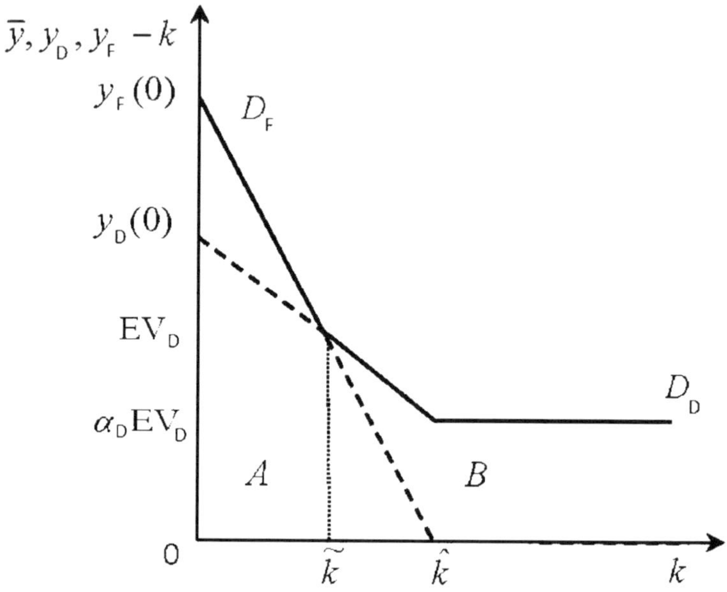

Figure 1. Traffickers' destination choice

shown, $y_D(k)$ decreases with search cost k, though at a rate strictly less than the slope of $y_F(k) - k$ with respect to k. Intuitively, the share of a victim's value $y_D(k)$ that a domestic trafficker commands depends in part on $y_F(k) - k$.[8] Since the trafficker's threat-point income in D, $y_F(k) - k$, declines with the cost he must incur to switch between buyer sources, the same trafficker's command on the value of a victim in D also declines with k. This continues until transnational trafficking is no longer a feasible option at $k \geq \hat{k}$. Thereafter, further increases in k have no impact on a domestic trafficker's share of the value of a victim, since his threat-point income is zero for $k \geq \hat{k}$. Now, since traffickers' types fall anywhere on the $(k, \bar{y})$ plane, how many will prefer transnational trafficking, domestic trafficking, or no trafficking in equilibrium?

2.2. Trafficking Equilibrium with Two-Way Bilateral Bargaining

A trafficking equilibrium with two-way bilateral bargaining is a combination $\{\mu_F, \mu_D\}$ representing the number of traffickers who engage, respectively, in

[8] Indeed, $y_D(k)$ is as may be expected a weighted average of EV_D and $y_F(k) - k$, or $y_D(k) = \alpha_D EV_D + (1 - \alpha_D)(y_F(k) - k)$ from equation (3).

transnational and domestic trafficking.[9] A trafficker engages in transnational trafficking if he belongs to area A of Figure 1, where $\{(k, \bar{y}_D) | y_F(k) - k = \max\{\bar{y}, y_F(k) - k, y_D(k)\}\}$. The cutoff $\tilde{k} = \alpha_F(EV_F - EV_D)$ gives the search cost of the marginal trafficker who is indifferent between transnational and domestic trafficking, or $y_F(\tilde{k}) - \tilde{k} = y_D(\tilde{k})$. Area B in Figure 1 illustrates the set of traffickers who engage in domestic trafficking $\{(k, \bar{y}_D) | y_D(k) = \max\{\bar{y}, y_F(k) - k, y_D(k)\}\}$. It follows that

$$\mu_F = \int_0^{\tilde{k}} \int_0^{y_F(k)-k} g(k, \bar{y}) d\bar{y} dk \tag{7}$$

and

$$\mu_D = \int_{\tilde{k}}^{\hat{k}} \int_0^{y_D(k)} g(k, \bar{y}) d\bar{y} dk + \int_{\hat{k}}^{\infty} \int_0^{\alpha_D EV_D} g(k, \bar{y}) d\bar{y} dk. \tag{8}$$

For potential traffickers with $(k, \bar{y})$ in neither A nor B, the fallback option of $\bar{y}$ is preferred. These individuals do not engage in either domestic or transnational trafficking.

We can now consider each of the policies a_F, ρ_F, and p_D in turn and their effects on transnational trafficking. Suppose for now that buyers' demand is sufficiently inelastic, and thus $\theta_a^F > 0$ and $\theta_\rho^F > 0$. In terms of foreign payoffs, a higher likelihood of discovery in the foreign country (due either to victim protection a_F or an increase in law enforcement ρ_F) raises a victim's value EV_F in F, raises the trafficker's share $y_F(k) - k$ from equation (6), and accordingly shifts the D_F schedule upward. In terms of domestic payoffs, a higher value of $y_F(k) - k$ raises the threat-point income of a domestic trafficker and shifts D_D upward as well since $y_D(k)$ increases with EV_F, from equation (7). The combined impacts on transnational trafficking are twofold. First, stronger foreign demand induced by stricter enforcement abroad increases the likelihood of transnational trafficking by raising the cutoff reservation income $y_F(k) - k$ among traffickers with an already low search cost ($< \tilde{k}$). This encourages transnational trafficking among those who previously prefer the fallback option $\bar{y}$. Second, the same increase in foreign demand also raises the cutoff search cost, $\tilde{k} = \alpha_F(EV_F - EV_D)$ with $\alpha_i > 0$. This encourages transnational trafficking among those who previously preferred domestic trafficking. Taken together, foreign legislation that raises the demand for trafficked victims unambiguously increases the likelihood of transnational trafficking, μ_F.

Consider instead an increase in law enforcement in the domestic country p_D. Assuming once again that demand is sufficiently inelastic ($\theta_p^D > 0$), we find that stricter domestic enforcement raises a victim's domestic value EV_D, raises the

[9] The number of middlemen that do not engage in trafficking is thus $1 - \mu_D - \mu_F$.

trafficker's share $y_D(k)$, and accordingly shifts the D_D schedule upward. This encourages domestic trafficking among some who would otherwise prefer transnational trafficking as the cutoff search cost $\tilde{k} = \alpha_F(EV_F - EV_D)$ moves to the left as D_D shifts upward. Using the by-now-familiar reasoning, we find that stricter domestic enforcement also increases the trafficker's share of EV_F in the foreign country, as his threat-point income $y_D(k)$ is now higher. This encourages transnational trafficking among those with $k \leq \hat{k}$ who would otherwise prefer the fallback option. These two effects run in opposite directions, and the net effect depends on whether there is sufficient probability mass among traffickers with a low search cost for the threat-point income effect to dominate, for example. To gauge the size of these two effects, denote

$$\mu_F^k = \int_0^{y_F(\tilde{k})-\tilde{k}} g(\tilde{k}, \bar{y})d\bar{y}$$

as the probability mass of traffickers with the cutoff search cost $\tilde{k}$. These are the first traffickers to switch away from transnational trafficking when the value of domestic trafficking rises. Meanwhile, denote

$$\mu_F^y = \int_0^{\tilde{k}} g(k, y_F(k) - k)dk$$

as the probability mass among transnational traffickers with the threshold reservation income $y_F(k) - k$, summing across all those with a search cost less than the cutoff. These are traffickers with sufficiently low search cost k but relatively high reservation income and as such are the first to engage in foreign trafficking when an increase in the value of domestic trafficking raises the threat-point income of foreign traffickers. The relative size of these two groups of traffickers determines the impact of domestic legislation on transnational trafficking. In what follows, we say that on net, a representative trafficker has considerable ease of mobility between D and F if the ratio μ_F^y/μ_F^k is sufficiently large. In particular,[10]

Proposition 1. For all $\alpha_i \in (0, 1)$, transnational trafficking μ_F increases with amnesty a_F and law enforcement ρ_F if and only if foreign buyers' demand is sufficiently inelastic ($\theta_a^1 > 0$, $\theta_\rho^1 > 0$). Transnational trafficking μ_F increases with domestic law enforcement p_D as well if and only if buyers' demand is sufficiently inelastic $\theta_p^D > 0$ and when traffickers enjoy considerable ease of mobility between D and F:

[10] To see the second part of the proposition, differentiate equation (8) with respect to p_D to obtain $\partial\mu_F/\partial p_D = \{-\alpha_F\mu_F^k + [\alpha_D(1-\alpha_F)/1-(1-\alpha_F)(1-\alpha_D)]\,\mu_F^y\}\,\theta_p^D$, and the second part of the proposition straightforwardly follows.

Table 1

Effects of a_F, ρ_F, and p_D on Transnational Trafficking

	$\mu_F^y/\mu_F^k < \bar{\alpha}$	$\mu_F^y/\mu_F^k > \bar{\alpha}$
Sufficiently inelastic demand: $\theta_a^F > 0$, $\theta_\rho^F > 0$, $\theta_p^D > 0$	+, +, −	+, +, +
All other demand elasticities: $\theta_a^F < 0$, $\theta_\rho^F < 0$, $\theta_p^D < 0$	−, −, +	−, −, −

$$\frac{\mu_F^y}{\mu_F^k} > \frac{\alpha_F[1-(1-\alpha_D)(1-\alpha_F)]}{\alpha_D(1-\alpha_F)} \equiv \bar{\alpha}.$$

Sufficiently inelastic demand and trafficker mobility facilitated by extensive cross-border buyer connection are thus two key conditions for foreign and domestic law-enforcement policies to mutually reinforce one another in expanding the scale of transnational trafficking.

Proposition 1 offers sharp empirical implications, summarized in Table 1 for the case of sufficiently inelastic demand and for all other demand elasticities. First, consistent with Becker, Murphy, and Grossman (2006), Table 1 demonstrates that the elasticity of demand is paramount. An increase in the incidence of transnational trafficking subsequent to improvements in the frequency of discovery $\rho_F + a_F$ in F is consistent only with sufficiently inelastic demand, while a reduction in the incidence of transnational trafficking is consistent with all other demand elasticities. This is true regardless of the cross-border reach of traffickers ($\mu_F^y/\mu_F^k > \bar{\alpha}$ or $\mu_F^y/\mu_F^k < \bar{\alpha}$).

Second, whether domestic and foreign law enforcement are found to be mutually reinforcing or run opposite to one another can shed light on the cross-border reach of middleman traffickers. In particular, law enforcement against illicit-sector activities in host (ρ_F) and source (p_D) countries that mutually reinforce one another in encouraging transnational trafficking is consistent only with traffickers who enjoy considerable ease of mobility between host and source countries ($\mu_F^y/\mu_F^k > \bar{\alpha}$). As displayed in Table 1, both $\rho_F + a_F$ and p_D have positive impacts on trafficking flows with sufficiently inelastic demand, while these same variables have negative impacts on trafficking flows with all other demand elasticities. Otherwise, with costly mobilities of traffickers, or $\mu_F^y/\mu_F^k < \bar{\alpha}$, the effects of $\rho_F + a_F$ and p_D on transnational trafficking bear opposite signs.[11]

2.3. Empirical Implications

Table 1 illustrates the difficulties that arise with attempts to coordinate an international response to mitigate against transnational trafficking. Clearly, information about demand elasticity and traffickers' mobility across countries is

[11] In Akee et al. (2011), we consider a number of extensions of the basic model in which we relax our assumption on the relative bargaining strength of the trafficker and differential penalties depending on whether discovery is a result of direct law enforcement or victim self-reporting. These results are available on request.

key to the design of such an international response. In what follows, the aim of our empirical investigation is precisely to try to understand these vital characteristics of the market for trafficking that are by nature difficult to directly estimate or proxy for. Our approach is to associate observed trafficking responses to policies in D and F to the relevant combination of demand elasticity and trafficker mobility using Table 1. But before we check the predictions of our comparative statics against the data, there are two sets of issues to consider.

2.3.1. Identification

The first issue concerns whether it is possible to identify the precise combination of demand elasticity and ease of trafficker mobility across countries on the basis of the comparative statics results alone. From Table 1, there are two consistent messages: all three policies mutually reinforce each other in influencing international trafficking flows only if there is significant trafficker mobility across countries, and given significant trafficker mobility, demand elasticity comes into play in determining the direction of the impact of all three policies on transnational trafficking. In particular, all three policies encourage trafficking if demand is sufficiently inelastic and discourage trafficking for all other demand elasticities. It follows, therefore, that there are two possible sets of comparative statics responses ($\{-, -, -\}$, $\{+, +, +\}$) that are each consistent with a unique combination of demand elasticity and ease of trafficker mobility. In both cases, traffickers enjoy significant ease of mobility. With positive trafficking responses to a_F, ρ_F, and p_D, the implication is thus that buyer demand is sufficiently inelastic. With negative trafficking responses to these same policies, all other elasticities, with the exception of sufficiently inelastic demand, apply.

2.3.2. Measurement

The second issue concerns the measurement of trafficked victims. By necessity, observed trafficking flow represents the number of victims discovered either through law enforcement or self-reporting rather than the actual number of trafficked victims. In the context of our model, denote observed transnational trafficking as μ_F^{Obs}:

$$\mu_F^{Obs} = (a_F + \rho_F)\mu_F = (a_F + \rho_F)\int_0^{\tilde{k}}\int_0^{y_F(k)-k} g(k, \bar{y})d\bar{y}dk,$$

where μ_F is the actual number of trafficked victims and $a_F + \rho_F$ denotes the probability that an individual victim of cross-border trafficking will be discovered. Our comparative-statics exercises presented in Table 1 are concerned with the impact of the three policies on actual trafficking flow $\partial\mu_F/\partial p_i$ and $\partial\mu_F/\partial a_F$. With regard to observed flows,

$$\frac{\partial\mu_F^{Obs}}{\partial a_F} = \mu_F + (a_F + \rho_F)\frac{\partial\mu_F}{\partial a_F}, \qquad \frac{\partial\mu_F^{Obs}}{\partial\rho_F} = \mu_F + (a_F + \rho_F)\frac{\partial\mu_F}{\partial\rho_F}$$

for policies initiated in the foreign (destination) country a_F, ρ_F, and

$$\frac{\partial \mu_F^{obs}}{\partial p_D} = (a_F + \rho_F)\frac{\partial \mu_F}{\partial p_D}$$

for policies initiated in the domestic (source) country p_D.

It follows, then, that comparative statics of observed flows with respect to foreign policies may falsely represent the direction of the comparative statics of actual flows. Intuitively, an increase in the likelihood of discovery can generate an increase in the observed flow of (discovered) trafficked victims, even when the total number of trafficked victims has declined.

The only exception to this complication is if the comparative statics are evaluated at the limit where $\mu_F \to 0$—the extensive margin—since

$$\lim_{\mu_F \to 0}\frac{\partial \mu_F^{Obs}}{\partial a_F} = (a_F + \rho_F)\frac{\partial \mu_F}{\partial a_F}, \qquad \lim_{\mu_F \to 0}\frac{\partial \mu_F^{Obs}}{\partial \rho_F} = (a_F + \rho_F)\frac{\partial \mu_F}{\partial \rho_F},$$

$$\lim_{\mu_F \to 0}\frac{\partial \mu_F^{Obs}}{\partial p_D} = (a_F + \rho_F)\frac{\partial \mu_F}{\partial p_D},$$

where the direction of the comparative-statics response based on observed flows is the same as that of the actual flow. Evaluated at $\mu_F \to 0$, Table 1 is thus applicable to both the actual flow of trafficked victims and the observed flow of trafficked victims. In the ensuing empirical analysis, we focus on this extensive margin.

3. Data on Human Trafficking

A paucity of reliable and comparable data has been a key factor hindering research on the forces that determine international trafficking. Research on the topic has so far been based primarily on information gathered from victims of trafficking.[12] While yielding valuable insights, these studies have a supply-side orientation that is not amenable to analysis of demand-side factors in host countries of trafficking, whether economic, demographic, legislative, or governance related, let alone the characteristics of the market of trafficking highlighted in Section 2.

[12] For example, the International Organization of Migration (IOM) has collected data since 1999 from persons assisted under its counter-trafficking programs. These data from the Counter-Trafficking Module Database of the IOM primarily cover trafficking originating from the Balkans (Salt 2005). More recently, a unique data set has been collected by the Special Action Program to Combat Forced Labour (SAP-FL) of the International Labour Organization (ILO). Based on questionnaires from 160 returned migrants in four origin countries (Albania, Romania, Moldova, and Ukraine), interviews with informants, focus-group discussions, and research in seven destination countries (France, Germany, Hungary, Japan, Russia, Turkey, and the United Kingdom), the SAP-FL database contains 298 entries of forced labor of which 186 are trafficked victims (see Andrees and van der Linden 2005). More recently, Mahmoud and Trebesch (2010) analyze IOM data from 5,513 households in Belarus, Bulgaria, Moldova, Romania, and Ukraine and show that migrant families in migration areas and with larger migrant networks are much more likely to be victims of trafficking.

For this paper, we compiled a dedicated data set based on the 2003 *TIP Report* (U.S. Department of State 2003) and the *HR Report* (TPP 2002). In terms of a global picture of the incidence of trafficking, the *TIP Report* and the *HR Report* are the two most extensive collections of cross-country trafficking information, to the best of our knowledge. The *TIP Report* provides extensive qualitative information on host and source countries of trafficking based on reports published in host countries and only for host countries where at least 100 cases of trafficking have been discovered in the past year, summing across all source countries identified for each host. The *HR Report* details trafficking routes as well as laws and legislation surrounding trafficking and prostitution in every country. In addition, the *HR Report* provides information about trafficking at a lower incidence threshold than the *TIP Report* data and therefore complements that data source.[13]

We combed through the sizeable and extensive country-by-country descriptive accounts in the *TIP Report* and the *HR Report* to obtain two sets of information for each country. First, we determine whether a country is a host country of trafficking, a source, both (a trafficking hub), or neither.[14] Second, for each country we identify its trafficking links, focusing on the extensive margin of trafficking. We do so by constructing a binary variable Traffic_{HS} for all potential host-source country pairs. The variable takes a value of one if trafficking from country S to country H has been reported and zero otherwise. The data in these reports are certainly not comprehensive, and clearly we cannot account for unreported cases of trafficking. Nevertheless, the data do contain information to support an analysis of broad patterns of trafficking and represent a first attempt at systematically using available information to analyze the interaction between host- and source-country legislation and incentives of traffickers.[15]

The Appendix lists the 187 countries included in our data set and their location

[13] For the annual *Trafficking in Persons Report* (*TIP Report*), see U.S. Department of State, Trafficking in Persons Report (http://www.state.gov/g/tip/rls/tiprpt). The report that we use to construct our data set (U.S. Department of State 2003) covers the period April 2002 to March 2003. The *Human Rights Report on Trafficking in Persons, Especially Women and Children* (*HR Report*), from The Protection Project (TPP 2002) provides information on legislation pertaining to trafficking and prostitution for the year 2002.

[14] We use the year 2002 as a cutoff, as our data on legislation on trafficking and prostitution from TPP (2002) pertain to that year. Furthermore, since 2003, a wave of national-level legislative reforms to crack down on international trafficking has reportedly taken place in response to the United Nations Protocol to Prevent, Suppress, and Punish Trafficking in Persons, Especially Women and Children. According to the United Nations Office on Drugs and Crime (UNODC 2009, p. 22), "most legislative frameworks on trafficking in persons have been developed only within the last few years. . . . The UN Protocol entered into force in December 2003. The data shows that the majority of countries did not have any sort of trafficking in persons legislation prior to that year and that most of the current laws criminalizing human trafficking were established after 2003." While the developments since 2003 raise intriguing empirical questions, we do not have access to information on the legislative reforms carried out at the individual country level since 2003.

[15] In addition, we estimate specifications based on a measure of trafficking that relies on only the *TIP Report* data and a measure of trafficking that relies on only the *HR Report* data. The results are qualitatively similar; however, as may be expected, estimates based on the more inclusive *HR Report*'s measure are more precise. These results are available on request.

in the four-part taxonomy: 37 are identified as source-only countries, 37 are host-only countries, 83 are hubs (or transit countries that act as both source and host), and 30 countries have no reported incidence of trafficking. To shed further light on the characteristics of the countries in each category, Table 2 provides category-specific information on a few key characteristics. All economic and demographic variables are taken from World Bank (2004) for the year 2000. All legislative- and law-enforcement-related variables are taken from TPP (2002). Variables capturing political stability, voice and accountability, and rule of law are from Kaufmann, Kraay, and Zoido-Lobaton (1999a, 1999b).[16]

4. Empirical Methodology

4.1. *Specification*

Our objective in what follows is to identify the push and pull factors that drive transnational trafficking. We pay close attention to the effect of two key policy-relevant variables—host-country victim protection through amnesty and host- and source-country legislation against prostitution, a sector that constitutes the lion's share of employment for trafficked victims.[17]

To identify the drivers of cross-border trafficking, we propose to estimate a modified gravity model. Such models have been widely used to examine trade flows and international migration. In its simplest form, in the migration context a gravity model specifies international migration flows between an origin and a destination country as a function of income and population in both locations and some measure of the physical distance between countries (see Sjaastad 1962; Greenwood 1975; Borjas 1987, 1989; Karemera, Oguledo, and Davis 2000). Both origin- and destination-country characteristics are included to control for the push and pull factors that drive the migration decision.

Drawing on this established literature, we specify and estimate an augmented gravity model. The outcome variable in our trafficking-flow model is a measure of whether there is any reported incidence of human trafficking from country S (source) to H (host). Following the standard approach, we specify trafficking as a function of per capita gross domestic product (PCGDP) in both the host and the source countries. To capture the cost of trafficking, we include a distance variable, a measure of whether countries share a border, and whether they are in a common region of the world.

In addition to the inclusion of distance, common-region, and common-border effects, we include other region-specific measures that may have a bearing on trafficking flows. These include for both host and source countries a variable

[16] The rule-of-law indicator is a composite index of voice and accountability, political stability, government effectiveness, regulatory framework, and rule of law and control of corruption. The indicator ranges from −3 (worst) to 3 (best).

[17] A recent study (UNODC 2009, p. 51) based on information provided by 52 countries shows that an overwhelming majority (79 percent) of the reported incidences of human trafficking involve sexual exploitation.

Table 2
Legislative, Economic, Demographic, and Labor Force Characteristics

Variable	Hub (N = 83)		Host Only (N = 37)		Source Only (N = 37)		No Trafficking (N = 30)	
	Mean	SD	Mean	SD	Mean	SD	Mean	SD
Grants legal status or amnesty to trafficked victims	.10	.30	.16	.37	.11	.32	0	0
Prohibits prostitution	.40	.49	.38	.49	.44	.50	.37	.49
Employment in agriculture (% of total)	18.78	17.74	8.00	7.04	32.58	20.37	11.86	11.69
Population density (people per square kilometer)	178.23	746.96	120.75	176.44	101.10	186.94	237.99	312.37
Mortality rate (under five deaths per 1,000 people)	82.19	75.72	19.43	27.94	89.86	70.65	38.04	43.47
Literacy rate (% of population)	77.33	21.27	87.42	9.91	77.73	21.92	82.46	18.40
Female unemployment rate	10.20	6.49	9.32	8.15	9.79	6.85	15.96	13.77
Male unemployment rate	9.14	6.17	6.50	6.02	8.61	5.58	11.58	9.58
Log GDP per capita (constant 1995 $U.S.)	7.26	1.45	9.33	1.17	7.70	1.74	7.66	1.18
Political stability	−.25	.91	.70	.71	−.07	1.01	.26	.89
Voice and accountability	−.18	.84	.65	1.00	.07	1.01	−.05	1.09
Rule of law	−.23	.81	.86	.79	−.03	.98	−.04	1.00
Legal origin: French	.44	.50	.46	.51	.30	.47	.25	.44
Legal origin: German	.03	.16	.09	.28	.06	.24	.00	.00
Legal origin: British	.33	.47	.31	.47	.39	.50	.36	.49
Legal origin: socialist	.21	.41	.00	.00	.21	.42	.32	.48
Legal origin: Scandinavian	.00	.00	.14	.36	.03	.17	.07	.26
Distaste for foreign neighbors	.20	.11	.17	.11	.18	.11	.09	.06
Justifiability of prostitution	2.39	.94	2.60	1.06	2.38	.93	4.13	.36
Settler mortality	304.56	574.05	47.86	32.11	164.87	156.28	38.47	52.01

Note. GDP = gross domestic product.

indicating whether the country is a transitional economy (from a socialist economy toward a market-based economy), one indicating whether the country is landlocked, and a set of regional fixed effects. Following some of the migration literature (Borjas 1987; Karemera, Oguledo, and Davis 2000), we also include a set of variables that reflect host and country political conditions. These are variables that capture rule of law, political stability and voice, and accountability in both host and source countries.

Finally, and most important, we include whether host and source countries have laws banning prostitution and laws that allow for the granting of amnesty to trafficked victims. A country that grants amnesty does not treat victims of trafficking as being in violation of immigration law and subject to deportation but offers them temporary or permanent residency status. The presence of host (source) country laws banning prostitution is the empirical counterpart of ρ_F (p_D), and having legal provisions allowing for amnesty is the empirical counterpart of a_F. We expect that countries that have laws banning prostitution are more likely to enforce laws related to trafficking (at least of women). While it is quite likely that there is a gap between legislation and enforcement, in the absence of actual information on law-enforcement activities, our use of laws banning prostitution as a proxy for law enforcement related to prostitution, given that it is a sector that accounts for the bulk of trafficked victims' employment, does not seem unreasonable.

The complete augmented gravity specification may be written as

$$\begin{aligned}\text{Traffic}_{HS} = {} & \text{PCGDP}_{H(S)} + \text{Distance}_{HS} + \text{Common Region} \\ & + \text{Common Border} + \text{Region}_{H(S)} \\ & + \text{Political Conditions}_{H(S)} + \text{Grants Legal Amnesty}_{H} \\ & + \text{Bans Prostitution}_{H(S)} + \varepsilon_{HS}.\end{aligned} \tag{9}$$

By way of interpretation, our earlier discussion of Table 1 serves as a guide to the lessons that we draw from the observed association between the three policies and Traffic_{HS}. Thus, what combination of buyer demand elasticity and trafficker ease of mobility is consistent with the observed empirical association between Grants Legal Amnesty_H and Traffic_{HS} and between Bans $\text{Prostitution}_{H(S)}$ and Traffic_{HS}?

4.2. Econometric Concerns and Estimation

Since Traffic_{HS} is a binary variable, assuming that ε_{HS} is normally distributed we begin by estimating several single-equation probit specifications of equation (9). Given that the main aim of the empirical work is to characterize the market for trafficking by examining the effects of amnesty in a host country and the effects of host- and source-country prostitution laws (as proxies for law enforcement with regard to trafficking), a relevant econometric concern is whether these three policy-related measures and trafficking flows are simultaneously determined. While laws pertaining to prostitution are less likely to be directly linked to trafficking flows, our main concern is about Grants Legal Amnesty, as it is probably the variable that is most susceptible to a two-way relationship. That is, a country may be more likely to grant amnesty if it experiences a large inflow of trafficking rather than trafficking flows being driven by the provision of amnesty.

An additional but related concern is that since we use a single cross section of data and cannot control for country-specific unobserved heterogeneity that may influence trafficking flows and laws, we may obtain biased estimates of the effect of amnesty-provision- and prostitution-related laws on trafficking. For example, unobserved country-specific characteristics and values such as tolerance and openness may influence trafficking flows and may also exert an effect on whether a country provides amnesty. In addition, the composition of the pattern of exploitation (for example, forced labor or sexual exploitation) inflicted on trafficked victims may also differ, and as such the relevance of law enforcement on specific illicit sectors of employment (for example, prostitution) can differ across countries. We adopt a range of estimation approaches in view of these econometric concerns.

4.2.1. Unobserved Country Values

An obvious approach to account for unobserved heterogeneity would be to use panel data and allow for country fixed effects. However, such data are not readily available, and even if they were, considering that amnesty- and prostitution-related variables are unlikely to display much variation over time, access to panel data is unlikely to aid identification of the effect of such laws on trafficking. As an alternative, in addition to the inclusion of the country-specific sociopolitical conditions in equation (9), to account for typically unobserved country values that may influence trafficking flows and the policy-relevant variables of concern, we estimate specifications that control for distaste for foreign neighbors and a country's views on prostitution.[18] These data are from the World Values Survey, a source that claims to provide a country-level representative assessment of values and the outlook of the residents in various countries (European Values Study Group and World Values Survey Association 2006).

4.2.2. Diverse Patterns of Exploitation

The next issue concerns the potentially diverse nature of trafficking subsumed under the binary variable $Traffic_{HS}$. While transport of women and children for the purpose of sexual exploitation is the predominant reason for trafficking

[18] The question on tolerance of foreign neighbors is "On this list are various groups of people. Could you please sort out any that you would not like to have as neighbors?" A positive response is recorded as 1, while a negative response is recorded as 0. The question for the justifiability of prostitution is "Please tell me for each of the following statements whether you think it can always be justified, never be justified, or something in between." A 10-point scale is given, with 1 equal to never justifiable and 10 equal to always justifiable.

(UNODC 2009), other forms of trafficking, such as forced labor and other forms of exploitation, are also known to exist. Arguably, as long as sexual exploitation is among the reasons for trafficking, we would expect laws banning prostitution to play a role, for example. Nonetheless, we make use of information (UNODC 2009) on regional variations in the patterns of exploitation. In particular, among western and central African countries, forced labor is reportedly a major form of trafficking, though trafficking for sexual exploitation is also observed. Among eastern African countries, information about the pattern of exploitation is scarce, and the details of the practice are largely unknown. In all other regions, sexual exploitation is reportedly the predominant form of trafficking. To see the potential impact that these differences in patterns of exploitation have on our estimates, we sequentially exclude countries with unknown patterns of exploitation and/or known patterns of exploitation that are largely not related to sexual exploitation.

4.2.3. Endogeneity and Credibility of Instruments

To allow for possible endogeneity between trafficking flows and amnesty, we adopt an instrumental variables (IV) approach and provide several IV estimates of equation (9). We endogenize amnesty and treat it as a function of the explanatory variables in equation (9) and a set of variables that are assumed to determine amnesty but not to have a direct bearing on trafficking (excluded from the trafficking equation). Following Vella (1993), we obtain generalized residuals from a first-stage probit regression of amnesty that are subsequently inserted in equation (9). This augmented probit equation provides consistent estimates, and a test of the null hypothesis that the coefficients on the generalized residuals are zero is a (Hausman) specification test for the exogeneity of amnesty.

While the estimation methodology is straightforward, a key concern while implementing IV estimation is the availability of credible instruments. To estimate the impact of amnesty on trafficking, we need variables that are correlated with the probability that a country grants amnesty but that, conditional on other controls, do not exert an effect on trafficking flows other than through their effect on amnesty provisions. A country's legal origins offer potentially relevant instruments.

In recent years, a large body of literature has shown that a country's legal origins have a direct bearing on its legal framework in several spheres and, through these laws, on economic and social outcomes.[19] In particular, LaPorta et al. (1997, 1998) use a country's legal origins as an instrument for its legal rules to identify the effect of laws on outcomes of interest. Taking a cue from this literature, we argue that laws regarding amnesty are likely to be influenced by a country's legal origins but are unlikely to exert a direct effect on trafficking

[19] For more details on the link between legal origins and laws in different spheres, including labor laws, corporate law, and security law, see LaPorta, Lopez-de-Silanes, and Shleifer (2008). For the link between legal origins and constitutional commitments to education, health, housing, and workers' rights, see Ben-Bassat and Dahan (2008).

patterns. While laws do evolve, the legal-origin theory argues that the origins of a legal system continue to exert a substantial influence on its current legal system and that each legal system is marked by an "ideology, that is, a religious or political conception of how economic or social life should be organized" (Zweigert and Kötz 1998, p. 72). Following Reynolds and Flores (1989), we classify each country in our data set into one of five groups (socialist, English common law, and civil law, further divided into French, Scandinavian, and German origin), and subsequently the set of variables indicating a country's legal origins is used to instrument amnesty.

While it is quite likely that a country's legal origins are correlated with the probability that it grants amnesty, the exclusion restriction that legal origins do not have a direct bearing on trafficking flows may be challenged. If legal origins are viewed as a general indicator of how economic and social life should be organized, then these instruments may capture country-level unobserved attitudes such as openness or tolerance and may indeed have a direct bearing on trafficking flows. To examine the extent to which our estimates may be driven by such omitted variables, we estimate several IV models that include specifications controlling for a number of variables that are likely to be correlated with trafficking flows and legal origin. These include measures of the rule of law, voice and accountability, and political stability.

5. Regression Results

5.1. Single-Equation Estimates

Single-equation estimates of several variants of equation (9) are provided in Table 3.[20] The first specification includes only the key variables of interest (amnesty and prostitution laws), while subsequent specifications expand the model to include additional regressors. In this regression and all subsequent regressions, we specifically omit the category of country (30 countries in all) for which we have no specific information on trafficking. We do so because inclusion of such countries would confound missing information on trafficking with no trafficking.[21] Specification (2) includes GDP and distance-related measures, while

[20] In an online appendix, we provide the corresponding single-equation estimates using trafficking variables calculated based on the *TIP Report* data alone and on the *HR Report* data alone. While qualitatively the results are quite similar to one another, using the more inclusive measure of trafficking (the *TIP Report* and the *HR Report* data) strengthens the observed result that granting amnesty by the host country increases the incidence of trafficking. The online appendix also provides single-equation estimates using a trafficking variable calculated based on both the *TIP Report* and the *HR Report* data and including also the 30 countries for which we have no information on trafficking activities as countries with no incidence of trafficking. Again, the results are qualitatively similar.

[21] For 26 of these countries, there are reports that document their legislative policies but state that there is no information on trafficking; for two of these countries there are no reports (Palestine and Niue); one (Jamaica) is classified as a transit country, and for another (New Zealand) information is limited to one case of trafficking in 1996. We also estimated the various specifications including these 30 countries. There are no qualitative differences from the results reported here. Estimates are available on request.

specification (3) also controls for landlocked and transitional economies. Specification (4) includes measures to control for regional fixed effects, while specifications (5) and (6) include controls for country-specific social and political conditions without and with regional fixed effects, respectively.

Focusing on the key variables of interest, as shown in Table 3, we note that the estimates indicate that the granting of amnesty by a host country is always positive in sign, and it is statistically significant in five of the six specifications. The marginal effect ranges from 9 to 1.1 percentage points, and while the inclusion of various regressors reduces the magnitude of the coefficient, it remains remarkably stable across the last five specifications. Except for specification (1), which includes only the key policy-relevant variables, the magnitude of the coefficient lies between 1.1 and 1.6 percentage points. Across the board we see that there is a positive link between host-country amnesty provision and trafficking flows, which suggests that a decrease in the probability of discovery (cost of trafficked individuals) does not hinder trafficking flows.

In terms of laws prohibiting prostitution, the estimates are also stable across specifications and display a positive link between host-country prostitution laws and the probability of trafficking. However, the estimates are small in magnitude and are not statistically significant. The coefficients on source-country prostitution laws are also positive, but they are statistically significant. The two sets of laws have a positive sign, which indicates that increases in law enforcement related to illicit-sector activities in both host and source countries mutually reinforce one another and are likely to increase rather than decrease trafficking flows. In light of the discussion in Section 2 and Table 1, the estimates related to amnesty and prostitution laws are jointly consistent with two characteristics of the market for transnational trafficking: inelastic buyer demand and relatively mobile middlemen with access to an internationally diverse buyer base and able to readily switch between domestic and foreign markets.

Table A1 displays single-regression estimates after controlling for potential unobserved heterogeneity in a country's attitudes toward foreign neighbors and toward prostitution. To account for the potentially diverse forms of exploitation subsumed under $Traffic_{HS}$, Tables A2, A3, and A4 successively exclude eastern African countries,[22] western and central African countries,[23] and eastern, western, and central African countries. While the number of observations is greatly reduced in some cases, the resulting estimates are evidently quite robust and uniformly display a positive link between amnesty, source-country prostitution laws, and host-country prostitution laws on trafficking. With these observations, in what follows we return to the full sample to carry out IV estimations.

[22] These include Burundi, Djibouti, Eritrea, Ethiopia, Kenya, Mauritius, Rwanda, Tanzania, and Uganda.

[23] These include Benin, Burkina Faso, Chad, Côte d'Ivoire, Gabon, Gambia, Ghana, Liberia, Mali, Mauritania, Niger, Nigeria, Senegal, Sierra Leone, and Togo.

Table 3
Probability of Trafficking: Probit Marginal Effect Estimates

Variable	(1)	(2)	(3)	(4)	(5)	(6)
Host country grants amnesty	.090**	.016	.015**	.011**	.016*	.011*
	(.027)	(.010)	(.0051)	(.0038)	(.0064)	(.0044)
Host-country prostitution laws	.0033	.0044	.0025	.0015	.0035	.0021
	(.0071)	(.0038)	(.0019)	(.0011)	(.0028)	(.0016)
Host-country log GDP per capita		.0073**	.0041**	.0023**	.0058**	.0032**
		(.0016)	(.00084)	(.00035)	(.0015)	(.00077)
Host country has transitional economy			−.0069**	−.0041**	−.0094**	−.0053**
			(.0011)	(.00066)	(.0013)	(.00077)
Host country landlocked			−.0055**	−.0030**	−.0064**	−.0033**
			(.0014)	(.00072)	(.0012)	(.00064)
Source-country prostitution laws	.012*	.0072**	.0038**	.0021**	.0045**	.0025**
	(.0059)	(.0022)	(.0012)	(.00068)	(.0013)	(.00079)
Source-country log GDP per capita		−.0047**	−.0038**	−.0019**	−.0041**	−.0019**
		(.00088)	(.00076)	(.00055)	(.0011)	(.00054)
Source country has transitional economy			.025**	.0042	.023**	.0047
			(.0079)	(.0026)	(.0060)	(.0029)
Source country landlocked			−.0039**	−.0021**	−.0052**	−.0023**
			(.0014)	(.00049)	(.0015)	(.00049)
Host and source in same region		.012	.018*	.011**	$.016^{+}$	.0091*
		(.011)	(.0078)	(.0037)	(.0088)	(.0040)
Host and source share border		.056**	.046**	.031**	.050**	.034**
		(.017)	(.0087)	(.0069)	(.015)	(.0089)
Distance (1,000 km)		−.0024**	−.0012**	−.00091**	−.0017**	−.0012**
		(.00082)	(.00021)	(.00015)	(.00026)	(.00015)
Source country in EAP				.13*		.19*
				(.057)		(.080)
Source country in ECA				$.071^{+}$		.069
				(.043)		(.045)

Source country in MENA				.0051		.0063
				(.0090)		(.011)
Source country in southern Asia				$.10^{+}$		$.11^{+}$
				(.054)		(.062)
Source country in SSA				.022		.028
				(.018)		(.024)
Source country in LAC				.048		.056
				(.034)		(.040)
Host-country political stability					.0010	.00024
					(.0013)	(.00081)
Host-country voice and accountability					.0012	.00092
					(.0015)	(.00079)
Host-country rule of law					−.0034	$-.0018^{**}$
					(.0021)	(.00068)
Source-country political stability					$.0020^{*}$	−.00067
					(.00087)	(.00043)
Source-country voice and accountability					.0019	.00086
					(.0016)	(.00056)
Source-country rule of law					$-.0052^{**}$	−.0011
					(.0020)	(.00075)
N	24,180	21,170	21,170	21,170	16,770	16,770
Pseudo-R^2	.051	.24	.29	.33	.29	.34
Log likelihood	−3,316	−2,430	−2,257	−2,124	−2,011	−1,878

Note. Robust standard errors are in parentheses. GDP = gross domestic product; EAP = east Asia and Pacific region; ECA = Europe and central Asia; MENA = Middle East and North Africa; SSA = sub-Saharan Africa; LAC = Latin America and the Caribbean.

$^{+}$ $p < .10$.
* $p < .05$.
** $p < .01$.

Table 4

Instrumental Variable Estimates of the Probability of Trafficking: Legal Origins

Variable	(1)	(2)	(3)	(4)	(5)	(6)
Host country grants amnesty	.34**	.028	.046**	.037*	.034	.029
	(.065)	(.026)	(.015)	(.016)	(.022)	(.018)
Host-country prostitution laws	.014	.0059	.0048^{+}	.0029^{+}	.0051^{+}	.0030*
	(.0099)	(.0053)	(.0026)	(.0015)	(.0027)	(.0015)
Source-country prostitution laws	.014*	.0084**	.0043**	.0026**	.0044**	.0024**
	(.0062)	(.0023)	(.0015)	(.00074)	(.0013)	(.00071)
Generalized residual	−.059**	−.0033	−.0061**	−.0037*	−.0044	−.0029
	(.013)	(.0049)	(.0018)	(.0014)	(.0031)	(.0019)

Note. Robust standard errors are in parentheses. N = 15,867.
$^{+}$ $p < .10$.
* $p < .05$.
** $p < .01$.

5.2. Instrumental Variables Estimates

Table 4 presents IV estimates based on the use of legal origins as an instrument. The first-stage estimates are provided in Table A5.

Before we turn to the second-stage estimates, a few comments on the first-stage estimates, in particular the strength of the instruments, are in order. Table A5 indicates that countries with French and German legal origins are more likely to provide amnesty than are countries with other legal origins. The greater likelihood of amnesty provisions in countries with a civil-law tradition is consistent with the findings of Ben-Bassat and Dahan (2008), who note that countries with a civil-law tradition tend to have a greater constitutional commitment to social rights than countries with a common-law tradition. The legal-origins variables are statistically significant, and a statistical test for excluding the instruments records a *p*-value less than .01.[24]

In some of the specifications reported in Table 4, the generalized residual is negative and statistically significant, which indicates that in the absence of this correction there would be a tendency to underestimate the effect of amnesty on trafficking. As in the case of the ordinary least squares (OLS) regression estimates, both host- and source-country prostitution laws exert a positive and mutually reinforcing effect on international trafficking.

Overall, qualitatively there is not much difference between the OLS estimates and the IV estimates. In both cases and across a variety of specifications, there is usually a positive, large and statistically significant effect of amnesty on trafficking flows. Across our empirical analysis, the effects of both host- and source-country prostitution laws remain positive and small, and the coefficients on these variables are statistically significant for the bulk of IV estimates.

[24] The strength of the instruments may be gauged by examining the *F*-statistic on the instruments in the first stage (see Stock, Wright, and Yogo 2002). In order to do so, we estimate the first-stage regression using a linear probability model. The first-stage *F*-statistic is 200.93, which may be compared with the benchmark of 10 for two-stage least squares to be reliable.

Our empirical findings are consistent with the coexistence of the following sets of characteristics of the market for trafficking: (1) buyer valuation exhibits a sufficiently inelastic demand, which suggests that stricter enforcement will raise the market value of trafficked victims, and (2) middleman traffickers exhibit a considerable degree of cross-border mobility. With point 1, the addition of point 2 suggests that domestic and foreign law-enforcement activities in illicit sectors of employment tend to have a positive and mutually reinforcing impact on the incidence of transnational trafficking.

6. Conclusion

We began this paper with two sets of questions—what is the trafficking impact of a crackdown on illicit activities in the source country if the bargaining position of transnational traffickers hinges on a threat to switch to a domestic buyer source? What about a similar increase in the likelihood of discovery in the foreign country? Our goal is to contribute to the debate on the coordination of international efforts to curb transnational trafficking by means of laws that directly act on the demand-side incentives that encourage individuals to engage in trafficking. Our theoretical model shows in the context of a two-way bilateral bargaining problem that the answers to these questions are nuanced. In particular, crackdowns on illicit employment of trafficked victims in the host and the source countries can be mutually reinforcing or can counteract one another, depending precisely on whether traffickers enjoy ready access to an internationally diverse buyer base and the demand elasticity of the demand for trafficked victims.

Using a novel data set of international trafficking, we empirically ascertain the drivers of cross-border trafficking, including victim-protection programs and law enforcement against prostitution. Our empirical assessment pays particular attention to the endogeneity of victim-protection legislation and country-specific unobserved heterogeneity. We present results from single-equation estimates and IV estimates using a country's legal origin as the instrument. In both cases, and across a variety of specifications, our findings show that the impacts of both host- and source-country legislation prohibiting prostitution on trafficking are positive. These findings are consistent with an inelastic demand for trafficked victims and considerable ease of access across domestic and foreign markets.

In terms of the debate concerning whether a heightened likelihood of discovery in illicit service sectors can stem the tide of transnational trafficking, these findings lend support to the view that with inelastic demand, heightened enforcement in the host country can raise the willingness to pay for trafficked victims in the host country, thus encouraging transnational trafficking. Meanwhile, with considerable ease of access between domestic and foreign markets, heightened enforcement in the source country can indeed "play into the hands of criminal networks" (Bureau of the Dutch National Rapporteur on Trafficking in Human Beings 2005, p. 6) by raising the (threat point) reservation price of trafficked victims and accordingly the profitability of transnational trafficking.

A number of other important questions remain unanswered. A key issue raised in this paper is that domestic and international trafficking activities are simultaneously determined. This suggests not only that domestic legislation can spill over to affect international trafficking but also that international enforcement of antitrafficking initiatives can affect domestic trafficking activities. This observation naturally suggests the need to empirically ascertain the link between trafficking-related policy measures and illicit domestic employment. In addition, the model that we explore is in fact equally applicable for illicit international trade in products such as drugs and antiquities. Empirical work on these alternative areas where middleman traffickers operate can be equally illuminating.

Appendix

A1. Countries and Status of Trafficking

No Trafficking. Andorra, Burundi, Comoros, Jamaica, Liechtenstein, Maldives, Malta, Marshall Islands, Mauritius, Micronesia, Monaco, Namibia, Nauru, New Zealand, Niue, Palau, Palestine, Papua New Guinea, Saint Kitts and Nevis, Saint Lucia, Saint Vincent and the Grenadines, Samoa, San Marino, São Tomé and Príncipe, Seychelles, Solomon Islands, Tonga, Tuvalu, Uruguay, and Vanuatu.

Host Only. Antigua, Australia, Austria, Bahamas, Bahrain, Belgium, Belize, Bosnia and Herzegovina, Botswana, Chile, Cyprus, Denmark, Djibouti, Egypt, Finland, Former Yugoslav Republic of Macedonia, France, Greece, Iceland, Italy, Japan, Kuwait, Lebanon, Libya, Luxembourg, Norway, Oman, Portugal, Qatar, Saudi Arabia, Spain, Suriname, Sweden, Switzerland, Trinidad and Tobago, United Arab Emirates, and United Kingdom.

Hub. Afghanistan, Albania, Algeria, Angola, Argentina, Benin, Brazil, Brunei, Bulgaria, Burkina Faso, Cambodia, Cameroon, Canada, Chad, China, Costa Rica, Côte d'Ivoire, Czech Republic, Democratic Republic of Congo, Dominican Republic, Ecuador, El Salvador, Equatorial Guinea, Estonia, Fiji, Gabon, Gambia, Germany, Ghana, Guatemala, Haiti, Hong Kong (Special Administrative Region), Hungary, India, Iran, Israel, Kazakhstan, Kenya, Kosovo, Kyrgyzstan, Liberia, Lithuania, Macau (Special Administrative Region), Malawi, Malaysia, Mali, Mexico, Nepal, Netherlands, Niger, Nigeria, Pakistan, Panama, Paraguay, Peru, Philippines, Poland, Romania, Russia Federation, Senegal, Singapore, Slovakia, South Africa, South Korea (Republic of Korea), Sri Lanka, Sudan, Swaziland, Syria, Taiwan, Tanzania, Thailand, Togo, Turkey, Uganda, Ukraine, United States, Uzbekistan, Venezuela, Vietnam, Yemen, Yugoslavia, Zambia, and Zimbabwe.

Source Only. Armenia, Azerbaijan, Bangladesh, Barbados, Belarus, Bhutan, Bolivia, Cape Verde, Central African Republic, Colombia, Croatia, Cuba, Eritrea, Ethiopia, Georgia, Guyana, Honduras, Indonesia, Iraq, Laos, Latvia, Lesotho, Madagascar, Mauritania, Moldova, Mongolia, Morocco, Mozambique, Myanmar, Nicaragua, Rwanda, Sierra Leone, Slovenia, Somalia, Tajikistan, Tunisia, and Turkmenistan.

A2. Additional Regressions

Table A1

Probit Marginal Effect Estimates Including Host-Country Values

Variable	(1)	(2)	(3)
Host country grants amnesty	.011**	.012**	.018**
	(.0021)	(.0023)	(.0053)
Host-country prostitution laws	.0015**	.0017**	.00014
	(.00050)	(.00054)	(.0020)
Source-country prostitution laws	.0021**	.0021**	.0019
	(.00056)	(.00058)	(.0015)
Host-country log GDP per capita	.0023**	.0024**	.0015**
	(.00030)	(.00031)	(.00042)
Host country has transitional economy	−.0041**	−.0041**	−.0073**
	(.00057)	(.00059)	(.00097)
Host country landlocked	−.0030**	−.0033**	−.0029**
	(.00053)	(.00058)	(.00053)
Source-country log GDP per capita	−.0019**	−.0019**	−.0017**
	(.00030)	(.00031)	(.00024)
Source country has transitional economy	.0042	.0040	.025**
	(.0038)	(.0038)	(.0043)
Source country landlocked	−.0021**	−.0023**	−.0021**
	(.00043)	(.00045)	(.00071)
Host and source are in same region	.011**	.010**	.0090*
	(.0018)	(.0019)	(.0039)
Host and source share border	.031**	.036**	.030**
	(.0065)	(.0074)	(.0090)
Distance (1,000 km)	−.00091**	−.00094**	−.00096**
	(.00013)	(.00014)	(.00025)
Source country in EAP	.13**	.14**	.18**
	(.037)	(.038)	(.034)
Source country in ECA	.071*	.075*	.040**
	(.032)	(.033)	(.0059)
Source country in MENA	.0051	.0055	.016**
	(.0044)	(.0047)	(.0057)
Source country in southern Asia	.10**	.10**	.16**
	(.037)	(.038)	(.027)
Source country in SSA	.022**	.024**	.037**
	(.0085)	(.0091)	(.0064)
Source country in LAC	.048**	.051**	.12**
	(.016)	(.017)	(.018)
Host country has French legal origin		−.00056	
		(.00045)	
Host country has German legal origin		.00017	
		(.00089)	
Host-country distaste for foreign neighbors			.0081
			(.0067)
Host-country justifiability of prostitution			.000030
			(.00048)
N	21,170	20,010	8,845
Pseudo-R^2	.33	.33	.31
Log likelihood	−2,124	−2,048	−872

Note. Robust standard errors are in parentheses. GDP = gross domestic product; EAP = east Asia and Pacific region; ECA = Europe and central Asia; MENA = Middle East and North Africa; SSA = sub-Saharan Africa; LAC = Latin America and the Caribbean.

* $p < .05$.

** $p < .01$.

Table A2

Probit Marginal Effect Estimates Excluding Eastern African Countries

Variable	(1)	(2)	(3)	(4)	(5)	(6)
Host country grants amnesty	.092**	.016	.015**	.011**	.016*	.011*
	(.027)	(.010)	(.0049)	(.0036)	(.0063)	(.0043)
Host-country prostitution laws	.0024	.0040	.0023	.0013	.0031	.0018
	(.0071)	(.0038)	(.0020)	(.0011)	(.0028)	(.0016)
Host-country log GDP per capita		.0072**	.0041**	.0023**	.0057**	.0032**
		(.0016)	(.00085)	(.00035)	(.0015)	(.00073)
Host country has transitional economy			−.0069**	−.0040**	−.0092**	−.0052**
			(.0011)	(.00068)	(.0013)	(.00080)
Host country landlocked			−.0055**	−.0030**	−.0064**	−.0033**
			(.0014)	(.00073)	(.0012)	(.00066)
Source-country prostitution laws	.013*	.0075**	.0039**	.0023**	.0042**	.0024**
	(.0059)	(.0021)	(.0012)	(.00065)	(.0011)	(.00075)
Source-country log GDP per capita		−.0050**	−.0040**	−.0019**	−.0042**	−.0017**
		(.00093)	(.00077)	(.00053)	(.0011)	(.00052)
Source country has transitional economy			.024**	.0041	.022**	.0044
			(.0076)	(.0025)	(.0056)	(.0027)
Source country landlocked			−.0040**	−.0021**	−.0053**	−.0022**
			(.0014)	(.00046)	(.0014)	(.00047)
Host and source in same region		.012	.017*	.010**	.015^{+}	.0088*
		(.011)	(.0080)	(.0038)	(.0089)	(.0040)
Host and source share border		.053**	.045**	.030**	.049**	.032**
		(.016)	(.0081)	(.0068)	(.014)	(.0085)
Distance (1,000 km)		−.0023**	−.0012**	−.00090**	−.0016**	−.0012**
		(.00080)	(.00021)	(.00016)	(.00025)	(.00016)
Source country in EAP				.13*		.19*
				(.054)		(.076)
Source country in ECA				.069^{+}		.067
				(.041)		(.043)

Source country in MENA				.0049		.0064
				(.0085)		(.011)
Source country in southern Asia				.10^{+}		.11^{+}
				(.053)		(.060)
Source country in SSA				.025		.030
				(.020)		(.027)
Source country in LAC				.047		.053
				(.032)		(.038)
Host-country political stability					.0013	.00040
					(.0014)	(.00085)
Host-country voice and accountability					.0010	.00083
					(.0015)	(.00077)
Host-country rule of law					−.0035^{+}	−.0019**
					(.0021)	(.00069)
Source-country political stability					.0020*	−.00065
					(.00087)	(.00047)
Source-country voice and accountability					.0020	.00096^{+}
					(.0017)	(.00057)
Source-country rule of law					−.0053*	−.0014*
					(.0022)	(.00073)
N	23,250	20,300	20,300	20,300	16,254	16,254
Pseudo-R^2	.052	.24	.29	.34	.29	.34
Log likelihood	−3,210	−2,340	−2,177	−2,049	−1,951	−1,819

Note. Robust standard errors are in parentheses. GDP = gross domestic product; EAP = east Asia and Pacific region; ECA = Europe and central Asia; MENA = Middle East and North Africa; SSA = sub-Saharan Africa; LAC = Latin America and the Caribbean.

$^{+}$ $p < .10$.
* $p < .05$.
** $p < .01$.

Table A3

Probit Marginal Effect Estimates Excluding Western and Central African Countries

Variable	(1)	(2)	(3)	(4)	(5)	(6)
Host country grants amnesty	.090**	.013	.013**	.0092**	.013*	.0087*
	(.027)	(.0085)	(.0047)	(.0034)	(.0059)	(.0040)
Host-country prostitution laws	.0039	.0047	.0029	.0017	.0039	.0023
	(.0073)	(.0039)	(.0021)	(.0012)	(.0033)	(.0019)
Host-country log GDP per capita		.0074**	.0045**	.0025**	.0067**	.0037**
		(.0016)	(.00088)	(.00032)	(.0015)	(.00067)
Host country has transitional economy			−.0061**	−.0035**	−.0082**	−.0047**
			(.00099)	(.00066)	(.0012)	(.00079)
Host country landlocked			−.0052**	−.0028**	−.0059**	−.0030**
			(.0014)	(.00069)	(.0014)	(.00071)
Source-country prostitution laws	.012^{+}	.0067**	.0037*	.0021**	.0044**	.0025**
	(.0069)	(.0022)	(.0015)	(.00073)	(.0015)	(.00079)
Source-country log GDP per capita		−.0048**	−.0038**	−.0018**	−.0041**	−.0017**
		(.00083)	(.00075)	(.00055)	(.0011)	(.00060)
Source country has transitional economy			.021**	.0040	.018**	.0039
			(.0067)	(.0025)	(.0051)	(.0031)
Source country landlocked			−.0036**	−.0018**	−.0044**	−.0018**
			(.0013)	(.00050)	(.0014)	(.00052)
Host and source in same region		.0075	.013	.0074*	.011	.0061
		(.010)	(.0084)	(.0035)	(.0094)	(.0039)
Host and source share border		.051**	.045**	.031**	.044**	.030**
		(.018)	(.011)	(.0091)	(.014)	(.0094)
Distance (1,000 km)		−.0021**	−.0011**	−.00085**	−.0016**	−.0012**
		(.00072)	(.00023)	(.00015)	(.00029)	(.00015)
Source country in EAP				.11*		.17*
				(.047)		(.069)
Source country in ECA				.057^{+}		.057
				(.034)		(.038)

Source country in MENA				.0043		.0056
				(.0076)		(.010)
Source country in southern Asia				.086⁺		.10⁺
				(.046)		(.055)
Source country in SSA				.022		.031
				(.019)		(.028)
Source country in LAC				.044		.050
				(.028)		(.032)
Host-country political stability					.00048	−.000064
					(.0017)	(.00100)
Host-country voice and accountability					.0015	.0011
					(.0018)	(.00099)
Host-country rule of law					−.0039⁺	−.0021*
					(.0022)	(.00084)
Source-country political stability					.0026**	−.00036
					(.00082)	(.00057)
Source-country voice and accountability					.0017	.00084
					(.0018)	(.00090)
Source-country rule of law					−.0058**	−.0015
					(.0018)	(.0010)
N	21,855	18,995	18,995	18,995	14,964	14,964
Pseudo-R^2	.053	.25	.29	.34	.29	.34
Log likelihood	−2,953	−2,132	−1,997	−1,871	−1,790	−1,667

Note. Robust standard errors are in parentheses. GDP = gross domestic product; EAP = east Asia and Pacific region; ECA = Europe and central Asia; MENA = Middle East and North Africa; SSA = sub-Saharan Africa; LAC = Latin America and the Caribbean.

⁺ $p < .10$.
* $p < .05$.
** $p < .01$.

Table A4

Probit Marginal Effect Estimates Excluding Eastern, Western, and Central African Countries

Variable	(1)	(2)	(3)	(4)	(5)	(6)
Host country grants amnesty	.092**	.013	.013**	.0089**	.012*	.0084*
	(.027)	(.0082)	(.0045)	(.0032)	(.0057)	(.0039)
Host-country prostitution laws	.0030	.0042	.0026	.0016	.0035	.0020
	(.0074)	(.0038)	(.0022)	(.0013)	(.0033)	(.0019)
Host-country log GDP per capita		.0072**	.0045**	.0025**	.0067**	.0037**
		(.0016)	(.00089)	(.00031)	(.0014)	(.00058)
Host country has transitional economy			−.0059**	−.0034**	−.0078**	−.0044**
			(.0011)	(.00069)	(.0013)	(.00083)
Host country landlocked			−.0052**	−.0027**	−.0059**	−.0029**
			(.0014)	(.00068)	(.0014)	(.00072)
Source-country prostitution laws	.014*	.0068**	.0038**	.0023**	.0040**	.0024**
	(.0069)	(.0020)	(.0014)	(.00064)	(.0014)	(.00073)
Source-country log GDP per capita		−.0051**	−.0040**	−.0017**	−.0043**	−.0014**
		(.00089)	(.00075)	(.00051)	(.00095)	(.00054)
Source country has transitional economy			.020**	.0037	.017**	.0033
			(.0062)	(.0024)	(.0048)	(.0028)
Source country landlocked			−.0036**	−.0017**	−.0046**	−.0015**
			(.0013)	(.00041)	(.0012)	(.00033)
Host and source in same region		.0067	.012	.0069*	.010	.0055
		(.0097)	(.0085)	(.0035)	(.0093)	(.0037)
Host and source share border		.047**	.042**	.029**	.041**	.027**
		(.017)	(.0099)	(.0086)	(.012)	(.0086)
Distance (1,000 km)		−.0021**	−.0011**	−.00084**	−.0016**	−.0012**
		(.00070)	(.00023)	(.00015)	(.00027)	(.00015)
Source country in EAP				.11*		.16*
				(.043)		(.065)
Source country in ECA				.055+		.055
				(.031)		(.036)

Source country in MENA				.0040		.0056
				(.0069)		(.0094)
Source country in southern Asia				$.084^{+}$		$.100^{+}$
				(.044)		(.052)
Source country in SSA				.025		.030
				(.022)		(.030)
Source country in LAC				.042		.046
				(.026)		(.029)
Host-country political stability					.00081	.00015
					(.0018)	(.0010)
Host-country voice and accountability					.0013	.0010
					(.0018)	(.00094)
Host-country rule of law					$-.0041^{+}$	$-.0023^{**}$
					(.0022)	(.00083)
Source-country political stability					$.0026^{**}$	−.00032
					(.00095)	(.00066)
Source-country voice and accountability					.0018	.0010
					(.0018)	(.00089)
Source-country rule of law					$-.0057^{**}$	$-.0020^{*}$
					(.0019)	(.00090)
N	20,925	18,125	18,125	18,125	14,448	14,448
Pseudo-R^2	.055	.25	.30	.34	.29	.34
Log likelihood	−2,848	−2,037	−1,915	−1,795	−1,728	−1,606

Note. Robust standard errors are in parentheses. GDP = gross domestic product; EAP = east Asia and Pacific region; ECA = Europe and central Asia; MENA = Middle East and North Africa; SSA = sub-Saharan Africa; LAC = Latin America and the Caribbean.
$^{+}$ $p < .10$.
* $p < .05$.
** $p < .01$.

Table A5
First-Stage Probit Estimates

	Host Country Grants Legal Amnesty	
Variable	Coefficient	SE
Host-country prostitution laws	.14**	.049
Host-country log GDP per capita	.54**	.039
Host country has transitional economy	1.23**	.081
Host country landlocked	−.32**	.062
Host-country political stability	.39**	.068
Host-country voice and accountability	1.03**	.060
Host-country rule of law	−.70**	.083
Source-country prostitution laws	−.0050	.043
Source-country log GDP per capita	.0045	.025
Source country has transitional economy	.0053	.22
Source country landlocked	.0090	.049
Source-country political stability	−.0031	.046
Source-country voice and accountability	−.0012	.036
Source-country rule of law	.0012	.059
Host and source in same region	−.23**	.065
Host and source share border	.27*	.13
Distance (thousands of km)	−.018**	.0060
Source country in EAP	.087	.094
Source country in ECA	−.011	.22
Source country in MENA	.0025	.094
Source country in southern Asia	.034	.14
Source country in SSA	.020	.10
Source country in LAC	.065	.089
Host country has French legal origin	.95**	.059
Host country has German legal origin	.62**	.071
Constant	−7.04**	.40

Note. GDP = gross domestic product; EAP = east Asia and Pacific region; ECA = Europe and central Asia; MENA = Middle East and North Africa; SSA = sub-Saharan Africa; LAC = Latin America and the Caribbean. N = 15,867.
* $p < .05$.
** $p < .01$.

References

Akee, Randall, Arnab Basu, Arjun Bedi, and Nancy Chau. 2011. Transnational Trafficking, Law Enforcement, and Victim Protection: A Middleman Trafficker's Perspective. Discussion Paper No. 6226. Institute for the Study of Labor, Bonn.

Andrees, Beate, and Mariska N. J. van der Linden. 2005. Designing Trafficking Research from a Labour Market Perspective: The ILO Experience. International Migration 43: 55–74.

Bales, Kevin. 1999. What Predicts Human Trafficking? Paper presented at the International Conference on New Frontiers of Crime: Trafficking in Human Beings and New Forms of Slavery. Verona, October 22-23.

———. 2004. Understanding the Demand behind Human Trafficking. Unpublished manuscript. University of Hull, Wilberforce Institute for the Study of Slavery and Emancipation, Hull. http://www.childtrafficking.com/Docs/bales_understanding_the_de.pdf.

Basu, Arnab K., and Nancy H. Chau. 2008. An Exploration of the Worst Forms of Child

Labor: Is Redemption a Viable Option? Pp. 37–76 in *Buying Freedom: The Ethics and Economics of Slave Redemption,* edited by Kwame Anthony Appiah and Martin Bunzel. Princeton, N.J.: Princeton University Press.

Becker, Gary S., Kevin M. Murphy, and Michael Grossman. 2006. The Market for Illegal Goods: The Case of Drugs. *Journal of Political Economy* 114:38–60.

Ben-Bassat, Avi, and Momi Dahan. 2008. Social Rights in the Constitution and in Practice. *Journal of Comparative Economics* 36:103–19.

Borjas, George J. 1987. Self-Selection and the Earnings of Immigrants. *American Economic Review* 77:531–53.

———. 1989. Economic Theory and International Migration. *International Migration Review* 23:457–85.

Bureau of the Dutch National Rapporteur on Trafficking in Human Beings. 2005. *Trafficking in Human Beings.* The Hague: Bureau of the Dutch National Rapporteur on Trafficking in Human Beings.

Busse, Matthias, and Sebastian Braun. 2002. Trade and Investment Effects of Forced Labour: An Empirical Assessment. Discussion Paper No. 200. Hamburg Institute of International Economics, Hamburg.

Danailova-Trainor, Gergana, and Patrick Belser. 2006. Globalization and the Illicit Market for Human Trafficking: An Empirical Analysis of Demand and Supply. Working Paper No. 78. International Labor Office Policy Integration Department, Geneva.

Dessy, Sylvain, and Stéphane Pallage. 2003. The Economics of Child Trafficking. Working Paper No. 03-23. University of Quebec, Center for Research on Economic Fluctuation and Employment, Quebec.

European Values Study Group and World Values Survey Association. 2006. European and World Value Surveys Four-Wave Integrated Data File, 1981–2004. Madrid and Tilburg: Análisis Sociológicos Económicos y Políticos and JD Systems.

Friebel, Guido, and Sergei Guriev. 2006. Smuggling Humans: A Theory of Debt-Financed Migration. *Journal of the European Economic Association* 4:1085–1111.

Greenwood, Michael. 1975. Research on Internal Migration in the United States: A Survey. *Journal of Economic Literature* 13:397–433.

ILO (International Labour Organization). 2005. *A Global Alliance against Forced Labour: Global Report under the Follow-up to the ILO Declaration on Fundamental Principles and Rights at Work.* Report of the Director General. Geneva: International Labour Office.

Kara, Siddharth. 2010. *Sex Trafficking: Inside the Business of Modern Slavery.* New York: Columbia University Press.

Karemera, David, Victor Iwuagwu Oguledo, and Bobby Davis. 2000. A Gravity Model Analysis of International Migration to North America. *Applied Economics* 32:1745–55.

Kaufmann, Daniel, Aart Kraay, and Pablo Zoido-Lobaton. 1999a. Aggregating Governance Indicators. Working Paper No. 2195. World Bank Policy Research Department, Washington, D.C.

———. 1999b. Governance Matters. Working Paper No. 2196. World Bank Policy Research Department, Washington, D.C.

La Porta, Rafael, Florencio Lopez-de-Silanes, and Andrei Shleifer. 2008. The Economic Consequences of Legal Origins. *Journal of Economic Literature* 46:285–332.

La Porta, Rafael, Florencio Lopez-de-Silanes, Andrei Shleifer, and Robert W. Vishny. 1997. Legal Determinants of External Finance. *Journal of Finance* 52:1131–50.

———. 1998. Law and Finance. *Journal of Political Economy* 106:1113–55.

Mahmoud, Toman Omar, and Christoph Trebesch. 2010. The Economic Drivers of Human Trafficking: Micro-evidence from Five Eastern European Countries. *Journal of Comparative Economics* 38:177–88.

TPP (The Protection Project). 2002. *Human Rights Report on Trafficking in Persons, Especially Women and Children: A Country-by-Country Report on a Contemporary Form of Slavery.* Washington, D.C.: Johns Hopkins University, Paul H. Nitze School of Advanced International Studies.

Reynolds, Thomas, and Arturo Flores. 1989. *Foreign Law: Current Sources of Basic Legislation in Jurisdictions of the World.* Littleton, Co.: Rothman.

Rogers, Carol Ann, and Kenneth A. Swinnerton. 2008. A Theory of Exploitative Child Labor. *Oxford Economic Papers* 60:20–41.

Salt, John. 2005. *Current Trends in International Migration in Europe.* Strasbourg: Council of Europe.

Sjaastad, L. A. 1962. The Cost and Returns of Human Migration. *Journal of Political Economy* 70:80–93.

Stock, James, Jonathan Wright, and Motohiro Yogo. 2002. A Survey of Weak Instruments and Weak Identification in Generalized Methods of Moments. *Journal of Business and Economic Statistics* 20:518–29.

UNODC (United Nations Office on Drugs and Crimes). 2009. *Global Report on Trafficking in Persons.* Vienna: UNODC.

U.S. Department of State. 2003. *Trafficking in Persons Report.* Washington, D.C.: U.S. Department of State.

———. 2007. *Trafficking in Persons Report.* Washington, D.C.: U.S. Department of State.

———. 2009. *Trafficking in Persons Report.* Washington, D.C.: U.S. Department of State.

Vella, Frank. 1993. A Simple Estimator for Simultaneous Models with Censored Endogenous Regressors. *International Economic Review* 34:441–57.

World Bank. 2004. *World Development Indicators* (CD-ROM). Washington, D.C.: World Bank.

Zweigert, Konrad, and Hein Kötz. 1998. *An Introduction to Comparative Law.* Translated by Tony Weir. 3d ed. New York: Oxford University Press.

Journal of Development Economics 121 (2016) 120–134

Contents lists available at ScienceDirect

Journal of Development Economics

journal homepage: www.elsevier.com/locate/devec

On sweatshop jobs and decent work☆

Nancy H. Chau *

Charles H. Dyson School of Applied Economics and Management, Cornell University, Ithaca, NY 14853, United States

ARTICLE INFO

Article history:
Received 21 July 2014
Received in revised form 1 December 2015
Accepted 22 February 2016
Available online 12 March 2016

Keywords:
Sweatshops
Efficiency
Job search capability

ABSTRACT

This paper argues that while rooting out sweatshop conditions raises unemployment, the potential gains include an increase in decent work employment, a pro-worker shift in distribution, and an improvement in overall efficiency. In a search model of employment inspired by firm- and household-level evidence about the harm that sweatshop conditions pose to workers' capability to be productive at work and to be vertically mobile, this paper unpacks the irony of job losses and efficiency gains by examining equilibria where, unless regulations are in place, employers tolerate unproductive sweatshop conditions, and where workers accept insufficiently compensating sweatshop wages.

"I start at about 6:30, after breakfast, and go until about 7 p.m.," explained one shy teenage girl.

"We break for lunch, and I take half an hour off then."

"You do this six days a week?"

"Oh, no. Every day." (Kristof and WuDunn, 2000).

" The [sweat]shops of Ciudad Hidalgo were not, however, efficient; they were having real trouble competing in the international marketplace; and the blatant violation of international standards was not helping matters, indeed quite the contrary ... One had to conclude that if the changes had been imposed by international labor standards, however imperialistic, they would have contributed to efficiency." (Piore, 2004).

1. Introduction

The proliferation of "no sweat" consumer merchandise in recent years reflects growing public protest against production settings where workers toil under sweatshop conditions. These include wholesale disregard for safety and health conditions and excessive overtime, with adverse impacts both on the work and on the worker (USGAO, 1988, Powell and Skarbek, 2006; Liu et al., 2011, Brown et al., 2015). This paper proposes a model of sweatshop job and decent work in which these adverse impacts are expressly stated as constraints on workers' capability, including their productivity at work, and their ability to seek better job prospects while on the sweatshop job. Can establishments bearing these features of a sweatshop thrive in the labor market? What are the employment, efficiency and distributional implications if sweatshop conditions meet a policy of indifference?

Originally coined in reference to the large pools of workers who arrived to work in cities in the wake of the Industrial Revolution (Engels, 1892), sweatshop establishments have continued to persist in developed countries in specific sectors (e.g., apparel), affecting particular segments of the working population (e.g., migrants) (USDOL, 1988; Esbenshade, 2004). Globalization of production has fueled the mass scale employment of sweatshop labor in developing countries, reinvigorating the sweatshop debate (Krugman, 1997; Elliott and Freeman, 2001; ILO, 2008).

Anti-sweatshop campaigners advocate in favor of a ban on sweatshop jobs on the grounds of excessively poor conditions and overtime despite meager wages (USGAO, 1988; USDOL, 2001; Ross, 2002). Others contend that sweatshop jobs present a market-based solution out of poverty, for why would workers accept a job unless it makes them better off, and why would employers select production conditions detrimental to profits? Banning sweatshop jobs, it is thus argued,

☆ I thank the co-editor of this journal and two anonymous referees for their insightful comments and suggestions. I am grateful to Arnab Basu, Kaushik Basu, Gary Fields, Mary Lovely, and Devashish Mitra for stimulating discussions. This research was initiated while I was a visiting fellow at the Institute for the Study of Labor (IZA). The hospitality of IZA and the financial support from the Alexander von Humboldt Foundation are gratefully acknowledged.

* Tel.: +1 607 255 4463.
E-mail address: hyc3@cornell.edu.

http://dx.doi.org/10.1016/j.jdeveco.2016.02.002
0304-3878/© 2016 Elsevier B.V. All rights reserved.

deprives developing countries of a win–win (Robinson, 1964; Bardhan, 2004, 2005 (ch. 12), Singh, 2003).[1]

This paper contributes to the sweatshop debate in two ways. First, this paper identifies and draws attention to three particularly salient features of sweatshop jobs based on an extensive survey of the evidence currently available (Section 2). To wit, sweatshop conditions exact a cost on (i) worker utility due to poor workplace conditions, (ii) job productivity due to neglect of safety and health, and (iii) vertical mobility as prospects for on-the-job search are reined in. All three features of sweatshop jobs are then incorporated in a model of on-the-job search (Mortensen, 1990; Burdett and Mortensen, 1998; Mortensen, 2000).[2] The model exhibits a number of other features relevant in the sweatshop debate. In particular, the model features a cost of hiring that accommodates labor market settings ranging from perfect competition to scenarios where sweatshop employers have been shown to possess market power (Harrison and Scorse, 2010).[3] Furthermore, in the model employers post wage offers that workers can freely accept or reject, consistent with the outright absence of individual/collective bargaining, another hallmark of sweatshop work.[4]

The model unveils the implications of a sweatshop option both at the employer level and in general equilibrium. Specifically, this paper argues that individual sweatshop employers, when they exist, offer jobs of bottom-rung lifetime value compared to employers of decent work. They do so because they see little need to pre-empt worker-induced job separation, as workers already face conditions hostile to search on-the-job. In general equilibrium, therefore, any increase in the share of sweatshop jobs induces a shift in the equilibrium distribution of wage offers in a way consistent with lower contract values and thus, lower wage expectations. This makes sweatshop workers even cheaper to hire, and results in a crowding-out of decent work opportunities.

Thus, while turning a blind eye to sweatshop conditions prevents sweatshop job losses, a central message here is that *more sweatshop jobs can paradoxically spell overall efficiency losses*. This arises when job creation is spurred by redistributing surplus from workers to employers at the cost of worker productivity and search capability, rather than by productive investments, for example. When the search capability deficit of a sweatshop job is sufficiently acute, a ban on sweatshop jobs does not deprive labor markets of a win–win. Quite the contrary, it is efficiency-improving.

All configurations of steady state equilibrium in the model are screened and two classes of equilibria emerge: a class of graduated labor markets with only decent work employers, and a class of labor markets with a mix of both sweatshop jobs and decent work. Graduation is deterred when workers have no better alternatives to turn to other than sweatshops due, for example, to poor unemployment protection (e.g., in the case of migrants),[5] and when there is high world demand for the final product regardless of labor conditions. The cost of hiring plays a critical and interestingly nuanced role. In most cases, it is shown that sweatshop employment tends to be the highest when the cost of hiring is neither too high (thus when workers are relatively plentiful to begin with), nor too low (when the competition for workers is so intense that inefficient employers do not survive).[6] Thus, far from offering a reliable cure, introducing competition via ease of entry in a piecemeal fashion can in fact encourage more inefficient sweatshops.

Graduation can be triggered by labor regulations as well. However, an all-out ban on sweatshop jobs may not be necessary. Indeed, small improvements in the condition of sweatshop jobs, such as the likelihood of job advancement while on the job, are shown to induce permanent discrete swings in the equilibrium shares of sweatshop jobs going from large positives to zero. This occurs around equilibria that can be characterized as unstable. Such equilibria arise in our setting as the emergence of bottom-rung sweatshop jobs displaces decent work, and shifts the distribution of wage offers to the left. Lower wage expectations give rise to lower reservation wages, which in turn spur further sweatshop entries.[7] In this context, labor regulations that safeguard a minimal level of workers' job search capability, for example by limiting mandatory overtime, can potentially eradicate sweatshops altogether by breaking the vicious cycle of sweatshops and low wages.

The economics literature related to sweatshop jobs and decent work is rich and longstanding, spanning diverse subjects including job search, international labor standards, exploitative labor, and dual labor markets. In the area of job search, our innovation lies in introducing a model where workers' on-the-job search capability is effectively chosen by employers. This complements models of job search in which the likelihood of receiving a job offer is endogenized as an investment decision by workers subject to a cost of job search (Rogerson et al., 2005, Benhabib and Bull, 1983).

A series of studies (OECD, 1996; Brown et al., 1997; Bagwell and Staiger, 2000; OECD, 2000, and Chau and Kanbur, 2006) have established the distribution and efficiency impacts of international labor standards in perfectly competitive labor market settings. Our on-the-job search setup begins with the competitive outcome with zero hiring cost as a special case, and explores the role of ease of entry by varying the cost of hiring as another potential contributor to the incidence of sweatshop jobs. The case of sweatshops considered here is also distinct from labor practices more often referred to as exploitative labor. These arise, for example, when employers lure workers into employment without providing full information (Rogers and Swinnerton, 2008). Set in a stage where lies and deceit whether willful or unwitting are absent, this paper asks whether a ban on sweatshop jobs can nonetheless be justified.

There is a long history of dual labor market models where different jobs for otherwise identical workers co-exist. A number of recent studies on good jobs and bad jobs focus on wage as the definitive characteristic, while work conditions, search capability, and/or worker productivity are kept constant and identical across jobs. In Acemoglu (2001), for example, different capital costs of job creation in equilibrium give rise to high- (good) and low-wage (bad) jobs. In Davis and Harrigan (2011), high- and low-wage jobs are made possible by firm heterogeneity à la Melitz (2003), and efficiency wage considerations as in Shapiro and Stiglitz (1984). In Basu and Chau (2004), wages are tied to the terms of an interlinked debt and labor contract. In studies related to informal employment, similar assumptions on exogenous wage differences but identical search capabilities are typically made (Fields,

[1] For example, Robinson (1964) famously stated that "The only thing worse than being exploited by a capitalist is not being exploited by a capitalist".

[2] For evidence of on-the-job search behavior in developed and developing countries, see, for example, Blau (1991) and Banerjee and Bucci (1995).

[3] While notoriously difficult to come by due to the clandestine nature of sweatshop jobs, China Labor Watch, (2015) (p. 10) presents rare evidence on the costs and wages of sweatshop jobs. This was accomplished by interviews conducted by researchers who disguised themselves as workers or by obtaining actual copies of sweatshop worker pay stubs, thus uncovering among many other facts the cost that sweatshop employers say they incur to hire workers through hiring intermediaries. In this case, they uncover hiring costs ranging from 600 to 1200 yuan per worker based on 60 interviews conducted in 2013–2014.

[4] See Section 2 for a review of evidence on this score based on a series of on-the-ground investigative reports on sweatshop conditions.

[5] This is consistent with the link frequently made between the prevalence of sweatshop jobs and illegal migrant inflow (USGAO, 1988).

[6] I show in Section 6 that this non-monotonicity applies whenever the search capability deficit associated with sweatshop work is not too acute.

[7] Multiple equilibria is a feature shared by a number of recent models of job search. In Acemoglu (2001), for example, a holdup problem arises because an employer who has sunk a high capital investment cost on creating a good job is forced to bargain against a higher wage. Multiple equilibria can prevail because the positive externality that capital investment has on workers are not internalized by employers. Burdett et al. (2003), in a model of crime and unemployment also illustrate the possibility of multiple equilibria, when more criminals increase the victimization rate, which in turn makes becoming a criminal relatively more attractive.

2005). In our model, wages are fully endogenous, and determined solely by sweatshop conditions.

The next section explores some common features of sweatshop work worldwide. Based on these features, Section 3 describes our on-the-job search model of sweatshop jobs and decent work, while Section 4 defines the steady state equilibrium. Section 5 addresses the labor market consequences of sweatshop jobs. Section 6 examines the various configurations of sweatshop equilibrium, and provides numerical simulations on the employment, distribution, and efficiency consequences of sweatshops. Section 7 concludes with a discussion on a number of extensions of the current setup.

2. Sweatshop facts

Notwithstanding the paucity of internationally comparable statistics on sweatshop employment, there has recently been a surge in worker- and firm-level surveys by civil society groups, and non-profit and government organizations. Together, the results of these surveys provide a rich account on the plight of sweatshop workers worldwide. Complementing earlier findings (e.g., USGAO, 1988; OECD, 1996), these recent studies identified what violations of labor standards tend to be prevalent in sweatshops. Other features of sweatshop work — hitherto underappreciated — have also been uncovered, specifically in regards to why sweatshop workers face difficulty resigning even when better job opportunities arise, whether sweatshop conditions adversely impact worker productivity and firm profitability, and whether sweatshop workers receive a compensating differential for the conditions they endure. Each of these features is discussed in turn.

2.1. Sweatshop conditions

In 2008, the ILO decent work agenda affirmed the need to monitor a set of decent work indicators worldwide (ILO, 2008).[8] In Bangladesh, for example, the ILO reports that over half of the workforce exceeds the limit on legal hours of work. Furthermore, total fatal injuries at work doubled between 2003 and 2011 (ILO, 2013). Widespread adoptions of sweatshop like condition exist in developed countries as well. A United States General Accounting Office (USGAO) report (USGAO, 1988) specifically defines a sweatshop as an establishment that violates both safety or health, and wage or child labor laws. At the conclusion of this 1988 GAO study, 40 of the 53 federal officials interviewed indicate sweatshop jobs are pervasive particularly in the apparel industry, meat packing and restaurant establishments. Violations are observed in 47 out of the 50 states surveyed.

At the firm level, the Fair Labor Association provides audit reports of factories under contract with companies that adopt voluntary codes of conduct.[9] Even in this arguably selective sample, the 59 audits that the FLA conducted globally in 2011, for example, yielded 596 findings of non-compliance, amounting to 10.6 findings of non-compliance per audit among FLA affiliated factories (FLA 2012). Most frequent violations occur in the area of health and safety (93% of all audits with at least one area of non-compliance), followed by hours of work (75%); wages, benefits and overtime (75%); and freedom of association (51%).[10] These relative rankings have been persistent since the earliest FLA report in 2006.

Unlike the FLA, the China Labor Watch (CLW) is a non-profit organization that investigates suspicious manufacturing operations and factories throughout China, regardless of whether stated codes of conduct apply. Based on over 400 individual assessments of labor conditions in Chinese factories,[11] violations with respect to overtime, and safety and health conditions appear in virtually every assessment.

2.2. Difficulty to search on the sweatshop job

Since its founding in 2000, the CLW has published over eighty reports on factory conditions.[12] With two exceptions (CLW, 2009a; CLW, 2009b), these reports document a plethora of employer strategies that deter voluntary resignations,[13] including wage deposits (CLW, 2001), explicit contractual limits on resignation (CLW, 2008), opaque resignation approval requirements (CLW, 2011), and late payment of wages and barriers to recovering back pay after resignation (CLW, 2012). It is important to note that these strategies compound circumstances already detrimental to sweatshop workers' ability to search on the job, for example, by creating psychological deterrents (Sen, 1993),[14] physical and health deterrents (Schöer and Leibbrandt, 2006),[15] and other demonstrated deterrents to earnings mobility in general among low-wage workers even in developed countries (Gottschalk, 1982; Neumark and Nizalova, 2007).

In addition to surveys targeting firms, a number of studies target sweatshop workers themselves (e.g., CLW, 2013). In fact, the CLW operates a worker hotline. Results of caller surveys indicate that in addition to wages (16%) and overtime (9%) violations, difficulty in resignations (12%) is a major challenge among sweatshop workers. A large-scale survey of migrants in the Pearl River Delta and the Yangtze River Delta corroborates these findings (Liu et al., 2011; Wan, 2011). This survey uncovered some of the most popular strategies employers use to deter resignation, including deduction of current month salary, charging deposits for employment, seizure of employment certifications, as well as verbal and physical threats, to name a few.

War on Want (2011) reports the results of a survey covering 1000 women workers in 41 garment factories in Bangladesh. 96% of the women surveyed indicated that overtime is a necessity to guarantee a basic salary. As high as 32% work 100–140 hours of overtime each month. In addition to highly publicized concerns associated with safety and health conditions in Bangladeshi garment factories (Bajaj, 2012), 67% of workers did not receive their wages on time. The report argues that most garment workers live on credit, and are thus particularly vulnerable to wage arrears. Late pay can also be a significant deterrent to search on the job, for resigning requires that workers forgo wages already earned by credit constrained households.

2.3. Sweatshop productivity

In a pioneering study, Brown et al. (2015) provides direct empirical evidence on the adverse productivity implications of sweatshop conditions. Using data from firms participating in Better Work Vietnam,[16] the study estimates a production function, and finds that the elasticity of the price cost margin with respect to the proxies of the various labor conditions is strictly positive. These findings reinforce earlier studies, which

[8] As of 2015, 18 country reports profile a diverse range of country experiences based on a list of decent work indicators.

[9] The Fair Labor Association is a tripartite organization connecting universities, civil society organizations and companies founded in 1999.

[10] The FLA code of conduct covers 8 broad categories of labor conditions including compensation, forced labor, freedom of association, harassment or abuse, child labor, discrimination, health and safety, and hours of work.

[11] These investigative reports cover 128 factories, 89 name brands, employing over 130,000 workers (China Labor Watch, 2013).

[12] A complete listing of these reports is available on the public domain at http://www.chinalaborwatch.org/reports (accessed June 16, 2015).

[13] These findings corroborate other reports of more extreme employer strategies including tightly controlled and monitored factory dormitory that restricts movement in and out of factory compounds, and forbids workers from outside contact, for example (Chan, 2000, 2003)

[14] Sen (1993) draws attention to a hitherto sparsely examined aspect of labor market — the capability set of the *employed* in the form of an inability to/a pessimistic attitude about the prospects of breaking free from the status quo: "*Our desires and pleasure-taking abilities adjust to circumstances... those who are persistently deprived... the routinely overworked sweatshop worker in exploitative conditions... tend to come to terms with their deprivation.*"

[15] Schöer and Leibbrandt (2006) demonstrate the importance of physical health and time constraint as key determinants of job search strategies in South Africa.

[16] Better Work is a partnership program between the International Labor Organization and the International Finance Committee to advance labor standards in global supply chains.

likewise suggest that a neglect on the conditions of work runs the risk of diminishing worker productivity (Piore, 2004; Singh, 2003). While rigorous empirical examinations in the area of sweatshop productivity are relatively nascent, this review has not encountered any study that provides robust evidence on sweatshop conditions that improve individual worker productivity.

2.4. Sweatshop wages

Finally, though much of the literature on sweatshop conditions argues that wages are too low given the harsh conditions workers face, there is in fact as yet no direct evidence on whether sweatshop workers fail to receive a compensating differential (Smith, 1776; Rosen, 1986). Powell and Skarbek (2006) comes closest to this point, and presents unconditional comparisons based on observed profiles of sweatshop and industry wages across a list of developing country apparel exporters, as reported in news and magazines. It is shown that average industry wage outstrips average sweatshop wage in most cases analyzed, suggesting that the average sweatshop worker is receiving an insufficiently compensating wage at best, despite the harsh conditions the worker faces.

In summary, three main characteristics of sweatshop jobs can be seen from this evidence: worker disutility in response to harsh workplace conditions, lower productivity due to the neglect of safety and health, and inferior vertical mobility as sweatshop job conditions challenge the worker's ability to effectively search for a job while on the job. Furthermore, sweatshop wages are meager, but cannot conclude from the evidence that wages are necessarily strictly lower in sweatshop jobs relative to decent work.[17] In what follows, this paper takes wages to be endogenously determined in a model that incorporates the three sweatshop characteristics, and explore the central role that this endogenous relationship between wages and sweatshop conditions plays in determining the employment, overall efficiency, and income distribution of a sweatshop option in the labor market.

3. A search model of sweatshop jobs and decent work

Consider a continuous time model of on-the-job search, in which free entering/exiting employers determine whether to offer sweatshop jobs or decent work, and select a corresponding wage offer. Workers decide whether to accept or reject any offer received, depending on the nature of work, the arrival rate of alternative job offers, and the wage distribution of these alternative offers conditional on receiving one. Throughout, the size of the pool of workers will be normalized at unity.

3.1. Workers

3.1.1. Worker participation and compensating differential

There are three states of employment (i): sweatshop jobs (s), decent work (d), and unemployment (u). Each worker chooses a plan to maximize the lifetime expected value of the stochastic stream of instantaneous utility, $E_0\int_0^\infty u(y(t),e(t))\exp(-rt)dt$, at rate of time preference r, where E_0 denotes expectation at time 0. Instantaneous utility $u(y(t),e(t))=y(t)-e(t)$ depends on earnings $y(t)$ and the disutility of work $e(t)$.

Since earnings ($y(t)$) and work disutility ($e(t)$) are parts and parcels of employment, let W denote the overall expected lifetime contract value of a job offer, and $F(W)$ the cumulative probability distribution of W on offer, with associated density $f(W)$ where the derivative exists. The range of W on $[0,\infty]$, along with the share and rank of sweatshop job and decent work offers according to $F(W)$ will need to be determined in equilibrium. For now, it is assumed simply that workers' choices are made taking into account the distribution $F(W)$, including the type of employment, d or s, required by any job offer.

Relative to decent work, sweatshop jobs exact poorer work conditions and longer hours of work. Assume therefore that the disutility of sweatshop employment is the highest, with $e_s>e_d\geq 0=e_u$. At unemployment income $b\geq 0$, the instantaneous utility of an unemployed worker is $u(b,0)=b\geq 0$.[18]

Job search – a random draw from the distribution $F(W)$ – takes place both on the job and while unemployed. Job arrival is governed by a Poisson process with an employment state-specific parameter α_i. Assume furthermore that sweatshop jobs exact inferior likelihood of job advancement, so that the frequency of job arrivals facing sweatshop workers is lower than the other two states: $\alpha_d=\alpha_u=\alpha$, and $\alpha_s=\varepsilon_s\alpha$, where ε_s is a non-negative fraction $\varepsilon_s\in[0,1)$. $1-\varepsilon_s$ thus measures the search capability deficit of sweatshop workers.

This is a common exogenous job destruction rate $\delta_s=\delta_d=\delta>0$. The following Bellman equations give the steady state contract values W_i of each type of employment at earnings y_i, $i=s,d$:

$$rW_s=y_s-e_s-\delta(W_s-W_u)+\alpha_s\int_{W_s}^{\infty}(W-W_s)dF(W), \tag{1}$$

$$rW_d=y_d-e_d-\delta(W_d-W_u)+\alpha\int_{W_d}^{\infty}(W-W_d)dF(W). \tag{2}$$

From Eqs. (1) and (2), the flow value of employment depends on instantaneous utility (y_i-e_i), the possibility of capital losses due to exogenous separations ((W_i-W_u) at rate δ), and capital gains through voluntary separation following successful on-the-job search ($\int_{W_d}^{\infty}(W-W_d)dF(W)$ at rate α).

The lower support of the range of job offers W coincides with the value of unemployment W_u for no workers will entertain any offer worse than unemployment. W_u solves:

$$rW_u=b+\alpha\int_{W_u}^{\infty}(W-W_u)dF(W). \tag{3}$$

It follows from Eqs. (1)–(2) that the minimal wage required to secure contract value $W\geq W_u$ can be expressed as $y_i(W)=\min\{y_i|W_i\geq W\}$:

$$y_s(W)=e_s+rW+\delta(W-W_u)-\alpha_s\int_W^{\infty}(x-W)dF(x), \tag{4}$$

$$y_d(W)=e_d+rW+\delta(W-W_u)-\alpha\int_W^{\infty}(x-W)dF(x). \tag{5}$$

where for a given W, $y_i(W)$ compensates workers for the disutility cost associated with employment, net of potential wage gains while employed through on-the-job search. Taking the difference between Eqs. (4) and (5) gives the compensating differential,

$$y_s(W)-y_d(W)=e_s-e_d+\alpha(1-\varepsilon_s)\int_W^{\infty}(x-W)dF(x)>0$$

for jobs that offer the same W. At this point of the analysis, it is not known whether sweatshop jobs and decent work span the same range of W. The above shows only that the differential is indeed strictly positive at given W since $e_s>e_d$, and $\alpha_s<\alpha$.

Furthermore, wage cost in s and d rises with contract value W, though at different rates depending only on job arrival rates α_s and α

[17] Our findings will in fact corroborate Powell and Skarbek (2006), in that sweatshop wages may be lower than decent wages, but need not be.

[18] b may also be interpreted as self-employment income for those who choose to opt out from the hired labor market altogether.

124 N.H. Chau / Journal of Development Economics 121 (2016) 120–134

respectively:

$$\frac{\partial y_s(W)}{\partial W} = r + \delta + \alpha_s(1 - F(W)) > 0, \frac{\partial y_d(W)}{\partial W} = r + \delta + \alpha(1 - F(W)) > 0. \tag{6}$$

3.2. Employers

Each one of the v number of employers has one vacancy to offer. Output can be produced under sweatshop or decent work conditions, though the implied revenue (p_i) and wage cost ($y_i(W)$) per worker differ. Denote $p_i = pq_i$ as the average revenue of a worker in i. p is an exogenously given relative price of the final output, and q_i gives the marginal product per worker in i, adjusted to account for any change in revenue per worker associated with the provision of better work conditions. Define instantaneous profit as $\theta_i(W) \equiv p_i - y_i(W)$ when output is positive and 0 otherwise.

A successful employer–worker match generates joint employer–worker instantaneous surplus $s_i \equiv p_i - e_i - b$.[19] Henceforth, assume that both technologies are viable, $s_i > 0$.

To capture the relative inefficiency of sweatshop work as discussed in Section 3, measure relative efficiency by

$$\rho \equiv \frac{p_d - e_d - b}{p_s - e_s - b} = \frac{s_d}{s_s},$$

and assume henceforth that $\rho > 1$.[20]

The problem of an employer with time rate of preference r, in choosing a plan to maximize the discounted expectation of the stream of profits involves two decisions: (i) which contract value W to post, and (ii) what work conditions to adopt given the cost of doing so $y_i(W)$. In (i), a higher contract value W impacts the recruitment of new workers, and in (ii), a higher contract value impacts worker retention post-recruitment. Each of these roles of W will be examined in turn, starting with the latter.

3.2.1. Contract value and retention

Denote $J_s(W)$ as the value function of a sweatshop employer who offers a contract valued at W. The flow value $rJ_s(W)$ of this sweatshop contract accounts for instantaneous profit, $\theta_s(W)$, net of possible capital losses due to exogenous and voluntary separation,[21] respectively at rates δ and $\alpha_s(1 - F(W))$:

$$rJ_s(W) = \theta_s(W) - \delta J_s(W) - \alpha_s(1 - F(W))J_s(W).$$

Rearranging,

$$J_s(W) = \frac{\theta_s(W)}{r + \delta + \alpha_s(1 - F(W))}, \tag{7}$$

the denominator, $r + \delta + \alpha_s(1 - F(W))$, reflects the effectiveness of raising contract value in improving retention in sweatshops, depending on the search capability of sweatshop workers ε_s. At the limit wherein sweatshop conditions are so severe that $\varepsilon_s = 0$, the usefulness of higher contract values to deter quits is replaced entirely by sweatshop conditions harsh enough to outright forbid on-the-job search.

The value function of a decent work employer is:

$$J_d(W) = \frac{\theta_d(W)}{r + \delta + \alpha(1 - F(W))}. \tag{8}$$

The difference $J_s(W) - J_d(W)$ gives the relative desirability of sweatshop conditions depending on contract value. A high-valuation job is costly as wages increase and profits $\theta_i(W) = p_i - y_i(W)$ decrease with W from Eq. (6). A high valuation job can nonetheless be desirable as such a job is better able to deter voluntary separation, since voluntary separation occurs at rate $\alpha_i(1 - F(W))$. Sweatshop conditions impact both these considerations since both the wage ($y_i(W)$) and retention ($\delta + \alpha_i(1 - F(W))$) implications of higher contract values depend critically on the search capability ε_s from Eqs. (4)–(6). Furthermore, sweatshop conditions have a direct impact on profits since $s_s < s_d$. On balance, therefore, will an employer issuing a relatively high valuation offer be more or less incentivized to resort to sweatshop conditions? Using Eqs. (7)–(8), a single crossing result obtains[22]:

Proposition 1. If sweatshop and decent work co-exist, an endogenous critical contract value $\overline{W} = max\{W | J_s(W) - J_d(W) \geq 0\} \geq W_u$ separates the two. Equilibrium sweatshop contract values are never higher than that of decent work.

The key observation here is that employers offering high-valuation contracts see little need to resort to costly ($y_s(W) > y_d(W)$, from Eqs. (4) and (5)) and inefficient ($s_s < s_d$) sweatshop conditions to deter separation. Proposition 1 accordingly pins down the value rank of sweatshop jobs and decent work. The relative shares of the two types of job offers can accordingly be simply characterized. Denote σ as the fraction of offers that exact sweatshop conditions. From Proposition 1, σ is given by the fraction of job offers with low contract values $W \leq \overline{W}$, or equivalently $F(\overline{W})$, and $1 - \sigma = 1 - F(\overline{W})$ is the fraction of decent work offers.

3.2.2. Contract value and recruitment

How do contract values impact recruitment? A contract valued at W_u is marginally attractive only to workers in the unemployment pool. A higher contract value ($W \in (W_u, \overline{W}]$) is attractive to some workers in sweatshops as well, while an even higher value ($W > \overline{W}$) can begin to entice workers in decent work (Proposition 1). The precise number of workers that find a contract value W acceptable will thus depend on the size of the unemployment pool, and the distribution of contract values among those who are employed.

Let n_i, $i = s, d, u$ be the fraction of workers in each of the three states of employment, with $n_s + n_d + n_u = 1$, and let $G(W)$ denote the distribution of contract values among the $1 - n_u$ employed workers. At any instant, there are effectively $\epsilon_s n_s + n_d + n_u$ number of job seekers, after for the search capability deficit of sweatshop workers. In a steady state, these values are given by the solution of a number of equilibrium relationships that balance inflows of workers with outflows at any given W. Accordingly, define separation rate $d_i(W)$ as the the sum of the exogenous and voluntary rates of separation facing an employer with a contract valued at W in $i = s, d$:

$$d_s(W) \equiv \delta + \alpha_s(1 - F(W)), d_d(W) \equiv \delta + \alpha(1 - F(W)).$$

To ensure that total outflows into unemployment (due to exogenous separation) equals inflows into the working population,

$$\delta(1 - n_u) = \alpha n_u.$$

[19] This sums instantaneous profit $\theta_i(W)$ and workers' pay $y_i(W)$ net of the discount and opportunity cost of work $e_i + b$.

[20] Note that a sufficient condition for $\rho > 1$ is that individual worker productivity is higher in decent work $q_d > q_s$. This model only requires that $\rho > 1$ however, for virtually all of the key results of this paper to hold. Thus, our assumption $\rho > 1$ accommodates situations where sweatshop conditions extract higher productivity from workers $q_d < q_s$, but are nonetheless inefficient $p_s - e_s - b < p_d - e_d - b$ once the correspondingly high disutility cost of work is accounted for.

[21] In case of separation, an employer can either exit or introduce a new job offer. With free entry, both options yield zero expected value ex ante. Thus, the capital loss associated with separation is $J_s(W)$.

[22] The proofs of this and subsequent propositions are relegated to Appendix A.

Next, to ensure that outflows from the pool of workers with sweatshop contracts $W(<\overline{W})$ is equal to inflow from the unemployment pool, set

$$d_s(W)G(W)(1-n_u)=\alpha F(W)n_u.$$

Finally, to ensure that outflows from the pool of workers with decent and sweatshop contracts valued at W ($>\overline{W}$) or less equals inflow from the unemployment pool, set

$$d_s(W)\,G(\overline{W})(1-n_u)+d_d(W)(G(W)-G(\overline{W}))(1-n_u)=\alpha F(W)n_u.$$

Solving these three steady state relationships simultaneously, the following expressions for employment and contract value distribution obtain:

$$n_u=\frac{\delta}{\alpha+\delta}, \tag{9}$$

$$G(W)=\frac{\delta F(W)}{d_s(W)},\ \text{for } W<\overline{W}, \tag{10}$$

$$G(W)=G(\overline{W})+\left(\frac{\delta(F(W)-\sigma)}{d_d(W)}\right)\left(\frac{\delta+\alpha_s}{d_s(\overline{W})}\right),\ \text{for } W\geq\overline{W} \tag{11}$$

where again, the job-arrival rate α and the equilibrium share of sweatshop jobs σ play a critical role. From these, sweatshop and decent work employment can also be explicitly expressed in terms of α and σ:

$$\begin{aligned} n_s&=(1-n_u)G(\overline{W})=\frac{\alpha}{\delta+\alpha}\frac{\delta\sigma}{d_s(\overline{W})},\ n_d=(1-n_u)(1-G(\overline{W}))\\ &=\frac{\alpha}{\delta+\alpha}\frac{(\delta+\alpha_s)(1-\sigma)}{d_s(\overline{W})}. \end{aligned} \tag{12}$$

Since a sweatshop offer $W\in[W_u,\overline{W})$ will be accepted by an unemployed worker (n_u), and by a sweatshop worker with contract values less than W ($\epsilon_s G(W)(1-n_u)$), but no other (Proposition 1), the match success likelihood of such an offer can be simply expressed as:

$$\begin{aligned} h(W)&=\frac{n_u+\epsilon_s G(W)(1-n_u)}{\epsilon_s n_s+n_d+n_u}\\ &=\frac{d_s(\overline{W})}{d_d(\overline{W})}\frac{\delta}{d_s(W)}\ \text{if } W\leq\overline{W}. \end{aligned} \tag{13}$$

For an employer who takes the job arrival rate α and the share of sweatshop jobs σ as given, success in recruitment is more likely with a higher W only when $\epsilon_s>0$ since $d_s(W)=\delta+\alpha_s(1-F(W))$, and otherwise with $\epsilon_s=0$, success in recruitment $h(W)=\delta/(\delta+\alpha(1-\sigma))$ is invariant to W. Intuitively, sweatshop employers cannot offer enough to lure away a worker in decent work (Proposition 1), while hiring another sweatshop worker is out of the question as $\epsilon_s=0$ to begin with.[23]

Analogously, a decent work offer $W\geq\overline{W}$ will be accepted by all unemployed workers, all job seekers currently in sweatshop jobs ($n_u+\epsilon_s n_s$), along with all workers in decent work with contracts outmatched by W ($(G(W)-G(\overline{W}))(1-n_u)$). The corresponding match success likelihood can also be simply expressed as:

$$\begin{aligned} h(W)&=\frac{n_u+\varepsilon_s n_s+(G(W)-G\overline{W})(1-n_u)}{\varepsilon_s n_s+n_d+n_u}\\ &=\frac{\delta}{d_d W}\ \text{if } W\geq W \end{aligned} \tag{14}$$

which again shows that success in recruitment is more likely with higher contract values.

3.2.3. Expected profits bridging retention and recruitment considerations

To close the model, let $\Psi(N,v)$ be a matching technology representing the total number of matches (Pissarides, 2000) between v offers (inclusive of sweatshop jobs and decent work) and N job seekers (inclusive of unemployed and employed workers). Assume that Ψ is homothetic, monotonically increasing in both arguments, with $\Psi(0,v)=\Psi(N,0)=0$. Both v and N are endogenous, where the effective number of job seekers is given by $N=\varepsilon_s n_s+n_d+n_u$.

For workers, the rate of job arrival is given by $\alpha=\Psi(N,v)/N=\Psi(1,v/N)$. For employers, the rate of an employer–worker match is $\alpha_e=\Psi(N,v)/v=\Psi(N/v,1)$. Both α and α_e depend on the ratio of job offers to job seekers v/N.[24]

The expected profit of an employer with a new vacancy offering W can now be specified:

$$\pi(W)=\max_{i=s,d}\pi_i(W)\equiv\alpha_e h(W)\max_{\{i=s,d\}}J_i(W),$$

which simultaneously accounts for the importance of setting the right contract value in recruitment (through the match likelihood $h(W)$), and in retention (through $J_i(W)=\theta_i(W)/(r+d_i(W))$), given a successful match.

4. Steady state equilibrium

Define a steady state equilibrium as a threshold contract value $\overline{W}^*$, a contract value distribution $F^*(W)$, a corresponding share of sweatshop offers $\sigma^*=F^*(\overline{W}^*)$, and an equilibrium job arrival rate α^* such that[25] (I) all sweatshop contracts yield the same expected profit π_s^*, and all decent work contracts yield the same expected profits πd^*, (II) employers are indifferent between offering sweatshop and decent work conditions at $\overline{W}^*$ if the two co-exist,

$$J_s^*(\overline{W}^*)=J_d^*(\overline{W}^*) \tag{15}$$

and (III) expected profit maximizing employers freely enter or exit subject to a per vacancy hiring cost c[26]:

$$\pi^*(W)=c. \tag{16}$$

In what follows, each of these equilibrium conditions will be examined, the joint solutions of which give the steady state equilibrium.

To solve the model, use (I) to express all endogenous variables in the model including wages and profits in terms of the overall job arrival rate α and the share of sweatshop jobs σ, along with all other exogenous parameters in the model. The indifference between sweatshop jobs

[23] As I will show in the following section, the search capability of sweatshop workers has a singularly important role to play in the equilibrium distribution of contract values throughout the labor market.

[24] Clearly, such a designation of job arrival rates satisfies "adding-up". In particular, the total number of workers with a match $\alpha n_u+\alpha n_d+\alpha\varepsilon_s n_s=\alpha N=\Psi(N,v)$. Likewise, the total number of matched vacancies $\alpha_e v=\Psi(N,v)$.

[25] With α^*, α_s^* is given by $\alpha^*\varepsilon_s$, while $\alpha_e^*=\Psi(N^*/v^*,1)$ where N^*/v^* can be derived from $\alpha^*=\Psi(1,v^*/N^*)$.

[26] As discussed in Section 2, hiring workers is not cost-free. This hiring cost, c common across sweatshop and decent work employers, is taken to be the cost it takes to present a job contract offer to a randomly selected worker.

and decent work in (II), and the free entry condition in (III) will then be simultaneously utilized to determine α^* and σ^* in a steady state.

4.1. Contract offer distribution

From (I), all sweatshop contracts ($W \in [W_u^*, \overline{W}^*]$) earn the same expected profit. The corresponding equilibrium contract value distribution exactly balances the cost of a higher contract value, against the increase in odds of hiring a new worker and retaining a hired worker: $\pi_s^*(W) = \pi_s^*(\overline{W}^*)$ for all $W \in [W_u^*, \overline{W}^*)$. To sharpen insights, consider henceforth the case where there is no discounting of the future. Setting r to zero, the equilibrium contract distribution can be expressed succinctly as

$$F^*(W) = \left(\delta + \alpha_s^* - d_s\left(\overline{W}^*\right)\sqrt{\theta_s(W)/\theta_s\left(\overline{W}^*\right)}\right)/\alpha_s^*, \tag{17}$$

for $W \in [W_u^*, \overline{W}^*)$. Since $\theta_s(W) = p_s - y_s(W)$ is strictly decreasing in W from (6), the contract offer distribution is strictly increasing in W.

Similarly, if all decent work contracts yield the same expected profit, then for all $W \geq \overline{W}^*$

$$F^*(W) = \left(\delta + \alpha^* - d_d\left(\overline{W}^*\right)\sqrt{\theta_d(W)/\theta_d\left(\overline{W}^*\right)}\right)/\alpha^*. \tag{18}$$

Taken together, $F^*(W)$ is continuous, piecewise differentiable with respect to W.[27] Let $f^*(W) = \partial F^*(W)/\partial W$ denote the associated density function where $F^*(W)$ is differentiable.[28]

The range of the support of $F^*(W)$, henceforth denoted $[W_u^*, W_{max}^*]$, can be ascertained as well. Integrating $f^*(W)$ over the contract value domains of sweatshop jobs $[W_u^*, \overline{W}^*)$ and decent work $[\overline{W}^*, W_{max}^*]$, for any given share of sweatshop offers $F^*(\overline{W}^*) = \sigma^*$:

$$\begin{aligned} \overline{W}^* - W_u^* &= 2\alpha_s^*\sigma^*\theta_s\left(\overline{W}^*\right)/d_s\left(\overline{W}^*\right)^2 \\ W_{max}^* - \overline{W}^* &= 2\alpha^*(1-\sigma^*)\theta_d\left(\overline{W}^*\right)/d_d\left(\overline{W}^*\right)^2. \end{aligned} \tag{19}$$

From Eqs. (17)–(19), the emergence of sweatshops evidently impacts *every worker* in the economy, as σ^* is subsumed in both the equilibrium distribution and the range of contract values. Respectively for sweatshop jobs and decent work, contract values are dispersed and the spread in contract values depends critically on profit levels $\theta_s(\overline{W}^*)$ and $\theta_d(\overline{W}^*)$, job-arrival rates α^* and α_s^*, and the share of sweatshop jobs α^*. The only exception is when $\varepsilon_s = 0$, where all sweatshop workers receive the same contract value W_u^* since employers offering higher-value sweatshop contracts do not benefit either from retention, or recruitment concerns ((7) and (13)).

4.2. Wages and profits

With the equilibrium offer distribution $F^*(W)$ explicitly introduced in Eqs. (17)–(19) as a function of instantaneous profits $\theta_i(W)$, we have now come full circle, for earlier in Eqs. (4)–(5), wages $y_i(W)$ and thus profits $\theta_i(W)$ were shown to be determined by $F^*(W)$. To obtain expressions for wages and profits in terms of α^* and σ^*, use Eqs. (4)–(5) and integrate using Eqs. (17)–(19). Wage cost evaluated at the marginal contract $\overline{W}^*$, $y_i(\overline{W}^*)$, can be expressed as a linear combination of the total costs of work as perceived by workers, $e_i + b$, and profits $\theta_i(\overline{W}^*)$:

$$y_d\left(\overline{W}^*\right) = e_d + b + \omega_s\theta_s\left(\overline{W}^*\right), \tag{20}$$

$$y_s\left(\overline{W}^*\right) = e_s + b + \omega_s\theta_s\left(\overline{W}^*\right) + \omega_d\theta_d\left(\overline{W}^*\right), \tag{21}$$

where the weights ω_s and ω_d are functions of α^* and σ^* among other exogenous parameters:

$$\omega_s \equiv \alpha^*\varepsilon_s\sigma^*\left(2d_d\left(\overline{W}^*\right) + \alpha^*\sigma^*\right)/d_s\left(\overline{W}^*\right)^2, \omega_d \equiv (1-\varepsilon_s)\left(1 - h\left(\overline{W}^*\right)\right)^2.$$

Intuitively, decent work employers with offer $\overline{W}^*$ compensate workers for the cost of work $e_d + b$ plus any additional wage increase required to raise the contract value from unemployment W_u^* to $\overline{W}^*$. From Eq. (19), this compensation is strictly positive if and only if $\varepsilon_s > 0$, for otherwise all sweatshop contracts will be identically valued at W_u^*. Meanwhile, sweatshop employers with offer $\overline{W}^*$ must also compensate workers for the expected wage gains that workers forgo ($\omega_d\theta_d(\overline{W}^*)$) as shown in Eq. (21), due to the search capability deficit of sweatshop jobs.

It follows directly that instantaneous profit at the margin $\theta_i(\overline{W}^*)$ is given by:

$$\theta_s\left(\overline{W}^*\right) = p_s - y_s\left(\overline{W}^*\right) = s_s - \omega_s\theta_s\left(\overline{W}^*\right) - \omega_d\theta_d\left(\overline{W}^*\right),$$

$$\theta_d\left(\overline{W}^*\right) = p_d - y_d\left(\overline{W}^*\right) = s_d - \omega_s\theta_s\left(\overline{W}^*\right).$$

This gives a system of two equations with two unknowns, $\theta_s(\overline{W}^*)$ and $\theta_d(\overline{W}^*)$. The solutions are:

$$\theta_s\left(\overline{W}^*\right) = \frac{s_s - \omega_d s_d}{1 + \omega_s(1 - \omega_d)}, \theta_d\left(\overline{W}^*\right) = \frac{s_d + \omega_s(s_d - s_s)}{1 + \omega_s(1 - \omega_d)}. \tag{22}$$

Using Eqs. (17) and (18), the above yields an expression for the equilibrium wage offer distribution $F^*(W)$, and from Eqs. (10)–(11), the equilibrium contract value distribution $G^*(W)$. These expressions can then be used to ascertain the labor market-wide outcomes associated with a sweatshop option.

5. Labor market consequences of sweatshop jobs

Two additional equations close the model. One is based on the free entry of firms (16), and the other is based on the selection between sweatshop jobs and decent works in Eq. (15); both are functions of α and σ. Before the conditions under which an interior solution (α^*, σ^*) to Eqs. (15)–(16) exists are discussed — a task undertaken in Section 6 — assume that at least one such equilibrium exists in this section, and proceed to examine the labor market consequences of sweatshop jobs in terms of impact on employment, wages, distribution and overall efficiency.

Specifically, henceforth compare a sweatshop equilibrium – any pair of α^* and $\sigma^* > 0$ that simultaneously solve Eqs. (15) and (16) — with a sweatshop free benchmark. Define a sweatshop free equilibrium as one in which σ is set to zero throughout the model, and where employers no longer have the option to choose between the two conditions of work. Thus, Eq. (15) no longer applies as an equilibrium condition in the sweatshop free benchmark. Throughout, use a superscript "^{o}" to denote sweatshop free equilibrium values. The detailed proofs are relegated to Appendix A.

5.1. Sweatshops and unemployment tradeoffs

A key question that confronts the sweatshop debate is whether the emergence of sweatshop jobs (i) creates jobs for the unemployed otherwise not available, or (ii) replaces decent jobs with sweatshop jobs.

---

[27] Note that $F^*(W)$ as defined in Eqs. (17) and (18) exhibits no gap at the threshold W^*, for $F^*(W^*) = \sigma$.

[28] The associated density functions are $f(W) = d_s(W^*)^2/(2\alpha_s^*\theta_s(W^*))$ if $W \in [W_u^*, W^*)$ and $f^*(W) = d_d(W^*)^2/(2\alpha^*\theta_d(W^*))$ otherwise.

Accordingly, we compare steady state employment allocations with or without sweatshops:

$$\begin{aligned} n_u^o &= \frac{\delta}{\delta+\alpha^o} > \frac{\delta}{\delta+\alpha^*} = n_u^* \\ n_d^o &= \frac{\alpha^o}{\delta+\alpha^o} > \frac{\alpha^*}{\delta+\alpha^*}\frac{(\delta+\alpha_s^*)(1-\sigma^*)}{\delta+\alpha^*(1-\sigma^*)} = n_d^* \\ n_s^o &= 0 < \frac{\alpha^*}{\delta+\alpha^*}\frac{\delta\sigma^*}{\delta+\alpha^*(1-\sigma^*)} = n_s^*. \end{aligned} \tag{23}$$

Proposition 2. *Starting from an equilibrium with $\sigma^* > 0$, a ban on sweatshop jobs gives rise to (i) the replacement of some sweatshop jobs by new decent work offers $n_d^* < n_d^o$, but simultaneously (ii) a higher unemployment rate as the ban has a net deterrent effect on the entry of new job offers $\alpha^* > \alpha^o$.*

To see this, consider the expected profit of an employer $\pi_d^*(\overline{W}^*)$:

$$\pi_d(\overline{W}^*) = \alpha_e^* h(\overline{W}^*)\frac{\theta_d(\overline{W}^*)}{d_d(\overline{W}^*)}.$$

At constant α^*, and hence α_e^*, lifting a ban on sweatshops always improves the match success rate of the marginal job since $h(\overline{W}^*) = \delta/(\delta + \alpha^*(1-\sigma^*))$. Furthermore, the increase in σ^* also improves the retention rate for the marginal job for $d_d(\overline{W}^*) = \delta + \alpha^*(1-\sigma^*)$. These two effects reinforce each other in raising discounted profits. Starting from an equilibrium with zero profits, there are two corresponding impacts: (i) higher profits encourage employer entry, and (ii) more entries disproportionately impact decent work employers as workers in decent work do not face impediments to on-the-job search. Consequently, sweatshop jobs strictly crowd out decent work opportunities.

5.2. Sweatshops and compensating differential

Are workers in sweatshop jobs adequately compensated for the disutility cost they incur relative to decent work? Making direct use of Eqs. (17)–(19), and the realized value distribution $G^*(W)$, the average wage of a worker employed in decent work net of the effort and opportunity cost of work $(e_d + b)$ can be expressed simply as

$$\begin{aligned} &\left(\int_{\overline{W}^*}^{W_{max}^*}(y_d(W)-e_d-b)dG^*(W)\right)/\left(1-G^*(\overline{W}^*)\right) \\ &= s_d - \frac{\delta\theta_d(\overline{W}^*)}{d_d(\overline{W}^*)} \equiv y_d^{avg} - e_d - b \end{aligned} \tag{24}$$

while the average wage of all sweatshop employees net of the effort and opportunity cost of work (e_s+b) can likewise be expressed as:

$$\begin{aligned} &\left(\int_{W_u^*}^{\overline{W}^*}(y_s(W)-e_s-b)dG^*(W)\right)/G^*(\overline{W}^*) \\ &= s_s - \frac{(\delta+\alpha_s^*)\theta_s(\overline{W}^*)}{d_s(\overline{W}^*)} \equiv y_s^{avg} - e_s - b. \end{aligned} \tag{25}$$

This allows for a direct comparison of the average earnings of a decent work employee, and a sweatshop worker. In Appendix A, the proof of the following will be provided:

Proposition 3. *In a steady state equilibrium with $\sigma^* > 0$, the average earnings difference $y_s^{avg} - y_d^{avg}$ always understates the disutility difference $e_s - e_d$, for*

$$(y_s^{avg} - e_s) - (y_d^{avg} - e_d) = s_s - s_d - \frac{\alpha_s^*\theta_s(\overline{W}^*)}{d_s(\overline{W}^*)} < 0.$$

Thus, sweatshop wages are always insufficiently compensating. From Proposition 3, the difference arises because sweatshop jobs are of inferior efficiency to begin with $(s_s < s_d)$, and because sweatshop jobs are bottom-rung jobs whenever $\alpha_s^* < \alpha^*$ from Proposition 1. That said, Proposition 3 also implies that

$$y_s^{avg} - y_d^{avg} = p_s - p_d - \frac{\alpha_s^*\theta_s^*}{d_s(\overline{W}^*)} < 0$$

if $p_s < p_d$. This sufficient condition requires that a sweatshop worker in fact produces less even accounting for the overtime and employers cost savings on work conditions, which is stronger than our standing assumption that $s_s < s_d$ since the disutility cost in sweatshop jobs is also higher. Thus, if $s_s < s_d$ but $p_s > p_d$, even though sweatshop wages continue to be insufficiently compensating, per worker sweatshop wage may well exceed per worker wage in decent work. As discussed earlier in Section 2, these observations are consistent with the rare evidence on sweatshop wages and industry wages presented in Powell and Skarbek (2006), where industry-wide average wages appear to outstrip sweatshop wages in some but not all cases.

5.3. Sweatshops and distribution

To assess the distributional consequences of equilibrium sweatshops between employers and workers, let ψ_i^* denote the steady state employer profit as a share of per worker surplus, $i = d, s$. Given Eqs. (17)–(19), using Eqs. (20)–(22) and the realized value distribution $G^*(W)$ yields:

$$\psi_d^* \equiv \frac{\int_{\overline{W}^*}^{W_{max}^*}\theta_d(W)dG^*(W)}{\left(1-G^*(\overline{W}^*)\right)s_d} = \frac{\delta}{s_d}\frac{\theta_d(\overline{W}^*)}{d_d(\overline{W}^*)}, \tag{26}$$

$$\psi_s^* \equiv \frac{\int_{W_u^*}^{\overline{W}^*}\theta_s(W)dG^*(W)}{G(\overline{W}^*)s_s} = \frac{\delta+\alpha_s^*}{s_s}\frac{\theta_s(\overline{W}^*)}{d_s(\overline{W}^*)}. \tag{27}$$

Likewise define the steady state employer profit as a share of per worker surplus in the absence of sweatshop jobs as

$$\psi_d^o \equiv \frac{\int_{W_u^o}^{W_{max}^o}\theta_s(W)dG^o(W)}{s_d} = \frac{\delta}{s_d}\frac{\theta_d^o(\overline{W}^o)}{d_d(\overline{W}^o)}. \tag{28}$$

Note that ψ_i^* and ψ_d^o depend critically on the level of discounted instantaneous profits $\theta_i(\overline{W}^*)/d_i(\overline{W}^*)$ and $\theta_d^o(W_u^o)/d_d^o(W_u^o)$ of the marginal employer. With free entry, the value functions of all jobs are identical in value. It follows from Eqs. (24)–(25) that $\psi_d^* < \psi_s^*$ always holds, consistent with sweatshop jobs being bottom-rung jobs. Furthermore,

Proposition 4. *In a steady state equilibrium with $\sigma^* > 0$,*

$$\psi_s^* > \psi_d^*.$$

If in addition ε_s is sufficiently small

$$\psi_s^* > \psi_d^* > \psi_d^o.$$

From Eq. (23), whenever $\varepsilon_s = 0$, the presence of sweatshops decreases the arrival rate of decent work since $\alpha^*(1-\sigma^*) < \alpha^o$ from Eq. (23). Consequently, the presence of sweatshops increases the discounted profits of decent work employers through a higher retention rate $(d_d(\overline{W}^*) = \delta + \alpha^*(1-\sigma^*) < \delta + \alpha^o = d_d(\overline{W}^o))$. Going in opposite direction, decent work employers must offer contract value strictly higher than the value of unemployment at $\overline{W}^* - W_u^* = 2\alpha_s^*\sigma^*\theta_s(\overline{W}^*)/d_s(\overline{W}^*)^2$ from Eq. (19). This raises the wage cost in decent work, and can potentially bring down the share of employer profits. Importantly, the strength of the latter wage cost effect depends on the search capability deficit of sweatshop workers. At the limit when $\varepsilon_s = 0$, $\overline{W}^* = W_u^*$ from Eq. (19). Propositions 4 accordingly shows that the profit share of decent work employers is in fact strictly higher in the presence of sweatshops when ε_s is sufficiently small.

5.4. Sweatshops and efficiency

From Eq. (23), the removal of sweatshops via a ban on sweatshops has two effects: (i) a replacement of sweatshop jobs by an increase in decent work opportunities, and (ii) an overall increase in unemployment as entry is deterred. A priori, therefore, the impact of sweatshop legislation in efficiency terms may seem uncertain.

As a gauge on efficiency, we follow Acemoglu (2001) in using net manufacturing surplus, to be defined as the sum of decent work and sweatshop surplus net of the total cost of hiring at any instant[29]:

$$S^* = n_d^* s_d + n_s^* s_s - v^* c.$$

Manufacturing surplus in the sweatshop free benchmark can be simply expressed as:

$$S^o = n_d^o s_d - v^o c = \left(\frac{\alpha^o}{\delta + \alpha^o}\right)^2 s_d \tag{29}$$

from Eqs. (12), (15) and (16). Intuitively, efficiency rises when job arrival rate α^o rises, and when the productivity of employed workers s_d rises. The corresponding expression when sweatshops prevail is shown in Appendix A. At one extreme, where no sweatshop workers are able to search on the job ($\varepsilon_s = 0$), the expression simplifies to

$$S^* = \left(\frac{\alpha^*(1-\sigma^*)}{\delta + \alpha^*(1-\sigma^*)}\right)^2 s_d \tag{30}$$

which shows that efficiency improves whenever decent job arrival rate $\alpha^*(1-\sigma^*)$ improves. From Proposition 2, decent work arrival decreases with the emergence of sweatshop jobs, and hence $\alpha^*(1-\sigma^*) < \alpha^o$ in this limiting case. It follows therefore that overall efficiency unambiguously improves with a ban on sweatshop jobs. Intuitively, when $\varepsilon_s = 0$, sweatshop conditions create jobs by redistributing income from workers to employers (Proposition 2). A comparison of Eqs. (29) and (30) using Eq. (23) shows that job creation spurred by such transfers necessarily lowers the arrival rate of decent work, and gives rise to an unambiguous decline in efficiency. More generally, it is shown in Appendix A that:

Proposition 5. *Starting from a steady state equilibrium with $\sigma^* > 0$, a ban on sweatshops leads to an unambiguous increase in net manufacturing surplus*

$$S^* < S^o$$

if ε_s is sufficiently small.

6. Graduation

Do labor markets graduate from sweatshop conditions when an all-out ban is not an option? This question can be investigated by juxtaposing the last two equilibrium conditions. Respectively, these require that employers are indifferent between the two types of work conditions, and expected profits are equal to zero accounting for hiring cost in equilibrium. We then summarize all job arrival and sweatshop incidence (α, σ) combinations that satisfy the indifference condition between the two types of work and refer to the resulting schedule as $\Delta\Delta$. We do the same for the zero expected profit condition and refer to the resulting schedule as OO. The interior intersection(s) of the $\Delta\Delta$ and the OO schedules, if they exist, constitute sweatshop equilibria where sweatshop jobs and decent work co-exist.

6.1. Schedule ΔΔ

In the choice between offering sweatshop jobs and decent work, employers consider the difference:

$$\Delta J^*\left(\overline{W}^*\right) = J_s^*\left(\overline{W}^*\right) - J_d^*\left(\overline{W}^*\right),$$

where from Eqs. (7)–(8), $\Delta J^*(\overline{W}^*) = 0$ if and only if

$$\rho - 1 = \theta_d\left(\overline{W}^*\right)(1-\varepsilon_s)\left(\left[1 - h\left(\overline{W}^*\right)\right] - \left[1 - h\left(\overline{W}^*\right)\right]^2\right)/s_s. \tag{31}$$

The dependence of $\theta_d(\overline{W}^*)$ on α^* and σ^* is given in Eq. (22), and the match success likelihood is by definition likewise a function of α^* and σ^*, with $h(W^*) = \delta/(\delta + \alpha^*(1-\sigma^*))$.

With $\rho > 1$ it is shown in Appendix B that the set of $\alpha^* > 0$ given $\sigma^* \in (0, 1]$ that solves Eq. (31) is non-empty only if ϵ_s is sufficiently small. Intuitively, it pays to adopt relatively inefficient sweatshop conditions only if the search capability deficit of sweatshop workers is sufficiently acute. In what follows, this condition is assumed to be satisfied.

Thus, denote $\Delta(\sigma^*; \epsilon_s, \rho) = \{\alpha^* | \Delta J^*(\overline{W}^*) = 0\}$ as the implicit solution of Eq. (31). Eq. (31) can be solved numerically, and three $\Delta(\sigma^*; \epsilon_s, \rho)$ schedules are plotted in Fig. 1a–c for successively lower levels of ϵ_s.[30] Henceforth, these are referred to as $\Delta\Delta$ schedules. The job arrival rate on the vertical axis is depicted in log scale. Thus $\Delta\Delta$ divides the $(\log(a), \sigma)$ quadrant with $\sigma \leq 1$ into two areas, one where $\Delta J^*(\overline{W}^*)$ is strictly positive and employers prefer sweatshop over decent work conditions, and the other where the opposite is true. Along $\Delta\Delta$, employers are indifferent between sweatshop and decent work conditions.

Note that $\Delta\Delta$ is non-monotonic – when job arrival α is small to begin with and competition for workers is thus not too intense, raising α increases the need to pre-empt quits as workers can more readily find work on-the-job. This tends to make sweatshop more lucrative. For higher levels of α, further increases in α improve job prospects for all workers including the unemployed. Thus, the wage increase that sweatshop employers must pay to make a sweatshop job worthwhile will accordingly increase. This tends to make decent work more lucrative, and results in a backward bending $\Delta\Delta$ schedule.[31]

Going across from Fig. 1a to c, where the $\Delta\Delta$ schedules are shown corresponding to successive reduction in the search capability ε_s of sweatshop workers, note that the range of α^* in which sweatshop profits strictly dominate decent work profits expands, and increasingly accommodates higher job arrival rates α and higher sweatshop incidence σ. In addition to ε_s, a change in the relative efficiency of decent work ρ will likewise shift the $\Delta\Delta$ schedule. From Eqs. (31), an decrease in ρ increases $\Delta J^*(W)$ for all σ. Equivalently, for all σ, a decrease in ρ will

[29] Total hiring cost v^*c can be obtained by noting from the definition of the matching function and Eq. (16) that $\alpha^*(n_u^* + n_d^* + \varepsilon_s n_s^*) = \alpha_e^* v^*$, and $\alpha_e^* \pi_d(\overline{W}^*) = c$ or $v_m^* c = \alpha^*(n_u^* + n_d^* + \varepsilon_s n_s^*)\delta\theta_d(\overline{W}^*)/(d_d(\overline{W}^*))^2$.

[30] Other parametric assumptions include $s_s = 1$ and $\delta = 0.5$.

[31] Note that the backward bending portion of $\Delta\Delta$ can in fact slope downward, as shown in Fig. 1b and c. In these cases, there are multiple values of σ^* that solve Eqs. (31) for any given α^*. Effectively, sweatshops have a tendency to beget more sweatshops for some parameter values. To see this, the non-linear term $(1-\varepsilon_s)[\alpha^*(1-\sigma^*)/(\delta+\alpha^*(1-\sigma^*)) - (\alpha^*(1-\sigma^*)/(\delta+\alpha^*(1-\sigma^*)))^2]$ in Eq. (31) rises with σ^* if and only if $-\delta + \alpha^*(1-\sigma^*) > 0$, and falls with σ^* if and only if $-\delta + \alpha^*(1-\sigma^*) < 0$. Thus, when competition for workers α^* is intense, and when σ^* is too small to begin with, more sweatshops can in fact locally raise the profitability of sweatshops.

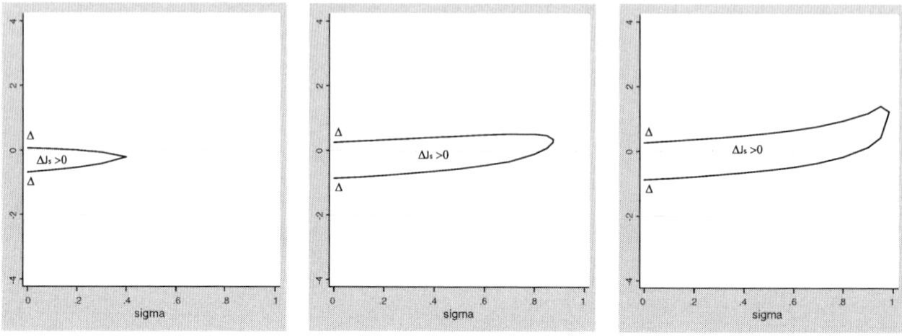

a) εs=0.2 b) εs=0.02 c) εs=0.0005

Fig. 1. The ΔΔ schedule, (ρ = 1.2).

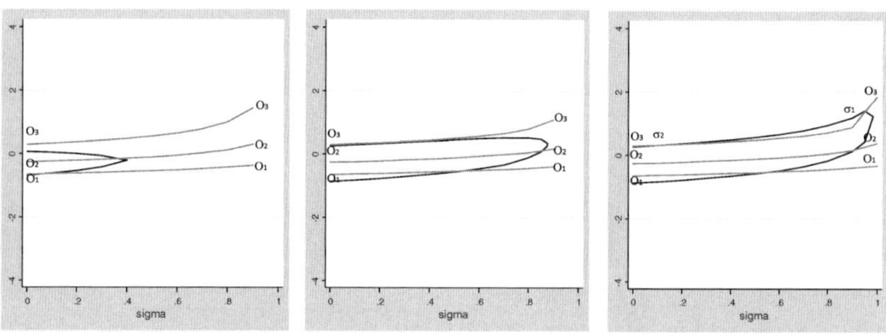

a) εs=0.2 b) εs=0.02 c) εs=0.0005

Fig. 2. The ΔΔ and OO schedules, (ρ = 1.2).

expand the range of α^* in which sweatshop profits dominate decent work profits.

6.2. Schedule OO

Turning now to the choice between entering the labor market or opting out, employers compare the expected profits from doing so with hiring costs. The zero expected profit condition requires:

$$\pi_d\left(\overline{W}^*\right) = \alpha_e h\left(\overline{W}^*\right)\frac{\theta_d\left(\overline{W}^*\right)}{d_d\left(\overline{W}^*\right)} - c = 0. \quad (32)$$

Denote $O(\sigma^*;\varepsilon_s,\rho,c) = \{\alpha^* | \pi_d(\overline{W}^*) = 0\}$ as the implicit solution of Eqs. (32) for given $\sigma^*, \varepsilon_s, \rho$ and c. Note that $O(\sigma^*;\varepsilon_s,\rho,c)$ is upward sloping, which reflects the fact that the higher the share of sweatshop jobs, the higher the retention likelihood $d_d(\overline{W}^*) = \delta + \alpha^*(1-\sigma^*)$ at constant α^*. To maintain zero profit, competition for workers through entry of new employers must intensify, or α^* must rise.

Fig. 2 presents numerical solutions of Eqs. (32) via a series of OO schedules for successively lower levels of hiring cost c, going from O_1O_1 to O_3O_3.[32] As before, the job arrival rate is in presented in log scale. Thus, OO divides $(\log(\alpha), \sigma)$ quadrant with $\sigma \le 1$ into two areas, one where $\pi(\overline{W}^*)$ is strictly positive and the other where the opposite is true. Along OO, employers earn zero expected profits. Note that as the cost of hiring decreases, the OO schedule is shifted upwards.

6.3. Sweatshop equilibrium

The intersection of the ΔΔ schedule and the OO schedule gives the steady state equilibrium in the labor market. The configuration of any particular steady state equilibrium depends on the characteristics of sweatshops relative to decent work subsumed in the ΔΔ schedule through the parameters ρ and ϵ_s, in addition to cost of hiring, which also controls OO among other parameters. The ensuing discussion is divided into three parts: (i) the role of relative decent work efficiency ρ, (ii) the role of the cost of hiring c, and (iii) the role of search capability deficit ϵ_s.

[32] To numerically simulate OO, I also assume that the match function $\Psi(v,N)$ is Cobb–Douglas and equal to $v^{0.5}N^{0.5}$. The parametric assumptions are similar to Fig. 1, and include $s_d = 1.2$, $s_s = 1$ and $\delta = 0.5$. The hiring costs are set respectively at $c = 5$, $c = 1$ and $c = 0.05$.

6.3.1. The role of relative decent work efficiency ρ

This is the most straightforward of all the three factors above. From Eq. (31), a solution with $\sigma^* > 0$ does not exist if ρ is sufficiently large. Intuitively, if decent work conditions overwhelmingly dominate sweatshop conditions in relative efficiency terms, equilibrium sweatshop jobs should not be expected. Since

$$\rho = \frac{s_d}{s_s} = \frac{pq_d - e_d - b}{pq_s - e_s - b}$$

it follows that

Proposition 6. *In a steady state equilibrium, sweatshop jobs prevail only if unemployment income b is sufficiently low, and/or if the world price p of the final output is sufficiently high in the presence of a productivity deficit of sweatshop jobs* $q_s < q_d$.

6.3.2. The role of the cost of hiring c

The role of c is highly nuanced in this setting. As noted earlier, when the cost of hiring is high consistent with a low job arrival rate to start, introducing competition via ease of entry increase the need for employers to retain workers. This tends to encourage sweatshop jobs, which further encourages entry for reasons already explained in our discussion of Eq. (31). This effect is evident in Fig. 2a–c, where a reduction in the cost of hiring, starting from O_1O_1 raises the equilibrium prevalence of sweatshops, as well as the equilibrium job arrival intensity.

Given added competition for workers as c decreases further, there are two possible scenarios. First where ϵ_s is not too low, employers turn to the more efficient decent work technology going from O_2O_2 to O_3O_3 to avoid paying the high wage cost of sweatshop work. In fact, sweatshop conditions vanish entirely in the case of Fig. 2a with $\epsilon_s = 0.2$, while sweatshop conditions likewise vanish in Fig. 2b with $\epsilon_s = 0.02$ but just barely.

However, when the search capability of sweatshop jobs is extremely low, as shown in Fig. 2c, for example, the same piecemeal increase in competition gives rise to multiple equilibria. In one equilibrium, call it σ_1, sweatshop conditions become even more acute in the labor market as σ^* increases going from O_2O_2 to O_3O_3. Another equilibrium exists at σ_2 as shown on Fig. 2c where O_3O_3 intersects with the upward sloping portion of the backward bending $\Delta\Delta$. It can be easily verified that this equilibrium is unstable in the Marshallian sense, in that immediately to the right of σ_2 on Fig. 2c, sweatshop profits exceed decent work profits indicating a tendency for sweatshops to beget more sweatshop jobs. Thus, in situations where the search capability deficit of workers is sufficiently low, a lower cost of entry generates more sweatshop jobs.

6.3.3. The role of search capability deficit

The role of ϵ_s can be clearly seen going from Fig. 2a to c. Not including the unstable equilibrium at σ_2 highlighted in Fig. 2c, successive worsening of the search capability of sweatshop workers increases the equilibrium prevalence of sweatshop jobs σ^*. However, and perhaps most intriguing, due to the tendency for multiple equilibria particularly when ϵ_s is extremely low, a slight improvement in the working condition of sweatshop workers, say going from $\epsilon_s = 0.0005$ in Fig. 2c to $\epsilon_s = 0.02$ in Fig. 2b can completely eradicate sweatshop jobs particularly in situations where the competition for workers are sufficiently intense to begin with; for example at O_3O_3.

The lesson that can be drawn from these observations is that small improvements in the search capability of sweatshop workers can eradicate the rationale for sweatshops altogether. From Proposition 5, such eradications can in fact be efficiency improving.

6.4. Employment, distribution, and welfare simulations

This section performs numerical simulations of the equilibrium outcomes given by the intersection of the $\Delta\Delta$ and the OO curves. To do so closed form solution for α^* given σ^* from Eq. (32) can be obtained by assuming that the match function takes the Cobb Douglas form,[33] with

$$\Psi(N, v) = N^a v^{1-a}, 0 < a < 1.$$

The sweatshop equilibrium pair (α^*, σ^*) simultaneously solves Eqs. (31) and (32). Given this solution, the equilibrium employment, distribution, and efficiency consequences of the emergence of sweatshops can be computed.

Three sets of simulations are performed, respectively corresponding to cases where ρ is set at 1.2, 1.05, and 1.001 in Table 1. Table 1 accounts for a full range of ϵ_s going from values close to zero, and values close to one, as well as a range of the one-time cost of hiring c going from 5% to 500% of the instantaneous surplus of sweatshop jobs. Table 1 reports the equilibrium job arrival rate, and the fraction of sweatshop offers with and without a ban on sweatshop jobs (α^o and α^*, and $\sigma^o = 0$ and σ^* respectively). The corresponding employment, distribution and efficiency consequences as reported in Propositions 2, 4 and 5 are then computed and reported.

Based on the findings in Table 1, five general observations can be made. To start, a policy of indifference to sweatshop jobs improves the job arrival rates $\alpha^* > \alpha^o$, increases total employment $n_d^* + n_s^* > n_d^o$, but crowds out employment in decent work $n_d^* < n_d^o$. These observations echo Proposition 2 which summarizes the employment consequences of sweatshops.

Second, these changes in job arrival rates, total employment, and employment in decent work are sensitive to the capability deficit of sweatshop work. The more severe the deficit, the larger these changes will be. Indeed, Table 1 (with $\rho = 1.2$) clearly shows that employers will only tolerate the relative inefficiency of sweatshop jobs if ϵ_s is sufficiently small.

Third, the share of per worker surplus that goes toward employer profits ψ_i^* likewise critically depends on ϵ_s. Consistent with Proposition 4, the emergence of sweatshops biases the distribution of income in favor of all employers, but particularly sweatshop employers, if ϵ_s is sufficiently small.

In terms of efficiency, Table 1 also reports the efficiency consequences of the emergence of sweatshop jobs. Where sweatshops are relatively inefficient ($\rho = 1.2$ and 1.05), the emergence of sweatshops leads to a decline in overall efficiency consistent with Proposition 5. When the relative inefficiency of sweatshops is very minor $\rho = 1.001$, the emergence of sweatshops nonetheless leads to a decline in overall efficiency if ϵ_s is sufficiently small. These results directly illustrate the efficiency benefits of safeguarding the on-the-job search capability of workers in sweatshop jobs, and show that overall efficiency can improve even when total employment decreases.

Finally, multiple equilibria can and do arise. One such possibility is shown in Table 1, when sweatshops are relatively inefficient ($\rho = 1.2$), when the search capability deficit is severe $\epsilon_s = 0.0005$, and when the cost of hiring c is small at 5% of s_s. Starting from such an equilibrium, even a minor improvement in the search capability of sweatshop workers ϵ_s (e.g., from 0.0005 to 0.4 for the case of $\rho = 1.2$),[34] can give rise to a sharp change in employment from predominantly sweatshop jobs to decent employment everywhere. Total employment in the labor market declines, but overall efficiency improves manifold. Furthermore, the share of production surplus going to workers likewise improves.

7. Concluding discussion

Sweatshop jobs embody a broad range of characteristics, including harsh conditions, long hours, and inferior health and safety standards, leading to lower worker productivity. Furthermore, sweatshop

[33] See Petrongolo and Pissarides (2001) for a survey of the wealth of empirical support for a Cobb Douglas matching function.

[34] Additional simulation results are available upon request. For example, sweatshops vanish completely with $\rho = 1.2$ for ϵ_s as small as 0.2, consistent with Fig. 2b.

Table 1
Simulating employment, distribution and efficiency changes.

Parameters		Job arrival		Sweatshop incidence		Employment			Profit share			Net surplus	
ε_s	c	α^o	α^*	σ^o	σ^*	n_d^o	$(n_d^*-n_d^o)/n_d^o \times 100\%$	$(n_u^o-n_u^*)/(1-n^o) \times 100\%$	ψ^o	ψ_d^*	ψ_s^*	S^o	$(S^*-S^o)/S^o \times 100\%$
$\rho=1.2$													
0.0005	0.05	1.969	**15.628**	0.000	**0.984**	0.797	**−98.0%**	**21.5%**	0.203	**0.492**	**0.600**	0.763	**−48.8%**
			2.149		**0.133**		**−11.8%**	**1.7%**		**0.212**	**0.254**		**−2.3%**
0.4			1.969		0.000		0.0%	0.0%		0.203	.		0.0%
0.8			1.969		0.000		0.0%	0.0%		0.203	.		0.0%
0.0005	1	0.547	**1.478**	0.000	**0.908**	0.523	**−86.9%**	**43.0%**	0.477	**0.783**	**0.941**	0.328	**−82.2%**
0.4			0.547		0.000		0.0%	0.0%		0.477	.		0.0%
0.8			0.547		0.000		0.0%	0.0%		0.477	.		0.0% [b]
0.0005	5	0.227	**0.298**	0.000	**0.550**	0.312	**−46.2%**	**19.7%**	0.688	**0.788**	**0.946**	0.117	**−54.0%**
0.4			0.227		0.000		0.0%	0.0%		0.688	.		0.0%
0.8			0.227		0.000		0.0%	0.0%		0.688	.		0.0%
$\rho=1.05$													
0.0005	0.05	1.870	**19.812**	0.000	**0.997**	0.789	**−99.7%**	**23.6%**	0.211	**0.519**	**0.556**	0.654	**−22.1%**
0.4			**2.122**		**0.630**		**−37.1%**	**2.6%**		**0.130**	**0.368**		**−0.2%**
0.8			1.870		0.000		0.0%	0.0%		0.211	.		0.0%
0.0005	1	0.512	**1.874**	0.000	**0.986**	0.506	**−97.8%**	**56.0%**	0.494	**0.940**	**0.989**	0.269	**−96.4%**
0.4			**0.645**		**0.800**		**−69.4%**	**11.3%**		**0.387**	**0.616**		**−4.5%**
0.8			**0.512**		**0.053**		**−2.8%**	**0.1%**		**0.483**	**0.924**		**−0.3%**
0.0005	5	0.209	**0.379**	0.000	**0.930**	0.295	**−89.8%**	**46.2%**	0.705	**0.949**	**0.997**	0.091	**−96.8%**
0.4			**0.248**		**0.728**		**−65.3%**	**12.4%**		**0.669**	**0.842**		**−21.3%**
0.8			0.209		0.000		0.0%	0.0%		0.705	.		0.0%
$\rho=1.005$													
0.0005	0.05	1.835	**20.857**	0.000	**0.999954**	0.786	**−99.99%**	**24.3%**	0.214	**0.523**	**0.534**	0.618	**−26.4%**
0.4			**2.544**		**0.995**		**−98.35%**	**6.3%**		**0.065**	**0.199**		**8.6%**
0.8			**1.980**		**0.975**		**−90.01%**	**1.6%**		**0.054**	**0.227**		**2.1%**
0.0005	1	0.500	**1.981**	0.000	**0.9997**	0.500	**−99.96%**	**59.7%**	0.500	**0.987**	**0.990**	0.250	**−96.9%**
0.4			**0.690**		**0.997**		**−99.37%**	**15.9%**		**0.349**	**0.543**		**6.2%**
0.8			**0.542**		**0.983**		**−96.74%**	**4.0%**		**0.276**	**0.515**		**2.2%**
0.0005	5	0.203	**0.385**	0.000	**0.999**	0.288	**−99.80%**	**50.8%**	0.712	**0.998**	**0.999**	0.083	**−99.6%**
0.4			**0.262**		**0.995**		**−99.30%**	**19.2%**		**0.654**	**0.792**		**−13.7%**
0.8			**0.217**		**0.979**		**−97.02%**	**4.8%**		**0.546**	**0.736**		**−2.2%**

Notes: 1. The following parametric assumptions are made: $s_s=1$, $\delta=0.5$, $\Psi(N,v)=N^{0.5}v^{0.5}$. 2. Figures in bold indicate steady state outcomes where sweatshop jobs and decent work co-exist.

conditions give rise to inferior prospects with regards to job advancement while on the job. By introducing search capability deficits of sweatshop jobs in a canonical model of on-the-job search, an extensive list of new insights concerning labor markets where sweatshop jobs, decent work, and unemployment co-exist emerge.

At the level of workers and firms, this paper traces the reasons why workers willingly undertake insufficiently compensating sweatshop jobs, while employers knowingly adopt workers conditions that are relatively inefficient. Throughout the labor market, the emergence of sweatshop jobs is shown to increase employment overall at the cost of decent work, biases the distribution of income against all workers in favor of employers, and reduces overall efficiency in the labor market when the search capability deficit is sufficiently acute.

In accordance with popular discussions, this paper finds that poor unemployment protection (e.g., as is the case with migrants) and high international price for products with no strings attached on worker condition are conditions favorable to sweatshops. However, much more nuanced results are also obtained. In particular, intense competition for workers coupled with legislations that safeguard the search capability of workers, even slightly, are shown to be capable of eradicating sweatshops altogether. However, the same intense competition for workers without any protection offered to workers creates the perfect environment for sweatshop jobs to thrive.

Many important questions remain. To begin with, the effectiveness of "no sweat" consumer activism can be of particular interest here, where decent work employers and sweatshop producers receive different prices for the goods they produce. Similarly, the role of foreign direct investment in the determination of sweatshop jobs is likewise of interest. In particular, they contribute to competition for workers among local employers and between local and foreign employers. Furthermore, foreign firms may carry codes of conduct that differ from local employers. In general equilibrium, the presence of these employers may thus impact the prevalence of sweatshop jobs among local firms in interesting ways. Finally, the role of internal migration of workers is also relevant here. Since the emergence of sweatshops increases job opportunities, does this itself fuel the migration of workers from rural areas to urban manufacturing centers? If so, what is the efficiency implication of sweatshop employment economy-wide? The basic model developed here provides a starting point for each of these questions to be addressed.

Appendix A

Proof of Proposition 1. I show that the difference $J_s(W) - J_d(W)$ has a single crossing at zero.

From Eq. (6), the difference $J_s(W) - J_d(W)$ is decreasing in W whenever $J_s(W) - J_d(W) = 0$, since

$$sgn\left\{\frac{\partial(J_s(W)-J_d(W))}{\partial W}\right\}\Bigg|_{J_s(W)=J_d(W)} = sgn\left\{-\alpha(1-\epsilon_s)(r+\delta)\right\} < 0.$$

Suppose that there exists at least two distinct crossings, and $W_1 < W_2$ are two such crossings with negative slopes and no other negatively sloped crossing in between. It follows that for $\varepsilon > 0$ small enough, $J_s(W_2 - \varepsilon) - J_d(W_2 - \varepsilon) > 0 > [J_s(W_1 + \varepsilon) - J_d(W_1 + \varepsilon)]$. By the intermediate value theorem, there exists $W \in [W_1 + \varepsilon, W_2 - \varepsilon]$ such that $J_s(W) - J_d(W) = 0$. Furthermore, by the mean value theorem, $J_s(W) - J_d(W)$ must have changed slope from negative at W_1 and W_2 to positive for at least one W. This contradicts the hypothesis that there are no other crossings between W_1 and W_2.

Proof of Proposition 2. I show that $\alpha^* > \alpha^o$, and furthermore, $n_d^* < n_d^o$. To see the former, note from Eq. (15) that self-selection of employers between sweatshop jobs and decent work implies:

$$
\begin{aligned}
J_s^*\left(\overline{W}^*\right) = J_d^*\left(\overline{W}^*\right) &\Leftrightarrow \frac{\theta_s\left(\overline{W}^*\right)}{d_s\left(\overline{W}^*\right)} = \frac{\theta_d\left(\overline{W}^*\right)}{d_d\left(\overline{W}^*\right)} \\
&\Leftrightarrow \frac{\theta_s\left(\overline{W}^*\right) - \theta_d\left(\overline{W}^*\right)}{d_s\left(\overline{W}^*\right)} = \theta_d\left(\overline{W}^*\right)\left(\frac{1}{d_d\left(\overline{W}^*\right)} - \frac{1}{d_s\left(\overline{W}^*\right)}\right) \\
&\Leftrightarrow \frac{s_s - s_d - \omega_d\theta_d\left(\overline{W}^*\right)}{d_s\left(\overline{W}^*\right)} = -\frac{\theta_d\left(\overline{W}^*\right)}{d_s\left(\overline{W}^*\right)} \frac{\alpha^*(1-\epsilon_s)(1-\sigma^*)}{d_d\left(\overline{W}^*\right)} \\
&\Leftrightarrow s_s - s_d = \theta_d\left(\overline{W}^*\right)\left((1-\epsilon_s)\left(1-h^*\left(\overline{W}^*\right)\right)^2 - (1-\epsilon_s)\left(1-h^*\left(\overline{W}^*\right)\right)\right) \\
&\Leftrightarrow \frac{\theta_d\left(\overline{W}^*\right)}{\left(d_d\left(\overline{W}^*\right)\right)^2} = \frac{s_d - s_s}{(1-\epsilon_s)\alpha^*(1-\sigma^*)\delta}
\end{aligned}
$$

From the free entry condition in Eq. (16),

$$
\alpha_e^*\delta\frac{\theta_d\left(\overline{W}^*\right)}{\left(d_d\left(\overline{W}^*\right)\right)^2} - c = \frac{\alpha_e^*(s_d - s_s)}{(1-\epsilon_s)\alpha^*(1-\sigma^*)\delta} - c = 0, \tag{33}
$$

Since α_e^* and α^* are inversely related by definition of the matching technology $\Psi(N, v)$, Eq. (33) shows that α^* is monotonically increasing in σ^*, and thus, $\alpha^* > \alpha^o$, equivalently, $n_{u*} < n_{uo}$. Furthermore, $\alpha_{e*} < \alpha_{eo}$, follows from $\alpha^* > \alpha^o$ and as such, $\alpha^*(1 - \sigma^*) < \alpha^o$.

With respect to employment in decent work, note from Eq. (12) that

$$
\begin{aligned}
n_d^* &= \frac{\alpha^*(1-\sigma^*)}{\delta + \alpha_s^*(1-\sigma^*)}\frac{\delta + \alpha_s^*}{\delta + \alpha^*} \\
&< \frac{\alpha^*(1-\sigma^*)}{\delta + \alpha^*(1-\sigma^*)} \\
&< \frac{\alpha^o}{\delta + \alpha^o}
\end{aligned}
$$

where the latter follows since $\alpha^*(1 - \sigma^*) < \alpha^o$ as shown earlier using Eq. (35).

Proof of Proposition 3. I obtain an expression for the average wage net of effort and opportunity costs in sweatshop jobs and decent work as displayed in Eqs. (24) and (25) and ascertain the size of the equilibrium compensating differential.

To arrive at an expression of total wages, first turn to profits. From the definition of $F^*(W)$ in Eqs. (17) and (19) and $G^*(W)$ in Eqs. (10)–(11), total sweatshop instantaneous profit can be simply expressed as:

$$
\begin{aligned}
\left(\int_{W_u^*}^{\overline{W}^*}\theta_s(W)dG^*(W)\right) &= \int_{W_u^*}^{\overline{W}^*}\sqrt{\frac{\theta_s\left(\overline{W}^*\right)}{\theta_s(W)}}\frac{\delta}{\alpha_s^*}\frac{\delta + \alpha_s^*}{\left(\overline{W}^*\right)}\frac{d_s(W)}{2} \\
&\int_{W_u^*}^{\overline{W}^*}\frac{\delta}{\alpha_s^*}\frac{\delta + \alpha_s^*}{\left(\overline{W}^*\right)}\frac{d_s\left(\overline{W}^*\right)}{2}dW \\
&= \frac{\delta(\delta + \alpha_s^*)}{2\alpha_s^*}\left(\overline{W}^* - W_u^*\right) \\
&= \delta(\delta + \alpha_s^*)\frac{\sigma^*\theta_s\left(\overline{W}^*\right)}{\left(d_s\left(\overline{W}^*\right)\right)^2}.
\end{aligned}
$$

An analogous approach using $F^*(W)$ in Eqs. (17) and (19) and $G^*(W)$ in Eqs. (10)–(11) yields total decent work instantaneous profits as:

$$
\left(\int_{W_u^*}^{\overline{W}^*}(\theta_d(W))dG^*(W)\right) = \delta(\delta + \alpha_s^*)\frac{(1-\sigma^*)\theta_s\left(\overline{W}^*\right)}{d_s\left(\overline{W}^*\right)d_d\left(\overline{W}^*\right)}.
$$

Since $y_i(W) - e_i - b = p_i - \theta_i(W) - e_i - b = s_i - \theta_i(W)$, while $G^*\left(\overline{W}^*\right) = \delta\sigma^*/d_s(\overline{W}^*)$, and $1 - G^*\left(\overline{W}^*\right) = (\delta + \alpha_s^*)(1-\sigma^*)/d_s(\overline{W}^*)$,

$$
\left(\int_{W_u^*}^{\overline{W}^*}(y_s(W) - e_s - b)dG^*(W)\right)/G^*\left(\overline{W}^*\right) = s_s - \frac{(\delta + \alpha_s^*)\theta_s^*\left(\overline{W}^*\right)}{d_s\left(\overline{W}^*\right)}, \tag{34}
$$

$$
\left(\int_{\overline{W}^*}^{W^*_{max}}(y_d(W) - e_d - b)dG^*(W)\right)/\left(1 - G^*\left(\overline{W}^*\right)\right) = s_d - \frac{\delta\theta_d^*\left(\overline{W}^*\right)}{d_d\left(\overline{W}^*\right)}. \tag{35}
$$

Furthermore, from Eq. (15), self-selection of employers between sweatshop jobs and decent work implies:

$$
J_s^*\left(\overline{W}^*\right) = J_d^*\left(\overline{W}^*\right) \Leftrightarrow \frac{\theta_s\left(\overline{W}^*\right)}{d_s\left(\overline{W}^*\right)} = \frac{\theta_d\left(\overline{W}^*\right)}{d_d\left(\overline{W}^*\right)}
$$

Proposition 4 obtains upon taking the difference between Eqs. (34) and (35).

Proofs of Proposition 4 and 5. I show here the share of producer profit in per worker surplus with and without sweatshops (Proposition 4), and the overall efficiency consequences of a ban on sweatshops (Proposition 5). I proceed in two steps. I first show that (I) for every $\rho > 1$, there exists an upper bound $\overline{\varepsilon}_s \in [0, 1)$ such that $\sigma^* > 0$ if and only if $\varepsilon_s < \overline{\varepsilon}_s$. I then show that (II) the relative ranking of producer shares and overall efficiency with and without sweatshops can be determined for values of ϵ_s sufficiently small in the range $[0, \overline{\varepsilon}_s]$.

I. Note from Eq. (15) that the self-selection of employers between sweatshop jobs and decent work implies:

$$
J_s^*\left(\overline{W}^*\right) \geq J_d^*\left(\overline{W}^*\right) \Leftrightarrow s_d - s_s \leq \theta_d\left(\overline{W}^*\right)\left((1-\varepsilon_s)\left(1-h^*\left(\overline{W}^*\right)\right)h\left(\overline{W}^*\right)\right). \tag{36}
$$

Since $h(\overline{W}^*) = \delta/d_d(\overline{W}^*)$ is a fraction, and $\theta_d^*(\overline{W}^*)$ evaluated at $\sigma^* = 0$ i is simply s_d from Eq. (22), it follows that the largest ϵ_s that can satisfy Eq. (31) evaluated at $\sigma^* = 0$ is

$$
1 \quad \frac{4(s_d - s_s)}{s_d} - \overline{\varepsilon}_s.
$$

II. From the Proof of Proposition 3:

$$
\begin{aligned}
\psi_d^* &\equiv \int_{\overline{W}^*}^{W_{max}}\theta_d(W)dG^*(W)/\left[\left(1 - G^*\left(\overline{W}^*\right)\right)s_d\right] = \frac{\delta}{s_d}\frac{\theta_d\left(\overline{W}^*\right)}{d_d\left(\overline{W}^*\right)}, \\
\psi_s^* &\equiv \int_{W_u^*}^{\overline{W}}\theta_s(W)dG^*(W)/\left[G^*\left(\overline{W}^*\right)s_s\right] = \frac{\delta + \alpha_s^*}{s_s}\frac{\theta_s\left(\overline{W}^*\right)}{d_s\left(\overline{W}^*\right)}.
\end{aligned}
$$

From the free entry condition,

$$\alpha_e^* h\left(\overline{W}^*\right)\frac{\theta_s\left(\overline{W}^*\right)}{d_s\left(\overline{W}^*\right)} = \alpha_e^* h\left(\overline{W}^*\right)\frac{\theta_d\left(\overline{W}^*\right)}{d_d\left(\overline{W}^*\right)},$$

or

$$\frac{\theta_s\left(\overline{W}^*\right)}{d_s\left(\overline{W}^*\right)} = \frac{\theta_s\left(\overline{W}^*\right)}{d_d\left(\overline{W}^*\right)}.$$

It follows immediately that $\psi_{d*} < \psi_{s*}$. In addition, from Eq. (22),

$$\frac{\theta_d\left(\overline{W}^*\right)}{d_d\left(\overline{W}^*\right)} = \frac{1}{d_d\left(\overline{W}^*\right)}\frac{s_d + \omega_s(s_d - s_s)}{1 + \omega_s(1 - \omega_d)}.$$

Thus,

$$\psi_d^*\big|_{\varepsilon_s=0} = \frac{\delta}{\delta + \alpha^*(1-\sigma^*)} > \frac{\delta}{\delta + \alpha^o} = \psi_d^o,$$
$$\psi_d^*\big|_{\varepsilon_s=\varepsilon_s} = \frac{\delta}{\delta + \alpha^o} = \psi_d^o.$$

It follows that there exists $\overline{\varepsilon}_s$ sufficiently smaller then ε_s such that $\psi_d^* \geq \psi_d^o$ for all $\varepsilon_s \leq \overline{\varepsilon}_s$.

Next, total output net of entry cost is given by:

$$S^* = n_d^* s_d + n_s^* s_s - \alpha^*(n_u^* + n_d^* + \varepsilon_s n_s^*)\delta\theta_d\left(\overline{W}^*\right)/\left(d_d\left(\overline{W}^*\right)\right)^2.$$

Substituting for equilibrium employment allocations using Eq. (12),

$$S^* = \frac{\alpha^*}{\delta + \alpha^*}\left(\frac{\delta + \alpha_s^*}{d_s\left(\overline{W}^*\right)}(1-\sigma^*)s_d + \frac{\delta\sigma^*}{d_s\left(\overline{W}^*\right)}s_s - \frac{\delta + \alpha_s^*}{d_s\left(\overline{W}^*\right)}\frac{\delta}{d_d\left(\overline{W}^*\right)}\theta_d\left(\overline{W}^*\right)\right).$$

Thus,

$$S^*\big|_{\varepsilon_s=0} = \frac{\alpha^*}{\delta + \alpha^*}\left((1-\sigma^*)s_d + \sigma^* s_s - \frac{\delta}{d_d\left(\overline{W}^*\right)}\theta_d\left(\overline{W}^*\right)\right)$$
$$= \left(\frac{\alpha^*(1-\sigma^*)}{\delta + \alpha^*(1-\sigma^*)}\right)^2 s_d < \left(\frac{\alpha^o}{\delta + \alpha^o}\right)^2 s_d = S^o,$$
$$S^*\big|_{\varepsilon_s=\varepsilon_s} = \left(\frac{\alpha^o}{\delta + \alpha^o}\right)^2 s_d = S^o.$$

where the second equality follows from the selection equation in (15). It follows that there exists $\tilde{\epsilon}_s$ sufficiently smaller then ϵ_s such that $S^* \leq S^o$ for all $\epsilon_s \leq \tilde{\epsilon}_s$.

Appendix B

I show here that as long as $\rho > 1$, the share of sweatshop jobs will always be strictly less than one. Furthermore, $\Delta(\sigma^*; \epsilon_s, \rho)$ is non-empty only if ϵ_s is sufficiently small

From Eq. (31), $\Delta J^*(\overline{W}^*) = 1 - \rho < 0$ evaluated at $\sigma^* = 1$. Intuitively, when all jobs are sweatshop jobs, the employer offering the highest value sweatshop contract $W_{\max}^*$ will always have an incentive to switch to decent work. Doing so does not change the separation rate $d_d(W_{\max}^*) = \delta + \alpha^*(1 - F(W_{\max}^*)) = \delta = \delta + \alpha_s^*(1 - F(W_{\max}^*)) = d_s(W_{\max}^*)$ since the employer already offers the highest value job, and faces no possibility of voluntary separation $F(W_{\max}^*) = 1$. Furthermore, the match success probability at recruitment $F(W_{\max}^*) = \delta/(\delta, +, \alpha^*, (1 - F, (W_{\max}^*)))$ is equal to unity regardless of the condition of work chosen. Consequently, the only difference between the two types of work is their relative productivity. If and only if $s_s < s_d$, decent work conditions maximize employer profits whenever $\sigma^* = 1$.

By inspection of Eq. (31), $\Delta J^*(\overline{W}^*)$ is non-negative only if ϵ_s is sufficiently smaller than one. In other words, a sweatshop equilibrium with $\sigma^* > 0$ is possible *only if* ε_s is sufficiently small. This observation reflects the fact that adopting sweatshops is in the end a costly move, due to the inferior surplus generated therein $s_s < s_d$. As such, the gains from an increase in retention and recruitment likelihood must be sufficiently large, or equivalently, ϵ_s must be sufficiently small.

References

Acemoglu, Daron, 2001. Good jobs versus bad jobs. J. Labor Econ. 19 (1), 1–21.

Bagwell, Kyle, Staiger, Robert W., 2000. The Simple Economics of Labor Standards and the GATT. In: Deardorff, A.V., Stern, R.M. (Eds.), Social Dimensions of U.S. Trade Policy. University Press, Ann Arbor, MI, pp. 195–231.

Bajaj, Vikas, 2012. Fatal fire in Bangladesh highlights the dangers facing garment workers. N. Y. Times A4 (November 26, 2012).

Banerjee, Biswajit, Bucci, Gabriella A., 1995. On-the-job search in a developing country: an analysis based on Indian data on migrants. Econ. Dev. Cult. Chang. 43 (3), 565–583.

Bardhan, Pranab, 2004. The Impact of Globalization on the Poor. In: Collins, S., Graham, C. (Eds.), Brookings Trade Forum: 2004, pp. 271–296.

Bardhan, Pranab, 2005. *Scarcity, Conflicts, and Cooperation*. MIT Press, Cambridge.

Basu, Arnab K., Chau, Nancy H., 2004. Exploitation of child labor and the dynamics of debt bondage. J. Econ. Growth 9, 209–238.

Benhabib, Jesse, Bull, Clive, 1983. Job search: the choice of intensity. J. Polit. Econ. 91 (5), 747–764.

Blau, David M., 1991. Search for non-wage job characteristics: a test of the reservation wage hypothesis. J. Labor Econ. 9 (2), 186–205.

Brown, Drusilla, Deardroff, Alan V., Stern, Robert M., 1997. Issues of Environmental and Labor Standards in the Global Trading System. Papers 97-10, Michigan - Center for Research on Economic and Social Theory.

Brown, Drusila, Dehejia, Rajeev, Robertson, Raymond, Domat, George, Veeraragoo, Selven, 2015. Are Sweatshops Profit-Maximizing? *Better Work Discussion Paper Series* No. 17

Burdett, Kenneth, Mortensen, Dale T., 1998. Wage differentials, employer size and unemployment. Int. Econ. Rev. 39, 257–273.

Burdett, Kenneth, Lagos, Ricardo, Wright, Randall, 2003. Crime, inequality, and unemployment. Am. Econ. Rev. 93 (5), 1764–1777.

Chan, Anita, 2000. Globalization, China's free (read bonded) labour market, and the Chinese Trade Union. Asia Pac. Bus. Rev. 6 (3 & 4), 260–281.

Chan, Anita, 2003. A race to the bottom: globalization and China's labour standards. China Perspect. 41–49 (No. 46 March–April).

Chau, Nancy H., Kanbur, Ravi, 2006. A race to the bottom from the bottom: labor standards competition among developing countries. Economica 73 (290), 193–228.

China Labor Watch, 2001. Merton Company Limited. http://www.chinalaborwatch.org/report/5.

China Labor Watch, 2008. Pumas Failure in CSR: Suppliers Critical Conditions. http://www.chinalaborwatch.org/report/21.

China Labor Watch, 2009a. Shattered Dreams: Underage Worker Death at Factory Supplying to Disney, Other International Brand. http://www.chinalaborwatch.org/report/30.

China Labor Watch, 2009b. KKR Reaps Profits from Sweatshop Labor: Illegal Conditions at Four Dollar General Supplier Factories. http://www.chinalaborwatch.org/report/36.

China Labor Watch, 2011. Dell, HP, and NEC Supplier Factory Case Study: MSI Computer (Shenzhen) Co., Ltd. http://www.chinalaborwatch.org/report/49.

China Labor Watch, 2012. Investigative Report of HTNS Shenzhen Co., Ltd. (Huizhou Branch). http://www.chinalaborwatch.org/report/67.

China Labor Watch, 2013. China Labor Watch 2013 Annual Report. http://chinalaborwatch.org/2013AnnualReportFINAL.pdf.

China Labor Watch, 2015. Analyzing labor conditions of Pegatron and Foxconn: apples low-cost reality. http://www.chinalaborwatch.org/report/107.

Davis, Donald R., Harrigan, James, 2011. Good jobs, bad jobs, and trade liberalization. J. Int. Econ. 84 (1), 26–36.

Elliott, Kimberly Ann, Freeman, Richard, 2001. White hats or Don Quixotes? Human rights vigilantes in the global economy. NBER Working Paper No. 8102.

Engels, Frederick, 1892. The Condition of the Working-Class in England in 1844. George Allen & Unwin Limited, London.

Esbenshade, Jill, 2004. *Monitoring Sweatshops: Workers, Consumers and the Global Apparel Industry*. Temple University Press, Philadelphia.

Fields, Gary S., 2005. A Guide to Multisector Labor Market Models. World Bank Social Protection Discussion Paper Series No. 0505.

Gottschalk, Peter, 1982. Earnings mobility: permanent change or transitory fluctuations? Rev. Econ. Stat. 64 (3), 45–56.

Harrison, Ann, Jason, Scorse, 2010. Multinationals and anti-sweatshop activism. Am. Econ. Rev. 100 (1), 247–273.

ILO, 2008. ILO Declaration on Social Justice for a Fair Globalization. ILO, Geneva.

ILO, 2013. *Decent Work Country Profile: Bangladesh*. ILO, Geneva.

Kristof, Nicholas D., WuDunn, Sheryl, 2000. Two cheers for sweatshops. N. Y. Times Mag. (September 24, 2000).

Krugman, Paul, 1997. In praise of cheap labor. Slate (March 21, 1997).

Liu, Linping, Yong, Xin, Shu, Binbin, 2011. Regional differences in labor rights: a survey of rural migrant workers in the Pearl River Delta and the Yangtze River Delta. Soc. Sci. China 2011-2, 107–123.

Melitz, Marc, 2003. The impact of trade on intra-industry reallocations and aggregate industry productivity. Econometrica 71, 1695–1725.

Mortensen, Dale T., 1990. Equilibrium Wage Distributions: A Synthesis. In: Hartog, J., Ridder, G., Theeuwes, J. (Eds.), Panel Data and Labor Market Studies. North-Holland, Amsterdam.

Mortensen, Dale T., 2000. Equilibrium Unemployment with Wage Posting: Burdett-Mortensen Meet Pissarides. In: Bunzel, Henning, Christensen, Bent J., Jensen, Peter, Kiefer, Nicholas M., Mortensen, Dale T. (Eds.), Panel Data and Structural Labour Market Models. Elsevier, Amsterdam, pp. 281–292.

Neumark, David, Nizalova, Olena, 2007. Minimum wage effects in the longer run. J. Hum. Resour. 42 (2), 435–452.

Organization for Exonomic Cooperation and Development (OECD), 1996D. *Trade, Employment, and Labour Standards: A Study of Core Workers' Rights and International Trade.* OECD, Paris.

Organization for Exonomic Cooperation and Development (OECD), 2000D. International Trade and Core Labour Standards. OECD, Paris.

Petrongolo, Barbara, Pissarides, Christopher A., 2001. "Looking into the black box: a survey of the matching function. J. Econ. Lit. 39, 390–431.

Piore, Michael, 2004. Rethinking International Labour Standards. In: Milberg, W. (Ed.), *Labour and the Globalization of Production: Causes and Consequences of Industrial Upgrading.* Palgrave, Baskingstoke, pp. 249–265.

Pissarides, C.A., 2000. Equilibrium Unemployment Theory. The MIT Press, Cambridge, MA.

Powell, Benjamin, Skarbek, David, 2006. Sweatshops and third world living standards: are the jobs worth the sweat? J. Lab. Res. 27 (2), 263–274.

Robinson, Joan, 1964. Economic Philosophy. Doubleday, Garden City NY.

Rogers, Carol Ann, Swinnerton, Kenneth A., 2008. A theory of exploitative child labor. Oxf. Econ. Pap. 60 (1), 20–41.

Rogerson, Richard, Shimer, Robert, Wright, Randall, 2005. Search-theoretic models of the labor market: a survey. J. Econ. Lit. 43 (4), 959–988.

Rosen, Sherwin, 1986. The Theory of Equalizing Differences. In: Ashenfelter, Orley, Layard, Richard (Eds.), Handbook of Labor Economics vol. I. North Holland, Amsterdam.

Ross, Robert, 2002. The New Sweatshops in the United States: How New, How Real, How Many, Why? In: Gereffi, Gary, Spencer, David, Blair, Jennifer (Eds.), *Free Trade and Uneven Development: The North American Apparel Industry.* Temple University Press, Philadelphia, pp. 100–122

Schöer, Volker, Leibbrandt, Murray, 2006. Determinants of job search strategies: evidence from the Khayelitsha/Mitchell's Plain Survey. S. Afr. J. Econ. 74 (4), 702–724.

Sen, Amartya, 1993. Capability and Well-Being. In: Nussbaum, Martha, Sen, Amartya (Eds.), The Quality of Life. Clarendon Press, Oxford, pp. 30–53.

Shapiro, Carl, Stiglitz, Joseph, 1984. Equilibrium unemployment as a worker discipline device. Am. Econ. Rev. 74 (3), 433–444.

Singh, Nirvikar, 2003. The History and Political Economy of International Labor Standards. In: Basu, Kaushik, et al. (Eds.), International Labor Standards. Blackwell Publishing, Oxford, pp. 9–83.

Smith, Adam, 1776. An Inquiry into the Nature and Causes of the Wealth of Nations. Methuen and Co., Ltd. Fifth edition, London.

U.S. Department of Labor (USDOL), 2001. *No Sweat: Garment Enforcement Reports.* October 1999–December 2000.

US General Accounting Office (USGAO), 1988. Sweatshops' in the U.S. Opinions on their Extent and Possible Enforcement Options. GAP/HRD-88-130BR.

Wan, Xiang Dong, 2011. "Comparison between Migrant Workers in Pearl River Delta and Yangtze River Delta," Mimeo. Sun Yat-Sen University. http://www.eu-china.net/upload/pdf/materialien/2011_Wan_Xiangdong-Comparison_Migrant_Workers_in_Pearl_and_Yangtze_River.pdf

War on Want, 2011. *Stitched Up: Women Workers in the Bangladeshi Garment Sector.* http://www.waronwant.org/attachments/StitchedUp.pdf.

THE
ECONOMIC
JOURNAL

The Economic Journal, **125** (*December*), 1534–1573. Doi: 10.1111/ecoj.12222 © 2014 Royal Economic Society. Published by John Wiley & Sons, 9600 Garsington Road, Oxford OX4 2DQ, UK and 350 Main Street, Malden, MA 02148, USA.

CONTRACTUAL DUALISM, MARKET POWER AND INFORMALITY*

Arnab K. Basu, Nancy H. Chau and Ravi Kanbur

We develop a search-theoretic model of contractual dualism in formal and informal labour markets. The model (*i*) provides the micro-underpinnings for endogenous determination of employer market power in the formal and informal sectors, (*ii*) offers a unified and coherent set-up whereby a host of salient features of developing country labour markets can be explained together and (*iii*) places for the first time the Stiglerian prescription of the optimal (unemployment minimising) minimum wage in the broader context of labour markets where formal job creation is costly, where employer market power is endogenous and where formal employment, informal employment and unemployment coexist.

Economic activities in developing countries are often classified as falling into either a state-regulated sphere or an unregulated sphere.[1] The labels 'formal' and 'informal' are often attached to these spheres or sectors, it being understood of course that in reality there is a continuum rather than a dichotomy. The dualistic formulation is nevertheless useful conceptually in capturing key characteristics for analytical or policy discourses. The literature on formality and informality is large and diverse, with many controversies, even down to whether the terms themselves are appropriate.[2] However, two features of these sectors, or rather two contrasts between them, seem to be generally accepted in different parts of the literature.

First, the informal sector is seen as being competitive, with no market power or dominance by a particular group/individual, in the absence of barriers inhibiting entry by actors from either side; the formal sector, on the other hand, is seen as having elements of market power, whether it be large firms or labour unions. Such characterisations are a staple of the development economics literature and have distinctive policy conclusions targeted towards the lack of competition in the formal sector.[3] Reducing union power in formal sector labour markets, or removing minimum wage legislation or other regulation in these markets, are typical policy conclusions that flow from such a perspective.[4]

* Corresponding author: Nancy Chau, Charles H. Dyson School of of Applied Economics and Management, Cornell University, Ithaca, NY 14853, UK. Email: hyc3@cornell.edu.

We thank Gary Fields, Santiago Levy and seminar participants at Cornell, the Federal Reserve Bank at St. Louis, the Inter-American Development Bank, the Institute for the Study of Labor (IZA), University of Sydney, University of New South Wales and Macquarie University for helpful comments and stimulating discussions. We also thank two anonymous referees and an editor of this Journal for their insightful comments and suggestions that have greatly improved this study.

[1] The pervasiveness of the unregulated sphere has been well documented. For example, Schneider and Enste (2000) find, using a multitude of methods, that the average size of the informal sector as a percentage of GDP ranges from 23% for transition countries to 39% for developing countries.

[2] See Guha Khasnobis *et al.* (2006) and Kanbur (2009) for the latest in many surveys of the literature.

[3] See for example Lipton (1984, pp. 198-201), in which the informal sector is seen to be characterised by 'prevalence of perfect, or rather ... near-perfect, competition', and 'largely [of] unincorporated enterprises, to which legal restrictions on employment (wage minima, regulations affecting working conditions, etc.) and on acquisitions of non-labour inputs (licences, quotas, etc.) do not apply'.

[4] For example, *The Economist* (11–17 September 2010, Available at: http://www.economist.com/node/16990967), in its survey of Latin America, notes: 'Thanks largely to baroque regulation, half the labour force toils in the informal economy, unable to reap the productivity gains that come from technology and greater scale'. See also Levy (2007). A classic exposition of such dualism is to be found in Harris and Todaro (1970).

Second, enforcement of contracts is seen as being particularly difficult in the informal sector. In developing countries, widespread incidence of wage arrears has been reported particularly in the informal sector (Lehmann and Wadsworth, 2001; Krstić and Sanfey, 2010; Fang and Lin, 2013).[5] This in turn leads to calls for extending the realm of formal regulation and law, which is seen as being able to 'unlock the economic potential' of the informal sector. Major policy initiatives, such as property titling in urban slums, flow from these initiatives.[6]

The basic contention of this article is that these two views – stated in sharp form as:

(*i*) the informal sector is competitive; and
(*ii*) contract enforcement is not possible in the informal sector – are incompatible.

Indeed, we argue that the lack of contract enforcement leads to the development of market power in equilibrium. We establish these claims by focusing on a model of limited commitment due to weak contract enforcement. In the model, wages are paid after work is done but employers cannot commit to wage contracts. A holdup problem thus arises because workers cannot be sure they will get paid for the work they have done. We argue that a self-enforcing equilibrium is characterised by employer market power even with free entry, because any attempts by newcomers to bid labour away with higher wages cannot be credible in the absence of enforceable contracts.

Consider now a situation where firms can choose between being in a regulated or an unregulated sector. In the unregulated portion of the economy, wage contracts are not enforceable by third parties, so that only those contracts that are self-enforcing are viable. In the regulated sector, firms face costly job creation/registration costs, in addition to a government-enforced minimum wage. In the conventional view of the formal sector, these government regulations are a costly burden for firms. But in our model, we offer an alternative interpretation. In a setting where a government's writ does not run throughout the economy, the costly act of signing up as a formal firm signals an employer's (state enforced) commitment to pay a high wage. In this setting, third party enforcement in the formal sector, sponsored, for example by a state-enforced minimum wage floor, alleviates the holdup problem and offers a *de facto* commitment device leading to greater efficiency, and contributes to greater equity as well. With this structure, we describe and characterise an equilibrium where the division of activity between the informal and formal sectors is determined endogenously. We show that market power of employers is greater in the informal sector than in the formal sector – informal is less competitive than formal despite, or actually because of, the need for self-enforcing contracts.

The importance of limited commitment in determining labour market outcomes, notably in developed country labour markets, has been discussed in a number of other settings. For example, Shapiro and Stiglitz (1984) study the implications of inability on the part of workers to make a prior commitment on effort. Chari *et al.* (2005) examine the implications of worker's inability to commit to staying on the job. Ramey and Watson (1997) derive the implications of two-sided limited commitments on the part of both workers and employers when shirking is a potential problem. The power of these and related studies lies in their ability to provide a coherent explanation for observed salient

[5] A number of studies additionally find wage arrears to one of the key determinants of the national wage distribution (Lehmann and Wadsworth, 2001; Krstić and Sanfey, 2010).
[6] The best known proponent of this position is de Soto (2003).

features of labour markets that are not easily explained in a setting otherwise free of commitment problems,[7] as well as in their ability to offer innovative policy conclusions.[8]

Complementing this earlier literature, we propose a model of contractual dualism in the formal and informal sectors that yields predictions consistent with five salient features of developing country labour markets that have received a good deal of attention, but are often difficult to explain together in a unified setting:

- skill levels in the formal and informal sectors overlap but the average skill level is higher in the formal sector (Thomas, 1992; Maloney, 1999, 2004; Gong and Van Soest, 2002; Gong *et al.*, 2004);
- given skill level, formal sector wages are higher than in the informal sector (Bargain and Kwenda, 2010; Charlot *et al.*, 2011);
- the national wage distribution has a spike at the minimum wage (Bell, 1997; Strobl and Walsh, 2001; Lemos, 2004; Maloney and Nunez, 2004; Cardoso and Portugal, 2006; Gindling and Terrell, 2006);
- some wages in the informal sector are above the formal sector minimum wage despite no requirement for them to be so;[9] and
- employment effects of minimum wage hikes are mixed, with evidence supporting a positive relationship (Carneiro and Corseuil, 2001; Fajnzylber, 2001), a negative relationship (Maloney and Nunez, 2004) and no significant relationship (Gindling and Terrell, 2007; Lemos, 2009).[10]

Our model is search theoretic in nature. As such, this study belongs to a recent class of models of the informal sector using a search-theoretic approach where match frictions play an important role in determining labour market outcomes subsequent to various policy interventions (Boeri and Garibaldi, 2007; Zenou, 2008; Albrecht *et al.*, 2009; Charlot *et al.*, 2011).[11] Departing from existing studies, this study introduces a

[7] Some of these include the existence of equilibrium unemployment (Shapiro and Stiglitz, 1984), seniority-based wages, high separation rates for low-skilled workers (Chari *et al.*, 2005) and countercyclical job destruction without real wage rigidities (Ramey and Watson, 1997).

[8] Shapiro and Stiglitz (1984) propose a tax on profits to fund wage subsidies, Chari, *et al.* (2005) propose raising firing costs to increase the duration of employer–worker matches and Ramey and Watson (1997) provide the rationale for a severance tax/tax on firms following good states, to finance firms following bad states.

[9] For studies that present kernel density plots and/or wage histograms of dispersed subminimum wage distribution, see for example Bell (1997) for Colombia, Maloney and Nunez (2004) for eight Latin American countries, Cardoso and Portugal (2006) for Portugal, Gindling and Terrell (2006) for Honduras, Strobl and Walsh (2001) for Trinidad and Tobago and Lemos (2004) for both the formal and informal sectors in Brazil. These studies also demonstrate wage dualism between the formal and informal sectors, the overlap of wage distributions in the two sectors and over compliance in the informal sector.

[10] Relatedly, co-movements of subminimum wages and the regulated minimum wage also show mixed patterns, including positive correlations, no significant correlations and negative correlations (Card and Krueger, 1995; Strobl and Walsh, 2001; Baanante, 2004; Lemos, 2004; Gindling and Terrell, 2009).

[11] For example, Zenou (2008) examines the employment impacts of unemployment benefits, wage subsidies and entry costs in the formal sector, and does so in a setting which assumes a frictionless informal labour market and a formal labour market characterised by search friction and unemployment. Albrecht *et al.* (2009) present a search and matching model of a regulated formal and an unregulated informal sector where the size, as well as skill composition of the formal and informal workforce adjust endogenously to severance and payroll taxes. Boeri and Garibaldi (2007) are likewise concerned with the skill composition of the formal and informal workforce, as well as the puzzling increase in size of the shadow economy despite improvements in detection technologies against tax evasion. Charlot *et al.* (2011) depart further from the standard search-theoretic setup by permitting product market price setting behaviour by formal and informal firms, and examine the impact of entry costs and workers' bargaining power on employment, unemployment and wage bargaining outcomes in the formal and informal sectors.

contractual perspective on wage formation and employer market power in the formal and the informal labour markets. We demonstrate that such a setting provides a coherent basis for understanding a wide variety of salient features related to differences in skill composition, wage distribution and regulation compliance commonly observed in the formal and informal sectors of developing countries that cannot be easily explained together.

In terms of policy implications, our setting yields a simple formula that revises the Stiglerian prescription of an optimal (unemployment minimising) minimum wage. The original prescription stipulates a skill-specific minimum wage, to be set at the marginal value product of labourers in an otherwise competitive labour market (Stigler, 1946). Our extension of the optimal minimum wage formula – in a setting with endogenous employer market power induced by contractual dualism in the formal and the informal sectors – takes the Stiglerian prescription as a special case and, more generally, incorporates the cost of creating a formal sector job as a key determinant of the height of such a minimum wage. Importantly, as has been recently demonstrated in Djankov *et al.* (2002), these costs of formal sector regulation can be substantial. Based on our formula, the corresponding downward revision required in setting the unemployment minimising minimum wage relative to the marginal value product of labour will accordingly be substantial as well. A novel implication of this analysis is thus that the cost of formal sector job creation puts a strict limit on the extent to which a government-enforced minimum wage can simultaneously achieve efficiency (raising employment) and distributional (raising wages) gains.[12]

In summary, the contributions of this article are threefold. It:

(*i*) provides the micro-underpinnings for endogenous determination of employer market power in the formal and informal sectors due to contractual dualism in the two sectors;
(*ii*) offers a unified and coherent set-up whereby a host of salient features of developing country labour markets can be explained together; and
(*iii*) places the original Stiglerian prescription of the optimal (unemployment minimising) minimum wage in the broader context of labour markets where formal job creation is costly, where employer market power is endogenous and where formal employment, informal employment and unemployment coexist.

The plan of the article is as follows. Section 1 develops the basic search framework where all labour contracts are subject to a no reneging constraint (NRC). A steady state equilibrium where formal and informal sectors coexist is then characterised and the features of this equilibrium are explored. Section 2 considers the special case of a non-intervention benchmark, where there is no minimum wage in the economy. In this case, the model collapses to a single sector. It is shown that in this equilibrium, employers have market power despite free entry, with consequent inefficiency of

[12] This article is also related to a large literature on the informal economy. Fields (2004) provides an excellent survey of multi-sectoral models of developing country labour markets where the implications of policy shifts for wage, formal and informal employment, and unemployment can be ascertained. This class of models typically assumes that labour markets in both the formal and informal sectors are competitive, thus effectively ruling out unemployment-reducing and equity-improving minimum wage reforms *à la* Stigler (1946).

outcomes, as well as distributional consequences. Section 3 focuses on minimum wage policy with contractual dualism. We show how the equilibrium changes with the minimum wage and, furthermore, how the lowest minimum wage that eliminates employer market power in fact coincides with the lowest minimum wage that minimises unemployment. Section 4 presents three extensions to the basic model bringing in non-wage benefits, mandated severance pay and partial reneging. Section 5 concludes.

1. The Model

We consider a labour market with match friction in discrete time. At each time period, $t = 0,1,2,\ldots,\infty$, there are three states of employment: formal, informal and unemployment. We begin with a description of workers and their preferences, as well as employers and their pay-offs in the formal and informal sectors.

1.1. *Workers and Preferences*

There is a large pool of workers ($\bar{N}$) with heterogeneous skills, parameterised by $a \geq 0$. The exogenously given number of workers with skill level a is $\bar{N}(a)$. The discounted lifetime utility of a worker over the infinite horizon starting at time τ, W_τ, takes the form:

$$W_\tau = \sum_{t=0}^{\infty} \beta_N^t y_{t+\tau},$$

where $y_{t+\tau}$ is income at time $t + \tau$ and $\beta_N \in (0,1)$ denotes workers' discount factor.

1.2. *Employers and Profits in the Formal and Informal Sectors*

There are $M(a)$ number of employers in search of workers of skill type a. The size of $M(a)$ as well as whether these employers are formal or informal will both be endogenously determined in what follows. The objective of every employer is to maximise the discounted sum of profits over the infinite horizon:

$$\pi_\tau = \sum_{t=0}^{\infty} \beta_E^t \pi_{t+\tau},$$

where β_E denotes the common employer discount factor.

All employers are price takers in the product market. A match between an employer and a skill type a worker in either sector generates revenue a per period regardless of sector of employment.[13] Differences between production in the two sectors arise with respect to production costs. First, a sector-specific fixed cost of job creation, $\rho_f a$ in the formal sector and $\rho_i a$ in the informal sector, applies for every period an employer is in search of a worker. This fixed cost covers the cost of worker search, registration tax and the cost of overcoming any other bureaucratic roadblocks that accompany job

[13] Even so, we will show in what follows that self-selection among matched pairs of employers and workers gives rise to systematic differences in per worker productivity, as well as wages, in the formal and informal sectors.

creation. We take ρ_i to be less than ρ_f to reflect the cost savings of operating informally. We also take the fixed cost of job creation to be increasing in the value of the final output a, where ρ_f and ρ_i are both strictly positive fractions.[14]

Employers face a government-mandated minimum wage $\bar{w}$.[15] We consider minimum wages in the range $(\bar{u}, a)$. The minimum wage is strictly enforced by third party government enforcement agencies in the formal sector but imperfectly enforced in the informal sector.[16] Employers are assumed to be risk neutral, so they compare the wage cost in the two sectors in expected terms. In the formal sector, the per period expected wage cost $w_f^e(w_f)$ at contracted formal sector wage w_f is:

$$w_f^e(w_f) = w_f + \max\{\bar{w} - w_f, 0\}. \tag{1}$$

With perfect enforcement, the expected formal wage is never less than the mandated minimum $\bar{w}$, for employers paying less than the minimum wage are discovered with certainty, and are required to pay $\max\{\bar{w} - w_f, 0\}$. In the informal sector, let $q \in [0,1)$ be the probability of detection of minimum wage violation.[17] The per period expected wage cost $w_i^e(w_i)$ at contracted informal sector wage w_i reflects this imperfect enforcement of the minimum wage as

$$w_i^e(w_i) = w_i + q\max\{\bar{w} - w_i, 0\}. \tag{2}$$

In each time period, a sequence of events ensues. At the start of each t, $M(a)$ new employers of skill type a workers pay the fixed cost of job creation corresponding to the sector of their choosing. Payment of the fixed cost entitles an employer to match with a randomly chosen worker from a common pool of unemployed a-type workers, to whom the employer then presents a wage offer. Employers who fail to consummate a contract with a worker do not produce any output. Workers who are not matched with an acceptable offer remain in the unemployment pool. Consummated matches lead to a job contract which produces output a, subject to the payment of the contracted wage and to the enforcement of the minimum wage depending on the sector of employment. Consummated matches that do not pay according to contract (e.g. less

[14] In Section 3, we discuss the relevance of ρ_f both in empirical studies on the cost of formal sector entry and in the determination of an optimal minimum wage in this set-up.

[15] In Section 4, we augment the analysis to include mandated severance pay as an example of other forms of strictly enforced policies in the formal sector.

[16] In many countries, the minimum wage is determined either directly or indirectly in consultation with unions through collective bargaining. In these cases, third party enforcement can also be facilitated through labour unions (Fine and Gordon, 2010). Although formal empirical studies of the role of union strength on labour standard enforcement are rare, Ronconi (2010) is one exception, which shows that evidence supporting such a link is not strong.

[17] In this article, we follow the convention set out in Ashenfelter and Smith (1979) and model imperfect minimum wage enforcement as a given probability of detection, as opposed to a given enforcement budget, for example. Our reason for doing so is twofold. First, in a model of minimum wage enforcement with a generalised government welfare function incorporating both efficiency and distribution concerns along with an associated endogenous enforcement budget, Basu *et al.* (2010) show in a rational expectation equilibrium with time consistent minimum wage enforcement that the decision problems of employers and workers strictly resemble the exogenous probability set-up. The only difference is that it is the time consistent detection probability that is to be taken as given. Second, if the government objective is instead to minimise unemployment, the focus of this study, then the unique unemployment minimising minimum wage for each skill level is in fact independent of the probability of detection in the informal sector and, hence, the budget cost required to elicit enforcement probability q. Subsection 3.3 contains a thorough discussion of this observation.

than the contracted wage) face worker initiated sanctions and associated output consequences discussed below. For all consummated matches, an exogenous separation probability $\delta \in (0,1)$ applies in each subsequent period. Separated employers may search again and separated workers join the unemployment pool. Henceforth, we focus on steady state values, so that the number of new employers, formal and informal employment, unemployment, along with the distribution of wage offers are all invariant over time.

To arrive at these steady state values, we turn next to a description of the specifics of the matching between workers and employers in the presence of search friction, and the associated contract valuations by workers and employers. These inform the wage offer decision of employers conditional on entry and, ultimately, the entry decision of employers in the two sectors.

1.3. *Matching with Search Friction*

Denote $U(a)$, $N_i(a)$ and $N_f(a)$ as the number of a-type workers respectively in three employment states: unemployment, informal employment and formal employment. Also let $N(a) \equiv N_i(a) + N_f(a)$ denote total employment of a-type workers. Due to sector-specific enforcement of the minimum wage, workers make comparisons between i and f based on the expected wage w^e. Thus, departing from the typical search friction set-up, we characterise wage offers in expected terms, along with the associated distribution of expected wage offers, inclusive of both formal and informal expected wage offers.[18] Specifically, at the start of each time period, an employer in search of an a-type worker chooses and proposes an expected wage offer w^e to one of $U(a)$ number of unemployed job seekers chosen at random. Let $F(w^e; a, \bar{w})$ be the cumulative distribution function of all such expected wage offers, including formal and informal offers, for given skill type a, and minimum wage $\bar{w}$. We assume that a job offer lasts at most one period and there is no possibility of recall of previously unaccepted offers.

Each job seeker rates any and all offers received, selects the best and rejects the rest. We assume that search friction prevents the job seeker from receiving the full set of offers. Instead, the likelihood that an unemployed job seeker is met with $z = 0, 1, 2, \ldots$ offers is given by a Poisson distribution with parameter $\lambda(a)=M(a)/U(a)$, or, $\Pr[z;\ \lambda(a)] = e^{-\lambda(a)}\lambda(a)^z/z!$ (Mortensen, 2003). Since the distribution of each such wage offer is $F(w^e; a, \bar{w})$, the cumulative distribution of the maximal offer received is:

$$H(w^e; a, \bar{w}) \equiv \sum_{z=0}^{\infty} \frac{e^{-\lambda(a)}\lambda(a)^z F(w^e; a, w)^z}{z!} = e^{-\lambda(a)[1-F(w^e;a,w)]}. \tag{3}$$

$H(w^e, a, \bar{w})$ gives the probability that the best offer that a skill type a worker receives is less than w^e. From an employer's perspective, $H(w^e; a, \bar{w})$ is thus the likelihood of consummating a match with a skill type a worker by offering w^e.

[18] With the aid of (1) and (2), the distribution of the actual wage offer w_f and w_i for each a can be straightforwardly inferred from the distribution of expected wage offers.

1.3.1. *Worker valuation of job contracts*

Denote $W(w^e, a, \bar{w})$ as the value function of an employed a-type worker at expected wage offer w^e and minimum wage $\bar{w}$, and $W^u(a, \bar{w})$ the value function of an a-type unemployed worker. Given current period expected wage w^e, and separation probability $\delta > 0$, the value function of an employed worker is

$$W(w^e, a, \bar{w}) = w^e + \beta_N[\delta W^u(a, \bar{w}) + (1-\delta) W(w^e, a, \bar{w})] \\ = \frac{w^e + \beta_N \delta W^u(a, \bar{w})}{1 - b_N}. \tag{4}$$

$b_N = \beta_N(1-\delta)$ henceforth denotes the separation risk-adjusted discount factor.

Given current period unemployment income $\bar{u} < a$,[19] an unemployed worker anticipates the choice between staying unemployed or accepting his best offer in the following period, with cumulative distribution $H(w^e; a, \bar{w})$ from (3). The value function of an unemployed skill type a worker is given by:

$$W^u(a, \bar{w}) = \bar{u} + \beta_N \int_{x \in \Omega^e(a, \bar{w})} \max\{W(x, a, \bar{w}), W^u(a, \bar{w})\} \mathrm{d}H(x; a, \bar{w}). \tag{5}$$

$\Omega^e(a, \bar{w})$ denotes the support of $H(w^e; a, \bar{w})$, the set of expected wage offers with positive density facing a-type workers.

From (4), $W(w^e, a, \bar{w})$ is monotonically increasing in w^e. Denote $w_r^e(a, \bar{w})$ as the reservation expected take-home pay – the lowest pay w^e such that a worker is better off working than remaining unemployed:

$$w_r^e(a, \bar{w}) = \min\{w^e | W(w^e, a, \bar{w}) \geq W^u(a, \bar{w})\}. \tag{6}$$

By monotonicity of $W(w^e, a, \bar{w})$ in w^e as shown in (4), $w_r^e(a, \bar{w})$ is uniquely defined given $W^u(a, \bar{w})$. We have[20]

$$W^u(a, \bar{w}) = \bar{u} + \beta_N \left\{ \int_{w_r^e(a,\bar{w})}^{\infty} W(x, a, \bar{w}) \mathrm{d}H(x; a, \bar{w}) + H\left[w_r^e(a, \bar{w}); a, \bar{w}\right] W^u(a, \bar{w}) \right\}.$$

An interior solution to (6) satisfies

$$w_r^e(a, \bar{w}) = \bar{u} + \frac{\beta_N}{1 - b_N} \int_{w_r^e(a,\bar{w})}^{\infty} \left[x - w_r^e(a, \bar{w})\right] \mathrm{d}H(x; a, \bar{w}). \tag{7}$$

The reservation offer $w_r^e(a, \bar{w})$ implicitly solves (7). Intuitively, $w_r^e(a, \bar{w})$ is equal to the unemployment income, plus the (separation risk adjusted) discounted income gains that an unemployed worker can expect upon delaying employment for one more period. With this in mind, we henceforth normalise $\bar{u}$ at zero.

[19] Though we refer to $\bar{u}$ as unemployment income throughout, $\bar{u}$ may also be interpreted as self-employment income, inclusive of any relevant government assistance available to unemployed/self-employed individuals.

[20] This follows from (4)–(6), where

$$W(w_r^e, a, \bar{w}) = \frac{w_r^e + \beta_N \delta W^u(a, \bar{w})}{1 - b_N} = W^u(a, \bar{w}) \Leftrightarrow W^u(a, \bar{w}) = w_r^e/(1 - \beta_N).$$

In other words, the lifetime discounted value of a stream of income equaling the reservation offer w_r^e gives the value function of the unemployed. The expression for $W^u(a, \bar{w})$ obtains upon substituting the above into (4).

1.3.2. *Employer valuation of job contracts*

Denote $V_j(w^e, a)$ as the employer value function associated with an existing contract with an a-type worker in sector $j = i, f$ at expected wage w^e, and $V_j^o(w^e, a, \bar{w})$ the value function of an employer in sector j prior to entry.

Given the expected wage cost w^e and separation probability δ, the value function of an employer with an existing contract is:

$$V_j(w^e, a) = a - w^e + \beta_E(1 - \delta)V_j(w^e, a) = \frac{a - w^e}{1 - b_E}, \tag{8}$$

where $b_E \equiv \beta_E(1 - \delta)$.

At fixed cost $\rho_j a$, we know from (3) that an expected wage offer w^e will be accepted with probability $H(w^e; a, \bar{w})$. The value function associated with an employer in search of a skill type a worker offering w^e in sector $j = i,f$ is

$$V_j^o(w^e, a, \bar{w}) = H(w^e; a, \bar{w})V_j(w^e, a) - \rho_j a. \tag{9}$$

With (8) and (9), the decision problem of an employer is made up of two parts:

(*i*) choose between offering a formal or an informal sector job; and
(*ii*) select an expected wage w^e to offer.

Solutions to these questions will give the equilibrium wage distribution at each skill level, the endogenous division of informal and formal sector jobs along the wage distribution and the associated reservation wage from (7). We proceed next to discuss the implications of three sets of demand side constraints facing employers in their wage offer choices.

1.4. *Three Wage Constraints*

The first constraint depicts the minimal expected wage offers in the two sectors in the presence of a minimum wage. Specifically, for all non-negative contracted formal wage w_f and w_i,

$$w_f^e = w_f + \max\{\bar{w} - w_f, 0\} \geq \bar{w}, w_i^e = w_i + q\max\{\bar{w} - w_i, 0\} \geq q\bar{w}. \tag{10}$$

Thus, the expected wage offer in the two sectors should never fall below the government-enforced expected wage respectively $\bar{w}$ and $q\bar{w}$ in the formal and informal sectors. Henceforth, we refer to (10) as the 'minimum wage constraints' (MWC). Figure 1 illustrates, showing the formal sector MWC at $\bar{w}$, and the informal sector MWC at $q\bar{w}$ due to imperfect enforcement.

The second constraint depicts the highest expected wage offers that employers can afford in the presence of free entry. Let $w_i^{FE}(a)$ and $w_f^{FE}(a)$ denote these skill specific maximal offers, if the maximal wage offer for a-type workers happen to occur in i and f respectively.

Starting with i, since there is by definition no other offer that outmatches $w_i^{FE}(a)$, the corresponding match likelihood of $w_i^{FE}(a)$ must be equal to unity, or $H[w_i^{FE}(a); a, \bar{w}] = 1$. Furthermore, with free entry, expected pre-entry employer valuation $V_i^o(w^e, a, \bar{w})$ evaluated at $w^e = w_i^{FE}(a)$ is equal to zero. It follows that

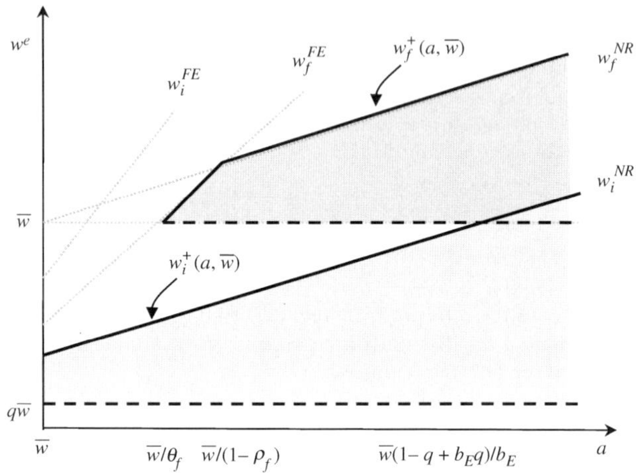

Fig. 1. *Wage Dualism*

$$V_i^o\left[w_i^{FE}(a), a, \bar{w}\right] = \frac{a - w_i^{FE}(a)}{1 - b_E} - \rho_i a = 0 \Leftrightarrow w_i^{FE}(a) = [b_E + (1 - b_E)(1 - \rho_i)]a \equiv \theta_i a.$$

By similar reasoning, if the maximal offer for *a*-type workers occurs in the formal sector, such a maximal offer must take the value $w_f^{FE}(a) = [b_E + (1 - b_E)(1 - \rho_f)]a \equiv \theta_f a$. Our second set of wage constraints requires simply that expected offers be no greater than these maximal values consistent with free entry

$$w_f^e \leq \theta_f a, \quad w_i^e \leq \theta_i a, \tag{11}$$

where both θ_f and θ_i are strictly positive fractions. Henceforth, we refer to (11) as the 'free entry constraints' (FEC). As shown in Figure 1, due to the higher cost of entry in the formal sector, the formal sector maximal wage offer at the break-even point, $\theta_f a$, is strictly less than that of informal sector, $\theta_i a$.

Unless there is perfect enforcement by third party agencies, credible labour contracting must also be self-enforcing, such that employers prefer paying the contracted wage over reneging on a labour contract that has been agreed upon. We assume that an employer who reneges on wage payment faces a worker-initiated termination of the employment relation in the following period.[21] The value function of a reneging informal employer is $a - q\bar{w}$, since he derives labour a from the contracted worker, pays $\bar{w}$ only if discovered by enforcement agencies (with probability q). Thus, an informal employer offering w_i^e and targeting a skill type a worker will not

[21] In Mukherjee and Ray (1995), for example, contract violation can have scarring effects. We abstract from such considerations in this article, since these effects would arguably impact both formal and informal sector employers. Instead, the NRC focuses on the additional enforcement that formal sector workers enjoy due to minimum wage enforcement.

renege if and only if $V_i(w_i^e, a) \geq a - q\bar{w}$.[22] Similarly, a formal employer offering w_f^e to a skill type a worker will prefer not to renege if and only if $V_f(w_f^e, a) \geq a - \bar{w}$. In effect[23]

$$\begin{aligned} V_i(w_i^e, a) &= \frac{a - w_i^e}{1 - b_E} \geq a - q\bar{w} \Leftrightarrow w_i^e \leq b_E a + (1 - b_E)q\bar{w} \equiv w_i^{NR}(a, \bar{w}); \\ V_f(w_f^e, a) &= \frac{a - w_f^e}{1 - b_E} \geq a - \bar{w} \Leftrightarrow w_f^e \leq b_E a + (1 - b_E)\bar{w} \equiv w_f^{NR}(a, \bar{w}). \end{aligned} \tag{12}$$

From (12), the maximal self-enforcing expected wage in the two sectors ($w_i^{NR}(a, \bar{w})$ and $w_f^{NR}(a, \bar{w})$) are weighted averages of worker productivity a and the government-enforced expected minimum wage in that sector $(q\bar{w}, \bar{w})$. In what follows, we refer to this last set of constraints as the NRC. In Figure 1, the formal sector NRC, $w_f^{NR}(a, \bar{w})$, is strictly higher than the informal sector NRC, $w_i^{NR}(a, \bar{w})$, as stricter formal sector enforcement of the minimum wage enables formal employers to issue a credible promise of higher wage payments than informal sector employers.

1.5 *Contractual Dualism and Wage Dualism*

Define $w_f^+(a, \bar{w})$ as the maximal formal sector expected wage offer, and $w_i^+(a, \bar{w})$ the maximal informal sector expected wage offer. The associated economy-wide wage upper bound is

$$w^+(a, \bar{w}) = \max\{w_i^+(a, \bar{w}), w_f^+(a, \bar{w})\}.$$

The three wage constraints in the formal sector constitute the bounds on the range of feasible formal wages at each skill level. In Figure 1, this range is given by the distance between the bold line labelled $w_f^+(a, \bar{w})$, the maximal formal sector expected wage offer and the dashed line at the minimum age $\bar{w}$. As shown, formal labour demand does not exist at sufficiently low skill levels $(a < \bar{w}/\theta_f)$ since at these skill levels, the minimum wage exceeds the break even wage $w_f^{FE}(a)$. For intermediate skill levels $a \in [\bar{w}/\theta_f, \bar{w}/(1 - \rho_f)]$, there is positive labour demand and employers can bid wages all the way up to the maximum break-even wage at $w_f^+(a, \bar{w}) = w_f^{FE}(a)$. At even higher skill levels $a > \bar{w}/(1 - \rho_f)$, there continues to be positive labour demand, however, the NRC now begins to bind as wages are high enough for wage reneging to be a concern. Consequently, the highest formal sector wage offer corresponds to the maximal self-enforcing wage $w_f^+(a, \bar{w}) = w_f^{NR}(a, \bar{w})$.

[22] Thus, we assume that the government enforces the minimum wage but not the contracted wage, which may be higher or lower than the government-mandated minimum wage. This is in keeping with the literature on minimum wage non-compliance starting from Ashenfelter and Smith (1979). Furthermore, this is also consistent with the intent of actual minimum wage laws. For example, the Minimum Wage Act of India in 1948 stipulates that 'the State Enforcement Machinery ... conduct regular inspections and in the event of detection of any case of non-payment or under-payment of minimum wages, they advise the employers to make payment of the shortfall of wages'.

[23] For expositional clarity, we focus here on the case of full reneging and complete suspension of effort. This assumption will be relaxed in Section 4, where we explicitly allow for any partial reneging on the part of the employer and corresponding partial effort on the part of the worker as punishment motivated by the fair wage–effort hypothesis of Akerlof and Yellen (1990). We show that:
(*i*) the current specification is in fact a special case of the Akerlof–Yellen fair wage–effort hypothesis; and
(*ii*) the NRC developed here continues to apply even upon allowing for partial reneging and partial effort.

Likewise, the three wage constraints in the informal sector put bounds on the range of feasible informal wages at each skill level. Given that imperfect third party enforcement of the minimum wage and lower fixed cost of entry are the key distinguishing features of the informal sector we have specified so far, we define contractual dualism is based on these factors:

DEFINITION 1. *For all $\bar{w} < a$, the labour market exhibits contractual dualism if and only if*

$$q < \min\left\{1 - \rho_i, \frac{1 - \rho_f - b_E}{(1 - \rho_f)(1 - b_E)}\right\}.$$

Definition 1 says that there is contractual dualism whenever the enforcement intensity in the informal sector q is sufficiently low. The threshold, $\min\{1 - \rho_i, (1 - \rho_f - b_E)/[(1 - \rho_f)(1 - b_E)]\}$, depends explicitly on the fixed costs of entry in the two sectors for reasons to be explained below.[24] Assuming that contractual dualism applies according to Definition 1, Figure 1 depicts the range of feasible informal wages as the distance between the bold line labelled $w_i^+(a, \bar{w})$ and the dashed line at the enforced minimum wage $q\bar{w}$.

We take away from Figure 1 four features that sharply distinguish between formal and informal wage determination in the presence of contractual dualism. First, with contractual dualism, the NRC is binding in the informal sector for all skill levels, since $w_i^{NR}(a, \bar{w}) < w_i^{FE}(a)$ whenever $q < 1 - \rho_i$ for all $\bar{w} < a$.[25] As such, the highest informal sector wage offer $w_i^+(a, \bar{w})$ is equal to the maximal self-enforcing wage $w_i^{NR}(a, \bar{w})$ for all a. This is contrary to the formal sector where full enforcement of the minimum wage implies that the NRC binds only for sufficiently highly skilled workers.

Second, the highest formal sector wage for any worker with skill a is strictly higher than the corresponding highest informal sector wage if the two types of work coexist.[26] This is despite the fact that the informal sector fixed cost $\rho_i a$ is less than the formal sector fixed cost $\rho_f a$. In our setting, a promise to raise the informal wage high enough to bring revenue net of wage and fixed cost of entry to zero violates the NRC and is thus ruled out in equilibrium.

Third, regardless of whether the FEC or the NRC is the binding constraint, formal and informal wages are segmented for a non-empty range of skill levels. In other words, a gap exists separating the lowest formal sector wage and the highest informal sector wage.[27] In Figure 1, at skill level $a = \bar{w}/(1 - \rho_f)$ for example, formal work pays $w^e = \bar{w}$,

[24] As stated, Definition 1 includes the special case where there is no enforcement at all in the informal sector, or where $q = 0$ so that the minimum wage legislation only applies to formal sector employers.

[25] Note from the definition of w_i^{NR} and w_i^{FE} that $w_i^{NR}(a, \bar{w}) - w_i^{FE}(a) = (1 - \rho_i)a - q\bar{w} > (1 - \rho_i - q)a > 0$ whenever there is contractual dualism according to definition 1 for all $\bar{w} < a$.

[26] Consider the range of skills $[\bar{w}/\theta_f, \bar{w}/(1 - \rho_f)]$. The highest formal sector wage is given by the FEC at $\theta_f a$. The highest informal sector wage is given by the NRC at $b_E a + (1 - b_E)q\bar{w}$. $\theta_f a > b_E a + (1 - b_E)q\bar{w}$ for $a > \bar{w}$ if $q < (1 - \rho_f)$, a condition that is satisfied if there is contractual dualism accordingly to Definition 1. Consider next the set of skills $a > \bar{w}/(1 - \rho_f)$. In this range, the NRC binds in both sectors. But from (12), the $w_f^{NR}(a, \bar{w}) > w_i^{NR}(a, \bar{w})$. Thus, the highest formal sector wage continues to dominate the highest informal sector wage.

[27] To see this, consider for example the skill level $a = \bar{w}/(1 - \rho_f)$. The lowest formal sector wage is $\bar{w}$ from the MWC, while the highest informal sector wage is given by the NRC as $w_i^{NR}(a, \bar{w}) = [b_E/(1 - \rho_f) + (1 - b_E)q]\bar{w}$. $\bar{w}$ is higher than $w_i^{NR}(a, \bar{w})$ if and only if $q < (1 - \rho_f - b_E)/[(1 - \rho_f)(1 - b_E)]$, which holds under contractual dualism in Definition 1.

but informal work can at maximum pay $w^e \leq w_i^{NR}(\bar{w}/(1-\rho_f), \bar{w}) < \bar{w}$ by Definition 1. Thus, contractual dualism implies segmented wages, with a wage spike at the minimum wage along the wage distribution.[28]

Finally, minimum wage over-compliance can occur in the informal sector. With contractual dualism, this occurs only for a subset of skill levels, and specifically when a is sufficiently high. In Figure 1, over-compliance in the informal sector occurs when the maximal informal self-enforcing wage w_i^{NR} exceeds the minimum wage $\bar{w}$, or when $a > \bar{w}(1 - q + b_E q)/b_E$.

Interestingly, of the five salient features of formal and informal labour markets discussed earlier in the Introduction, the implications of contractual dualism highlighted above are consistent with the first four, namely:

(*i*) higher average skill levels in the formal sector;
(*ii*) higher average wages in the formal sector conditional on skills;
(*iii*) a spike at the minimum wage along the wage distribution; and
(*iv*) over-compliance in the informal sector for some skill levels.

In what follows, we examine the properties of a steady state labour market equilibrium with contractual dualism. Doing so allows us to verify the fifth feature noted in the Introduction, which deals with the equilibrium unemployment response to minimum wage hikes.

1.6. *Steady State Equilibrium*

Define a steady state equilibrium as:

(*i*) an expected wage offer distribution $H^*(w^e; a, \bar{w})$ for each skill type a;[29]
(*ii*) a set of equilibrium wage offers with positive density $(\Omega^e(a, \bar{w}))$, inclusive of formal $(\Omega_f^e(a, \bar{w}))$ and informal expected wage offers $\Omega_i^e(a, \bar{w}))$, where $\Omega^e(a, \bar{w}) = \Omega_f^e(a, \bar{w}) \cup \Omega_i^e(a, \bar{w})$; and
(*iii*) levels of equilibrium unemployment $U^*(a, \bar{w})$, informal employment $N_i^*(a, \bar{w})$ and formal employment $N_f^*(a, \bar{w})$,

such that the following four sets of equilibrium requirements are simultaneously met.

The first includes the three wage constraints facing employers in the two sectors: MWC, FEC and NRC. The second deals with labour supply, and requires that no wage offer is lower than the reservation offer $w_r^e(a, \bar{w})$. Equivalently, for all $w^e \in \Omega_f^e(a, \bar{w})$, $w^e \geq w_r^e(a, \bar{w})$ and likewise for all $w^e \in \Omega_i^e(a, \bar{w})$, $w^e \geq w_r^e(a, \bar{w})$. A third equilibrium

[28] This is in sharp contrast to the continuous wage distributions typically implied by canonical search models (Burdett and Mortensen, 1998). The height of such a spike in the wage distribution for any given a, or the economy wide distribution aggregated across all skill types, are both endogenously determined in this setting. We turn to these issues in subsection 3.2.

[29] Note that the equilibrium distribution of offers $F^*(w^e; a, \bar{w})$, and the ratio of recruiting employers to unemployed workers $\lambda^*(a) = M^*(a)/U^*(a)$ can be obtained once $H^*(w^e; a, \bar{w})$ and the reservation wage $w_r^e(a, \bar{w})$ in (6) are both determined. Specifically, from (3),

$$H^*(w^e; a, \bar{w}) = \mathrm{e}^{-\lambda^*(a)[1-F^*(w^e;a,\bar{w})]}, \quad H^*[w_r^e(a, \bar{w}); a, \bar{w}] = \mathrm{e}^{-\lambda^*(a)}.$$

It follows that $F^*(w^e; a, w) = -(\ln[H^*(w^e; a, \bar{w})] - \ln\{H^*[w_r^e(a, \bar{w}); a, \bar{w}]\})/\ln\{H^*[w_r^e(a, \bar{w}); a, \bar{w}]\}$ and $\lambda^*(a) = -\ln\{H^*[w_r^e(a, \bar{w}); a, \bar{w}]\}$.

requirement allows employers to freely choose their sector of operation. Thus, all formal and informal contracts with positive probability density yield the same expected profits in equilibrium:

$$V_i^o(\hat{w}^e, a, \bar{w}) = V_f^o(\bar{w}^e, a, \bar{w}) \tag{13}$$

for any $\hat{w}^e$ in $\Omega_i^e(a, \bar{w})$ and $\bar{w}^e$ in $\Omega_f^e(a, \bar{w})$ if formal and informal employers coexist. Otherwise if there are only formal employers, then for any w^e and $\bar{w}^e$ in $\Omega_f^e(a, \bar{w})$,

$$V_f^o(w^e, a, \bar{w}) = V_f^o(\bar{w}^e, a, \bar{w}) \tag{14}$$

and if only informal employers exist, then for any w^e and $\hat{w}^e$ in $\Omega_i^e(a, \bar{w})$,

$$V_i^o(w^e, a, \bar{w}) = V_i^o(\hat{w}^e, a, \bar{w}). \tag{15}$$

The final requirement pins down equilibrium labour allocations. Let $p_f(a, \bar{w}) \equiv \int_{w^e \in \Omega_f^e(a,\bar{w})} \mathrm{d}H^*(w^e; a, \bar{w})$ refer to the fraction of unemployed workers accepting a formal sector job at any time period in a steady state, and $p_i(a, \bar{w}) \equiv \int_{w^e \in \Omega_i^e(a,\bar{w})} \mathrm{d}H^*(w^e; a, \bar{w})$ the fraction accepting an informal sector job. In a steady state, inflows into any state of employment must equal outflows:

$$\begin{aligned} p_f(a, \bar{w})U^*(a, \bar{w}) &= \delta N_f^*(a, \bar{w}), \\ [p_f(a, \bar{w}) + p_i(a, \bar{w})]U^*(a, \bar{w}) &= \delta[N_f^*(a, \bar{w}) + N_i^*(a, \bar{w})]. \end{aligned} \tag{16}$$

Solving (16), and accounting for adding up, $\bar{N}(a) = N_f^*(a, \bar{w}) + N_i^*(a, \bar{w}) + U^*(a, \bar{w})$, we obtain:

$$\begin{aligned} U^*(a, \bar{w}) = \frac{\delta \bar{N}(a)}{\delta + p_i(a, \bar{w}) + p_f(a, \bar{w})}, \quad N_i^*(a, \bar{w}) = \frac{p_i(a, \bar{w})\bar{N}(a)}{\delta + p_i(a, \bar{w}) + p_f(a, \bar{w})}, \\ N_f^*(a, \bar{w}) = \frac{p_f(a, \bar{w})\bar{N}(a)}{\delta + p_i(a, \bar{w}) + p_f(a, \bar{w})}. \end{aligned} \tag{17}$$

Thus, the higher the separation frequency δ, all else equal, the larger will be the equilibrium unemployment pool. Meanwhile, informal and formal sector employment additionally depend on the fractions $p_i(a, \bar{w})$ and $p_f(a, \bar{w})$ of unemployed accepting respectively an informal and a formal job.

2. The No-intervention Benchmark

As a useful benchmark, we begin with an examination of a steady state equilibrium in which there is no minimum wage ($\bar{w} = 0$) and thus no need for minimum wage enforcement ($q = 0$). Of the three wage constraints, the MWC is no longer relevant. Furthermore, from (12) the NRC for the formal and informal sectors coincide at $w_i^{NR}(a, 0) = w_f^{NR}(a, 0) = b_E a$ in the absence of a minimum wage. Consequently, being formal implies only a higher cost of entry but no other gains such as contract credibility. It follows that competition will drive all employers to be informal in this no-intervention benchmark

We investigate two baseline cases with zero minimum wage:

(*i*) employers can fully commit *ex ante* to wage contracts for reasons exogenous to the model; and (*ii*) employers cannot commit *ex ante* and wage contracting must obey the self-enforcement constraint.

In each case, we are interested in the steady state equilibrium configuration of employer market power, wage distribution and equilibrium unemployment.

2.1. *Market Power*

If employers are able to commit *ex ante* to any wage offer, the NRC is no longer required to maintain contract credibility and the FEC is the only remaining wage constraint. It follows by definition of the FEC that the expected profit associated with having contracted a worker, $V_i^o(w_i^{FE}(a), a)$, will be driven to zero in equilibrium for all a and all employers, and as such no employer has market power as measured by strictly positive excess profit.

By contrast, if all contracts are self-enforcing, the NRC applies. By definition of the NRC, wages offers higher than $w_i^{NR}(a,0) = b_E a$ will ultimately be reneged upon. At the maximal self-enforcing wage, $w_i^{NR}(a,0)$, the expected profit of an employer is

$$V_i^o\left[w_i^{NR}(a,0), a\right] = \frac{a - w_i^{NR}(a,0)}{1 - b_E} - \rho_i a = a(1-\rho_i) > 0. \tag{18}$$

Equation (18) shows that self-enforcing labour contracting breeds employer market power. Equilibrium expected profits will not dissipate despite the absence of explicit entry barriers. Employers with an existing labour contract earn positive profits but new entrants who may aspire to profit from hiring workers and bidding up wages cannot credibly do so without violating the NRC. Henceforth, we define the strictly positive level of expected profit $a(1-\rho_i)$ in the absence of a minimum wage as $\bar{V}(a,0)$, where the zero stands for zero minimum wage.

2.2. *Wage Distribution*

When employers freely choose wage offers, the distribution $H^*(w^e; a, 0)$ reflects the balance that needs to be struck in equilibrium between the cost of a higher wage offer w^e and the benefits of a higher match likelihood from (15). Expected profit equalisation (15) along with (9) together imply that for an informal employer offering $w^e \in \Omega_i^e(a,0)$:[30]

$$H^*(w^e; a, 0) = \frac{(1-b_E)[\rho_i a + \bar{V}(a,0)]}{a - w^e}. \tag{19}$$

Equilibrium market power, with positive $\bar{V}(a,0) = a(1-\rho_i)$ instead of zero expected profits gives rise to a shift in the entire match likelihood function consistent with a lower first-order stochastic order from (19):

[30] To see this, note from (15) that $V_i^o(w^e; a, 0) = \bar{V}(a,0) \Leftrightarrow H^*(w^e; a,0)(a - w^e)/(1-b_E) - \rho_i a = \bar{V}(a,0)$. Rearranging using (9), the unique solution is displayed in (19). It can be easily verified that $H^*(\hat{w}^e; a, 0) > 0$ is well-defined for every non-negative $\hat{w}^e$ that does not exceed the NRC. In particular, evaluated at the maximum defined by $w^e = w_i^{NR}(a,0) = b_E a$, $H^*(b_E a; a, 0) = (1-b_E)a/(a - b_E a) = 1$.

$$H^*(w^e;a,0)=\frac{(1-b_E)[\rho_i a+\bar{V}(a,0)]}{a-w^e}=\frac{(1-b_E)a}{a-w^e}>\frac{(1-b_E)\rho_i a}{a-w^e},$$

where the latter, $(1-b_E)\rho_i a/(a-w^e)$, would have been the equilibrium match likelihood function had expected profits $\bar{V}(a,0)$ been driven down to zero. The effect of employer market power thus reverberates along the entire match likelihood function, consistent with a more pessimistic but nonetheless rational outlook about job prospects.

To complete the characterisation of the wage distributions with and without the ability on the part of employers to commit to wage contracts, we specify the range of expected wages with positive support $\Omega^e(a,0)$. $\Omega^e(a,0)$ is bounded above by the break-even wage $w_i^{FE}(a)=[b_E+(1-b_E)(1-\rho_i)]a$ if employers can commit to wage contracts *ex ante*.[31] Otherwise, the maximal self-enforcing minimum wage $w_i^{NR}(a,0)=b_E a$ serves instead as the upper bound of $\Omega^e(a,0)$. From (11) and (12), $w_i^{FE}(a)>w_i^{NR}(a,0)$.

The lower bound of $\Omega^e(a,0)$ is given by the reservation wage $w_r^e(a,0)$ from (7).[32] $w_r^e(a,0)$ is endogenous, and depends in particular on the wage distribution $H^*(w^e;a,0)$ itself. From (7), it can be shown that the market-induced shift in the distribution of wage offers due to employer market power has the effect of decreasing the reservation wage $w_r^e(a,0)$.[33] In summary, employer market power shifts the entire wage distribution, as well as the range of expected wage offers with positive support to the left.

2.3. *Unemployment*

From (17), equilibrium unemployment $U^*(a,0)$ depends on the fractions $p_i(a,0)$ and $p_f(a,0)$ of the unemployed accepting respectively an informal and a formal job. Since there are only informal employers in the absence of a minimum wage, $p_f(a,0)=0$. For an unemployed worker, an acceptable offer is received with probability $p_i(a,0)=1-H^*[w_r^e(a,0);a,0]$ evaluated at the reservation wage $w_r^e(a,0)$. Thus,

$$U^*(a,0)=\frac{\delta\bar{N}(a)}{1+\delta-H^*[w_r^e(a,0);a,0]}. \tag{20}$$

By inspection, employer market power has two opposing effects on $U^*(a,0)$. First, as shown in (20), employer market power shifts the wage distribution function $H^*[w_r^e(a,0);a,0]$ to the left. This contributes to raising unemployment at constant reservation pay w_r^e. Second, employer market power also leads workers to revise downwards their reservation wage from (7).[34] This has a tendency to decrease

[31] Since there are only informal employers in this no-intervention regime, $\Omega_i^e(a,0)=\Omega^e(a,0)$.

[32] An interior solution of $w_r^e(a,0)$ to (7) always applies. To see this, note that the right-hand side of (7) is strictly positive for all $w_r^e\in[0,w_i^{NR}(a,0)]$. And as such, the corner solution of a zero reservation wage never applies in equilibrium.

[33] See Appendix A for a proof of this claim.

[34] As noted, a proof of this claim is available in Appendix A.

unemployment. From (7), the reservation wage effect on $w_r^e(a, 0)$ will be weak if workers' discount factor β_N is low.[35]

Summarising, wage contracting with self-enforcement leads to employer market power (18). The presence of market power in turn shifts the wage distribution in a way consistent with lower expected wages (19). With a sufficiently low workers' discount factor, β_N, the need for self-enforcing contracts furthermore gives rise to higher unemployment relative to an equilibrium where employers can *ex ante* commit to any wage offers (20). Based on these observations, in terms of distribution, the need for self-enforcing contracts shifts income distribution in favour of employers with an existing worker as expected profits turn positive and wages decline. In terms of efficiency, the need for self-enforcing contracts lowers total output as unemployment increases.

Thus, policy measures that aim at improving upon this no-intervention baseline can be targeted towards allaying distributional inequities between employers and workers, towards improving efficiency or as the case may be, both. In the next Section, we examine a minimum wage policy, and thus the possibility of formalisation, as a potential candidate. Our goal is to explore the role of a minimum wage on:

(*i*) expected employer profits, which we have taken as a gauge on the extent of employer market power despite the absence of explicit barriers;
(*ii*) the equilibrium distribution of expected offers $H^*(w^e; a, \bar{w})$; and
(*iii*) the equilibrium allocation of employed and unemployed workers.

3. Minimum Wage Policy

Assume as before that contractual dualism according to Definition 1 applies. Figure 2 reorganises the information presented in Figure 1, so as to highlight how successively higher levels of the minimum wage impact formal and informal labour demand as given by the joint application of the MWC, the FEC and the NRC.

The upward sloping lines in Figure 2 mark four areas of interest discussed earlier in subsection 1.5. The area marked A_f^{NR} depicts an area of relatively low minimum wages and relatively high skill levels $a \geq \bar{w}/(1-\rho_f)$. With the government enforced minimum wage still relatively low, the NRC in the formal sector is binding. A_f^{NR} is further divided into two parts by an upward sloping dotted line at $\bar{w} = b_E a/(1 - q + b_E q)$. For all $(a, \bar{w})$ pairings below this line, the minimum wage is sufficiently low for there to be over-compliance in the informal sector. For all other $(a, \bar{w})$ pairings, formal and informal wages are segmented if both types of jobs coexist. Next, the area marked A_f^{FE} covers higher levels of minimum wage $a \in [\bar{w}/\theta_f, \bar{w}/(1-\rho_f)]$. Government enforcement of this higher minimum wage now improves the credibility of formal contracts so much so that the formal NRC no longer binds and the FEC takes its place. Further raising this minimum wage to A_i^{NR} results in

[35] To see this, recall that

$$w_r^e(a, 0) = \bar{u} + \frac{\beta_N}{1 - b_N} \int_{w_r^e(a)}^{\infty} [x - w_r^e(a, 0)] \mathrm{d}H(x; a, 0).$$

The role of $H^*(w^e; a, 0)$ on the reservation offer depends critically on the size of β_N.

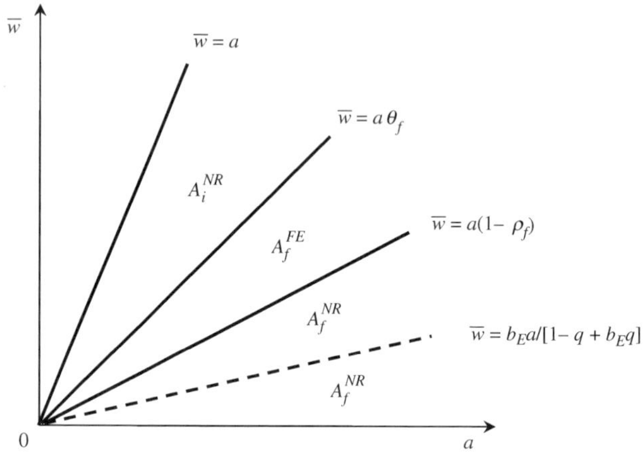

Fig. 2. *Minimum Wage, the FEC and the NRC*

a complete exodus of employers out of the formal sector in favour of informality, where enforcement of the high minimum wage is relatively lax ($a \in [\bar{w}/\theta_f, \bar{w})$).[36]

3.1. *Market Power*

How does employer market power change as the minimum wage increases, starting from A_f^{NR} where the formal NRC is binding, to A_f^{FE} where the formal FEC is binding, and then finally to A_i^{NR} where the informal NRC is binding?

For any $(a, \bar{w})$ in A_f^{NR}, the highest wage offer is given by the formal sector NRC at $w_f^{NR}(a, \bar{w}) = b_E a + (1 - b_E)\bar{w}$. In equilibrium, all employers earn the same expected profit as the employer who offers the highest wage, namely:

$$\bar{V}(a, \bar{w}) = V_f^o[w_f^{NR}(a, \bar{w}), a] = \frac{a - b_E a - (1 - b_E)\bar{w}}{1 - b_E} - \rho_f a, \tag{21}$$

where the minimum wage can be seen to adversely impact expected profits. Now for $(a, \bar{w})$ in A_f^{FE}, the highest wage offer is given by the formal sector FEC at $w_f^{FE}(a) = b_E a + (1 - b_E)(1 - \rho_f)a$. The corresponding expected profit is given by:

$$\bar{V}(a, \bar{w}) = V_f^o[w^{FE}(a), a] = \frac{a - b_E a - (1 - b_E)(1 - \rho_f)a}{1 - b_E} - \rho_f a, \tag{22}$$

where the explicit dependence of expected profits on the minimum wage no longer applies.

Finally, for all $(a, \bar{w}) \in A_i^{NR}$, the highest expected wage is offered in the informal sector at $w_i^{NR}(a, \bar{w})$. Expected profit is given by:

[36] Minimum wages in the remaining area are strictly higher than a and are thus outside of the feasible range $(\bar{u}, a) = (0, a)$.

$$\bar{V}(a,\bar{w}) = V_i^o[w_i^{NR}(a,\bar{w}),a] = \frac{a - b_E a - (1-b_E)q\bar{w}}{1-b_E} - \rho_i a. \tag{23}$$

Applying (21)–(23), we obtain:

PROPOSITION 1. *With contractual dualism,*

- *Expected profit $\bar{V}(a,\bar{w}) = a - \bar{w} - \rho_f a$ is strictly positive for all $(a,\bar{w}) \in A_f^{NR}$ despite no explicit barriers to entry. A further increase in $\bar{w}$ lowers $\bar{V}(a,\bar{w})$.*
- *Expected profit $\bar{V}(a,\bar{w})$ is at zero for all $(a,\bar{w}) \in A_f^{FE}$. A further increase in $\bar{w}$ has no local effect on $\bar{V}(a,\bar{w})$.*
- *Transitioning from A_f^{FE} to A_i^{NR}, there is a discrete upward jump in expected profits at $\bar{w} = a/\theta_f$ as all formal employers exit and all remaining employers choose informality. A further increase in $\bar{w}$ will decrease expected profit $\bar{V}(a,\bar{w}) = a - q\bar{w} - \rho_i a$ if and only if $q > 0$. Otherwise, $\bar{V}(a,\bar{w})$ is invariant to $\bar{w}$ with $q = 0$.*

The relationship between employer profits and the minimum wage is thus non-monotonic and U-shaped. Figure 3(*a*) and (*b*) illustrates this U-shaped relationship respectively for the cases of $q > 0$ and $q = 0$. Note that these relationships imply the existence of a smallest minimum wage for every a that completely eliminates employer market power in the formal sector at $\bar{w} = a(1 - \rho_f)$. Sufficiently higher minimum wages can paradoxically increase expected profits as employers turn to informality. The smallest minimum wage that gives rise full informality is $\bar{w} = \theta_f a$.

3.2. *The Wage Distribution*

From (13)–(15), the match likelihood function associated with wage offers $\hat{w}^e \in \Omega_i^e(a,\bar{w})$ in the informal sector, and $\tilde{w}^e \in \Omega_f^e(a,\bar{w})$ in the formal sector, if they exist, are respectively:

$$H^*(\hat{w}^e; a,\bar{w}) = \frac{(1-b_E)[\rho_i a + \bar{V}(a,\bar{w})]}{a - \hat{w}^e}, \quad H^*(\tilde{w}^e; a,\bar{w}) = \frac{(1-b_E)[\rho_f a + \bar{V}(a,\bar{w})]}{a - \tilde{w}^e}.$$

Similar to the no-intervention benchmark, rising equilibrium employer profits $\bar{V}(a,\bar{w})$ is associated with leftward shifts in the entire match likelihood function, consistent with lower average expected wage offers. Since Proposition 1 shows that the impact of the minimum wage on equilibrium employer profits is U-shaped, changes in the minimum wage can have interesting and non-monotonic impact on the wage offer distribution $H^*(w^e; a,\bar{w})$.

Consider, therefore, the equilibrium match likelihood function $H^*(w^e; a,\bar{w})$ associated with each of the four areas (A_f^{NR} (with $\bar{w} \le b_E a/(1 - q + b_E q)$, or $\bar{w} > b_E a/(1 - q + b_E q)$), A_f^{FE}, and A_i^{NR}). Starting with A_f^{NR} and $\bar{w} < b_E a/(1 - q + b_E q)$, the NRC is binding in the formal sector and some informal employers overcomply with the minimum wage. We have from Proposition 2 that expected profits is $\bar{V}(a,\bar{w}) = a - \bar{w} - \rho_f a$. From (13)–(15), expected profit equalisation implies the following equilibrium match likelihood function:[37]

[37] With higher job creation cost in the formal sector, an offer generates higher informal profits than formal profits so long as w^e is feasible, or $w^e \le w_i^{NR}(a,\bar{w})$ since $V_i^o(w^e,a,\bar{w}) = H^*(w^e;a,\bar{w})V_i(w^e,a) - \rho_i a < H^*(w^e;a,\bar{w})V_f(w^e,a) - \rho_f a = V_f^o(w^e,a,\bar{w})$. Thus, all employers offering less than $w_i^{NR}(a,\bar{w})$ are informal employers

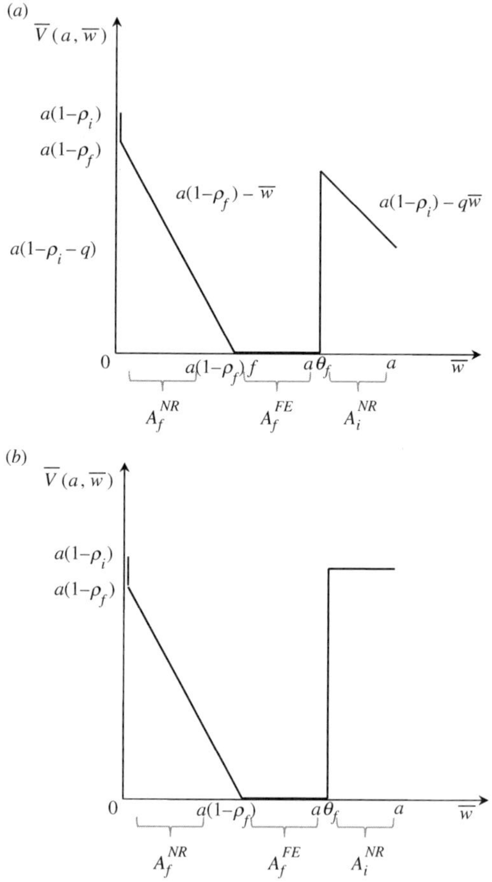

Fig. 3. *(a) Expected Profits and the Minimum Wage (q > 0) (b) Expected Profits and the Minimum Wage (q = 0)*

$$H^*(w^e; a, \bar{w}) = \begin{cases} H_i^*(w^e; a, \bar{w}) = \dfrac{(1 - b_E)[a - \bar{w} - (\rho_f - \rho_i)a]}{a - w^e}, & w^e \leq w_i^{NR}(a, \bar{w}) \\ H_f^*(w^e; a, \bar{w}) = \dfrac{(1 - b_E)(a - \bar{w})}{a - w^e}, & w^e \in (w_i^{NR}(a, \bar{w}), w_f^{NR}(a, \bar{w})]. \end{cases}$$

The two segments respectively give the match likelihoods facing informal sector workers at low wages $w^e \leq w_i^{NR}(a, \bar{w})$ and formal sector workers at wages higher than $w_i^{NR}(a, \bar{w})$. From Proposition 2, a minimum wage hike $\bar{w}$ in this range decreases employer expected profits. Accordingly, the same minimum wage hike gives rise to a first order stochastically dominating (rightward) shift in the match likelihood function consistent with higher wage offer expectations.

To complete the specification of this wage distribution, we characterise the range of $H^*(w^e; a, \bar{w})$, or $\Omega^e(a, \bar{w})$. There are two issues to note. First, $\Omega^e(a, \bar{w})$ is bounded above by $w_f^{NR}(a, \bar{w})$, and below by the reservation wage defined in (6). Henceforth, we will assume throughout that the interior solution of the reservation wage in (7) applies. Furthermore, in order to focus on situations where there is positive informal sector employment, we will also assume that this reservation wage does not exceed the maximal self-enforcing wage in the informal sector. In Appendix B, we show that the reservation wage is given by the interior solution in (7) if minimum wage enforcement in the informal sector q is sufficiently lax. In Appendix C, we show that the reservation wage lies below the informal self-enforcing wage and, as such, there is always positive informal employment if β_N is sufficiently small. In all of our analysis to follow, we will assume that these two sets of conditions are met.

Turning now to solve for $H^*(w^e; a, \bar{w})$ for the next set of (a, w) pairs such that $a(1 - \rho_f) > \bar{w} > b_E a/(1 - q + b_E q)$ in A_f^{NR}, we have from (13)–(15), as well as Proposition 2, that

$$H^*(w^e; a, \bar{w}) = \begin{cases} H_i^*(w^e; a, \bar{w}) = \dfrac{(1 - b_E)[a - \bar{w} - (\rho_f - \rho_i)a]}{a - w^e}, & w^e \leq w_i^{NR}(a, \bar{w}) \\ H_o^*(w^e; a, \bar{w}) = \dfrac{a - \bar{w} - (\rho_f - \rho_i)a}{a - q\bar{w}}, & w^e \in (w_i^{NR}(a, \bar{w}), \bar{w}) \\ H_f^*(w^e; a, \bar{w}) = \dfrac{(1 - b_E)(a - \bar{w})}{a - w^e}, & w^e \in [\bar{w}, w_f^{NR}(a, \bar{w})]. \end{cases}$$

The intermediate segment $H_o^*(w^e; a, \bar{w}) = H_i^*[w_i^{NR}(a, \bar{w}); a, \bar{w}]$ for $w^e \in [w_i^{NR}(a, \bar{w}), \bar{w}]$ represents the range of wages too high for informal employers but too low for formal employers with a mandated minimum wage. The height of the minimum wage spike is given by $H_f^*(\bar{w}; a, \bar{w}) - H_i^*[w_i^{NR}(a, \bar{w}); a, \bar{w}] = 1 - b_E - [a - \bar{w} - (\rho_f - \rho_i)a]/(a - q\bar{w})$.

Table 1 summarises the rest of the match likelihood functions obtained in analogous fashion. Proposition 2 below summarises the wage offer distribution impact of the minimum wage, which reflects directly the expected profit impact of a minimum wage already seen in Proposition 1:

PROPOSITION 2. *With contractual dualism,*

- *For $(a, \bar{w}) \in A_f^{NR}$ and $\bar{w} \leq b_E a/(1 - q + b_E q)$, some informal employers over-comply $(w_i^{NR}(a) > \bar{w})$. An increase in $\bar{w}$ shifts $H^*(w^e; a, \bar{w})$ to the right.*
- *For $(a, \bar{w}) \in A_f^{NR}$ and $\bar{w} \in [b_E a/(1 - q + b_E q), a(1 - \rho_f)]$, $H^*(w^e; a, \bar{w})$ exhibits a spike at $\bar{w}$. An increase in $\bar{w}$ shifts the match likelihood function $H^*(w^e; a, \bar{w})$ to the right.*
- *For all $(a, \bar{w}) \in A_f^{FE}$, $H^*(w^e; a, \bar{w})$ exhibits a spike at $\bar{w}$. An increase in $\bar{w}$ gives rise to a single crossing shift of $H^*(w^e; a, \bar{w})$ if and only if $q > 0$, and a rightward shift of $H^*(w^e; a, \bar{w})$ otherwise with $q = 0$.*
- *Transitioning from A_f^{FE} to A_i^{NR} there is a discrete shift in the distribution leftwards as all formal employers become informalised. Further increases in $\bar{w}$ will shift $H^*(w^e; a, w)$ to the right if and only if $q > 0$, and $H^*(w^e; a, \bar{w})$ is invariant to $\bar{w}$ otherwise with $q = 0$.*

Table 1

*The Minimum Wage and the Match Likelihood Function**

$(a, \bar{w}) \in A_f^{NR}$ and $\bar{w} \le b_E a/(1 - q + b_E q)$

$$H^*(w^e;a,\bar{w}) = H_i^*(w^e;a,\bar{w}) = (1 - b_E)[a - \bar{w} - (\rho_f - \rho_i)a]/(a - w^e), \quad w^e \le w_i^{NR}$$
$$H_f^*(w^e;a,\bar{w}) = (1 - b_E)(a - \bar{w})/(a - w^e), \quad w^e \in (w_i^{NR}, w_f^{NR}).$$

$(a,\bar{w}) \in A_f^{NR}$ and $\bar{w} > b_E a/(1 - q + b_E q)$

$$H^*(w^e;a,\bar{w}) = H_i^*(w^e;a,\bar{w}) = (1 - b_E)[a - \bar{w} - (\rho_f - \rho_i)a]/(a - w^e), \quad w^e \le w_i^{NR}$$
$$H_o^*(w^e;a;\bar{w}) = [a - \bar{w} - (\rho_f - \rho_i)a]/(a - q\bar{w}), \quad w^e \in (w_i^{NR}, \bar{w})$$
$$H_f^*(w^e;a,\bar{w}) = (1 - b_E)(a - \bar{w})/(a - w^e), \quad w^e \in [\bar{w}, w_f^{NR}].$$

$(a,\bar{w}) \in A_f^{FE}$

$$H^*(w^e;a,\bar{w}) = H_i^*(w^e;a,\bar{w}) = (1 - b_E)\rho_i a/(a - w^e), \quad w^e \le w_i^{NR}$$
$$H_o^*(w^e;a,\bar{w}) = \rho_i a/(a - q\bar{w}), \quad w^e \in (w_i^{NR}, \bar{w})$$
$$H_f^*(w^e;a,\bar{w}) = (1 - b_E)\rho_f a/(a - w^e), \quad w^e \in [\bar{w}, w_f^{FE}].$$

$(a, \bar{w}) \in A_i^{NR}$

$$H^*(w^e;a,\bar{w}) = H_i^*(w^e;a,\bar{w}) = (1 - b_E)(a - q\bar{w})/(a - w^e), \quad w^e \le w_i^{NR}(a).$$

Note. $^*A_f^{NR} = \{(a, \bar{w}) | a \ge \bar{w}/(1 - \rho_f)\}$; $A_f^{FE} = \{(a, \bar{w}) | a \ge \bar{w}/\theta_f\}$ and $A_i^{NR} = \{(a, \bar{w}) | a \in [\bar{w}/\theta_f), \bar{w}\}$.

Thus, the minimum wage can have impact throughout the entire match likelihood function both above and below the minimum wage in very nuanced ways. Figure 4(a)–(c) displays these findings assuming a given a and $q > 0$. To start, H^o, H^1 and H^2 in Figure 4(a) are match likelihood functions with successively higher minimum wages and a binding formal NRC. Respectively, the three match likelihood functions correspond to the case of zero minimum wage $\bar{w}^0 = 0$, over-compliance in the informal sector $[0 < \bar{w}^1 < b_E a/(1 - q + b_E q)]$, and full non-compliance in the informal sector and a spike at the minimum wage $[\bar{w}^2 > b_E a/(1 - q + b_E q)]$. Since an increase in the minimum wage lowers expected employer profits (Proposition 2), rising minimum wage shifts the match likelihood function to the right first from H^o to H^1 and then from H^1 to H^2. Along the way, the maximal formal and informal expected wages $w_f^{NR}(a, \bar{w})$ and $w_i^{NR}(a, \bar{w})$ are shifted to the right from $w_i^{NR_1}$ and $w_f^{NR_1}$ to $w_i^{NR_2}$ and $w_f^{NR_2}$ as well.

In Figure 4(b), the FEC binds and the match likelihood functions H^3 and H^4 correspond to successively higher minimum wages $\bar{w}^3$ and $\bar{w}^4$. Note that there is a spike at the minimum wage associated with each of the match likelihood functions. While an increase in the minimum wage from $\bar{w}^3$ to $\bar{w}^4$ shifts the minimum wage spike to the right, the rest of the match likelihood $H^*(\bar{w}; a, \bar{w})$ evaluated at the new minimum wage remains exactly the same, consistent with zero expected profits both before and after the spike. With positive enforcement, the maximal informal wage $w_i^{NR}(a, \bar{w})$ increases

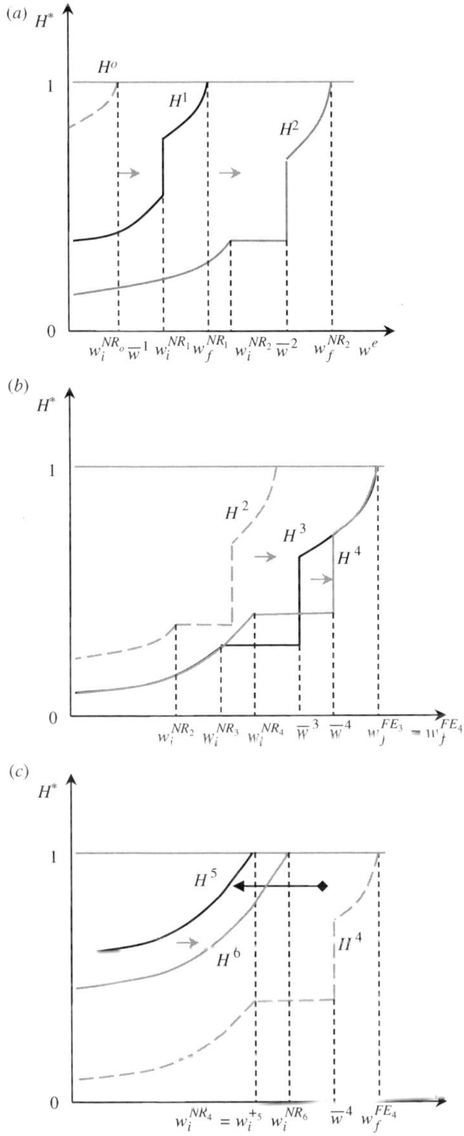

Fig. 4. *(a) Minimum Wage with a Binding Formal NRC and Binding Informal NRC ($q > 0$) (b) Minimum Wage with a Binding Formal FEC and Binding Informal NRC ($q > 0$) (c) Minimum Wage with a Binding Informal NRC ($q > 0$)*

with $\bar{w}$ from $w_i^{NR_3}$ to $w_i^{NR_4}$. The result is a single-crossing shift in $H^*(w^e; a, \bar{w})$ as stated in Proposition 2.

Raising the minimum wage further will eventually lead to a discrete transition to a match likelihood function with informal offers only, or $(\bar{w}, a) \in A_i^{NR}$. In Figure 4($c$), we consider the two match likelihood functions (H^4 and H^5) respectively before and after the transition evaluated at the marginal minimum wage $\bar{w}^4 = a\theta_f$. Thereafter, further increases in the minimum wage with $q > 0$ lower the expected informal profits, and shifts the match likelihood from H^5 to H^6 and the maximal informal wage from $w_i^{NR_5}$ and $w_i^{NR_6}$ in Figure 4(c).

In Figure 5(a)–(c), we illustrate the same sequence of minimum wage increases as in Figure 4(a)–(c) when informal enforcement q is set at 0. Note that with $q = 0$, the NRC in the informal sector $w^e \leq w_i^{NR}(a, \bar{w}) = b_E a$ is invariant to the minimum wage. This is shown in Figure 5 as $w_i^{NR}(a, \bar{w}) = w_i^{NR_0}$ which remains constant at $b_E a$ regardless of the level of the minimum wage. When the formal NRC binds as in Figure 5(a), an increase in the minimum wage decreases employer profits and shifts the match likelihood to the right. When the FEC binds as in Figure 5(b), an increase in the minimum wage simply raises the minimal formal sector wage, pushing the wage spike to the right and otherwise has no impact on the match likelihood function. For even higher minimum wages so that only informal firms remain, the wage distribution reverts to the no-intervention benchmark H^0, as shown in Figure 5(c), and is henceforth invariant to $\bar{w}$.

3.3. *Unemployment*

From (7) and (17), steady state unemployment is given by

$$U^*(a, \bar{w}) = \frac{\delta \bar{N}(a)}{1 + \delta - H^*[w_r^e(a, \bar{w}); a, \bar{w}]}.$$

Thus, a minimum wage hike can potentially impact unemployment in two distinctive ways. First, from Proposition 1, an increase in the minimum wage impacts market power in a non-monotonic fashion, which in turn gives rise to shifts in the wage offer distribution $H^*(w_r^e; a, \bar{w})$ at constant reservation wage w_r^e as summarised Proposition 2. Second, an increase in the minimum wage also changes the reservation wage $w_r^e(a, \bar{w})$ via (7). This will directly impact unemployment as $H^*(w_r^e(a, \bar{w}); a, \bar{w})$ evaluated at the reservation wage gives the likelihood that an unemployed individual will not receive an acceptable wage offer.

These two forces associated with a minimum wage hike can run in opposite directions. Specifically, when an increase in the minimum wage raises the credibility of high offers (such as in A_f^{NR} and A_i^{NR} if $q > 0$), $H^*(w^e; a, \bar{w})$ shifts to the right, thus improving the match likelihood of unemployed workers. Going in opposite direction, a higher minimum wage leads to higher wage expectations through shifts in the wage distribution $H(w^e; a, \bar{w})$. This raises the reservation wage through (7). Unemployment thus tends to increase as workers are encouraged to wait for a better job. The second effect is particularly pronounced if the discount factor of workers β_N is high.

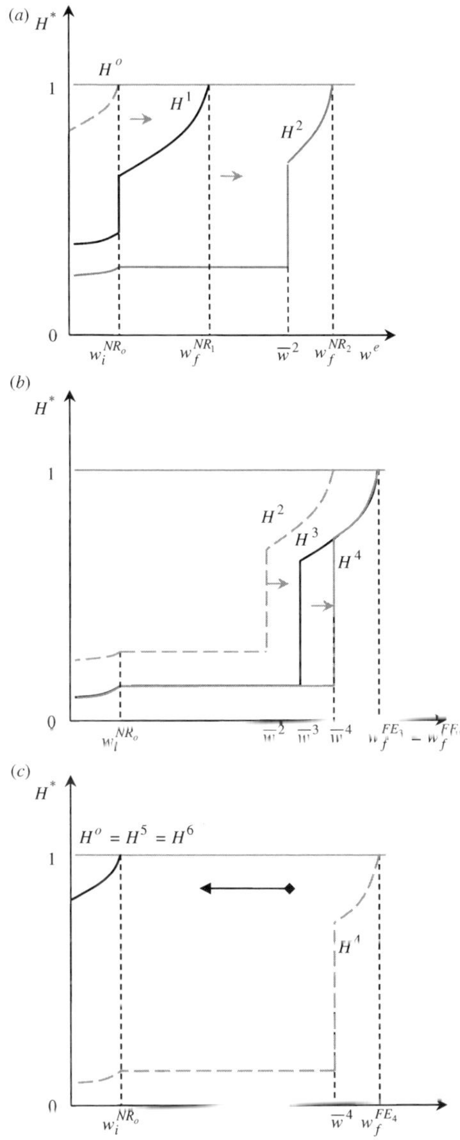

Fig. 5. *Minimum Wage with a Binding Formal NRC and Binding Informal NRC ($q = 0$) (b) Minimum Wage with a Binding Formal FEC and Binding Informal NRC ($q = 0$) (c) Minimum Wage with a Binding Informal NRC ($q = 0$)*

The comparative statics response of equilibrium unemployment with respect to the minimum wage across the different regions of A_f^{NR}, A_f^{FE} and A_i^{NR} are summarised in Table 2.[38] This is done based on the following set of assumptions. First, the enforcement intensity of the minimum wage in the informal sector, q, is assumed to be sufficiently small, so that the reservation wage is an interior solution as shown in (7) (Appendix B). Second, the discount rate β_N is not too high, so that informal and formal employment coexist (Appendix C) and also so that the impact of future wage expectations on current reservation offer is not too high ((7)).

From Table 2, there is a U-shaped relationship between equilibrium unemployment $U^*(a, \bar{w})$ and the minimum wage. This is consistent with the last of our five salient features of formal and informal labour markets discussed in the Introduction. Indeed, these results imply the existence of an the unemployment minimising minimum wage, which coincides with the smallest minimum wage that eliminates employer market power, $a(1 - \rho_f)$. But raising the minimum wage too high runs the risk of encouraging informalisation, where lax enforcement there once again accommodates employer market power and a return to a low wage–high unemployment equilibrium.[39]

For completeness, Table 2 also displays the comparative statics responses of equilibrium informal employment, formal employment, as well as the number of workers paid at exactly the minimum wage, $\bar{N}_f(a; \bar{w})$, with respect to a minimum wage hike. Table 2 shows that these comparative statics responses are non-monotonic, depending in particular on:

(*i*) whether the NRC, or the FEC binds; and
(*ii*) whether formal and informal sector employers coexist.

3.4. *The Optimal Minimum Wage*

The model presented here generates sharp implications concerning the choice of a minimum wage. From our discussion above in subsections 3.1 and 3.3, the minimum wage that minimises employer expected profits, while maximising total informal and formal employment follows a remarkably simple and intuitive formula: $\bar{w}^* \equiv a(1 - \rho_f)$. In the absence of a fixed cost of entry in the formal sector, the minimum wage $\bar{w}^* = a$ coincides with the Stigler (1946) prescription, where the employment maximising minimum wage is simply the marginal value product of labour in an otherwise competitive labour market. Thus, the higher the productivity, the higher the minimum wage should be. But with a positive cost of formalisation, $\bar{w}^*$ rules out full marginal productivity pricing. Being based both on productivity and the fixed entry costs, this formula implies that $\bar{w}^*$ need not even meet the poverty line. To the best of our knowledge, this article is the first that a provides a link between the cost

[38] The detailed derivations that lead to Table 2 are provided in Appendix C.

[39] As alluded to earlier in the Introduction, these nuanced employment effects of the minimum wage, depending on the size of the minimum wage relative to the productivity a, echo the findings of a large empirical literature, which points to very mixed evidence on how the minimum wage affect employment in the two sectors (Carneiro and Corseuil, 2001; Fajnzylber, 2001; Maloney and Nunez, 2004; Gindling and Terrell, 2007; Lemos, 2009).

Table 2

Expected Profits, Equilibrium Labour Allocation and the Minimum Wage

	Coexistence of informal and employment		Transition from coexistence to informal only	Informal employment only
	$(a, \bar{w}) \in A_f^{NR}$ $\bar{w} < (1-\rho_f)a$	$(a, \bar{w}) \in A_f^{FE}$ $\bar{w} \in [(1-\rho_f)a, \theta_f a)$	$\bar{w} = \theta_f a$	$(a, \bar{w}) \in A_i^{NR}$ $\bar{w} \in (\theta_f a, a]$
$\bar{V}(a, \bar{w})$	<0	no change	$\lim_{\epsilon \to 0}[\bar{V}(a, \theta_f a + \epsilon) - \bar{V}(a, \theta_f a - \epsilon)] > 0$	<0 if $q > 0$ no change if $q = 0$
$U^*(a, \bar{w})$	<0	>0	$\lim_{\epsilon \to 0}[U^*(a, \theta_f a + \epsilon) - U^*(a, \theta_f a - \epsilon)] > 0$	<0 or no change if $q > 0$ no change if $q = 0$
$N_i^*(a, \bar{w})$	<0	>0	$\lim_{\epsilon \to 0}[N_i^*(a, \theta_f a + \epsilon) - N_i^*(a, \theta_f a - \epsilon)] > 0$	pos. if $q > 0$ no change if $q = 0$
$N_f^*(a, \bar{w})$	>0	<0	$\lim_{\epsilon \to 0}[N_f^*(a, \theta_f a + \epsilon) - N_f^*(a, \theta_f a - \epsilon)] < 0$	–
$\bar{N}_f^*(a, \bar{w})$	>0[†]	>0	$\lim_{\epsilon \to 0}[\bar{N}_f^*(a, \theta_f a + \epsilon) - \bar{N}_f^*(a, \theta_f a - \epsilon)] < 0$	–

Notes. The equilibrium employer profits $\bar{V}(a, \bar{w})$ has been demonstrated in Proposition 2. Furthermore, equilibrium labour allocations are given by: $U^*(a, \bar{w}) = \delta/\Delta$, $N_i^*(a, \bar{w}) = \{H_i^*[w_i^{NR}(a, \bar{w}); a, \bar{w}] - H_i^*[w_r^e(a, \bar{w}); a, \bar{w}]\}/\Delta$, $N_f^*(a, \bar{w}) = \{1 - H_i^*[w_i^{NR}(a, \bar{w}); a, \bar{w}]\}/\Delta$, and $\bar{N}_f^*(a, \bar{w}) = \{H_f^*(\bar{w}; a, \bar{w}) - H_i^*[w_i^{NR}(a, \bar{w}); a, \bar{w}]\}/\Delta$ where $\Delta = \{1 + \delta - H^*[w_r^e(a, \bar{w}); a, \bar{w}]\}/\bar{N}(a)$. [†]If $\bar{w} > b_E a/[1 - (1 - b_E)q]$.

of formalisation ρ_f and the formulation of an optimal minimum wage that eliminates employer market power and maximises employment.

To establish a raw gauge on the importance of entry cost in the determination of the optimal minimum wage, consider for example data collected regarding the regulation cost of entry of start-up firms in 85 developed and developing countries from Djankov *et al.* (2002). The data cover the number of procedures, official time and official cost that a start-up must bear before it can operate legally. The direct and time cost of entry is expressed as a fraction of GDP *per capita* in 1999 – a proxy of our ρ_f. As reported in Djankov *et al.* (2002), these entry costs are indeed substantial in many countries, with an average ρ_f of 0.66 and median ρ_f of 0.40. Thus, the optimal minimum wage that minimises unemployment is indeed substantially smaller than the Stiglerian prediction.

4. Extensions

In this Section, we consider a number of extensions to the basic model. In particular, we consider introducing:

(*i*) non-wage benefits of formal employment *vis-à-vis* informal employment;
(*ii*) government policies other than the minimum wage; and
(*iii*) modes of reneging beyond the no reneging or full reneging dichotomy.

In each case, the difference that these new considerations make to the MWC, the FEC and the NRC constraints, and thus the workings and predictions of the basic model will be explained. Furthermore, the implications that these changes can have on the formulation of an optimal minimum, if any, will also be assessed.

4.1. *Non-wage Benefits*

It has been argued that workers typically strictly prefer formal employment to informal employment, even when wages are equal, due for example to better labour standards in formal employment (Rogers and Swinnerton, 2003; Kucera and Roncolato, 2008).[40] Importantly, when wages are not the only criterion based on which workers select between employment options, dispersion in wages alone is not sufficient to characterise the dispersion in well-being across workers. In the context of the basic model presented so far, let the income equivalent of the per period non-wage benefits from formal and informal employment respectively as $n_f > n_i = 0$, normalising non-wage informal benefits at 0. The discounted lifetime utility (W_τ) of a worker now takes the form:

$$W_\tau = \sum_{t=0}^{\infty} \beta_N^t (u_{t+\tau}), \quad u_{t+\tau} = y_{t+\tau} + n_{t+\tau},$$

which sums the wage and non-wage benefits of employment.

[40] In addition to better on-the-job benefits, formal workers may also enjoy better benefits even after involuntary separation. Unemployment insurance financed in part by worker and employer contributions is one such example. These programmes typically have time limits, and as such they can distort job search incentives (Gerard and Gonzaga, 2011). Furthermore, in countries with large informal sectors where separated workers receiving benefits may find employment without getting caught, these programmes are administratively very costly to monitor (Vodopivec, 2013). Thus, introducing unemployment insurance raises whole new considerations that are beyond the scope of this study but are clearly worthy of attention in future research.

From a formal employers' perspective, the per period wage cost y_j that an employer in sector j will need to pay to offer an employment opportunity with per period utility u_j, is given simply by $y_j = u_j - n_j$, which is strictly decreasing in the size of the non-wage benefit. With this observation, it follows that given any accepted employment opportunity offering expected utility u^e, the employer earns current period expected profit $a - u^e + n_j$, with expected discounted profits:

$$V_j(u^e, a) = \frac{a - u^e + n_j}{1 - b_E}.$$

In expected utility terms, therefore, the minimal expected utility that a formal worker will receive is equal to the sum of the minimum wage and non-wage benefits of formal work:

$$u_f^e \geq \bar{w} + n_f.$$

This is the expected utility analogue of the MWC. The expected utility analogue of the FEC is given by:

$$V_j(u_f^{FE}, a) = \frac{a - u^e + n_j}{1 - b_E} \geq 0 \Leftrightarrow u_f^e \leq \theta_f a + n_f.$$

Finally, the NRC will also need to be revised, to guarantee that the expected profits from continuing an employment contract exceeds that from reneging:

$$\frac{a - u_f^e + n_f}{1 - b_E} \geq a - \bar{w} \Leftrightarrow u_f^e \leq b_E a + (1 - b_E)\bar{w} + n_f.$$

Relative to (10)–(12), the introduction of non-wage benefits simply shifts the three constraints upwards by exactly the size of the non-wage benefit. Effectively, the introduction of non-wage benefits of formal employment implies that the range of former worker utility shifts upwards by the amount n_f. The threshold skill levels at the point where formal employment becomes viable $\bar{w}/\theta_j$, and where the NRC begins to bind $\bar{w}/(1 - \rho_f)$, remain exactly the same. As such, the rest of the analysis can proceed in exactly the same manner as before, so that the equilibrium dispersion of expected utility (as opposed to expected wage in the absence of non-wage benefits) across workers can be described, and the comparative statics analysis undertaken in the same fashion.

In terms of policy, the invariance of the threshold skill levels with respect to non-wage benefits also implies that the smallest minimum wage that eliminates market power, $a(1 - \rho_f)$, remains exactly the same. The introduction of non-wage benefits in the formal sector accordingly leaves the optimal minimum wage prescription unchanged.[41]

[41] One can also consider formal–informal asymmetries from a producer's perspective. For example, formal employers may benefit from a productivity bonus, all else equal, due to more and better sources of formal finance. By contrast, formal employers may also see additional costs, if a revenue tax is levied on formal firms. Suppose that the sum total of these influences means that skill type a worker generates revenue $a(1 + \lambda)$ in the formal sector and a in the informal sector, where λ is a fraction that can be positive or negative depending on the magnitudes of the two effects. It is straightforward to show that the optimal minimum wage in this setting is equal to $a(1 + \lambda - \rho_f)$. Despite the inclusion of the λ term, the interpretation is exactly the same – the optimal minimum wage is given by worker productivity (adjusted for taxes and productivity bonus in the formal sector) net of the fixed cost of entry.

4.2. *Mandated Severance Pay*[42]

A mandated minimum wage is but one amongst a range of possible policies that a government can impose on formal employers. Holzmann *et al.* (2011) provides the first comprehensive account of severance pay programmes in 183 countries and finds that in all but seven countries, severance pay programmes for formal sector workers exist. The employer cost of these programmes is in fact found to be more burdensome in low to middle income countries. In our context, we ask, does mandated severance pay alter employer commitment to pay higher self-enforcing wages? Furthermore, how does mandated severance pay impact the formulation of an unemployment minimising minimum wage?

Denote $\bar{s}$ as a one-time mandated severance pay, over and above the mandated minimum wage, that a formal employer is obliged to pay the worker to terminate an employment relationship. We assume that a mandated severance pay in the formal sector is always in force for as long as exogenous separation has not yet taken place to break up the employer–worker match. The discounted expected profit facing a formal employer who intends to continue a formal employment relationship at expected wage w^e is thus the same as before at

$$V_f(w^e, a) = a - w^e + \beta_E(1-\delta)V_f(w^e, a) = \frac{a - w^e}{1 - b_E}. \tag{24}$$

The discounted expected profit facing a formal employer who terminates a formal employment relationship after work has been done is thus

$$a - \bar{w} - \bar{s}. \tag{25}$$

We can now write down the MWC, the FEC and the NRC in the presence of mandated severance pay. First, the MWC continues to simply require that the expected pay in the formal sector be bounded below by $\bar{w}$:

$$w_f^e \geq \bar{w}. \tag{26}$$

Next, the FEC also continues to require that the expected profits $V_f(w^e, a)$ associated with a decision to continue an employment relationship is strictly positive, or

$$V_f(w^e, a) \geq 0, \Leftrightarrow w_f^e \leq \theta_f a. \tag{27}$$

Thus, neither of these two conditions is subject to change upon introducing severance pay considerations. Turning now to the NRC, which requires that the continuation expected profits is no less than that of a formal employer who terminates a contract before exogenous separation accounting for the mandated minimum wage and severance pay package, we have:

$$V_f(w^e, a) \geq a - \bar{w} - \bar{s} \Leftrightarrow w_f^e \leq b_E a + (1 - b_E)(\bar{w} + \bar{s}). \tag{28}$$

Thus, the maximal self-enforcing wage in the formal sector is in fact strictly increasing in the mandated severance pay. By limiting the profits that a reneging employer can expect, an increase in the mandated severance pay has the ability to

[42] We thank an anonymous referee for encouraging us to pursue an extension of the model to demonstrate the self-enforcement implications of mandated severance pay.

increase the credibility of a firm to offer a higher wage formal contract since w_f^e is strictly increasing in $\bar{s}$ along the NRC.

We now turn to the question of an optimal minimum wage in the presence of a mandated severance pay. Provided that the non-reneging constraint is satisfied, workers rationally expect that employers will refrain from reneging on their wage offers. Following the rest of the analysis in Sections 1 and 3 in analogous fashion, the optimal minimum wage formula can once again be shown to be the smallest minimum wage that eliminates employer market power, or in other words when the NRC augmented with severance pay (28) and the FEC (27) coincide. Equivalently, the unemployment minimising minimum wage is now

$$\bar{w} = a(1 - \rho_f) - \bar{s}.$$

The role of severance pay on the optimal minimum wage formula turns out to be remarkably simple – the unemployment minimising minimum wage decreases dollar for dollar with mandated severance pay. Intuitively, $\bar{w} + s$ together gives the cost to an employer attempting to terminate an employment relationship. The higher this sum, the higher will be the wage that employers can credibly commit to pay and, accordingly, the lower the market power. This result reinforces the intuition developed earlier, that the rationale behind the minimum wage is to increase the cost to an employer who terminates employment relationships after work has been done.

4.3. *Partial Reneging*

Consistent with much of the literature on labour contracting in developing country labour markets (Mukherjee and Ray, 1995; Caselli, 1997; Basu, 2002), the NRC is based on two sets of assumptions:

(*i*) employers can either renege fully and pay zero wage, or not renege at all; and
(*ii*) workers, as a matter of social norm, react to any employer attempts to reneging by terminating the employment relationship altogether.

Here, we extend both (*i*) and (*ii*) to respectively to incorporate the possibility of a full range of possible reneging and a full range of possible withdrawals of worker effort depending on the extent of reneging.

In the extension, we follow the Akerlof–Yellen (1990) fair wage–effort hypothesis.[43] In its original formulation, any wage underpayment relative to the fair wage is immediately faced with a contemporaneous withdrawal of worker effort, where the fair wage is an arbitrary weighted average between the equilibrium wage of a predetermined reference group, and the market clearing wage. In order to adopt this hypothesis to our setting, we make two changes. First, effort is withdrawn with a one period lag subsequent to any reneging attempt, consistent with a setting where wages are paid after work is done. Second, we assume that worker-initiated punishment in the form of effort suspension is

[43] This work has inspired a large literature including models of imperfect labour market and equilibrium unemployment in trade models (Kreickemeier and Nelson, 2006) and experimental evidence on reciprocal relationships and social exchange (Gächter and Thöni, 2010).

directed towards failure on the part of an employer to pay the expected wage difference over and above what government enforcement already guarantees.

Specifically, let y_j^e, $j = i, f$ be the actual expected wage offer and y_j be the actual wage in sector j respectively, where

$$y_i^e(y_i) = y_i + q\max\{\bar{w} - y_i, 0\}, \quad y_f^e(y_f) = y_f + \max\{\bar{w} - y_f, 0\}.$$

To recall, w_j^e, $j = i, f$ denotes the contracted expected wage and w_j the contracted wage, where

$$w_i^e(w_i) = w_i + q\max\{\bar{w} - w_i, 0\}, \quad w_f^e(w_f) = w_f + \max\{\bar{w} - w_f, 0\}.$$

Thus, whenever the actual wage y_j is less than the contracted wage w_j, the expected wage y_j^e is less than the contracted expected wage w_j^e.

The fair wage–effort hypothesis posits that any one time underpayment of the contracted wage leads to worker reprisal in the form of a proportionate reduction in effort $E_j \in [0, 1]$ in subsequent periods such that the fraction of producer surplus lost due to effort reduction on the part of workers is equal to the fraction of wage lost due to employer reneging:

$$\frac{aE_i - y_i^e}{a - w_i^e} = \frac{y_i^e - q\bar{w}}{w_i^e - q\bar{w}}, \quad \frac{aE_f - y_f^e}{a - w_f^e} = \frac{y_f^e - \bar{w}}{w_f^e - \bar{w}}.$$

It can easily be seen now that the all or nothing reneging that we have been considering so far is but a special case, where full reneging by the employer, setting $y_i^e - q\bar{w} = 0$ in i, or $y_f^e - \bar{w} = 0$ in f, leads to zero profit and thus effectively a termination of the employment relationship in subsequent periods.

Based on the above, the expected discounted profits of employers who pay y_j^e each period despite a contracted expected wage w_j^e in the two sectors respectively are given by[44]

$$\begin{aligned} V_f^r(y_f^e, w_f^e, a) &= a - y_f^e + \frac{b_E}{1 - b_E}(a - w_f^e)\frac{y_f^e - \bar{w}}{w_f^e - \bar{w}}, \\ V_i^r(y_i^e, w_i^e, a) &= a - y_i^e + \frac{b_E}{1 - b_E}(a - w_i^e)\frac{y_i^e - q\bar{w}}{w_i^e - q\bar{w}}. \end{aligned} \tag{29}$$

The NRC requires that the expected discounted profits in (29) above are no greater than when there is no reneging. Specifically, we have

$$\begin{aligned} V_f(w_f^e, a) - V_f^r(y_f^e, w_f^e, a) \geq 0 \quad &\text{iff} \quad \left[b_E a + (1 - b_E)\bar{w} - w_f^e\right](w_f^e - y_f^e) \geq 0, \\ V_i(w_i^e, a) - V_i^r(y_i^e, w_i^e, a) \geq 0 \quad &\text{iff} \quad \left[b_E a + (1 - b_E)q\bar{w} - w_i^e\right](w_i^e - y_i^e) \geq 0. \end{aligned} \tag{30}$$

for all $w_j^e \geq y_j^e$. Thus, if the NRC as stated in (12) is satisfied, or equivalently, if $w_f^e \leq b_E a + (1 - b_E)\bar{w}$ and $w_i^e \leq b_E a + (1 - b_E)q\bar{w}$ respectively in the formal and informal sectors, employers strictly prefer no reneging to any level of reneging, partial ($0 < y_i^e - q\bar{w} < w_i^e - q\bar{w}$ in i and $0 < y_f^e - \bar{w} < w_f^e - \bar{w}$ in f), or in full ($0 = y_i^e - q\bar{w} < w_i^e - q\bar{w}$ in i and $0 = y_f^e - \bar{w} < w_f^e - \bar{w}$ in f). As such, our analysis

[44] In writing (29), we assume that the MWC is satisfied, so for any $y_f \geq \bar{w}$ and $w_f \geq \bar{w}$.

concerning labour market outcomes as well as our optimal wage prescription remain strictly robust to this extension allowing for variable degrees of reneging and punishment.

5. Conclusion

This study models the confluence of three strands of the literature on formality and informality in developing countries – the degree of competition in the labour market, the ease of labour contract enforcement and government regulation of wages. We present an equilibrium where workers and firms sign contracts that will not be reneged upon; and firms can choose between the formal sector, where minimum wage regulations are strongly enforced, and the informal sector, where they are only weakly enforced. We show that this model is able to account for a number of stylised facts on wage distribution and labour allocations in developing countries. We demonstrate conditions under which employer power is greater in the informal sector due to the need for self-enforcing contracts. In the formal sector enforcement of minimum wage regulation indirectly provides a partial commitment technology, thereby improving efficiency and equity over some ranges of the minimum wage. Finally, we derive the optimal minimum wage taking into account the full equilibrium repercussions in both sectors.

To conclude, let us emphasise again that two conventional characterisations of the informal sector – that it is more competitive and that it has greater difficulty of contract enforcement – are incompatible with each other. Greater difficulty of contract enforcement in our model leads to greater employer power in the informal sector. Paradoxical as it may seem, government regulation in the formal sector mitigates the potential for employer power by providing a technology of third party enforcement, whose effects spill over to the informal sector and can lead to greater efficiency and greater equity in the economy as a whole.

Appendix A. Proof of Claim in Section 2.2 – The Reservation Wage Decreases with Employer Market Power

We demonstrate here that in the absence of a minimum wage legislation, heightened employer market power in the presence of a binding NRC decreases the reservation wage as defined in (7). To this end, suppose to begin with that employers are able to commit *ex ante* to refrain from reneging on an agreed upon wage contract. The NRC is no longer warranted, and employer profits are driven to zero from the FEC. It follows, therefore, from (19) that

$$H^*(w^e; a, 0) = \frac{(1-b_E)\rho_i a}{a - w^e}.$$

Furthermore, in the absence of an NRC,

$$w_i^+(a, 0) = w_i^{FE}(a) = b_E a + (1-b_E)(1-\rho_i)a.$$

Let the corresponding reservation wage be $\hat{w}_r^e(a, \bar{w})$, where from (7), upon integrating by parts:

$$\hat{w}_r^e(a) = \frac{\beta_N}{1-\beta_N}\left\{\left[w_i^{FE}(a) - \hat{w}_r^e(a, \bar{w})\right] - \int_{\hat{w}_r^e(a,\bar{w})}^{w_i^{FE}} \frac{(1-b_E)\rho_i a}{a - w^e} \mathrm{d}w^e\right\}.$$

Suppose instead that employers are unable to commit, and the NRC is binding. It follows that

$$w_i^+(a,0) = w_i^{NR}(a,0) = b_E a.$$

Employer profits are now strictly positive, and

$$H^*(w^e; a, 0) = \frac{(1-b_E)a}{a-w^e}.$$

Let the corresponding reservation wage be $\tilde{w}_r^e(a)$, where:

$$\tilde{w}_r^e(a,\bar{w}) = \frac{\beta_N}{1-b_N}\left\{\left[w_i^{FE}(a) - \Delta - \hat{w}_r^e(a,\bar{w})\right] - \int_{\hat{w}_r^e(a,\bar{w})}^{w_i^{FE}-\Delta} \frac{(1-b_E)\rho_i a + \Delta}{a-w^e}\mathrm{d}w^e\right\},$$

where $\Delta \equiv (1-b_E)(1-\rho_i)a > 0$. It follows immediately upon routine differentiation that $\tilde{w}_r^e(a,\bar{w})$ is strictly decreasing in Δ, or equivalently, a binding NRC, and the corresponding employer market power implies a strict reduction in the reservation wage. Indeed,

$$\frac{\partial\tilde{w}_r^e(a,\bar{w})}{\partial\Delta} = -\frac{\beta_N}{1-b_N}\left[\int_{\hat{w}_r^e(a,\bar{w})}^{w_i^{FE}-\Delta} \frac{1}{a-w^e}\mathrm{d}w^e\right]$$

is proportional to β_N, all else equal. Thus, the higher the discount factor β_N, the larger will be the reduction in the reservation offer in the presence of employer market power.

Appendix B. Proof of Claim in Section 3.2 – The Equilibrium Reservation Wage Solves (7) if Minimum Wage Enforcement in the Informal Sector q is Sufficiently Lax

In this Appendix, we show the condition under which the reservation wage $w_r^e(a,\bar{w})$ as specified in (6) is an interior solution given (7). An interior solution rules an informal job which offers exactly an expected wage of $q\bar{w}$ as strictly unacceptable. Such an informal job pays the minimum wage in the event of government enforcement (with probability q), and pay zero otherwise. From (7), an interior solution w_r^e solves

$$[w_r^e | w_r^e - \frac{\beta_N}{1-b_N}\int_{w_r^e}^{\infty}(x-w_r^e)\mathrm{d}H(x;a,\bar{w}) = 0].$$

Since the smallest informal sector expected wage satisfying the three wage constraints is $q\bar{w}$, it can be ready verified that $w_r^e - (\beta_N/1-b_N)\int_{w_r^e}^{w_i^{NR}(a,\bar{w})}(x-w_r^e)\mathrm{d}H(x;a,\bar{w})$ evaluated at $w_r^e = q\bar{w}$ is strictly negative if q is sufficiently small, with

$$q < \frac{\beta_E + (1-b_E)\ln(1-b_E)}{1+\beta_E+(1-b_E)\ln(1-b_E)},$$

and strictly positive evaluated the upper bound $w_r^e = w_i^{NR}(a,\bar{w})$. Since the difference is monotonically increasing in w_r^e, we conclude that an interior solution with $w_r^e(a,\bar{w}) > q\bar{w}$ applies whenever q is sufficiently small.

Appendix C. Proof of Claim in Section 3.2 – Formal and Informal Employment: Co-existence Proof and Comparative Statics

We begin with the following result:

LEMMA 1.

1. *There exists a* $\hat{\beta}_N \in [0,1]$ *such that for all* $\beta_N < \hat{\beta}_N$, $\Omega_i^e(a,\bar{w})$ *is non-empty and* $w_r^e(a,\bar{w}) < w_i^{NR}(a,\bar{w})$.
2. *The reservation offer* $w_r^e(a,\bar{w})$ *is always monotonically increasing in* $\bar{w}$ *for* $(a,\bar{w}) \in A_f^{NR}(\bar{w})$, $A_i^{NR}(\bar{w})$, *and monotonically increasing in* $\bar{w}$ *for* $(a,\bar{w}) \in A_f^{FE}(\bar{w})$ *if* q *is sufficiently small.* 3. *For any* $(a,\bar{w})$ *pair,* $\partial w_r^e(a,\bar{w})/\partial\bar{w} \to 0$ *as* $\beta_N \to 0$.

Proof.

1. Denote the right-hand side of (7) as $\Phi(w_r^e)$:

$$\Phi(w_r^e) \equiv \frac{\beta_N}{1-b_N}\int_{w_r^e}^{w^+(a,\bar{w})}(x-w_r^e)\mathrm{d}H(x;a,\bar{w}).$$

Three observations follow: (i) $\Phi(w_r^e)$ is monotonically decreasing in w_r^e and β_N respectively, (ii) $\Phi[w^+(a,\bar{w})] = 0$, and (iii) $\Phi(0) > 0$. Thus,

$$w^+(a,\bar{w}) - \Phi[w^+(a,\bar{w})] > 0, \quad \text{and} \quad 0-\Phi(0)<0.$$

It follows that the implicit solution to (7), $w_r^e(a,\bar{w})$, is unique, and lies in the interval $[0, w^+(a,\bar{w})]$. Furthermore, routine differentiation shows that $w_r^e(a,\bar{w})$ is monotonically increasing in β_N, with $w_r^e(a,\bar{w}) \to 0$ as $\beta_N \to 0$. Define

$$\hat{\beta}_N = \max\{\beta_N \in [0,1] | w_r^e(a,\bar{w}) \leq w_i^{NR}(a,\bar{w})\}.$$

By monotonicity of $w_r^e(a,\bar{w})$ with respect to β_N, $\hat{\beta}_N$ is uniquely defined. Furthermore, for any $\beta < \hat{\beta}_N$, $w_r^e(a,\bar{w}) < w_i^{NR}(a,\bar{w})$, and $\Omega_i^e(a) = [w_r^e(a,\bar{w}), w_i^{NR}(a,\bar{w})]$ is thus non-empty.

2. Assuming first that $\beta_N < \hat{\beta}_N$ so that informal and formal employment coexist from Lemma 1.1, it follows from (7) upon integrating by parts that for $(a,\bar{w}) \in A_f^{NR}(\bar{w})$,

$$sgn\left\{\frac{\partial w_r^e(a,\bar{w})}{\partial\bar{w}}\right\} = sgn\left\{\beta_N\int_{w_r^e}^{w_i^{NR}}\frac{1}{a-w^e}\mathrm{d}w^e + \beta_N\int_{w_i^{NR}}^{w^+}\frac{1}{a-w^e}\mathrm{d}w^e\right\} \geq 0 \qquad \text{(C.1)}$$

if and only if $\beta_N \geq 0$. The cases of $(a,\bar{w}) \in A_i^{NR}(\bar{w})$, $A_i^{FE}(\bar{w})$ and $A_i^{NR}(a)$ can be analogously obtained by routine differentiation, upon integration (7) by parts.

3. This follows directly from (C.1) above, where by inspection $\partial w_r^e(\cdot)/\partial\bar{w} \to 0$ if $\beta_N \to 0$.

Proof of Table 2. We consider β_N sufficiently small, and in particular $\beta_N < \hat{\beta}_N$, such that $\Omega_i^e(a,\bar{w})$ is non-empty and $w_r^e(a,\bar{w}) < w_i^{NR}(a,\bar{w})$.

Furthermore, recall that $w_i^+(a,\bar{w}) = w_i^{NR}(a,w)$. Thus,

$$p_i(a,\bar{w}) = \int_{w^e\in\Omega_i^e(a,\bar{w})}\mathrm{d}H^*(w^e;a,\bar{w}) = H_i^*[w_i^{NR}(a,\bar{w}),a,\bar{w}] - H_i^*[w_r^e(a,\bar{w});a,\bar{w}],$$

$$p_f(a,\bar{w}) = \int_{w^e\in\Omega_f^e(a,\bar{w})}\mathrm{d}H^*(w^e;a,\bar{w}) = 1 - H_i^*[w_i^{NR}(a,w);a,\bar{w}].$$

From (17),

$$U^*(a,\bar{w}) = \frac{\delta}{\Delta}, \quad N_i^*(a,\bar{w}) = \frac{H_i^*[w_i^{NR}(a,\bar{w});a,\bar{w}] - H_i^*[w_r^e(a,\bar{w});a,\bar{w}]}{\Delta}, \qquad \text{(C.2)}$$

$$N_f^*(a,\bar{w}) = \frac{1 - H_i^*[w_i^{NR}(a,\bar{w}); a, \bar{w}]}{\Delta}, \tag{C.3}$$

where $\Delta = \{1 + \delta - H^*[w_r^e(a,\bar{w}); a, \bar{w}]\}/\bar{N}(a)$. In addition, the number of workers paid exactly the minimum wage is given by

$$\bar{N}_f^*(a,\bar{w}) = \frac{H_f^*(\bar{w}; a, \bar{w}) - H_i^*[w_i^{NR}(a,\bar{w}); a, \bar{w}]}{\Delta}, \tag{C.4}$$

when formal and informal employment coexist, and when $\bar{w} > b_E a/(1 - q + b_E q)$.

Our objective is to confirm, entry-by-entry, the comparative statics responses displayed in Table 2. The expected employer profits response to a minimum wage has already been shown in Proposition 1. What remain to be demonstrated are the responses of unemployment $U^*(a,\bar{w})$, informal employment $N_i^*(a,\bar{w})$, formal employment $N_f^*(a,\bar{w})$ and the equilibrium size of the spike at the minimum wage $\bar{N}_f^*(a,\bar{w})$ subsequent to a minimum wage hike.

In what follows, we demonstrate the comparative statics responses displayed in the second and fourth column of Table 2, respectively $(a,\bar{w}) \in A_f^{NR}$, and the transition from coexistence to informal employment only. The comparative statics responses displayed in the third and fifth column can be shown in analogous fashion and are available upon request.

C.1. *Coexistence of Formal and Informal Employment* (A_f^{NR})

To begin with, consider minimum wages that are sufficiently small, so that $(a,\bar{w}) \in A_f^{NR}$, or $\bar{w} < a(1 - \rho_f)$. From Table 1, we have

$$H^*(w^e; a, \bar{w}) = \begin{cases} H_i^*(w^e; a, \bar{w}) = (1 - b_E)[a - \bar{w} - (\rho_f - \rho_i)a]/(a - w^e), & w^e \leq w_i^{NR} \\ H_f^*(w^e; a, \bar{w}) = (1 - b_E)(a - \bar{w})/(a - w^e), & w^e \in (w_i^{NR}, w_f^{NR}]. \end{cases}$$

C.2. *Unemployed Workers*

From Table 1,

$$H_i^*[w_r^e(a,\bar{w}); a, \bar{w}] = \frac{(1 - b_E)[a - \bar{w} - (\rho_f - \rho_i)a]}{a - w_r^e(a,\bar{w})}. \tag{C.5}$$

Now from (C.5) and Lemma 1.3, $H^*[w_r^e(a,\bar{w}); a, \bar{w}]$ is strictly decreasing in the minimum wage $\bar{w}$ if β_N is sufficiently small. From (C.2), it follows that $U^*(a,\bar{w})$ is likewise strictly decreasing in $\bar{w}$.

Taken together, equilibrium unemployment is always strictly decreasing with respect to $\bar{w}$ for all $(a,\bar{w}) \in A_f^{NR}$ so long as β_N is sufficiently small.

C.3. *Informal Workers*

Note first of all from Lemma 1 that,

$$\begin{aligned} p_i(a,\bar{w}) &= H_i^*[w_i^{NR}(a,\bar{w}); a, \bar{w}] - H_i^*[w_r^e(a,\bar{w}); a, \bar{w}] \\ &= \frac{(1 - b_E)[a - \bar{w} - (\rho_f - \rho_i)a]}{a - w_i^{NR}(a,\bar{w})} - \frac{(1 - b_E)[a - \bar{w} - (\rho_f - \rho_i)a]}{a - w_r^e(a,\bar{w})}. \end{aligned} \tag{C.6}$$

From Lemmas 1.2 and 1.3, $p_i(a, \bar{w})$ is strictly decreasing with respect to $\bar{w}$ if β_N is sufficiently small. It follows from (C.6) that $N_i^*(a, \bar{w})$ is strictly decreasing with respect to w for all $(a, \bar{w}) \in A_f^{NR}$ so long as β_N is sufficiently small.

C.4. *Formal Employment*

From (C.2) and (C.3) above, since equilibrium unemployment and informal employment are both decreasing with respect to $\bar{w}$, formal employment must rise with the minimum wage.

C.5. *Minimum Wage Workers*

As shown in Section 4 and Figure 1, a spike at the minimum wage occurs whenever $\bar{w} > b_E a/(1 - q + b_E q)$. From (C.3) and (C.4), the number of workers earning higher than the minimum wage is

$$N_f^*(a, \bar{w}) - \bar{N}_f^*(a, \bar{w}) = \frac{1 - H_f^*(\bar{w}; a, \bar{w})}{\Delta} = \frac{b_E}{\Delta}. \tag{C.7}$$

From (C.7), it follows straightforwardly that the number of workers earning higher than the minimum wage $N_f^*(a, \bar{w}) - \bar{N}_f^*(a, \bar{w})$ is strictly decreasing in $\bar{w}$. Since $N_f^*(a, \bar{w})$ rises with the minimum wage as shown above, it must be the case that the number of workers earning exactly the minimum wage rises with the minimum wage.

C.6. *Transition*

As the minimum wage rises beyond the critical threshold $a\theta_f$, there is full informalisation. To determine the direction of the discrete change in equilibrium labour allocation, use Table 1 to ascertain the following difference:

$$\begin{aligned}&\lim_{\epsilon \to 0} H_i^*[w_r^e(a, a\theta_f + \epsilon); a, a\theta_f + \epsilon] - H_i^*[w_r^e(a, a\theta_f - \epsilon); a, a\theta_f - \epsilon] \\ &= (1 - b_E)(a - a\theta_f q)/[a - w_r^{e+}(a, a\theta_f)] - (1 - b_E)\rho_i a/[a - w_r^{e-}(a, a\theta_f)],\end{aligned} \tag{C.8}$$

where the reservation wage $w_r^{e-}(a, \bar{w})$ evaluated based on $\lim_{\epsilon \to 0} H_i^*(w^e; a, a\theta_f - \epsilon)$ solves

$$w_r^{e-}(a, \bar{w}) = \lim_{\epsilon \to 0} \frac{\beta_N}{1 - b_N} \int_{w_r^{e-}(a, \bar{w})}^{\infty} [x - w_r^{e-}(a, \bar{w})] \mathrm{d}H(x; a, a\theta_f - \epsilon),$$

and the reservation wage $w_r^{e+}(a, \bar{w})$ evaluated based on $\lim_{\epsilon \to 0} H_i^*(w^e; a, a\theta_f + \epsilon)$ solves

$$w_r^{e+}(a, \bar{w}) = \lim_{\epsilon \to 0} \frac{\beta_N}{1 - b_N} \int_{w_r^{e+}(a, \bar{w})}^{\infty} [x - w_r^{e+}(a, \bar{w})] \mathrm{d}H(x; a, a\theta_f + \epsilon).$$

From (C.2), there is a discrete increase in equilibrium unemployment as the minimum wage rises beyond $a\theta_f$ if and only if (C.8) is strictly positive. To this end, note that by contractual dualism, the numerator of the first term $(a - a\theta_f q)$ strictly exceeds the numerator of the second term $\rho_i a$. Furthermore, if β_N is sufficiently small, it follows from the definition of the reservation wage that the change from $w_r^{e+}(a, a\theta_f)$ in the denominator of the first term to $w_r^{e-}(a, a\theta_f)$ in the denominator of the second term will accordingly be small. It follows that there is a discrete increase in equilibrium unemployment as the minimum wage rises beyond $a\theta_f$, with $\lim_{\epsilon \to 0} U^*(a\theta_f + \epsilon) - U^*(a, a\theta_f - \epsilon) > 0$.

Now turning to informal employment, consider now the following difference, supposing once again that β_N is sufficiently small, so that $w_r^e(a,\bar{w}) \leq q\bar{w}$:

$$\lim_{\epsilon\to 0}\frac{\{H_i^*[w_i^{NR}(a,a\theta_f+\epsilon)]-H_i^*[w_r^{e+}(a,a\theta_f);a,a\theta_f+\epsilon]\}}{1+\delta-H_i^*[w_r^{e+}(a,a\theta_f);a,a\theta_f+\epsilon]}$$

$$-\lim_{\epsilon\to 0}\frac{\{H_i^*[w_i^{NR}(a,a\theta_f-\epsilon)]-H_i^*[w_r^{e-}(a,a\theta_f);a,a\theta_f-\epsilon]\}}{1+\delta-H_i^*[w_r^{e-}(a,a\theta_f);a,a\theta_f+\epsilon]}$$

$$=\frac{(1-b_E)(a-q\theta_f a)/[a-w_i^{NR}(a,\theta_f a)]-(1-b_E)(a-q\theta_f a)/[a-w_r^{e+}(a,\theta_f a)]}{1+\delta-(1-b_E)(a-q\theta_f a)/[a-w_r^{e+}(a,\theta_f a)]}$$

$$-\frac{(1-b_E)(\rho_i a)/[a-w_i^{NR}(a,\theta_f a)]-(1-b_E)(\rho_i a)/[a-w_r^{e-}(a,\theta_f a)]}{1+\delta-(1-b_E)(\rho_i a)/[a-w_r^{e-}(a,\theta_f a)]}. \quad \text{(C.9)}$$

From (C.2), there is a discrete increase in equilibrium informal employment as the minimum wage rises beyond $a\theta_f$ if and only if (C.9) above is strictly positive. Using arguments similar to our proof regarding, the change in unemployment above in (C.9), we note that by contractual dualism, $(a - a\theta_f q)$ strictly exceeds $\rho_i a$. Furthermore, if β_N is sufficiently small, the change from $w_r^{e+}(a,a\theta_f)$ to $w_r^{e-}(a,a\theta_f)$ will be small. Under these assumptions, there is a discrete increase in equilibrium informal employment as the minimum wage rises beyond $a\theta_f$, with $\lim_{\epsilon\to 0} U^*(a\theta_f+\epsilon) - U^*(a,a\theta_f-\epsilon) > 0$.

Cornell University, IZA, ZEF
Cornell University, IZA, ZEF
Cornell University, CEPR, IZA

Accepted: 9 September 2014

References

Akerlof, G.A. and Yellen, J.L. (1990). 'The fair wage-effort hypothesis and unemployment', *Quarterly Journal of Economics*, vol. 105(2), pp. 255–83.
Albrecht, J., Navarro, L. and Vroman, S. (2009). 'The effects of labor market policies in an economy with an informal sector', ECONOMIC JOURNAL, vol. 119(539), pp. 1105–29.
Ashenfelter, O. and Smith, R.S. (1979). 'Compliance with the minimum wage law', *Journal of Political Economy*, vol. 87(2), pp. 333–50.
Baanante, M.J. (2004). 'Minimum wage effects under endogenous compliance: evidence from Peru', *Económica*, vol. 50(1–2), pp. 85–123.
Bargain, O. and Kwenda, P. (2010). 'Is informality bad? Evidence from Brazil, Mexico and South Africa', Discussion Paper No. 4711, IZA.
Basu, A.K. (2002). 'Oligopsonistic landlords, segmented labor markets and the persistence of tied-labor contracts', *American Journal of Agricultural Eocnomics*, vol. 84(2), pp. 438–53.
Basu, A.K., Chau, N.H. and Kanbur, R. (2010). 'Turning a blind eye: costly enforcement, credible commitment and minimum wage laws', ECONOMIC JOURNAL, vol. 120(543), pp. 244–69.
Bell, L. (1997). 'The impact of minimum wages in Mexico and Columbia', *Journal of Labor Economics*, vol. 15 (3), pp. S102–35.
Boeri, T. and Garibaldi, P. (2007). 'Shadow sorting', in (J. Frankel and C. Pissarides, eds.), *NBER International Seminar on Macroeconomics 2005*, pp. 125–63, Cambridge, MA: MIT Press.
Burdett, K. and Mortensen, D.T. (1998). 'Wage differentials, employer size, and unemployment', *International Economic Review*, vol. 39(2), pp. 257–73.
Card, D. and Krueger, A.B. (1995). *Myth and Measurement: The New Economics of the Minimum Wage*, Princeton, NJ: Princeton University Press.

Cardoso, A.R. and Portugal, P. (2006). 'Disentangling the minimum wage puzzle: an analysis of worker accessions and separations', *Journal of the European Economic Association*, vol. 4(5), pp. 988–1013.

Carneiro, F.G. and Corseuil, C. (2001). 'Minimum wage effects on wages and employment: evidence from time series and longitudinal data', Working Paper No. 849, December, Institute for Applied Economic Research (IPEA), Brazil.

Caselli, F. (1997). 'Rural labor and credit markets', *Journal of Development Economics*, vol. 54(2), pp. 235–60.

Chari, V.V., Restuccia, D. and Urrutia, C. (2005). 'On-the-job training, limited commitment and firing costs', Working Paper, Federal Reserve Bank of Minneapolis.

Charlot, O., Malherbet, F. and Terra, C. (2011). 'Product market regulation, firm size, unemployment and informality in developing economies', Discussion Paper No. 5519, IZA.

de Soto, H. (2003). *The Mystery of Capital: Why Capitalism Triumps in the West and Fails Everywhere Else*, New York: Basic Books.

Djankov, S., La Porta, R., Lopez-de-Silanes, F. and Shleifer, A. (2002). 'The regulation of entry', *Quarterly Journal of Economics*, vol. 117(1), pp. 1–37.

Fajnzylber, P. (2001). 'Minimum wage effects throughout the wage distribution: evidence from Brazil's formal and informal sectors', Working Paper No. 151, CEDEPLAR.

Fang, T. and Lin, C. (2013). 'Minimum wages and employment in China', Discussion Paper No. 7813, IZA.

Fields, G. (2004). 'A guide to multisector labor market models', Working Paper No. 11-1-2004, Cornell University School of Industrial and Labor Relations.

Fine, J. and Gordon, J. (2010). 'Strengthening labor standards enforcement through partnerships with workers organizations', *Politics and Society*, vol. 38(4), pp. 552–85.

Gächter, S. and Thöni, C. (2010). 'Social comparison and performance: experimental evidence on the fair wage-effort hypothesis', Discussion Paper No. 4687, IZA.

Gerard, F. and Gonzaga, G. (2011). 'Social insurance under imperfect monitoring: labor market and welfare impacts of the Brazilian UI program', mimeo, U.C. Berkeley.

Gindling, T.H. and Terrell, K. (2006). 'Minimum wages, globalization and poverty in Honduras', Discussion Paper No. 2497, IZA.

Gindling, T.H. and Terrell, K. (2007). 'The effects of multiple minimum wages throughout the labor market: the case of Costa Rica', *Labour Economics*, vol. 14(3), pp. 485–511.

Gindling, T.H. and Terrell, K. (2009). 'Minimum wages and employment in various sectors in Honduras', *Labour Economics*, vol. 16(3), pp. 291–303.

Gong, X. and Van Soest, A. (2002). 'Wage differentials and mobility in the urban labour market: a panel data analysis for Mexico', *Labour Economics*, vol. 9(4), pp. 513–29.

Gong, X., Van Soest, A. and Villagomez, E. (2004). 'Mobility in the urban labor market: a panel data analysis for Mexico', *Economic Development and Cultural Change*, vol. 53(1), pp. 1–36.

Guha-Khasnobis, B., Kanbur, R. and Ostrom, E. (2006). *Linking the Formal and Informal Economy Concepts and Policies*, Oxford: Oxford University Press.

Harris, J.R. and Todaro, M.P. (1970). 'Migration, unemployment and development: a two-sector analysis', *American Economic Review*, vol. 60(1), pp. 126–42.

Holzmann, R., Pouget, Y., Vodopivec, M. and Weber, M. (2011). 'Severance pay programs around the world: history, rationale, status, and reforms', Discussion Paper No. 5731, IZA.

Kanbur, R. (2009). 'Conceptualising informality: regulation and enforcement', *Indian Journal of Labour Economics*, vol. 52(1), pp. 33–42.

Kreickemeier, U. and Nelson, D. (2006). 'Fair wages, unemployment and technological change in a global economy', *Journal of International Economics*, vol. 70(2), pp. 451–69.

Krstić, G. and Sanfey, P. (2010). 'Earning inequality and the informal economy: evidence from Serbia', Working Paper No. 114, European Bank for Reconstruction and Development.

Kucera, D. and Roncolato, L. (2008). 'Informal employment: two contested policy issues', *International Labour Review*, vol. 147(4), pp. 321–48.

Lehmann, H. and Wadsworth, J. (2001). 'Wage arrears and the distribution of earnings in Russia'. Discussion Paper No. 410, IZA.

Lemos, S. (2004). 'The effects of the minimum wage in the formal and informal sectors in Brazil', Discussion Paper No. 1089, IZA.

Lemos, S. (2009). 'Minimum wage effects in a developing country', *Labour Economics*, vol. 16(2), pp. 224–37.

Levy, S. (2007). *Good Intentions, Bad Outcomes: Social Policy, Informality, and Economic Growth in Mexico*, Washington, DC: Brookings Institution Press.

Lipton, M. (1984). 'Family, fungibility and formality: rural advantages of informal non-farm enterprise versus the urban-formal state', in S. Amin (ed.), *Human Resources, Employment and Development, 5: Developing Countries*, pp. 189–242, London: MacMillan, for International Economic Association.

Maloney, W.F. (1999). 'Does informality imply segmentation in urban labor markets? Evidence from sectoral transitions in Mexico', *World Bank Economic Review* vol. 13(2), pp. 275–302.

Maloney, W.F. (2004). 'Informality revisited', *World Development* vol. 32(7), pp. 1159–78.

Maloney, W.F. and Nunez, J. (2004). 'Measuring the impact of minimum wages: evidence from Latin America', in J. Heckman and C. Pagés (eds.), *Law and Employment. Lessons from Latin America and the Caribbean*, pp. 109–30, Cambridge, MA: NBER.
Mortensen, D.T. (2003). *Wage Dispersion. Why Are Similar Workers Paid Differently?* Cambridge, MA: MIT Press.
Mukherjee, A. and Ray, D. (1995). 'Labor tying', *Journal of Development Economics*, vol. 47(2), pp. 207–39.
Portugal, P. and Cardoso, A.R. (2002). 'Disentangling the minimum wage puzzle: an analysis of worker accessions and separations', Discussion Paper No. 544, IZA.
Ramey, G. and Watson, J. (1997). 'Contractual fragility, job destruction, and business cycles', *Quarterly Journal of Economics*, vol. 112(3), pp. 873–911.
Rogers, C.A. and Swinnerton, S. (2003). 'A model of informal sector labor markets', mimeo, Georgetown University.
Ronconi, L. (2010). 'Enforcement and compliance with labor regulations', *Industrial and Labor Relations Review*, vol. 63(4), pp. 719–36.
Schneider, F. and Enste, D.H. (2000). 'Shadow economies: size, causes, and consequences', *Journal of Economic Literature*, vol. 38(1), pp. 77–114.
Shapiro, C. and Stiglitz, J.E. (1984). 'Equilibrium unemployment as a worker discipline device', *American Economic Review*, vol. 74(3), pp. 433–44.
Stigler, G.J. (1946). 'The economics of minimum wage legislation', *American Economic Review*, vol. 36(3), pp. 358–65.
Strobl, E. and Walsh, F. (2001). 'Minimum wage and compliance: the case of Trinidad and Tobago', *Economic Development and Cultural Change*, vol. 51(2), pp. 427–50.
Thomas, J.J. (1992). *Informal Economic Activity* (LSE Handbooks in Economics), Ann Arbor, MI: The University of Michigan Press.
Vodopivec, M. (2013). 'Introducing unemployment insurance to developing countries', *IZA Journal of Labor Policy*, vol. 2(1), pp. 1–23.
Zenou, Y. (2008). 'Job search and mobility in developing countries: theory and policy implications', *Journal of Development Economics*, vol. 86(2), pp. 336–55.

On Footloose Industries and Labor Disputes with Endogenous Information Asymmetry

*Nancy H. Chau and Ravi Kanbur**

Abstract

If capital becomes internationally mobile but labor does not, are outcomes of labor disputes tilted in favor of workers or employers? In this paper, we show that the answer depends critically on how the information structure of the dispute changes endogenously with capital mobility, and in addition, whether international investment incentives selectively favor the outflow of capital from the most or the least productive firms. In doing so, this paper brings together three strands of literature that are not often seen together—incentive compatible contracting, wage and unemployment outcomes of labor disputes, and international capital mobility with heterogeneous firms.

1. Introduction

If capital becomes internationally mobile but labor does not, are outcomes of labor disputes tilted in favor of workers or employers? Recent years have witnessed many high profile incidents of worker strikes in developing countries, featuring demands for higher pay and/or working conditions in the presence of footloose multinationals. For example, in China, a worker strike in a Honda plant in Guangdong province involved coordinated walk-outs by thousands of workers, only to be followed later on by similar walk-outs in Yunnan, Henan, Gansu, Shandong and Jiangsu provinces (*China Daily*, 2010). In Lesotho, demands for better pay and better working conditions likewise led to a strike in a Taiwanese garment factory which is part of a global production network in Taiwan, Nigeria, and Mexico (De Haan and Stichele, 2007). In Tunisia, thousands of workers in a German cable company went on strike to demand better wage compensations (Tunisialive, 2012).

In each of these cases, concerns were raised regarding the possibility that union demands for higher wages and working conditions will trigger a shift of production by the multinational to a different location with lower cost of production. A simple model that most clearly illustrates this concern is Rodrik (1997). In its simplest form, the model shows that a footloose industry exhibits a higher elasticity of labor demand, as wage demands from a labor union depress employment via two distinct and mutually reinforcing routes in the presence of capital mobility; (i) the traditional wage effect that represents a movement along a *ceteris paribus* labor demand schedule, and (ii) an additional effect that accounts for the outflow of capital serves to depress employment even further. Cast in a standard wage bargaining framework, workers

* Chau: Charles H. Dyson School of Applied Economics and Management, Cornell University, Ithaca NY 14853. Tel: +1-607-255 4463, Fax. +1-607-255-9984, Email: hyc3@cornell.edu. Kanbur: Charles H. Dyson School of Applied Economics and Management and Department of Economics, Cornell University, Ithaca NY 14853, USA. We are grateful to seminar participants at the Midwest International Economics Group Meeting, Cornell University, University of Cambridge, and an anonymous referee for useful comments and suggestions.

are necessarily worse off in both wage and employment terms once capital becomes mobile, even when workers are given a free hand to make wage and employment demands by moving first.

This partial equilibrium perfect information framework has been criticized in the literature for in equilibrium, strikes occur with zero probability. This is an obvious violation of empirical reality. In this paper, we address the issue of labor disputes with a footloose industry by augmenting a canonical model of labor strikes (Card, 1990) with a footloose firm. A well-known problem in the economics of labor disputes where strikes are involved is that strikes may be seen to be an out-of-equilibrium phenomenon (Farber, 2001; Ashenfelter and Johnson, 1969). This is because all parties are no worse off accepting the bargaining outcome without incurring the cost of a strike. Card (1990) develops an equilibrium model of labor strikes. The model has three main features. First, there is asymmetric information about the profitability of the firm. This information advantage allows the firm to depress wages. Second, being imperfectly informed, the union designs a downward sloping wage-strike duration schedule to entice higher productivity firms to willingly select to pay higher wage demands in order to avoid a costly and drawn out strike, and to entice low productivity firms to select to pay lower wages at the cost of a longer strike duration. Finally, unlike the efficient bargaining model where the union and the firm jointly select an efficient combination of wages and employment, or the right to manage model in which the firm selects a profit maximizing level of employment given the negotiated wage, this model of labor strikes with asymmetric information features a worker initiated inefficient level of employment, lower than that which would prevail in the absence of asymmetric information. The rationale here is that strikes are used as a (costly) means for the union to screen out high productivity firms from low productivity ones.

There are two distinct dimensions to the literature laid out so far: labor disputes with and without capital mobility, and labor disputes with and without information asymmetry. Given perfect information, wage and employment outcomes are predicted to worsen as labor demand elasticity increases going from capital immobility to capital mobility (Rodrik, 1997). Given the extent of capital mobility, and thus the elasticity of labor demand, wage and employment outcomes are likewise predicted to worsen as one moves from a world with perfect information, to one with information asymmetry (Card, 1990). In this paper, we provide an answer to an important question that remains: [1]given a pre-existing distortion in the form of asymmetric information, so that strikes are accordingly a real possibility, are wage and employment outcomes for workers worsened when capital becomes internationally mobile?

As a second contribution of this paper, we demonstrate that the relationship between the productivity of the footloose firm at home and abroad plays a critical role in formulating our answer. In particular, are more productive firms at origin likewise more productive abroad? To this end, Caves (1999) provides a classification particularly for developed to developing country capital flows, separating situations where host country productivity is independent of the productivity of the multinational because

> traditions of interpersonal relationships . . . resist conformance within a business hierarchy. (p. 4)

from situations where host country productivity rises with the productivity of the multinational when, for example, host country managerial talent is in constrained supply.

More generally, however, the relationship between multinational productivity in the source and host countries for South–South investment flows, or reverse flows from South to North have yet to be explored in the empirical literature. In the absence of a definitive answer to the issue of how firm level productivity at home and abroad tend to co-move, our model sets out a framework that accommodates a wide range of possible relationships between relative incentives to invest abroad and firm level productivities.

For an intuitive account of the problem and of our approach, consider a canonical setting under perfect information where the union makes a "take it or leave it" employment-wage offer. If the employer accepts then the negotiation is complete. If the employer does not, neither side gets the benefit of production. The union will thus make a employment-wage offer that is (i) efficient in the sense that workers' reservation wage is set equal to the marginal value product of labor (MVPL), and (ii) just attractive enough for the employer to accept. In such a setting a key determinant of the outcome is the elasticity of the labor demand. The larger is this elasticity, the less favorable will be the outcome for the union. The role of capital mobility can now be seen clearly. Allowing capital to be mobile increases the elasticity of labor demand, since production activities can now be relocated in response to higher wages, and this makes the union worse off.[2]

The picture changes as asymmetric information is introduced. Suppose now that the employer is fully informed about the total factor productivity of the firm but the union is not. Then in a closed economy, and an otherwise identical setup of labor dispute, the union fashions a wage–employment schedule for each level of possible productivity. Defining equilibrium strike duration as any increase in union unemployment over and above the efficient level set in the perfect information benchmark, strikes occurs in equilibrium (Card, 1990; McConnell, 1989). Moreover, the union cannot now be as well off as before, since the firm earns an informational rent from the fact that the union cannot perfectly tailor its offer to a known marginal value product of labor (MVPL) curve. Here, information asymmetry introduces a distortion in the form of an excessive level of labor strikes, and accordingly a deviation of the MVPL from the reservation wage of the workers. The size of this deviation, and accordingly the reduction in union employment through strikes, depends critically on the extent of informational asymmetry as measured by the spread of MVPL. Indeed, the greater the spread of MVPL, that is, the greater the asymmetry of information, the worse off will the union be.

Finally, suppose now that investing abroad is an option for the firm after it sees the union offer. Will the union be better off or worse off, compared with the closed economy asymmetric information benchmark? There are now three forces in play. First, as before, this openness increases the elasticity of labor demand at each level of productivity, and this tends to have all of the effects discussed in the perfect information setting. The interplay between the rise in labor demand elasticity and information asymmetry gives rise to a second effect. Namely, for any given degree of information asymmetry, and hence the size of the difference between the MVPL and the reservation wage required for incentive compatibility, a larger distortion in union employment arises subsequent to openness by virtue of the rise in labor demand elasticity. Clearly, this second effect reinforces the first in lowering union employment through strikes even further. Finally, a third effect arises owing to the endogenous interplay between capital mobility and information asymmetry, and directly impacts the spread of MVPLs. In particular, if capital mobility increases this spread, in other words, if it widens the gap in MVPL for any given gap in productivity, it worsens the union's position by increasing the informational rent extractable by the employer. If it decreases the spread then it effectively reduces the asymmetric information and thereby strengthens the union's hand.

The object of this paper is to elaborate upon these informational consequences of capital mobility, and to bring together three strands of literature that are not often seen together—incentive compatible contracting, wage and unemployment consequences of labor disputes, and international capital mobility. We develop a model in which the competing forces affecting the negotiation outcome can be brought into sharp relief, and their relative strengths can be analyzed in detail. Our findings suggest that not only is it the case that capital mobility can systematically affect the spread of the MVPLs, but whether the impact on spread strengthens the union or the employer's hand depend critically on whether capital mobility favors the outflow of the most productive firms, or the least productive firms. Specifically, if capital productivity mobility exhibits *home bias*, in the sense high productivity firms earn proportionately higher revenue at home than abroad, so that the least productive firms are the ones most prone to exporting jobs abroad, we show that capital mobility strictly increases the spread of the MVPLs. Effectively, capital mobility makes information asymmetry even more acute, and the union is necessarily worse off with a footloose industry.

By contrast, if the nature of capital mobility is such that the most productive firms are also the most prone to export jobs abroad, our findings accordingly show that the spread of the MVPL, or the degree of information asymmetry weakens. As can be expected, this informational role of capital mobility can have important empirical implications, particularly with respect to the wage, employment and welfare consequences of capital mobility. As our analysis ensues, we show that by changing the informational environment in which a union negotiates with an employer, capital mobility can eliminate at least partly the need for wasteful strike induced unemployment, and raise the welfare of the union.

This paper provides the theoretical underpinnings that can aid in the understanding of a small but growing empirical literature on the relationship between the strike-proneness and foreign ownership.[3] Both at the industry level (Creigh and Makeham, 1978), and at the firm level (Cousineau et al., 1991; Enderwick and Buckley, 1982; Forsyth, 1973; Gennard and Steuer, 1971; Kelly and Brannick, 1988; Millward, 1979; and Budd, 1994), where so far the results have been mixed with some showing that foreign-owned firms are more strike-prone (Enderwick and Buckley, 1982; Forsyth, 1973; Kelly and Brannick, 1988), less strike-prone (Cousineau et al., 1991; Gennard and Steuer, 1971), or not significantly different from their locally owned counterparts (Budd, 1994; Creigh and Makeham, 1978; Millward, 1979; Ng and Maki, 1988). None of these papers attempt to control for the possible correlation between firm level productivity at origin and at the host country, which, based on our study, can potentially shed light on these mixed empirical findings.

This paper is also related to a recent literature on the role of firm heterogeneity in foreign direct investment is the subject of interest in a number of recent studies. See for example, Helpman et al. (2004), which models foreign direct investment by assuming that a more productive firm at home is automatically more productive abroad. Bagwell and Staiger (2003) shows that when there is informational asymmetry about costs among rival multinationals, foreign direct investment decisions will be based not just on the impact on actual costs, but also on the perception of cost held by rivals. Neither of these studies directly deal with the question of labor disputes subsequent to capital mobility, which is the subject of this paper.

Finally, this paper complements a series of recent studies on the role of union bargaining power in the host country as a determinant of foreign direct investment (Naylor, 2003, Naylor and Santoni, 2003) depending on whether wage bargaining is centralized or decentralized (Bughin and Vannini, 1995; Cooke, 1997; Cooke and Noble, 1998; Traxler and Woitech, 2000). Mezzetti and Dinopoulos (1991) shows that the international mobility of multinational production improves the fall back position of the firm, and thus leads to a lower negotiated wage with the union. Zhao (1995) extends this line of reasoning and finds that firms' incentives to invest abroad are enhanced precisely because of the impact the mobility of production can have on the negotiated wage. Eckel and Egger (2009) revisits this question in a setting with heterogeneous firms where firms self-select into those that engage in FDI, and those that do not, and confirm the existence of wage advantages that a production facility abroad can confer to the multinational. This paper complements this literature by introducing a setting where wage and employment outcomes are subject to information asymmetry, and where strikes do occur in equilibrium.

The rest of the paper is organized as follows. Section 2 introduces the basic notation and model. Sections 3–5 derive the basic results. Section 6 concludes.

2. The Model

Consider a firm and a union as the two parties of a labor dispute. There is asymmetric information in the sense that the true productivity of the firm at home and the true productivity of the firm abroad are both unknown to the union. What is known to the union, however, is the correlation between the productivity of the firm at home and abroad. This correlation, which we will refer to as the degree of home bias of the productivity of capital, is assumed to take on one among a wide range of values. Within this basic setting, we assume, as in Card (1990), that the union fashions a wage–employment schedule that elicits truth-telling on the part of the firm based on the schedule of strike duration that the wage–employment schedule implies. Our objective is to compare the employment, strike, and wage outcomes of this problem with and without capital mobility.

In what follows, we first address the two central issues already discussed in the introduction: (i) the nature the firm's labor demand adjusted for capital mobility, and (ii) the information environment facing the two parties depending on capital mobility. These will inform the design of the wage–employment schedule that elicits truth-telling in the presence of capital mobility in section 3. We then compare the employment and strike outcomes with the solution to the union's problem without capital mobility in section 4. In section 5, we discuss the change in wage bill and profits with and without capital mobility.

Mobility Adjusted Labor Demand

The firm is endowed with $\bar{K}$ units of capital, and hires laborers from a pool of labor union members to produce an output. We assume that the firm faces an exogenous price for its output, normalized to unity. Let $R(\sigma, k, \ell) = \sigma k^{\beta}\ell^{\alpha}$ denote the revenue function, with α, $\beta \subset (0,1)$ and $\alpha + \beta < 1$. $\sigma > 0$ denotes the productivity of the firm. The range of σ is given by $[\underline{\sigma}, \bar{\sigma}]$.

The labor union is made up of $\mathcal{L}$ members, each with one unit of labor time. A contract between the union and the firm stipulates a wage–employment pair, respectively, w and ℓ, where $w/\mathcal{L}$ denotes wage per union member. Each union member earns a reservation wage income, to be denoted as $\bar{W}$, in the event of unemployment. The preferences of the labor union are represented by a utility function that embodies the full income of all $\mathcal{L}$ number of union members, $U(w,\ell)=w+\bar{W}(\mathcal{L}-\ell)$. We use lowercase ℓ and w to indicate the values of employment and wage bill in the presence of capital mobility, and uppercase L and W to indicate these same values in the absence of capital mobility. Thus, without capital mobility, union welfare will be denoted as $U(W,L)=W+\bar{W}(\mathcal{L}-L)$.

Let us begin with the simplest problem with capital immobility, and perfect information. Here, endowed with information about the productivity of the firm, and the knowledge that capital will always remain in the home country, the union makes a wage–employment offer that maximizes union welfare $U(W,L)=W+\bar{W}(\mathcal{L}-L)$ subject to the constraint that the firm's profit is non-negative. This individual rationality constraint can be stated as:

$$R(\sigma,\bar{K},L)-W\geq 0.$$

Accounting for this constraint in maximizing union welfare $U(W,L)=W+\bar{W}(\mathcal{L}-L)$, the level of employment (L_0) that maximizes the $U(W,L)$ equates the reservation wage $\bar{W}$ with the marginal value product of labor $R_L(\sigma,\bar{K},L)\equiv V(\sigma,\bar{K},L)=\alpha\sigma L^{\alpha-1}\bar{K}^{\beta}$ at

$$L_0(\sigma,\bar{K})=\{L|\bar{W}=V(\sigma,\bar{K},L)\}=\left(\frac{\alpha\sigma\bar{K}^{\beta}}{\bar{W}}\right)^{\frac{1}{1-\alpha}}. \tag{1}$$

The corresponding union welfare maximizing wage proposal follows directly from the individual rationality constraint as $W_0=R(\sigma,\bar{K},L_0(\sigma,\bar{K}))$. Thus, with capital immobility and perfect information, it is to the best interest of the union to maximize the "size of the pie" by selecting an efficient level of employment, which equates the marginal value product of labor with the reservation wage $\bar{W}$.

Let us now turn to the case where capital is internationally mobile, while retaining the assumption of perfect information. Here, the union proposes a wage–employment offer to the firm, with the knowledge that the firm is footloose, and can accordingly relocate its capital upon receiving the union proposal. To examine this possibility, we introduce more structure to the model, and let demand for capital in the rest of the world be perfectly elastic, offering unit returns $r_\sigma^*=r^*\sigma^\delta$, with $r^*>0$, for capital originating from firms with productivity σ in the home country.[4] We assume throughout that parameters $\bar{W}$, $\bar{K}$, and r^* take on values that permit outward foreign investment, with $\partial R(\sigma,K,\ell)/\partial K|_{K=\bar{K}}=R_K(\sigma,\bar{K},\ell)\leq r_\sigma^*$, when employment level (ℓ) in the home country equates the marginal value product of labor with the opportunity cost of labor $\bar{W}$.[5]

δ denotes the location specificity of capital in the production process. The value of δ is of clear interest since it governs the nature of selection among employers with different productivity types in their relative incentive to export jobs abroad. When $\delta=0$, for example, all employers regardless of productivity type (σ) at home are equally productive abroad, earning r^*. As δ rises, rising productivity at home implies rising productivity abroad.[6] In Appendix A, we provide two very simple examples, in which δ is shown to be respectively strictly greater than, and equal to unity, depending simply on the elasticity of substitution between capital and foreign labor.[7] More specifically, define

Definition 1. *The productivity of capital exhibits home bias if and only if*

$$\delta = \frac{\partial \log r_\sigma^*(\bar{K}-k)}{\partial \log \sigma} < \frac{\partial \log R(\sigma, k, \ell)}{\partial \log \sigma} = 1.$$

Thus, when the productivity of capital is subject to home bias ($\delta < 1$), raising the productivity of the firm, σ, leads to higher (proportionate) revenue gains at home than abroad.

As stated earlier, the sequence of events begins with a union initiated wage–employment proposal in the first stage. In the second stage, the firm allocates capital between the home country (k) and the rest of the world ($\bar{K}-k$), taking union employment ℓ, and wage proposal w as given. Beginning our analysis from the second stage, the restricted home profit function of the firm $\pi(\sigma, \ell)$ is given by the maximal home revenue net of opportunity cost of capital, $R(\sigma, k, \ell) - r_\sigma^* k$ by choice of k, with

$$\pi(\sigma, \ell) \equiv \max_k \{R(\sigma, k, \ell) - r_\sigma^* k\}. \tag{2}$$

Let $k^*(\sigma, \ell)$ denote the capital allocation that solves the above problem, with

$$k^*(\sigma, \ell) = \arg\max_k \{R(\sigma, k, \ell) - r_\sigma^* k\} = \left(\frac{\beta \sigma \ell^\alpha}{r_\sigma^*}\right)^{\frac{1}{1-\beta}}. \tag{3}$$

Substituting into (2), the restricted home profit function is given by

$$\begin{aligned} \pi(\sigma, \ell) &\equiv R(\sigma, k^*(\sigma, \ell), \ell) - r_\sigma^* k^*(\sigma, \ell), \\ &= (1-\beta)\left(\sigma \left(\frac{\beta}{r_\sigma^*}\right)^\beta \ell^\alpha\right)^{\frac{1}{1-\beta}}. \end{aligned} \tag{4}$$

By standard arguments, the restricted home profit function is increasing and quasi-convex in σ. Meanwhile, π is decreasing and quasi-concave in $r_\sigma^* = r^* \sigma^\delta$. Since both of these effects depend critically on σ, we rearrange the restricted home profit function to highlight the key role of the location specificity of capital by defining:

$$\begin{aligned} \pi(\sigma, \ell) &= \phi \ell^{\frac{\alpha}{1-\beta}}. \\ \phi \equiv \phi(\sigma) &= (1-\beta)\left(\sigma^{1-\delta\beta}\left(\frac{\beta}{r^*}\right)^\beta\right)^{\frac{1}{1-\beta}} \end{aligned} \tag{5}$$

will henceforth be referred to as the mobility-adjusted productivity of the firm in the home country. As may be expected, ϕ rises with σ if and only if productivity improvements lead to proportionate revenue gains abroad that are not too much higher than that attainable in the home country. This requires $\delta < 1/\beta$.

The mobility adjusted productivity of the firm determines (i) the restricted profit of the firm at home, (ii) the value of marginal product of labor in the home country, (iii) employment level and (iv) total profits of the firm in much the same way as σ does in the absence of capital mobility. To see this, we have already noted in equation (5) that given ℓ, restricted profit at home $\pi(\cdot)=\phi\ell^{\alpha/(1-\beta)}$ rises proportionately with $\phi>0$. Similarly, the marginal value product of labor $v(\cdot)=\partial\pi(\sigma,k^*,\ell)/\partial\ell$ in the home country adjusted for capital mobility is given by

$$\begin{aligned} v(\phi,\ell) &= R_\ell(\sigma,k^*,\ell)+(R_K(\sigma,k^*,\ell)-r_\sigma^*)\frac{\partial k^*}{\partial\ell} \\ &= V(\sigma,k^*,\ell)+(R_K(\sigma,k^*,\ell)-r_\sigma^*)\frac{\partial k^*}{\partial\ell}. \end{aligned}$$

Once again using lowercase to denote capital mobility and uppercase to denote capital immobility, the marginal value product of labor with capital mobility $v(\phi,\ell)$ is made of two parts. The first part is the *ceteris paribus* marginal value product of labor when capital is immobile, $V(\sigma,k^*,\ell)$, given the amount of capital employed at home k^*:

$$V(\sigma,k^*,\ell)=\alpha\sigma\ell^{\alpha-1}(k^*)^\beta \tag{6}$$

evaluated at the restricted home profit maximizing $k^*=k^*(\sigma,\ell)$.

The second part, $(R_K(\sigma,k^*,\ell)-r_\sigma^*)\frac{\partial k^*}{\partial\ell}$, accounts for any profit impact of changing home country labor employment on profit maximizing capital allocation in the home country, k^*. From equation (2), $R_K(\sigma,k^*,\ell)$ will be set at r_σ^* because of profit maximization and hence

$$\begin{aligned} v(\phi,\ell) &= V(\sigma,k^*(\sigma,\ell),\ell) \\ &= \frac{\alpha}{1-\beta}\phi\ell^{\frac{\alpha}{1-\beta}-1} \end{aligned} \tag{7}$$

and like the monotonic relationship between σ and $V(\sigma,k^*,\ell)$ when capital is immobile, the mobility adjusted $v(\phi,\ell)$ rises proportionately with ϕ as well.

We are now in a position to examine the union's problem in the first stage, which involves the determination of a wage–employment offer that maximizes union wage income $w+\bar{W}(\mathcal{L}-\ell)$, subject to the constraint that the firm's total profit, while operating at least partially at home, is no less than if the firm allocates all $\bar{K}$ units of capital abroad, or:

$$R(\sigma,k^*,\ell)-w+r_\sigma^*(\bar{K}-k^*(\sigma,\ell))\geq r_\sigma^*\bar{K}.$$

Accounting for this constraint, the level of employment (ℓ_0) that maximizes the union's welfare equates the reservation wage with the *mobility adjusted marginal value product of labor*, $v(\phi,\ell)$. From equation (7), therefore,

$$\ell_0(\phi)=\{\ell|\bar{W}=v(\phi,\ell)\}=\left(\frac{\alpha\phi}{(1-\beta)\bar{W}}\right)^{\frac{1-\beta}{1-\alpha-\beta}}. \tag{8}$$

It follows that the union's employment choice continues to be efficient, in the sense that it equates the union reservation wage $\bar{W}$ with the marginal value product of labor, now adjusted for the possibility of capital reallocation that occurs conditional on the union proposal.

Comparing employment with (ℓ_0) and without (L_0) openness, but with perfect information throughout, three points are evident. First, it can be easily verified that whenever $R_K(\sigma, \bar{K}, L_0(\sigma, \bar{K})) \leq r_\sigma^*$, so that outward foreign direct investment is profitable, $L_0(\sigma, \bar{K}) \geq \ell_0(\phi)$. In other words, capital outflow leads inevitably to a decline in employment in a perfect information setting. Second, ℓ_0 and L_0 are respectively increasing in ϕ and σ, confirming the similar roles played by ϕ and σ in determining employment levels with and without openness. Third, note also from (6) and (7) that the implied price elasticity of labor demand changes discretely with openness. In the absence of information asymmetry, our setup is thus consistent with Rodrik (1997), in that the implied price elasticity of labor demand is higher when capital is mobile $((1-\beta)/(1-\alpha-\beta))$ than when it is not $(1/(1-\alpha))$.

Finally, the total profit function of the firm is simply

$$R(\sigma, k^*, \ell) - w + r_\sigma^*(\bar{K} - k^*(\sigma, \ell)) = \phi \ell^{\frac{\alpha}{1-\beta}} - w + r^* \sigma^\delta \bar{K}, \tag{9}$$

where ϕ plays once again a key role, and pins down in particular how total profit to be attributed to production in the home country depends on the productivity of the firm σ. These observations prompt us to define

DEFINITION 2. *Foreign direct investment gives rise to productivity rank reversal in the home country if and only if ϕ is strictly decreasing with respect to σ, or equivalently, if and only if $\delta > 1/\beta$.*

In the sequel, we will focus solely on the case wherein foreign direct investment does not give rise to productivity rank reversal. The case where δ is greater than $1/\beta$ is analogous, and can be similarly worked out. Any key modifications that may be required will be noted in what follows.

Mobility Adjusted Informational Environment

We turn now to a description of the informational environment facing workers and employers. In particular, while the firm is perfectly aware of its productivity type, the union's belief on σ is represented by a cumulative probability distribution function $F(\sigma)$ on $[\underline{\sigma}, \bar{\sigma}]$, with an associated density function $F'(\sigma) = f(\sigma) > 0$. Also let the hazard rate $f(\sigma)/(1 - F(\sigma))$, or equivalently, the elasticity of the incidence of high productivity firms with respect to σ ($\varepsilon^f(\sigma) \equiv -(d \log(1 - F(\sigma)))/d \log \sigma$), be increasing in σ.[8]

By definition of the mobility adjusted productivity ϕ in (5), with

$$\phi = (1-\beta)\left(\sigma^{1-\delta\beta}\left(\frac{\beta}{r^*}\right)^\beta\right)^{\frac{1}{1-\beta}}$$

the induced cumulative distribution function and the density function of the mobility adjusted productivity of the firm ϕ, $G(\phi)$ and $g(\phi)$, are given respectively by[9]

$$G(\phi) = F\left(\left(\frac{\phi}{(1-\beta)\left(\frac{\beta}{r^*}\right)^\beta}\right)^{\frac{1-\beta}{1-\delta\beta}}\right), \quad g(\phi) = \frac{\partial G(\phi)}{\partial \phi}. \tag{10}$$

While the productivity σ ranges from $[\underline{\sigma},\bar{\sigma}]$, the corresponding range of ϕ, $[\underline{\phi},\bar{\phi}]$, is just $\left[(1-\beta)\left(\underline{\sigma}^{1-\delta\beta}\left(\frac{\beta}{r^*}\right)^{\beta}\right)^{\frac{1}{1-\beta}},(1-\beta)\left(\bar{\sigma}^{1-\delta\beta}\left(\frac{\beta}{r^*}\right)^{\beta}\right)^{\frac{1}{1-\beta}}\right]$. The associated elasticity $-d\log(1-G(\phi))/d\log\phi$ will be denoted as $\varepsilon^g(\phi)$.

By inspection, the spread of the mobility adjustment productivity of capital $[\underline{\phi},\bar{\phi}]$, as well as the elasticity of the incidence of high (mobility adjusted) productivity firms $\varepsilon^g(\phi)$, both depend critically on the location specificity of capital, δ. These expressions, in turn, reveal the extent of informational asymmetry that the union faces, or equivalently the information advantage of the firm. Making use of (10), we have the following result:

Lemma 1.

(1) *As δ increases, the size of the range of mobility adjusted productivity levels, $\bar{\phi}-\underline{\phi}$, decreases. At the limit, as δ tends to $1/\beta$, $G(\phi,\delta)$ puts unit mass on $\phi=(1-\beta)(\beta/r^*)^{\frac{\beta}{1-\beta}}$.*

(2) *If and only if $\delta\geq 1$, so that the productivity of capital does not exhibit home bias, the elasticity of the incidence of high productivity firms (ε^g) is higher with the introduction of openness, than without (ε^f) for given σ*

$$\varepsilon^g(\phi(\sigma))=\frac{1-\beta}{1-\delta\beta}\left(\frac{\sigma f(\sigma)}{1-F(\sigma)}\right)\geq\varepsilon^f(\sigma).$$

At the limit, as δ tends to $1/\beta$, $1/\varepsilon^g(\phi(\sigma))=0$ for all $\sigma\in[\underline{\sigma},\bar{\sigma}]$.

Whenever δ is greater than unity, the implied location specificity of the productivity of capital favors the investment of capital by relatively high productivity firms in the foreign country, or low productivity firms at home. This effectively weakens the informational advantage of high productivity firms, with a corresponding narrowing of the range $[\underline{\phi},\bar{\phi}]$, and a higher elasticity of the incidence of firms with high *mobility adjusted productivity* subsequent to openness. Analytically, this shows up in the form a restricted home profit function that is strictly concave in σ (equation (2)). Indeed, as δ tends to $1/\beta$, productivity differences of capital in the home country are exactly balanced by productivity differences abroad. The union thus effectively operates in an environment where information asymmetry is no longer an issue, and $G(\phi)$ puts unit mass on $(1-\beta)(\beta/r^*)^{\frac{\beta}{1-\beta}}$, even though the true value of σ remains unknown to the union.

However, if δ is less than unity indicating relatively strong home bias, low productivity firms are more likely to export higher amounts of capital abroad. In sharp contrast, therefore, home bias strengthens the informational advantage of high productivity firms. This is indicated by a widening of the range of mobility adjusted productivity, $[\underline{\phi},\bar{\phi}]$, a lower elasticity $\varepsilon^g(\sigma)$ subsequent to openness as shown in Lemma 1.

Figure 1 illustrates, and plots the relationship between $\phi(\sigma)=(1-\beta)\left(\sigma^{1-\delta\beta}\left(\frac{\beta}{r^*}\right)^{\beta}\right)^{\frac{1}{1-\beta}}$ and σ, depending on home bias, and accordingly the range of the mobility adjusted

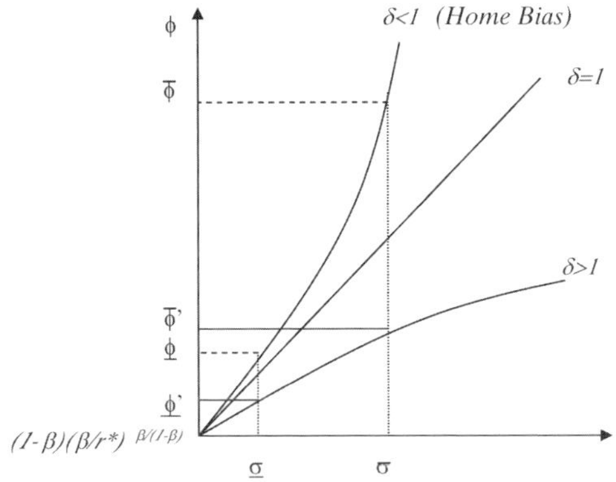

Figure 1. Mobility Adjusted Productivity With or Without Home Bias

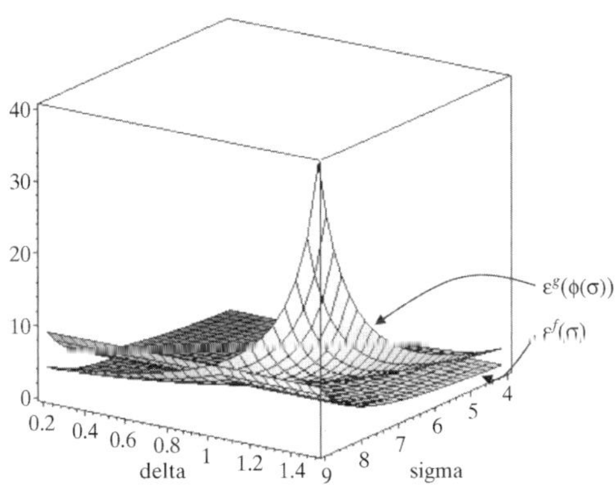

Figure 2. Information Imperfection With or Without Capital Mobility

productivity of the firm $[\underline{\phi}-\overline{\phi}]$. Assuming, for example, that the cumulative distribution function $F(\sigma)$ is uniform and $\beta = 0.6$,[10] Figure 2 plots the elasticity of the induced cumulative distribution function $G(\phi(\sigma))$, $\varepsilon^g(\phi(\sigma))$, as well as $\varepsilon^f(\sigma)$ as a function of both δ and σ. As shown in Lemma 1, $\varepsilon^g \geq (<) \varepsilon^f$ whenever there is home bias, or when $\delta \geq (<)1$. In addition, as δ tends to $1/\beta = 1.666$ in this simulation, ε^g tends to infinity as expected.

3. Labor Dispute with a Footloose Industry

In the rest of this paper, we utilize the insights of our analysis developed up to now to examine the consequences of capital mobility in labor disputes with asymmetric information. The sequence of events is the same as before: the union begins with a wage-employment proposal in the first stage.[11] In the presence of information asymmetry, the union proposal is in the form of a wage–employment schedule, one for each mobility adjusted productivity of capital. In the second stage, the firm may (i) accept the union offer by selecting one pairing of wage and employment along the union proposed schedule, and adjust its allocation of capital conditional on this choice of union offer, or (ii) reject the union offer in which case no output will be produced and workers resort to their reservation employment income, and adjust its allocation of capital conditional on a negotiation breakdown with the union.

Define $w(\phi)$ and $\ell(\phi)$ as the wage and employment schedules to be proposed by the union, targeting a firm with mobility adjusted productivity type ϕ. Also let $y(\phi, \hat{\phi})$ be the variable part of the profit function in (9), when a firm with mobility adjusted productivity ϕ chooses a union contract that targets $\hat{\phi}$:

$$y(\phi, \hat{\phi}) = \phi \ell(\hat{\phi})^{\frac{\alpha}{1-\beta}} - w(\hat{\phi}), \quad y(\phi, \phi) = y(\phi).$$

In the presence of a wage–employment schedule that elicits truth-telling, a firm with mobility adjusted productivity ϕ willingly chooses a union contract $(w(\phi), \ell(\phi))$ that targets ϕ. Accordingly, define $\ell_0(\phi) - \ell(\phi)$ as the extent of equilibrium strike induced unemployment in the presence of capital mobility. Thus, the amount of time that a union spends on strikes is defined as the increase in union unemployment to elicit truth-telling ($(L - \ell(\phi)) - (L - \ell_0(\phi))$, over and above the efficient level of unemployment which would otherwise occur in a perfect information setting (section 2). To determine the equilibrium duration of strikes, we appeal to the revelation principle, which requires that a contract that elicits truth-telling satisfies (i) incentive compatibility, and (ii) individual rationality.

In particular, incentive compatibility requires that for any two distinct mobility adjusted productivity levels, ϕ and $\hat{\phi}$, the firm with mobility adjusted productivity ϕ prefers $(w(\phi), \ell(\phi))$ to $(w(\hat{\phi}), \ell(\hat{\phi}))$, and the firm with mobility adjusted productivity $\hat{\phi}$ prefers $(w(\hat{\phi}), \ell(\hat{\phi}))$ to $(w(\phi), \ell(\phi))$. Equivalently, the variable profit of the firm is higher with truth-telling:

$$y(\phi) \geq y(\phi, \hat{\phi}), \quad y(\hat{\phi}) \geq y(\hat{\phi}, \phi),$$

or,

$$(\phi - \hat{\phi}) \ell(\phi)^{\frac{\alpha}{1-\beta}} \geq y(\phi) - y(\hat{\phi}) \geq (\phi - \hat{\phi}) \ell(\hat{\phi})^{\frac{\alpha}{1-\beta}}. \tag{11}$$

Thus, employment is strictly higher in firms with higher mobility adjusted productivity: $\phi > \hat{\phi} \Rightarrow \ell(\phi) > \ell(\hat{\phi})$. In addition, the variable profit function $y(\phi)$ consistent with incentive compatibility is convex in ϕ, differentiable almost everywhere from (11), and satisfies the follow property:

$$\dot{y}(\phi) = \ell(\phi)^{\frac{\alpha}{1-\beta}}. \tag{12}$$

Turning now to individual rationality with capital mobility, a firm with mobility adjusted productivity ϕ should earn no less profit operating at least in part at home compared with locating abroad altogether, or,

$$
\begin{aligned}
R(\sigma, k^*(\sigma, \ell(\phi)), \ell(\phi)) - w(\phi) + r_\sigma^*(\bar{K} - k^*(\sigma, \ell(\phi))) &\geq r_\sigma^* \bar{K} \\
\Leftrightarrow \phi \ell(\phi)^{\frac{\alpha}{1-\beta}} - w(\phi) &\geq 0 \\
\Leftrightarrow y(\phi) &\geq 0
\end{aligned}
$$

requiring thus that variable profit $y(\phi)$ is non-negative. Note that individual rationality for the firm with the lowest mobility adjusted productivity $\phi = \underline{\phi}$, along with incentive compatibility, is sufficient for individuality rationality for $\phi > \underline{\phi}$, since

$$
\begin{aligned}
&\underline{\phi}\ell(\underline{\phi})^{\frac{\alpha}{1-\beta}} - w(\underline{\phi}) + r^* \underline{\sigma}^\delta \bar{K} \geq r^* \underline{\sigma}^\delta \bar{K} \\
&\quad \Leftrightarrow 0 \leq y(\underline{\phi}) \leq y(\phi, \underline{\phi}) \leq y(\phi),
\end{aligned}
$$

for any $\phi \geq \underline{\phi}$.

The optimization problem of the union is thus subject to four constraints: (I) $y(\underline{\phi}) \geq 0$; (II) $\dot{y}(\phi) - \ell(\phi)^{\frac{\alpha}{1-\beta}}$; (III) $\ell(\phi)$ is non-decreasing in ϕ, and finally, (IV) $\ell(\phi) \leq L$. As will become apparent in the sequel, constraints (III) and (IV) are not binding. Thus, the Hamiltonian for the optimal control problem of the union is simply:

$$
H = \left(\phi \ell^{\frac{\alpha}{1-\beta}} + \bar{W}(L - \ell) - y \right) g(\phi) + \eta(\phi) \ell^{\frac{\alpha}{1-\beta}}, \tag{13}
$$

where $\eta(\phi)$ is the costate variable. The necessary conditions for optimization are given by the following:

$$
\frac{\alpha}{1-\beta} \ell(\phi)^{\frac{\alpha}{1-\beta}-1} (\phi + \eta(\phi)) - \bar{W} = 0
$$

$$
-\eta'(\phi) = -g(\phi)
$$

$$
\eta(\bar{\phi}) = 1.
$$

Routine manipulations yield the following expression that gives the employment schedule in the optimal contract:

$$
\frac{\alpha}{1-\beta} \phi \ell(\phi)^{\frac{\alpha}{1-\beta}-1} \left(1 - \frac{1}{\varepsilon^g(\phi)} \right) = \bar{W}. \tag{14}
$$

Thus, the solution to the union's problem drives a wedge between the marginal value product of labor, as shown in equation (7), and the reservation wage of the union. The size of this wedge depends on the elasticity $\varepsilon^g(\phi)$.

Recall that employment in the absence of information asymmetry ($\ell_0(\phi)$)—one which allows the union to equate the opportunity cost of employment with the firm $\bar{W}$ and the derived (inverse) demand for labor $v(\phi, \ell)$—is simply

$$
\ell_0(\phi) = \left(\frac{\alpha}{1-\beta} \frac{\phi}{\bar{W}} \right)^{\frac{1-\beta}{1-\alpha-\beta}}.
$$

It thus follows that for the firm with the highest mobility adjusted productivity, employment level is efficiently set by the union with

$$\ell(\bar{\phi}) = \left(\frac{\alpha}{1-\beta}\frac{\bar{\phi}}{\bar{W}}\right)^{\frac{1-\beta}{1-\alpha-\beta}} = \ell_0(\bar{\phi})$$

as $G(\bar{\phi}) = 1$ and thus $1/\varepsilon^g(\bar{\phi}) = 0$. Thus, for the firm with the highest mobility adjusted productivity, there will be no union initiated strikes.

Making use of the definition of $\ell_0(\phi)$, and that of ϕ, a more intuitive way of presenting $\ell(\bar{\phi})$ above can be had by a change of variables. In particular, denote $\ell^*(\sigma)$ as $\ell(\phi(\sigma))$, and $\ell_0^*(\sigma)$ as $\ell_0(\phi(\sigma))$. The definition of $G(\phi)$ can be used to yield a simplified expression for $\ell(\phi)$, with

$$\ell(\phi(\sigma)) = \ell^*(\sigma) = \ell_0^*(\sigma)\left(1 - \frac{1-\delta\beta}{1-\beta}\frac{1}{\varepsilon^f(\sigma)}\right)^{\frac{1-\beta}{1-\alpha-\beta}}, \tag{15}$$

which states that total union employment is almost always only a fraction of that which can be achieved when information asymmetry is not an issue. Put differently, the extent of strike induced unemployment is given by:

$$\ell_0^*(\sigma) - \ell^*(\sigma) = \ell_0^*(\sigma)\left(1 - \left(1 - \frac{1-\delta\beta}{1-\beta}\frac{1}{\varepsilon^f(\sigma)}\right)^{\frac{1-\beta}{1-\alpha-\beta}}\right). \tag{16}$$

As shown in Lemma 1, the spread of the mobility adjusted productivity of the footloose firm decreases with δ. Correspondingly, strike induced unemployment is decreasing in δ, as shown in (16) above.

4. Openness and Union Employment

To examine how union employment changes with the mobility of capital, we require an analogous expression for union employment in the absence of capital mobility under information asymmetry. In addition, we also need to have a gauge on how the distortion induced by information asymmetry—in the form of a wedge between the marginal value product of labor and the reservation wage $\bar{W}$—ultimately feeds back to changes in employment levels with and without capital mobility.

But as may be expected, the problem of the union when capital is immobile is very similar. The details of the proof is thus relegated to Appendix B. We show that compared with the case with capital mobility, the solution to the union's problem with capital immobility has two main differences. First, the productivity level σ, rather than the mobility adjusted productivity ϕ serves as the relevant random variable. Second, the marginal value products of labor, with and without capital mobility, were expressed in equations (6) and (7) as

$$v(\phi) = \frac{\alpha}{1-\beta}\phi\ell^{\frac{\alpha}{1-\beta}-1}, \quad V(\sigma, \ell, k) = \alpha\sigma\ell^{\alpha-1}k^{\beta}.$$

Thus, as noted already, the price elasticity of the derived labor demand rises from $1/(1-\alpha)$ to $(1-\beta)/(1-\alpha-\beta)$, implying therefore a larger employment distortion owing to the same wage distortion, when capital market opens up. Specifically, let $L(\sigma)$ be the level of union employment that solves the optimal control problem of the union when capital is immobile, we have

$$L(\sigma) = L_0(\sigma)\left(1 - \frac{1}{\varepsilon^f(\sigma)}\right)^{\frac{1}{1-\alpha}} \leq L_0(\sigma). \tag{17}$$

To recall, $L_0(\sigma)$ is simply the level of union employment when both information asymmetry and capital mobility are absent (equation 1).

As in section 3, define $L_0(\sigma) - L(\sigma)$—the decline in employment solely because of labor contracting in the presence of information asymmetry—as the extent of strike induced unemployment in the absence of capital mobility. Since strike induced unemployment depends critically on the information advantage of the firm, the impact of openness on union employment $\ell^*(\sigma) - L(\sigma)$, should depend, among other things, on the extent to which openness impacts the informational advantage of the firm. To this end, we have the following result:

Proposition 1. *The change in union employment subsequent to openness when information is asymmetric is given by:*

$$\begin{aligned}\log \ell^*(\sigma) - \log L(\sigma) &= \log \ell_0^*(\sigma) - \log L_0(\sigma) \\ &\quad + \left(\frac{1-\beta}{1-\alpha-\beta} - \frac{1}{1-\alpha}\right)\log\left(1 - \frac{1}{\varepsilon^f(\sigma)}\right) \\ &\quad + \frac{1-\beta}{1-\beta-\alpha}\left(\log\left(1 - \frac{1-\delta\beta}{1-\beta}\frac{1}{\varepsilon^f(\sigma)}\right) - \log\left(1 - \frac{1}{\varepsilon^f(\sigma)}\right)\right).\end{aligned} \tag{18}$$

Thus, union employment may in fact increase with openness if δ is sufficiently large.

The change in union employment once the option of capital mobility opens depends on the interaction of three effects. First, $\log \ell_0^*(\sigma) - \log L_0(\sigma)$ represents the change in union employment when information asymmetry is not an issue. The size of this difference depends on whether there is excess supply of capital $\bar{K}$ in the home country, given r^* and $\bar{W}$. Second, since information asymmetry in effect drives a wedge between the reservation wage and the marginal product of labor, the more elastic is the demand for labor, the larger will be the corresponding impact on employment. Now, as the elasticity of demand for labor rises from $1/(1-\alpha)$ to $(1-\beta)/(1-\alpha-\beta)$ when the capital market opens up, this second effect has an unambiguous negative effect on the right-hand side of equation (16), since $1 - \frac{1}{\varepsilon^f(\sigma)} < 1$. Finally, openness can nevertheless imply a net positive impact on union employment, if the third term on the right hand side of equation (18), which represents the *informational* role of capital mobility, is sufficiently large.

In particular, if $\delta < 1$, and hence $\varepsilon^g(\phi(\sigma)) > \varepsilon^f(\sigma)$ (Lemma 1), the productivity of capital exhibits home bias. In turn, capital mobility strengthens the informational advantage of the firm, and union employment necessarily falls at given σ. If $\delta \geq 1$, however, the third term of the right-hand side of equation (18) is strictly positive. Clearly, the larger δ is, the more likely it is that employment can in fact increase with openness. The question, however, is whether there is a clearly identifiable range of δs that can accomplish this in equilibrium. To this end:

Proposition 2. *There exists $\delta^* \in (1,1/\beta)$ such that the proportionate change in employment as a result of capital mobility is larger in the presence of informational asymmetry than when information is perfect, or:*

$$\frac{\ell^*(\sigma)-L(\sigma)}{L(\sigma)} > \frac{\ell_0^*(\sigma)-L_0(\sigma)}{L_0(\sigma)}$$

for all δ greater than δ^*, and $\sigma<\bar{\sigma}$.

Proof. Making use of equations (15) and (17), it can be readily confirmed that $(\ell^*(\sigma)-L(\sigma))/L(\sigma)$ is strictly increasing in δ. Note, in addition, evaluated at $\delta=1/\beta$,

$$\frac{\ell^*(\sigma)-L(\sigma)}{L(\sigma)} - \frac{\ell_0^*(\sigma)-L_0(\sigma)}{L_0(\sigma)} = \frac{\ell_0^*(\sigma)}{L_0(\sigma)}\left[\frac{1}{\left(1-\frac{1}{\varepsilon^f(\sigma)}\right)^{\frac{1}{1-\alpha}}}-1\right]>0.$$

Evaluated at $\delta=1$,

$$\frac{\ell^*(\sigma)-L(\sigma)}{L(\sigma)} - \frac{\ell_0^*(\sigma)-L_0(\sigma)}{L_0(\sigma)} = \frac{\ell_0^*(\sigma)}{L_0(\sigma)}\left[\frac{\left(1-\frac{1}{\varepsilon^f(\sigma)}\right)^{\frac{1-\beta}{1-\alpha-\beta}}}{\left(1-\frac{1}{\varepsilon^f(\sigma)}\right)^{\frac{1}{1-\alpha}}}-1\right]<0.$$

The proposition thus follows from the intermediate value theorem.

Intuitively, Proposition 2 states that as long as δ is sufficiently large, and close to $1/\beta$, capital mobility deteriorates the informational advantage of the firm. Consequently, any reduction in employment owing to directly to the impact of capital mobility on capital allocation or the elasticity of labor demand is mediated by the informational role of capital mobility. It then follows that any proportionate change in employment owing to capital mobility is strictly *more positive* when information is asymmetry, than when information is perfect.

Furthermore, with proposition 1, the following observations are immediate.

Corollary 1. *If the productivity of capital exhibits home bias ($\delta<1$), openness can never increase union employment in the presence of information asymmetry.*

Corollary 2. *If $\ell_0^*(\sigma)=L_0(\sigma)$ when information asymmetry is not an issue, at the borderline case where the firm is indifferent about exporting jobs abroad since $R_K(\sigma,\bar{K},L_0(\sigma,\bar{K}))=r_\sigma^*$ with perfect information, then openness gives rise to*

(1) *strictly higher union employment when information is asymmetric*

$$\ell^*(\sigma) - L(\sigma) > 0$$

for all $\sigma < \bar{\sigma}$ *and* $\delta > \delta^*$, *despite the fact that*

(2) *equilibrium capital outflow is strictly positive,* $k(\sigma, \ell^*(\sigma)) < \bar{K}$ for $\sigma < \bar{\sigma}$.

Assuming $\ell_0^*(\sigma) = L_0(\sigma)$ as in Corollary 2, we have thus the following employment ranking in the two capital mobility and the two information regimes

$$L(\sigma) < \ell^*(\sigma) < \ell_0^*(\sigma) = L_0(\sigma).$$

Since information asymmetry leads to a reduction in employment given any one of the two capital mobility regimes, $L(\sigma) < L_0(\sigma)$ and $\ell^*(\sigma) < \ell_0^*(\sigma)$. However, since $\delta > \delta^*$, capital mobility reduces the degree of information asymmetry confronting the union. Indeed, the conditions of Corollary 2 guarantee that employment rises with capital mobility in the presence of information asymmetry, or, $L(\sigma) < \ell^*(\sigma)$.

The second observation in the proposition follows upon substituting the expression for $\ell^*(\sigma)$ into $k(\sigma, \ell)$. Since strike induced unemployment ($\ell^*(\sigma) < \ell_0^*(\sigma)$) decreases the returns to capital in the home country, there is strictly positive capital outflow even when none exists in the absence of asymmetric information.

5. Openness, Profits and Wages

Consider now the profit of the firm. Constraint (II), equation (14), and the definition of $y(\phi)$ jointly imply that total profit is equal to

$$y(\phi(\sigma)) + r^*\sigma^\delta \bar{K} \equiv y^*(\sigma) + + r^*\sigma^\delta \bar{K} = \int_{\underline{\sigma}}^{\sigma} \frac{1-\delta\beta}{1-\beta} \ell^*(t)^{\frac{\alpha}{1-\beta}} \frac{\phi(t)}{t} dt + + r^*\sigma^\delta \bar{K}. \quad (19)$$

Meanwhile, total union wage earning is given, from the individual rationality constraint, by:

$$w^*(\sigma) = \phi(\sigma)\ell^*(\sigma)^{\frac{\alpha}{1-\beta}} - y^*(\sigma). \quad (20)$$

As should be apparent, the location specificity of capital is key here once again. In particular, as δ tends to $1/\beta$, informational asymmetry effectively vanishes, and $y(\phi(\sigma))$ accordingly tends to zero, for any firm type σ. Thus,

PROPOSITION 3. *As* δ *increases and tends to* $1/\beta$,

(1) *total profits of the firm approaches* $r_\sigma^* \bar{K}$ *for all* $\sigma \in [\underline{\sigma}, \bar{\sigma}]$,

(2) *the welfare of union members approaches the perfect information benchmark with capital mobility,* $w_0^*(\sigma) + \bar{W}(\mathcal{L} - \ell_0^*(\sigma))$,

The first part of the proposition follows by inspection of equation (19). The second part of the proposition follows since $y^*(\sigma) = 0$ when $\delta = 1/\beta$, and $\ell^*(\sigma) = \ell_0(\sigma)$ from equation (15), so that employment level reverts back to the no informational asymmetry level. More generally, however, the wage (and hence profit) impact of openness depends on the interaction of the following effects:

PROPOSITION 4. *In the absence of productivity rank reversal, the change in union wage income subsequent to openness is given by:*

$$\begin{aligned}\log w^*(\sigma) - \log W(\sigma) = {}& \log w_0^*(\sigma) - \log W_0(\sigma) \\ & + \left(\frac{\alpha}{1-\alpha-\beta} - \frac{1}{1-\alpha}\right)\log\left(1 - \frac{1}{\varepsilon^f(\sigma)}\right) \\ & + \frac{\alpha}{1-\beta-\alpha}\left(\log\left(1 - \frac{1-\delta\beta}{1-\beta}\frac{1}{\varepsilon^f(\sigma)}\right) - \log\left(1 - \frac{1}{\varepsilon^f(\sigma)}\right)\right) \\ & + \log\left(1 - \frac{1-\delta\beta}{1-\beta}\int_{\underline{\sigma}}^{\sigma}\left(\frac{t}{\sigma}\right)^{\frac{1-\delta\beta}{1-\alpha-\beta}}\frac{1}{t}\Omega^g(t)dt\right) \\ & - \log\left(1 - \int_{\underline{\sigma}}^{\sigma}\left(\frac{t}{\sigma}\right)^{\frac{1}{1-\alpha}}\frac{1}{t}\Omega^f(t)dt\right) \end{aligned} \quad (21)$$

$$\Omega^g(t) = \left(\left(1 - \frac{1-\delta\beta}{1-\beta}\frac{1}{\varepsilon^f(t)}\right)\Big/\left(1 - \frac{1-\delta\beta}{1-\beta}\frac{1}{\varepsilon^f(\sigma)}\right)\right)^{\alpha/(1-\alpha-\beta)} < 1$$

and

$$\Omega^f(t)) = \left(\left(1 - \frac{1}{\varepsilon^f(t)}\right)\Big/\left(1 - \frac{1}{\varepsilon^f(\sigma)}\right)\right)^{\alpha/(1-\alpha)} < 1.$$

Thus, the change in union wage earnings once the option of capital mobility opens depends on the interaction of four effects. The first three of these effects are analogous to the factors governing the corresponding change in union employment displayed in Proposition 2. In particular, $\log w_0^*(\sigma) - \log W_0(\sigma)$ represents the change in wage earnings in the absence of information asymmetry. As discussed, this is unambiguously negative as soon as the option of capital mobility opens up. The second effect is likewise strictly negative, as higher labor demand elasticity in the presence of capital mobility exacerbates the negative output impact of the proportionate wage gap $1 - 1/\varepsilon^f(\sigma)$. The third effect concerns the size of the wage gap required to elicit truth-telling, and is strictly negative (positive) whenever the productivity of capital exhibits (does not exhibit) home bias.

A final effect (the last two terms in equation (21)) concerns the informational rent of the firm, $y^*(\sigma)$ and $Y(\sigma)$. In particular, if $\delta = 1/\beta$, capital mobility deprives the firm completely of its informational advantage, and the difference displayed in the last two terms of equation (21) is strictly positive.

6. Conclusion

It has long been recognized that greater openness in foreign investment regimes is likely to disadvantage workers in their negotiations with employers because it increases the elasticity of labor demand. This paper has highlighted a hitherto underappreciated informational role of openness in affecting wage and employment outcomes in a world of asymmetric information. Openness can reduce or increase the variability of the marginal value product of labor curve, and hence the informational rent that the firm can extract from the union. Whether it does so or not depends crucially on whether the most productive firms domestically are also the most likely to move jobs abroad, or equivalently, if foreign returns to capital is highly positively correlated with domestic returns to capital.

If foreign returns are indeed such that the most productive firms are also those with the most incentive to invest abroad, we show that openness to foreign investment will reduce the spread of MVPL and hence improve the outcome for workers in a world with asymmetric information. This effect will counteract the conventional negative effect on workers of an increase in the elasticity of the MVPL curve as a result of greater openness. However, if foreign returns to capital favor the outflow of capital from only the least productive firms, then the spread of MVPL increases and workers are disadvantaged all round by greater openness.

Apart from bringing together capital mobility, incentive compatibility and the economics of labor disputes together in a way that they are not usually brought together, our analysis has highlighted the importance of home bias of capital—the precise relationship between domestic returns and foreign returns in a cross section of firms. By disentangling the potential elasticity and informational consequences of capital mobility, our framework can be readily employed to decompose and flesh out comparative labor market consequences of footloose industry in a variety of more nuanced contexts. In particular, a regime change in an economy going from full capital immobility to full capital mobility can in general entail both the aforementioned elasticity and informational effects on labor market outcomes. In contrast, a regime change going from capital mobility to a select group of countries, to capital mobility with a larger selection of host countries of foreign direct investment, may have drastically different implications, depending specifically on whether relatively high or low productivity firms are systematically selected in the group of firms that export jobs to the newly emerging host countries of investment.

With these general lessons in mind, our analysis can be extended to incorporate other, to date, rarely studied factors that may ultimately impact the wage and unemployment outcome of labor disputes in the presence of footloose industries. To name one such example, while the impact of taxation on the location of firms has been a longstanding area of active research,[12] the importance of international differences in the *progressivity* of corporate tax rates, for example, in impacting the wage and unemployment outcomes of labor disputes in the presence of footloose industries remains a largely open question, but such differences in tax rate progressivities can readily translate to differential degrees of correlation between foreign and domestic returns on capital as highlighted in this paper. The precise manner in which corporate taxation can indeed contribute to determining the outcomes of labor disputes is an interesting area of future research.

Appendix A

In this Appendix, we illustrate with two simple examples that whether the productivity of capital exhibit home bias depend ultimately on the specific environment in which international capital flows that place. As a first example, suppose that capital outflow enables the production of a foreign output R^* via the production function $\sigma(\bar{K}-k)^{1-\lambda}(\ell^*)^{\lambda}$, with $0<\lambda<1$. $K-k$ denotes the size of the capital outflow, and ℓ^* refers to foreign labor. Assume in addition that foreign labor is available in unlimited supply, at reservation wage W^*. Maximizing profits abroad yields

$$\max_{\ell^*} \sigma(\bar{K}-k)^{1-\lambda}(\ell^*)^{\lambda} - W^*\ell^*,$$

$$\Leftrightarrow r_{\sigma}^*(\bar{K}-k) = \sigma^{\frac{1}{1-\lambda}}C(\bar{K}-k)$$

$$\Leftrightarrow \delta = \frac{1}{1-\lambda} > 1$$

where C is a positive constant. This is of course simply a reiteration of a standard property of profit functions, requiring that maximal profits be quasi-convex in σ, at given input prices. Thus, an increase in the productivity of the capital leads to higher proportionate revenue gains abroad $r_{\sigma}^*(\bar{K}-k)$ than at home ($R(\sigma, k, \ell)$). In addition, $\delta = 1/(1-\lambda)$ is strictly increasing in foreign labor share λ.

Instead, suppose now that the revenue from production abroad is given by $R^* = \min\{\sigma(\bar{K}-k), \ell^*\}$, and capital and foreign labor are now perfect complements. With unlimited supply of foreign labor, and the same reservation wage W^*, profit abroad is just

$$R^* - W^*\ell^* = r_{\sigma}^*(\bar{K}-k) = \sigma(\bar{K}-k)(1-W^*),$$

implying $\delta = 1$ as long as production abroad yields positive profits $(1 - W^* > 0)$.

Appendix B

In this Appendix, we briefly describe the solution to the optimal control problem of the union when capital is immobile. We seek a wage bill and an employment schedule, respectively $W(\sigma)$ and $L(\sigma)$, that jointly maximize expected union welfare while satisfying incentive compatibility, and individual rationality. Since the profit function is given by $Y(\sigma, \hat{\sigma}) = \sigma\bar{K}^{\beta}L(\hat{\sigma})^{\alpha} - W(\hat{\sigma})$, with $Y(\sigma, \sigma) = Y(\sigma)$. It can be readily verified that incentive compatibility requires that $(\sigma-\hat{\sigma})\bar{K}^{\beta}L(\sigma)^{\alpha} \geq Y(\sigma) - Y(\hat{\sigma}) \geq (\sigma-\hat{\sigma})\bar{K}^{\beta}L(\hat{\sigma})^{\alpha}$. In addition, $Y(\sigma)$ is convex, and differentiable almost everywhere, with

$$\dot{Y}(\sigma) \equiv \frac{dY(\sigma)}{d\sigma} = \bar{K}^{\beta}L(\sigma)^{\alpha}.$$

If the contract yields non-negative profits for a firm with $\sigma = \underline{\sigma}$,

$$0 \leq Y(\underline{\sigma}) \leq Y(\sigma, \underline{\sigma}) \leq Y(\sigma, \sigma), \quad \sigma > \underline{\sigma}$$

where the inequalities follow respectively since $Y(\sigma, \hat{\sigma})$ is monotonically increasing in σ and since incentive compatibility is satisfied.

Thus, the decision problem of the union is subject to four constraints: (i) $Y(\underline{\sigma})$ is non-negative; (ii) $\dot{Y}(\sigma) = \bar{K}^{\beta}L(\sigma)^{\alpha}$; (iii) $L(\sigma)$ is non-decreasing with respect to σ and finally, (iv) $L(\sigma) \leq \mathcal{L}$. Setting up the Hamiltonian as in equation (12), the union welfare maximizing contract requires that

$$V(\sigma, \bar{K}, L(\sigma))\left(1 - \frac{1}{\varepsilon^f(\sigma)}\right) = \bar{W}. \tag{22}$$

Rearranging terms, we obtain, making use of the definition of $L_0(\sigma, k)$ in equation (6),

$$L(\sigma) = L_0(\sigma)\left(1 - \frac{1}{\varepsilon^f(\sigma)}\right)^{\frac{1}{1-\alpha}} < L_0(\sigma). \tag{23}$$

References

Ashenfelter, O. and G. E. Johnson, "Bargaining Theory, Trade Unions and Industrial Strike Activity," *American Economic Review* 59 no. 1 (1969):35–49.

Bagwell, K. and R. Staiger, "Informational Aspects of Foreign Direct Investment and the Multinational Firm," *Japan and the World Economy* 15 no. 1 (2003):1–20.

Bond, E. and T. Gresik, "Regulation of Multinational Firms with Two Active Governments: A Common Agency Approach." *Journal of Public Economics* 59 no. 1 (1996):33–53.

Budd, J. W., "The Effect of Mutinational Institutions on Strike Activity in Canada," *Industrial and Labor Relations Review* 47 (1994):401–66.

Bellak, C., "Multinational Enterprises, and their Domestic Counterparts: Past Research, Current Issues and Future Directions," Vienna University of Economics and Business Administration Working Paper Series No. 18 (2001).

Bughin, J. and S. Vannini, "Strategic Direct Investment Under Unionised Oligopoly," *International Journal of Industrial Organisation* 13 (1995):127–45.

Calzolari, G., K. Diaw, and J. Pouyet, "Regulatory Competition and Exclusion in an International Context," GREMAQ, Université des Sciences Sociales de Toulouse, mimeo (2002).

Card, D., "Strikes and Wages: A Test of an Asymmetric Information Model," *Quarterly Journal of Economics* 105 (1990):625–59.

Caves, R. E., "Spillovers from Multinationals in Developing Countries: the Mechanisms at Work," William Davidson Institute working paper 247, Stephen M. Ross Business School, University of Michigan, Ann Arbor (1999).

China Daily, "Strikes signal end to cheap labor," 3 June 2010. Available at http://www.chinadaily.com.cn/cndy/2010–06/03/content_9926008.htm.

Cooke, W. N., "The Influence of Industrial Relations Factors on U.S. Foreign Direct Investment Abroad," *Industrial and Labor Relations Review* 51 (1997):3–17.

Cooke, W. N. and D. S. Noble, "Industrial Relations Systems and US Foreign Direct Investment Abroad," *British Journal of Industrial Relations* 36 (1998):581–609.

Cousineau, J. M., R. Lacroix, and D. Vachon, "Foreign Ownership and Strike Activity in Canada," *Relations Industrielles* 46 (1991):616–30.

Creigh, S. W. and P. Makeham, "Foreign Ownership and Strike-Proneness: A Research Note," *British Journal of Industrial Relations* 16 (1978):369–72.

De Haan, E. and M. V. Stichele, "Footloose Investors: Investing in the Garment Industry in Africa. SOMO, Center for Research on Multinational Corporations, Amsterdam (2007).

Devereux, M. P., "The Impact of Taxation on the Location of Capital, Firms and Profit: A Survey of Empirical Evidence," Oxford University Centre for Business Taxation working paper 07/02 (2007).

Doms, M. E. and J. B. Jensen, "Comparing Wages, Skills, and Productivity between Domestically and Foreign-owned Manufacturing Establishments in the United States," in R. E. Baldwin, R. E. Lipsey, and J. D. Richardson (eds), *Geography and Ownership as Bases for Economic Accounting*, Studies in Income and Wealth, Chicago, IL: University of Chicago Press (1998).

Eckel, C. and H. Egger, "Wage Bargaining and Multinational Firms," *Journal of International Economics* 77 (2009):206–14.

Enderwick, P. and P. J. Buckley, "Strike Activity and Foreign Ownership: An Analysis of British Manufacturing, 1971–1973," *British Journal of Industrial Relations* 20 (1982):308–21.

Farber, H., "Notes on the Economics of Labor Unions," Princeton University, Industrial Relations Section, working paper 452 (2001).

Forsyth, D. J. C., "Foreign-owned Firms and Labour Relations: A Regional Perspective," *British Journal of Industrial Relations* 11 no. 1 (1973):20–8.

Gennard, J. and M. D. Steuer, "The Industrial Relations of Foreign Owned Subsidiaries in the United Kingdom," *British Journal of Industrial Relations* 9 (1971):143–59.
Helpman, E., M. J. Melitz, and S. R. Yeaple, "Export versus FDI with Heterogeneous Firms," *American Economic Review* 94 (2004):300–16.
Kelly, A. and T. Brannick, "Explaining The Strike-Proneness of British Companies in Ireland," *British Journal of Industrial Relations* 26 (1988):37–55.
McConnell, S., "Strikes, Wages and Private Information: An Empirical Study," *American Economic Review* 79 (1989):801–15.
Mezzetti, C. and E. Dinopoulos, "Domestic Unionization and Import Competition," *Journal of International Economics* 31 (1991):79–100.
Millward, N., "Research Note: The Strike Record of Foreign-owned Manufacturing Plants in Great Britain," *British Journal of Industrial Relations* 17 (1979):99–104.
Naylor, R., "Economic Models of Trade Union Behaviour," in J. T. Addison and C. Schnabel, (eds), *International Handbook of Trade Unions*, Cheltenham: Edward Elgar (2003).
Naylor, R. and M. Santoni, "Foreign Direct Investment and Wage Bargaining," *Journal of International Trade and Economic Development* 12 (2003):1–18.
Ng, I. and D. R. Maki, "Strike Activity of U.S. Institutions in Canada," *British Journal of Industrial Relations* 26 (1988):63–73.
Prusa, T., "An Incentive Compatible Approach to the Transfer Pricing Problem," *Journal of International Economics* 28 (1990):155–72.
Rodrik, D., *Has Globalization Gone Too Far?* Washington, DC: Institute for International Economics (1997).
Slaughter, M. J., "International Trade and Labor Demand Elasticities," NBER working paper 6282 (1997).
Traxler, F. and B. Woitech, "Transnational Investment and National Labour Market Regimes: A Case of 'Regime Shopping?" *European Journal of Industrial Relations* 6 (2000):141–59.
Tunisialive, "Leoni's Mateur Plant Resumes Operations After Three Days of Closure," 13 February 2012. Available at http://www.tunisia-live.net/2012/02/13/leonis-mateur-plant-resumes-operations-after-three-days-of-closure/ (2012).
Zhao, L., "Cross-hauling Direct Foreign Investment and Unionized Oligopoly," *European Economic Review* 39 (1995):1237–53.

Notes

1. There is also a burgeoning literature on foreign direct investment under asymmetric information. See Bond and Gresik (1996), Calzolari et al. (2002), Prusa (1990) for example, that examine investment policy formation with asymmetrically informed government/governments and perfectly informed multinationals. Also see Bagwell and Staiger (2003) for the informational role of the locational choice of multinationals.
2. Using US data, Slaughter (1997) investigates whether there is indeed a positive relationship between labor demand elasticity and openness, and finds mixed empirical support.
3. Bellak (2001) discusses both sides of the argument relating foreign ownership with strike-proneness. Supporting a positive link, Bellak (2001) argues that information about a foreign-owned firm may be deemed less credible to unions, resulting in more frequent strikes in foreign-owned firms. Supporting a negative link, foreign-owned firms may pay higher wages (Doms and Jensen, 1998), adhere more firmly to labor standard legislations, and invest in reducing information asymmetries that can eventually speed up negotiations.
4. We model foreign demand for capital as perfectly elastic for two reasons. First, we are interested in investment behavior by the individual firm, and hence the lack of market power in world market for capital would seem to be a reasonable assumption. Second, while the absence of investment opportunities (a perfectly inelastic foreign demand for capital at zero capital flow) represents one extreme, the case of perfectly elastic demand represents the other, wherein a union's ability to command high wages is likely to be affected the most.

5. This requires that $r_{\sigma}^{*}\bar{K} \geq \beta\left[\left(\frac{\alpha}{\bar{W}}\right)^{\alpha} \sigma \bar{K}^{\beta}\right]^{\frac{1}{1-\alpha}}$.

6. See also Helpman et al. (2004), in which more productive firms at home are equally as productive abroad, after accounting for the fixed cost of foreign direct investment.
7. In addition to location specificity, the size of δ can depend on a variety of additional factors, ranging from the nature of the production/revenue function abroad, the existence of expropriation risks in the foreign country, and correspondingly the risk attitudes of the entrepreneurs in question, for example. What is important to note here is that *a priori*, δ can exhibit a full range of values, and is likely also specific to the industry in question.
8. As is well-known, the assumption of an upward sloping hazard rate is satisfied by a wide range of probability distribution functions, including for example the normal and the uniform distributions.
9. With productivity rank reversal, ϕ is monotonically decreasing with respect to σ. The induced cumulative distribution function of ϕ is thus $1 - F\left(\left(\frac{\phi}{(1-\beta)\left(\frac{\beta}{r^*}\right)^{\beta}}\right)^{\frac{1-\beta}{1-\delta\beta}}\right)$. In addition, the range of ϕ is given by $\left[(1-\beta)\left(\bar{\sigma}^{1-\delta\beta}\left(\frac{\beta}{r^*}\right)^{\beta}\right)^{\frac{1}{1-\beta}}, (1-\beta)\left(\underline{\sigma}^{1-\delta\beta}\left(\frac{\beta}{r^*}\right)^{\beta}\right)^{\frac{1}{1-\beta}}\right]$.

10. The range of σ used in this simulation is [1, 10], and r^* is normalized to 1.
11. Of course, the outcome will change if the employer moves first by proposing a wage and employment schedule. In this case, the solution trivially reduces to one in which the employer pays exactly the reservation wage regardless of capital mobility, and hires as many as it wishes at that wage depending on capital mobility. For one thing, this is inconsistent with the oft-noted inverse relationship between strike incidence and wages. Another way of understanding this strand of the literature on wage bargaining adopted here is that the model outcome illustrates the opposite benchmark, and shows the maximal extractable surplus that the union can hope to achieve.
12. See Devereux (2007) for a recent survey.

Guaranteed Manufactured without Child Labor: The Economics of Consumer Boycotts, Social Labeling and Trade Sanctions

*Arnab K. Basu, Nancy H. Chau, and Ulrike Grote**

Abstract

Does labeling products "Child-Labor Free" provide a market-based solution to the pervasive employment of child labor? This paper explores the promise of social labeling in the context of its four oft-noted objectives: child labor employment, consumer information, welfare, and trade linkages, when competition between the North and South is based both on comparative cost advantage, and the use of child labor as a hidden product attribute. We show that (i) social labeling benefits consumers and Southern producers, whereas children and Northern producers are worse off; (ii) trade sanctions on unlabeled products deteriorates Southern terms of trade, but leaves the incidence of child labor strictly unaffected; and (iii) a threat to sanction imports of unlabeled Southern products *discourages* the South from maintaining a credible social labeling program. We also explore the question of whether social labeling should be viewed as a transitory or a permanent institution in developing economies.

1. Introduction

Debates over the design of an appropriate trade policy response to the employment of child labor in export industries have ranged from the inclusion of a "Social Clause" in the World Trade Organization (WTO), to calls for import bans to be imposed on products made with child labor.[1] Concurrently, social labeling initiatives—aimed at providing information on the adoption of acceptable labor standards, such as whether child laborers are employed in the production process—has gained currency particularly as a voluntary and industry-based initiative to combat the problem of child labor. Social labeling has origins that can be traced back to the White Label in the US as early as 1899,[2] and draws on the success of more recent eco-labeling initiatives that promotes environmentally friendly production methods (Hilowitz, 1997a).[3] Table 1 lists some of the key attributes of six social labeling programs already in existence worldwide.

These pioneering initiatives have attracted considerable attention, and the arguments, both for and against, can be categorized, respectively, under four oft-noted objectives of social labeling. These include: (i) child labor employment; (ii) consumer information; (iii) welfare; and (iv) trade linkages. First, social labeling is market-based (Hilowitz, 1997a; Freeman, 1994; Harvey, 1996), and its impact on child labor depends first and foremost on the willingness of producers to voluntarily impose self-restraints

* Basu: Department of Economics, College of William and Mary, Williamsburg, VA 23187. Tel: (757) 221-1318; Fax: (757) 221-1175; E-mail: akbasu@wm.edu. Chau: Department of Applied Economics and Management, Cornell University, Ithaca NY 14853. Tel: (607) 255-4463; Fax: (607) 255-9984; E-mail: hyc3@cornell.edu. Grote: Center for Development Research (ZEF), University of Bonn, Walter-Flex-Str. 3, D-53113, Bonn, Germany. Tel: 49-228-73-1883; Fax: 49-228-73-1869; E-mail: u.grote@uni-bonn.de. This is a revised version of Cornell AEM-Working Paper #2000-14. The comments of an anonymous referee, Assefa Admassie, Ron Balvers, Subhayu Bandyopadhyay, Richard Barnett, Kaushik Basu, Joachim von Braun, Patrick Conway, Amy Glass, Ron Jones, Ali Khan, Devashish Mitra, Tim Mount, Yana Rodgers, Russ Sobel, and participants at the XII-IEA World Congress, Cornell, West Virginia, CityU HK, Southeast and Midwest International Economics Meetings, and World Bank GDN-conference are gratefully acknowledged.

on the employment of children. With very little government support (RUGMARK and KALEEN) in some cases, and the complete absence of support in others (CARE & FAIR, STEP, ABRINQ, DIP), participating producers typically also pay a levy, used to fund the education of children displaced by the labeling program (Birdsall, 1998; Brown, 2000). As a justification for these costs of participation, labeling exploits the increase in public awareness in developed and developing economies about child labor, and provides the bridge that allows producers to internalize consumers' willingness to pay (Basu, 1999a, b; Srinivasan, 1996; Maskus, 1997).

Second, from the perspective of developing countries, of central concern is the difficulty inherent in monitoring and maintaining the reliability of the information that social labels convey (Basu, 1999b).[4] Indeed, despite the alleged gains in producer revenue for developing countries, sponsorships of social labeling initiatives have largely originated from major consumer markets (Table 1).[5] Meanwhile, participating producers may not be subject to on-site monitoring and inspections in selected programs. The KALEEN label, sponsored by the Indian government is one such example. These observations are particularly relevant in light of Maskus (1997), Basu (1999b), and Brown (2000), in which a warning is raised that market-based incentives meant to discourage the employment of child labor can in fact be misused, resulting instead in widespread practice of false-labeling.

Third, consumer boycotts of products made with child labor facilitated by social labeling programs, even those that are credibly enforced, may not translate to an improvement in the welfare of children. Indeed, simply removing children from the work place may benefit adult labor employers at the expense of children, and risks displacing children in developing countries from poverty to destitution (Birdsall, 1998; Basu, 1999b, 2001). This is in keeping with the growing literature on the supply-side determinants of child labor, and the potential problems associated with a host of policies that deem the eradication of child labor as an end in itself.[6]

Finally, explicit labeling renders unlabeled products particularly vulnerable to allegations of unfair trade practice, and provides a possible lever for interest groups in developed countries to advocate restrictions on market access. The proposal for a Child *Labor Deterrence Act* in the United States, for example, sought to eliminate child labor employment in the export sectors of developing countries by prohibiting the imports of goods known to be so produced.[7]

As a first objective of this paper, we propose a North–South model that synthesizes the insights and discussions in Srinivsan (1996), Maskus (1997), Hilowitz (1997a, b) and Basu (1999a, b; 2001) in terms of the four objectives of social labeling. We do so by identifying four groups of stakeholders: (i) consumers in the North whose preferences are characterized by a desire to boycott employers of child labor; (ii) producers in the South whose choice of production techniques depends on the trade-off between cost-savings and revenue losses associated with employing child labor, (iii) producers in the North who compete with Southern producers for market share; and (iv) Southern households who account for the derived demand and opportunity cost of sending their children to work.

The basic analysis makes plain that social labeling should be more appropriately understood as a corrective policy that targets the lack of complete information for *consumers* who cannot otherwise reveal their preferences on the use of child labor as a production input. The choice of monitoring intensity in social labeling programs, likewise, should be understood as a corrective policy that mitigates the moral hazard problem associated with the practice of false labeling. Of course, whether labeling combined with enforcement ultimately benefit children depends critically on whether unfettered child

Table 1. Social Labeling Initiatives

	Year	*Producer countries*	*Consumer markets*	*Aims at removing child labor*	*Sponsorship*	*Receives government support*	*On-site monitoring*	*Collect levies*
RUGMARK	1994	India and Nepal	Germany and US	Yes	Private foundation (Germany)	Germany	Yes	Yes
KALEEN	1996	India	Germany	Yes	National government (India)	Yes	No	Yes
CARE and FAIR	1994	India and Nepal	Germany	No	Retail association	No	No	Yes
STEP	1995	India Nepal and Pakistan	Switzerland	Gradually	NGOs	No	Some	Yes
ABRINQ	1995	Brazil	Brazil	Yes	Private foundation	No	Yes	Yes
DIP	1995	Kenya India	Switzerland	Yes	Private	No	Yes	Yes

Source: Hilowitz, (1997b): Labeling Child Labour Products; ILO.

labor employment can otherwise be deemed *excessive*. In keeping with second-best argumentation of policy reforms (Grootaert and Kanbur, 1995; Bhagwati, 1995), our analysis underscores the potential for the good intentions of social labeling to produce outcomes that go against not just the welfare of children, but also the developing country in question. In particular, as the basic analysis unfolds, we provide formal arguments that point to circumstances under which the following claims are *false*:

- By eliminating unfair competitive advantages that Southern producers enjoy, credible social labeling programs are expected to confer damages to producers in the South and benefits to producers in the North.
- Trade barriers against the import of unlabeled products facilitate (i) the employment objective of social labeling by lowering the incidence of child labor, and (ii) the welfare objective of social labeling by increasing the rewards for adult labor employers.
- The anticipation of trade sanctions against unlabeled products biases the incentive of Southern governments in favor of initiating a credible social labeling program.

Intuitively, social labeling is but a means of product differentiation, without which rational consumers in the North can only differentiate between products from different country of origins, but not between products made with and without child labor. If child labor is a non-issue in the North, but pervasive in the South, consumers' willingness to pay in a (semi-)pooling equilibrium without social labeling can only reflect consumer perceptions on country-specific child labor employment in the aggregate, rather than producer-specific child labor use at the firm level. A *credible* social labeling program corrects for this informational bias favoring Northern producers. Consequently, the alleged gains for Northern producers subsequent to labeling need not be realized.

Precisely by differentiating products, social labeling also exposes *unlabeled* Southern products by rendering them synonymous with products that are made with child labor. Labeling thus opens the door for discriminatory trade sanctions to be imposed on imports of unlabeled products from the South. Unless there is a corresponding increase in monitoring intensity in the South, a trade sanction on unlabeled product simply induces false-labeling. In equilibrium, therefore, the incidence of child labor may remain strictly unaffected subsequent to a trade sanction. Our earlier observation that developing countries appear reluctant to institute social labeling programs can accordingly be better understood once the threat of trade sanctions on unlabeled products—which accomplish little other than a deterioration of Southern terms of trade—is taken into account.

With these important caveats in place, we extend the basic model to circumstances under which social labeling raises Southern welfare. This may be due, for example, to (i) significant external diseconomies associated with unfettered child labor employment, and (ii) the crowding-out of adult employment opportunities, particularly when adult wages depend negatively on economy-wide child labor employment. The paper concludes by examining the question: suppose indeed that social labeling benefits the South, will labeling become a permanent institution, in the sense that all else equal, child labor employment has a tendency to bounce back to its pre-labeling level just as soon as the labeling program is removed? Based on a standard dynamic adjustment process, we find that a no social labeling equilibrium may well be dynamically unstable. As such, a labeling induced price premium can also be understood as a temporary device that serves to initiate a virtuous process of successive reduction in child labor, effective even after the price premium from social labeling has long vanished.

2. A Model of Social Labeling

There are two countries, the North and the South. We envisage an asymmetric production structure, wherein the export sector of the South produces an output that employs child labor, whereas the corresponding import competing sector in the North only employs adult laborers. The basic analysis takes four groups of individuals as building blocks: Northern consumers, producers in the South and the North, and Southern households.

Demand for Child Labor

Northern consumers Consumers in the North are characterized by their preferences and income. Each of N Northern consumers allocates their disposable income E between a numeraire commodity, y, which does not accommodate child labor employment, and another commodity x. Let d^y denote the quantity of demand for y, and d_i^x, $i = a, k$, suitably subscripted, the quantity demand for Southern products made with and without child labor (d_k^x and d_a^x). The same commodity x is also produced in the North with adult labor only, and we denote d^X with an upper case superscript as the corresponding quantity demand. The utility function of a representative consumer is given by:

$$U(d_a^x, d_k^x, d^X, d^y) = \alpha \log D(d_a^x, d_k^x, d^X) + (1-\alpha)\log d^y.$$

$\alpha > 0$ and $(1 - \alpha)$ denote the weight allotted to the consumption of commodities x and y. $D(d_a^x, d_k^x, d^X)$ is a sub-utility index (Dixit and Stiglitz, 1977) with $D(d_a^x, d_k^x, d^X) = a_a(d_a^x + d^X) + a_k d_k^x$. The parameters a_i embody the preference rankings of consumers between products that are produced by adult and child labor, with $a_a/a_k \equiv a > 1$. The interpretation of such preference rankings can be quite general, and embodies consumers' desire to penalize exporting firms who employ child laborers, or to reward firms that choose to employ only adult laborers (Maskus, 1997), for example. In either case, $a > 1$ stipulates that the marginal rate of substitution between products made without and with child labor is strictly greater than one.[8] Also let p_ℓ (p_u) be the price of a labeled (an unlabeled) product originating from the South. Northern variables are denoted by upper case symbols. Since there is no child labor in the North, all d^X is sold at a uniform price P.

The limits of labeling as a screening device We assume that consumers have rational expectations and incorporate the possibility of false labeling into their consumption decision calculus. Let λ be the probability that a labeled Southern product is produced by adult labor. By standard arguments (Dixit and Stiglitz, 1977), the utility maximizing solution of the consumer's decision problem is given by an expenditure share α $(1 - \alpha)$ devoted to the consumption of commodity x (y), demand functions $d_i^x(p_\ell, p_u, P)$ $i = \ell, u$ for Southern imports, and a demand function for Northern production of the same commodity, $d^X(p_\ell, p_u, P)$.[9] Demand is positive for both labeled and unlabeled products originating from South if and only if

$$\frac{p_\ell}{p_u} = \lambda a + (1-\lambda) < a; \quad \text{and} \quad \frac{P}{p_u} = a.$$

Thus,

$$\frac{p_\ell}{p_u} - 1 = \lambda(a-1) \leq a - 1 = \frac{P}{p_u} - 1, \tag{1}$$

whenever $\lambda \leq 1$. Naturally, false labeling decreases the premium that consumers are willing to pay for labeled goods.

In addition, if labeled and unlabeled products co-exist, (i) the price of labeled products exceeds that of unlabeled products if and only if $\lambda > 0$, and (ii) the relative price premium (p_ℓ/p_u) precisely reflects consumers' relative willingness to pay for (the marginal rate of substitution (a)) child labor free products if and only if false labeling does not prevail, i.e., when $\lambda = 1$.

In stark contrast, a uniform price p^o (P^o) applies to all Southern (Northern) producers in the absence of social labeling. Note that the two prices p^o and P^o need not coincide since consumers can still account for the pooling of producers in the South with heterogeneous input choices, by resorting to the country-of-origin of a product.[10] To see this, note that if $\gamma \in [0, 1]$ denote the fraction of Southern exports produced using adult labor, and only adult laborers are employed in the North, demand for output x in both the South and the North is positive if and only if

$$\frac{\gamma a_a + (1-\gamma)a_k}{p^o} = \frac{a_a}{P^o},$$

or equivalently,

$$\frac{P^o}{p^o} = \frac{a}{1+\gamma(a-1)} > 1. \tag{2}$$

Thus, a proportionate price premium prevails even in the absence of labeling, with the country-of-origin of a product serving as a signal of the input choice of the average Southern producer.[11]

Production in the North and South Two sectors y and x constitute the production side of the North and the South. Production of the composite numeraire y in the South takes as input of production, adult laborers L_y, with $y = \omega L_y$. Similarly, output of y in the North is given by $Y = \Omega L_y$. Since ω and Ω denote both the average and marginal productivity of adult labor, the economy-wide rewards to labor is given by ω for n_a number of adult laborers in the South and Ω for N number of adult laborers in the North. Competitive producers in sector x constitute a small subset of the economy in both countries, and accordingly take the economy-wide adult wage rate as given.[12]

There are M producers in the North who produce X using only adult laborers, with $X = \min\{K, \mathcal{L}_a\}$, where K and $\mathcal{L}_a$ denotes, respectively, capital and labor inputs employed by each of the M producers. In the South, there are m producers engaged in the production of commodity x. To focus on the choice of technique on the part of producers, the production functions of good x using child and adult laborers are:[13]

$$x_k = \min\left\{\kappa, \frac{\ell_k}{b_k}\right\}; \quad x_a = \min\left\{\kappa, \frac{\ell_a}{b}\right\},$$

where κ denotes capital input accessible to each of the m Southern producers. ℓ_i, $i = a, k$, respectively, denotes the number of adult and child laborers employed, and whereas b and b_k capture the productivity of adult and child laborers. We assume that firms have differential access to cost saving technologies, and $\mu(b)$ characterizes the cumulative distribution of the m firms in the range $[b^-, b^+]$. The cumulative distribution $\mu(\cdot)$ is taken to be continuously differentiable over $[b^-, b^+]$ with a strictly positive density function $\mu' > 0$.[14] In addition, each child labor produces only a fraction of the output of an adult, with $b_k > b^+$.[15] Let the wage income of a child laborer be denoted as ω_k and

$\tau > 0$ the per unit levy (or license fee) applied to firms that voluntarily participate in the labeling scheme.

The decision problem of Southern producers is a two-stage problem: (i) whether or not to employ child labor, and (ii) whether or not to participate in the social labeling scheme. We begin with the second stage.

For an adult labor employer, participation in the social labeling scheme implies unit revenue $p_\ell - \tau$, and p_u otherwise. Equation (3) expresses the participation constraint, with the interpretation that adult labor employers benefit from signaling their type, given τ, via labeling if and only if:

$$p_\ell - p_u \geq \tau. \tag{3}$$

Now let $\phi > 0$ be the probability associated with the discovery of false labeling, which captures the monitoring intensity to be determined endogenously by the Southern government. Child labor employers do not benefit from (falsely) signaling their choice of input if and only if:

$$[(1-\phi)p_\ell + \phi p_u - \tau]\kappa \leq p_u\kappa \Leftrightarrow p_\ell - p_u \leq \frac{\tau}{(1-\phi)}. \tag{4}$$

The false labeling constraint in equation (4) gives the maximal price premium on labeled products that can be maintained without inducing more producers to practice false labeling. Also, in light of Hilowitz (1997b), equation (4) implies that employers whose false labeling practices are discovered are simply delicensed.

Figure 1 summarizes these observations. First, note that if the participation constraint is violated, social labeling is a matter of irrelevance to producers ($x_\ell = 0$), a uniform price p^o applies to all producers. Meanwhile, strictly positive supplies of both labeled and unlabeled products prevail whenever the price premium falls within the range $[\tau, \tau/(1-\phi)]$. Clearly, as $\phi \to 1$, any social labeling scheme that satisfies the participation constraint belongs to this range. With $\phi = 0$, at the other extreme, the false labeling and participation constraints coincide. Finally, *everyone labels* whenever

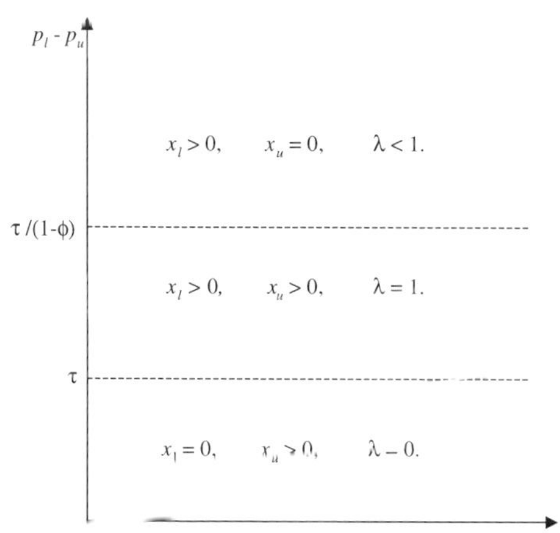

Figure 1. Participation and False-Labeling Constraints

the price premium for labeled products exceeds $\tau/(1-\phi)$, and whether or not child laborers are employed.

Turning now to the first stage problem, producers derive higher profits by participating in a labeling scheme and employing adult labor if and only if

$$(p_\ell - \omega b - \tau)\kappa \geq (p_u - \omega_k b_k)\kappa$$
$$\Leftrightarrow p_\ell - p_u - \tau \geq \omega b - \omega_k b_k.$$

Thus, the price premium attached to labeled products $(p_\ell - p_u)$, along with the wage cost savings that the employment of child labor entails, $(\omega b - \omega_k b_k)$, dictate the self-selection among producers into employers of child and adult labor. Define

$$b^*(p_\ell, p_u, \omega_k) \equiv \frac{p_\ell - p_u + \omega_k b_k - \tau}{\omega}. \tag{5}$$

Southern producers with $b > b^*$ are better off employing child labor. As should be expected, at any given price premium, relatively cost inefficient producers will choose to employ child labor.

The definition of b^* above implies an aggregate (derived) demand curve for child labor $L_k^d = (1 - \mu(b^*))b_k\kappa m$. L_k^d is inversely (positively) related to the supply price of child labor (adult labor), and is strictly decreasing in the price premium attached to labeled goods. The absence of social labeling is but a special case of equation (5), wherein $p_\ell - p_u - \tau = 0$, and the marginal producer in the South is characterized by $b^o \equiv \omega_k^o b_k/\omega$.

We now turn to a description of the equilibrium conditions in child labor and output markets, and demonstrate how the satisfaction of the participation and the false labeling constraints are in fact central to the determination of the welfare and employment of children.

Supply of Child Labor

There are a large number n_k of potential child laborers available for work in sector x. Child labor supply is determined by an opportunity cost schedule $R(\theta)h(L_k)$, with $R'(\cdot) > 0$. The parameter $\theta \in [\theta^-, \theta^+]$ is taken to be a function of exogenous factors specific to each child and may include the subsistence income of the household (Basu and Van, 1998), the number of children in the household (ILO, 1996b), the effective borrowing interest rate to finance education (Grote et al., 1998; Baland and Robinson, 2000; Jafarey and Lahiri, 2002), or the expected returns to education (Akabayashi and Pscharopoulos, 1999). The above specification of the child labor supply function allows for a possible divergence between the private and the social marginal benefits of child labor (Grootaert and Kanbur, 1995). Accordingly, let the scale factor $h(\cdot)$ be strictly positive, with $h'(\cdot) \leq (>)0$, representing scale economies of human capital accumulation (congestion diseconomies associated with the next best alternative of child labor employment in sector x).

Taking as given the stock of child laborers, a child is better off working if and only if

$$\theta \leq \bar{\theta}(\omega_k, L_k) \equiv \{\theta \mid R(\theta)h(L_k) = \omega_k\}.$$

In addition, if the distribution of θ among the n children is given by the cumulative distribution function $\nu(\theta)$, the aggregate supply of child labor in sector x is simply given by $L_k^s(\omega_k) = n_k\nu(\bar{\theta})$. We restrict ourselves to the case where the scale effect associated with human capital accumulation is not too large, with $\partial L_k^s/\partial \omega_k > 0$ or equivalently, the own-price supply schedule of child labor is positively sloped.[16]

Turning now to the North, we assume that the incidence of child labor is a non-issue for Northern households. Purely from the viewpoint of the supply side of the market for child labor, such asymmetries between the labor markets of the North and the South apply whenever the North is characterized by: (i) returns to human capital that are sufficiently high; (ii) a marginal product of child labor that is too small; (iii) credit markets that are better equipped to accommodate human capital undertaking of the poor; or (iv) households that enjoy income levels too high to justify putting children to work. Thus, aggregate Northern supply of child labor-free products, X, is given by KM.

3. Social Labeling as a Market-based Solution to Child Labor

To close the model, two market clearing conditions will be applied. For output market clearing, total consumer expenditure on the output of the Southern x sector and the Northern X sector, is equal to aggregate revenue received by Southern and Northern producers if

$$\begin{aligned}\alpha EN &= \left[p_\ell^* \frac{\mu(b^*)}{\lambda^*} + p_u^*\left(1 - \frac{\mu(b^*)}{\lambda^*}\right)\right]\kappa m + P^* KM \\ &= p_u^*\left(\left[1 + \mu(b^*)\frac{p_\ell - p_u}{\lambda^* p_u}\right]\kappa m + aKM\right) \\ &= p_u^*([1 + \mu(b^*)(a-1)]\kappa m + aKM),\end{aligned}$$

where the third equality follows since consumers equate the marginal rate of substitution with relative prices (equation (1)), and an asterisk represents equilibrium values. Rearranging,

$$p_u^* = \frac{\alpha EN}{([1 + \mu(b^*)(a-1)]\kappa m + aKM)}.$$

Now, from equation (1) we have $\lambda(a-1) = p_\ell/p_u - 1$. Substituting for p_u^* yields,

$$p_\ell^* - p_u^* = \frac{\lambda^*(a-1)\alpha EN}{[1 + \mu(b^*)(a-1)]\kappa m + aKM}. \tag{6}$$

As should be expected, the higher the fraction of true labels (λ^*), the higher will be the equilibrium price premium attached to labeled Southern imports by Northern consumers.

Figure 2 highlights the consequences of false labeling in terms of the equilibrium price premium and child labor employment. The EE schedule represents producer response to the price premium in equation (5). Starting from $p_\ell - p_u - \tau = 0$, b^o coincides with the marginal employer in the absence of labeling. The D^iD^i ($i = 0, 1, 2$) schedules in Figure 2 depict the negative relationship between the $p_\ell^* - p_u^*$ and $\mu(b^*)$ in equation (6), taking as given consumer's expectation that $\lambda = 1$. In addition, D^oD^o, D^1D^1 and D^2D^2 represent successively: (i) higher shares of consumer income devoted to x and X (α); (ii) higher levels of consumer's willingness to pay (a); and (iii) lower levels of x and X sector output combined (κm and KM).

Thus, D^oD^o demonstrates the case where the equilibrium price premium as given by the intersection of D^oD^o and EE does not justify the levy imposed on labeling τ ($p_\ell - p_u < \tau$). As such, equilibrium child labor employment is given by $(1 - \mu(b^o))\kappa m$. Curve D^1D^1, on the other hand, is consistent with rational expectation and labeled

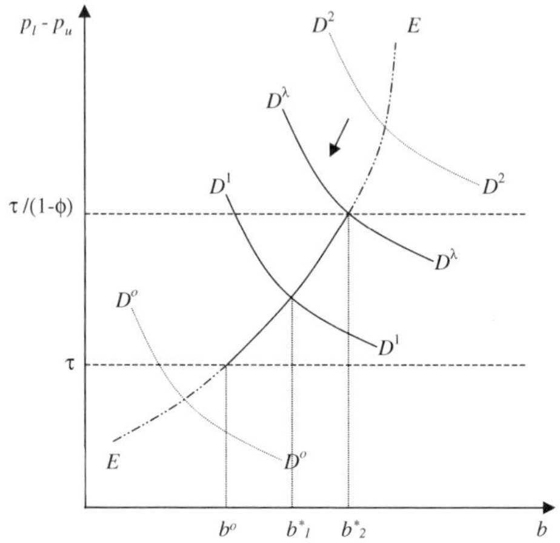

Figure 2. Equilibrium Price Premium and Child Labor Demand

products are synonymous with goods that are made solely with adult labor. As such, b_1^* represents the marginal employer in the South who is just indifferent between hiring adult and child labor. Finally, curve D^2D^2 intersects EE at a point which violates rational expectations as the number of firms with false labels is strictly positive. It follows, therefore, that the fraction of true labels in the pool of Southern exports must be lower than 1 and D^2D^2 shifts to the left until the false labeling constraint is just binding ($D^\lambda D^\lambda$). At this point, the marginal employer of adult laborers is characterized by $b = b_2^*$.

Figure 2 yields a number of observations that prove to be useful in the sequel. To begin with, note that whenever the participation constraint is satisfied, for all $\phi \geq 0$, social labeling always decreases the equilibrium share of child labor employers $b^* \geq b^o$.[17] In addition, when the false labeling constraint is binding, child labor employment $(1 - \mu(b^*))\kappa m$ is determined by the intersection of the false labeling constraint and the EE curve. As such, the endogenous link between demand side considerations (the D^iD^i curves) and the equilibrium number of child laborers employed is severed. Finally, an increase in the monitoring intensity (ϕ) shifts the false labeling constraint upwards. It follows that equilibrium share of child labor employers falls, while the price premium increases.

A second market equilibrium condition requires that ω_k^* equates child labor demand and supply, with

$$[1 - \mu(b^*)]\kappa m b_k - L_k^s(\omega_k^*) = 0. \quad (7)$$

In what follows, we summarize a number of key observations regarding the effectiveness of social labeling based on the four objectives enumerated in section 1. Formal proofs of these results can be found in the Appendix.[18]

Welfare of Consumers

Social labeling reveals information that would otherwise be unknown to consumers. Indeed, the indirect utility of Northern consumers subsequent to labeling can be expressed as:

$$U^* = -\alpha(\log p_u^* - \log a_k) + \log E + \log \alpha^\alpha (1-\alpha)^{1-\alpha}$$
$$= \alpha \log \frac{(1+\mu(b^*)(a-1))\kappa m + KM}{\alpha EN} + C,$$

where $C = \alpha \log a_k + \log E + \log \alpha^\alpha (1-\alpha)^{1-\alpha}$ and the second equality follows from product market clearing. Thus, consumers' welfare is strictly decreasing in the proportion of Southern producers using child labor, $1 - \mu(b^*)$, whenever $a > 1$.

In comparison, if consumers must resort to a product's country-of-origin as a signal, and there exists pooling of child and adult labor employers in the South, the welfare of consumers in the North is given simply by:[19]

$$U^o = \alpha \log \frac{(1+\mu(b^o)(a-1))\kappa m + aKM}{\alpha EN} + C. \tag{8}$$

Clearly, $U^o < U^*$ if and only if $\mu(b^o) < \mu(b^*)$. Taking into account the observations corresponding to Figure 2 above, we have

PROPOSITION 1.
(i) *Social labeling benefits Northern consumers if and only if the participation constraint is satisfied.*
(ii) *If the false labeling constraint is binding, an increase in monitoring intensity unambiguously increases the welfare of Northern consumers.*

Welfare of Producers

By allowing consumers to differentiate between producers depending on their choice of inputs, social labeling can also be shown to create revenue consequences for producers in the South and in the North that go in opposite directions:[20]

PROPOSITION 2.

$$P^o > P^*, \quad \text{and} \quad p^o > p_u^*$$

if and only if the participation constraint is satisfied. In addition,

$$p_\ell^* > p^o$$

if and only if the fraction of true labels λ^* is no less than $\mu(b^o)$.

Southern adult labor employers are rewarded through a higher price level ($p_\ell^* > p^o$) whenever the fraction of child labor free products in the pool of labeled Southern exports is no less than that which applies in the absence of labeling.[21] Meanwhile, Southern employers of child labor can no longer free ride on the uniform price that consumers are willing to pay in the absence of social labels and as a result, receive a strictly lower price $p^o > p_u^*$. Perhaps more interestingly, beginning from a regime where country-of-origin labels represents the only source of information available to consumers, social labeling negatively impact Northern producer revenue, since labeling in the South implies that Northern producers no longer constitute the only source of products made only by adult workers.

To make the case of the positive consequences of social labeling on producer revenues in the South even stronger, it can be readily verified that the levels of total producer revenue G in the South (child labor and adult labor employers inclusive), respectively, without and with social labeling are:

$$G^o = \alpha EN\kappa m\left(\kappa m + \frac{aKM}{1+\mu(b^o)(a-1)}\right)^{-1}, \quad G^* = \alpha EN\kappa m\left(\kappa m + \frac{aKM}{1+\mu(b^*)(a-1)}\right)^{-1}.$$

Thus, Southern producer revenue rises unambiguously subsequent to social labeling in the South if and only if $b^* > b^o$. In addition, since Northern producer revenue is given by the residual demands $\alpha EN - G^o$ and $\alpha EN - G^*$, respectively, without and with labeling, Northern producer revenue is negatively impacted by social labeling. The intuition is straightforward. Note that whereas social labeling has negative revenue consequences on child labor employers, this is but a first round effect. The transition from a pooling to a semi-separating regime via labeling biases Southern producers' incentives against the use of child labor. As such, the *average* willingness to pay for Southern products unambiguously rises. Summarizing these arguments, we have

PROPOSITION 3.

(i) *Social labeling (strictly) increases the average revenue of Southern exports* ($(G^* - G^o)/\kappa m > 0$), *and (strictly) decreases the average revenue of Northern product* ($[(\alpha EN - G^*) - (\alpha EN - G^o)]/KM < 0$), *if and only if the participation constraint is satisfied and* $\phi \geq (>) 0$.

(ii) *If the false labeling constraint is binding, an increase in monitoring intensity increases the unit revenue of Southern exports, and decreases the unit revenue of Northern output X.*

Propositions 2 and 3 reiterate our introductory remarks, and show that a social labeling program targets information imperfection on the consumption side, and corrects for the moral hazard problem on the production side. In the following sections, we consider how these corrective policies may spillover to affect the welfare of children in the South, and how social labeling-induced changes in producer profits affect national welfare.

Incidence of Child Labor

Referring to Figure 2 once more, social labeling strictly decreases the incidence of child labor whenever the participation constraint is satisfied, or equivalently, whenever $b^* > b^o$. Simply put, an increase in the price premium $p^*_\ell - p^*_u$ discourages Southern producers from employing child labor. However, the presence of false labels in the pool of Southern labeled products implies that employers of adult laborers cannot reap the full benefits of social labeling as the proportionate price premium of labeled products is strictly decreasing in $1 - \lambda^*$ (equation (6)). Thus, the promise of social labeling in securing children away from the work place is subject to the intensity of monitoring, with $\partial L^*_k/\partial\phi < 0$ whenever the false labeling constraint is binding.[22]

PROPOSITION 4.

(i) *Social labeling (strictly) reduces the incidence of child labor in sector x if and only if the participation constraint is satisfied.*

(ii) *If the false labeling constraint is binding, an increase in monitoring intensity decreases the incidence of child labor in sector x.*

Welfare of Children

Moving beyond the employment objective of social labeling per se, the full income of children in the South G^*_k, plus transfers from producers via the producer levy τ, is

$$G_k^* + \mu(b^*)\kappa m\tau = n_k \omega_k^* v(\bar{\theta}) + n_k \int_{\bar{\theta}(\omega_k^*, L_k^*)}^{\theta^+} R(\theta) h(L_k^*) dv(\theta) + \mu(b^*)\kappa m\tau,$$

where the first term represents the wage income of child laborers and the second term is the joint reservation income of children who do not work, and $\mu(b^*)\kappa m\tau$ represents the contribution to the welfare of children via the producer levy. We take G_k^* as a measure of the potential contribution of children to household income, taking into account both the wage income of children in sector x, along with the opportunity cost of child labor for those who are not put at work as a child. Since child labor market clearance requires $L_k^* = n_k v(\bar{\theta}(w_k^*, L_k^*)) = (1 - \mu(b^*))\kappa m b_k$ from equation (7), we have

$$\frac{\partial G_k^*}{\partial b^*} = \left(n_k v(\bar{\theta}) \frac{\partial \omega_k^*}{\partial L_k^*} + (\omega_k^* - R(\bar{\theta})h(L_k^*)) + n_k \left(\int_{\bar{\theta}(\omega_k^*, L_k^*)}^{\theta^+} R(\theta) dv(\theta) \right) h'(L_k^*) \right) \frac{\partial L_k^*}{\partial b^*}$$

$$= \left(n_k v(\bar{\theta}) \frac{\partial \omega_k^*}{\partial L_k^*} + n_k \left(\int_{\bar{\theta}(\omega_k^*, L_k^*)}^{\theta^+} R(\theta) dv(\theta) \right) h'(L_k^*) \right) \frac{\partial L_k^*}{\partial b^*}, \quad (9)$$

where the second equality follows since ω_k^* is equal to the opportunity cost of child labor at $\theta = \theta$. Thus, a labeling-induced decline in producers' incentives to employ child labor has two effects on the full income of children in the South. First, and as should be expected, demand shifts that favor adult labor usage puts downward pressure on the wage income of existing child laborers if and only if the supply schedule of child labor is upward sloping $(\partial\omega_k^*/\partial L_k^* = v'(\bar{\theta}(w_k^*, L_k^*))/(R'(\bar{\theta})h(L_k^*) + v'(\bar{\theta})R(\bar{\theta})h(L_k^*)) > 0)$. Meanwhile, for given w_k^*, if human capital accumulation exhibit scale economies (diseconomies) $(h'(L_k^*) < (>)0)$, social labeling provides a market mechanism which narrows the gap between the social opportunity cost of child labor $(\partial G_k^*/\partial L_k^*)|_{w_k^* cons.}$ and the private opportunity cost of the marginal child labor $R(\bar{\theta})h(L_k^*) = w_k^*$. The second term in equation (9) in parenthesis expresses the size of this gap, with $n_k \int_{\bar{\theta}(w_k^*, L_k^*)}^{\theta^+} R(\theta) dv(\theta) h'(L_k^*)(\partial L_k^*/\partial b^*) > (<)0$, if and only if $h'(L_k^*) < (>)0$ as L_k^* is inversely related to the share of adult employers $\mu(b^*)$. We have,

PROPOSITION 5. *If the participation constraint is satisfied, a necessary (though not sufficient) condition for social labeling to improve the pre-transfer full income of children (G_k^*) is that the social opportunity cost of child labor be strictly greater than the private opportunity cost of child labor.*

Put differently, with congestion diseconomies associated with the next best alternative to child labor, the application of social labeling in sector x can indeed imply that children are doubly worse off. Proposition 5 singles out what social labeling can achieve other than simply as a means of income transfer made possible through producer levy τ. Indeed, Proposition 5 shows that if the social opportunity cost is no greater than the private opportunity cost of child labor, the objective of promoting the welfare of children can be better served by a direct income transfer from producers to children through taxation and redistribution.

Trade Sanctions

Social labeling also opens up a host of possibilities regarding the choice of trade policies that the North may undertake in the face of unlabeled Southern imports, particularly since these are goods that compete with Northern producers who follow the practice of hiring only adult laborers. In this light, consider an import tax t_u levied on unlabeled imports. The market clearing equation (6) above should be accordingly rewritten as:

$$\alpha E(t_u)N = (p_u^* + t_u)\{[1 + \mu(b^*)(a-1)]\kappa m + aKM\},$$

where $E(t_u) = E + t_u(1 - \mu(b^*)/\lambda^*)\kappa m/N$ represents the disposable income of Northern consumers upon accounting for tariff revenue. In the appendix, we show that

Proposition 6. *If the false labeling constraint is not binding, a (small) move away from free trade due to an import tax levied on unlabeled Southern imports leads to:*

(i) *a reduction in the incidence of child labor;*
(ii) *a decline in the price of unlabeled products;*
(iii) *a decline in the price of labeled products, originating either from the South or the North, if the elasticity of supply of unlabeled products* $-d\log(1-\mu(b^*))/d\log(p_\ell - p_u)$ *is greater than 1/a; and*
(iv) *under the same supply elasticity restriction, an import tariff* t_u *increases the welfare of Northern consumers.*

The first item of the above proposition should not be too surprising, particularly since a discriminatory trade sanction lowers the willingness of Northern consumers to pay for unlabeled goods.[23] The resulting increase in the supply of labeled products can in fact ensure that the price of labeled products decreases as well, so long as the positive supply response of labeled products with respect to the change in price premium is sufficiently large. Interestingly, therefore, producers of labeled *and* unlabeled products, regardless of their country-of-origin, can suffer from revenue losses subsequent to a trade sanction imposed on unlabeled products.

Finally, the dual effects of declining prices *and* a decrease in the total supply of products made by child labor guarantee that Northern consumers to be unambiguously better off. These conclusions should be contrasted with the case where the monitoring intensity is sufficiently small:

Proposition 7. *If the false labeling constraint is binding, a (small) move away from free trade due to an import tax levied on unlabeled Southern imports at constant* ϕ*:*

(i) *leaves the incidence of child labor unchanged;*
(ii) *leads to a decline in the price of both labeled and unlabeled products for Southern producers. Meanwhile, the price of the Northern output increases unambiguously; and*
(iii) *improves the welfare of Northern consumers.*

As a first round impact of trade sanctions, child labor employers are faced with an increase in the price premium for labeled products. With the probability of detection by monitoring agencies unchanged, this translates into an increase in the incentive to apply false labels. In Figure 3, an increase in import tariff is illustrated by a shift of the *DD* curve upwards at constant λ. As stated earlier, a point like *A* violates rational expectations, since the pool of labeled products originating from the South is now contaminated with false labels. Thus, quite contrary to the original intent of trade sanctions against unlabeled products, an increase in t_u only results in a further increase in the share of false labels in the pool of Southern labeled imports, and equilibrium child labor employment is strictly unaffected as the $D'D'$ curve shifts all the way back to *DD*, or until the false labeling constraint just binds.

Meanwhile, with rising incidence of false labeling among Southern imports, consumers accordingly adapt their expectations λ, and adjusts their willingness to pay for Southern labeled imports downwards. It follows, therefore, that even though the price

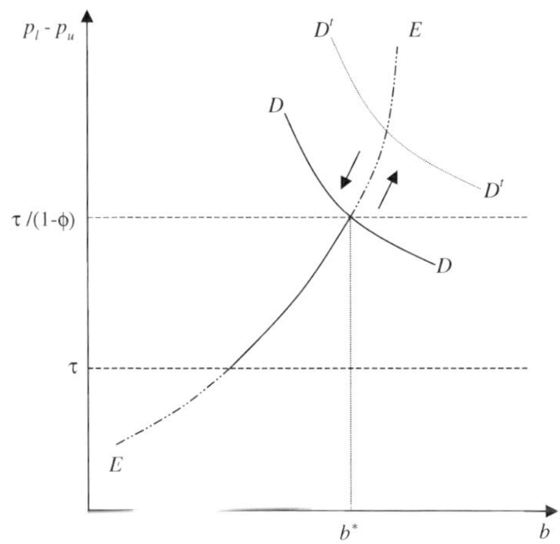

Figure 3. Trade Sanctions with No Impact on the Incidence of Child Labor

premium on labeled products remains unaltered ($p_\ell^* - p_u^* = \tau/(1-\phi)$), an import tariff succeeds in lowering both p_ℓ and p_u by identical amounts. Consequently, a trade sanction on unlabeled goods has an adverse effect on both adult and child labor employers in the South. In stark contrast to the regime with perfect monitoring, however, trade sanctions that raise the fraction of false labels in the South confer revenue benefits to the North, as consumers resort to demand Northern child labor free products, and P^* rises unambiguously.

Finally, although there is no change in child labor employment, consumers nevertheless enjoy an improvement in welfare associated with the income gain via the collection of tariff revenue, at the expense of Southern producers.

4. Gains from Social Labeling

Having discussed the relative gains and losses associated with social labeling, a question still remains as to whether the joint welfare of each of the individual constituents of the South, including child laborers, adult workers, and producers of both the x and y sectors, stand to gain from social labeling. Consider, therefore the welfare of the South,

$$\begin{aligned} V^* = {} & G^* - \mu(b^*)\kappa m\tau - \left[\int_{b^-}^{b^*} \omega b\, d\mu(b) + \omega_k b_k(1-\mu(b^*)\right]\kappa m \\ & + G_k^* + \mu(b^*)\kappa m\tau + \omega n_a \\ & - \left[p_\ell^* \frac{\mu(b^*)}{\lambda^*} + p_u^*\left(1 - \frac{\mu(b^*)}{\lambda^*}\right)\right]\kappa m - \left[\int_{b^-}^{b^*} \omega b\, d\mu(b) + \omega_k b_k(1-\mu(b^*)\right]\kappa m \\ & + n_k\omega_k^* v(\bar{\theta}) + n_k\int_{\bar{\theta}}^{\theta^+} R(\theta)h(L_k^*)dv(\theta) + \omega n_a \qquad (10) \\ = {} & \left[\alpha E(t) - P^*KM - t_u\left(1 - \frac{\mu(b^*)}{\lambda^*}\right)\kappa m\right] + \omega L_y^* + n_k\int_{\bar{\theta}}^{\theta^+} R(\theta)h(L_k^*)dv(\theta). \qquad (11) \end{aligned}$$

The first expression in equation (10) denotes producer profits in sector x, representing the total revenue G^* net of the aggregate wage bill for child labor, adult labor along with the producer levy τ for those participating in the labeling program. G_k^*, to recall, is the full income of children which include the wage income and opportunity costs of child labor and transfers from producers $\mu(b^*)m\tau$. ωn_a is the total wage income of adult a workers in the South. The second equality in equation (10) follows directly from product market clearance. Note that we do not include any resource cost that the South may incur in monitoring producers. Our purpose here is to determine whether the South may benefit from a labeling scheme, even when it is not responsible for the monitoring costs involved (Table 1). We have,

$$\frac{\partial V^*}{\partial \phi}\Big|_{\phi=0} = -KM\frac{\partial P^*}{\partial \phi} + (1-\alpha)t_u \kappa m \frac{\partial \mu(b^*)/\lambda^*}{\partial \phi} + n_k\left[\int_{\bar{\theta}}^{\theta^+} R(\theta)dv(\theta)\right]h'(L_k^*)\frac{\partial L_k^*}{\partial \phi}. \tag{12}$$

Thus, in addition to the desire to improve export revenue (or equivalently, to decrease the market share of Northern producers, P^*KM), and to narrow the gap between social and private returns to human capital accumulation, the incentives of the South to maintain a credible social labeling scheme depends on factors that are indigenous to the South, along with trade policies originating from the North. In particular, since $\partial L_k^*/\partial\phi < 0$ from Proposition 4, the right-hand side of equation (12) is strictly decreasing in $\int_{\bar{\theta}}^{\theta^+} R(\theta)dv$. Recall that θ depends on a vector of supply side determinants of child labor, so that an increase in θ is tantamount to an increase in the reservation wage required to induce each household to send its child to work. It follows, therefore, that in the presence of scale economies of human capital accumulation, economies where individual perceives low expected rewards to human capital accumulation $R(\theta)h(L_k)$ due, for example, to high borrowing rates of interest and relatively low parental income, have relatively little to gain from labeling schemes.

In addition, the right-hand side of equation (12) is strictly *decreasing* in t_u if and only if $(\mu(b^*)/\lambda^*)\kappa m$—total Southern supply of labeled products, regardless of whether child laborers are employed—*decreases* with monitoring. In other words, high import barriers on unlabeled products can in fact discourage the South to maintain a credible social labeling program. To see the intuition behind this rather surprising incentive consequence of trade sanctions, note that whenever false labeling prevails, Southern employers can avoid being subject to an import tariff via one of two means: (i) substituting adult laborers for child laborers; or (ii) applying false labels. In other words, economies where a majority of firms do not have access to cost saving technologies—$\mu(\cdot)$ is skewed with a fat right tail—are further discouraged from social labeling precisely because of a threat of trade sanctions, provided that at any given rate of import tariff, the number of adult labor employers $\mu(b^*)m$ increases at a much slower pace than the decline in false labeling.

PROPOSITION 8. *The South optimally sets $\phi = 0$ if:*

(i) *social opportunity cost of child labor is no greater than the private opportunity cost of child labor;*
(ii) *the South monopolizes the world market for product x ($KM = 0$);*
(iii) *the return to human capital is sufficiently small; and*
(iv) *the tax on unlabeled import is sufficiently high and $\mu(b^*)/\lambda^*$ is decreasing in ϕ.*

5. Social Labeling as a Transitional Institution

The questions of whether social labeling indeed benefits the South, and whether incentives—either via the market-based price premium, or extra-national threat of trade sanctions—to promote a credible social labeling program are solutions to the *problem* of child labor have been the focus of our analysis so far. In particular, we find that whether there are external diseconomies of child labor that individual households do not internalize in their child labor supply decision-making, is key to whether social labeling solves the problem of the potential over-supply of child labor.

However, a question still remains as to whether social labeling should be viewed as a permanent institution in poor economies, or should it be viewed as a step that initiates a process, by facilitating individuals to recognize the external diseconomies associated with child labor. To this end, a number of possibilities can be considered, such as embedding our basic setup in a growth theoretic framework or by introducing political institutions that endogenize the policy making process. Here, we adopt a direction which is closer in spirit with the current literature on child labor, and focus on the interaction between adult wages and the incidence of child labor (Baland and Robinson, 2000, Basu and Van, 1998; Grote, Basu, and Weinhold, 1998).

Let production in the y sector of the South be governed by a neoclassical production function: $y = f(n_a - L_a)$, with positive and diminishing marginal product. n_a denotes total Southern endowment of adult laborers, and L_a denotes adult labor employment in sector x. Profit maximizing calculus in adult labor hiring on the part of y sector producers yields a reservation wage schedule of adult laborers ($\omega(L_a)$) facing producers in sector x.

$$\omega = f'(n_a - L_a) \leftrightarrow L_a = L_a^s(\omega),$$

$L_a^s(\omega)$ is thus the supply of adult labor, which depends on the prevailing market wage for adults. Since b^* denotes the marginal Southern producer who is just indifferent between hiring adult or child laborers, market clearance in the adult labor market requires:

$$\left(\int_{b^-}^{b^*} b d\mu(b)\right)\kappa m = L_a^s(\omega). \tag{13}$$

As should be expected, ω is increasing in the fraction of producers who employ adult laborers, $\mu(b^*)$.

Meanwhile, let the reservation wage schedule of child labor be given by $R(\theta, \omega)h(L_k)$ an increase in the wage of adults ω increases the reservation wage $R(\theta, \omega)$ for all θ. It follows that a child is better off working in the x sector if $\theta \leq \bar{\theta}(\omega_k, L_k, \omega) \equiv \{\theta | R(\theta, \omega)h(L_k) = \omega_k.\}$. Thus, the supply of child labor schedule can be written as $L_k^s = L_k^s(\omega_k, \omega)$, with $\partial L_k^s/\partial\omega < 0$. In concert with standard arguments of the supply side determinants of child labor, an increase in the wage income of adult members of the household reduces the need to put children to work.

It follows that market clearance for the employment of child labor requires:

$$(1 - \mu(b^*))b_k\kappa m = L_k^s(\omega_k, \omega). \tag{14}$$

Thus, an increase in the fraction of child labor employers $(1 - \mu(b^*))$ go hand-in-hand with either an increase in ω_k, or a reduction in the adult wage ω, or both.

In addition, recall from equation (5) that the marginal producer is endogenously defined by:

$$\omega b^* - \omega_k b_k = p_\ell - p_u - \tau, \tag{15}$$

which equates the cost savings of hiring child labor with the revenue losses in the presence of social labeling. Thus, holding the adult wage constant, the cost savings gap of hiring child labor $\omega b^* - \omega_k b_k$ is strictly decreasing in the fraction of child labor employers $(1 - \mu(b^*))$, since from equation (14) above, an increase in child labor demand bids up wages ω_k, closing the cost savings gap.

With adult wages now endogenously determined, equations (13)–(15) can be used to yield the following result:

PROPOSITION 9. *The cost savings gap of hiring child labor is strictly increasing in the fraction of child labor employers* $(1 - \mu(b^*))$ *if and only if the elasticity of child labor supply with respect to the adult wage* $\varepsilon^s_{ka} = -d \log L^s_k/d \log \omega$ *is sufficiently large.*

The proof of this result is relegated to the Appendix, although the intuition of how child labor employment can create its own demand can be readily understood by noting that if the problem of child labor is pervasive, and crowds out adult employment opportunities, the resulting downward pressure on adult wages (equation (13)) is but a first round effect. In particular, if a reduction in adult wage income induces a large enough labor supply response (equation (14)), the lower the adult wage ω, the *higher* will be the cost savings associated with hiring child labor $\omega b^* - \omega_k b_k$ in general equilibrium. The result is thus a second round increase in child labor demand, and the cumulative causation of events implies that the cost savings gap of hiring child labor is in fact strictly increasing in child labor employment.

In the context of our graphical analysis in Figures 2 and 3, Proposition 9 implies that the *EE* schedule, which requires that cost savings of child labor employment be equal to the price premium $p_\ell - p_u$, is downward sloping.[24] For our purpose, which involve the question of whether social labeling is a transitional institution that can guide the South away from the oversupply of child labor, consider the following dynamic adjustment process:

$$\dot{b}^* = \psi[\max\{p^*_\ell - p^*_u - \tau, 0\} - (\omega b^* - \omega_k b_k)], \quad \psi > 0, \quad \text{if } b^* \in [b^-, b^+], \tag{16}$$

where $\dot{b}^*$ denotes derivative with respect to time. The price premium (*EE* curve), or $p_\ell - p_u$ is given by product market clearance in equation (6), taking the intensity of monitoring ϕ as given. In addition, $\max\{p_\ell - p_u - \tau, 0\} = p_\ell - p_u - \tau$ whenever the participation constraint is satisfied. Otherwise, no producer participate in social labeling, and all producers receive the same price p^o.

Note that equation (16) simply requires that the fraction of adult labor employers rises whenever the price premium net of the employer levy τ is greater than the cost savings of employing child labor. Starting from any $b^* \in [b^-, b^+]$, $\tilde{b}^*$ is an equilibrium based on the adjustment process if $\dot{b}^*|_{\tilde{b}^*} = 0$ for $\tilde{b}^* \in (b^-, b^+)$, or $\dot{b}^* \leq 0$ for $\tilde{b}^* = b^-$, and $\dot{b}^* \geq 0$ for $\tilde{b}^* = b^+$. We are now in a position to state:

PROPOSITION 10. *Starting from* $b^* = b^o$ *in the absence of labeling, if a social labeling program satisfies the participation constraint, then* $\tilde{b}^* = b^+$ *if* ε^s_{ka} *is sufficiently large.*

Figure 4 illustrates. The downward sloping *EE* curve that is steeper than the *DD* curve reflects the fact that ε_{ka} is large enough. As indicated in section 3, starting from the initial equilibrium with $b^* = b^o$, a social labeling program that satisfies the participation constraint implies that *DD* lies above the $p_\ell - p_u - \tau(=0)$ at $b^* = b^o$. The labeling induced price premium encourages Southern producers to employ adult workers, with $\dot{b}^* > 0$ since $p^*_\ell - p^*_u - \tau - (\omega b^* - \omega_k b_k) > 0$. This marks the beginning of a virtuous

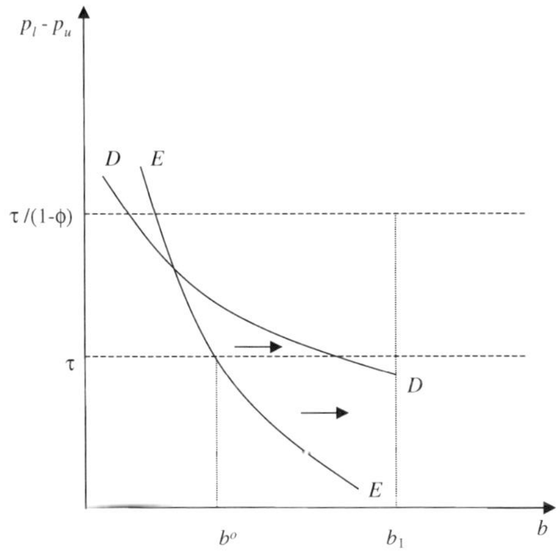

Figure 4. Dynamics of Child Labor Employment and Social Labeling

process, throughout which the cost savings associated with child labor employment fall continuously. Note that this process continues despite the fact that after some point (b_1 in figure 4), the participation constraint is violated, and a uniform price applies to employers of both adult and child laborers. To see this, note that in the absence of labeling, the absence of a price premium implies that cost savings of hiring child labor is equal to zero at the original equilibrium point b^o. Therefore, as long as ε^s_{ka} is sufficiently large, proposition 9 guarantees that the cost savings associated with child labor employment is strictly negative for all $b^* > b^o$. Thus, child labor employment continues to decline even when *no employer* participates in the social labeling program for $b \in [b_1, b^+]$.[25]

6. Conclusion

The purpose of this paper has been two-fold: to develop a theoretical model to formalize the arguments in the descriptive literature concerning the potential merits and problems associated with social labeling in a general equilibrium framework; and to argue that social labeling should be viewed as a potential aid to the welfare of children in poor countries only in so far as it may serve as a *second best* policy.

Based on our framework, we obtain a number of additional insights which emphasize that the employment objective of social labeling depends critically on the level of monitoring in place and that the information objective of social labeling can favor both consumers and Southern producers once labels provide the appropriate linkage between consumer preferences and producers' input choices. In contrast, as soon as one recognizes that producers in both countries compete not just in prices, but also in hidden product attributes such as the degree of child labor usage in the production process, shifting Southern producers to costlier production methods (adult labor employment) need not render Northern producers better-off. From the viewpoint of the welfare of the children, rather than viewing the incidence of child labor as an end in itself, of particular relevance seems to be the underlying characteristics of Southern labor markets that make child employment *excessive*. These include the need to secure subsistence, credit market imperfections, and the prospects of education. We also find that a more prudent look into the question of whether trade sanctions can indeed assist in promoting the welfare of children absent other alternatives, or whether the mere threat of trade sanctions is sufficient to provide incentives for the South to uphold a given version of labor standards, is called for. Indeed, discriminatory barriers to trade may in fact discourage the South from initiating the monitoring required to maintain a credible social labeling program.

Finally, we took a first step in understanding social labeling as a transitional institution, aimed as assisting individuals in poor economies to recognize, where they exist, the potential external economies of the alternatives to child labor, such as education. In this context, we find that if the extent of child labor is so pervasive as to crowd out adult employment opportunities, and adult wages are strictly decreasing in child labor employment as in Basu and Van (1998), then a no social labeling equilibrium may well be dynamically unstable. Indeed, the labeling induced price premium can serve as a temporary device which eventually eradicates child labor, even after the price premium of social labeling itself vanishes with excess supply of products that are guaranteed manufactured without child labor.

Appendix

Proof of Propositions 1 and 4

Making use of equation (7), and denote $p_\ell^* - p_u^* \equiv \Delta p^*$, $\partial L_k^s / \partial \omega_k \equiv L_{kk}^s$, we have

$$\omega \frac{\partial b^*}{\partial(\Delta p^* - \tau)} = \frac{\partial(\Delta p^* - \tau + \omega_k^* b_k)}{\partial(\Delta p^* - \tau)} = \frac{L_{kk}^s}{L_{kk}^s + \mu' \kappa m b_k^2 / \omega} > 0. \tag{17}$$

It follows that b^* is uniquely determined by $\Delta p^* - \tau$. Specifically, since the satisfaction of the participation constraint implies that $\Delta p^* - \tau > 0$, and b^* is strictly increased in $\Delta p^* - \tau$ from equation (17) above, we have $b^* > b^o$. Substituting this into the indirect utility function of Northern consumer yields the desired result.

To show that consumers welfare improve with the degree of monitoring, observe from the definition of U^* that this is equivalent to a positive relationship between b^* and ϕ. To see this, note that if the false labeling constrained is just binding, we have, in addition, that $\Delta p^* = \tau/(1 - \phi)$. Substituting this into equation (7), we have

$$\left(1 - \mu\left(\frac{\frac{\phi\tau}{1-\phi} + \omega_k^* b_k}{\omega}\right)\right)\kappa m b_k = L_k^s(\omega_k^*).$$

It follows that equilibrium child labor employment is uniquely determined by monitoring intensity, with $\partial\omega_k^*/\partial\phi < 0$ whenever L_k^s is upward sloping. Equivalently, $L_k^*(\omega_k^*)$, and hence $(1 - \mu(b^*))$ is strictly decreasing in ϕ.

Proof of Proposition 2

Denote $B^* \equiv 1 + \mu(b^*)(a - 1)$, $B^o \equiv 1 + \mu(b^o)(a - 1)$ and $B^\lambda \equiv 1 + \lambda^*(a - 1)$, we have, from product market clearance and footnote (19),

$$\frac{P^o}{P^*} = \frac{B^*\kappa m + aKM}{B^o\kappa m + aKM} > 1, \quad \frac{p^o}{p_u^*} = B^o \frac{B^*\kappa m + aKM}{B^o\kappa m + aKM} > 1.$$

In addition,

$$\frac{p^o}{p_\ell^*} = \frac{B^o}{B^\lambda}\frac{B^*\kappa m + aKM}{B^o\kappa m + aKM} = \frac{B^*\kappa m + aKM}{B^\lambda \kappa m + (B^\lambda aKM/B^o)} < \frac{B^*\kappa m + aKM}{B^\lambda\kappa m + aKM} < 1,$$

where the first inequality holds whenever $\lambda^* > \mu(b^o)$, and the second inequality follows whenever total supply of unlabeled products is positive $(1 - \mu(b^*)/\lambda^*) > 0$.

Proof of Proposition 3

Observe from product market clearing that

$$P^o = \alpha aEN(B^o\kappa m + aKM)^{-1}, \quad P^* = \alpha aEN(B^*\kappa m + aKM)^{-1}.$$

The expression for G^o and G^* can be readily obtained by observation that $G^o = \alpha EN - P^o KM$ and likewise, $G^* = \alpha EN - P^* KM$.

Proof of Proposition 6

If the participation constraint is satisfied, and all Southern products bears true labels, we have

$$p_u^* + t_u = \frac{\alpha(E + t_u(1 - \mu(b^*)\kappa m))}{(1 + \mu(b^*)(a-1))\kappa m + aKM} \equiv G(\Delta p^*, t_u) \tag{18}$$

$$\Leftrightarrow \Delta p^* = p_\ell^* - p_u^* = (a-1)G(\Delta p^*, t_u) + t_u,$$

with $G_1 < 0$ and $1 > G_2 > 0$. By routine manipulation, $G_1 + G_2 < 0$ if and only if the elasticity of supply of unlabeled products with respect to Δp, $\eta = d\log(1 - \mu(\Delta p^* + \omega_k b_k))/d\log \Delta p^*$, holding ω_k constant, is strictly greater than $1/a$.

Equation (18) above implicitly defines the equilibrium price premium on labeled goods Δp in terms of the size of the import tax t_u. In particular,

$$\frac{\partial \Delta p}{\partial t_u} = \frac{(a-1)G_2 + 1}{1 - (a-1)G_1} > 0, \quad \frac{\partial p_u^*}{\partial t_u} = \frac{G_2 - 1 + aG_1}{1 - (a-1)G_1} < 0, \quad \frac{\partial p_\ell^*}{\partial t_u} = a\frac{G_1 + G_2}{1 - (a-1)G_1} < 0.$$

Thus, an import tax widens the price gap and decreases the price of unlabeled goods. In addition, if the elasticity of supply η of unlabeled products is sufficiently large, the price of labeled products is similarly decreasing in t_u. Substituting these results in the indirect utility function of consumers, it can be readily verified that consumers' welfare is increased by deviating from a free trade.

Proof of Proposition 7

From equations (1), (4) and (18), aggregate supply of unlabeled products can be written as

$$\left(1 - \frac{\mu(b^*)}{\lambda^*}\right)\kappa m = \left(1 - \frac{\mu(b^*)(a-1)(p_u^* + t_u)}{(\tau/(1-\phi)) - t_u}\right)\kappa m.$$

Denote tariff revenue $t_u(1-\mu(b^*)/\lambda^*)\kappa m = T(p_u^*, t_u)$. It can be readily verified that starting with $t_u = 0$,

$$T_1 < 0; \quad (1+\mu(b^*)(a-1))\kappa m + aKM > T_2(p_u^*, 0) > 0.$$

From product market clearance, and the false labeling constraint,

$$p_u^* + t_u = \frac{\alpha(E+T(p_u^*, t_u))}{(1+\mu(b^*)(a-1))\kappa m + aKM} \Leftrightarrow P^* = a\frac{\alpha(E+T(p_u^*, t_u))}{(1+\mu(b^*)(a-1))\kappa m + aKM}$$
$$\Delta p^* = \frac{\tau}{1-\phi}. \tag{19}$$

From equation (19), equilibrium price premium is invariant to t_u, as such, an import tax has no influence on b^*, or equivalently, the incidence of child labor. In addition,

$$\frac{\partial p_u^*}{\partial t_u} = \frac{\Gamma - \alpha T_2}{\alpha T_1 - \Gamma} < 0, \quad \frac{\partial p_\ell^*}{\partial t_u} = \frac{\partial(p_u^* + \tau/(1-\phi))}{\partial t_u} = \frac{\partial p_u^*}{\partial t_u} < 0, \quad \frac{\partial P^*}{\partial t_u} = a\alpha\frac{T_1 - T_2}{\alpha T_1 - \Gamma} > 0,$$

where $\Gamma \equiv (1 + \mu(b^*)(a-1)\kappa m + aKM > T_2$. Thus, an import tax on decreases the price of all Southern products, while it increases that of the North.

Proof of Proposition 9

Denote $\partial L_a^i/\partial\omega$ as L_{aa}^i and $\partial L_k^i/\partial\omega$ as L_{ka}^i, $i = s, d$, market clearance for adult and child labor (equations (13) and (14)) can be used to obtain:

$$\frac{\partial\omega}{\partial b^*} = \frac{\mu'(b^*)b^*\kappa m}{L_{aa}^s}, \quad \frac{\partial\omega_k}{\partial b^*} = -\frac{\mu'(b^*)\kappa m}{L_{kk}^s}\left(b_k + b^*\frac{L_{ka}^s}{L_{aa}^s}\right).$$

As indicated in the discussion of proposition 9, the adult wage is bided upwards whenever b^* rises, but since child labor supply is decreasing in ω ($L_{ka}^s < 0$), the child labor wage may well be increasing in b^* as well, as long as L_{ka}^s is sufficiently large. In addition, from the definition of b^* in equation (5), along with that of the demand for adult and child laborers in section 2, we have

$$\frac{\partial L_k^d}{\partial\omega_k} = -\frac{\mu'(b^*)b_k^2\kappa m}{\omega} \equiv -\varepsilon_{kk}^d\frac{L_k^d}{\omega_k}$$
$$\frac{\partial L_a^d}{\partial w} = -\frac{\mu'(b^*)(b^*)^2\kappa m}{\omega} \equiv -\varepsilon_{aa}^d\frac{L_a^d}{\omega}$$
$$\frac{\partial L_a^d}{\partial\omega_k} = \frac{\mu'(b^*)b^*b_k\kappa m}{\omega} \equiv \varepsilon_{ak}^d\frac{L_a^d}{\omega_k},$$

where $\varepsilon_{ij}^d > 0$, $i = a, k$ and $j = a, k$ are elasticities of labor demand of L_i with respect to a change in the wage of adult, and child labor. Also let $\varepsilon_{ij}^d > 0$, $i = a, k$ and $j = a, k$ as elasticities of the supply of L_i with respect to ω and ω_k, it follows that the cost savings of hiring child labor narrows, as the fraction of employers who hire only adult workers increase:

$$\frac{\partial\omega b^* - \omega_k b_k}{\partial b^*} = \omega\left(1 + \frac{\varepsilon_{aa}^d}{\varepsilon_{aa}^s} + \frac{\varepsilon_{kk}^d}{\varepsilon_{kk}^s} - \frac{\varepsilon_{ak}^d}{\varepsilon_{kk}^s}\frac{\varepsilon_{ka}^s}{\varepsilon_{aa}^s}\right) \le 0$$
$$\Leftrightarrow \varepsilon_{ka}^s \ge \frac{\varepsilon_{kk}^s\varepsilon_{aa}^s + \varepsilon_{aa}^d\varepsilon_{kk}^s + \varepsilon_{kk}^d\varepsilon_{aa}^s}{\varepsilon_{ak}^d}.$$

Proof of Proposition 10

Note that the slope of the *EE* curve in figure 4 is given by totally differentiating equation (6) which defines the price premium $p_\ell - p_u$ that consumers are willing to pay. In particular, $p_\ell - p_u$ is strictly decreasing with the supply of products made by adults $(\mu(b^*)\kappa m)$, Meanwhile, the slope of the *DD* curve is given by equation (15), which equates the cost savings of employing child labor with the price premium. From the proof of Proposition 9, *DD* is decreasing in b^* if ε^s_{ka} is sufficiently large. In addition, the larger is ε^s_{ka}, the steeper the slope of the *DD* curve.

The original equilibrium point b^o is unstable if and only if $p_\ell - p_u - (\omega b^* - \omega_k b_k)$ is increasing in b^*. In terms of figure 4, if ε^s_{ka} is sufficiently large so that *DD* is steeper than *EE*, $\max\{p_\ell - p_u - \tau, 0\} - (\omega b^* - \omega_k b_k)$ is strictly positive and increasing in b^* for all $b^* > b^o$. Making use of equation (16), it follows that $b^* > 0$ for $b^* > b^o$, and $\tilde{b}^* = b^+$.

References

Akabayashi, Hideo and George Psacharopoulos, "The Trade-off between Child Labour and Human Capital Formation: a Tanzanian Case Study," *The Journal of Development Studies* 35 (1999):120–40.

Baland, Jean-Marie and James Robinson, "Is Child Labor Inefficient?" *Journal of Political Economy* 108 (2000):662–79.

Basu, Arnab and Nancy H. Chau, "Asymmetric Country-of-Origin Effects on Intra-Industry Trade and the International Quality Race," *Review of Development Economics* 2 (1998):140–66.

Basu, Kaushik, "International Labor Standards and Child Labor," *Challenge* 42 (1999a):80–93.

Basu, Kaushik, "Child Labor: Cause, Consequence, and Cure with Remarks on International Labor Standards," *Journal of Economic Literature* (September) (1999b):1083–119.

Basu, Kaushik, "Compacts, Conventions, and Codes: Initiatives for Higher International Labor Standards," *Cornell International Law Journal* 34 (2001):487–500.

Basu, Kaushik and Pham Hoang Van, "The Economics of Child Labor," *American Economic Review* 88 (1998):412–27.

Bhagwati, Jagdish, "Trade Liberalization and 'Fair Trade' Demands: Addressing Environmental and Labor Standards Issues," *World Economy* 18 (1995):745–59.

Birdsall, Nancy, "Life is Unfair: Inequality in the World," *Foreign Policy* (Summer) 87 (1998):76–93.

Brown, Drusilla, "Can Consumer Product Labels Deter Foreign Child Labor Exploitation?" Working Paper, *Department of Economics, Tufts University, Boston, MA* (2000).

Dixit, Avinash and Joseph E. Stiglitz, "Monopolistic Competition and Optimum Product Diversity," *American Economic Review* 67 (1977):297–308.

Freeman, Richard B., "A Hard Headed Look at Labor Standards," in US Department of Labor, Bureau of International Labor Affairs, International Labor Standards and Global Economic Integration: Proceedings of a Symposium, Washington DC (1994).

Grootaert, Christiaan and Ravi Kanbur, "Child Labor: an Economic Perspective," *International Labor Review* 134 (1995):187–203.

Grote, Ulrike, Arnab Basu, and Diana Weinhold, "Child Labor and the International Policy Debate: the Education-Child Labor Trade-off and the Consequences of Trade Sanctions," Working Paper No 1, *Center for Development Research (ZEF), University of Bonn, Germany* (1998).

Harvey, Pharis J., *Rugmark After One Year: Appraisal of a New Effort at Social Marketing in the Interests of Children.* Washington DC: International Labor Rights Fund (1996).

Hilowitz, Janet, "Social Labeling to Combat Child Labor: Some Considerations," *International Labor Review* 136 (1997a):215–32.

Hilowitz, Janet, "Labeling Child Labor Products—A preliminary Study," Washington DC: International Labor Organization, http://www.ilo.org/public/english/standards/ipec/publ/policy/papers/labelling/index.htm (accessed May 2006).

ILO., "Is Child Labor Really Necessary in India's Carpet Industry," Geneva, ILO, http://www.ilo.org/public/english/standards/ipec/publ/policy/papers/carpet/carpet1.htm (accessed May 2006).

ILO., "Child Labour: Targeting the Intolerable," Geneva, ILO, http://www.ilo.org/public/english/standards/ipec/publ/clrep96.htm (accessed May 2006).

Jafarey, Saqib and Sajal Lahiri, "Will Trade Sanctions Reduce Child Labor? The Role of Credit Markets," *Journal of Development Economics* 68 (2002):137–56.

Krueger, Alan, "International Labor Standards and Trade," in Michael Brumo and Boris Pleskovic (eds), *Proceedings of the Annual World Bank Conference on Development Economics 1996*. Washington DC: World Bank (1997).

Maskus, Keith, "Should Core Labor Standards be Imposed through International Trade Policy?" Policy Research Working Paper No. 1817. Washington DC: World Bank (1997).

Srinivasan, T.N., "International Trade and Labor Standards from an Economic Perspective," in P. van Dyck and G. Faber (eds), *Challenges to the New World Trade Organization*. Amsterdam: Kluwer Publishers (1996).

Notes

1. In a recent article, Basu (1999a) classifies these efforts into three categories: (i) *Intra-National* efforts comprise legislations enacted by developing countries to discourage child labor employment within domestic boundaries; (ii) *Supra-National* efforts made by the ILO, WTO and UNICEF which encourage countries to enact intra-national legislations; and (iii) *Extra-National* efforts, including those legislations that prohibits the import of goods from developing countries that are made with child labor.

2. The White Label was sponsored and monitored by the National Consumers League, it guaranteed manufacturers' compliance with the maintenance of decent working conditions and the employment of no child labor. See Hilowitz (1997a) for other early attempts at social labeling in the US.

3. The first social labels that aimed directly at the mitigation of child labor employment in developing countries are "RUGMARK" and "CARE & FAIR". RUGMARK was established in 1994 to guarantee German and US consumers that hand-knotted carpets made in India and Nepal were child-labor free.

4. These criteria range from the complete elimination of child labor usage in the production process enforced through random inspection by independent agencies in some cases (RUGMARK, KALEEN, ABRINQ, DIP), to the adoption of company codes of conduct that aims at improving work conditions with self-monitoring (CARE & FAIR, STEP).

5. In section 3, we present a formal argument that supports this conjecture.

6. See Basu (1999a), Basu and Van (1998), Baland and Robinson (2000), and Goorteart and Kanbur (1995).

7. In its latest version, the Harkin's bill proposed that legislation should be enacted to protect adult worker's wages in the developed countries against unfair competition from lower priced imports made with child labor. It is argued that the loss of export markets would then act as an incentive for developing countries to enact and enforce stricter laws against child labor employment. The debate over whether the underlying motivation of trade sanctions are driven by a desire to protect domestic import competing interests, or the welfare of children, is ongoing. See, for instance Krueger (1997) for findings in support of the latter.

8. Basu (1999a) points out that policy recommendations based solely on consumer attitudes may confuse the incidence of child labor with child welfare. In light of this, Sections 3.1 to 3.4 examines the impact of social labeling, respectively, on the well-being of children, of producers in the North and South, along with that of consumers.

9. More specifically, $d_a^x(p_\ell, p_u, P) = \alpha E/p_\ell$ if $a_\lambda/p_\ell > a_k/p_u$; and $a_\lambda/p_\ell > a_a/P$, and zero if $a_k/p_u > a_\lambda/p_\ell$; or; $a_a/P > a_\ell/p_\ell$. Also, $d_u^x(p_\ell, p_u, P) = \alpha E/p_u$, if $a_\lambda/p_\ell < a_k/p_u$; and $a_a/P < a_a/p_u$ and zero if $a_\lambda/p_\ell > a_k/p_u$; or $a_a/P > a_k/p_u$, where $a_\lambda \equiv \lambda a_a + (1 - \lambda)a_k$. Likewise, the demand schedule for Northern production of x is given by $d^X(p_\ell, p_u, P) = \alpha E/P$, if $a_\lambda/p_\ell < a_a/P$; and $a_k/p_u < a_a/P$ and zero if $a_\lambda/p_\ell > a_a/P$; or $a_a/P < a_k/p_u$.

10. Alternatively, and even in the absence of a country-of-origin label, we can further extend our model to incorporate Northern producers' decision to institute a social label, specific to Northern producers. In this context, our current setup can also be interpreted as one in which a credible social labeling program is in place in the North. Since child labor is a non-issue, all Northern producers participate, and the uniform price P^o applies when the South does not have a labeling program, and P otherwise.

11. See Basu and Chau (1998) for an analysis of the determination of North–South terms-of-trade when consumers statistically discriminate against products based on the country-of-origin labels.

12. We relax this assumption in section 5, and show that endogenizing the adult wage rate can make the case for social labeling even stronger.

13. The fixed coefficient technology allows us to focus on the choice between adult and child labor on the part of individual producers. With a more general production technology, the three-stage decision of (i) technology choice, (ii) input demand given market returns to labor, for example, and finally, (iii) to label or not, will each need to be considered. See footnote 23 for a brief discussion.

14. We take firm-specific differences in adult productivity as the selection criteria for child labor employers. Alternatives such as the transaction costs required for the subcontracting of work to child labor employers, and other geographical determinants such as firm location can also be considered. The results of this paper remain robust, so long as a positive fraction of Southern producers are child labor employers responding to the price incentives of social labeling.

15. Field studies presented in ILO (1996a) find that the so-called *nimble fingers* argument is fallacious in the carpet industry, that is, children are not relatively more productive as compared to adult laborers.

16. More specifically, this requires that $|h'|$ be small enough so that $\partial(L_k^s - n_k v(\bar{\theta}))/\partial L_k^s = 1 + n_k v'(\bar{\theta}) R(\bar{\theta}) h'(L_k^s)/(R'(\bar{\theta}) h(L_k^s)) > 0$.

17. In the absence of monitoring, labeled firms are rewarded with a price premium that is just equal the levy imposed on labeled products. As such, the unit revenue of labeled and unlabeled firms is identical. Simply put, labeling in the complete absence of monitoring has no bearing on child labor employment.

18. Assuming that the false labeling constraint is not binding, and hence $\lambda^* = 1$, equations (5), (6), and (7) can be used to solve for b^*, ω_k^* and $p_\ell^* - p_u^*$. The rest of the unknowns can be had by observing that $p_\ell^* = P^* = ap_u^*$ from equation (1) whenever $\lambda^* - 1$. If, however, the false labeling constraint is binding, and hence $p_\ell - p_u = \tau/(1 - \phi)$ will serve as an additional constraint, but λ^* now endogenous, as $\lambda^*(a - 1) = p_\ell^* - p_u^*$ again from equation (1).

19. To see this, note that product market clearance require $\alpha EN = p^o \kappa m + P^o KM$, or

$$\alpha EN = p^o\left(\kappa m + \frac{KM}{\frac{1}{a} + \left(1 - \mu(b^o)\left(1 - \frac{1}{a}\right)\right)}\right) \Leftrightarrow p^o = \frac{\alpha EN}{\kappa m + (1 + \mu(b^o)(a-1))^{-1} aKM}.$$

Equation (8) follows from substituting p^o into the utility function of Northern households.

20. Alternatively, one may also think of these results as comparing (i) both the North and the South has social labeling programs (at prices P^*, p_ℓ^* and p_u^*), and (ii) only the North instituted one (at equilibrium prices P^o and p^o). We thank an anonymous referee for pointing out the importance of this interpretation to us.

21. Note that in general, λ^* may be greater than or less than $\mu(b^o)$. In the proof of proposition 2, we show that $\lambda^* > \mu(b^o)$ holds whenever the unit output levy τ is sufficient large so as to deter false labeling in the absence of perfect monitoring.

22. Indeed, if the false labeling constraint is not binding, and the production technology is of the variable coefficient variety, the price incentives ($p_u^* < p^o$ and $p_\ell^* > p^o$) generated through labeling affect child labor employment in two ways: (i) the share of child labor employers declines (Proposition 4); (ii) employers who continue to employ child labor (adult) laborers respond by reducing (increasing) their labor demand, if the derived demand labor curve is monotonically increasing in output price. The two effects thus reinforce each other, and child labor falls even further. If instead, the false labeling constraint binds, the same price incentives can increase the employment of child labor producing falsely labeled product. The net effect will depend on the relative magnitude of these three sets of forces.
23. To see this, note that labeled and unlabeled goods coexist if and only if

$$\frac{p_u}{p_\ell} < \frac{a_k}{a_a} = \frac{p_u + t_u}{p_\ell}.$$

24. There are, of course, other possible configurations of *EE* and *DD* whenever both these schedules are downward sloping, involving multiple equilibria when *EE* and *DD* intersect more than once, or non-existence of equilibrium when foreign demand is too weak so that *DD* lies below *EE*.
25. From Figure 4, it should also be clear that Proposition 10 holds even when the false labeling constraint is binding. To see this, simply shift the *DD* curve upwards so that *DD* and *EE* intersect at $\tau/(1-\phi)$. The dynamics that follows upon instituting a labeling program likewise imply a virtuous process with $\tilde{b}^* = b^+$.

J Econ Inequal (2016) 14:81–108
DOI 10.1007/s10888-015-9314-2

Middlemen, fair traders, and poverty

Nancy H. Chau[1] · Hideaki Goto[2] · Ravi Kanbur[3]

Received: 18 January 2013 / Accepted: 7 July 2015 / Published online: 7 August 2015

Abstract We propose a spatial model of producer market access where local middlemen reap market power due to match friction, and fair traders enter to present an alternative. The model features location as a key determinant of the impact of fair trader entry on the market share of fair traders, the distribution of consumer willingness to pay between middlemen and producers, and intra- / inter-regional poverty incidence. For governments who wish to minimize the poverty gap, our results support directing resources to subsidize fair trade organizations, and/or to producers with no access to markets, rather than to local middlemen intermediaries.

Keywords Middlemen · Fair traders · Poverty · Market access

Electronic supplementary material The online version of this article (doi:10.1007/s10888-015-9314-2) contains supplementary material, which is available to authorized users.

✉ Nancy H. Chau
hyc3@cornell.edu

Hideaki Goto
h-goto@iuj.ac.jp

Ravi Kanbur
sk145@cornell.edu

1 Charles H. Dyson School of Applied Economics and Management, Cornell University, Ithaca, NY 14853, USA

2 Graduate School of International Relations, International University of Japan, Niigata 949-7277, Japan

3 Charles H. Dyson School of Applied Economics and Management and Department of Economics, Cornell University, Ithaca, NY 14853, USA

1 Introduction

Middlemen, trading entrepreneurs who link the backwaters of developing countries to emerging markets nationally and especially globally, seem to be universally reviled despite the economic service they provide. Without their capital, specialized knowledge and information, consumer demand in growing markets might be outside the reach of the small holder in the rural area, or of the home-based artisan in the urban slum. By bridging this gap, albeit for profit, surely they help to alleviate poverty?

And yet it is this profit motive, and the claim that these middlemen make "excessive profits" because of market power, that is at the root of much of the concern. Thus, for example, McMillan et al. (2004) study the case of cashews in Mozambique, and report that cashew growers only receive 40 % to 50 % of the border price, even after border taxes are allowed for. They go on to note:

> "it is clear that the marketing channels for raw cashew nuts remain imperfectly competitive. Farmers' incomes are depressed not only by transport and marketing costs, but also by the market power exercised by the traders." (p 120).

Many social movements in developing countries address themselves to providing an alternative channel to the market for poor producers. For example, the Self Employed Women's Association (SEWA) in India has set up the SEWA Trade Facilitation Center (STFC):

> "...the artisan women though skilled in hand embroidery had to forcibly migrate in search of work, or undertake earth digging work. The trade of their old valuable embroidered trouso would typically occur during distressed time. This would occur with traders and middlemen since the artisans had access to a very limited market. Moreover they only had their traditional skills but still required products which they could sell in the market. Lack of market information hindered artisans from building a strong relationship with the buyers. With the inception of STFC, integrated supply chain mechanism was created and the production became organized." (SEWA Trade Facilitation Center 2015).

Some organizations in the fair trade business promise a number of outcomes, including an improved outcome for the impoverished producers of the products being sold.[1] According to the Fair Trade Federation:

> "...Fair trade organizations work directly with producers, cutting out middlemen, so they can keep products affordable for consumers and return a greater percentage of the price to the producers." (Fair Trade Federation 2015).

The juxtaposition of middlemen trading for profit and fair traders with explicit goals to assist poor producers raises interesting and important analytical and policy issues. What determines equilibrium share of producers served by middlemen and fair traders? Does fair trader entry reinforce the poverty impact of market access by changing the middlemen markup as well as the extent of market price pass-through? What precisely is the impact of

[1] Over 1.2 million individual farmers and workers in 58 producing countries are involved in producing Fairtrade certified products in 2009 according to the Fairtrade Labelling Organizations International. Fairtrade products are sold in over 70 countries, and in some national markets, Fairtrade accounts for as high as 20 %–50 % of total market share (Fairtrade Labelling Organizations International 2010a, 2010b).

fair traders on poverty when the full round of market repercussions, including entry and exit of middlemen and of fair traders, is taken into account? Should a government interested in poverty reduction subsidize the entry of fair traders, or should it perhaps subsidize the entry of middlemen?

These are the questions to which this paper is directed, and they are questions to which we believe the literature provides only a partial answer. To do so, we work with a model that exhibits three features. First, we focus on situations where producers rely on middlemen to deliver their products to market. As such, price pass-throughs depend critically on the market power of the middleman, and the associated markup. Second, we posit that match friction exists between producers and middlemen. The resulting information asymmetry about price offers received by other producers induces endogenous middlemen market power and price dispersion at the farm gate level even with free entry. Third, we examine the equilibrium at each point along a spatial continuum by allowing middlemen market power to vary endogenously across locations. The resulting framework yields middlemen market power, dispersion in farm gate prices, and an endogenous price pass-through that jointly depend on a producer's location along the spatial continuum.

Within this setting, we introduce fair traders motivated by a concern for poverty either on behalf of the final consumers they serve via a location specific price premium, or the preferences of the fair traders themselves. These fair traders act as an alternative intermediary other than traditional middlemen linking markets and individual producers.[2] Like many models of voluntary contribution and of altruistic behavior, this concern for poverty will be expressed in the form of price shifter via a warm glow effect (Andreoni 1990), which applies whenever the fair trader operates in locations where poverty is known to be pervasive.[3]

Thus, this paper brings together two so far distinctive areas of research inquiry: (i) the role of middlemen and market power in determining price behavior and as such intra- and interregional poverty in a spatial setting, and (ii) the role of fair traders in facilitating price pass-throughs, and in providing a market based mechanism for expressing consumer concerns for the plight of marginalized producers along the locational continuum.

The role of middlemen and market power in determining price pass-throughs has been widely commented upon (Arndt et al. 2000; Hertel and Winters 2005; Thapa and Pokhrel 2007). This paper contributes to the literature by explicitly modeling match friction *à la* Mortensen (2003) due to farmers' imperfect knowledge about price offers by middlemen to producers in the same location. In doing so, we depart from the multi-tiered marginalization approach used for example in McMillan et al. (2004), and consider instead a setting that can accommodate heterogeneity in the distribution of the export surpluses between middlemen and producers within a given region. In addition, we also depart from the familiar match friction setting by introducing a spatial dimension to the model. Consistent with a number of recent empirical empirical studies, market equilibrium is characterized by price dispersion among otherwise identical producers given location, and heterogeneity in price distribution across locations (Svensson and Yanagizawa 2009; Goyal 2010; Mookherjee et al. 2013).

[2]Lewin et al. (2004) finds that only about 20 % of global fair trade production capacity is sold at fair trade prices. The prevailing world price plays a key role in determining farmers' choice between fair traders and local intemediaries (Renard and Pèrez-Grovas 2007).

[3]Examples abound: The Fairtrade Foundation cooperates with growers in remote villages where the poorest coffee farmers are typically located (Global Exchange 2015). Economic Development Imports is another organization that works with local artisans in the most remote parts of East and West Africa by providing access to world markets (World Inquiry 2015).

Furthermore, we show that across locations and accounting for producers operating in increasingly remote areas, middlemen market power intensifies.[4] This endogenous variation in middlemen market power across location further dictates the extent of imperfect price transmission. Indeed, we find that producers in more remote locations are more susceptible to an unequal division of the size of the market surplus.

More generally, the functioning of middlemen intermediaries has been shown to span a number of distinctive categories (Spulber 1996a), including (i) price setting and market clearing (McMillan et al. 2004), (ii) inventory holding and liquidity provision (Clower and Leijonhufvud 1975; Spulber 1985), (iii) suppliers and buyers matching (Rubinstein and Wolinsky 1987; Spulber 1996b; Rauch and Watson 2004; Antràs and Costinot 2011), and (iv) performance monitoring and quality guarantees (Biglaiser 1993; Biglaiser Friedman 1994; Bardhan et al. 2013). The introduction of fair traders in our model contributes to this literature by introducing heterogeneity in motivations between competing middlemen as an additional line of research, allowing for differential policy prescription targeting middlemen depending on motivations. Furthermore, we show that the introduction of fair traders impact middlemen market share as well as pricing behavior, and the strength of such impacts depends in particular on producer locations.

The plan of the paper is as follows. Section 2 sets up the framework and equilibrium with middlemen only. Section 3 introduces fair traders and characterizes equilibrium when both types of intermediaries can enter. Section 4 takes up the policy questions – who exactly should the government subsidize? Section 5 offers a number of extensions of the model presented. Section 6 concludes.

2 The model and equilibrium with middlemen

2.1 The basic setup

We consider a spatially dispersed economy, in which production takes place at a range of distances $x \in [\underline{x}, \bar{x}]$ away from a transport hub. At each location x there is a large number of identical producers, N. Each producer has a unit of output for sale. Any output bound for market must be transported to the hub. For each unit sold, let p^* be the unit market price, and $p \leq p^*$ the farm gate price. Output not bound for market can be used for own-consumption, and the revenue equivalent of any output not marketed is c. We assume that $0 \leq c < p^*$ for there to be a potential for gains from trade.

2.2 Middlemen: the Bertrand benchmark

Transportation is carried out by middlemen, who incur a location-specific transportation cost tx per unit output.[5] If free entry and frictionless Bertrand price competition prevail among middlemen, the equilibrium producer price $p^* - tx$ is strictly location-specific at

[4] Where markets are competitive with minimal entry costs, extortionary middlemen markups have not been found (Fafchamps et al. 2005; Osborne 2005; Minten et al. 2013; de Janvry et al. 2015). But in remote areas, studies show rural households confront higher transport cost and middlemen with market power (Goetz 1992; Sexton et al. 1991; Nicita 2004; Hertel and Winters 2005; Hertel and Winters 2005; Fafchamp and Minten 2012).

[5] A Samuelson iceberg type transportation cost can similarly be imposed, by assuming for example that $t = \tau p^*$, $\tau > 0$, without affecting the qualitative implications of the model.

each x, as long as $p^* - tx$ is greater than the reservation value c.[6] All middlemen thus earn zero profit: they sell output at price p^* at the hub, after having incurred tx as transportation cost, and $p^* - tx$ as payment to producers. This simple framework yields a stark set of predictions regarding the volume of marketed output, the distribution of income between middlemen and producers, as well as the incidence of poverty among producers.

In terms of marketed volume, all producers located at $x \leq (p^* - c)/t \equiv x_o^+$ market all of their output since $p^* - tx \leq c$ whenever $x \leq x_o^+$. In what follows, we assume that there exist at least some locations where bringing output to market generates strictly positive surplus $p^* - tx - c > 0$. Equivalently, we assume that $\underline{x} < x_o^+$. To furthermore accommodate the possibility of incomplete coverage and location as a binding constraint on sales for at least some producers, we assume in addition that $\bar{x} \geq x_o^+$.

In terms of producer prices, Bertrand competition implies a perfect one-to-one pass-through of the net market price $p^* - tx$ to producers, and the full market surplus $p^* - tx - c$ at each location x, accounting for opportunity cost c, is captured by the producer. Consequently, inequality in the distribution of revenue among producers is a strictly inter-regional phenomenon. At any given location $x \leq x_o^+$, all producers earn identically $p^* - tx$. Across locations, producer price is decreasing in x. For $x > x_o^+$, market price p^* is insufficient to cover the full cost $tx + c$, and producers receive the own consumption value c per unit.

Let $\bar{p}$ denote the minimal producer price required to sustain private consumption at a level no less than an exogenously given poverty line, with $\bar{p} > c$ so poverty among at least some producers is a real possibility. With Bertrand competition among middlemen, poverty incidence as measured by the share of producers living under the poverty line is discontinuous along the locational continuum: for $x \leq (p^* - \bar{p})/t \equiv x_o^p (< x_o^+)$, no one is poor, but immediately thereafter, every producer is poor.

In summary, there are two critical threshold locations, x_o^p and x_o^+. For $x \leq x_o^p$, access to market at price $p^* - tx$ completely eradicates poverty. For $x \in (x_o^p, x_o^+)$, unit revenue lies strictly between c and the poverty line $\bar{p}$. Producers at locations even more distant than x_o^+ from the hub have effectively no access to markets. Figure 1 summarizes, and shows the equilibrium producer price along the location continuum.

2.3 Middlemen market power

We depart now from the Bertrand assumption, where every producer is perfectly aware of each and every middlemen price offer, and consider instead an arguably more realistic scenario in which there is match friction between producers and middlemen (Mortensen 2003). We are interested in exploring how middlemen market power impacts price information arrival rates, middlemen profit margins, and the distribution of realized producer prices. In our spatial setup, we can also ascertain differences in price information arrival, middlemen profit margin, and the distribution of realized producer price across the spatial continuum as middlemen market power changes endogenously.

Specifically, match friction arises whenever producers are aware of only a partial set of price offers made by middlemen in a given location. Let the likelihood that a producer comes across $z = 0, 1, 2, \ldots$ offers be given by a Poisson distribution with parameter $\lambda_x = M_x/N$,

[6] This is consistent with Fafchamps et al. (2005) who find evidence supporting constant returns to scale in agricultural trade including transportation cost.

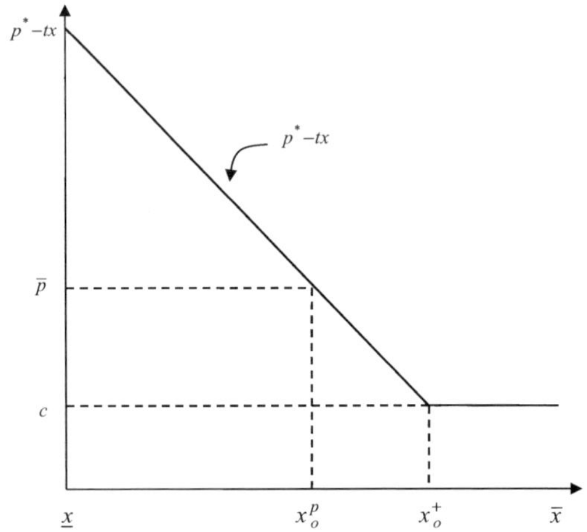

Fig. 1 Producer price and location with Bertrand competition

or, $\Pr(z;\ \lambda_x) = e^{-\lambda_x}\lambda_x^z/z!$,[7] where M_x denotes the endogenous number of middlemen in location x with a price offer $p \geq c$. This formulation allows the probability distribution of price information arrival to be location-specific, and the average number of price offers a producer in location x receives is equal to λ_x. λ_x measures the location-specific middleman market power. Whether producers in more remote locations tend to receive more or less price information is thus endogenously determined via λ_x as a function of x in our setup.

In this setting, each of the M_x middlemen proposes an offer to one of the N producers chosen at random. Let $F_x(p)$ be the cumulative distribution function of middlemen price offers at location x. Each producer ranks any and all offers received this way, accepts the highest offer, and rejects the rest. Since the distribution of each such price offer is $F_x(p)$, the cumulative distribution of the maximal offer received is:

$$H_x(p) \equiv \sum_{z=0}^{\infty} \frac{e^{-\lambda_x}\lambda_x^z F_x(p)^z}{z!} = e^{-\lambda_x(1-F_x(p))}. \tag{1}$$

With match friction, producers are only aware of a subset of price offers in each location, and thus the middleman margin $p^* - tx - p$ need not be driven to zero in equilibrium. Indeed, the likelihood that any price offer $p \geq c$ out-competes all other offers received by a randomly selected producer is given by $H_x(p)$ in Eq. 1. For any given price offer p,

[7]As is well-known, the Poisson distribution is the limit of the binomial distribution with parameter λ_x as the number of trials approaches infinity.

therefore, middlemen expected profit is $H_x(p)(p^* - tx - p) - K$, where $K \geq 0$ is a fixed search cost per producer contacted. Each middleman's problem is simply:

$$\Pi_x = \max_p H_x(p)(p^* - tx - p) - K \tag{2}$$

The solution to Eq. 2 gives the following equilibrium price offer distribution:

$$F_x(p) = \frac{1}{\lambda_x} \ln\left(\frac{p^* - tx - c}{p^* - tx - p}\right), \qquad f_x(p) = \frac{1}{\lambda_x(p^* - tx - p)}. \tag{3}$$

Naturally, $F_x(c) = 0$ for no producer will accept a price offer less than c. Meanwhile, the highest price offer given across all middlemen p_x^+ at location x can be found by setting $F_x(p_x^+) = 1$, or equivalently:

$$p_x^+ = (1 - e^{-\lambda_x})(p^* - tx) + e^{-\lambda_x}c, \tag{4}$$

a weighted average of the net market price $(p^* - tx)$, and the domestic value (c). The relative weights depend only on the extent of middlemen market power, λ_x. As $\lambda_x \to \infty$, $F_x(p)$ puts unit mass on $\lim_{\lambda_x \to \infty} p_x^+ = p^* - tx$. However, as $\lambda_x \to 0$, p_x^+ tends to the domestic price c.

Let there be free entry of middlemen in each location x. Doing so drives expected profits Π_x to zero, and implies that the *realized* distribution of producer prices for all $p \geq c$, is given by

$$H_x(p) = \min\left\{\frac{K}{p^* - tx - p}, 1\right\}. \tag{5}$$

In particular, $H_x(c) = \min\{K/(p^* - tx - c), 1\}$ gives the fraction of producers who are left out of markets, and $H_x(p) - H_x(c)$ the fraction for whom output is bound for market, and who fetch a price at p or less from their middlemen. The maximal price offer is $p_x^+ = \max\{p^* - tx - K, c\}$. From Eqs. 1 and 5 evaluated at $p = c$, endogenous entry implies equilibrium market power at:

$$\lambda_x = M_x/N = \max\{\ln((p^* - tx - c)/K), 0\}. \tag{6}$$

Equation 6 gives the equilibrium market power as parameterized by λ_x as determined by the interplay between search cost K, and the market surplus $p^* - tx - c$. Thus, if $K \to 0$, middlemen market power vanishes as $\lambda_x \to \infty$ and $H_x(p)$ puts positive mass only on $p = p^* - tx$. Now for $K > 0$, equilibrium $\lambda_x = M_x/N$ increases with market price p^* reflecting more intense competition among middlemen. Furthermore, λ_x decreases with distance x reflecting a deepening of middlemen power along the location continuum. In the end, with positive search cost, λ_x is positive only in the range $x \leq (p^* - c - K)/t \equiv x^+$. In comparison with the Bertrand outcome with no match friction, $x_o^+ = (p^* - c)/t > x^+$, producers in locations $(x^+, x_o^+]$ are no longer serviced by middlemen, and as such they do not have access to market.

2.4 Farm gate price and pass-through

Recall that in the absence of match friction, all farmers in location x receive the same price $p^* - tx$. By contrast, from Eq. 5, match friction additionally gives rise to location-specific dispersion of realized farm gate prices $H_x(p)$. The expected farm gate price conditional on receiving at least one acceptable price offer (Ep_x) can be expressed as:

$$Ep_x \equiv \int_c^{p_x^+} \frac{pdH_x(p)}{1 - H_x(c)} = (1 - \gamma_x)(p^* - tx) + \gamma_x c < p^* - tx. \tag{7}$$

Ep_x is thus a weighted average of the net market price ($p^* - tx$) and the domestic value c, where $\gamma_x \equiv \lambda_x e^{-\lambda_x}/(1 - e^{-\lambda_x})$. Since $p^* - tx - c$ represents net market surplus, the share that goes, on average, to middlemen is thus:

$$\frac{p^* - tx - Ep_x}{p^* - tx - c} = \gamma_x \equiv \frac{\lambda_x e^{-\lambda_x}}{1 - e^{-\lambda_x}}$$

γ_x thus captures the extent of unequal division of the market surplus between middlemen and producers. Evidently, this division depends systematically on middlemen market power λ_x, and as such the division of surplus varies endogenously along the locational continuum. From Eq. 6, it can be verified that γ_x rises with distance for middlemen market power strengthens with distance. Producers at farther away locations are accordingly left with a smaller slice of the market surplus.

Using Eqs. 6 and 7, the average farm gate price with endogenous entry can also be expressed as:

$$Ep_x = p^* - tx - K \ln\left(\frac{p^* - tx - c}{K}\right) \frac{p^* - tx - c}{p^* - tx - c - K}. \tag{8}$$

The expected middlemen markup

$$p^* - tx - Ep_x = K \ln\left(\frac{p^* - tx - c}{K}\right) \frac{p^* - tx - c}{p^* - tx - c - K} > 0$$

is strictly positive whenever the search cost is strictly positive $K > 0$. The size of this markup, accounting for endogenous entry, is strictly increasing in the net market price $p^* - tx$. Intuitively, a higher net market price encourages entry (λ_x) and simultaneously increases the number of middlemen who fail to strike a successful match $M_x - N(1 - H_x(c)) = N(\lambda_x - (1 - e^{\lambda_x}))$ as they are outbid by other middlemen. To justify this risk, the markup $p^* - tx - Ep_x$ for those who succeed in striking a match must also rise in tandem.

Using Eq. 8, the average revenue of all producers at x, regardless of whether they succeed in marketing their products, can be expressed simply as the weighted average:

$$ER_x = (1 - H_x(c))Ep_x + H_x(c)c = p^* - tx - (1 + \lambda_x)K. \tag{9}$$

where $\lambda_x = \ln(p^* - tx - c) - \ln K$ from Eq. 6. The responsiveness as measured by

$$\frac{\partial ER_x}{\partial(p^* - tx)} = 1 - \frac{K}{p^* - tx - c} = 1 - e^{-\lambda_x} < 1 \tag{10}$$

gives the extent of price pass-through along the spatial continuum. From Eq. 10, the revenue of the average producer at location x rises less than one for one with net market price precisely because middlemen market power as captured by λ_x. The extent of this imperfect pass-through due to middlemen market power worsens endogenously with distance from

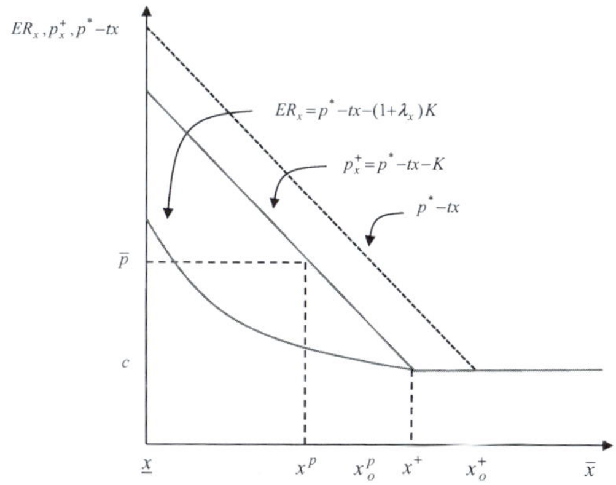

Fig. 2 Average producer revenue with endogenous middlemen market power

Eq. 6, all the way up until the point is reached where $x \geq x^+$ and thus $\lambda_x = 0$. Producers located here and beyond are by definition untouched by forces of markets. Figure 2 illustrates, and shows the range of middlemen price offer $[c, p_x^+]$ at each location, as well as the average revenue of all local producers along the location continuum.

2.5 Intra- and inter-regional poverty

With price dispersion both within region through $H_x(p)$, and across regions as $H_x(p)$ varies with x, the incidence of poverty has both an intra- and an inter-regional dimension. These are shown in Fig. 3, for three successively more remote regions (from H^1 to H^p and then to H^2), and accordingly three producer price distributions that can be rank ordered in the sense of first order stochastic dominance.

Define $P^m_{x,\alpha}$ and $P^c_{x,\alpha}$ as the poverty of producers who gain access to markets through middlemen, and the poverty of all other producers at location x. We adopt the Foster-Greer-Thorbecke (1984) poverty indicator:[8]

$$P^c_{x,\alpha} = \left(\frac{\bar{p} - c}{\bar{p}}\right)^{\alpha} \geq \int_c^{\min\{\bar{p}, p_x^+\}} \left(\frac{\bar{p} - p}{\bar{p}}\right)^{\alpha} \frac{dH_x(p)}{1 - H_x(c)} = P^m_{x,\alpha} \tag{11}$$

where $(\bar{p} - p)/\bar{p}$ is the poverty gap ratio, and $\alpha \geq 0$ parameterizes the extent of poverty aversion. As shown in Eq. 11, of the two groups of producers living under the poverty

[8] As a poverty indicator, the Foster-Greer-Thorbecke measure represents a class of poverty indicators that satisfies the subgroup consistency axiom. This axiom guarantees that if poverty of some groups have changed and others have not, then poverty of the changing subgroup and total poverty move in the same direction. This property is particularly relevant in our context where total economy-wide poverty is both inter regional and intra-regional.

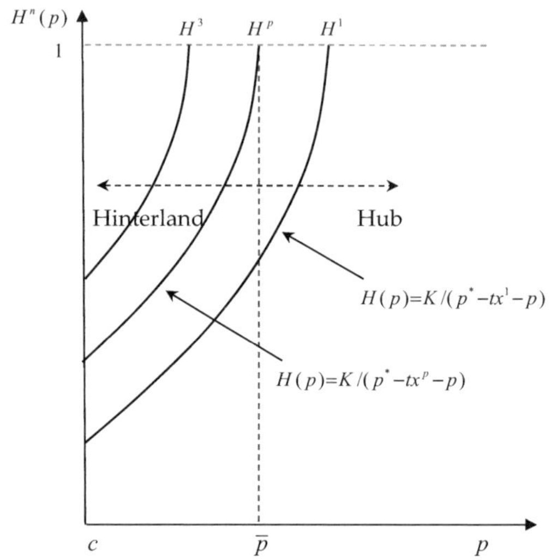

Fig. 3 Producer price distribution

line, the first group is poor because they fail to bring output to market because no offers greater than the reservation value c arrives. The number of these producers is $NH_x(c)$. A second group remains poor despite access to market for they receive a price lower than $\bar{p}$. The number of this second group of producer is $N(H_x(\min\{\bar{p}, p_x^+\}) - H_x(c))$. Between the two, producers who fail to bring output to market are poorer since $P_{x,\alpha}^c \geq P_{x,\alpha}^m$ whenever $\alpha \geq 0$. Naturally, overall poverty at location x can be expressed as the weighted sum:

$$P_{x,\alpha} = H_x(c)P_{x,\alpha}^c + (1 - H_x(c))P_{x,\alpha}^m. \tag{12}$$

As long as some producers are non-poor, or $p_x^+ > \bar{p}$, a small increase in the market price p^*, all else equal, decreases the share of producers with no access to markets $H_x(c) = K/(p^* - tx - c)$ and thus alleviates poverty due to lack of market access from Eq. 5. The same increase in market price p^* also decreases poverty among producers who do have access to markets, for the distribution of price offers $H_x(p) = \min\{K/(p^* - tx - p), 1\}$ improves with p^* from Eq. 5. Furthermore, as competition heightens between middlemen (an increase in λ_x) either because of increases in p^*, or a reduction in K, $\lambda_x \to \infty$ as $K/(p^* - tx - c) \to 0$ approaching the Bertrand outcome. At the limit, therefore, the first source of poverty $H_x(c)$ vanishes with the disappearance of match friction as long as the net market price $p^* - tx$ exceeds the poverty line $\bar{p}$, while the measure of the second $H_x(\bar{p}) - H_x(c)$ likewise approaches zero, since no middlemen can offer less than the full $p^* - tx$ and get away with it in the absence of match friction.

Inter-regional differences in poverty arise for two reasons in our setup. First, remote locations are naturally disadvantaged for the net market price $(p^* - tx)$ is lower there. Second, remote locations are in fact made doubly worse off for middlemen market power also deepens along the locational continuum from Eq. 5. Taken together, poverty worsens with distance, and indeed from Eq. 13, the poverty indicator can be re-expressed to reflect directly the impact of location on poverty:

$$P_{x,\alpha} = \frac{\alpha}{\bar{p}} \int_{c}^{\bar{p}} \left(\frac{\bar{p} - p}{\bar{p}} \right)^{\alpha - 1} \frac{K}{p^* - tx - p} dp.$$

for locations where there are at least some producers who are non-poor. The threshold distance, call it x^p, beyond which producers are universally living below the poverty line is reached when the maximal price offer p_x^+ can no longer cover $\bar{p}$, or equivalently $\min\{\bar{p}, p_x^+\} = p_x^+$. From Eqs. 4 and 6,

$$\begin{aligned} x \geq x^p &\equiv \left(p^* - \bar{p} - e^{-\lambda_x}(p^* - tx - c)\right)/t = (p^* - \bar{p} - K)/t \qquad (13) \\ &\leq \frac{p^* - \bar{p}}{t} = x_o^p. \end{aligned}$$

Consequently, middlemen market power deepens the incidence of poverty along both the intensive ($P_{x,\alpha} > 0$) and extensive ($x^p < x_o^p$) margins (Fig. 2). For $x > x^p$, all producers are poor, and thus,

$$P_{x,\alpha} = \frac{\alpha}{\bar{p}} \int_{c}^{p_x^+} \left(\frac{\bar{p} - p}{\bar{p}} \right)^{\alpha - 1} \frac{K}{p^* - tx - p} dp + \left(\frac{\bar{p} - p_x^+}{\bar{p}} \right)^{\alpha}$$

and $P_{x,\alpha}$ continues to worsen with distance x (say from H^p to H^3 in Fig. 3). Henceforth, we assume that x^p exceeds at least the lower bound $\underline{x}$, in order to examine the set of factors that effect changes along the extensive margin.

We have so far demonstrated location as a key determinant of middlemen market power. In addition, we have demonstrated the implications of such a link in terms of markups, pass-through, and intra-and inter-regional poverty. In this context, how does the introduction of fair traders impact middlemen market power along the locational continuum? And what about the related issues of markup and pass-through, as well as intra- and inter-regional poverty?

3 Fair traders

There are many different ways in which fair traders contract with producers on the ground. Some organizations contract directly with producer cooperatives (Develtere and Pollet 2005). Others alternative trading organizations contract directly with individual producers (Abufarha 2013; Fair Trade USA 2012). As the case may be, the N producers at each location x can be interpreted as N producer cooperatives or N individual producers in a similar location. Their ability to command a higher price depend on the price offers they receive. As before, match friction dictates the likelihood of price offer arrival to each producer / producer cooperative, depending on middlemen market power which will now need to be adjusted to reflect the presence of fair traders.

Specifically, like profit-maximizing middlemen, fair traders serve producers by bringing output to markets at transportation cost tx. But as the various examples in the introduction demonstrate, unlike profit-maximizing middlemen, fair traders are additionally motivated by location-specific factors that impact poverty and access to the world market among producers. We incorporate these concerns by a location specific price premium $p_x^n - p^* > 0$, where p_x^n is the valuation that fair traders put on striking a contract with a producer at location x.[9] Our restriction on $p_x^n - p^*$ is mild, and our objective is simply to capture a concern by fair traders or final consumers for producers in locations otherwise characterized by high markups and / or isolation from world markets. Specifically, we assume $p_x^n - p^* = a^n + ax$ where $a \geq 0$ captures the overall strength of the poverty and locational concerns of the fair trader, while a^n captures locationally invariant consumer preference for particular attributes associated with fair trade products.[10] In what follows, we further assume that the dependence of the price premium on x is not overly strong, so that the net market price accounting for transportation costs, tx, continues to indicate remoteness as a deterrence to trade, or equivalently $p_x^n - tx = p^* + a^n - (t - a)x$ is decreasing in x.[11]

In terms of fair trader fixed costs, contracting with producers can be more expensive relative to local middlemen due for example to fair traders' cost disadvantage relative to longstanding middlemen, and other costs of monitoring and certification required to justify the final consumer price premium.[12] We reflect these considerations by assuming that the fixed cost applicable to fair traders K^n is strictly greater than K.

For producers, contracting with fair traders can be costlier relative to contracting with local middlemen either because of the fixed cost required to join and / or maintain a cooperative, to set up contracts, or to abide by internationally recognized product or environmental standards (Loureiro and Lotade 2005). Thus, let $d^n \geq 0$ represent the fixed cost of contracting with fair traders facing each producer.[13] The cost of any product standards required by middlemen will be normalized at zero here. Furthermore, let ρ be the price offer, and p the price offer net of the cost of compliance, or in other words, $p = \rho - d^n$.

Due to the fixed cost of contracting d^n, the actual cost to the fair trader based on a net price offer p is equal to $\rho = p + d^n$.[14] For notational economy, we henceforth denote the difference between the additional cost of fair trade production and consumer preference for fair trade attributes $d^n - a^n$ as δ^n. δ^n may be positive or negative depending on the relative importance of cost and consumer preference considerations associated with fair trade production for each producer. The combined (money equivalent) gains to a fair trader who serves a producer located at x, and offers a net price offer p (accounting for the cost of contracting), thus continues to be location-specific

$$p_x^n - d^n - tx - p = p^* + ax - \delta^n - tx - p.$$

[9]Empirical work on the willingness to pay for fair trade products is a nascent field of research. The importance of the poverty impact of the program on consumer's willingness to pay, as we have assumed here, has been demonstrated by Basu and Hicks (2008, 2009) in a diverse set of experimental settings, where test subjects compare different versions of the fair trade coffee label with differing degrees of promised impact on grower wellbeing.

[10]There are often other provisions such as in the fair trade including the adoption of sustainable practices or organic farming.

[11]The linearity of the price premium in x assumed here can be easily relaxed to accommodate any monotonically increasing function $a(x)$ without affecting the results to follow, as long as $tx - ax$ is increasing in x and distance continues to deter trade.

[12]The opposite scenario where $K^n < K$ can be easily inferred from the analysis to follow.

[13]Meanwhile, contracting with fair traders can also lead the way to skill acquisition, and other technology transfers (Abufarha 2013; Fair Trade USA 2012). In these cases, the parameter d^n introduced here will then take on a negative value.

[14]Recall that total output is normalized at unity, and thus p gives the total revenue of a producer.

In what follows, we assume that $ax - \delta^n > 0$ for all $x \in [\underline{x}, \bar{x}]$, in order to reflect a strictly positive price premium associated with fair trade products. Otherwise, the baseline solution of the model with no fair traders trivially applies.

3.1 Equilibrium with middlemen and fair traders

Like the baseline scenario with no fair traders, producers / cooperatives have information on only a subset of the net price offers made by middlemen and fair traders. They make contract decisions by comparing all net price offers p received inclusive of those from fair traders and middlemen, select the best, and reject the rest. Denote $F_x^n(p)$, $p \geq c$, as the cumulative distribution of price offers inclusive of both fair traders and middlemen. Let $H_x^n(p) = e^{-\lambda_x^n(1-F_x^n(p))}$ be the cumulative distribution of the realized producer price distribution, where λ_x^n is now the ratio $(m_x^n + M_x^n)/N$, and m_x^n and M_x^n respectively denote the endogenous number of fair traders and middlemen.

The problem of fair traders is otherwise similar to that of a middleman: they account for the net (price premium augmented) gains from serving a producer $(p_x^n - d^n - tx - p)$, adjusted appropriately to reflect the likelihood of successfully striking a match, $H_x^n(p)$, in the face of competing price offers from other middlemen:

$$\pi_x^n = \max_p H_x^n(p)(p_x^n - d^n - tx - p) - K^n \tag{14}$$

$$\Pi_x^n = \max_p H_x^n(p)(p^* - tx - p) - K. \tag{15}$$

Since the premium adjusted gains from a match is higher for a fair trader $p_x^n - d^n - tx - p = p^* + ax - \delta^n - tx - p > p^* - tx - p$ for any given price offer, it is straightforward to show that the equilibrium range of fair trader price offers, if non-empty, is always higher than that of profit-maximizing middlemen.[15] Put another way, the entry of fair traders effectively confines profit maximizing middlemen to service producers who are not matched with fair traders.

Accordingly, let $\hat{p}_x$ be an endogenous price offer threshold, dividing the range of middlemen and fair trader price offers. $F_x^n(\hat{p}_x)$ thus gives the share of price offers from private profit maximizing middlemen $(M_x^n/(m_x^n + M_x^n))$, and $1 - F_x^n(\hat{p}_x)$ the share from fair traders. For any $p \leq \hat{p}_x$, Eq. 15 implies

$$F_x^n(p) = \frac{1}{\lambda_x^n} \ln\left(\frac{p^* - tx - c}{p^* - tx - p}\right) \tag{16}$$

[15] To see this, suppose that $\tilde{p}^n$ and $\tilde{p}$ are solutions to Eqs. 14 and 15 respectively. By virtue of profit maximization, it must be the case that

$$\frac{p_x^n - d^n - tx - \tilde{p}^n}{p_x^n - d^n - tx - \tilde{p}} \geq \frac{H_x^n(\tilde{p})}{H_x^n(\tilde{p}^n)} \geq \frac{p^* - tx - \tilde{p}^n}{p^* - tx - \tilde{p}},$$

with

$$ax - \delta^n \geq 0.$$

It follows that $\tilde{p}^n \geq \tilde{p}$.

and otherwise with $p > \hat{p}_x$ for fair traders, Eqs. 15 and 16 give

$$F_x^n(p) = F_x^n(\hat{p}_x) + \frac{1}{\lambda_x^n} \ln\left(\frac{p_x^n - tx - \hat{p}_x - d^n}{p_x^n - tx - p - d^n}\right). \tag{17}$$

The threshold $\hat{p}_x$ is determined via Eq. 17 as soon as the share of middlemen at location x, $F_x^n(\hat{p})$, is known. This important share is endogenized here by way of simultaneous endogenous entry of profit maximizing middlemen and fair traders respectively:

$$e^{-\lambda_x^n}(p^* - tx - c) = e^{-\lambda_x^n(1-F_x^n(\hat{p}_x))}(p^* - tx - \hat{p}_x) = K, \tag{18}$$

$$e^{-\lambda_x^n(1-F_x^n(\hat{p}_x))}(p_x^n - d^n - tx - \hat{p}_x) = e^{-\lambda_x^n(1-F_x^n(p))}(p_x^n - d^n - tx - p) = K^n \tag{19}$$

where the marginal fair trader $\lambda_x^n(1 - F^n(\hat{p}_x)) = m_x^n/N$ equates the price premium augmented expected market surplus $e^{-\lambda_x^n(1-F_x^n(\hat{p}_x))}(p_x^n - d^n - tx - \hat{p}_x)$ and the cost of entry K^n from Eq. 20, and the marginal middlemen $\lambda_x^n = (m_x^n + M_x^n)/N$ then equates the expected market surplus $(e^{-}\lambda_x(p^* - tx - c))$ with the cost of entry K from Eq. 19. Thus for interior solutions $F_x^n(\hat{p}_x) \in (0, 1)$, the threshold price offer dividing middlemen and fair traders is:

$$\hat{p}_x = p^* - tx - \frac{(ax - \delta^n)k}{1-k} \tag{20}$$

where k denotes the ratio of fixed costs $K/K^n < 1$. Clearly, the higher the price premium ax, the narrower the range of middlemen price offers $[c, \hat{p}_x]$. Meanwhile, the greater the fair trader's (fixed) cost disadvantage $K^n/K = 1/k$, the higher the middlemen's maximal price offer. Furthermore, the higher the fixed cost associated with fair trade production relative to consumer gains δ^n, the wider the range of middleman price offers. These show interestingly the tendency for middlemen to optimally charge a higher markup on average to producers they continue to serve, the higher the fair traders' price premium. At the other end of the price offer spectrum, the maximal fair trader price offer is given by:

$$p_x^{n+} = p^* + ax - \delta^n - tx - K^n \tag{21}$$

from Eq. 20 evaluated at $F_x^n(p_x^+) = 1$. The larger the price premium, the higher of course will be the maximal fair trader offer in equilibrium.

From Eqs. 18 and 19, the number of fair traders (m_x^n) and the number of middlemen (M_x^n) at an interior equilibrium are respectively,

$$m_x^n = N\lambda_x^n(1 - F_x^n(\hat{p}_x)) = N \ln\left(\frac{ax - \delta^n}{K^n - K}\right) \tag{22}$$

$$M_x^n + m_x^n = N\lambda_x^n = N \ln\left(\frac{p^* - tx - c}{K}\right). \tag{23}$$

Thus, the equilibrium number of middlemen rises with market price p^*. This is consistent with evidence in Renard and Pèrez-Grovas (2007, pp. 143), who find that there are *opportunistic* growers who switch in favor of local intermediaries in periods of high world prices.

Making use of Eqs. 1, 16 and 17 as well as Eqs. 22 and 23, the realized price distribution associated with middlemen mediated trade $p \leq \hat{p}_x$ is

$$H_x^n(p) = \min\left\{\frac{K}{p^* - tx - p}, 1\right\}$$

and for $p > \hat{p}_x$ associated with fair trader mediated trade,

$$H_x^n(p) = \min\left\{\frac{K^n}{p_x^n - d^n - tx - p}, 1\right\}.$$

It remains to be shown whether the threshold price $\hat{p}_x$ is an interior solution in the range of prices so that both middlemen and fair traders co-exist, or if in fact equilibrium accommodates either middlemen or fair traders. We turn to these questions next.

3.2 Farm gate price and pass-through

Depending on the price premium, fixed costs, as well as the market surplus, it follows from Eqs. 22 and 23 that there are three possible equilibrium configurations, respectively when there exist only middlemen, only fair traders, and when the two coexist:

Proposition 1 *By introducing fair traders with price premium* $a \geq t(K^n + \delta^n - K)/(p^* - c - K)$*, producers are served*

1. *entirely by middlemen at locations closest to the hub* $x < (K^n + \delta^n - K)/a$
2. *by a mix of both middlemen and fair traders, for* $x \in [(K^n + \delta^n - K)/a, [(1-k)(p^* - c) + \delta^n k]/(ka + (1-k)t))$
3. *entirely by fair traders, for* $x \in [[(1-k)(p^* - c) + \delta^n k]/(ka + (1-k)t), (p^* - c - K^n - \delta^n)/(t - a)]$.

Producers at even farther away locations are not served by either middlemen or fair traders.

We relegate the details of the proof to the Online Appendix, and describe here the intuitions behind the classification shown in Proposition 1. The proposition begins with a requirement that fair trader profit $(p^* + ax - tx - p - \delta^n - K^n)$ is higher than that of middlemen profit $(p^* - tx - p - K)$ in at least some locations where middlemen operate $x \leq x^+ \equiv (p^* - c - K)/t$. This gives the condition $a \geq t(K^n + \delta^n - K)/(p^* - c - K)$ as shown.

Now, at locations sufficiently close to the hub, fair traders fail to out-compete middlemen if the price premium ax is too small to cover the added fixed cost $K^n - K$. Region I of Fig. 4 illustrates all (x, a) combinations consistent with this equilibrium, and $x^1(a) \equiv (K^n + \delta^n - K)/a$ denotes the threshold distance, depending on a, beyond which at least some producers will be served by fair traders in equilibrium.

At the other extreme, a no-middlemen equilibrium applies at sufficiently remote locations $(x > [(1-k)(p^* - c) + \delta^n k]/(ka + (1-k)t) = x^2(a))$, but not too remote $(< (p^* - c - K^n - \delta^n)/(t - a) \equiv x^{n+}(a))$ for even fair traders cannot make ends meet in these locations. These two restrictions are illustrated in Fig. 4 by region III including all combinations of (x, a) bounded respectively to the left and right by schedules $x^2(a)$ and $x^{n+}(a)$. Recall from Eq. 6 that x^+ denotes the threshold location beyond which there will be no more middleman in an equilibrium in the absence of fair traders. Thus, as shown in Fig. 4, region III can be further divided into two parts. The first part $x \subset [x^2(a), x^+)$ represents all locations wherein fair traders take over and middlemen are completely displaced. The second include all other locations where fair traders now serve as brand new links to markets where previously none existed.

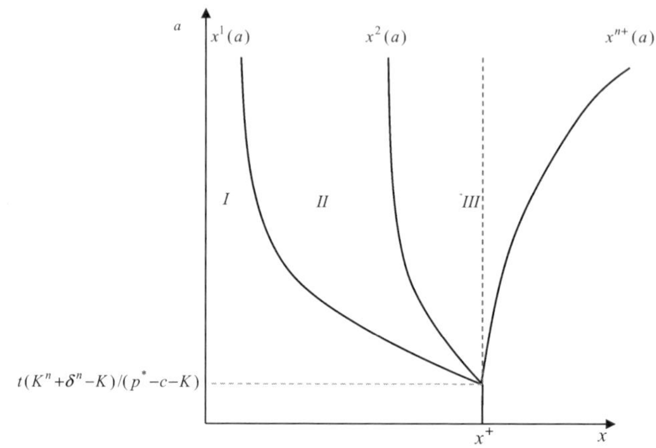

Fig. 4 Middlemen and fair traders *I*: middlemen only *II*: coexistence *III*: fair traders only

In between these two extremes, middleman and fair traders coexist. Region II in Fig. 4 illustrates this intermediate range.

Depending on the equilibrium combination of middlemen and fair traders in a particular location x as shown in Proposition 1, we can use Eqs. 16–23 to determine the impact of the introduction of fair traders on the farm gate price distribution, the corresponding average farm gate price, and the responsiveness of the average local producer revenue to market price changes. In particular

Proposition 2 *For all* $x \leq x^{n+}(a)$, *the introduction of fair traders with price premium* $a \geq t(K^n + \delta^n - K)/(p^* - c - K)$

1. *gives rise to a first order stochastically dominating shift in the producer price distribution as* $H_x^n(p) \leq H_x(p)$,
2. *raises the average farm gate price since* $E^n p_x \geq E p_x$, *and*
3. *improves the responsiveness of average local producer revenue, inclusive of those who have access to markets and those who do not, to market price changes since* $\partial E^n R_x / \partial(p^* - tx) \geq \partial E R_x / \partial(p^* - tx)$.

Proof See the Online Appendix. □

To see what drives these results, we will utilize the region by region summary of the impact of fair trader entry in Fig. 4. We will also reference Fig. 5, in which a family of realized price distributions is shown going from distances nearest to the hub, to more remote locations deeper into the hinterland, based on the realized price distribution derived in Section 3.1.

Starting with Region I of Fig. 4, where there exists no fair traders in equilibrium, the distribution of realized prices is naturally unaffected by the entry of fair traders. Consequently, the average producer price, the responsiveness of average producer revenue to world price

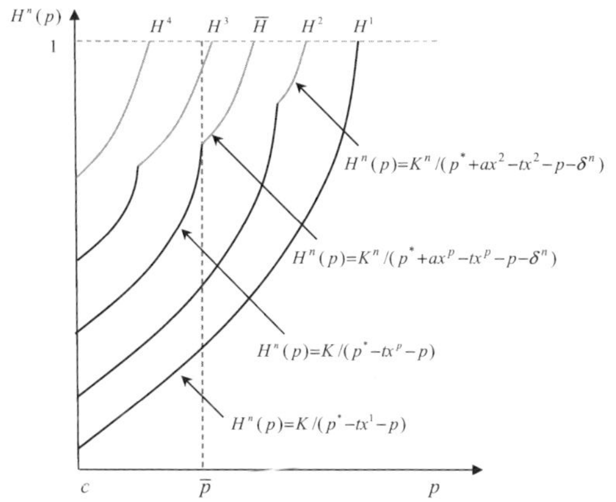

Fig. 5 Producer price distribution with fair traders and middlemen

changes, along with intra-regional poverty, all remain untouched by the possibility of fair trader entry. In Fig. 5, H^1 is example of such a price distribution.

In region III of Fig. 4, there are only fair traders here where a is relatively higher in locations sufficiently far away from the hub. In terms of price distribution, H^4 in Fig. 5 is one such example. We know from earlier discussion in Eqs. 6 and 8 that higher market prices lead to a first order stochastically dominating shift in the farm gate price distribution consistent with an improvement in the average farm gate price. Furthermore, we also know from earlier discussion following (6) that as λ_x rises with higher prices, the responsiveness of producer revenue with respect to changes in $p^* - tx$ rises as well. Thus, the entry of fair traders shifts the distribution of farm gate prices, raises the average farm gate price, and improves the responsiveness of farm gate price to market price changes.

Finally in region II of Fig. 4, fair traders and middlemen co-exist. For each location x, the price distribution at the range of prices that middlemen continues to offer remain strictly unchanged. However, the price distribution at the range of (higher) prices the fair traders offer has changed to represent a first order stochastically dominating shift consistent with higher price offers by fair traders. H^2 and H^3 in Fig. 5 are examples of this mix. These changes implies that the entry of fair traders raises the associated average farm gate price.

What is particularly interesting is that in this region where fair traders and middlemen compete, fair trader entry displaces existing middlemen. In fact, from Eq. 6

$$\lambda_x^n = \frac{m_x^n + M_x^n}{N} = \ln(p^* - tx - c) - \ln(K) = \frac{M_x}{N} = \lambda_x.$$

All else constant, therefore, the entry of one more fair trader has the effect of directly displacing a middleman. While this result is of interest in its own right, it also suggests that the responsiveness of the average farm gate price to market price $p^* - tx$ remains unchanged despite the introduction of fair traders since market power as parameterized by λ_x^n remains unchanged.

In summary, Region I in Fig. 4 exhibits invariance of farm gate price distribution despite the possibility of fair trader entry. In the intermediate Region II overall producer revenue rises thanks to the entry of fair traders, but the degree of market price pass-through remains untouched. The final region III encompasses locations where fair traders completely displace middlemen, and locations in which fair traders facilitate trade where isolation from world markets was the norm. At these locations, both overall producer revenue, and the extent of market price pass-through improve with fair traders. Proposition 2 presents a summary of these points.

3.3 Intra- and inter-regional poverty incidence

The poverty implications of fair trader entry are illustrated in Fig. 5. Of particular interest is the cutoff distribution $\bar{H}$. For locations closer to the hub relative to $\bar{H}$, the poor are served by middlemen only, and fair traders offer a price higher than the poverty line $\bar{p}$, or

$$\hat{p} \geq \bar{p} \quad \Leftrightarrow \quad x \leq \frac{p^* - \bar{p} - k\delta^n/(1-k)}{t + ak/(1-k)} \equiv \bar{x}^n(a). \tag{24}$$

Since the poor remains untouched by fair traders, the introduction of fair traders at these locations naturally leave poverty unchanged at:

$$P^n_{x,\alpha} = \frac{\alpha}{\bar{p}} \int_c^{\bar{p}} \left(\frac{\bar{p}-p}{\bar{p}}\right)^{\alpha-1} \frac{K}{p^* - tx - p} dp = P_{x,\alpha}.$$

By contrast, for locations further into the hinterland than $\bar{H}$, either some (for $x \in [\bar{x}^n(a), x^2(a))$, or all of the poor ($x \in [x^2(a), x^{n+}(a))$) will be served by fair traders. At all locations where there are at least some non-poor, $\bar{p} \leq p^{n+}$, poverty declines with the entry of fair traders:

$$\begin{aligned} P^n_{x,\alpha} &= \frac{\alpha}{\bar{p}} \int_c^{\bar{p}} \left(\frac{\bar{p}-p}{\bar{p}}\right)^{\alpha-1} H^n_x(p)dp \\ &\leq \frac{\alpha}{\bar{p}} \int_c^{\bar{p}} \left(\frac{\bar{p}-p}{\bar{p}}\right)^{\alpha-1} H_x(p)dp. = P_{x,\alpha} \end{aligned}$$

which follows since $H^n_x(p)$ first order stochastically dominate $H_x(p)$ from Proposition 1. In the Online Appendix, we discuss all of the remaining cases, depending on (i) whether all producers are poor, and (ii) whether middlemen and fair traders co-exist. But in all:

Proposition 3 *At the national level, averaging across all locations $x \in [\underline{x}, \bar{x}]$, the introduction of fair traders*

1. *reduces overall average poverty ($P^n_{x,\alpha} \leq P_{x,\alpha}$) if $a \geq t(K^n + \delta^n - K)/(p^* - c - K)$, and remains unchanged otherwise,*
2. *pushes back towards the hinterland the threshold location beyond which all producers are poor if in addition $a \geq t(K^n + \delta^n - K)/(p^* - \bar{p} - K)$; otherwise the threshold location remains unchanged.*

Proof See the Online Appendix. □

To see the intuition behind the second part of the proposition, note that the maximal fair trader price offer $p^* + ax - tx - \delta^n - K^n$ from Eq. 21 is below the poverty line

$$x \geq \frac{p^* - \bar{p} - \delta^n - K^n}{t - a} \equiv x^{np}(a) \geq x^p = \frac{p^* - \bar{p} - K}{t} \tag{25}$$

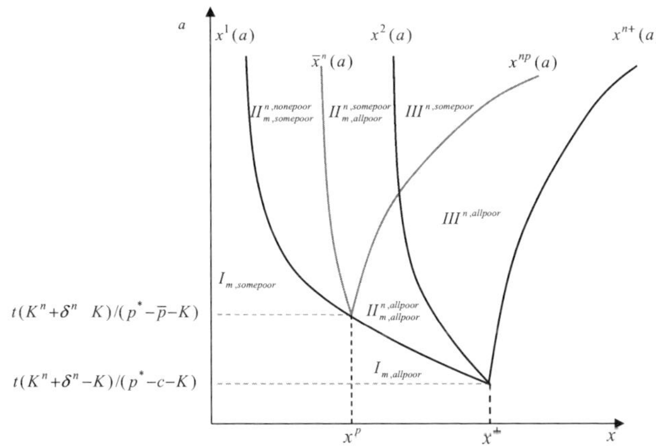

Fig. 6 Intra- and Inter- regional poverty *I*: middlemen only *II*: coexistence *III*: fair traders only

if and only if $a \geq t(K^n + \delta^n - K)/(p^* - \bar{p} - K)$ as stated based on Eq. 13. With the help of Eqs. 24–25, Fig. 6 illustrates the full array of possibilities in our model of middlemen and fair traders. Depending on the size of the premium a, there are two main classes of outcomes.[16] The first class involves a at relatively low levels, between $t(K^n+\delta^n-K)/(p^*-c-K)$ and $t(K^n + \delta^n - K)/(p^* - \bar{p} - K)$. In this range of price premia, fair trader can emerge and do so in regions $\text{II}^{n,allpoor}_{m,allpoor}$ where they co-exist with middlemen, and $\text{III}^{n,allpoor}$ where fair traders only serve as producers' link to markets. Importantly, with price premia this low, in no location are fair traders able to price above the poverty line.

The second class of cases involves relatively high price premia $a \geq t(K^n + \delta^n - K)/(p^* - \bar{p} - K)$. For each a in this range, there are as many as five distinctive equilibrium middlemen-fair trader configurations, depending on whether middlemen and fair traders coexist (regions I, II or III), and whether at least some of the producers served are non-poor. Interestingly, therefore, at a given price premium, a, the mean poverty of producers served by fair traders across all locations:

$$P_\alpha^n = \frac{\int_{x^1(a)}^{x^2(a)} \int_{\hat{p}_x}^{\min\{\bar{p},p_x^{n+}\}} [(\bar{p}-p)/\bar{p}]^\alpha dH_x^n(p)dx + \int_{x^2(a)}^{x^{n+}(a)} \int_c^{\min\{\bar{p},p_x^{n+}\}} [(\bar{p}-p)/\bar{p}]^\alpha dH_x^n(p)dx}{\int_{x^1(a)}^{x^2(a)} 1 - H_x^n(\hat{p}_x)dx + \int_{x^2(a)}^{x^{n+}(a)} 1 - H_x^n(c)dx} \tag{26}$$

may well be *higher* or *lower* than the mean poverty of producers served by middlemen:

$$P_\alpha^m = \frac{\int_{\underline{x}}^{x^1(a)} \int_c^{\min\{\bar{p},p_x^+\}} [(\bar{p}-p)/\bar{p}]^\alpha dH_x^n(p)dx + \int_{x^1(a)}^{x^2(a)} \int_c^{\min\{\bar{p},\hat{p}_x\}} [(\bar{p}-p)/\bar{p}]^\alpha dH_x^n(p)dx}{\int_{\underline{x}}^{x^1(a)} 1 - H_x^n(c)dx + \int_{x^1(a)}^{x^2(a)} H_x^n(\hat{p}_x) - H_x^n(c)dx} \tag{27}$$

[16] An additional class has a smaller than $t(K^n + \delta^n - K)/(p^* - c - K)$ and as shown in Fig. 5, a is too small for fair traders to ever emerge in equilibrium.

since there are regions (say $\text{II}^{n,allpoor}_{m,allpoor}$) where fair traders offer strictly higher prices compared to middlemen in the same location, but there are also locations (say, $\text{III}^{n,allpoor}$) where some fair traders offer strictly lower prices compared to middlemen in other locations (say, region $\text{I}_{n,somepoor}$). These can be contrasted against the average poverty of producers who continue to have no access to markets,

$$P^c_\alpha = \frac{\int_{\underline{x}}^{\bar{x}} [(\bar{p} - c)/\bar{p}]^\alpha H^n_x(c)dx}{\int_{\underline{x}}^{\bar{x}} H^n_x(c)dx} = \left(\frac{\bar{p} - c}{\bar{p}}\right)^\alpha. \tag{28}$$

In what follows, we offer an observation comparing the three.

Lemma 1 *For all $a \geq t(K^n + \delta^n - K)/(p^* - c - K)$ where either middlemen, fair traders, or both can emerge in equilibrium depending on location, poverty among producers who do not have access to market is the greatest but the poverty ranking between producers served by middlemen and fair traders is in general ambiguous:*

$$P^c_\alpha \geq \max\{P^m_\alpha, P^n_\alpha\}.$$

In the special case of poverty head count with $\alpha = 0$, and price premia in the range $a \in [t(K^n + \delta^n - K)/(p^* - c - K), t(K^n + \delta^n - K)/(p^* - \bar{p} - K)]$

$$1 = P^c_0 = P^n_0 > P^m_0$$

all producers who have no access to market and all producers served by fair traders are poor, but some producers served by middlemen are not.

There are two opposing forces at work here. With a price premium, fair traders do indeed offer higher prices (Propositions 2 and 3). But with poverty aversion, fair traders tend to work in remote locations where producers are poorer (Proposition 1). Consequently, the relative poverty of producers served by middlemen and fair traders is indeed ambiguous. As we will see, however, this particular ranking turns out to be key in the determination of poverty reducing strategies.

4 Policy for poverty reduction

We have by now seen the full range of possibilities in the absence of government interventions, in terms of the equilibrium share of middlemen and fair traders, the impact of fair traders on markup and pass-through, as well as the equilibrium poverty implication of fair traders. We now address a final question: Should a government interested in poverty reduction subsidize fair traders, or should it perhaps subsidize middlemen? This is particularly important for in many cases such fair traders receive direct support from governments and other donors. DFID (2009, pp. 44–45), for example, reports for one of the most recent government commitments to support fair trade through direct investment and procurements. Suppose that the objective of the government is the mitigation of overall poverty. Should government use the same budget to subsidize indigenous middlemen instead?

With three groups of producers served respectively by middlemen, fair traders, and no intermediaries at all, there are three corresponding direct mechanisms of intervention: (i) a subsidy on trade mediated by middlemen s^m; (ii) a subsidy on trade mediated by fair traders

s^n, and (iii) a direct subsidy to producers who have no access to markets s^c. The first option effectively raises the market price for middlemen from p^* to $p^* + s^m$. The second option effectively raises the premium adjusted market price facing fair traders from p^n to $p_x^n + s^n$. The final option raises producers' opportunity cost of bringing output to market from c to $c + s^c$. The revised expected profits of fair traders and middlemen are:

$$\pi_x^n = \max_p H_x^n(p)(p_x^n + s^n - d^n - tx - p) - K^n,$$

$$\Pi_x^n = \max_p H_x^n(p)(p^* + s^m - tx - p) - K.$$

Since the reservation value facing producers is now $c + s^c$ in the presence of the direct subsidy s^c, the minimum price offer from any middlemen must now be $c + s^c$. Like before, let $\hat{p}_x$ be the price offer threshold separating fair traders and middlemen, the distribution of middlemen price offers $p \leq \hat{p}_x$, accounting for the three subsidies is:

$$F_x^n(p) = \frac{1}{\lambda_x^n} \ln\left(\frac{p^* + s^m - tx - c - s^c}{p^* + s^m - tx - p}\right). \tag{29}$$

Thus, an increase in s^m shifts the price offer distribution via a first order stochastically dominating change, reflecting an on average higher offer from middlemen to producers. Likewise, an increase in s^c has a similar effect, literally since the minimum offer rises in tandem with s^c. Now for fair trader price offers with $p > \hat{p}_x$,

$$F_x^n(p) = F_x^n(\hat{p}_x) + \frac{1}{\lambda_x^n} \ln\left(\frac{p_x^n + s^n - tx - \hat{p}_x - d^n}{p_x^n + s^n - tx - p - d^n}\right), \tag{30}$$

and as such an increase in the subsidy s^n shifts the price offer distribution again via a first order stochastically dominating change, raising the average fair trader price offer even further. Each of these observations are important from a distributional standpoint, since the poverty head count $H_x^n(\bar{p})$ ultimately depends on the price offer distribution $F_x^n(p)$:

$$H_x^n(p) = e^{-\lambda_x^n(1-F_x^n(p))}.$$

Now, the threshold price offer $\hat{p}_x$ separating middlemen and fair traders is determined once again obtained by observing that with simultaneous and endogenous entry of profit maximizing middlemen and fair traders:

$$\begin{aligned} e^{-\lambda_x^n}(p^* + s^m - tx - c - s^c) &= e^{-\lambda_x^n(1-F_x^n(\hat{p}_x))}(p^* + s^m - tx - \hat{p}_x) \\ &= K, \end{aligned} \tag{31}$$

$$\begin{aligned} e^{-\lambda_x^n(1-F_x^n(\hat{p}_x))}(p_x^n + s^n - d^n - tx - \hat{p}_x) &- e^{-\lambda_x^n(1-F_x^n(p))}(p_x^n + s^n - d^n - tx - p) \\ &= K^n \end{aligned} \tag{32}$$

and thus for interior solutions where $F_x^n(\hat{p}_x) \in (0, 1)$ where middlemen and fair traders co-exist:

$$\begin{aligned} \hat{p}_x &= p^* - tx - \frac{(ax - \delta^n + s^n)k}{1 - k} + \frac{s^m}{1 - k} \\ \frac{m_x^n}{N} &= \lambda_x^n(1 - F_x^n(\hat{p}_x)) = \ln\left(\frac{ax - \delta^n + s^n - s^m}{K^n - K}\right) \\ \frac{M_x^n + m_x^n}{N} &= \lambda_x^n - \ln\left(\frac{p^* - tx - c + s^m - s^c}{K}\right). \end{aligned} \tag{33}$$

Evidently, any difference in $s^n - s^m > 0$, reflecting policy discrimination favoring fair traders, directly impacts fair trader entry and thus the equilibrium number of fair traders m_x^n. Meanwhile, any difference in $s^m - s^c$, will directly impact middlemen entry, and thus the equilibrium number of middlemen, at constant $s^n - s^m$.

For any given price premium $a > t(K^n + \delta^n - K)/(p^* + s^m - c - s^c - K)$ in Fig. 6 so that fair traders emerge in some locations,[17] let β^m, and β^n denote the share of producers served by middlemen and fair traders respectively, across all locations:

$$\beta^m = \frac{\int_{\underline{x}}^{x^1(a)}(1 - H_x^n(c))dx + \int_{x^1(a)}^{x^2(a)}(H_x^n(\hat{p}_x) - H_x^n(c))dx}{\bar{x} - \underline{x}},$$

$$\beta^n = \frac{\int_{x^1(a)}^{x^2(a)}(1 - H_x^n(\hat{p}_x))dx + \int_{x^2(a)}^{x^{n+}(a)}(1 - H_x^n(c))dx}{\bar{x} - \underline{x}}.$$

We can now express overall poverty, accounting for all locations, as:

$$P_\alpha = \beta^m P_\alpha^m + \beta^n P_\alpha^n + (1 - \beta^m - \beta^n)P_\alpha^c,$$

and the budget cost $\bar{B}$ of the three subsidies as:

$$\bar{B}^m + \bar{B}^n + \bar{B}^c = [\beta^m s^m + \beta^n s^n + (1 - \beta^m - \beta^n)s^c](\bar{x} - \underline{x})N \tag{34}$$

where $\bar{B}^i = s^i\beta^i(\bar{x} - \underline{x})N$, $i = m, n, c$. Consider therefore a small increase in subsidy budget $\bar{B}^n$ directly towards subsidizing fair traders, $s^n\beta^n(\bar{x} - \underline{x})N$. In the Online Appendix, we show that starting from $s^n = 0$, the marginal impact of a small increase in the fair trader subsidy budget on total poverty P_α,

$$\frac{\partial P_\alpha}{\partial \bar{B}^n} = -\frac{\alpha}{\bar{p}N(\bar{x} - \underline{x})}P_{\alpha-1}^n, \tag{35}$$

is proportional to the poverty indicator $P_{\alpha-1}^n$ among producers served by fair traders. This echoes Besley and Kanbur (1988), where the national poverty impact (P_α) of a regional food subsidy is shown to be the highest by targeting a region with the highest $P_{\alpha-1}$. This very insight continues to hold despite several key difference between setups: the prevalence of both intra- and inter-regional heterogeneity in producer income here, and the fact that middlemen, fair traders, or both, can and do partake in the income gains made possible by the corresponding subsidy program because of imperfect pass-through.

In similar fashion, the marginal impact of a middlemen subsidy, and a domestic price support are respectively given by:

$$\frac{\partial P_\alpha}{\partial \bar{B}^m} = -\frac{\alpha P_{\alpha-1}^m}{\bar{p}N(\bar{x} - \underline{x})} \text{ and } \frac{\partial P_\alpha}{\partial \bar{B}^c} = -\frac{\alpha P_{\alpha-1}^c}{\bar{p}N(\bar{x} - \underline{x})}.$$

From Lemma 1, we know that the relative ranking of $P_{\alpha-1}^m$, and $P_{\alpha-1}^n$ is in general ambiguous for any given price premia, and thus the relative ranking of the marginal impacts of a fair trader subsidy and a middlemen subsidy is accordingly ambiguous. But for the special case of $\alpha = 1$, we know from Lemma 1 that in fact $1 = P_0^c = P_0^n > P_0^m$ based on the poverty head count, we have thus:

[17] Figure 6 shows equilibrium configuration when all three subsidies are evaluated at zero.

Proposition 4 *The marginal impacts of respectively a small increase in* s^n, s^m, *and* s^c *on the overall poverty gap ratio* P_1 *can be ranked as follows:*

$$\left|\frac{\partial P_1}{\partial \bar{B}^c}\right| = \left|\frac{\partial P_1}{\partial \bar{B}^n}\right| > \left|\frac{\partial P_1}{\partial \bar{B}^m}\right|$$

if the price premium is in the range $a \in [t(K^n + \delta^n - K)/(p^* - c - K), t(K^n + \delta^n - K)/(p^* - \bar{p} - K)]$.

Interestingly, and intuitively, with an objective to minimize overall poverty (P_1) at $\alpha = 1$, one way to maximize the marginal impact of the subsidy program (36) is to target fair traders, if the price premium a is small and in fact all producers served by fair traders are living below the poverty line. Alternatively, the marginal impact of a domestic price support is similar in magnitude, because producers who do not have access to markets are likewise poor across the board.

5 Discussion

In this section, we relax a number of assumptions. They are concerned with three aspects of the model. First, from a producer perspective, we incorporate variations in the number of producers by distance from the hub. Next, as an alternative government policy, we introduce the possibility of investment in information flows, such as through enhanced communication networks.[18] Finally, we ask whether consumers interested in poverty reduction can play a role in choosing the right form of intervention, either through a direct price premium on purchases as assumed so far, or a fund that subsidize the fixed cost of fair traders.

5.1 Remoteness and producer density

Throughout, we have maintained the assumption that transportation cost and consumer willingness to pay for fair trade commodities are the only variables that vary across location. Nonetheless, evidence suggests that remoteness in agriculture is associated with systematic differences in input (e.g. labor input, land quality) and output (e.g. productivity) indicators (Stifel et al. 2003). Depending on the variable of interest, there is rich set of possibilities for extending the basic model to accommodate locational heterogeneity. In this extension, we relax an assumption arguably most pertinent to the issue of match friction and middlemen market power, namely, the density of farmers by location. Indeed, departing from our earlier assumption that the density of producers is constant through the locational continuum, assume instead that the number of producers can be heterogeneous across locations, say N_x. From the endogenous entry condition (7), the equilibrium number of middlemen is now given by:

$$M_x = N_x \max\{\ln((p^* - tx - c)/K), 0\}$$

Thus, changing $N_x > 0$ has a scaling effect on the equilibrium number of middlemen M_x. However, the ratio M_x/N_x, which critically determines the market power λ_x of middlemen

[18] We are grateful to an anonymous referee for suggesting this possibility.

remains unchanged. As such, the equilibrium distribution of price offers $H_x(p)$, continues to depend only on the search cost K, as well as the net market price $p^* - tx$. Thus, the rest of the results in this paper remain strictly unaffected even as the number of producers varies across location.

5.2 Investment in communication networks

Since middlemen enjoy market power due to match friction in our setup, a natural candidate for policy intervention is investment in communication networks and technologies, that increases the number of offers that a producer can receive, given the same number of middlemen in a given location (Jensen 2007; Aker 2008). Muto and Yamano (2009) demonstrates the importance of mobile phones in assisting farmers particularly in remote locations to gain access to markets. To model this possibility, let the Poisson rate of offer arrival λ_x be given by

$$\lambda_x \equiv (1+\theta)\frac{M_x}{N_x}, \quad \theta \geq 0.$$

It follows that at constant middlemen to producer ratio, the number of offers a producer will receive increases as θ rises. Of course, if there are no middlemen, or $M_x = 0$, the Poisson parameter is equal to zero. Consider therefore a government investment that increases θ in a given location. What impact will this have on equilibrium producer wellbeing? A priori, if the endogenous ratio of middlemen to producer remains unchanged, such an improvement in communication technology will clearly benefit producers since, as we have shown, the price distribution $H_x(p)$, the average farm gate price, and the responsiveness of this price (Proposition 2) are dependent on λ_x. However, if an improvement in communication technology makes competition among middlemen sufficiently acute so that rising θ in fact displace the number middlemen in equilibrium, the potential for an increase in θ to benefit producers can be muted, or even canceled out.

In the context of our model, by appropriate incorporating θ into Eq. 6,

$$\lambda_x = (1+\theta)\frac{M_x}{N_x} = \max\{\ln((p^* - tx - c)/K), 0\}.$$

From the above, an improvement in communication technology through θ drives out middlemen in the market, in such a way that the equilibrium offer arrival rates λ_x depends only on the search cost K, and the market surplus $p^* - tx - c$. It follows, in fact, that only investing in θ without changing the search cost parameter K has no impact on equilibrium price distribution, and producer wellbeing. While sharp, this finding points usefully to the importance of accounting for endogenous middlemen entry in evaluating the benefits of using communication technologies to improve market access.

5.3 Consumer subsidies

In this final section, we investigate whether subsidizing production via a price premium $p_x^n > p$ is a sensible strategy for consumers interested in raising the welfare of producers at large. A natural candidate to compare with is a subsidy on fair trader entry. Thus, let S^a and S^k represent respectively subsidies to supplement the fair trader premium from ax to $ax + S^a$, and subsidized fair trader entry, so that the fixed cost is reduced from K^n to $K^n - S^k$. Denote

$$m^n(a) = \int_{x^1(a)}^{x^2(a)} \lambda_x^n (1 - F_x^n(\hat{p}_x)) N dx + \int_{x^2(a)}^{x^{n+}(a)} \lambda_x^n N dx$$

as the total number of fair traders across all locations at given a. The budget costs of the two subsidies can now be expressed as:

$$\bar{B}^a = N\beta^n(\bar{x} - \underline{x})S^a, \quad \bar{B}^k = m^n(a)S^k.$$

where $N\beta^n(\bar{x} - \underline{x})$ as before gives the total number of producers served by fair traders. Consider therefore a small increase in the direct entry subsidy, starting from $S^k = 0$, the associated impact

$$\frac{\partial P_\alpha}{\partial \bar{B}^k} = -\frac{\beta^m P_\alpha^n}{m^n(a)K^n}$$

whereas the marginal poverty impact of a small increase in $\bar{B}^n$ has already been shown to be

$$\frac{\partial P_\alpha}{\partial \bar{B}^a} = -\frac{\alpha}{\bar{p}N(\bar{x} - \underline{x})} P_{\alpha-1}^n.$$

The relative effectiveness of the two reduces to the sign of the difference

$$\left|\frac{\partial P_\alpha}{\partial \bar{B}^k}\right| - \left|\frac{\partial P_\alpha}{\partial \bar{B}^a}\right| \tag{36}$$

which is ambiguous in general. But to gain further intuitive insights, we note that $P_\alpha^n \leq P_{\alpha-1}^n(\bar{p}-c)/\bar{p}$ since $\bar{p}-c$ is the largest possible poverty gap. Now, the sign of the difference in (37) reduces to a simple sufficient condition:

Proposition 5 *The overall poverty impact of a consumer subsidy on the price premium is greater than a direct subsidy on fair trader entry if*

$$\alpha \geq \frac{\beta^m N(\bar{x} - \underline{x})(\bar{p} - c)}{m^n(a)K^n}.$$

Proposition 5 is intuitive. It says that raising the per unit price premium has a larger overall impact on poverty if the poverty gap $\beta^m N(\bar{x} - \underline{x})(\bar{p} - c)$ is sufficiently greater than the cost of entry $m^n(a)K^n$, and in addition, if poverty aversion α is sufficiently acute.

6 Conclusion

Let us return to the questions posed in the introduction. What determines equilibrium share of producers served by middlemen and fair traders? We have provided a full characterization of when only middlemen will enter, when only fair traders will enter, and when both middlemen and fair traders exist in equilibrium. In the last of these cases, locations closest to the hub, the most advantaged, are served by middlemen; locations farthest away, the least advantaged, are served by fair traders; but in between are locations which are served by both middlemen and fair traders.

Does fair trader entry reinforce the poverty impact of market access by changing the middlemen markup as well as the extent of market price pass-through? The answer depends on the location. Close to the hub, where only middlemen operate even after the entry of fair traders, nothing has been changed by entry of fair traders, including markup and pass-through. Farthest from the hub, where only fair traders operate, we show that both the average market price, as well as the responsiveness of producer revenue to market price changes is now greater than if only middlemen had operated. However, we show that in intermediate locations, where middlemen and fair traders co-exist, the average producer price rises with the entry of fair traders, but the pass-through remains unchanged.

What precisely is the impact of fair traders on poverty when the full round of market repercussions, including entry and exit of middlemen and of fair traders, is taken into account? We show that the introduction of fair traders pushes back the distance from the hub beyond which all producers are poor. Essentially, fair traders serve the distant locations which are not profitable for middlemen to serve. We also show that under certain conditions, which capture whether the concern of the fair trader for poverty is strong enough, the introduction of fair traders reduces national poverty.

Finally, should a government interested in poverty reduction subsidize the entry of fair traders, or should it perhaps subsidize the entry of middlemen? We address this question and add a new possibility, that the government invests to improve the opportunity cost of selling to either middlemen or fair traders (for example through improving local infrastructure). We provide a detailed analytical characterization, and we get sharp results for specific cases. If the government's objective is to minimize the poverty gap measure P_1, we show the conditions under which subsidizing the entry of middlemen is ranked lowest in terms of policy effectiveness. Subsidizing the entry of fair traders and subsidizing the opportunity costs are equal in effectiveness, but both are superior to subsidizing the entry of middlemen.

We believe that we have just begun the formal analysis of a range of markets that are prevalent in developing countries; where middlemen earn profits that are considered "excessive"; where remoteness exacerbates imperfect pass-through; where fair traders come in to help the poor in the face of what they see as exploitation by these middlemen; where governments are faced with a policy problem of whether and how much to help fair traders or sanction middlemen; and where consumers are asked to pay a price premium for products marketed by fair traders on behalf of poor producers, and to support the creation and entry of such fair traders into these markets. The model structure we have developed allows us to ask and answer a number of key questions in the debate on middlemen and fair traders. A rich research agenda awaits.

Acknowledgments We are grateful to two Editors of this journal and two anonymous referees for insightful remarks and suggestions.

References

Abufarha, N.: Alterntive trade organizations and the fair trade movements (2013). http://fairworldproject.org/voices-of-fair-trade/alternative-trade-organizations-and-the-fair-trade-movement

Aker, J.C.: Does digital divide or provide? The impact of cell phones on grain markets in Niger. BREAD working paper no. 177 (2008)

Andreoni, J.: Impure altruism and donations to public goods: a theory of warm-glow giving. Econ. J. **100**, 464–477 (1990)

Antràs, P., Costinot, A.: Intermediated trade. Q. J. Econ. **126**, 1319–1374 (2011)

Arndt, C., Jensen, H.T., Robinson, S., Tarp, F.: Marketing margins and agricultural technology in Mozambique. J. Dev. Stud. **37**(1), 121–137 (2000)

Bardhan, P., Mookherjee, D., Tsumagari, M.: Middlemen, margins and globalization. Am. Econ. J.: Microeconomics **5**(4), 81–119 (2013)

Basu, A.K., Hicks, R.L.: Label performance and the willingness to pay for fair trade coffee: a cross-national perspective. Int. J. Consum. Stud. **32**(5), 470–478 (2008)

Basu, A.K., Hicks, R.L.: Aversion to poverty and relative deprivation? An analysis of consumers' willingness to pay for fair trade coffee. Working Paper, Department of Economics, College of William and Mary, Williamsburg, VA (2009)

Besley, T., Kanbur, R.: Food subsidies and poverty alleviation. Econ. J. **98**, 701–719 (1988)

Biglaiser, G.: Middlemen and experts. Rand J. Econ. **24**(2), 212–23 (1993)

Biglaiser, G., Friedman, J.: Middlemen as guarantors of quality. Int. J. Ind. Organ. **12**, 509–531 (1994)

Clower, R., Leijonhufvud, A.: The coordination of economic activities: a Keynesian perspective. Am. Econ. Rev. **65**, 182–188 (1975)

de Janvry, A., McIntosh, C., Sadoulet, E.: Fair trade efficiency: can a disequilibrium market serve as development tool? Rev. Econ. Stat. **97**(3), 567–573 (2015)

Department for International Development (DFID): Eliminating world poverty: building our common future. Report presented to parliament by the secretary of state for international development by command of her majesty. The Stationary Office Limited, United Kingdom (2009). https://www.gov.uk/government/uploads/system/uploads/attachment_data/file/229029/7656.pdf

Develtere, P., Pollet, I.: Cooperatives and fair trade. Katholieke Universiteit Leuven (2005). http://www.copac.coop/about/2005/cooperatives-and-fair-trade-final.pdf

Fafchamps, M., Gabre-Madhin, E., Minten, B.: Increasing returns and market efficiency in agricultural trade. J. Dev. Econ. **78**(2), 406–442 (2005)

Fafchamps, M., Minten, B.: Impact of Sms-based agricultural information on Indian farmers. World Bank Econ. Rev. **26**(3), 383–414 (2012)

Fairtrade Labelling Organizations International: Annual Report 2009-2010 (2010a). http://www.fairtrade.net/fileadmin/user_upload/content/2009/resources/FLO_Annual-Report-2009_komplett_double_web.pdf

Fairtrade Labelling Organizations International: Fairtrade at a Glance (2010b) http://www.fairtrade.net/fileadmin/user_upload/content/2009/resources/2010-03_Fairtrade_at_a_Glance.pdf

Fair Trade Federation: https://www.fairtradefederation.org/fair-trade-myths/. Cited 12 Jan 2015 (2015)

Fair Trade USA: Fair Trade for All: Delivering Fair Trade to More People (2012). http://fairtradeusa.org/sites/all/files/wysiwyg/filemanager/Fair_Trade_for_All/Fair_Trade_for_All_Overview_July_2012.pdf

Foster, J., Greer, J., Thorbecke, E.: A class of decomposable poverty measures. Econometrica **52**(3), 761–766 (1984)

Global Exchange: http://www.globalexchange.org/fairtrade/cocoa/cooperatives. Cited 12 Jan 2015 (2015)

Goetz, S.: A selectivity model of household food marketing behavior in Sub-Saharan Africa. Am. J. Agric. Econ. **74**, 444–452 (1992)

Goyal, A.: Information, direct access to farmers and rural market performance in Central India. Am. Econ. J.: Appl. Econ. **2.3**, 22–45 (2010)

Hertel, T., Winters, A.: Poverty and the WTO: impacts of the Doha development agenda. Palgrave Macmillan, New York, World Bank, Washington DC (2005)

Jensen, R.: The digital provide; information (technology), market performance, and welfare in the South Indian fisheries sector. Q. J. Econ. **122**(3), 879–924 (2007)

Lewin, B., Giovannucci, D., Varangis, P.: Coffee markets: new paradigms in gobal supply and demand. World Bank Agriculture and Rural Development Discussion Paper 3 (2004)

Loureiro, M.L., Lotade, J.: Do fair trade and eco-labels in coffee wake up the consumer conscience? Ecol. Econ. **53**, 129–138 (2005)

McMillan, M.S., Welch, K.H., Rodrik, D.: When economic reform goes wrong: cashew in Mozambique. Brookings Trade Forum-2003, pp. 97–151 (2004)

Minten, B., Tamru, S., Engida, E., Kuma, T.: Using evidence in unraveling food supply chains in Ethiopia: the supply chain of Teff from major production areas to Addis Ababa. Ethiopia Strategy Support Report II. IFPRI (2013)

Mookherjee, D., Mitra, S., Torero, M., Visaria, S.: Asymmetric information and middleman margins: an experiment with West Bengal potato farmers. MIT (2013). http://economics.mit.edu/files/8720

Mortensen, D.T.: Wage dispersion. Why are similar workers paid differently? MIT Press, Cambridge MA (2003)

Muto, M., Yamano, T.: The impact of mobile phone coverage expansion on market participation: panel data evidence from Uganda. World Dev. **37**(12), 1887–1896 (2009)

Nicita, A.: Who benefited from trade liberalization in Mexico? Measuring the effects on household welfare. World Bank Working Papers 3265 (2004)

Osborne, T.: Impertect competition in agricultural makrets: evidence from Ethiopia. J. Dev. Econ. **76**, 405–428 (2005)

Rauch, J., Watson, J.: Network intermediaries in international trade. J. Econ. Manag. Strateg. **13**(1), 69–93 (2004)

Renard, M.-C., Pèrez-Grovas, V.: Fair trade coffee in Mexico: at the center of the debates. In: Raynolds, L.T., Murray, D., Wilkinson, J. (eds.) Fair Trade: The Challenges of Transforming Globalization, pp. 139–156. Routledge, London and New York (2007)

Rubinstein, A., Wolinsky, A.: Middlemen. Q. J. Econ. **102**(3), 581–594 (1987)

SEWA Trade Facilitation Center: http://www.sewa.org/Sewa%20Trade%20Facilitation%20Centre.asp. Cited 12 Jan 2015 (2015)

Sexton, R.J., Kling, C.L., Carman, H.F.: Market integration, efficiency of arbitrage, and imperfect competition: methodology and application to U.S. celery market integration, efficiency of arbitrage, and imperfect competition: methodology and application to U.S. celery. Am. J. Agric. Econ. **73**, 568–580 (1991)

Spulber, D.F.: Risk sharing and inventories. J. Econ. Behav. Organ. **6**, 55–68 (1985)

Spulber, D.F.: Market microstructure and intermediation. J. Econ. Perspect. **10**(3), 135–152 (1996a)

Spulber, D.F.: Market making by price-setting firms. Rev. Econ. Stud. **63**(4), 559–580 (1996b)

Stifel, D., Minten, B., Dorosh, P.: Transaction costs and agricultural productivity: implications of isolation for rural poverty in Madagascar. MSSD Discussion Paper no. 56. IFPRI, Washington DC (2003)

Svensson, J., Yanagizawa, D.: Getting prices right: the impact of the market information service in Uganda. J. Eur. Econ. Assoc. **7**(2-3), 435–445 (2009)

Thapa, G.B., Pokhrel, D.M.: Are marketing intemediaries exploiting mountain farmers in Nepal? A study based on market price, marketing margin and income distribution analyses. Agric. Syst. **94**, 151–164 (2007)

World Inquiry: http://worldinquiry.case.edu/bankInnovationView.cfm?idArchive=1078. Cited 12 Jan 2015 (2015)

J Econ Inequal (2013) 11:1–34
DOI 10.1007/s10888-011-9179-y

Impact of rural employment guarantee schemes on seasonal labor markets: optimum compensation and workers' welfare

Arnab K. Basu

Received: 17 February 2008 / Accepted: 18 April 2011 / Published online: 15 May 2011

Abstract The recent enactment of the National Rural Employment Guarantee Act in India has been widely hailed as a policy that provides a safety net for the rural poor with the potential to boost rural income, stabilize agricultural production and reduce rural-urban migration. This paper models the impact of such employment guarantee schemes in the context of an agrarian economy characterized by lean season involuntary unemployment as a consequence of tied-labor contracts. Specifically, we examine labor and output market responses to a *productive* rural Employment Guarantee Scheme (EGS) and determine the optimal compensation to public work employees consistent with the objectives of (i) productive efficiency in agriculture and (ii) welfare maximization of the laborers. Our framework provides a theoretical framework for the evaluation of a number of (sometimes) conflicting observations and empirical results on the impact of an EGS on agricultural wages, employment and output, and underscores the importance of the relative productivity of workers in the EGS program *vis-à-vis* their counterparts engaged in agricultural production in determining the success of these programs.

Keywords Labor contracts · Rural unemployment · Employment guarantee schemes · Public input · Optimal wage

JEL Classification J3 · O38 · Q12

A. K. Basu (✉)
Department of Economics, College of William & Mary, Williamsburg, VA 23185, USA
e-mail: akbasu@wm.edu

A. K. Basu
Center for Development Research (ZEF), Rheinische-Friedrich-Wilhelms Universität, Bonn, Germany

A. K. Basu
Institute for the Study of Labor (IZA), Bonn, Germany

1 Introduction

Guaranteed employment at a pre-determined wage aimed at providing income security to the otherwise unemployed has been a longstanding staple policy for governments worldwide. Starting with the Poor Employment Act of 1817 in Britain, and later on the New Deal Programs in the United States in the 1930s, government intervention in the labor market as an employer of the last resort has been adopted as an integral feature of labor market policies in many developing countries over the last few decades [35]. Recent examples of the latter include public work programs in India, Bangladesh, Pakistan, Philippines, Egypt, Botswana, Kenya and Chile [35, 53].

Amongst developing countries, no public works program has been empirically studied as extensively as the *Employment Guarantee Scheme* (EGS) in the State of Maharashtra, India.[1] It is not surprising, therefore, that the recent enactment of the National Rural Employment Guarantee Act of India in 2005 (since renamed the Mahatma Gandhi National Rural Employment Guarantee Act) has generated renewed interest in the effectiveness of EGS programs to provide an economic safety net to the rural poor [40]. The National Rural Employment Guarantee Scheme (NREGS) following the Act of 2005 has, with minor modifications, broadened the coverage and enacted into law the EGS in existence since the 1960's in the State of Maharashtra in India. In turn, the origins of the Maharashtra EGS in India and its counterpart, the Rural Public Works (RPW) program in Bangladesh, can be traced back to the *Famine Codes* established in British India in the 1880's where direct action in the form of public work programs was the central feature of famine relief strategy.

It is now widely recognized that labor market interventions through rural EGS programs generate income support for the poor and also raise agricultural productivity over the long run [22]. As examples, the EGS in Maharashtra has been credited with averting a famine during the drought of 1970–73 and alleviating poverty [20, 22], while the *Rural Public Works* (RPW) program in Bangladesh has been commended for its contribution to rural development and increased agricultural production through the creation and maintenance of rural infrastructure [2]. In this context, the NREGS can be thought of as a policy to boost rural income, stabilize agricultural production and reduce rural-urban migration.

The NREGS is initially applicable in 200 rural districts and encompasses all rural areas of India including the Fifth and Sixth Schedule areas, except the State of Jammu and Kashmir. Some of the provisions of the NREGS are: (i) every household in the rural areas of India shall have a right to at least 100 days of guaranteed employment every year for at least one adult member for doing casual manual labour at the rate of Rupees 60 per day (approximately US $1.30 per day); (ii) only productive works shall undertaken: the identification of projects will be based on the economic, social and environmental benefits of different types of works, their contribution to social equity, and their ability to create permanent assets; and (iii)

[1] See for example, Ravallion [45, 46] and Ravallion et al. [47].

employment will be provided within a radius of 5 km of the village where the applicant resides at the time of applying. Moreover, the NREGS allows for any existing EGS to be deemed as the action plan for purposes of the Act. Existing EGS programs, however, have stricter workfare guidelines as compared to the broader scope of the NREGS elucidated above. For instance, the EGS in Maharashtra specifies that (a) large scale employment is to be provided to landless laborers during the lean (or slack) seasons, thereby preventing the out-migration of laborers to the urban regions, (b) to construct and maintain rural infrastructure, viz, irrigation facilities, flood control measures and roads, (c) to encourage farmers to invest in cultivation so as to fulfill the objective of self-sufficiency in foodgrains, and (d) public works employment should not affect the availability of agricultural labor at lawful minimum wages [19].

Although the design and efficacy of public works programs as an instrument for poverty alleviation has been a subject of extensive theoretical research,[2] the effect of such programs on rural labor market outcomes and agricultural production decisions has received surprisingly little attention. Notable exceptions to the latter has been the work of Ravallion [46] and Khan [34], which recognizes that EGS programs have ramifications in both the output as well as the labor markets. However, both these papers analyze market responses to EGS programs in the context of a dual economy characterized by a perfectly competitive rural labor market and urban unemployment à la Harris-Todaro.[3] While agrarian relations in rural India exhibit a variety of labor hiring arrangements—from active casual markets in both seasons, to tied-labor/implicit contracts to collective bargaining between laborers and landlords—the explicit and implicit objectives of the EGS and NREGS programs (highlighted above respectively) is to target those laborers that are either involuntarily unemployed in the agricultural lean season or those that are desperate to escape the vicious cycle of poverty and debt. Thus, competitive rural labor market framework, given the program objectives highlighted above, is hardly the suitable one for the purpose of analyzing agricultural labor market outcomes in the presence of either an NREGS or an EGS.

Two types of laborers, those either vulnerable to debt-bondage (through interlinked credit-labor contracts) or potential participants in tied-labor contracts (which generates involuntary unemployment in the lean season), fit best as the intended beneficiaries of the NREGS and EGS programs. Consider the institution of debt bondage first. Absent formal credit markets in rural areas, debt-bondage is a phenomenon where poor laborers borrow from richer landlords to finance subsistence consumption in the lean season with the pledge to repay the loan through labor services in the peak season. While these contracts are entered into voluntarily

[2]Some of the studies that revolve around the poverty alleviation aspect of EGS programs are: (a) the incentive argument of public works programs, specifically, the self-targeting and screening potential of these programs [14], (b) the use of means-tested and universal schemes in the alleviation of poverty [13], (c) schemes aiming at wide coverage at low wages and restricted coverage at higher wages [45], (d) transfer benefits from public works employment [21] and (e) the relative benefits of payments in cash or kind through these programs [7, 9].

[3]Following Harris and Todaro's [31] classic formulation.

by poor laborers, usurious interest rates force them into a vicious cycle of debt. Frequently these laborers have no choice but to pledge the labor services of their children (in addition to their own labor services) in order to repay these loans. The phenomenon of debt-bondage for adult laborers has been studied by Genicot [30], and for adult and child laborers by Basu and Chau [10, 11]. Basu and Chau [10] explicitly consider the impact of an EGS program to alleviate debt-bondage, and show that while an EGS program may well be effective in targeting *potential* laborers from entering into such repressive credit-labor arrangements, a policy of subsidized credit may well be a more effective instrument in targeting potential and existing laborers vulnerable to debt-bondage.

The discussion above leaves the framework of two-tiered labor markets as the remaining one that is yet to be used for the evaluation of labor market outcomes in the presence of employment guarantee programs. To begin with, labor tying is usually observed where agricultural production exhibits seasonality as defined by low labor demand during the lean/slack season (dominated by activities like soil preparation, tilling and sowing) and *usually* high labor demand during the peak season (when the crop is harvested, threshed and stored/marketed) [5]. The presence of this production uncertainty, in turn, induces landlords to lock-in of a certain number of laborers at a pre-determined wage over both seasons to minimize production costs. Such locking-in of laborers still allows for the option to supplement tied-laborers with casual ones at the competitive wage in the peak season if actual peak season production does end up exceeding the anticipated level in the lean season [3, 4].[4] A direct consequence of labor-tying (with an inactive casual labor market in the lean season) is involuntary unemployment—the explicit target group for the EGS and the implicit target of the NREGS to provide a hundred days of guaranteed employment.

Indeed, evidence suggests that tied-labor contracts (with accompanying involuntary unemployment) still exist in rural India. Although historically the Indian States of Bihar (including the State of Jharkhand) and Uttar Pradesh (including the State of Uttaranchal) had some of the highest incidence of attached or tied labor [4], more recently tied labor is shown to be more pervasive in the Indian States of Andhra Pradesh, Madhya Pradesh, Rajasthan and Punjab. Using data from the Consumption Expenditure of Rural Labour Households survey of the Government of India (1999–2000), Deshingkar and Farrington [24] show that in the State of Andhra Pradesh attached laborers are on yearly contracts and the demographic profile is almost exclusively male and between the ages of 10–70. The primary reason for a high percentage of attached or tied labor in Andhra Pradesh is due to a poor household's need for credit to pay off outstanding debt. Further, these attached labor

[4]Bardhan [3] posits that labor tying arrangements of this nature stem from the landlords' motive to minimize recruitment costs in the peak season when labor demand is usually high. Bardhan [4] provides an alternative hypothesis in that production uncertainty, coupled with the absence of insurance markets, enables landlords to offer contracts that ensure a certain income for risk-averse laborers. A third hypothesis revolves around the notion that laborers have an incentive to shirk, and hence contractual arrangements that guarantee a remuneration above a laborers' opportunity income may elicit loyalty [26].

contracts are entered into voluntarily and their incidence increases during the periods of draught, which points to these contracts as an insurance mechanism. A similar pattern of attached labor is also found in Madhya Pradesh, where feudal agrarian relations have led to the bonded labor contracts called *Hali*. These contracts entail an advance of a full-season's wages in lieu of a laborer working a certain number of hours for a particular landlord, and these wage advances are positively correlated with the prevailing agricultural wage. Attached labor contracts are also observed amongst the lower caste landless households in Rajasthan [15] as well as amongst migrant laborers in Punjab who are on annual contracts. Incidentally, in Punjab, although the proportion of attached laborers to casual laborers is less than one, this proportion increases with the size of the land holdings [51]. Finally, village level studies by Motiram [37] in the Telangana region of South India and by Rawal [48] in rural Haryana also point to the existence of tied and attached laborers in these regions.

Unfortunately, comprehensive studies aimed at identifying the percentage of tied labor across individual rural districts within the various States of India, and the corresponding district level implementation of the NREGS programs to ascertain the degree to which these programs are targeted towards tied laborers, do not yet exist. Nevertheless, it is important to map the concentration of NREGS programs across the Indian states to check whether a relatively higher number of these programs have, at the very least, been instituted in those States where the institution of tied labor has been reported by existing studies. In this regard, Chakraborty [18] provides a comprehensive picture of the number of NREGS districts in each Indian State. The highest concentration of NREGS programs are in Bihar (23 districts), Uttaranchal (22 districts), Jharkhand (20 districts), Orissa (19 districts), Madhya Pradesh (18 districts), Andhra Pradesh (13 districts), Maharashtra (12 districts), West Bengal (10 districts), and Rajasthan, Kerala and Gujarat (6 districts each). Interestingly, Andhra Pradesh is also the State with one of the highest reported incidence of debt-bondage along with the States of Orissa, Uttar Pradesh and Karnataka for both agricultural and non-agricultural rural workers. Debt bondage, however, is observed to a lesser extent in Madhya Pradesh, Rajasthan and Punjab [52].

In light of the above, the main objective in this paper is to trace out the labor and output market responses to an EGS program instituted in the lean season to hire the rural unemployed and produce a public input. We consider a model of labor-tying that is a generalization of Bardhan's [3] model in which monopsonistic landlords minimize recruitment costs by offering tied-labor contracts. In our model, risk-neutral, oligopsonistic landlords hire risk-averse, landless laborers to produce a single crop. The production of this crop is spread over two seasons, the lean and the peak, with the peak season output subject to fluctuations in *weather*. Based on their expectation about peak season output, landlords choose the number of laborers to be hired as attached or permanent laborers at a fixed wage over the two seasons thereby giving rise to the institution of tied-labor contracts. If the peak season weather turns out to be better than expected, landlords supplement the need for additional labor through the hiring of casual laborers at the prevailing spot market wage.

The intuition behind the persistence of tied-labor contracts in the above setting follows from the fact that landlords, by accounting for the trade-off between the number of permanent hires and the peak season recruitment cost in their expected profit maximization calculus, offer permanent contracts at a wage that equates the value of the expected marginal revenue product of labor with the marginal cost of hiring over both seasons. Consequently, the permanent wage and the number of contracts offered is less than what obtains under a competitive setting leading to involuntary unemployment in the lean season.[5] In the absence of any alternative employment opportunities, laborers who fail to get permanent contracts rely solely on the competitive casual labor market to find agricultural employment in the peak season.[6] In the lean season, a *productive* EGS program fulfills the first of its three objectives by employing this group of otherwise unemployed laborers. Naturally, government hiring of unemployed laborers would affect labor allocations across both seasons directly through its effect on the wages and indirectly through its effect on peak season output.

A second important dimension of these EGS programs, hitherto neglected in the literature when accounting for market responses to public interventions, relates to their productive nature. It can be argued, inter alia, that productive assets or infrastructure created through an EGS program in the rural sector will have a direct impact on agricultural productivity as a *public input*. Indeed, if EGS were to undertake projects on irrigation or flood control measures in areas prone to droughts or flooding, it is only natural that output and labor hiring decisions take into account the effect of these projects in mitigating such factors as weather fluctuations which customarily plague agricultural production. In fact, empirical studies by Binswanger et al. [16] and Fan et al. [27] strongly suggest a positive relationship between government investment in infrastructure and agricultural output.[7] Additionally,

[5]Tied labor contracts can also be generated in other settings, such as Eswaran and Kotwal's [26] model where tied-contracts circumvent shirking by laborers. However, since the focus of our paper is about EGS programs that are the employer of the last resort, it is difficult to justify that landless laborers, with no alternative source of income, have an incentive to shirk if they find regular agricultural employment. Second, the choice of our framework is dictated by the observation that EGS programs guarantee jobs for *only* those unemployed in the agricultural sector and hence, unlike Mukherjee and Ray [39], our framework precludes the existence of an active casual labor market in the lean season. It should also be noted that the assumption regarding output uncertainty in this model is based on the realistic production environment in South Asia and is not necessary for the emergence and persistence of tied-labor contracts. The assumption of oligopsony is sufficient for this purpose. In fact, in our model output uncertainty by itself will not lead to the prevalence of tied-labor contracts in an unfettered economy, unless additional assumptions are made regarding the production technology (see, for example, [4, 6]).

[6]We assume that laborers in this economy have no other source of income except from that of an agricultural laborer or of an EGS employee. This assumption follows from the fact that EGS programs are directed primarily towards the rural landless, as evidenced by the implementation of the *Rural Landless Employment Guarantee Scheme* under the seventh five-year plan (1985–1990) in India as well as a number of other programs such as the *Jawahar Rozgar Yojana* in 1989. Further, the extent of unemployment amongst landless agricultural laborers is significant in India [32, 36].

[7]Binswanger et al. [16] points out that private agricultural investment and input use is more profitable the better the government infrastructure. Fan et al. finds that investments in rural roads and agricultural research have the highest impact per rupee spent than any other government investment on agricultural productivity. Further evidence linking agricultural productivity with investment in rural infrastructure can be found in Thomas [54] which suggests that yearly yields of paddy had increased as a result of the Rural Public Works program in Bangladesh. See also Narayana et al. [41] for an empirical analysis of the costs and benefits of EGS programs in India.

Sathe [49] reports that 91% of ex-EGS laborers find that rural employment guarantee schemes contributed to formal agricultural activity through work on protective irrigation to otherwise dry lands, and that these assets created through EGS employment had led to positive developments in agricultural and rural non-agricultural activities.

In effect, our theoretical framework allows for an evaluation of a number of (sometimes) conflicting observations and empirical results on the impact of an EGS on agricultural wages, employment and output, as well as underscores the importance of the relative productivity of workers in the EGS program *vis-à-vis* their counterparts engaged in agricultural production in determining the success of these programs. As examples, Osmani and Chowdhury [43] and Basu [8] posit for Bangladesh and India respectively that an EGS program exerts upward pressure on agricultural wages, while Ravallion [46] and Ahmad and Hossain [1] show that an EGS displaces laborers from agricultural employment. We show that while the institution of an EGS program increases the permanent wage and displaces some permanent laborers into the pool of casual ones, the impact of an EGS program on the casual wage in the peak season may well be positive depending upon the relative productivity of the EGS laborers *vis-à-vis* their agricultural counterparts.

The final objective of our paper concerns the determination of the *optimum* wage to be paid in an EGS program taking into account its public good aspect. Although the NREGS stipulates Rupees 60 as the daily renumeration for EGS workers, this pre-determined wage may well be inconsistent with one of the following three objectives: (i) screening the poor from the not-so-poor insofar as who gets employed in the program, (ii) maximizing expected agricultural output and (iii) maximizing the welfare of the laborers in the economy. The first objective has received extensive treatment elsewhere. Our concern is therefore with the second and the third objectives. It should be noted that the objective of expected agricultural output maximization is of utmost importance not only because entitlement failures are the consequence of the loss of employment associated with bad harvests, but also because assessments of harvest quality form the basis of the *annewari* system of early warning in India.[8] Our findings indicate that the optimum wage consistent with expected agricultural output maximization almost always conflicts with the one consistent with the objective of welfare maximization of the laborers. Thus, even though a pre-determined wage for EGS workers may accidentally fulfill one of the objectives, it is guaranteed to be in conflict with the other.

The plan of the paper is as follows. Section 2 develops the model and explains its workings. Section 3 analyzes market responses to EGS programs while Section 4 focuses on the determination of the optimum wage. Section 5 provides a sketch of the impact of public works programs in alternative labor market settings. Finally, Section 6 offers some concluding remarks.

[8]See Drèze [22]

2 The model

2.1 Landlords

Consider an economy with N identical, risk neutral, oligopsonistic landlords and a large number, $\mathcal{L}$, of homogeneous, risk averse landless laborers.[9] The total amount of land is fixed and equally divided amongst the landlords who maximize profit over an infinite horizon by hiring landless laborers to produce a single crop. During each time period, the production of this crop is spread over two seasons, the lean and the peak. Given expectations about weather conditions in the peak season, an individual landlord maximizes profit by choosing a fraction of the laborers to be hired as permanent or tied laborers at a fixed wage over the two seasons at the beginning of any time period. In the peak season, landlords hire casual laborers at the ongoing spot market wage to supplement permanent laborers.[10] Further, casual and permanent laborers perform the same task in the peak season.

Specifically, lean season output for the ith landlord, Q^i_L, is given by,

$$Q^i_L = \beta L^i_P; \quad \beta > 0 \tag{1}$$

where β is a technology parameter affecting lean season output and denotes both the average and the marginal productivity of permanent laborers in the lean season.

The remaining laborers, i.e., the ones who fail to get permanent contracts in the lean season, are absorbed by a productive EGS program at a pre-determined wage, $\bar{w}$, for the creation and maintenance of rural infrastructure.[11] We focus on EGS programs that are in effect only over the duration of the lean season based on (i) the observation that governments try to avoid competition with farmers over casual labor in the peak season when agricultural labor demand is usually high [46] and (ii) the guarantee of one hundred days of employment under the NREGS, which most likely will be accessed by the rural poor when the private labor market is inactive during the lean season.[12]

[9]According to Sathe [49], data collected through village level surveys in Maharashtra between 1987–1989 for 62 villages and 14,345 households shows that half the job seekers in the EGS program were from the backward castes. In addition, 31% of the sample laborers were landless while 50% were marginal farmers, and 79% of the respondents alluded to the lack of alternative employment opportunities as the reason for choosing EGS work. In a recent study on the characteristics of job seekers in the NREGS programs in the State of Rajasthan, Jha et al. [33] also show that members of the scheduled tribes and landless agricultural workers are the primary beneficiaries of these programs.

[10]Unlike Osmani [42] and Mukherjee and Ray [38], laborers in this model do not have bargaining power in the casual labor market.

[11]Following Basu [9], we assume that the government hires, at a pre-determined wage, *all* laborers unable to find permanent contracts. Whether *all* workers seeking employment in EGS programs actually manage to find employment in Maharashtra has recently been studied by Ravallion et al. [47].

[12]Dev [25, p. 126] reports that EGS and agricultural employment are complementary in the sense that EGS employment is high in the lean season (April–July) and low in the peak season (October–January). For instance, in two villages within Maharashtra (Shirapur and Kanzara), the EGS and agricultural employment profiles for male agricultural laborers show negative correlations of −0.68 and −0.33 respectively.

Let the shadow cost of public funds used for the EGS program be $\Pi > 0$. In other words, each dollar spent by the government on direct job creation through an EGS program is either (a) raised through distortionary taxes and costs society $(1 + \Pi)$ dollars[13] or (b) the opportunity cost of a dollar of foreign aid, not specifically tied to job creation through an EGS program, is $(1 + \Pi)$ dollars.[14]

The production function for the EGS program is given by

$$Q_G = \alpha L_G; \quad \alpha > 0, \tag{2}$$

where α denotes both the marginal and average productivity of labor in this EGS program. By virtue of the employment guarantee scheme, the allocation of laborers across the EGS program and private production for the landlords in the lean season must satisfy:

$$L_G + NL_P^i = \mathcal{L} \tag{3}$$

where NL_P^i is the total number of permanent contracts offered by the landlords.

Denote $A \in [\underline{A}, M]$ as the weather outcome in the peak season, where $\underline{A}$ and M are respectively the *worst* and the *best* possible weather outcomes. Let $F(A)$ be the cumulative distribution function associated with the random variable A with $f(A) = F'(A) > 0$ as the density function.[15] We shall assume that the expectation of A $(= \int_{\underline{A}}^{M} Af(A)dA)$, equals unity. Now, total output in the peak season depends on three inputs: (i) lean season output, $A\beta L_P^i$, comprised of the work done by permanent laborers, (βL_P^i denoting the amount of seeds planted etc.) along with the actual weather condition at the beginning of the peak season, (A denoting the amount of rainfall); (ii) the amount of work done in the peak season itself and (iii) the output of the EGS program, $\bar{Q}_G$, which plays the role of a public input affecting agricultural production in the peak season. Therefore, *actual* peak season output for an individual landlord is written as follows:

$$Q_H^i = g\left(\bar{Q}_G\right) H\left(A\beta L_P^i,\ L_a^i\right); \quad E(A) = 1; \quad H_1,\ H_2 > 0,\ H_{11},\ H_{22} < 0 \tag{4}$$

We shall assume that $H(\cdot,\cdot)$ is twice continuously differentiable, exhibits constant returns to scale and diminishing marginal productivity with respect to both inputs and $g(0) = 1$ and $g' > 0$, $g'' < 0$. Note that $L_a^i = L_P^i + L_C^i = \frac{\mathcal{L}}{N}$ is the total amount of labor employed by an individual landlord in the peak season with L_C^i as the number of casual laborers hired.[16]

Accordingly, a landlord's labor hiring decision follows a two-stage maximization problem. In the lean season, employment of permanent labor is determined. In the peak season, casual labor employment is determined given the prevailing spot wage, w_C, the amount of lean season output, $A\beta L_P^i$, and the amount of the EGS output, $\bar{Q}_G$.

[13] We are in effect assuming that ideal lump-sum taxation is not available and higher the inefficiency of tax collection by the government the higher the value of Π.

[14] For instance, the Food-for-Work program in Bangladesh was financed by U.S aid under the PL-480 agreement, and is an example of foreign aid tied specifically to job creation programs (see [2]).

[15] A $'$ denotes the first derivative of the variable in question.

[16] The total number of laborers in this economy, $NL_P^i + NL_C^i = NL_a^i = \mathcal{L}$, with NL_C^i is the total number of casual laborers in the peak season.

With the price of the agricultural output exogenously given and normalized to unity, we shall begin with the peak season maximization problem of a typical landlord. Given $A\beta L_P^i$ and $\bar{Q}_G$, let w_C^i be the wage offer of the ith landlord and $l_C^i(w_C^1, ..., w_C^j, ..., w_C^N)$ be the corresponding casual labor supply to this landlord. Clearly, $w_C^i = w_C^j$ for all landlords since a lower wage offer by any landlord would result in a zero casual labor supply in return. Further, $w_C^i = w_C^j = w_C$ is the competitive wage for the economy in the peak season due to the fact that under constant return to scale technologies, Bertrand competition by oligopsonistic landlords leads to a symmetric competitive outcome. Once w_C is determined, the number of casual laborers employed by an individual landlord is given as a solution to

$$\max_{L_C^i} \quad g\left(\bar{Q}_G\right) H\left(A\beta L_P^i,\ L_P^i + L_C^i\right) - w_C^i L_C^i; \quad s.t \quad L_C^i \leq l_C^i\left(w_C^1, ..., w_C^N\right)$$

The equilibrium casual wage is thus given by

$$w_C = g\left(\bar{Q}_G\right) H_2\left(A\beta L_P^i,\ L_P^i + L_C^i\right)$$

As a first step, we need to identify how the number of permanent contracts offered at the begining of the lean season affects the casual wage in the peak season. To this end, we need to pin down whether permanent and casual laborers are substitutes or complements of one another in the peak season. Thus, totally differentiating the above equation yields,

$$\frac{\partial L_C^i}{\partial L_P^i} = -\frac{\left(-\alpha N g' H_2 + g A\beta H_{21} + g H_{22}\right)}{g H_{22}}$$

Since $H(\cdot, \cdot)$ exhibits constant returns to scale, we utilize the fact that $L_P^i H_{21} + L_C^i H_{22} = 0$, and noting that $-\frac{\alpha N g' L_P^i}{g} = \epsilon_{L_P^i}^g < 0$ is the elasticity of the EGS input with respect to permanent labor while $\frac{H_2}{H_{22} L_C^i} = \epsilon_{L_C^i}^{H_2} < 0$ is the elasticity of peak season agricultural output with respect to casual labor we can rewrite the above equation as,

$$\frac{\partial L_C^i}{\partial L_P^i} = -\frac{\epsilon_{L_P^i}^g}{\epsilon_{L_C^i}^{H_2}} \frac{L_C^i}{L_P^i} + A\beta \frac{L_C^i}{L_P^i} - 1$$

The right hand side of the above can be either positive or negative implying that permanent and casual laborers can be either complements or substitutes of one another in the peak season production process. As we show in Appendix A.1, if (i) $\epsilon_{L_P^i}^g$ is small, (ii) weather outcome (A) is distinctly favorable, (iii) agricultural productivity (β) in the lean season is large and (iv) the number of permanent laborers relative to the total labor force in the economy is small, then permanent and casual laborers complement one another. The economic intuition is simple: If the hiring of an additional permanent laborer has (i) a negligible adverse effect on the output of the EGS program and hence on the peak season agricultural output, (ii) revealed weather in the peak season is very good and (iii) if the marginal productivity of permanent laborers is very high (implying a large intermediate input for the peak season production function), then the hiring of an additional permanent laborer raises the productivity of all laborers in the peak leading to an increased need for casual laborers.

Thus, even though the casual labor market clears in the peak season at the prevailing market wage, the choice of permanent contracts will impinge upon the actual casual wage once weather conditions are revealed in the peak. In particular,

$$w_C(A) = g\left(\bar{Q}_G\right) H_2\left(A\beta L^i_P, \frac{\mathcal{L}}{N}\right) \tag{5}$$

where the right hand side of the above equation denotes the inverse demand function for casual labor. Assuming point expectation, i.e., a unique w_C for every possible revelation of A, it is easy to see that the casual wage, w_C, is increasing in (i) the number of permanent contracts, L^i_P, (ii) the productivity of permanent laborers, β, (iii) the amoumt of EGS input generated in the lean season, $\bar{Q}_G$ and (iv) the revealed weather in the peak season, A.

The aggregate labor demand by all landlords across the peak and the lean season therefore satisfy

$$(N-1)\left[L^j_P + L^j_C\left(w_C, L^j_P, A\right)\right] + L^i_P + L^i_C\left(w_C, L^i_P, A\right) = \mathcal{L}, \tag{6}$$

where L^j_P and L^j_C are, respectively, the demand for permanent and casual laborers for all landlords excluding the ith one. Totally differentiating Eq. 6 we have

$$\frac{dw_C}{dL^i_P} = -\frac{\left(1 + \frac{\partial L^i_C}{\partial L^i_P}\right)}{(N-1)\frac{\partial L^j_C}{\partial w_C} + \frac{\partial L^i_C}{\partial w_C}} = -\frac{\left[-\frac{\epsilon^g_{L^i_P}}{\epsilon^{H_2}_{L^i_C}}\frac{L^i_C}{L^i_P} + A\beta\frac{L^i_C}{L^i_P}\right]}{(N-1)\frac{\partial L^j_C}{\partial w_C} + \frac{\partial L^i_C}{\partial w_C}}$$

Since $\frac{\partial L^j_C}{\partial w_C}$ and $\frac{\partial L^i_C}{\partial w_C}$ are both negative, a low value of $\epsilon^g_{L^i_P}$ is sufficient to guarantee that the hiring of an additional permanent laborer raises casual labor demand thereby generating a positive relationship between the number of permanent hires in the lean season and the revealed casual wage in the peak season.[17]

2.2 Laborers

We start by focusing on the availability of permanent and casual labor jobs in the economy and the corresponding lifetime utilities of the laborers from these jobs. Our framework for the determination of the lifetime utilities of permanent and casual laborers follows closely that of Mukherjee and Ray [39] and Basu [6]. Consider therefore a typical laborer in this economy at the beginning of the lean season. This laborer has the possibility of either (i) getting a permanent contract, available with probability p, and an associated wage w_P paid at the end of each season or (ii) not get a permanent contract with probability $(1-p)$ and work in the EGS program for wage $\bar{w}$ in the lean season and work as a casual laborer for wage $w_C(A)$ in the peak.[18]

[17] We shall assume that $\frac{d^2 w_C}{d(L^i_P)^2} < 0$. Note also that by virtue of symmetry, all landlords hire the same number of permanent laborers.

[18] We do not consider the issue of access for laborers to the EGS program. In other words, all laborers willing to work for an EGS can do so without incurring any transaction costs. Basu et al. [12] consider the scenario where a government may use an EGS program as a rationing device by choice of location.

Denoting V_* as the lifetime utility of a laborer and W_* as the lifetime utility of a laborer *conditional* on getting a permanent contract at the beginning of the lean season, we have:

$$V_* = pW_* + (1-p)\left[U(\bar{w}) + \rho \int_{\underline{A}}^{M} U\left(w_C\left(A,\ L_P^i,\ \beta\right)\right) f(A)dA + \rho^2 V_*\right], \quad (7)$$

$$W_* = (1+\rho)U(w_P) + \rho^2(1-q)W_* + \rho^2 q V_*, \quad (8)$$

where $U(\cdot)$ is strictly concave and twice differentiable with $U' > 0$ and $U'' < 0$. $\rho \in (0, 1)$ is the rate at which laborers discount future utility and q is an exogenously given quit rate from a permanent contract at the end of the "year".[19] Solving simultaneously for W_* and V_* we get,

$$V_* = \frac{1}{|Q|}\left[p(1+\rho)U(w_P) + (1-p)\left(1-(1-q)\rho^2\right)\hat{U}\right],$$

and

$$W_* = \frac{1}{|Q|}\left[\left(1-(1-p)\rho^2\right)(1+\rho)U(w_P) + \rho^2 q(1-p)\hat{U}\right],$$

where $|Q| = (1-\rho^2)[(1-\rho^2) + \rho^2(q + p(1-q))] > 0$ and $\hat{U} = U(\bar{w}) + \int_{\underline{A}}^{M} U(w_C) f(A)dA$.

For a permanent contract to be acceptable to a laborer, it must be the case that $W_* \geq V_*$. Therefore, the *acceptability* constraint implies

$$(1+\rho)U(w_P) \geq U(\bar{w}) + \rho \int_{\underline{A}}^{M} U\left(w_C\left(A,\ L_P^i,\ \bar{Q}_G,\ \beta\right)\right) f(A)dA,$$

otherwise tied labor contracts will never be accepted. However, note that the permanent wage in the peak season is lower than the expected casual wage since the permanent wage in the peak season is the certainty equivalent wage offered by landlords, and given that laborers are risk averse, must be less than the expected casual wage.

Consider now the following possibilities: (1) after having accepted a contract, a permanent laborer may quit and choose to remain unemployed in the lean season and (2) after having worked as a permanent laborer in the lean season, a permanent laborer may choose to join the casual labor pool in the peak season, particularly, when the revealed casual wage is high. The acceptability constraint guarantees that a permanent laborer will not choose option (1). For option (2) we again follow Mukherjee and Ray [39] and Basu [6] and assume that (i) in the case of such a deviation, the landlord terminates the contract without any pay for the peak season and the laborer is returned to the pool of casual laborers and (ii) a permanent laborer who reneges on a contract is *scarred*, i.e., the worker has a lower probability $\tilde{p}$ of obtaining a permanent contract the following "year". The extent to which $\tilde{p}$ differs from p depends on the ease with which information regarding a reneger

[19] q is the exogenous probability of nonrenewal of a contract rather than a quit from an *ongoing* contract (see [39]).

diffuses amongst landlords. Denoting the ease of information diffusion by $0 < \mu < 1$, a constant, we have $\tilde{p} = (1-\mu)p$. Even though landlords prefer a honest laborer to a reneger, a reneger's reputation is laundered once he finds a permanent contract. Thus, the lifetime utility of a reneger, R_*, at the beginning of the lean season is

$$R_* = \tilde{p}W_* + (1-\tilde{p})\left[U(\bar{w}) + \rho \int_{\underline{A}}^{M} U(w_C) f(A) dA + \rho^2 R_*\right]. \tag{9}$$

First note that $V_* \geq R_*$ and $W_* \geq R_*$. To ensure that a permanent laborer does not have the incentive to renege, landlords must offer a contract that is *incentive-compatible*. In other words, the incentive compatibility constraint must guarantee that the lifetime utility of a honest permanent worker (W_*) is at least as high as that of a reneger, (R_*). To this end, denote w_C^+ as the maximum possible casual wage in the beginning of *any* peak season consistent with the best possible weather outcome for a given number of permanent contracts. The discounted lifetime of a reneger in this scenario is $U(w_C^+) + \rho R_*$ while the discounted lifetime utility of a permanent laborer who chooses not to renege is $U(w_P) + \rho W_*$. The incentive-compatibility constraint must therefore guarantee that

$$U(w_P) + \rho W_* \geq U\left(w_C^+\right) + \rho R_*.$$

Substituting for W_* and R_* in the above equation and rearranging yields:[20]

$$[1 + \nu(1+\rho)]U(w_P) \geq \nu U(\bar{w}) + \nu\rho \int_{\underline{A}}^{M} U(w_C) f(A) dA + U\left(w_C^+\right), \tag{10}$$

where

$$\nu = \frac{\rho(1-\tilde{p})\left(1-(1-p)\rho^2\right)}{\left(1-(1-\tilde{p})\rho^2\right)\left[\left(1-\rho^2\right) + \rho^2(q + p(1-q))\right]} > 0$$

is the factor by which lifetime utility of a permanent worker is discounted. It follows that the discount factor ν is endogenously determined, depending on L_P^i, p and q. In the sequel we shall assume that

Assumption 1 $\frac{\partial \nu}{\partial p} < 0$.

The reason behind Assumption 1 is as follows. For a laborer with a permanent contract over two seasons, the discounted present value of lifetime utility of remaining a permanent laborer ($= \rho[W_* - V*]$), is lower if the probability of being hired as a permanent laborer is high. Another way to interpret Assumption 1 would be that the current period utility from reneging from a permanent contract ($= U(w_C^+) - U(w_P)$), is higher if the probability of being hired as a permanent laborer is high at the beginning of any lean season.[21]

Before focusing on the determination of the terms of permanent contracts in the presence of an EGS, a few observations are in order. First, the incentive compatibility

[20] Appendix A.2 provides a formal derivation of the acceptability and incentive compatibility constraints.

[21] Appendix A.3 provides a proof of this result.

constraint accounts for all possible revelations of w_C for a given number of permanent contracts. Second, it can be easily checked that if the incentive-compatibility binds then W_* is strictly greater than V_* or the lifetime utility of a permanent laborer is strictly greater than that of a casual one. Third, Eq. 10 ensures that the permanent wage is the lowest possible incentive compatible wage and therefore laborers will not be *able* to undercut the permanent wage, while full employment in the peak season ensures that laborers will not be *willing* to undercut the casual wage.[22] Fourth, $\int_{\underline{A}}^{M} w_C f(A)dA > w_P > \bar{w}$, i.e., the wage paid at the EGS program is the lowest in the economy. Finally, the probability of getting a permanent contract at the beginning of any time period or "year" is given simply as the ratio between the number of vacancies to the total pool of job seekers, i.e.,

$$p = \frac{qNL^i_P}{\mathcal{L} - (1-q)NL^i_P}. \tag{11}$$

Therefore, the proportion of tied labor in equilibrium is given by

$$\frac{NL^i_P}{\mathcal{L}} = \frac{p}{q + p(1-q)}.$$

Noting that the incentive-compatibility constraint implies the acceptability constraint, the maximization problem pertaining to each individual landlord at the beginning of the lean season is:

$$\max_{L^i_P,\, w^i_P} \frac{1}{(1-\rho)} \int_{\underline{A}}^{M} \left(\rho g\left(\bar{Q}_G\right) H\left(A\beta L^i_P,\ L^i_P + L^i_C\right) - (1+\rho) w_P L^i_P - \rho TC^2\right) f(A)dA;$$

subject to the following constraints,

(i) $L^i_P \le l^i_P\left(w^1_P, \ldots\ldots\ldots, w^N_P\right)$

(ii) $[1 + \nu(1+\rho)]U(w_P) = \nu U(\bar{w}) + \nu\rho \int_{\underline{A}}^{M} U(w_C) f(A)dA + U\left(w^+_C\right)$

where the peak season casual wage cost is given by

$$TC^2 = w_C L^i_C = g\left(\bar{Q}_G\right) H_2\left(A\beta L^i_P,\ \frac{\mathcal{L}}{N}\right)\left[\frac{\mathcal{L}}{N} - L^i_P\right]$$

The first order conditions with respect to L^i_P, w_P and the Lagrange multiplier λ are:

$$\frac{\rho}{(1-\rho)} \int_{\underline{A}}^{M} \left[A\beta H_1 - \alpha N g' H + w_C - \frac{dw_C}{dL^i_P}\left(\frac{\mathcal{L}}{N} - L^i_P\right)\right] f(A)dA$$
$$- \frac{(1+\rho)}{(1-\rho)} w_P = \lambda\Omega \tag{12}$$

$$\frac{(1+\rho)L^i_P}{(1-\rho)[1+\nu(1+\rho)]U'(w_P)} = \lambda \tag{13}$$

[22] The interested reader is referred to Mukherjee and Ray [39] for a detailed discussion of the incentive-compatibility problem that arises when laborers are averse to income fluctuations. As a comparison, Mukherjee and Ray develop their model of labor-tying within a framework characterized by perfectly competitive landlords, absence of uncertainty and an active casual labor market in the lean season.

$$[1 + \nu(1 + \rho)]\,U(w_P) - \nu U(\bar{w}) - \nu\rho \int_{\underline{A}}^{M} U(w_C) f(A) dA - U\left(w_C^+\right) = 0 \qquad (14)$$

where

$$\Omega = \nu\rho \int_{\underline{A}}^{M} U'(w_C) \frac{dw_C}{dL_P^i} f(A) dA - \frac{\partial v}{\partial L_P^i}[W_* - V_*] + U'\left(w_C^+\right) \frac{dw_C^+}{dL_P^i}$$

The formalization of our model is now complete. We have nine unknowns w_P, w_C, L_P^i, L_C^i, λ, Q_G, Q_L^i, Q_H^i and p which can be solved using Eqs. 1–6 and Eqs. 11–13. First, Eqs. 12 and 13 can be solved simultaneously to obtain the values for L_P^i and w_P after substituting for λ into Eqs. 12 from 13. Once L_P^i is known, Eq. 1 determines Q_L^i, Eq. 2 determines L_G and therefore Eq. 3 determines Q_G while Eq. 11 determines p. Given L_P^i, w_P and p, λ is determined from Eq. 13. With L_P^i given, w_C as a function of A is determined from Eq. 5, and hence L_C^i is determined from Eq. 6. Finally, given L_C^i and L_P^i, Eq. 4 can be used to determine Q_H^i as a function of A. We are now in a position to discuss the labor market response to a government intervention through an EGS program.

3 Labor market response to an EGS program

In this section we analyze the labor market response to a (i) change in the wage paid at the government EGS program (an increase in $\bar{w}$), (ii) productivity increase of workers in the EGS program (an increase in α) and (iii) productivity increase (technological improvement) in the agricultural sector that affects lean season output (an increase in β). We begin with the following proposition:[23]

Proposition 1 *An increase in $\bar{w}$ leads to an increase in w_P, a decrease in L_P, a decrease in Q_L and an increase in Q_G. The casual wage in the peak season w_C and expected agricultural output, $\mathcal{E}Q_H$, increases (decreases) if and only if the elasticity of the EGS input in the peak season production function with respect to permanent labor ($|\epsilon^g_{L_P^i}|$), is greater than the elasticity of expected agricultural output with respect to permanent labor ($\epsilon^{\mathcal{E}Q_P}_{L_P^i}$).*

The intuition behind Proposition 1 is as follows: *ceteris paribus*, an increase in the wage paid in the EGS program implies, via the incentive compatibility constraint, an increase in the permanent wage. This in turn implies a decline in the number of permanent contracts offered and hence an increase in the pool of laborers seeking casual employment in the peak season. However, the impact of an EGS wage increase on the peak season casual wage as well as on expected agricultural output is determined by two opposing forces at play. On one hand, the displacement of permanent laborers deepens the casual labor pool and would tend to have a negative impact on both the casual wage as well as expected agricultural output due to loss in lean season input engendered through the displacement of permanent labor into the

[23] Proofs of all propositions in Section 3 are presented in Appendix B.1. Further, in the notations that follow, $L_P = NL_P^i$, $Q_L = NQ_L^i$ and $L_C^d = NL_C^i$ etc., denoting aggregate levels of the variables.

casual pool. This is the *displacement* effect of an EGS wage increase. On the other hand, a productive EGS has a positive impact on casual labor demand and expected agricultural output in the peak season for every value of A through the increase in the EGS input in the lean season. This is the *productivity* effect. Recalling that $w_C = g(\bar{Q}_G)H_2(A\beta L^i_P, \frac{\mathcal{L}}{N})$ from Eq. 5, if the elasticity of the EGS input with respect to permanent labor (in absolute value) is greater than the elasticity of expected agricultural output with respect to permanent labor, the loss in expected agricultural output (due a decline in lean season output when the number of contracts fall in response to an increase in $\bar{w}$) is dominated by the increase of the EGS input into the peak season production function due to an increase in the number of laborers seeking EGS employment in the lean season. Labor demand in the peak season and casual wages along with expected agricultural output therefore increases in response to an EGS wage increase.

Proposition 1 is consistent with studies which indicate that implementation of EGS programs (any positive wage offered for alternative employment) exerts upward pressure on average agricultural wages [43] and displaces workers from agricultural employment [1, 46]. More specific to Proposition 1, there are empirical studies subsequent to the May 1988 EGS wage increase in Maharashtra that shed light on the forces that might be at play in a two-tiered agricultural labor market. The question of whether this EGS wage hike had an impact on formal agricultural wages and employment is studied by Dev [25]. According to Dev [25] average EGS wage in 1976/77 was Rs.2.81 and much less than the average agricultural wage of Rs.13.20. After the EGS wage increase in 1989/90 the average EGS wage of Rs.15.53 exceeded the average agricultural wage of Rs.11.80 in Maharashtra. Sathe [49] and Dev [25] posit that the EGS wage increase in 1988 might have led to an upward pressure on agricultural wages while Sathe [49] concludes that agricultural employment increased after the post-EGS wage hike although this increase might have been generated due to increased agricultural productivity as a result of the assets created through EGS work. In the event that the agricultural sector indeed exhibited a two-tiered labor market, an increase in the EGS wage would increase the permanent wage and decrease number of permanent contracts. However, focusing on just the competitive casual labor market, the ensuing increase in the pool of casual laborers would depress the casual wage as a first round effect but the subsequent increase in agricultural productivity due to the impact of EGS work could well dominate this first round effect to show an overall increase in the casual wage in the peak season.[24]

Nevertheless, it bears emphasis that empirical studies conducted after the EGS wage increase in Maharashtra in 1988 implicitly assume a competitive agricultural labor market even though a variety of labor hiring arrangements are likely to be

[24]However, Datt and Ravallion [21] found that the average monthly expenditure on EGS programs fell after the wage hike and employment in these programs fell by a third pointing to employment rationing in the EGS programs after the wage increase and that the increase in the EGS wage did not have an impact on agricultural wages. The issue of rationing in EGS employment is analyzed theoretically by Basu et al. [12] where the government jointly maximizes the EGS wage and access to EGS employment given an aggregate employment target. Basu et al. show that the credibility of such an employment target is endogenously determined by a host of factors (distributional concern of the planner and private sector productivity, amongst others). An explicit model of employment rationing in EGS programs either through access or changes in budgetary outlay is beyond the scope of this paper.

prevalent within the State of Maharashtra. As such, the empirical results delineated above after the 1988 EGS wage increase should not be interpreted as either a reinforcement or a rejection of our theoretical findings based on a two-tiered labor market structure. However, our proposition above with regards to the impact of an EGS wage increase on just the *peak* season competitive agricultural wage and employment can well be observationally consistent with the above empirical studies. It is worth noting here that even in the absence of or a minimal impact on agricultural productivity in the peak season through EGS work done in the lean season, demand for casual labor may well increase due to a positive weather shock—a variable ignored by prior empirical studies/surveys that aimed at estimating the impact of an EGS wage on agricultural wages and employment.

We next turn to the question of how productivity changes in the EGS program, and in the agricultural sector impact labor market responses. First, consider an increase in the productivity of laborers in the EGS program. As a starting point, suppose that $\epsilon_{\alpha}^{Q_G} > 0$, or the output elasticity of the EGS program is positive with respect to a technological change. In this case, seasonal labor markets and agricultural output responds according to,

Proposition 2 *An increase in* α *increases* w_P, L_P, Q_L, *and increases* w_C *if the elasticity of the marginal product of EGS input in peak season agricultural production with respect to* Q_G ($\epsilon_{Q_G}^{g'}$) *is close to negative unity. If in addition, the elasticity of expected agricultural output with respect to permanent labor* $\epsilon_{L_P^i}^{\mathcal{E}Q_P}$ *is greater than the elasticity of the EGS input in the peak season production function with respect to permanent labor* $|\epsilon_{L_P^i}^{g}|$, *then* $\mathcal{E}Q_H$ *increases.*

Proposition 2 indicates that a yield-increasing improvement in technology originating from the government project increases the number of permanent contracts if $\epsilon_{Q_G}^{g'} \to -1$. The reason being that if landlords hire less permanent workers in the lean season under the above sufficient condition, the negative impact of the lean season agricultural output dominates the positive impact of an increase in the productivity of the EGS output on agricultural production in the peak season. This results in a decline in expected agricultural output. Therefore, the number of permanent contracts must rise in response to productivity increases in the EGS program to prevent a decline in expected agricultural output. The increase in the number of permanent contracts increases lean season agricultural output, and tightens the pool of casual laborers which causes an increase in the casual wage. Furthermore, the increase in the casual wage entails an increase in the permanent wage via the incentive compatibility constraint.

Consider now the impact of a productivity increase affecting lean season agricultural production on labor hiring decisions and expected agricultural output. Suppose that at the beginning of the lean season there is, say, an increase in the usage of inputs such as fertilizers and/or increased mechanization that has a positive effect on the productivity of permanent workers. Then[25]

[25] We shall assume for simplicity that $\epsilon_{\beta}^{Q_L}$, the elasticity of lean period output with respect to technological change affecting its output is positive.

Proposition 3 *An increase in β increases w_P, L_P, decreases Q_G and increases w_C if (i) $\epsilon^{g}_{L^i_P} > -1$ and (ii) the elasticity of the marginal product of lean season output (in the peak season) with respect to permanent labor ($\epsilon^{H_1}_{L^i_P}$) is close to zero. If in addition, the elasticity of expected agricultural output with respect to permanent labor $\epsilon^{\mathcal{E}Q_P}_{L^i_P}$ is greater than the elasticity of the EGS input in the peak season production function with respect to permanent labor $|\epsilon^{g}_{L^i_P}|$, then $\mathcal{E}Q_H$ increases.*

Suppose that $\epsilon^{H_1}_{L^i_P} \to 0$ and $\epsilon^{\mathcal{E}Q_P}_{L^i_P} > |\epsilon^{g}_{L^i_P}|$. Now if $\epsilon^{g}_{L^i_P}$ is sufficiently large, then an increase in β leads to an increase in expected agricultural output even when the number of permanent contracts fall. This happens because the increase in the EGS input into the peak season agricultural production due to a larger number of laborers seeking EGS employment is more than sufficient to outweigh the fall in peak season agricultural production caused by a decline in lean season agricultural output due to a fewer number of permanent laborers. A fewer number of permanent laborers in turn increases the pool of casual laborers and depresses the casual wage for every value of A. For the incentive-compatibility constraint to hold in equilibrium, a decline in the casual wage implies a fall in the permanent wage as well. On the other hand, for $\epsilon^{g}_{L^i_P} > -1$, the number of permanent laborers hired increases, and the subsequent increase in the lean season output overweighs the fall in the EGS input leading to an increase in expected agricultural output. In the event where $\epsilon^{g}_{L^i_P} > -1$, Proposition 3 is consistent with the empirical findings of Bardhan [4] which demonstrates a positive correlation between land productivity and the number of permanent contracts.

The labor and output market responses to changes in the above three parameters has interesting implications for policy formulations. Conditional on the way in which labor demand in the two seasons vary in accordance with changes in the policy instruments, a natural question arises as to whether by directly improving the income of the rural unemployed or indirectly through (a) raising the productivity of EGS programs and/or (b) inducing technological change in the agricultural sector, will the interests of the poor be best served. We conjecture that an indirect mechanism in the form of inducing technological improvement in the agricultural sector increases the income of the laborers relative to a direct policy such as raising the wage paid in the EGS program provided, (i) $\epsilon^{H_1}_{L^i_P} \to 0$, (ii) $\epsilon^{g}_{L^i_P} > -1$ and (iii) $\epsilon^{g'}_{Q_G} \to -1$. If there remains an element of uncertainty as to whether induced technological improvement will in fact take place,[26] raising the productivity of laborers in the EGS program through an increase in α would have the same desired effect. In fact, productivity increases in the EGS program is a superior policy vis-à-vis wage increases in the program both in terms of improving the employment opportunities of the laborers

[26]It might very well be the case that landlords voluntarily refuse to undertake technological change affecting lean season output since such an increase corresponds to a higher wage bill and might end up reducing the profit margin. For instance, Braverman and Stiglitz [17] analyzes whether such technological innovations are undertaken by landlords in the context of share tenancy contracts.

as well as through its ability to increase agricultural production. As Propositions 1 and 2 underscore, indirect intervention through an improvement in the productivity of a EGS program has a positive impact on agricultural production as compared to a direct increase in the EGS wage if the elasticity of expected agricultural output with respect to permanent labor ($\epsilon_{L_P^i}^{\mathcal{E}Q_P}$) is greater than the elasticity of the EGS input in the peak season production function with respect to permanent labor ($|\epsilon_{L_P^i}^{g}|$). Indeed, as we shall point out in the next section, even when funds for an EGS program are unlimited, indirect intervention might prove to be a better option.

4 Determination of the optimum wage

Existing theoretical models due to Ravallion [46] and Khan [34] analyze market responses to EGS programs by assuming that laborers working in an EGS project are paid the ongoing wage in the agricultural sector. Basu [9], on the other hand, has shown that wages paid at the EGS in Maharashtra and the RPW program in Bangladesh has been too low and ought to be raised to the point where the minimum compensation to an EGS employee equates the *potential employment schedule*[27] with the labor supply schedule for the EGS program. A minimum wage determined in this fashion, while guaranteeing self-selection amongst the poor and not-so-poor in so far as the question of who should be employed in an EGS program is concerned, may be inadequate to achieve the objective of, say, agricultural output maximization. Clearly then, the nature of such an *appropriate* wage depends on the objective which the government wishes to pursue.

As stated in Section 1, an important objective of EGS programs that is particularly relevant in the context of poverty alleviation is to maximize agricultural production that ensures the availability of food and reduces the dependence on imports. Thus, a wage $\bar{w}_o$, which achieves the goal of expected agricultural output maximization net of the shadow cost of public funds may serve as one criterion for an optimal compensation for an EGS employee. Accordingly consider,

$$\max_{\bar{w}_o} \; \rho \int_{\underline{A}}^{M} NQ_P^i g(Q_G) f(A) dA - (1+\Pi)\bar{w} NL_C^i,$$

where $NQ_P^i = NH(A\beta L_P^i,\ L_P^i + L_C^i)$ is the total *private* output of the economy; $NL_C^i = \mathcal{L} - NL_P^i = L_G$ and $g(Q_G) = g(\alpha(\mathcal{L} - NL_P^i))$ is the EGS input in agricultural production. Provided that the second order conditions are fulfilled, the first order condition corresponding to the foregoing maximization problem follows,

$$\rho \int_{\underline{A}}^{M} NQ_P^i g(Q_G) f(A) dA \left(\epsilon_{L_P^i}^{\mathcal{E}Q_P} + \epsilon_{L_P^i}^{g}\right) \frac{dL_P^i}{d\bar{w}} \frac{\bar{w}}{L_P^i} - (1+\Pi)\bar{w} NL_C^i \left(1 + \epsilon_{\bar{w}}^{L_C^i}\right) = 0$$

[27] If the total amount of funds available for relief work is X, then given a wage G the maximum number of laborers that can be employed is simply X/G. The schedule that traces out this relationship for different values of G is the potential employment schedule.

Thus the optimal wage $\bar{w}_o$ must be set at a level such that,

$$\frac{\left(\epsilon_{L_P^i}^{\mathcal{E}Q_P}+\epsilon_{L_P^i}^{g}\right)}{\left(1+\epsilon_{\bar{w}}^{L_C^i}\right)}\epsilon_{\bar{w}}^{L_P^i}=\frac{(1+\Pi)\bar{w}NL_C^i}{\rho\int_{\underline{A}}^{M}NQ_P^i g(Q_G)f(A)dA}\equiv\delta^R, \tag{15}$$

where $\delta^R > 0$ if and only if $\bar{w} > 0$ and equals the share of EGS outlays per unit of expected agricultural output. Note also that,

- $\epsilon_{L_P^i}^{\mathcal{E}Q_P}$ is the elasticity of the expected agricultural output with respect to permanent labor and is positive,
- $\epsilon_{L_P^i}^{g}$ is the elasticity of the EGS output with respect to permanent labor and is negative (the higher the number of permanent laborers hired, the lower the number of laborers hired in the EGS program and hence lower the amount of the EGS output),
- $\epsilon_{\bar{w}}^{L_C^i}$ is the elasticity of casual labor with respect to the EGS wage and is positive (the higher the EGS wage the lower the number of permanent laborers hired by virtue of the incentive-compatibility constraint, resulting in a larger number of casual laborers seeking employment in the peak season),
- $\epsilon_{\bar{w}}^{L_P^i}$ is the elasticity of permanent hires with respect to the EGS wage and is negative.

Two comments are in order. First, Eq. 15 captures the fact that an EGS program should pay a positive wage if and only if $(\epsilon_{L_P^i}^{\mathcal{E}Q_P}+\epsilon_{L_P^i}^{g})$ is negative. Second, Eq. 15 also captures the fact that if the elasticity of expected agricultural output with respect to permanent labor is low then, as indicated by our results in Proposition 1, the wage compensation to EGS laborers should be relatively high so as to attract a larger number of laborers to the EGS program and vice versa when the expected elasticity of output with respect to permanent labor is high. It can easily be checked that the optimal level of productivity for an EGS and for the agricultural sector (α and β) respectively that maximizes expected output is given by same condition as in Eq. 15.

A second, yet perhaps more direct objective to follow is one which maximizes the ex-ante expected lifetime welfare of a new laborer joining the labor market in the economy. Such a laborer could either become a permanent laborer with probability p or a casual laborer with probability $(1-p)$. The expected lifetime utility of such a laborer is given by

$$V_* = \frac{1}{|Q|}\left[p(1+\rho)U(w_P)+(1-p)\left(1-(1-q)\rho^2\right)\hat{U}\right]$$

where $\hat{U}=U(\bar{w})+\rho\int_{\underline{A}}^{M}U(w_C)f(A)dA$ and $|Q|=(1-\rho^2)[(1-\rho^2)+\rho^2(q+p(1-q))]>0$.

The optimum wage $\bar{w}_v$ then can be obtained as a solution to the following condition,[28]

$$\left[\left(\frac{\epsilon^{u}_{w_P}\epsilon^{w_P}_{\bar{w}}}{\epsilon^{p}_{L_P}\epsilon^{L_P}_{\bar{w}}}\right)+1\right]$$
$$+\ (1-p)\left(1-(1-q)\rho^2\right)\left[U(\bar{w}_v)\epsilon^{u}_{\bar{w}}+\rho\int_{\underline{A}}^{M}U(w_C)f(A)dA\left(\frac{\epsilon^{u}_{w_C}\epsilon^{w_C}_{L_P}\epsilon^{L_P}_{\bar{w}}}{\epsilon^{p}_{L_P}\epsilon^{L_P}_{\bar{w}}}\right)\right]$$
$$=\frac{\left[\rho^2\left(1-\rho^2\right)(1-q)p\right]V_*}{p(1+\rho)U(w_P)}, \tag{16}$$

where

- $\epsilon^{u}_{j} > 0$; $j = w_P, w_C$ and $\bar{w}$ is the elasticity of utility with respect to the permanent, casual and the EGS wage respectively,
- $\epsilon^{w_P}_{\bar{w}}$ is the elasticity of the permanent wage with respect to the EGS wage and is positive since an increase in the wage paid at the EGS program engenders an increase in the permanent wage to preserve the incentive compatibility constraint,
- $\epsilon^{p}_{L_P}$ is the elasticity of the probability of finding employment as a permanent laborer with respect to the number of permanent laborers and is positive. Note that the probability of finding employment as a permanent laborer is denoted simply as the ratio of the number of vacancies to the number of laborers seeking employment as a permanent laborer. Therefore, an increase in the number of permanent hires, given a fixed quit rate, increases the number of vacancies while simultaneously reducing the number of job seekers which, in turn, increases the probability of finding employment as a permanent laborer.
- $\epsilon^{L_P}_{\bar{w}}$ is the elasticity of permanent hires with respect to the EGS wage and is negative since an increase in the EGS wage leads to an increase in the permanent wage and hence a reduction in the number of permanent laborers hired,
- $\epsilon^{w_C}_{L_P}$ is the elasticity of the casual wage with respect to the number of permanent laborers and is positive since an increase in the number or permanent hires tightens the casual labor market and leads to an increase in the market clearing casual wage.

Equation 16 captures the fact that the optimum wage consistent with the maximization of the ex-ante expected lifetime welfare of a laborer must account for two distinct labor market responses on the ex-post expected lifetime welfare of a laborer. First, those laborers who find employment as permanent ones are better-off since the permanent wage increases in response to an increase in the EGS wage. However, the probability of finding employment as a permanent laborer falls since the decline in the number of permanent hires subsequent to an increase in the permanent wage implies fewer vacancies in equilibrium. Second, the ensuing increase in the number of casual laborers implies a lower market clearing casual wage in the peak season

[28]Please refer to the Appendix B.2 for a detailed derivation of Eq. 16.

which, depending upon the elasticity of the casual wage with respect to permanent labor and the elasticities of the utility function with respect to the casual and the EGS wage, may actually make a casual laborer worse-off. For instance, if both the elasticity of the probability of employment as a permanent laborer with respect to the number of permanent hires and the elasticity of the number of permanent hires with respect to the EGS wage are large, then there is a large displacement of permanent laborers caused by an increase in the EGS wage. This displacement effect coupled with a high elasticity of the casual wage with respect to the number of permanent hires would tend make a casual laborer worse-off. In this case $\bar{w}_v$ should be kept very low in order to ensure that the number of permanent laborers displaced is very small.

As a third objective, the government might want to maximize the expected welfare of casual workers (the *poorest* in this economy) at any given time period. Such an optimum government wage, $\bar{w}_u$, consistent with the objective of expected welfare maximization of casual workers can be deduced as a solution to

$$U(\bar{w}_u)\epsilon^{u}_{\bar{w}} = -\rho \int_{\underline{A}}^{M} U(w_C) f(A) dA \left(\epsilon^{u}_{w_C} \epsilon^{w_C}_{\bar{w}}\right). \tag{17}$$

That $\bar{w}_o$, $\bar{w}_v$ and $\bar{w}_u$ may not be consistent with the objectives of maximizing expected agricultural output and the ex-ante expected lifetime welfare of a laborer (either a potentially new entrant to the labor force or a casual one) should be clear from Eqs. 15–17. To see this, consider for instance the extreme case where the EGS program is unproductive, i.e., the government hires the rural unemployed in the lean season to build roads and bridges which get washed away. In terms of our model, peak season output Q_H is then independent of $\bar{Q}_G$. It is easy to see that the optimum wage paid for the EGS program consistent with the objective of maximizing expected output, in this case, should satisfy the condition $\frac{\epsilon^{\varepsilon Q_P}_{L^i_P}}{(1+\epsilon^{L^i_C}_{\bar{w}})}\epsilon^{L^i_P}_{\bar{w}} = \delta^R$. Since $\epsilon^{L^i_P}_{\bar{w}}$ is negative, the optimum wage should be zero. This is what one should expect since an unproductive EGS program only serves to displace laborers away from agriculture and hence agricultural output must fall as the EGS program competes with landlords for laborers. On the other hand, a zero wage for instance, which is perfectly justifiable in the event where the EGS program should not interfere with agricultural production decisions, cannot be one which simultaneously maximizes the welfare of a laborer in this economy.

A final criteria that a government might wish to pursue through the institution of EGS programs is to explicitly address poverty alleviation—specially for the casual laborers whose annual income is subject to considerable income variability in the presence of production uncertainty. Consider therefore the Foster et al. [29] P_α index of poverty for the casual laborers in the economy (see also [28]).

$$P_\alpha = \frac{L_C}{\mathcal{L}} \left\{ \frac{z - (\bar{w} + w_C)}{z} \right\}^{\alpha}$$

where z is the poverty line, $(\bar{w} + w_C)$ is the annual income of the casual laborers from EGS and peak season employment combined and $\frac{L_C}{\mathcal{L}}$ is the fraction of the casual laborers in the economy. Differentiating the above equation with respect to the EGS wage $\bar{w}$ and simplifying we have

$$\frac{dP_\alpha}{d\bar{w}} = \frac{P_\alpha L_C}{\bar{w}\mathcal{L}}\left[\epsilon_{\bar{w}}^{L_C} - \frac{\alpha\bar{w}}{z-(\bar{w}+w_C)}\left(1+\frac{dw_c}{d\bar{w}}\right)\right] > (<)\ 0$$

In general the impact of an EGS wage increase on the poverty index of casual laborers is indeterminate since the elasticity of casual labor supply with respect to the EGS wage, $\epsilon_{\bar{w}}^{L_C}$, is negative while $\frac{dw_c}{d\bar{w}}$ can be either positive or negative. However, if the if the elasticity of the EGS input in the peak season production function with respect to permanent labor ($|\epsilon_{L_P^i}^{g}|$), is greater than the elasticity of expected agricultural output with respect to permanent labor ($\epsilon_{L_P^i}^{\mathcal{E}Q_P}$) then casual wages increase with an increase in the EGS wage, and the poverty index for casual laborers unambiguously falls. Once again, the relative productivity of EGS laborers *vis-à-vis* their agricultural counterparts play a crucial role in determining how effective an EGS program is in alleviating poverty.

5 NREGS/EGS in alternative labor market settings

Given that a variety of labor hiring arrangements exist in rural India, we sketch the the potential impact of an EGS on agricultural employment and wages under some alternative labor hiring mechanisms.

Collective bargaining In a recent paper, Dasgupta [23] models an economy with two labor unions (an advanced and a backward class) simultaneously contesting a legislated minimum wage against a single employer and higher employment shares against each other. Such a model, at least within India, is more applicable to Indian States like Kerala where labor unions are strong and collective bargaining laws are enforced more regularly as compared to Indian States like Bihar and Orissa. In fact, an empirical study undertaken by Shanmugam and Vijayalakshmy [50] in Palakkad district in Kerala and Nagapattinam district of Tamil Nadu shows that education and income from non-agricultural activities were the most significant factors influencing the labor union participation by the laborers. Nevertheless, the key idea in Dasgupta [23] is that a landlord hires workers from both the advanced and backward caste groups, and the maximum per-worker wage that a landlord can pay, $\bar{W}$, is greater than the reservation wage of the both the advanced (w_A) and backward (w_B) caste workers (or $\bar{W} > w_A > w_B$). Consider now the case of a government mandated minimum wage w which a landlord would like to evade, and hire only workers from the backward caste with the lower reservation wage w_B. However, both the advanced and the backward caste unions contest this minimum wage against the common employer, as well as against each other to increase the employment share for members within each union.

Such a wage contestation model between two groups of workers for a higher share of employment at a mandated minimum wage provides some interesting propositions. First, an increase in the reservation wage of either group of workers benefits the other group in terms of a higher share of employment at the minimum wage w. Second, an increase in the minimum wage w itself benefits workers of the advanced caste as the expense of the backward caste in terms of a higher employment share. In order to understand these propositions in a parsimonious way, Dasgupta's model assumes the minimum wage to belong within the range of the maximum wage that a landlord is willing to pay a worker and the reservation wage of the advanced caste, or $w \in [w_A, \bar{W}]$. Workers belonging to each caste invest a fraction of the difference between the minimum wage and their reservation wage to contest non-cooperatively against each other, and against the landlord for a higher employment share. Since, $w - w_A < w - w_B$, the union representing the backward caste workers contest the minimum wage relatively more intensely.

In Dasgupta's framework above, consider now the case of an EGS that not only guarantees a wage but also employment to workers of either caste. Depending on the EGS wage, w^e, relative to the reservation wage of the two groups of workers we can sketch some cursory results:

(i) $w^e < w_B < w_A < \bar{W}$: This is a trivial case where the institution of an EGS at a wage lower than the reservation wage of the backward caste workers has no effect on class conflict. Both unions will still invest in contesting the other and the landlord for a higher employment share at the agricultural wage $\bar{W}$.

(ii) $w_B \leq w^e < w_A < \bar{W}$: When the EGS wage is greater than or equal to the reservation wage of the backward caste, the advanced caste benefits in terms of a higher employment share in agricultural work. The result follows from the fact that the union representing the backward caste will invest less in contesting the agricultural wage both because the gap between $\bar{W} - w^e$ is smaller and they can also find guaranteed EGS employment at $w^e \geq w_B$.

(iii) $w_B < w_A \leq w^e < \bar{W}$: When the EGS wage is greater than or equal to the reservation wage of the advanced class workers, both unions reduce their investment in contesting the agricultural wage (with a relatively greater reduction for the backward caste workers). This situation also benefits the advanced caste in terms of a higher share of employment in agricultural work.

Thus an EGS has the potential to attract backward class workers and reduce inter-caste conflict but it also has the potential for increasing the employment share of the advanced caste in agricultural work. Nevertheless, extension of this basic model to a situation where unions representing the advanced and backward classes contest the agricultural wage in the presence of seasonal labor markets (in the lean as well as the peak) requires accounting for the trade-off of employment shares across the two seasons by the unions. In such a situation, reduction in inter-caste conflict during the lean season thanks to an EGS, specially case (iii) above, might well imply an escalation of conflict in the peak season if unions can divert resources saved in the lean season towards intensifying contestation of the agricultural wage in the peak. Perhaps more interesting is the case where absent collective bargaining laws, an EGS by providing a threat point can induce lobby formation amongst workers to negotiate higher wages with landlords. Needless to say, a formal analysis of the above is beyond the scope of this paper.

Aside from selected areas in the States of Kerala and Tamil Nadu, collective bargaining laws in rural India are seldom enforced, and workers have little recourse to contesting the mandated minimum wage. Yet, as Osmani [42] notes, agricultural wages in rural India are sometimes higher than the competitive wage, and more interestingly workers resist this wage to be pushed down to the competitive level even in the presence of unemployment.

Implicit contracts Osmani [42] models a situation where workers bid for a wage from a given distribution of wages, and an individual worker's wage bid depends on his perception of the probability of finding employment at that wage. The probability of finding employment for an individual worker depends, in turn, on how many workers actually bid a lower wage. In other words, the probability of finding employment for an individual worker depends on the wage bids by all workers. Thus an individual worker's payoff (P) from a wage bid (w_i) equals

$$P_i(\tilde{w}) = \theta_i(\tilde{w})\, w_i + (1 - \theta_i(\tilde{w})\, c_i$$

where $\tilde{w}$ is the distribution of wage bids, θ_i is the probability of finding employment and c_i is the opportunity income for this worker. Assuming all workers are identical and have the same opportunity income, a non-cooperative infinite period game with punitive actions in the future (trigger strategy) by workers against an individual who undercuts the equilibrium wage in any given period yields a Nash equilibrium wage that is higher than the competitive one (which equals the opportunity income, c, of the workers). Needless to say, the afore-mentioned equilibrium Nash outcome generates random involuntary unemployment for any worker at any given period. Yet, and because of the trigger strategy, no worker has the incentive to undercut the ongoing wage. In this case, institution of an EGS that pays the involuntarily unemployed a little more than the opportunity income c will lead to an upward pressure on the agricultural wage as all workers adjust their wage bids upward.

Co-existence of permanent and casual contracts in both seasons Based on the observation that in some areas of rural India, permanent and casual contracts co-exist in both the lean and the peak season, Mukherjee and Ray [39] and Pal [44] posit that the existence of tied labor contracts are an outcome of landlord's minimizing hiring costs in the casual market in each season. In other words, labor *hoarding* through tied contracts is a way to circumvent high casual season labor costs. The situation considered (see [44], for instance) is one where casual wages are low in the lean season and high in the peak season in a seasonal labor market. If casual wages are very low in the lean season then the rural labor market would be characterized by just a competitive casual labor market in each season. However, as lean season competitive wages increase and/or the anticipated casual wage in the peak season is very high, landlords find it cheaper to offer tied labor contracts to some laborers across both seasons. In equilibrium the permanent wage in each season is greater than the casual wage in the lean season but lower than the casual wage in the peak season. In other words, $w_c^{\text{lean}} < w_p < w_c^{\text{peak}}$ where w_p is the permanent wage in each season and w_c^{lean} and w_c^{peak} are the casual wages in the lean and the peak season respectively. In this case, an EGS that offers guaranteed employment at a wage greater than the lean season casual wage will induce landlords to favor *more* permanent contracts as laborers would refuse to participate in the lean season casual labor market for any wage less than the EGS wage.

6 Conclusion

This paper examines the labor and output market responses to a productive rural public works program and determines the optimum compensation to program employees. By accounting for the seasonality in agricultural production and the institution of permanent labor contracts, we have shown that technological change and productivity increases in EGS programs tend to make laborers better-off as compared to a direct increase in the wage paid at the relief program. Further, an optimal wage that maximizes expected agricultural output may be in conflict with the one that maximizes the expected lifetime utility of laborers. Trade-offs thus exist between different policy objectives. In the event where the elasticity of the EGS input with respect to permanent laborers is high, a specific subsidy targeted towards the hiring of permanent laborers best serves the twin objectives of increased expected agricultural productivity and increased welfare for the laborers. Finally, we extend our analysis to account for the impact of EGS programs on a number of other labor hiring mechanisms and point out that an EGS (by introducing contestability in the agricultural labor market) can yield a host of interesting implications for the wage and employment patterns of the rural poor.

Acknowledgements Research support from the Alexander von Humboldt Foundation, Germany and the Freeman Grant from the Reves Center at the College of William and Mary is gratefully acknowledged. I thank three anonymous referees for their comments and Iryna Dovgel for able research assistance. Part of the research was completed while the author was visiting the School of Industrial and Labor Relations, Cornell University, and special thanks to Gary Fields for his hospitality and insightful observations on the structure of labor markets in developing countries.

Appendix A

A.1 Relationship between permanent and casual laborers

An individual landlord maximizes peak season profit, for a given number of permanent laborers, to choose the number of casual laborers, i.e.,

$$\max_{L_C^i} \; g\left(\bar{Q}_G\right) H\left(A\beta L_P^i,\ L_P^i + L_C^i\right) - w_C^i L_C^i; \quad s.t \quad L_C^i \leq l_C^i\left(w_C^1, \ldots\ldots, w_C^N\right)$$

Therefore,

$$w_C = g\left(\bar{Q}_G\right) H_2\left(A\beta L_P^i,\ L_P^i + L_C^i\right)$$

Totally differentiating the above equation yields,

$$\frac{\partial L_C^i}{\partial w_C} = \frac{1}{g(\bar{Q}_G) H_{22}} < 0$$

and

$$\frac{\partial L_C^i}{\partial L_P^i} = -\frac{\left(-\alpha N g' H_2 + g A\beta H_{21} + g H_{22}\right)}{g H_{22}}$$

Since $H(\cdot,\cdot)$ exhibits constant returns to scale, we utilize the fact that $L^i_P H_{21} + L^i_C H_{22} = 0$ and noting that $-\frac{\alpha N g' L^i_P}{g} = \epsilon^g_{L^i_P} < 0$ is the elasticity of the EGS input with respect to permanent labor while $\frac{H_2}{H_{22} L^i_C} = \epsilon^{H_2}_{L^i_C} < 0$. Therefore,

$$\frac{\partial L^i_C}{\partial L^i_P} = -\frac{\epsilon^g_{L^i_P}}{\epsilon^{H_2}_{L^i_C}} \frac{L^i_C}{L^i_P} + A\beta \frac{L^i_C}{L^i_P} - 1$$

Since $NL^i_P + NL^i_C = \mathcal{L}$ substituting above yields

$$\frac{\partial L^i_C}{\partial L^i_P} = \left[-\frac{\epsilon^g_{L^i_P}}{\epsilon^{H_2}_{L^i_C}} + A\beta \right] \left[\frac{\mathcal{L}}{NL^i_P} - 1 \right] - 1$$

Thus in addition to a low value of $\epsilon^g_{L^i_P}$ and high values of A and β, the larger the ratio of the total labor force to the total number of tied contracts offered, the greater is the possibility that permanent and casual laborers are complements of one another.

It remains to be shown that if $H(A\beta L^i_P, L^i_a)$ exhibits constant returns to scale then $L^i_P H_{21} + L^i_C H_{22} = 0$. Consider the following Cobb-Douglas form for $H(\cdot,\ \cdot)$: $Q_H = (A\beta L_P)^\phi (L_P + L_C)^{(1-\phi)}$. Therefore, $\frac{\partial Q_H}{\partial L_P} = \frac{\phi Q_H}{L_P} + \frac{(1-\phi)Q_H}{(L_P + L_C}$ and $\frac{\partial Q_H}{\partial L_C} = \frac{(1-\phi)Q_H}{(L_P+L_C)}$. As a result, $L_P \frac{\partial Q_H}{\partial L_P} + L_C \frac{\partial Q_H}{\partial L_C} = 0$. Again, $\frac{\partial^2 Q_H}{\partial (L_C)^2}$ (equivalent to H_{22}) equals $-\frac{\phi(1-\phi)Q_H}{(L_P+L_C)^2}$ and $\frac{\partial^2 Q_H}{\partial L_C \partial L_P}$ (equivalent to H_{21}) equals $\frac{\phi(1-\phi)Q_H}{(L_P+L_C)(L_P)} - \frac{\phi(1-\phi)Q_H}{(L_P+L_C)^2}$. Consequently, $L_C H_{22} + L_P H_{21} = 0$.

Finally, totally differentiating Eq. 6 and substituting for $\frac{\partial L^i_C}{\partial L^i_P}$ we have

$$\frac{dw_C}{dL^i_P} = -\frac{1 + \frac{\partial L^i_C}{\partial L^i_P}}{(N-1)\frac{\partial L^j_C}{\partial w_C} + \frac{\partial L^i_C}{\partial w_C}} = -\frac{\left[-\frac{\epsilon^g_{L^i_P}}{\epsilon^{H_2}_{L^i_C}} \frac{L^i_C}{L^i_P} + A\beta \frac{L^i_C}{L^i_P} \right]}{(N-1)\frac{\partial L^j_C}{\partial w_C} + \frac{\partial L^i_C}{\partial w_C}}$$

and

$$\frac{d^2 w_C}{d\left(L^i_P\right)^2} = -\frac{1}{(NgH_{22})^2} \left[-\frac{\mathcal{L} N g H_{22}}{\left(L^i_P\right)^2} \left(1 + \epsilon^g_{L^i_P}\right) + \frac{2N(\alpha N g')^2 H_2}{g} - N(\alpha N)^2 g'' H_2 - \frac{\alpha N g' L^i_C}{L^i_P} \right] > (<) 0$$

Further,

$$\frac{d}{d\beta}\left(\frac{dw_C}{dL^i_P}\right) = -\frac{A\alpha N g' H_{21} L^i_P}{N(gH_{22})^2} < 0$$

and

$$\frac{d}{d\alpha}\left(\frac{dw_C}{dL_P^i}\right) = \frac{-1}{(NgH_{22})^2}\left[N^2 g' H_2\left(1+\epsilon_{Q_G}^{g'}\right) - \frac{NH_2\alpha N(g')^2 L_G}{gH_{22}}\right.$$
$$\left. - \left(1+\frac{L_C^i}{L_P^i}\left(1-\frac{|\epsilon_{L_P^i}^{g}|}{|\epsilon_{L_C^i}^{H_2}|}\right)\right) Ng' L_G H_{22}\right]$$

The right hand side of the above equation is negative if (i) $|\epsilon_{Q_G}^{g'}| \geq 1$ and (ii) $\frac{dw_C}{dL_P^i} > 0$.

A.2 Acceptability and incentive-compatibility

First, define $\hat{U} = U(\bar{w}) + \rho \int_{\underline{A}}^{M} U(w_C) f(A) dA$ and rewrite Eqs. 7 and 8 as

$$\left[1-(1-p)\rho^2\right] V_* = pW_* + (1-p)\hat{U},$$

and

$$\left[1-(1-q)\rho^2\right] W_* = (1+\rho)U(w_P) + \rho^2 q V_*.$$

Now solving the above two equations simultaneously from the matrix below

$$\begin{bmatrix} (1-(1-p)\rho^2) & -p \\ -\rho^2 q & (1-(1-q)\rho^2) \end{bmatrix}\begin{bmatrix} V_* \\ W_* \end{bmatrix} = \begin{bmatrix} (1-p)\hat{U} \\ U(w_P)+\hat{U} \end{bmatrix}$$

we get

$$V_* = \frac{1}{|Q|}\left[p(1+\rho)U(w_P) + (1-p)\left(1-(1-q)\rho^2\right)\hat{U}\right],$$

and

$$W_* = \frac{1}{|Q|}\left[\left(1-(1-p)\rho^2\right)(1+\rho)U(w_P) + \rho^2 q(1-p)\hat{U}\right],$$

where $|Q| = (1-\rho^2)[(1-\rho^2)+\rho^2(q+p(1-q))] > 0$. Therefore the acceptability constraint ($W_* \geq V_*$) implies that $(1+\rho)U(w_P) \geq \hat{U}$. Now define the lifetime utility of a reneger as

$$R_* = \frac{\tilde{p}}{(1-(1-\tilde{p})\rho^2)} W_* + \frac{(1-\tilde{p})}{(1-(1-\tilde{p})\rho^2)}\hat{U}.$$

Therefore,

$$V_* - R_* = \frac{(1-\rho^2)\mu p}{(1-(1-p)\rho^2)(1-(1-\tilde{p})\rho^2)}\left[W_* - \frac{\hat{U}}{(1-\rho^2)}\right] \geq 0,$$

$$W_* - R_* = \frac{(1-\rho^2)(1-\tilde{p})}{(1-(1-\tilde{p})\rho^2)}\left[W_* - \frac{\hat{U}}{(1-\rho^2)}\right] \geq 0.$$

To show that the incentive-compatibility constraint implies the acceptability constraint we rewrite the incentive-compatibility constraint, $(U(w_P) + \rho W_* \geq U(w_C^+) + \rho R_*)$, as

$$\nu\left[(1+\rho)U(w_P) - \hat{U}\right] \geq \left[U\left(w_C^+\right) - U(w_P)\right].$$

Note that the right hand side of the above equation is strictly positive and therefore the left hand side, denoting the acceptability constraint and given by $(1+\rho)U(w_P) - \hat{U}$, is also > 0.

Rearranging the incentive-compatibility constraint we get

$$[U(w_P) - U(\bar{w})] \geq \frac{1}{\nu}\left[U\left(w_C^+\right) - U(w_P)\right] + \rho\left[\int_{\underline{A}}^{M} U(w_C)f(A)dA - U(w_P)\right].$$

Again, since the right hand side of the above equation is strictly positive and as a result, $U(w_P) > U(\bar{w})$ or $w_P > \bar{w}$.

We now need to show that $w_P < \int_{\underline{A}}^{M} w_C f(A)dA$. Consider the incentive-compatibility constraint from the beginning of the lean season. Landlords, in this case must choose to offer a permanent wage such that

$$(1+\rho)U(w_P) + \rho^2 qV_* + (1-q)\rho^2 W_* \geq U(w_P) + \rho\int_{\underline{A}}^{M} U(w_C)f(A)dA + \rho^2 R_*.$$

Substituting for W_*, V_* and R_* we get

$$(1+\nu(1+\rho))U(w_P) \geq (1+\nu\rho)\int_{\underline{A}}^{M} U(w_C)f(A)dA,$$

$$U(w_P) \geq \frac{(1+\nu\rho)}{(1+\nu(1+\rho))}\int_{\underline{A}}^{M} U(w_C)f(A)dA.$$

Define

$$U(\tilde{w_C}) = \frac{1+\nu\rho}{1+\nu(1+\rho)}U\left(w_C\left(L_P^i,\ A,\ \bar{Q}_G,\ \beta\right)\right) + \frac{1+\nu\rho}{1+\nu(1+\rho)}U(0).$$

Noting that U is strictly concave and applying Jensen's inequality we have

$$\tilde{w_C} < \frac{1+\nu\rho}{1+\nu(1+\rho)}w_C\left(L_P^i,\ A,\ \bar{Q}_G,\ \beta\right) < w_C\left(L_P^i,\ A,\ \bar{Q}_G,\ \beta\right),$$

since $\frac{(1+\nu\rho)}{(1+\nu(1+\rho))} < 1$. In addition, since $\int_{\underline{A}}^{M} U(\tilde{w_C})f(A)dA = U(w_P)$ if the incentive-compatibility constraint is binding, invoking Jensen's inequality once again results in

$$w_P < \int_{\underline{A}}^{M} \tilde{w_C}\left(L_P^i,\ A,\ \bar{Q}_G,\ \beta\right)f(A)dA < \int_{\underline{A}}^{M} w_C\left(L_P^i,\ A,\ \bar{Q}_G,\ \beta\right)f(A)dA$$

A.3 $\frac{\partial\nu}{\partial \mathbf{L}_\mathbf{P}^\mathbf{i}} < \mathbf{0}$

First note that ν is given by

$$\nu = \frac{\rho\left(1-\rho^2\right)(1-\tilde{p})\left(1-\rho^2(1-p)\right)}{|Q|\left(1-(1-\tilde{p})\rho^2\right)}.$$

Substituting for $|Q|$ and in the above equation and defining $u = \rho(1-\tilde{p})(1-(1-p)\rho^2)$ and $v = (1-(1-\tilde{p})\rho^2)[(1-\rho^2)+\rho^2(q+p(1-q))]$ we get

$$\frac{\partial u}{\partial p} = -(1-\mu)\left(1-(1-p)\rho^2\right)+(1-\tilde{p})\rho^2 > (<)0$$

$$\frac{\partial^2 u}{\partial p^2} = -2(1-\mu)\rho^2 < 0$$

$$\frac{\partial v}{\partial p} = \left[(1-\rho^2)+\rho^2(q+p(1-q)\right](1-\mu)\rho^2+\left(1-(1-\tilde{p})\rho^2\right)\rho^2(1-q) > 0$$

$$\frac{\partial^2 v}{\partial p^2} = 2(1-q)(1-\mu)\rho^4 > 0$$

Now

$$\frac{\partial \nu}{\partial p} = \frac{1}{v^2}\left[v\frac{\partial u}{\partial p} - u\frac{\partial v}{\partial p}\right].$$

Therefore $\frac{\partial \nu}{\partial p} < 0$ if $\mu \to 1$.

Again,

$$\frac{\partial^2 \nu}{\partial p^2} = \frac{1}{v^2}\left(v\frac{\partial^2 u}{\partial p^2} - u\frac{\partial^2 v}{\partial p^2}\right) - \frac{2}{v}\frac{\partial v}{\partial p}\frac{\partial \nu}{\partial p} < 0.$$

if $\frac{\partial v}{\partial p} \to 0$ which is the case if (i) $\mu \to 1$ and (ii) $q \to 1$.

Now

$$\frac{\partial p}{\partial L_P^i} = \frac{qN}{(1-(1-q)NL_P^i)} > 0,$$

$$\frac{\partial^2 p}{\partial \left(L_P^i\right)^2} = \frac{2q(1-q)N^2}{\left(1-(1-q)NL_P^i\right)^3} > 0.$$

Therefore $\frac{\partial \nu}{\partial L_P^i} < 0$ and $\frac{\partial^2 \nu}{\partial (L_P^i)^2} < 0$.

Appendix B

B.1 Market responses to an EGS program

Totally differentiating Eqs. 12 and 14 after substituting for λ from Eq. 13 into Eq. 12 and using Cramer's rule we get

$$\begin{bmatrix} Z & -Y \\ N & -M \end{bmatrix}\begin{bmatrix} dL_P \\ dw_P \end{bmatrix} = \begin{bmatrix} -Sd\alpha - Rd\beta \\ -Jd\bar{w} \end{bmatrix}$$

where

$$Z = \frac{d^2 EQ^i_H}{d\left(L^i_P\right)^2} - \frac{d^2 TC^2}{d\left(L^i_P\right)^2} - \Psi_P$$

$$Y = \frac{(1+\rho)}{(1-\rho)} - \lambda(1+\rho)U'(w_P)\frac{\partial \nu}{\partial L^i_P}\left[1 + \frac{\epsilon^{\lambda}_{w_P}}{\epsilon^{U}_{w_P}}\right] > 0$$

$$M = (1 + \nu(1+\rho))U'(w_P) > 0$$

$$N = \nu\rho \int_{\underline{A}}^{M} U'(w_C)\frac{dw_C}{dL^i_P} f(A)dA - [W_* - V_*]\frac{\partial \nu}{\partial L^i_P} > 0$$

$$R = \frac{\rho}{(1-\rho)} \int_{\underline{A}}^{M} \left[AgH_1 \frac{L^i_C}{\mathcal{L}} \epsilon^{H_1}_{L^i_P} + AgH_1\left(1 + \epsilon^{g}_{L^i_P}\right) + \frac{dw_C}{d\beta} - \frac{d}{d\beta}\left(\frac{dw_C}{dL^i_P}\right)\left(\frac{\mathcal{L}}{N} - L^i_P\right)\right] f(A)dA$$
$$-\lambda\rho \int_{\underline{A}}^{M} U'(w_C)\frac{dw_C}{d\beta}\frac{\partial \nu}{\partial L^i_P} f(A)dA$$
$$-\lambda\left[U''\left(w^+_C\right)\frac{dw^+_C}{d\beta}\frac{dw^+_C}{dL^i_P} + U'\left(w^+_C\right)\frac{d}{d\beta}\left(\frac{dw^+_C}{dL^i_P}\right)\right]$$
$$-\lambda\nu\rho \int_{\underline{A}}^{M} \left[U''(w_C)\frac{dw_C}{d\beta}\frac{dw_C}{dL^i_P} + U'(w_C)\frac{d}{d\beta}\left(\frac{dw_C}{dL^i_P}\right)\right] f(A)dA$$

$$S = \frac{\rho}{(1-\rho)} \int_{\underline{A}}^{M} \left[A\beta g' L_G H_1 + Ng'H\left(1 + \epsilon^{g'}_{Q_G}\right) + \frac{dw_C}{d\alpha} - \frac{d}{d\alpha}\left(\frac{dw_C}{dL^i_P}\right)\left(\frac{\mathcal{L}}{N} - L^i_P\right)\right] f(A)dA$$
$$-\lambda\rho \int_{\underline{A}}^{M} U'(w_C)\frac{dw_C}{d\alpha}\frac{\partial \nu}{\partial L^i_P} f(A)dA$$
$$-\lambda\left[U''\left(w^+_C\right)\frac{dw^+_C}{d\alpha}\frac{dw^+_C}{dL^i_P} + U'\left(w^+_C\right)\frac{d}{d\alpha}\left(\frac{dw^+_C}{dL^i_P}\right)\right]$$
$$-\lambda\nu\rho \int_{\underline{A}}^{M} \left[U''(w_C)\frac{dw_C}{d\alpha}\frac{dw_C}{dL^i_P} + U'(w_C)\frac{d}{d\alpha}\left(\frac{dw_C}{dL^i_P}\right)\right] f(A)dA$$

$$J = \nu U'(\bar{w}) > 0$$

where

$$\frac{d^2 EQ^i_H}{d\left(L^i_P\right)^2} = \frac{\rho}{(1-\rho)} \int_{\underline{A}}^{M} \left[(A\beta)^2 gH_{11} - 2A\beta\alpha Ng'H_1 + (\alpha N)^2 g''H\right] f(A)dA$$

$$\frac{d^2 TC^2}{d\left(L^i_P\right)^2} = -\frac{\rho}{(1-\rho)} \int_{\underline{A}}^{M} \left[\frac{dw_C}{dL^i_P}\left(2 + \epsilon^{(w_C)'}_{L^i_P}\right) + \frac{d^2 w_C}{d\left(L^i_P\right)^2}\left(\frac{\mathcal{L}}{N}\right)\right] f(A)dA$$

$$\Psi_P = -\Omega\frac{\partial\lambda}{\partial L^i_P} - \lambda[W_* - V_*]\frac{\partial^2 \nu}{\partial (L^i_P)^2} + 2\lambda\rho\frac{\partial \nu}{\partial L^i_P}\int_{\underline{A}}^{M} U'(w_C)\frac{dw_C}{dL^i_P} f(A)dA$$
$$+\lambda U''(w^+_C)\left(\frac{dw^+_C}{dL^i_P}\right)^2\left[1 - \frac{\epsilon^{(w^+_C)'}_{L^i_P}}{r_{w^+_C}\epsilon^{w^+_C}_{L^i_P}}\right]$$
$$+\lambda\nu\rho\int_{\underline{A}}^{M}\left\{U''(w_C)\left(\frac{dw_C}{dL^i_P}\right)^2\left[1 - \frac{\epsilon^{(w_C)'}_{L^i_P}}{r_{w_C}\epsilon^{w_C}_{L^i_P}}\right]\right\} f(A)dA$$

where $\epsilon^{(j)'}_{L^i_P} = \frac{d^2 j}{d(L^i_P)^2}\frac{L^i_P}{\frac{dj}{dL^i_P}} > 0,\ j = w^+_C, w_C$; ϵ^m_n is the elasticity of m with respect to $n, m = U, g, g', w_C, w^+_C, \lambda; n = L^i_P, Q_G, w_P$ and r_j is the relative risk aversion with respect to the casual wage. It can easily be checked that $\frac{\partial\lambda}{\partial n}, n = L^i_P, w_P$ are both positive.

The sign of Z is in general indeterminate. We shall assume, however, that $\frac{d^2 Q^i_H}{d(L^i_P)^2} - \frac{d^2 TC^2}{d(L^i_P)^2} - \Psi_P$ is negative by the second order condition of profit maximization. With the determinant of the above matrix $|\mathcal{H}| = -ZM + YN > 0$, we have therefore:

(i) $\frac{dL^i_P}{d\bar{w}} < 0$, $\frac{dw_P}{d\bar{w}} > 0$ and $\frac{dw_C}{d\bar{w}} > 0$ iff $|\epsilon^g_{L^i_P}| > \epsilon^{\mathcal{E}Q_P}_{L^i_P}$.

(ii) $\frac{dL^i_P}{d\alpha} > 0$, $\frac{dw_P}{d\alpha} > 0$ and $\frac{dw_C}{d\alpha} > 0$.

(iii) $\frac{dL^i_P}{d\beta} > 0$, $\frac{dw_P}{d\beta} > 0$ and $\frac{dw_C}{d\beta} > 0$.

B.2 Determination of the optimum wage

Optimum wage consistent with the maximization of the welfare of the laborers is derived by totally differentiating

$$V_* = \frac{1}{|Q|}\left[p(1+\rho)U(w_P) + (1-p)\left(1-(1-q)\rho^2\right)\hat{U}\right]$$

with respect to $\bar{w}_v$; we get

$$\frac{dV_*}{d\bar{w}} = \frac{1}{|Q|}\left\{p(1+\rho)U'(w_P)\frac{dw_P}{d\bar{w}}\right.$$
$$\left. + (1-p)(1-(1-q)\rho^2)\left[U'(\bar{w}) + \rho\int_{\underline{A}}^{M} U'(w_C)\frac{dw_C}{dL_P}\frac{dL_P}{d\bar{w}} f(A)dA\right]\right\}$$
$$+\frac{1}{|Q|}(1+\rho)U(w_P)$$
$$-(1-(1-q)\rho^2)\left[u(\bar{w}) + +\rho\int_{\underline{A}}^{M} U(w_C)f(A)dA\right]\frac{dp}{dL_P}\frac{dL_P}{d\bar{w}}$$
$$-\frac{1}{|Q^2|}\left\{p(1+\rho)U(w_P) + (1-p)(1-(1-q)\rho^2)[\hat{U}]\right\}(1-\rho^2)\rho^2(1-q)$$
$$\times\frac{dp}{dL_P}\frac{dL_P}{d\bar{w}} = 0.$$

Rearranging the above equation and substituting for V_* yields Eq. 16.

References

1. Ahmad, Q.K., Hossain, M.: An evaluation of selected policies and programmes for the alleviation of rural poverty in Bangladesh. In: Islam, R. (ed.) Strategies for Alleviating Poverty in Rural Asia. ILO, Bangkok (1985)
2. Alamgir, M.: A review of the public rural works programme of Bangladesh 1960–78. Bangladesh Dev. Stud. **11**, 13–40 (1983)
3. Bardhan, P.K.: Wages and unemployment in a poor agrarian economy: a theoretical and empirical analysis. J. Polit. Econ. **87**, 479–500 (1979)
4. Bardhan, P.K.: Labor-tying in a poor agrarian economy: a theoretical and empirical analysis. Q. J. Econ. **98**, 501–514 (1983)
5. Bardhan, P.K., Rudra, A.: Terms and conditions of labor contracts in agriculture: results of a survey in West Bengal, 1979. Oxf. Bull. Econ. Stat. **43**, 89–111 (1981)
6. Basu, A.K.: Oligopsonistic landlords, segmented labor markets and the persistence of tied-labor contracts. Am. J. Agric. Econ. **84**, 438–453 (2002)
7. Basu, K.: Food for work programmes: beyond roads that get washed away. Econ. Polit. Wkly. **16**, 37–40 (1981)
8. Basu, K.: Food for work. Some economic and political consequences. Rev. Agric. Econ. Polit. Wkly. **17**, A9–A14 (1982)
9. Basu, K.: The elimination of endemic hunger in South Asia. some policy options. In: Drèze, J., Sen, A. (eds.) The Political Economy of Hunger. Clarendon, Oxford (1990)
10. Basu, A.K. Chau, N.H.: Targeting child labor in debt bondage: evidence theory and policy prescriptions. World Bank Econ. Rev. **17**, 255–281 (2003)
11. Basu, A.K., Chau, N.H.: Exploitation of child labor and the dynamics of debt bondage. J. Econ. Growth **9**, 209–238 (2004)
12. Basu, A.K., Chau, N.H., Kanbur, R.: A theory of employment guarantees: contestability, credibility and distributional concerns. J. Public Econ. **93**, 482–497 (2009)
13. Besley, T.: Means testing versus universal provision in poverty alleviation programmes. Economica **57**, 119–129 (1990)
14. Besley, T., Coate, S.: Workfare versus welfare: incentive arguments for work requirements in poverty alleviation programs. Am. Econ. Rev. **82**, 249–261 (1992)
15. Bhasin, V.: Economic pursuits and strategies of survival among Damor of Rajasthan. J. Hum. Ecol. **16**, 1–16 (2004)
16. Binswanger, H.P., Khandker, S.R., Rosenzweig, M.R.: How infrastructure and financial institutions affect agricultural output and investment in India. J. Dev. Econ. **41**, 337–366 (1993)
17. Braverman, A., Stiglitz, J.: Landlords, tenants and technological innovations. J. Dev. Econ. **23**, 313–332 (1986)
18. Chakraborty, P.: Implementation of the National Rural Employment Guarantee Act in India: Spatial Dimensions and Fiscal Implications. Working paper No. 505, The Levy Institute of Bard College, Annandale-on-Hudson, NY (2007)
19. Dandekar, K., Sathe, M.: Employment guarantee scheme and food for work programme. Econ. Polit. Wkly. **15**, 707–713 (1980)
20. Dandekar, V.M.: Agriculture, employment and poverty. Rev. Agric. Econ. Polit. Wkly. **21**, A90–A100 (1986)
21. Datt, G., Ravallion, M.: Transfer benefits from public works employment: evidence for rural India. Econ. J. **104**, 1346–1369 (1994)
22. Drèze, J.: Famine prevention in India. In: Drèze, J., Sen, A. (eds.) The Political Economy of Hunger. Clarendon, Oxford (1990)
23. Dasgupta, I.: 'Living' wage, class conflict and ethnic strife. J. Econ. Behav. Organ. **72**, 750–765 (2009)
24. Deshingkar, P., Farrington, J.: Rural Labour Markets and Migration in South Asia: Evidence from India and Bangladesh. Background Paper for the World Development Report 2008. http://siteresources.worldbank.org/INTWDR2008/Resources/2795087-1191427986785/DeshingkarP&Farrington.pdf (2006)
25. Dev, M.: India's (Maharashtra) employment guarantee scheme: lessons from long experience. In: von Braun, J. (ed.) Employment for Poverty Reduction and Food Security, pp. 108–143. International Food Policy Research Institute (IFPRI), Washington, DC (1995)
26. Eswaran, M., Kotwal, A.: A theory of two-tier labor markets in agrarian economies. Am. Econ. Rev. **75**, 162–177 (1985)

27. Fan, S., Hazell, P., Thorat, S.: Government spending, growth and poverty in rural India. Am. J. Agric. Econ. **82**, 1038–1051 (2000)
28. Fields, G., Kanbur, R.: Minimum wages and poverty with income sharing. J. Econ. Ineq. **5**, 135–147 (2007)
29. Foster, J., Greer, J., Thorbecke, E.: A class of decomposable poverty measures. Econometrica **52**, 761–776 (1984)
30. Genicot, G.: Bonded labor and serfdom: a paradox of voluntary choice. J. Dev. Econ. **67**, 101–127 (2002)
31. Harris, J.R., Todaro, M.P.: Migration, unemployment and development: a two-sector analysis. Am. Econ. Rev. **60**, 126–142 (1970)
32. India Rural Development Report (1999). National Institute for Rural Development, Hyderabad, India
33. Jha, R., Bhattacharyya, S., Gaiha, R., Shankar, S.: 'Capture' of anti-poverty programs: an analysis of the national rural employment guarantee program in India. J. Asian Econ. **20**, 456–464 (2009)
34. Khan, M.A.: Trade and development in the presence of an informal sector: a four-factor model. In: Basu, K., Majumdar, M., Mitra, T. (eds.) Capital, Investment and Development. Blackwell, Cambridge (1993)
35. Lipton, M.: Success in Anti-Poverty. Issues in Development, Discussion Paper 8. International Labour Organization, Geneva (1996)
36. Mearns, R. Access to Land in Rural India. World Bank Policy Research Working Paper, No. 2123. The World Bank, Washington, DC (2000)
37. Motiram, S.: Attached labour contracts in agriculture: results and analysis from a survey in South India. Can. J. Dev. Res. **28**, 99–117 (2007)
38. Mukherjee, A., Ray, D.: Wages and involuntary unemployment in the slack season of a village economy. J. Dev. Econ. **37**, 227–264 (1992)
39. Mukherjee, A., Ray, D.: Labor tying. J. Dev. Econ. **47**, 207–239 (1995)
40. The National Rural Employment Guarantee Act of 2005. The Gazette of India, Ministry of Law and Justice, No. 48
41. Narayana, N., Parikh, K., Srinivasan, T.: Rural works programs in India: costs and benefits. J. Dev. Econ. **29**, 131–156 (1988)
42. Osmani, S.R.: Wage determination in rural labor markets: the theory of implicit co-operation. J. Dev. Econ. **34**, 3–23 (1991)
43. Osmani, S.R., Chowdhury, O.H.: Short run impacts of food for work programme in Bangladesh. Bangladesh Dev. Stud. **11**, 135–190 (1983)
44. Pal, S.: Segmentation of rural labour contracts: some further evidence. Bull. Econ. Res. **54**(2), 151–180 (2002)
45. Ravallion, M.: On the coverage of public employment schemes for poverty alleviation. J. Dev. Econ. **34**, 57–79 (1991)
46. Ravallion, M.: Market responses to anti-hunger policies: effects on wages, prices and employment. In: Drèze, J., Sen, A. (eds.) The Political Economy of Hunger. Clarendon, Oxford (1990)
47. Ravallion, M., Datt, G., Chaudhuri, S.: Does Maharashtra's "employment guarantee scheme" guarantee employment? Econ. Dev. Cult. Change **41**, 251–276 (1993)
48. Rawal, V.: The labour process in rural Haryana (India): a field-report from two villages. Journal of Agrarian Change **6**, 538–583 (2006)
49. Sathe, M.D.: Rural Employment and Employment Guarantee Scheme in Maharashtra. Vijayanagar, Pune and Mahrashtra Development Group (1991)
50. Shanmugam, T.R., Vijayalakshmy, K.: Determinants of agricultural labour participation in organisation in India. Agric. Trop. Subtrop. **38**, 51–55 (2005)
51. Singh, L., Singh, I., Ghuman, R.S.: Changing Character of Rural Economy and Migrant Labour in Punjab. Munich Personal RePEc Archive, Paper No. 6420. http://mpra.ub.uni-muenchen.de/6420/ (2007)
52. Srivastava, R.: Bonded labour in India: its incidence and pattern. In: InFocus Programme on Promoting the Declaration on Fundamental Principles and Rights at Work. International Labour Office, Geneva (2005)
53. Subbarao, K.: Public works as an anti-poverty program: an overview of cross-country experience. Am. J. Agric. Econ. **84**(2), 678–683 (1999)
54. Thomas, J.W.: The rural public works programme and rural development in East Pakistan. In: Falcon, W.P., Papanek, G.F. (eds.) Development Policy II: The Pakistan Experience. Harvard University Press, Cambridge (1971)

Economica (2006) **73**, 193–228
doi:10.1111/j.1468-0335.2006.00483.x

The Race to the Bottom, from the Bottom

By NANCY H. CHAU† and RAVI KANBUR†‡

†*Cornell University* ‡*CEPR*

Final version received 10 March 2005.

The dominant perspective in discussions of labour and environmental standards and globalization is that of North–South competition and its impact on Northern standards. This paper presents an alternative perspective, that of South–South competition to export to the North and its impact on Southern standards. It develops a simple model of Southern competition, and demonstrates that whether a Southern race to the bottom is possible depends intricately on the Northern demand curve, the size of large exporters relative to each other and the relative size of the competitive fringe of small exporters. The possibility that Northern trade protectionism may undermine Southern standards is also examined.

INTRODUCTION

Does Chinese trade competition pose a threat to labour and environmental standards in other large developing countries such as India? Are standards in India and China pulled down by standards in small countries such as Myanmar, Honduras or South Africa? Does trade protectionism in the United States protect standards in developing countries, or undermine them?

These are questions of extraordinary and growing importance to poor countries in a globalizing world. Yet one finds very little in the way of analysis that speaks to them. This is because the dominant perspective in present discussions is one of trade competition between the rich North and the poor South, and the consequences of this for standards in the North:

> Labour unions and human rights activists in developed countries argue that market access in the North should be conditioned on raising labour standards in the South to prevent social dumping and a 'race to the bottom' in wages and benefits. Trade sanctions imposed in response to violations of labour standards are sometimes referred to as a 'social clause'. Developing countries tend to view such clauses as disguised protectionism and have fought vigorously against initiatives by the United States and other developed countries to give the WTO a role in the area of labour standards.
>
> (Kahn 2000)

Thus, even the well worn phrase 'race to the bottom' has typically come to be seen in terms of downward pressure on Northern standards as a result of competition with the South. It should be clear that this dominant perspective cannot address the questions posed above. Recently, therefore, some commentators have begun to call for the shift of perspective that these questions demand—to a perspective that highlights South–South competition for export market share and its impact on Southern standards.

> Consider the celebrated soccer ball industry. . . . The top five suppliers were Pakistan, China, Indonesia, India and Thailand, which together supplied 96.9 percent of soccer balls imported by the United States. It is also worth keeping in mind that the United

> States does not produce any soccer balls. If any of these countries is banned from exporting to the United States, it is highly unlikely that the demand will shift to another industrialized nation. It will be some other developing country that picks up the slack. ... [L]abor standards are a great concern within the developing country. This concern is combined with a fear that any action on this front by any one country will cause a shift in production to some other developing country. Indians point out that China's lack of democracy enables it to use forms of forced labour, such as prison labour, that would not be feasible in India. China, on the other hand, worries about India's greater poverty pushing wages down and sending large numbers of children into forced labour.
>
> (Basu 1999)

Not surprisingly, the dominant perspective has produced a large analytical literature.[1] The perspective of South–South trade competition and its impact on Southern standards has produced far less. There are isolated references in the literature to this perspective on the race to the bottom, from the bottom; for example, Brown *et al.* (1996) discuss possible collusion among developing countries to raise standards. But there is very little analysis of the problem. Indeed, in their recent review Rollo and Winters (2000) note that 'so far this argument has not figured at all in the debate'.

Once the focus is shifted to trade competition among developing countries, it is no longer appropriate to treat them as an undifferentiated homogeneous group. In particular, there are large and small exporters in any commodity category. Basu's (1999) example of soccer balls shows exports to United States dominated by five 'big' exporters. Similar size distribution patterns are present in exports to all countries, and in several commodity categories, as shown in Table 1. The sizeable shares of developing countries in major export markets indicate that there are potential price consequences when standards improve and output changes. In particular, the suggestion by Brown *et al.* (1996) that developing countries collude on labour standards is based precisely on the possible terms-of-trade effects of collusion between such countries. However, while big exporters compete against each other, they also compete against smaller exporters who could take away market share. There have been dramatic instances of shifts of production—away from Iran in carpets and towards textiles in Bangladesh, for example—which highlight the threat that the big exporters face. The thought that follows is that, while big exporters will worry about the terms-of-trade consequences of their choice of standards, and indeed about standards elsewhere, small ones will not. To extend Basu's (1999) analogy, while the competition between an India and a China in exports of soccer balls is important and needs to be analysed, equally important is the interaction between this competition and the competition that the Indias and Chinas as a group face from the South Africas and the Hondurases of the world.

One of the key features of the dominant perspective is the focus on the role of Northern protectionism and whether or not it is justified in light of North–South competition on standards. There is a fierce debate on whether requirements for higher standards in the South, as a part of trade agreements, are disguised protectionism, and whether Northern trade protection through tariffs is an appropriate response to a presumed downward pull on Northern standards. But the question that is not addressed in the dominant perspective is

TABLE 1
LABOUR INTENSIVE EXPORTS AND DEVELOPING COUNTRIES

Country	Textiles US$m. 1997	Country	Carpets US$m. 1998	Country	Balls* US$m. 1998
China	4954.14	China	216.70	Pakistan	1754.59
India	3141.01	India	168.76	China	1680.25
Korea, Rep. of	2341.05	Mexico	65.20	Thailand	596.22
Pakistan	2138.06	Israel	62.34	India	348.57
Turkey	1995.85	Egypt	47.27	Indonesia	79.61
Canada	1618.41	Turkey	46.37	Vietnam	66.12
Indonesia	1433.83	Australia	30.54	Mexico	48.42
Mexico	1312.85	Brazil	30.30	Philippines	38.79
Israel	851.57	South Africa	20.22	Dominican Rep.	28.13
Thailand	844.66	Indonesia	19.14	Malaysia	20.17
Czech Rep.	634.57	Morocco	11.89	Brazil	17.85
Iran, Islamic Rep. of	633.94	Thailand	11.07	Morocco	12.35
Egypt	515.34	Hungary	10.14	Panama	11.35
Poland	413.92	Pakistan	8.13	Czech Rep.	11.13
Brazil	359.28	Czech Rep.	6.93	Belarus	10.63
Malaysia	345.99	Saudi Arabia	6.27	Paraguay	6.35
Tunisia	272.73	Poland	5.31	Colombia	5.49
Hungary	232.54	Colombia	4.09	Peru	4.48
Slovak Rep.	198.10	Chile	3.18	Poland	3.93
Slovenia	194.87	Argentina	3.00	Romania	2.96
Bangladesh	184.31	Sri Lanka	2.57	Hungary	2.37
Nepal	170.17	Vietnam	2.50	Saudi Arabia	1.81
Philippines	167.28	Malaysia	2.28	Uruguay	1.77
Sri Lanka	165.75	Russian Federation	2.11	Estonia	1.74

TABLE 1
CONTINUED

Country	Textiles US$m. 1997	Country	Carpets US$m. 1998	Country	Balls* US$m. 1998
Romania	131.91	Panama	1.45	Turkey	1.11
Russian Federation	129.68	Romania	1.41	Argentina	1.05
South Africa	117.16	Estonia	0.81	Sri Lanka	0.94
Estonia	112.85	Venezuela	0.73	Chile	0.83
Morocco	99.32	Philippines	0.63	South Africa	0.70
Lithuania	95.85	Nepal	0.57	Guatemala	0.59
Bulgaria	92.69	Lebanon	0.38	Venezuela	0.56
Viet Nam	84.24	Kazakhstan	0.36	Israel	0.44
United Arab Emirates	67.93	Belize	0.34	Ukrainian	0.42
Australia	59.82	Bangladesh	0.27	Costa Rica	0.23
Croatia	59.19	Slovenia	0.27	Ecuador	0.20
Peru	44.40	Turkmenistan	0.27	Egypt	0.18
Dominican Republic	40.12	Tunisia	0.26	Latvia	0.16
Colombia	36.76	Peru	0.20	Mauritius	0.14
El Salvador	25.82	Ecuador	0.16	Russian Federation	0.12
Costa Rica	19.15	Uruguay	0.14	Honduras	0.12
Guatemala	15.55	Zimbabwe	0.14	Nepal	0.11
Uruguay	7.00	Guatemala	0.13	Jamaica	0.10

*excl. tennis and golf balls.
Source: WTO (1998); UNCTAD–(2000).

whether Northern trade protectionism hurts or benefits Southern standards, when the countries of the South are competing against each other in export markets. This is the third of the questions posed above, and on which there is again very little analysis.

The purpose of this paper is to develop a simple model that can begin to provide insight into this perspective on the race to the bottom as seen from the bottom, and to provide preliminary answers to the three questions posed at the beginning. Section I sets out the elements of a model of Ricardian trade, in which 'big' and 'small' Southern countries export into a Northern demand curve. Countries have the choice of adopting a high or a low 'standard', which we will think of as a labour standard but which could equally be an environmental standard. The essential point is that there is an intervention that could enhance welfare directly but would also raise labour costs and hence reduce output and exports.

Section II explores the incentives that different countries have to adopt the high standard. Big exporters take into account the terms-of-trade effects and standards in other countries, while the 'competitive fringe' of small exporters do not. Given these incentives, Section III characterizes Nash equilibria in standards as a function of the Northern demand curve, the size of the big exports relative to each other and the size of the competitive fringe. It provides a precise and complete characterization of when high-standards and low-standards equilibria arise as the parameters vary.

Section IV turns to welfare and asks if and when there exists the possibility of welfare-improving coordination on high standards when the Nash equilibrium is a low-standards equilibrium. Section V considers the consequences of a Northern tariff for the outcome of South–South competition on standards. In particular, it looks at whether the Northern tariffs increase or decrease the likelihood of low-standards equilibrium in the South. It shows that the answer depends critically on the timing of whether the tariff is chosen before the standards are set in the South, or after.[2] Section VI concludes. It revisits the three questions that motivated this paper, examines the answers that this paper provides and suggests areas for further research.

I. The Model

We develop the simplest trade model in which standards and competition among exporting countries can be analysed. Let there be two internationally traded commodities, indexed by $j = 1, 2$, and a single internationally immobile but domestically mobile factor, labour. A single developed country imports good 1 from developing countries. The developing countries can be divided into two types. The first group of countries, labelled $i = 0$, is made up of many identical small open economies which take the world price of their exports as given. Without loss of generality, we normalize the number of these small countries to unity. The second group of exporters consists of two developing economies labelled $i = 1, 2$. We will refer to them as large exporters, in the sense that they take into account the terms-of-trade consequences of any changes in their exports. The Northern importing country is denoted by $*$.

Each exporting country, large and small, has the choice of a level of domestic standard s^i, where

(1) $$s^i = \{s^-, s^+\}; s^+ > s^-_, \; i = 0, 1, 2,$$

so that s^+ denotes the higher standard. We think of this as a labour standard, but it could equally well be interpreted as an environmental standard. Choice of standard s^i affects production costs and the utility of workers in the country. Let us begin with the production costs story. Production technologies in the exporting and importing countries are assumed to be given by

(2) $$\phi(s^i)a_j x_j = L_j, \; j = 1, 2, i = 0, 1, 2,$$

(3) $$a_j^* x_j^* = L_j^*, \; j = 1, 2,$$

where L_j denotes labour employed in sector j, x_j is the output of sector j, a_j is the input–output coefficient and ϕ is a coefficient showing the cost consequences of adopting different standards. (We focus solely on standards in the exporting countries.) We assume that

(4) $$s^- = 1; \; \phi(s^-) = 1; \; \phi(s^+) > 1.$$

Thus, we normalize the lower standard at unity, and normalize its effect on labour cost at neutrality. The higher standard lowers output per worker in each sector.

With technology as described by (2) and (3), the production frontiers of the exporting countries and the importing country are given by

(5) $$\phi(s^i)a_1 x_1^i + \phi(s^i)a_2 x_2^i = L^i, \; i = 0, 1, 2,$$

$$a_1^* x_1^* + a_2^* x_2^* = L^*,$$

where L^i denotes the labour endowment of country i. We assume that

(6) $$\frac{a_1^*}{a_2^*} > \frac{a_1}{a_2},$$

so that developing countries have comparative advantage in the production of good 1. Let good 2 be the numeraire, and let p be the world price of good 1 relative to good 2. It is well known that, if p lies in the range

(7) $$\frac{a_1^*}{a_2^*} > p > \frac{a_1}{a_2},$$

then $i = 0, 1, 2$ will specialize in the production of good 1 and $*$ will specialize in the production of good 2. We will focus on this range of outcomes. With this pattern of specialization, revenue functions can be written as

(8) $$R^i(p, s^i) = \frac{pL^i}{\phi(s^i)a_1},$$

(9) $$R^*(p) = \frac{L^*}{a_2^*}.$$

The production costs of higher standards are thus reflected in lower revenues, as shown in (8), since $\phi(s^+) > \phi(s^-) = 1$. The revenue losses associated with higher standards are to be set against the potential utility gains. We characterize these effects through the utility function

$$(10) \qquad U^i(c_1, c_2, s^i) = \alpha \log c_1 + (1-\alpha)\log c_2 + \log s^i, \; i = 0, 1, 2,$$

where c_1 and c_2 represent consumption of the two commodities. Thus, when $s^i = s^- = 1$, we have the base case of no effect on utility; but the higher-standard $s^i = s^+ > 1$ raises utility directly. This utility function is of course restrictive. For example, it implies that the marginal rate of substitution in consumption between c_1 and c_2 is independent of the standard. But, as will be seen, the special form used in (10) serves to simplify the analytics and to provide sharp characterizations of equilibria.[3]

For exporting countries, maximizing (10) subject to the revenue constraint in (8) gives the indirect utility function

$$(11) \qquad V^i(p, s^i) = K + \log \frac{s^i L^i}{\phi(s^i)a_1} + (1-\alpha)\log p, i = 0, 1, 2,$$

where $K = \alpha \log \alpha + (1-\alpha) \log (1-\alpha)$ is a constant in the analysis. The export supply functions are given by

$$(12) \qquad X_1^i = (1-\alpha)\frac{L^i}{\phi(s^i)a_1}, i = 0, 1, 2.$$

Notice from (12) that exports fall with the adoption of high standards, since $\phi(s^+) > 1$. For the importing country, denote utility, indirect utility and the inverse import demand function by

$$(13) \qquad U^* = U^*(c_1, c_2), \;\; V^* = V^*(p, R^*), \;\; p = p^*(c_1^*, R^*).$$

In what follows we drop the subscript representing commodity 1, it being understood that the focus is on exports and imports of $j = 1$. We also drop the superscript $*$ from $p^*(\cdot)$, it being understood that $p(\cdot)$ represents the inverse Northern import demand function for good 1.

From (12), it is clear that total exports depend critically on how many workers in the developing world fall under a high-standards regime. Denote by ℓ the number of workers in all the exporting countries that have $s = s^+$. Also, define

$$(14) \qquad L = L^1 + L^2$$

as the labour endowment of the two big exporting countries. Then total exports can be written as

$$(15) \qquad X_1(\ell) = \sum_{i=0,1,2} X_1^i = \frac{1-\alpha}{a_1}\left[L^0 + L - \ell\left(1 - \frac{1}{\phi(s^+)}\right)\right].$$

World trade equilibrium is given by a market clearing relative price p, such that

$$(16) \qquad p = p(X(\ell)),$$

where we have suppressed the dependence of p on R^*. Notice that

$$(17)\qquad \frac{\partial X}{\partial \ell} = -\frac{1-\alpha}{a_1}\left(1 - \frac{1}{\phi(s^+)}\right) < 0$$

since $\phi(s^+) > 1$. As more and more workers come under the high-standards regime, production costs rise and output falls, as do exports. We assume that $p(\cdot)$ is downward sloping. Hence

$$(18)\qquad \frac{\partial p}{\partial \ell} = \frac{\partial p}{\partial X}\frac{\partial X}{\partial \ell} > 0.$$

In words, higher standards lead to an improvement in the terms of trade for exporters.

We can thus characterize world trade equilibrium when ℓ of the workers in the developing world come under the high-standards regime. But what determines ℓ? The next section considers the incentives for each country to adopt or not adopt the high standard, and provides a precise characterization of the patterns of incentives as country size and import demand varies.

II. Incentives for Adopting Standards

We assume that country i adopts the higher standard if its welfare V^i with $s^i = s^+$, denoted V^{i+}, is greater than welfare with $s^i = s^- = 1$, denoted V^{i-}. Let the number of workers other than those of country i who have the higher standard be ℓ^{-i}. Then country i's adoption of the higher standard increases ℓ from ℓ^{-i} to $\ell^{-i} + L^i$. From (11), the gain in welfare from adopting the high standard is[4]

$$(19)\qquad \begin{aligned} \Delta^i(\ell^{-i}, \ell^{-i} + L^i) &= V^{i+} - V^{i-} \\ &= \log\frac{s^+}{\phi(s^+)} + (1-\alpha)\log\left(\frac{p(X(\ell^{-i} + L^i))}{p(X(\ell^{-i}))}\right), \quad i = 0, 1, 2, \end{aligned}$$

where $p(X(\ell^{-i} + L^i))$ and $p(X(\ell^{-i}))$ are the equilibrium terms of trade from (16), as different numbers of workers come under the higher standard.

Expression (19) captures the different forces acting on welfare. First is the direct effect on welfare through s^+. Second is the production cost effect through $\phi(s^+)$. Third is the terms-of-trade effect $\log(p(X(\ell^{-i} + L^i))/p(X(l^{-i})))$. Since p is increasing in ℓ from (18), the terms-of-trade effect is always positive. It follows that, if the direct utility effect of the standard s^+ is greater than the production cost effect $\phi(s^+)$, it is always worth adopting the higher standard. In this case all countries would choose $s = s^+$ and there would be nothing left to analyse on choice of standard. To focus attention on the problems we are interested in, therefore, we make the following assumption.

Assumption 1.

$$(20)\qquad \log\frac{s^+}{\phi(s^+)} < 0.$$

Thus, the production cost effect has to be traded off against direct gains in utility and terms of trade gains.

The assumption in (20) immediately determines the outcome in our model for 'small' exporters, i.e. those who take the terms of trade as given. For these countries $p(\ell^{-0}+L^0)$ is *perceived* to be the same as $p(\ell^{-0})$, so from (19) and (20)

$$\Delta^0 < 0 \tag{21}$$

and we have our first proposition.

Proposition 1. Small exporters always adopt the lower standard.

For small exporters, expanding market share improves welfare, so they always stick to the lower standard. As we shall see, the relative weight of small exporters in overall exports critically affects, in turn, the choice of standard in the big exporting countries.

We assume that the big exporting countries, $i = 1, 2$, fully perceive and take into account the terms-of-trade effect in evaluating the gains from adopting the higher standard. From (19), this gain depends on ℓ^{-i} and $\ell^{-i}+L^i$. A central issue is whether Δ^i increases or decreases with ℓ^{-i}, the number of workers in other countries who are already under the high standard. To this end, we propose the following definition.

Definition 1. Standards are complements (substitutes) if the net gain to a country from adopting the high standard increases (decreases) with the number of workers in other countries who are already under the high standard.

Complementarity or substitutability of standards, as defined above, will prove a crucial determinant of incentives and of equilibrium outcomes.[5] Since X is linear and decreasing in ℓ^{-i},

$$\frac{\partial \Delta^i(\ell^{-i}, \ell^{-i}+L^i)}{\partial \ell^{-i}} \gtrless 0 \text{ according as } \log p(X) \text{ is } \left\{ \begin{matrix} \text{convex} \\ \text{concave} \end{matrix} \right\}. \tag{22}$$

Expression (22) immediately gives us the following proposition.

Proposition 2. Standards are complements (substitutes) if and only if the inverse import demand function is logconvex (logconcave).

Logconcavity and logconvexity of the demand function can be related to standard demand functions as follows.

Lemma 1. (i) If $p(X)$ is a constant elasticity function, it is logconvex.

(ii) If $p(X)$ is linear, it is logconcave.

The proof of this lemma is straightforward, but what it shows is that two commonly used demand functions give diametrically opposite answers to the question of whether standards are complements or substitutes and thus, as we shall see in the next section, lead to very different equilibrium outcomes in patterns of standards.

Having delineated when gains from high standards increase or decrease with other adoptions of high standards, we are now in a position to characterize incentives in each of the two large exporting countries to adopt the high standard, conditional on the other country having, or not having, done so. We will be particularly interested in how their relative size affects these incentives. To this end, recall from (14) that $L = L^1 + L^2$ is the total labour endowment of the big exporters, and define

$$(23) \qquad L^1 = \frac{L}{2} + \delta,\ L^2 = \frac{L}{2} - \delta.$$

Thus, as δ varies between $(-L/2, L/2)$, it measures the size of country 1 relative to that of country 2.

First of all, consider the gain for country 1 of adopting the high standard when country 2 has not done so. We denote this by Δ^1_-, where the superscript refers to the country in question and the subscript denotes the level of standard in the other country ($-$ or $+$). Since from Proposition 1 the small exporters never adopt the high standard, in this case, $\ell^{-1} = 0$ and $\ell^{-1} + L^1 = L^1 = L/2 + \delta$. From the definition of total exports $X(\ell)$ in (15), we have

$$X(\ell^{-1}) = X(0) = \frac{1-\alpha}{a_1}(L^0 + L)$$

$$X(\ell^{-1} + L^1) = X(L^1) = \frac{1-\alpha}{a_1}\left[L^0 + L - \left(\frac{L}{2} + \delta\right)\left(1 - \frac{1}{\phi(s^+)}\right)\right].$$

Thus, from (19),

$$(24) \qquad \Delta^1_- = \Delta^1\left(0, \frac{L}{2} + \delta\right) = \log\frac{s^+}{\phi(s^+)} + (1-\alpha)\left(\log\frac{p(X(\frac{L}{2} + \delta))}{p(X(0))}\right).$$

Now consider the gain for country 1 from adopting the high standard when country 2 has already done so. Denote this Δ^1_+. In this case $\ell^{-1} = L^2 = L/2 - \delta$, and $\ell^{-1} + L^1 = L^2 + L^1 = L$:

$$X(\ell^{-1}) = X(L^2) = \frac{1-\alpha}{a_1}\left[L^0 + L - \left(\frac{L}{2} - \delta\right)\left(1 - \frac{1}{\phi(s^+)}\right)\right],$$

$$X(\ell^{-1} + L^1) = X(L) = \frac{1-\alpha}{a_1}\left[L^0 + L - L\left(1 - \frac{1}{\phi(s^+)}\right)\right].$$

So from (19),

$$(25) \qquad \Delta^1_+ = \Delta^1\left(\frac{L}{2} - \delta, L\right) = \log\frac{s^+}{\phi(s^+)} + (1-\alpha)\left(\log\frac{p(X(L))}{p(X(\frac{L}{2} - \delta))}\right).$$

By similar reasoning, we can derive the gains for country 2 from adopting higher standards when country 1 has not done so, denoted Δ^2_+ and when country 1 has already done so, denoted Δ^2_-:

$$\Delta_+^2 = \Delta^2\left(0, \frac{L}{2} - \delta\right) = \log\frac{s^+}{\phi(s^+)} + (1-\alpha)\left(\log\frac{p(X(L))}{p(X(\frac{L}{2} - \delta))}\right). \tag{26}$$

$$\Delta_-^2 = \Delta^2\left(\frac{L}{2} + \delta, L\right) = \log\frac{s^+}{\phi(s^+)} + (1-\alpha)\left(\log\frac{p(X(L))}{p(X(\frac{L}{2} + \delta))}\right). \tag{27}$$

Consider how the gains from adopting higher standards vary with two key parameters: L^0, the weight of small exporters as a group, and δ, which captures the size of the two big exporters relative to each other.[6] Inspection of (24) shows that as L^0 increases Δ_-^1 increases or decreases according as $p(X)$ is logconvex or logconcave. In fact, inspection of (25), (26) and (27) shows that the same is true for Δ_+^1, Δ_+^2 and Δ_-^2. This leads to our next proposition.

Proposition 3. As the weight of small exporters increases, the gain to the large exporters from adopting high standards increases if the inverse demand function is logconcave and decreases if it is logconvex.

The intuition behind this follows from Proposition 2. An increase in L^0 increases the number of workers falling under the low-standards regime. If standards are complements ($p(\cdot)$ is logconvex) this will reduce incentives for others to adopt high standards. If on the other hand standards are substitutes ($p(\cdot)$ is logconcave), lower standards elsewhere will increase the incentive for the big exporters as a group to adopt high standards.

Let us turn to variations in δ for fixed L^0. Inspection of (24) shows that, since $\phi(s^+) > 1$ and $p(\cdot)$ is a decreasing function, Δ_-^1 is increasing in δ. The intuition is as follows. With country 2 fixed at the low standard, when country 1 adopts the low standard the total number of workers in the low standard regime is zero, independent of δ. But when country 1 adopts the high standard the number of workers in the low-standard regime is reduced by $(L/2 + \delta)$. This reduction is greater, output is lower and price and welfare is higher, the bigger is δ. Hence the gains from country 1 adopting the higher standard are increasing in δ. Similar reasoning, or direct inspection of (25), (26) and (27), shows that Δ_+^1 is increasing in δ and Δ_+^2 and Δ_-^2 are decreasing in δ. These are all captured in the following proposition.

Proposition 4. As the relative size of a big exporter grows, its gain from adopting the higher standard increases.

Propositions 3 and 4 describe when the gains from adopting a high standard increase or decrease as L^0 and δ vary parametrically. But actual adoption or otherwise depends on whether the gains are positive or negative. To partition the (δ, L^0) space into regions where the high standard yields positive or negative benefits, we need the following four loci:

$$\Delta_-^1 = 0 \Leftrightarrow \delta = \delta_-^1(L^0) \tag{28}$$

$$\Delta_+^1 = 0 \Leftrightarrow \delta = \delta_+^1(L^0) \tag{29}$$

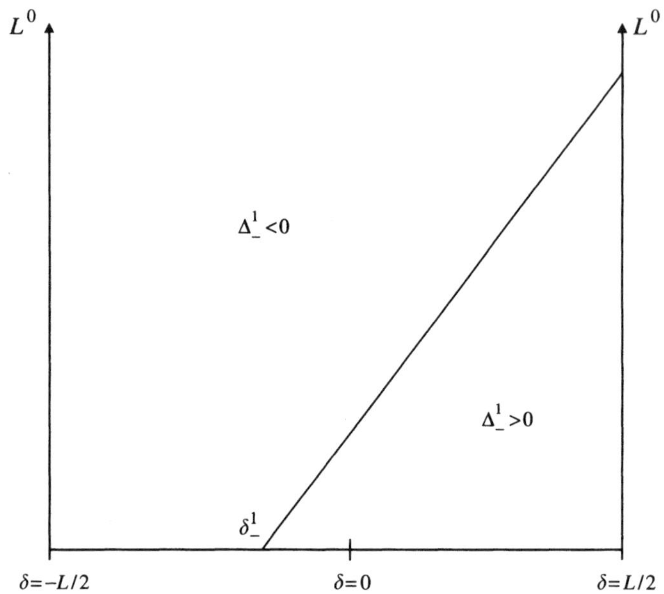

FIGURE 1. Incentives for country 1 under complementarity when country 2 has low standard.

$$(30) \qquad \Delta^2_- = 0 \Leftrightarrow \delta = \delta^2_-(L^0)$$

$$(31) \qquad \Delta^2_+ = 0 \Leftrightarrow \delta = \delta^2_+(L^0)$$

Proposition 3 suggests strongly that any partitioning of (δ, L^0) space will depend crucially on whether the inverse import demand curve is logconvex or logconcave. Let us develop the partitioning first of all for the case of logconvexity, that is, complementarity of standards. It follows immediately that the locus $\delta^1_-(L^0)$ is upward sloping in (δ, L^0) space, and that below this locus $\Delta^1_- > 0$ and above it $\Delta^1_- < 0$, as shown in Figure 1. To see the reasoning behind the partition shown there, start from a point on the locus, so that $\Delta^1_- = 0$. Then from Proposition 4, increasing δ makes $\Delta^1_- > 0$ and decreasing it makes $\Delta^1_- < 0$. And from Proposition 3, starting from a point on the locus and increasing L^0 makes $\Delta^1_- < 0$ and decreasing L^0 makes $\Delta^1_- > 0$, given the assumption of complementarity (logconvexity of the demand function). It is then also easy to see that $\delta^1_-(L^0)$ must be upward sloping, as shown.

Figure 2 adds a partitioning into positive or negative gains for country 1 when country 2 has already adopted the higher standard, still under complementarity. By the same reasoning as before, using Propositions 3 and 4, the locus $\delta^1_+(L^0)$ is also upward sloping. But it must also lie above $\delta^1_-(L^0)$, except when $\delta = L/2$ as shown in Figure 3. To see this, start from any point on

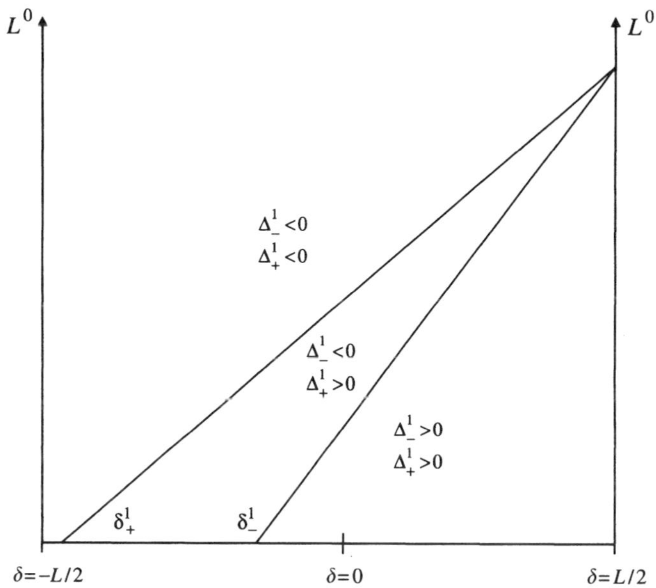

FIGURE 2. Incentives for country 1 under complementarity.

the $\delta^1_-(L^0)$ locus, so that Δ^1_- in (24) is zero. At this point Δ^1_+ in (25) must be positive for $\delta < L/2$ because adding the amount

$$-\left(\frac{L}{2} - \delta\right)\left(\frac{1}{\phi(s^+)} - 1\right)$$

to each of the terms,

$$L^0 + L - \left(\frac{L}{2} + \delta\right)\left(1 - \frac{1}{\phi(s^+)}\right)$$

and $L^0 + L$ in (24) converts it to (25). However, by logconvexity of $p(\cdot)$, it follows that if (24) is zero (25) must be positive for $\delta < L/2$. Now if $\delta = L/2$, $\Delta^1(L/2 - \delta, L) = \Delta^1(0, L) = \Delta^1(0, L/2 + \delta)$. Thus, the $\delta^1_-(L^0)$-locus and $\delta^1_+(L^0)$-locus coincide exactly at $\delta = L/2$. Intuitively, there is just one large country when $\delta = L/2$, and country 2's decision to adopt a high or low standard has no impact on the net benefits of high standards to country i.

Thus, with complementarity Figure 2 gives the exact partitioning of (δ, L^0)-space into regions where country 1's gains from adopting high standards are positive or negative. It is seen that, with L^0 low enough and δ large enough, country 1 benefits from adopting high standards no matter what country 2 does. With L^0 high enough and δ small enough, country 1 loses from the high standard no matter what country 2 does. In between these extremes, whether country 1 gains or loses from high standards depends on what country 2 does.

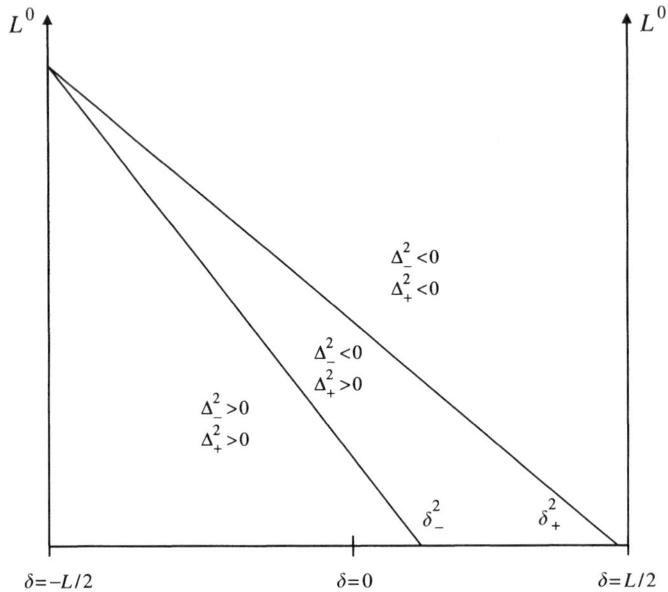

FIGURE 3. Incentives for country 2 under complementarity.

By reasoning similar to that which led to Figure 2, Figure 3 plots the loci $\delta_-^2(L^0)$ and $\delta_+^2(L^0)$. It can be shown that $\delta_-^2(L^0)$ and $\delta_+^2(L^0)$ are downward sloping and that $\delta_+^2(L^0)$ strictly lies above $\delta_-^2(L^0)$ for $\delta > -L/2$ under complementarity. In addition, $\delta_+^2(L^0)$ and $\delta_-^2(L^0)$ coincides at $\delta = -L/2$. Finally, Figures 2 and 3 can be overlaid to give Figure 4, which provides a complete account of the gains and losses for the two countries from adopting high standards under complementarity. As can be seen, even our very simple model leads to a complex pattern of incentives for each country, conditional on the behaviour of the other country.

The patterns may be complex, but they have an intuitive explanation based on the reasoning leading up to Figure 4. Consider first of all regions *A*, *B* and *C* at the top of the figure, where L^0 is 'large'. In these regions the predominant thrust of the incentives is in favour of the low standard, either because both countries will lose from the high standard no matter what the other country does (region *A*), or because one country will lose from the high standard no matter what the other country does and the other country will lose from the high standard if the first country has a low standard (regions *B* and *C*). By similar and symmetric reasoning, in regions *D*, *E* and *F*, where L^0 is 'small', the thrust of the incentives is in favour of the high standard.

In regions *G* and *H*, the incentives are dramatically opposite for the two countries depending on size. When country 1 is large enough, in region *H*, it has the incentive to adopt high standards no matter what country 2 does, while

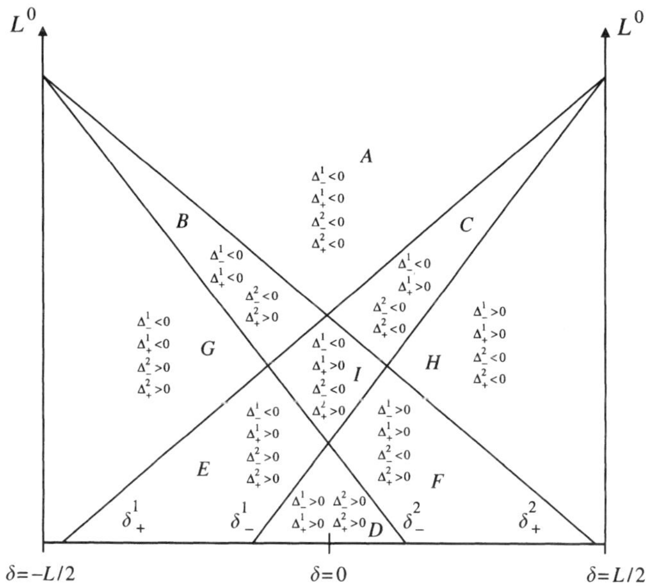

FIGURE 4. Incentives under complementarity.

country 2 has the incentive to adopt low standards irrespective of what country 1 does. The situation is reversed in region G, where country 2 is the relatively large one. Regions G and H illustrate Proposition 4 further—relative largeness helps incentives for high standards for a big exporter.

This leaves region I, where neither of the two big exporters is very large relative to the other, and the 'small exporters' group is neither very large nor very small. In this intermediate region, incentives for either country to adopt the high standard are positive only if the country also adopts the high standard—otherwise the incentive is negative.

All of the above discussion pertains to the case of complementarity, or logconvexity of the inverse import demand function. How is the partitioning affected when standards are substitutes and the demand function is logconcave? The answer is that the reasoning is modified at several crucial steps, leading to a very different type of partitioning of (δ, L^0)-space. To illustrate this, consider what the locus $\delta^1_-(L^0)$ would look like under substitutability. This is shown in Figure 5, which graphs $\delta^1_-(L^0)$ as a downward-sloping curve such that above the curve $\Delta^1_- > 0$ and below it $\Delta^1 < 0$. To see this, start from a point on this locus, where by definition $\Delta^1_- = 0$, and increase L^0 while holding δ constant. From Proposition 3, $\Delta^1_- > 0$ under logconcavity. Since standards are now substitutes, having more workers elsewhere with lower standards increases the benefit to country 1 from adopting the higher standard. Also, Proposition 4 tells us that increasing δ

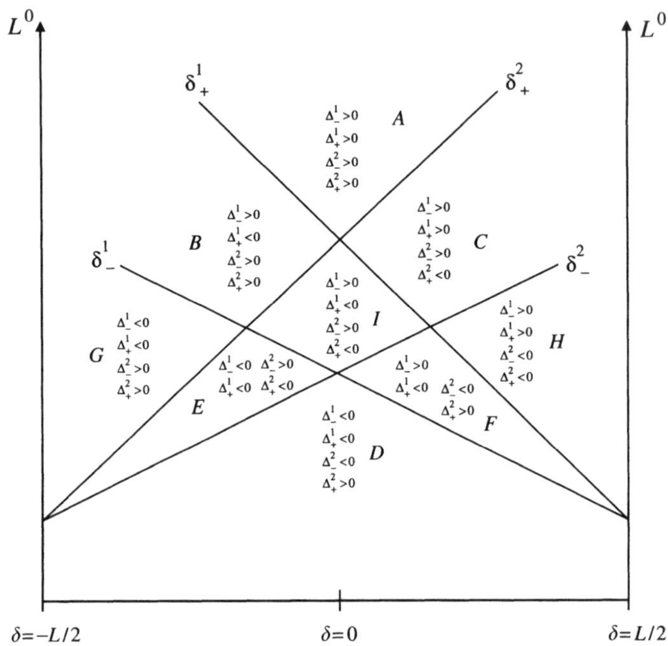

FIGURE 5. Incentives under substitutability.

from the locus will make $\Delta^1_- > 0$. These two features together establish that the locus $\delta^1_-(L^0)$ is downward sloping.

With country 2 having the high standard, $\delta^1_+(L^0)$ partitions the (δ, L^0)-space into regions of positive or negative gains for country 1. Reasoning similar to that used for Figure 2, but this time using logconcavity, establishes that $\delta^1_+(L^0)$ is downward slopping and lies above $\delta^1_-(L^0)$, and $\delta^2_-(L^0)$ lies above $\delta^2_+(L^0)$. $\delta^2_-(L^0)$ and $\delta^2_+ L^0$ characterize the incentive patterns for country 2 under the assumption of substitutability of standards analogously to Figure 3, and complete the characterization of incentives under substitutability for the two large countries.

Figure 5 presents some striking contrasts to Figure 4. In its region A, where L^0 is high enough, the incentives are all skewed in favour of the high standard. This contrasts with the corresponding region A in Figure 4, where with high enough L^0 the incentives are all in favour of the low standard. A similar reversal is seen by comparing regions D in the two figures. This diametrically opposite outcome is one of the most striking consequences of the assumption of logconcavity or logconvexity of the demand curve.

With complementarity, in Figure 4 regions B and C presented a congruent thrust of incentives in favour of high standards, in the sense that, while one country had positive gains from the high standard no matter what, the other country had positive gains from the high standard only if the first country had the high standard. But regions B and C in Figure 5 do not present such congruence. In region C, for example, country 1 has positive gains from adopting the high standard no matter what country 2 does, but country 2 has positive gains from the high standard only if country 1 adopts the *low* standard. A similar incongruence is found in region B and in regions E and F in Figure 5, in contrast to the congruence in incentives in these regions in Figure 4.

Regions G and H are the two regions where incentive patterns are similar in the two figures. One country has the clear incentive to adopt the high standard, while the other country has the clear incentive to adopt the low standard in these regions, in both figures. But the intermediate region I in Figure 5 again presents a contrast with the corresponding region in Figure 4. In Figure 4 each country has the incentive to adopt the high standard if and only if the other country also adopts the high standard. However, in Figure 5 each country has the incentive to adopt the high standard if and only if the other country adopts the *low* standard. As might be guessed, these incentive patterns have major consequences for the patterns of standards that emerge as an equilibrium under strategic interaction.

We have shown that the incentives for adoption of high standards depend intricately not only on the nature of the import demand function, but also on the size structure of exporting countries—the number of 'small' exporters, who take price as given, and the relative sizes of the 'large' exporters, who take into account the terms-of-trade consequences of their action. We are now ready to apply these results to an analysis of strategic interaction and equilibrium in the choice of standards.

III. EQUILIBRIUM

Consider the following simultaneous decision problem of the two large countries. Let $(q^i, 1-q^i)$ denote the mixed strategy in which country i adopts the high standard with probability q^i, and the low standard with the complementary probability $1-q^i$. The expected welfare of country i, $i=1$, 2, is given by

$$\text{(32)}\quad \begin{aligned} EV^i(q^i,q^j) &= q^i\left[q^jV^{i+}(p(X(L))) + (1-q^j)V^{i+}(p(X(L^i)))\right] \\ &\quad + (1-q^i)\left[q^jV^{i-}(p(X(L^j))) + (1-q^j)V^{i-}(p(X(0)))\right],\ i \neq j, \end{aligned}$$

where E is the expectation operator. Making use of (24)–(27) and (32) simplifies this expression to

$$\text{(33)}\quad \begin{aligned} EV^i(q^i,q^j) &= q^i\left(q^j\Delta^i_+ + (1-q^j)\Delta^i_-\right) \\ &\quad + \left[q^jV^{i-}(p(X(L^j))) + (1-q^j)V^{i-}(p(X(0)))\right]. \end{aligned}$$

Differentiating EV^i with respect to q^i, we have

$$\text{(34)}\quad EV^i_{q^i} = q^j\Delta^i_+ + (1-q^j)\Delta^i_-,\ i \neq j, i = 1, 2.$$

TABLE 2

INCENTIVE PATTERNS AND NASH EQUILIBRIUM UNDER COMPLEMENTARITY

	$\Delta^2_+ > 0$ $\Delta^2_- > 0$	$\Delta^2_+ > 0$ $\Delta^2_- < 0$	$\Delta^2_+ < 0$ $\Delta^2_- < 0$
$\Delta^1_+ > 0$ $\Delta^1_- > 0$	$D(+, +)$	$F(+, +)$	$G(+, -)$
$\Delta^1_+ > 0$ $\Delta^1_- < 0$	$E(+, +)$	$I(+, +)(-, -)$	$C(-, -)$
$\Delta^1_+ < 0$ $\Delta^1_- < 0$	$H(-, +)$	$B(-, -)$	$A(-, -)$

Note: Rows show country 1 incentives; columns, country 2 incentives. Cell labels *A* to *I* correspond to the regions in Figure 4. The first entry in $(\cdot, \cdot)$ refers to country 1's standard, the second entry to country 2's standard. A + denotes high standard in equilibrium, a − denotes low standard. Region *I* also has a mixed strategy equilibrium, but it is unstable under the standard adjustment process.

TABLE 3

INCENTIVE PATTERNS AND NASH EQUILIBRIUM UNDER SUBSTITUTABILITY

	$\Delta^2_+ > 0$ $\Delta^2_- > 0$	$\Delta^2_+ < 0$ $\Delta^2_- > 0$	$\Delta^2_+ < 0$ $\Delta^2_- < 0$
$\Delta^1_+ > 0$ $\Delta^1_- > 0$	$A(+, +)$	$C(+, -)$	$H(+, -)$
$\Delta^1_+ < 0$ $\Delta^1_- > 0$	$B(-, +)$	$I(-, +)(+, -)$	$F(+, -)$
$\Delta^1_+ < 0$ $\Delta^1_- < 0$	$G(-, +)$	$E(-, +)$	$D(-, -)$

Note: Rows show country 1 incentives; columns, country 2 incentives. Cell labels *A* to *I* correspond to the regions in Figure 8. The first entry in $(\cdot, \cdot)$ refers to country 1's standard, the second entry to country 2's standard. A + denotes high standard in equilibrium, a − denotes low standard. Region *I* also has a mixed strategy equilibrium, but it is unstable under the standard adjustment process.

The sign of (34) thus depends crucially on combinations of $\Delta^i_+ > (<) 0$ and $\Delta^i_- > (<) 0$, $i = 1, 2$. Some combinations can be ruled out, given the structure of the problem. Thus, complementarity rules out $\Delta^i_+ < 0$ and $\Delta^i_- > 0$, $i = 1, 2$, since it requires that the gains from adopting the high standard be greater when the other country has already adopted the high standard. By analogous reasoning, substitutability rules out $\Delta^i_+ > 0$ and $\Delta^i_- < 0$, $i = 1, 2$.

Let us start with the complementarity case. Table 2 sets out all nine possible sign patterns in this case. The cell labels *A*–*I* correspond exactly to regions *A*–*I* of Figure 4. In the cells are entries $(+, +)$, $(+, -)$, $(-, +)$ and $(-, -)$. These depict the Nash equilibrium outcomes. The first entry is for country 1, the second for country 2. A + depicts high standard, and − a low standard.

Table 3 provides a complete characterization of stable Nash equilibria. The reasoning is as follows. Whenever $\Delta^i_+ > 0$ and $\Delta^i_- > 0$, then $q^i = 1$, from (34), and the high standard is the dominant strategy. This is why the first entries in the cells of the first row of Table 1 are all +, and the second entries in the cells of the first column are also +. By analogous reasoning, whenever $\Delta^i_+ < 0$, and $\Delta^i_- < 0$, then the low standard is the dominant strategy. Putting these together, we get that (,) is the unique Nash equilibrium for cell A (and therefore region *A* of Figure 4), while $(+, +)$ is the corresponding equilibrium for cell *D*.

If the combination of sign patterns is $\Delta^i_+ > 0$ and $\Delta^i_- > 0$, $\Delta^j_+ < 0$ and $\Delta^j_- < 0, i \neq j$, i.e. a pattern of 'opposing dominant strategies', then clearly we will get an equilibrium with

$$q^i = 1 = 1 - q^j, \ i \neq j.$$

Hence the asymmetric sign patterns in cells G and H. But if the sign patterns are $\Delta^i_+ > 0$ and $\Delta^i_- > 0$, $\Delta^j_+ > 0$ and $\Delta^j_- < 0$, $i \neq j$, then from (34) $q^i = 1$ and, considering (34) with i and j switched around, $q^j = 1$. Hence in this case both countries will end up with high standards, as shown in cells E and F. By similar reasoning, if $\Delta^i_+ < 0$ and $\Delta^i_- > 0$, $\Delta^j_+ > 0$ and $\Delta^j_- > 0, i \neq j$, then $q^i = q^j = 0$, as shown in cells B and C.

This leaves the sign pattern in cell I: $\Delta^i_+ > 0$ and $\Delta^i_- < 0, i = 1, 2$. From (34), by standard arguments there exists a unique $\tilde{q}^j$, such that

$$EV^i_{q^i} = \tilde{q}^j \Delta^i_+ + (1 - \tilde{q}^j)\Delta^i_- = 0.$$

In addition, by complementarity, $EV^i_{q^i}$ is monotonically increasing in q^j since

$$(35) \qquad EV^i_{q^i q^j} = \Delta^i_+ - \Delta^i_- > 0.$$

Thus, for all $q^j > \tilde{q}^j$, $EV^i_{q^i} > 0$. The best-response function of country i, $q^i(q^j)$ is given by

$$(36) \qquad q^i(q^j) = \begin{cases} 0 & \text{if } q^j < \tilde{q}^j, \\ [0,1] & \text{if } q^j = \tilde{q}^j \\ 1 & \text{otherwise.} \end{cases}$$

By standard arguments, there are three possible equilibrium outcomes, involving: (i) low standards in both countries, (ii) high standards in both countries, and (iii) a mixed strategy equilibrium with

$$(37) \qquad \tilde{q}^i = \frac{-\Delta^j_-}{\Delta^j_+ - \Delta^j_-}, \ i = 1, 2, \ i \neq j,$$

It is easy to show that this mixed strategy equilibrium is unstable via the standard adjustment process. We therefore show only the two pure strategy equilibria in cell I of Table 2.

Figure 6 translates Table 2 back on to (δ, L^0)-space. It shows the pattern of Nash equilibria across different regions A–I, which correspond exactly to the regions in Figure 4 and the cells in Table 2. There are five possible equilibrium configurations of standards, depending on δ and L^0. In particular, when L^0 is sufficiently small (region D), both countries benefit from adopting high standards, depicted $(+, +)$. Another symmetric outcome indicates the opposite scenario, with $(-, -)$ when the market share of big exporters is sufficiently small relative to small countries (region A). Finally, asymmetries in labour endowments in the two large countries likewise imply asymmetries in the equilibrium strategies, with $q^i = 1 - q^j = 1$ whenever country i possesses significantly more market power than country j (regions G and H), depicted $(-, +)$ and $(+, -)$.

When export competition with the group of small countries with low standards is not too intense (L^0 is sufficiently small), regions E and F admit the symmetric Nash equilibrium $(+, +)$, even though the high standard is a dominant strategy for only one of the two countries. The intuition follows from strategic complementarity, as a high standard in country i raises the benefits of a high standard in j enough to justify setting $q^j = 1$. Similarly, as soon as export

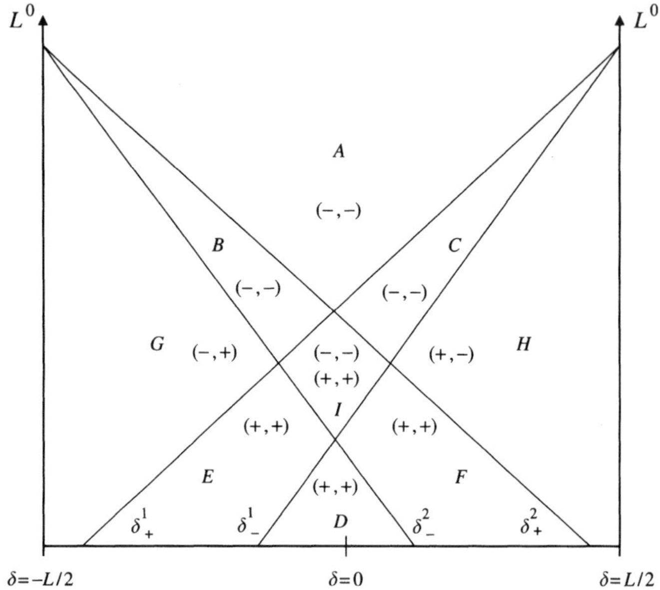

FIGURE 6. Nash equilibria under complementarity.

competition comes increasingly from countries with low standards, regions *B* and *C* admit yet another symmetric Nash equilibrium (– , –), even though low standard is a dominant strategy for only one of the two countries. Finally, in region *I*, where L^0 and δ are of intermediate magnitude, there are two pure strategy equilibria wherein both of the above symmetric Nash equilibrium are possible.

We turn now to the case where standards are substitutes. Table 3 lays out the patterns of Δ^i_+, Δ^i_-, the cells of the table corresponding exactly to the regions in Figure 5. As in the discussion of the complementarity case, when

$$\Delta^i_+ > 0 \text{ and } \Delta^i_- > 0,\ i = 1, 2;\ \text{or } \Delta^i_+ < 0 \text{ and } \Delta^i_- < 0,\ i = 1, 2,$$

we get a dominant strategy equilibrium and the outcomes (+ , +) and (– , –) respectively, as shown in cells *A* and *D*. When there are opposing dominant strategies, i.e.

$$\Delta^i_+ > 0 \text{ and } \Delta^i_- > 0;\ \text{or } \Delta^j_+ < 0 \text{ and } \Delta^j_- < 0,\ i \neq j,$$

then as before we get asymmetric Nash equilibria (+ , –) and (– , +) as shown in cells *G* and *H*.

When only one of the countries has a dominant strategy, i.e. when

$$\Delta^i_+ > 0 \text{ and } \Delta^i_- > 0;\ \text{or } \Delta^j_+ > 0 \text{ and } \Delta^j_- < 0,\ i \neq j,$$

then from (34) $q^i = 1$. Switching i and j in (34), and setting $q^i = 1$ gives us, $q^j = 0$, since $\Delta^j_+ < 0$. Thus, in cells B and C, we get $(-,+)$ and $(+,-)$ as the outcomes. Similarly, when

$$\Delta^i_+ < 0 \text{ and } \Delta^i_- < 0; \text{ or } \Delta^i_+ < 0 \text{ and } \Delta^i_- > 0, \ i \neq j,$$

we get the asymmetric equilibria $(+,-)$ and $(-,+)$ in cells F and E.

Finally, consider cell I, with sign pattern $\Delta^i_+ < 0$ and $\Delta^i_- > 0$, $i = 1, 2$, In this case there exists a unique $\tilde{q}^j$ such that

$$EV^i_{q^i} = \tilde{q}^j \Delta^i_+ + (1 - \tilde{q}^j)\Delta^i_- = 0.$$

Also, by substitutability,

$$EV^i_{q^i q^j} = \Delta^i_+ - \Delta^i_- < 0. \tag{38}$$

Thus, for all $q^j > \tilde{q}^j$, $EV^i_{q^i} < 0$. The best-response function of country i, $q^i(q^j)$, is given by

$$q^i(q^j) = \begin{cases} 0 & \text{if } q^j > \tilde{q}^j, \\ [0,1] & \text{if } q^j = \tilde{q}^j \\ 1 & \text{otherwise.} \end{cases} \tag{39}$$

Note that, since $q^i(q^j)$ is downward sloping, there are three Nash equilibria, with $q^1 = 1 = 1 - q^2$, $q^2 = 1 = 1 - q^1$ and $q^1 = \tilde{q}^1$ and $q^2 = \tilde{q}^2$. But the mixed strategy equilibrium $(\tilde{q}^i, \tilde{q}^j)$ is unstable, with $\tilde{q}^i$ and $\tilde{q}^j$ given by (37). So we show only the $(+,-)$ and $(-,+)$ pure strategy equilibria in cell I of Table 3.

Figure 7 translates Table 3 into (δ, L^0) space for the substitutability case, with regions $A - I$ in Figure 7 corresponding exactly to cells $A - I$ in Table 2 and regions $A - I$ in Figure 5. Starting from (δ, L^0) combinations such that δ is neither too large nor too small, note that, by substitutability, the symmetric Nash equilibrium $(+,+)$ applies for (δ, L^0) combinations in region A of Figure 7 when L^0 is large enough. However, $(-,-)$ applies in region D only, when L^0 is sufficiently small. Region I admits two asymmetric Nash equilibria. Thus, contrary to the case of strategic complementarity, export competition from small countries with low standards in fact prompts both countries to adopt high standards. As such, under substitutability there is no presumption that export competition induces a race to the bottom in standards as competition arises from countries with low standards

In contrast, combinations of (δ, L^0) in region G (H) are the circumstances under which the market power country 1 (2) is large enough, relative to country 2 (1), that the dominant strategies of the two countries are diametrically opposed, with $q^1 = 1 = 1 - q^2$ ($q^2 = 1 = 1 - q^1$), shown as $(+,-)$ (or $(-,+)$). Note also that strategic interactions between the two countries yield asymmetric Nash equilibria even when one of the two countries does not have dominant strategy. In particular, in regions F and C, where δ is relatively large, $q^1 = 1$ and $q^2 = 0$, shown as $(+,-)$. The intuition follows from strategic substitutability, as a high standard in country 1 is sufficient to deter country 2 from raising its standard. Regions E and F depicts the opposite scenario, and $q^1 = 0$ and $q^2 = 1$, shown as $(-,+)$

Figures 6 and 7 provide a precise and complete characterization of equilibrium in the choice of standards as a function of the size of the big

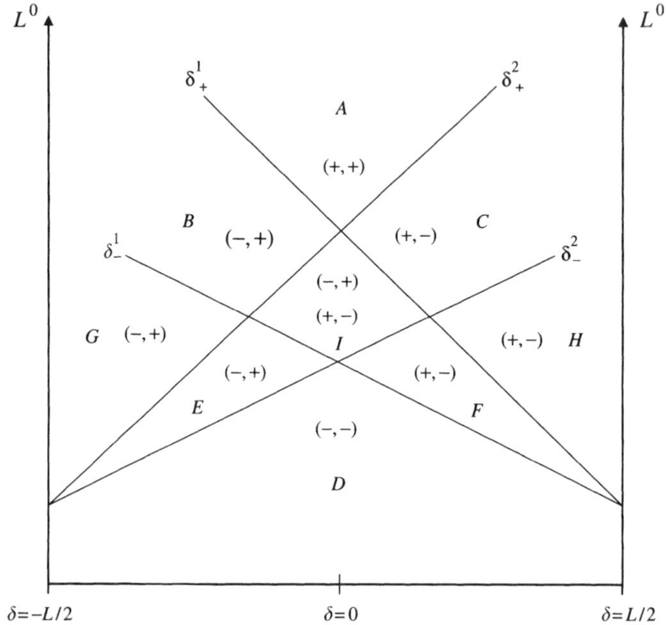

FIGURE 7. Nash equilibria under substitutability.

exporters relative to each other (δ), the size of the competitive fringe of small exporters (L^0) and the Northern demand curve (whether it is logconvex, or logconcave, leading to Figures 6 and 7, respectively). Consider first of all the effect of varying δ on the nature of the equilibrium. In Figure 6, as δ increases, the tendency is to move from region G to region H, moving from $(-,+)$ through $(+,+)$ or $(+,-)$ to $(+,-)$. The same is true in Figure 7. In this sense, a higher δ makes $(+,-)$ outcomes 'more likely'. These observations lead to the following proposition.

Proposition 5. As one of the big exporters becomes larger relative to the other, the likelihood of equilibria, in which the larger exporter has high standards and the other exporter has low standards, increases.

This outcome should not be too surprising, since the larger exporter increasingly acts as a single exporter and adopts higher standards not only for its direct benefit but also because output restriction is beneficial in the face of a downward-sloping demand curve. More generally, since we have already established in Proposition 1 that the smallest exporters adopt low standards, Proposition 5 strengthens the argument that there should be positive correlation between market share and standards.

Consider now the impact of the size of the competitive fringe on equilibrium outcomes. As discussed earlier, when L^0 increases, the general movement is from region D to region A, moving from $(+,+)$ through $(+,-)$ or $(-,+)$, to $(-,-)$. This is the sense in which a larger L^0 makes the low standards outcome 'more likely'. The opposite is true in Figure 7, where the movement is from $(-,-)$, through $(+,-)$ or $(-,+)$, to $(+,+)$. We capture these observations in the following proposition.

Proposition 6. As the size of the competitive fringe of small Southern exporters grows, the likelihood of low standards equilibria increases if Northern demand is logconvex (so that standards are complements) and decreases if Northern demand is logconcave (so that standards are substitutes).

That increasing competition from small countries, which have low standards and care only about expanding output, may not put downward pressure on the standards of big exporters is at first sight a surprising conclusion. But when the role of substitutability is made clear, it is not surprising at all. What is remarkable is that substitutability is not a curiosum but the implication of some commonly used demand functions which fit the data (e.g. linear demand). Moreover, the fact that the curvature of the demand curve plays such a key role highlights the need for parameterizing and estimating the degree of curvature of the demand curves for specific exports of developing countries.

Our analysis so far identifies circumstances under which strategic responses to export competition induce one or both countries to adopt lower standards. It should be noted, however, that a low standard need not imply low welfare, particularly when terms of trade adjustments and direct utility benefits are small, relative to the increase in production costs that higher standards necessitate. Accordingly, an equilibrium in which both countries select low standards need not necessarily imply a *coordination failure*. We turn to this question in the next section, and investigate the potential welfare gains that can be achieved via South–South cooperation in standards.

IV. Welfare and Coordination

In the previous section we have shown that low-standards equilibria are not inevitable. We have provided a precise characterization of circumstances in which high-standards equilibria can arise—for example combinations of logconvexity of demand and a small enough competitive fringe, or logconcavity of demand and a large enough competitive fringe. But low standards equilibria do arise, and in such cases an important question is whether welfare could be improved by both countries adopting high standards and whether such an outcome could be sustainable. This section considers, therefore, issues of welfare and coordination in standards.

Let us start by noting that in our model the small exporters always adopt low standards. If the small exporters as a group were to adopt high standards, they might benefit. But, by assumption, small exporters are too small individually to perceive any benefits from coordination. Our analysis will therefore focus on coordination between the big exporters. Suffice it to say that, when the big exporters adopt high standards, the small exporters benefit indirectly through the terms-of-trade gains.

There are two cases to consider in which both of the big exporters do not have high standards:—symmetric equilibria with $(-,-)$, and asymmetric equilibria with $(+,-)$ or $(-,+)$. We begin with the symmetric equilibria. The first question is whether either or both countries are better off with a $(+,+)$ outcome than with the actual outcome of $(-,-)$. Note from (19) that the gain to each country from both countries going to $(+,+)$, so that the number of workers in the world under the high standards regime goes from $\ell=0$ to $\ell=L$, is given by

$$\begin{aligned}\Delta^1(0,L) &= \Delta^2(0,L) = \Delta(0,L)\\ &= \log\frac{s^+}{\phi(s^+)} + (1-\alpha)[\log(p(X(L)))\log(p(X(0)))].\end{aligned} \tag{40}$$

In other words, if country 1 is better off when both countries switch from low to higher standards, country 2 must also be better off, regardless of the distribution of resources in the two countries. When, if at all, do the two countries benefit from coordinating on high standards? The answer depends on whether standards are substitutes or complements. Starting with complementarity, and recalling that in this case $\Delta^i(\ell^{-i},\ell^{-i}+L^i)$ is decreasing in L^0, it follows that

$$\begin{aligned}&0\leqslant \Delta^1(0,L)\\ \Leftrightarrow\ &0\leqslant \Delta^1\left(0,\frac{L}{2}+\delta\right) \quad \text{if } \delta=\frac{L}{2},\\ \Leftrightarrow\ &0\leqslant \Delta^1\left(\frac{L}{2}-\delta,L\right) \quad \text{if } \delta=\frac{L}{2},\\ \Leftrightarrow\ &L^0\leqslant \left\{L^0|\delta^1_-(L^0)=\delta^1_+(L^0)=\frac{L}{2}\right\}\equiv \bar{L}^0.\end{aligned}$$

L^0 thus denotes the critical level of labour endowment in small countries such that, for all $L^0\leqslant\bar{L}^0$, country 1 is strictly better off when both countries switch from low to high standards. By similar reasoning,

$$0\leqslant\Delta^2(0,L)\quad\Leftrightarrow L^0\geqslant\{L^0|\delta^2_+(L^0)=\delta^2_-(L^0)=-\frac{L}{2}\}\equiv\bar{L}^0.$$

$\bar{L}^0$ divides the (δ, L^0) space into two regions. For all $L^0\geqslant\bar{L}^0$, $\Delta^i(0,L)\leqslant 0$, $i=1$, 2, and $\Delta^i(0,L)>0$ otherwise. $\bar{L}^0$ is shown in Figure 8. Thus (δ, L^0)-combinations in all of regions B, C and I and a subset of region A guarantee welfare improvements for both countries whenever the two countries move from the low-standards equilibria in these regions to adopt high standards.

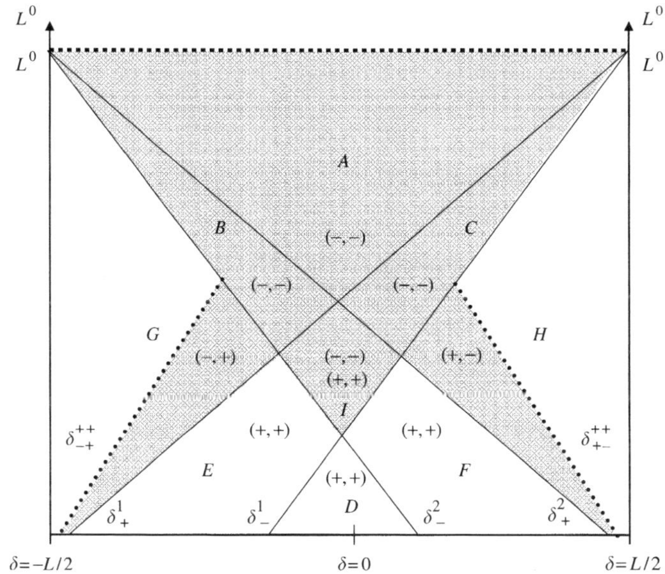

FIGURE 8. Areas of welfare improvement from joint adoption of high standards under complementarity.

Turning now to the case of substitutability, and using reasoning similar to above, we can define

$$\underline{L}^0 \equiv \left\{L^0|\delta^1_-(L^0) = \delta^1_+(L^0) = \frac{L}{2}\right\}, \text{ and } \underline{L}^0$$
$$\equiv \left\{L^0|\delta^2_+(L^0) = \delta^2_-(L^0) = -\frac{L}{2}\right\}.$$

Thus, $\underline{L}^0$ divides the (δ, L^0)-space into two regions, and, by virtue of strategic substitutability, $\Delta^i(0, L) < (\geqslant)0$ whenever $L^0 < (\geqslant)\underline{L}^0$. The possibility of a welfare gain when both countries switch from low to high standards is therefore assured whenever L^0 is larger than $\underline{L}^0$. $\underline{L}^0$ is shown in Figure 9. Thus, (δ, L^0)-combinations in all of region D guarantee welfare improvements for both countries whenever the two countries move from the low standards to high standards.

So much for symmetric low standards equilibria (− , −). What about asymmetric equilibria in which one of the two countries has a high standard and the other a low standard? Can a move from (+ , −) or (− , +) to (+ , +) lead to a welfare improvement? Clearly, such a move cannot lead to both countries being better off, since the country with the low standards in equilibrium prefers low standards when the other country has high standards. A Pareto improvement is thus ruled out. We can however consider a general utilitarian welfare function from (11):

$$
\begin{aligned}
W &= \sum_{i=1,2} V^i(p, s^i) \\
&= 2K + \sum_{i=1,2} \log \frac{s^i L^i}{\phi(s^i) a_1} + 2(1-\alpha) \log p(X(\ell)).
\end{aligned} \tag{41}
$$

Note once again that we are focusing attention on the joint welfare of the two big exporters—the small exporters will always benefit when the two big exporters adopt successively higher standards.

There are two cases to consider: $(-, +)$ and $(+, -)$. The welfare gain in moving from $(-, +)$ to $(+, +)$ is given by

$$
\begin{aligned}
\Delta_{-+}^{++} &= W^{++} - W^{-+} \\
&= \log \frac{s^+}{\phi(s^+)} + 2(1-\alpha) \left[\log p(X(L)) - \log p\left(X\left(\frac{L}{2} - \delta \right) \right) \right].
\end{aligned} \tag{42}
$$

Similarly, the welfare gain in moving from $(+, -)$ to $(+, +)$ is given by

$$
\begin{aligned}
\Delta_{+-}^{++} &= W^{++} - W^{+-} \\
&= \log \frac{s^+}{\phi(s^+)} + 2(1-\alpha) \left[\log p(X(L)) - \log p\left(X\left(\frac{L}{2} + \delta \right) \right) \right].
\end{aligned} \tag{43}
$$

Expressions (42) and (43) can be used to partition the (δ, L^0)-space into regions of welfare improvement in the two cases. As might be expected, the partitioning is different for the cases of complementarity and substitutability. Starting with complementarity, consider the locus

$$
\Delta_{-+}^{++} = 0 \Leftrightarrow \delta = \delta_{-+}^{++}(L^0). \tag{44}
$$

Above the locus, $\Delta_{-+}^{++} < 0$, and below it $\Delta_{-+}^{++} > 0$. Comparing (42) with (25), it is clear that with complementarity the locus $\delta_{-+}^{++}(L^0)$ will be upward sloping in (δ, L^0)-space and lie everywhere above the locus δ_+^1. Now consider the locus

$$
\Delta_{+-}^{++} \Leftrightarrow \delta = \delta_{+-}^{++}(L^0). \tag{45}
$$

Comparing (45) with (27) establishes that $\delta_{+-}^{++}(L^0)$ will be downward sloping and lie everywhere above the locus δ_+^2. Above the locus, $\Delta_{+-}^{++} < 0$, and below it $\Delta_{+-}^{++} > 0$.

The same analysis can be repeated for substitutability. In this case the locus $\delta_{-+}^{++}(L^0)$ will be downward sloping and lie everywhere below the locus δ_+^1, while $\delta_{+-}^{++}(L^0)$ will be upward sloping and lie everywhere below the locus δ_+^2. Moreover, above the loci there will be welfare improvement, below them a welfare decrease.

Putting together the analysis for the symmetric and asymmetric case, Figures 8 and 9 provide a complete characterization of when welfare improvement occurs in moving from $(-,-)$, $(+,-)$ or $(-,+)$ to the

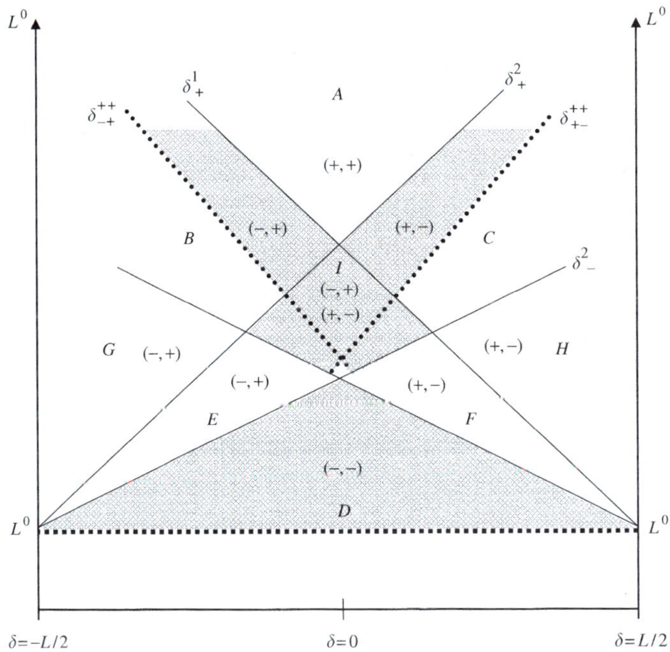

FIGURE 9. Areas of welfare improvement from joint adoption of high standards under substitutability

high-standards outcome (+ , +), respectively, for the case of complementarity and substitutability. The shaded areas give us (δ, L^0)-combinations where such improvements are possible; note that when the starting equilibrium is symmetric (− , −) the welfare improvement is moreover a Pareto improvement.

Looking at Figures 8 and 9, the role of L^0 and δ in determining whether a welfare improvement is possible in moving from low to high standards should be clear. Consider the regions *A*, *H*, *G*, *B*, *C* and *I* in Figure 8 (the low-standards regions under complementarity); starting from any point in these regions, for given L^0, a move of δ closer to 0 increases (or does not decrease) the likelihood of getting to an area where welfare improvement is possible as a result of high-standards adoption by both countries. The same is true of regions *D*, *E*, *F*, *G*, *H*, *B*, *C* and *I* in Figure 9 (the low-standards regions under substitutability). These observations prompt the following proposition.

Proposition 7. Starting from an equilibrium in which at least one country has low standards, the joint adoption of high standards is more likely to improve joint welfare the more equal the two countries are in size.

Where Proposition 5 shows that greater disparity in size is more likely to lead to an equilibrium in which one of the countries has high standards and the other low standards, Proposition 7 argues that greater disparity also makes it more unlikely that adoption of common high standards will lead to a welfare improvement.

Now consider variations in L^0. Starting from any point in region A, H, G, B, C, or I in Figure 8, a decrease in L^0 that leaves the countries in the same region increases (or does not decrease) the likelihood of their getting into an area where joint high standards lead to a joint welfare improvement. However, in Figure 9, starting from any point in regions D, E, F, G, H, B, C or I, an increase in L^0 that leaves the countries in the same region increases (or does not decrease) the likelihood of their getting into an area of joint welfare improvement through joint high standards. These observations lead to the following proposition.

Proposition 8. Starting from an equilibrium in which at least one country has low standards, joint adoption of high standards is more likely to lead to a joint improvement of welfare in the big exporters if (i) the competitive fringe gets a little smaller in the case of logconvex demand, or (ii) the competitive fringe gets a little larger in the case of logconcave demand.

Proposition 8 brings out the interaction between the nature of Northern demand and the size of Southern small exporters as a group, in determining the benefits from coordination to the big exporters. When the shape of the Northern demand curve makes Southern standards complements, a decrease in the relative weight of the small (low-standards) exporters increases the benefits of coordinating on high standards. But when the shape of the Northern demand curve makes Southern standards substitutes, the opposite is the case. Once again, this highlights the importance of getting good empirical estimates of the curvature of the demand curve for specific commodities.

In each of the shaded areas in Figures 8 and 9, the Nash equilibrium outcome is welfare-dominated by a coordinated outcome with high standards in both countries. But can this coordinated outcome itself be sustained? Clearly, it cannot be sustained as a static Nash equilibrium. But it is well known that coordinated outcomes can sometimes be sustained in the context of repeated games where deviation from the coordinated outcome is punished appropriately. We focus on a game structure where, if both countries cooperate and adopt high standards up to time t, each country adopts high standards; otherwise, each country adopts the pure Nash equilibrium standard. With multiple pure strategy equilibria, we allow for any one of the pure strategy equilibria to be chosen. As always, small exporters stick to low standards.

The discounted welfare of country i over the infinite horizon is given by

$$\sum_{t=0}^{\infty} r^t V^i,$$

where $0<r<1$ is the common subjective discount factor. We look for the conditions under which there is a subgame-perfect Nash equilibrium that supports $q^1 = q^2 = 1$, given the static Nash equilibrium choices of standards elaborated in Section IV.

Let us start with asymmetric Nash equilibria. Suppose we have $(-,+)$. Then deviation from $(+,+)$ by country 1 to the lower standard will certainly increase its welfare in the period of deviation. By the hypothesis of Nash reversion, in the period after the deviation the countries play $(-,+)$ as strategies, but this is the same as the outcome in the period of deviation. Country 1 therefore always benefits from deviation and $(+,+)$ cannot be sustained as a subgame-perfect Nash equilibrium when $(-,+)$ is the asymmetric Nash equilibrium. A similar argument holds for the case when $(+,-)$ is a Nash equilibrium. We thus have the following proposition.

Proposition 9. When the size of the competitive fringe and the relative sizes of the big exporters are such as to produce an asymmetric equilibrium in standards, the joint high-standards outcome cannot be sustained as a subgame-perfect Nash equilibrium (under conventional assumptions) even when it leads to higher joint welfare.

Consider now symmetric equilibria $(-,-)$ and the prospects for cooperating to achieve $(+,+)$. Starting from $(+,+)$ if country i deviates its change in welfare in the deviation period is simply $-\Delta^i_+$, $i = 1, 2$, that is, minus the gain from adopting the high standard when the other country sticks to the high standard. In subsequent periods, the loss to the deviating country is the welfare loss from being at a $(-,-)$ rather that a $(+,+)$ outcome.

From (40), this is simply $\Delta(0, L)$ for the two countries. Thus, country i will not deviate from $(+,+)$ if

$$-\Delta^i_+ - \frac{r}{1-r}\Delta(0, L) < 0.$$

Using the fact, from (25), (27) and (40), that $\Delta^i_+ < \Delta(0, L)$, this can be rewritten as

$$(46) \qquad r > \hat{r}^i = \frac{\Delta^i_+}{\Delta^i_+ - \Delta^i(0, L)}.$$

It follows that

$$(47) \qquad r > \max\{\hat{r}^1, \hat{r}^2\}$$

ensures that neither country deviates from the $(+,+)$ outcome. Now, notice that at $\delta = 0$, $\Delta^1_+ = \Delta^2_+$, and therefore $\hat{r}^1 = \hat{r}^2$. A small change in δ starting from zero introduces a gap between $\hat{r}^1$ and $\hat{r}^2$ and therefore reduces the range of r in (47) which allows the dynamic equilibrium to be sustained. In fact, it can be shown that the gap between Δ^1_+ and Δ^2_+, increases monotonically in δ, so this range of r is reduced as δ goes further and further away from zero. These observations lead to the following proposition.

Proposition 10. When the size of the competitive fringe and the relative size of the big exporters are such as to produce a symmetric low-standards equilibrium, a welfare-improving joint high-standards outcome can be sustained as a dynamic equilibrium (under conventional assumptions) provided that countries are patient enough. As the two big exporters become more asymmetric in size, the permissible range of patience shrinks, making it less likely that the joint high standards outcome can be sustained.

Propositions 9 and 10 highlight the damaging impact that size asymmetry between the two big exporters can have on the possibility of sustaining a high-standards outcome. Starting from equality, and assuming the weight of the competitive fringe to be such that there is a symmetric low-standards equilibrium, Proposition 10 shows that as the disparity grows the range of patience required to sustain the welfare-improving high-standards outcome shrinks, making it less likely. Beyond a certain point, the disparity is so great that there is an asymmetric-standards equilibrium. But then, from Proposition 9, the joint high-standards outcome is not sustainable at all, even when it would improve joint welfare.

V. Northern Protectionism and Southern Standards

The question of whether Northern trade protectionism could or should protect Northern standards is at the heart of the current controversies on globalization. But, whatever its impact on Northern standards, does Northern protection protect Southern standards, or does it undermine them? Does it put a floor under a Southern race to the bottom, or does it accelerate the race?

The model and analysis developed so far can be put to further work to answer these questions. Let t be a specific tariff levied by the North on the exports of the South. Recalling that the Northern inverse import demand function is $p(X, R^*)$, where R^* is the Northern revenue function, with a specific tariff t the new terms of trade are given by

$$p(X(\ell), R^* + tX(\ell)) - t,$$

where $X(\ell)$ is Southern exports as a function of ℓ, the number of Southern workers under the high-standards regime. It is easy to check from (15) that Southern exports are unaffected by the tariff.

With the tariff in place, the incentives for country i to adopt high standards, the analogous expression to (19), is now given by

$$\begin{aligned}\Delta^1(\ell^{-i}, \ell^{-i} + L^i, t) = \log\frac{s^+}{\phi(s^+)} &+ (1-\alpha)[\log(p(X(\ell^{-i} + L^i), R^* \\ &+ tX(\ell^{-i} + L^i)) - t) \\ &- \log(p(X(\ell^{-i}), R^* + tX(\ell^{-i})) - t)],\end{aligned} \tag{48}$$

and therefore

$$\frac{\partial\Delta^i(\ell^{-i}, \ell^i + L^i)}{\partial t} = (1-\alpha)\left[\frac{m(\ell^{-i} + L^i) - 1}{p(\ell^{-i} + L^i) - t} - \frac{m(\ell^{-i}) - 1}{p(\ell^{-i}) - t}\right], \tag{49}$$

where

$$(50) \qquad m(X(\ell)) = \frac{\partial(pX(\ell))}{\partial R*}$$

is the marginal propensity to import in the North. We make the following standard assumption.

Assumption 2. The Northern propensity to import as its income increases is less than one and decreasing in total imports.

With this assumption, it follows immediately from (49) that $\partial\Delta^i/\partial t > 0$. In other words, a Northern tariff increases Southern incentives to adopt high standards.

To see the intuition here, note that the marginal export revenue of country i is given by $p_x(X(\ell))X^i + p(X) - t$; that is, marginal export revenue decreases one-for-one with the import tariff. Thus, the extent of export revenue gains that can be achieved by expanding exports is lower, the higher is the import tariff, regardless of whether standards are strategic complements or substitutes. In addition, import restrictions also generate an income effect, via the tariff revenue. In particular, the income effect reinforces incentives to raise standards (lower exports), so long as the marginal propensity to consume is decreasing in total exports.

Since a tariff increases the incentives to adopt high standards, it might be expected that the likelihood of low standards equilibria would increase. In Figure 6, the loci δ^1_+, δ^1_-, δ^2_+ and δ^2_- all shift upwards. The effect on the size of regions G and H (the regions of asymmetric equilibria) is ambiguous. Region I contracts, but both $(+, +)$ and $(-, -)$ equilibria are possible here. However, regions A, B and C (low standards) contract and regions D, E and F (high standards) expand. In Figure 7 the loci δ^1_+, δ^1_-, δ^2_+ and δ^2_- all shift downwards. Thus, region D in this figure (the region of low standards in both countries) contracts and region A (the region of high standards) expands. It is in this sense, i.e. the expansion of $(+, +)$ regions and the contraction of $(-, -)$ regions, that an import tariff makes the emergence of high standards more likely.

Moreover, from (46),

$$(51) \qquad \frac{\partial \hat{r}^i}{\partial t} = \frac{1}{\Delta^i_+ - \Delta^i(0, L)}\left((1 - \hat{r}^i)\frac{\partial \Delta^i_+}{\partial t} + \hat{r}^i\frac{\partial \Delta^i(0, L)}{\partial t}\right) < 0$$

since $\Delta^i_+ - \Delta^i(0, L) < 0$ and

$$\frac{\partial \Delta^i_+}{\partial t} > 0 \text{ and } \frac{\partial \Delta^i(0, L)}{\partial t} > 0,$$

from (49) and Assumption 2. In other words, using Proposition 10, a sustainable welfare-improving joint high-standards outcome becomes more likely, in the sense that the range of r for which this occurs is expanded.

It would appear, then, that Northern protectionism aids the emergence of high standards in the South. However, the implicit assumption in the previous analysis is that the importing country will not further vary t, once the standard choices of the two large exporters are made. But this is not entirely credible. We might expect the North to set its tariff optimally, given the outcomes in the South. In particular, consider the following scenario. The importing and exporting countries play a two-stage game. In the first stage exporting countries compete in setting standards. In the second stage the importing country has the liberty to maximize the national welfare by selecting an optimal import tariff, taking into account Southern choices. What happens in this case?

Beginning with the second-stage, recall from (7) and (5) that aggregate export supply is a step function, with

$$(52)\qquad X(\ell) = \begin{cases} 0 & \text{if } p < a_1/a_2, \\ [0, (1-\alpha)[L^0 + L + \ell(1/\phi - 1)]/a_1] & \text{if } p = a_1/a_2, \\ (1-\alpha)[L^0 + L + \ell(1/\phi - 1)]/a_1 & \text{otherwise.} \end{cases}$$

Let the optimal import tariff be $t(p, \ell)$, where p is the market-clearing world price of good 1. Thus, as long as a positive amount of trade takes place between the two countries,

$$(53)\qquad t(p, \ell) = \begin{cases} 0 & \text{if } p = a_1/a_2, \\ p(\ell) - a_1/a_2 & \text{if } p > a_1/a_2, \end{cases}$$

corresponding respectively to the perfectly elastic and perfectly inelastic segments of the export supply curve. It follows, therefore, that the terms of trade that the two exporting countries can anticipate, given ℓ, is just $p(\ell) - t(p, \ell)$.

Turning to the first-stage problem of the two large countries, the gain to country i ($i = 1, 2$) from adopting the high standard with probability q^i, $EV^{i+} - EV^{i-}$, is

$$\log\frac{s^i L^i}{\phi(s^+)a_1} + (1-\alpha)q^i\left[q^j \log(p(L) - t(p, L)) + (1 - q^j)\log\left(p(L) - t(p, L^i)\right)\right]$$

$$-\log\frac{L^i}{a_1} + (1-\alpha)(1-q^i)\left[q^j \log\left(p(L^j) - t(p, L^j)\right) + (1-q^j)\log(p(0) - t(p, 0))\right],$$

where q^j is the probability that country j ($i \neq j$) will adopt the high standard and $t(p, \ell)$ is the Northern tariff. Using (53), the gain from adopting the high standard becomes

$$EV^{i+} - EV^{i-} = \log\frac{s^+}{\phi(s^+)} < 0.$$

We therefore have the remarkable result that in this case all incentives to adopt the high standard are removed. It follows that the only possible equilibria are low standards for all in the South.

Whether Northern protectionism protects or undermines Southern standards is therefore a subtle matter. We summarize our analysis in the following proposition.[7]

Proposition 11. When Southern standards are set after Northern tariffs are imposed, Northern protectionism makes high-standards equilibria more likely, and coordination on high standards more likely to be sustainable. But when

Northern tariffs are chosen optimally after Southern standards are set, the choice of these tariffs will be such as to totally eliminate high-standards equilibria in the South.

If Northern tariffs are set optimally in the Northern interest, therefore, they are no friend of Southern standards. In this case, far from protecting them, Northern protectionism undermines Southern standards.

VI. Conclusion

Let us return to the three questions posed at the start of this paper. Does Chinese trade competition pose a threat to environmental and labour standards in India, and vice versa? Propositions 5, 7 and 9 clarify the sense in which this might be the case. The equilibrium outcome and welfare consequences depend on the size of the exporters relative to each other. Proposition 5 says that, as one country becomes relatively large, it is that country which is more likely to adopt high standards.

Proposition 7 tells us that the greater the disparity in size, the more unlikely it is that the joint adoption of high standards will lead to an improvement in joint welfare; and Proposition 9 concludes that it is less likely that the joint high-standards outcome can be sustained as a dynamic equilibrium. The answer to the question depends entirely, therefore, on the relative size of 'China and India'. The bigger country will tend to have higher standards, but asymmetry in size is more likely to lead to outcomes detrimental to joint welfare.

Are standards in India and China pulled down by standards in small countries such as Myanmar, Honduras or South Africa? Proposition 1 tells us that the competitive fringe of small exporters always adopt low standards. But do these act as a drag on big exporters' standards? Proposition 6 says that the answer depends on very specific properties of the Northern demand curve. In a general sense, a larger competitive fringe of small exporters is detrimental to standards of the big exporters if standards are complements, but is beneficial if they are substitutes.

In the specific model, this depends on whether the Northern demand curve is logconvex or logconcave. More generally, it depends on the curvature of the demand curve. A larger competitive fringe is also less likely to lead to situations where joint adoption of high standards by the big exporters will lead to (i) an increase in joint welfare if demand is logconvex, and (ii) a decrease in joint welfare if demand is logconcave (Proposition 8). That central properties on equilibrium outcomes and welfare should depend on such specific properties of the demand curve is in one sense no surprise. But what this does is to highlight the need for empirical work on parameterizing and estimating the curvature of commodity-specific Northern import demand functions. Also important, so long as a detailed account of these properties of the import demand function is yet to be had, the presumption of a 'race to the bottom' in standards should likewise treated as suspect.

Does trade protectionism in the United States protect standards in developing countries, or does it undermine them? Proposition 11 provides a surprisingly sharp, but intuitively clear, answer to this question. When

Southern standards are set after Northern tariffs, these tariffs aid the adoption of high standards because they reduce the potential revenue gain to any Southern country from undercutting standards to increase exports. However, if Northern tariffs are chosen after Southern standards are set, and moreover are chosen optimally to advance Northern interests, then the situation is completely reversed: all incentive to set high standards in the South is creamed off by the optimal tariff. Since the more likely scenario is that the North will choose Northern tariffs in the Northern interest, we reach our final conclusion: Northern protection undermines Southern standards.

The model we have developed is rich enough to allow certain key questions to be posed, but simple enough to allow specific answers to be given and intuitions to be further sharpened. Clearly, the direct applicability of the model is limited by its special assumptions. But it does suggest areas for empirical research. For example, it calls for an investigation of the correlation between market share in exports and standards, the estimation of demand curvature for developing country exports and the connection between tariffs in the importing country and standards in the exporting country. Further research is called for not only in testing the robustness of our theoretical results in more general models, but also in empirical investigations of export competition and standards in developing countries.

ACKNOWLEDGMENTS

We thank Raji Jayaraman for research assistance in the preparation of this paper. We also thank Kaushik Basu, Gary Fields, Henry Wan, an anonymous referee and seminar participants at Cornell University and the University of Edinburgh for helpful comments.

NOTES

1. Some recent contributions on labour standards are Ehrenberg (1994), Bhagwati (1996), Brown *et al.* (1996), Kuruvilla (1996), OECD (1996), Rodrik (1996), Krueger (1997), Krugman (1997), Mah (1997), Maskus (1997), Bagwell and Staiger (1998), Srinivasan (1998), Brown (2000). See Nordstrom and Vaughan (2000) for an excellent survey on the literature on environmental standards. Kanbur *et al.* (1995) and Wilson (1996) examine the possibility of a race to the bottom in environmental regulations when capital is internationally mobile. Basu and Chau (2001) analyse the race to the top in environmental standards in the presence of green consumerism.
2. Bagwell and Staiger (2001) point out that an import tariff and a lower labour standard are, in a specific sense, policy substitutes, as the former raises the price of imports while the latter lowers labour costs. Both policies thus provide relief to import-competing sectors by putting downward pressure on world prices by, respectively, reducing import demand, and raising domestic supply. The question posed in our analysis differs, and seeks instead to unveil how Northern tariffs affect the incentive of Southern countries to adopt high standards, in the absence of international negotiations specifically targeting labour standards and trade policies.
3. Without a doubt, standards are multifaceted (Fields 2000). Brown *et al.* (1996) point out that most labour standards are labour-using, and effectively reduce the labour endowment of the country imposing the standard. In our model these production effects of higher standards are subsumed under the term $\phi(s^i)$.
4. One might further argue that, like labour standards, an export tax may similarly influence the terms of trade. Unlike labour standards in (19), however, an export tax additionally generates costly allocative inefficiency by distorting consumption decisions. Thus, the larger the anticipated degree of (import) consumption distortion, the smaller will be the scope for such a tax, even when optimally set, to raise the country's welfare. Our analysis can thus be viewed as one in which either (i) the use of trade policy instruments is bound, by, say, a trade agreement, or (ii) the exporting countries in question are highly import dependent, and the

income share of import consumption $(1 - \alpha)$ is sufficiently large. We are grateful to an anonymous referee and an associate editor for pointing this out to us.

5. The discussion here is closely related to that of strategic complementarity and substitutability as in Bulow *et al.* (1985).
6. The basic thrust of the propositions of this paper is unaltered if we consider not L^0 but the share $L^0/(L^0 + L^1 + L^2)$.
7. It can be shown that the thrust of the proposition holds also for the case of an *ad valorem* tariff.

REFERENCES

BAGWELL, K. and STAIGER, R. W. (1998). The simple economics of labour standards and the GATT. In A. V. Deardorff and R. M. Stern (eds.), *Social Dimensions of US Trade Policies*. Ann Arbor: University of Michigan Press, pp. 195–231.

——— and ——— (2001). Domestic policies, national sovereignty, and international economic institutions. *Quarterly Journal of Economics*, **111**, 519–62.

BASU, K. (1999). International labour standards and child labour. *Challenge*, September–October, 80–93.

BASU, A. K. and CHAU, N. H. (2001). *Market Access Rivalry and Eco-Labeling Standards: Are Eco-Labels Non-Tariff Barriers in Disguise?* Department of Applied Economics and Management, Cornell University Working paper 2001–15.

BHAGWATI, J. (1996). The demands to reduce domestic diversity among trading nations. In J. Bhagwati and R. Hudec (eds.), *Fair Trade and Harmonization: Prerequisites for Free Trade?*, Vol. 1, Cambridge, Mass.: MIT Press.

BROWN, D. K. (2000). *International Trade and Core Labour Standards: A Survey of Recent Literature*. OECD Occasional Papers, WD(2000) 4. Paris: OECD.

———, DEARDORFF, A. V. and STERN, R. M. (1996). International labour standards and trade: a theoretical analysis. In J. Bhagwati and R. Hudec (eds.), *Harmonization and Fair Trade: Prerequisites for Free Trade?* Cambridge, Mass.: MIT Press.

BULOW, J. I., GEANAKOPLOS, J. D. and KLEMPERER, P. D. (1985). Multimarket oligopoly: strategic substitutes and complements. *Journal of Political Economy*, **93**, 488–511.

EHRENBERG, R. (1994). *Labour Markets and Integrating National Economies*. Washington, DC: Brookings Institution.

FIELDS, G. S. (2000). The role of labour standards in US trade policies. In A. V. Deardorff and R. M. Stern (eds.), *Social Dimensions of US Trade Policies*. Ann Arbor: University of Michigan Press, pp. 167–88.

KAHN, J. (2000). Multinationals sign un pact on rights and environment. *New York Times*, 27 July.

KANBUR, R., KEEN, M. and VAN WIJNBERGEN, S. (1995). Industrial competitiveness, environmental regulations and direct foreign investment. In I. Goldin and L. A. Winters (eds.), *The Economics of Sustainable Development*. Cambridge: Cambridge University Press.

KRUEGER, A. (1997). Observations on international labour standards and trade. In *Proceedings of the World Bank Annual Conference on Development Economics* 1996. Washington, DC: World Bank, pp. 281–302.

KRUGMAN, P. R. (1997). What should trade negotiators negotiate about? *Journal of Economic Literature*, **35**, 113–20.

KURUVILLA, S. (1996). Linkages between industrialization strategies and industrial relations/human resource policies: Singapore, Malaysia, the Philippines and India. *Industrial and Labour Relations Review*, **49**, 635–57.

MAH, J. S. (1997). Core labour standards and export performance in developing countries. *World Economy*, **20**, 773–85.

MASKUS, K. (1997). *Should Core Labour Standards be Imposed through International Trade Policy?* World Bank Policy Research Working Paper no. 1817.

NORDSTROM, H. and VAUGHAN, S. (2000). *Trade and Environment*. WTO Special Studies 4. Geneva: WTO Publications.

OECD (1996). *Trade, Employment and Labour Standards: A Study of Core Workers' Rights and International Trade*. Paris: OECD.

RODRIK, D. (1996). Labour standards in international trade: do they matter and what do we do about them? In R. Z. Lawrence, D. Rodrik and J. Whalley (eds.), *Emerging Agenda for Global*

Trade: High States for Developing Countries. Overseas Development Council Essay No. 20. Baltimore: Johns Hopkins University Press.

ROLLO, J. and WINTERS, A. L. (2000). Subsidiarity and governance challenges for the WTO: environmental and labour standards. *World Economy*, **23**, 561–76.

SRINIVASAN, T. N. (1998). Trade and human rights. In A. V. Deardorff and R. M. Stern (eds.), *Constituent Interests and US Trade Policies*. Ann Arbor: University of Michigan Press, pp. 225–53.

WILSON, J. D. (1996). Capital mobility and environmental standards: is there a theoretical basis for a race to the bottom? In J. N. Bhagwati and R. E. Hudec (eds.), *Fair Trade and Harmonization*, Vol. 1, Cambridge Mass.: MIT Press, pp. 393–472.

WTO (1998). *World Trade Organization Annual Report*. Washington, DC: WTO.

UNCTAD (2000). Trade analysis and information system. At http://www.leman.com/~kuwahara/services.htm.

NANCY H. CHAU
Cornell University
RAVI KANBUR
Cornell University

The Adoption of International Labor Standards Conventions: Who, When, and Why?

In the empirical literature on labor standards and economic performance, the adoption of international labor standards is measured by the ratification of International Labor Organization (ILO) conventions and is treated as an exogenous variable that explains labor costs, growth, exports, or inward foreign direct investment. For example, OECD attempts to relate aggregate and labor intensive exports to the ratification of ILO conventions.[1] No relationship is found, which is interpreted by some as suggesting that there are no economic costs to the adoption of labor standards. But Mah, who also investigates the role of labor standards on export performance, finds a negative association between the ratification of certain "core" ILO conventions and performance.[2] Rodrik tries to explain manufacturing labor costs and finds that the number of conventions ratified is statistically significant.[3] Palley finds a positive association between economic growth and the ratification of the Freedom of Association Convention.[4] But Rama argues that the number of ILO conventions ratified is not significant as a determinant of growth performance in Latin America.[5]

Throughout this empirical literature, therefore, the ratification of ILO conventions is assumed to provide information on labor standards adopted and

The authors thank Leonid Fedorov and Raji Jayaraman for research assistance in the preparation of this paper. We also thank Kaushik Basu, Susan Collins, Kim Elliot, Ann Harrison, Gary Fields, Peter Morici, Kevin O'Rourke, Dave Richardson, Dani Rodrik, and Dan Tarullo for helpful comments.

1. OECD (1996).
2. Mah (1997).
3. Rodrik (1996).
4. Palley (1999).
5. Rama (1995).

Table 1. Core ILO Conventions and Dates of Entry into Force

Freedom of Association and the Right to Collectively Bargain	
	Freedom of Association and the Protection of the Right to Organize Convention, 1950 (Convention 87)
	Right to Organize and Collective Bargaining Convention, 1951 (Convention 98)
The Elimination of Forced and Compulsory Labor	
	Forced Labor Convention, 1932 (Convention 29)
	Abolition of Forced Labor Convention, 1959 (Convention 105)
The Elimination of Employment Discrimination	
	Equal Remuneration Convention, 1953 (Convention 100)
	Discrimination (Employment and Occupation) Convention, 1960 (Convention 111)
The Abolition of Child Labor	
	Minimum Age Convention, 1976 (Convention 138)
	Worst Forms of Child Labor Convention, 2000 (Convention 182)

Source: ILO (2001).

implemented in a country. This paper's object is to investigate the determinants of ratification directly and, indirectly, the determinants of labor standards. It presents an empirical analysis of the time patterns and determinants of ratification. Despite the relative lack of emphasis on enforcement and punishments associated with these conventions, we find evidence suggesting a process of self-selection and matching in which the probability of ratification depends on country characteristics. For example, we find that peer effects are in play. For some conventions the probability of ratification depends on how many other countries in a peer group have already ratified that convention.

The following section of this paper introduces the ILO core conventions that are the focus of interest, presents basic data on their ratification, and begins the discussion on basic time patterns in ratification. Next, the paper develops an analytical framework for the empirical analysis by considering the ratification decision and its determinants. This is followed by econometric results and a conclusion.

ILO Core Conventions: Who Ratifies and When

ILO conventions are international treaties, subject to ratification by member states. There are now more than 180 conventions on a wide array of subjects. But the ILO itself has established a set of core labor standards. These standards are laid out in the ILO Declaration on Fundamental Principles and Rights at Work under four main headings, as shown in table 1.[6] These constitute the eight fundamental conventions of the ILO.

6. See www.ilo.org/public/english/standards/decl/declaration/index.htm.

However, the decision to ratify any of these conventions remains the right of each member nation, and it reflects willingness on the part of the ratifying country to enact legislation, and put in place mechanisms that facilitate implementation in practice. On the part of the ILO, three types of mechanisms are in place to ensure compliance. First, systems of supervision are in place to improve transparency and to oversee compliance.[7] A second component of ILO activities that facilitates improvements of labor standards takes the form of technical assistance and financial support, especially for the poorest countries. Finally, in cases of violation where recommendations are not responded to, Article 33 of the ILO constitution provides that the ILO Governing Body may recommend "action as it may deem wise and expedient to secure compliance therewith" against the violating country.

These mechanisms outline the extent to which there may be explicit costs and benefits associated with ratifying ILO conventions. But what is repeatedly stressed in policy and popular writings is that sanctions against noncomplying members have very rarely been invoked. And it is generally agreed that the ILO lacks "teeth" to enforce implementation of conventions that have been ratified.[8] Allegations have also been raised regarding the ILO supervisory system.[9] In particular, as measures against violating countries are typically based either on complaints by employers and union representatives, or reports from the country in question, violations in countries that forbid union complaints, or are late in complying with reporting requirements, face the risk of remaining undetected.[10]

However, if it were true that countries faced no costs whatsoever (explicit or implicit) of complying, one might expect all countries to ratify every convention, assuming even a minuscule benefit of signing on. At least we would

7. See Elliot (2001) for an in-depth discussion of the three basic tools—referred to therein as "sunshine," "carrots," and "sticks" employed to enforce labor standards by the ILO.

8. In a recent high profile case, the governing body of the ILO invoked Article 33 (Failure to carry out recommendation of the Commission of Inquiry or International Court of Justice) in November 2000 for the very first time, and approved a resolution in condemnation of the government of Myanmar. The resolution condemned Myanmar's failure to comply with Convention 29 (forced labor convention), and the country's failure to take actions in response to the recommendation of the Commission of Inquiry regarding the use of forced labor. But the unusualness of this illustrates the lack of explicit enforcement of the ILO conventions.

9. Charnovitz (1997).

10. The question of whether the ILO is the most appropriate international organization to promote and protect labor standards remains a heated debate. See, for example, Cappuyns (1998), Charny (2001), and Srinivasan (1998) for discussions on the relative merit of the World Trade Organization—endowed with the authority to employ trade related punitive measures—and the ILO in enforcing international core labor standards.

not expect any systematic connection between ratification and actual domestic standards, in which case the common use of ratification data in the empirical literature on labor standards would be questioned.

This paper will show that there are indeed systematic determinants of ratification for some conventions, and that for these conventions there is evidence to suggest that ratification of an international standard is an indicator of the domestic level of that standard. But that will come in subsequent sections. As a buildup to that analysis we consider now the broad time patterns of ratification of four selected core conventions—one from each category in table 1. Of the eight core conventions, the last one, on Worst Forms of Child Labor, 2000 (Convention 182, henceforth C182), is too recent to provide useful information on time patterns of ratification, so we choose C138 from the last category. The economic data used in the Empirical Framework and Results section of this paper go back to 1950 and cannot cover the early period of the Forced Labor Convention, 1932 (C29), so we choose C105 from the second category. Of the other two categories, we choose the later conventions. This gives us C98 (Right to Organize), C105 (Abolition of Forced Labor), C111 (Discrimination), and C138 (Minimum Age) as the four core conventions that are the focus of this study.

Table 2 lists ratification dates for each convention from the ILOLEX database, and date of independence where relevant for the ninety-four countries in our data set.[11] Table 2 shows some interesting features. For example, the United States and Canada have not signed the Right to Organize Convention. In fact the United States has only signed one of the four conventions listed. European countries were early signatories to the Right to Organize Convention, except Switzerland, which waited till 1999. In general there seems to be a fair amount of variation in who ratified which convention and when.

Figure 1 plots frequency distributions of ratification by year of ratification. For C98, C105, and C111 the peak frequency comes near the start, while for C138 the frequency is low and constant in the first two decades. For all four conventions, there was clearly a surge of ratification from the second half of the 1990s onwards. As elaborated in ILO (2000), this might be attributed to the ILO campaign launched in May 1995 following the World Summit on Social Development.[12] Another development since 1995 with a similarly "supply-side" orientation was the declaration of the WTO Ministerial Conference in Singapore in 1996, which underscored the commitment of participating

11. ILO (2001).
12. ILO (2001).

Table 2. Ratification of ILO Core Conventions

Country	Convention C98[a] (1951)	C111[b] (1960)	C105[c] (1959)	C138[d] (1976)	Developing[e]	Independence	Legal origin	Exports[f]
Algeria	1962	1969	1969	1984	X	1962	French	Fuel
Austria	1951	1973	1958	2000		...	German	Diversified
Bangladesh	1972	1972	1972	N.R.	X	1971	British	Diversified
Belgium	1953	1977	1961	1988		...	French	Diversified
Benin	1968	1961	1961	1997	X	1960	British	Services
Bolivia	1973	1977	1990	1993	X	...	French	Primary
Botswana	1997	1997	1997	1997	X	1966	French	Primary
Brazil	1952	1965	1965	N.R.	X	...	French	Diversified
Cameroon	1962	1988	1962	N.R.	X	1960	French	Diversified
Canada	N.R.	1964	1959	N.R.		...	British	Manufactures
Central African Republic	1964	1964	1964	1999	X	1960	French	Diversified
Chad	1961	1966	1961	N.R.	X	1960	French	Primary
Chile	1999	1971	1999	1999	X	...	French	Primary
China	N.R.	N.R.	N.R.	1999	X	...	Socialist	Manufactures
Colombia	1976	1969	1963	2001	X	...	French	Diversified
Congo	1999	1999	1999	1999	X	1960	French	Primary
Costa Rica	1960	1962	1959	1976	X	...	French	Diversified
Denmark	1955	1960	1958	1999		...	Scandinavian	Diversified
Dominican Republic	1953	1964	1958	2000	X	...	French	Services
Ecuador	1959	1962	1962	1999	X	...	French	Diversified
Egypt	1954	1960	1958	1999	X	...	French	Services
El Salvador	N.R.	1995	1958	1996	X	...	French	Services
Ethiopia	1963	1966	1999	1999	X	...	French	Primary
Fiji	1974	N.R.	1974	N.R.	X	1970	French	Services
Finland	1951	1970	1960	1976		...	Scandinavian	Manufactures
France	1951	1981	1969	1990		...	French	Diversified

Table 2. Ratification of ILO Core Conventions (continued)

	Convention							
Country	*C98*[a] *(1951)*	*C111*[b] *(1960)*	*C105*[c] *(1959)*	*C138*[d] *(1976)*	*Developing*[e]	*Independence*	*Legal origin*	*Exports*[f]
Gabon	1961	1961	1961	N.R.	X	1960	French	Fuel
Gambia	2000	2000	N.R.	N.R.	X	1965	French	Services
Germany, West	1956	1961	1959	1976		...	German	Manufactures
Guatemala	1952	1960	1959	1990	X	...	French	Primary
Guinea-Bissau	1977	1977	1977	N.R.	X	1973	French	Primary
Guyana	1966	1975	1966	1998	X	1966	French	Primary
Honduras	1956	1960	1958	1980	X	...	French	Primary
India	N.R.	1960	2000	N.R.	X	...	British	Diversified
Iran	N.R.	1964	1959	N.R.	X	1979	French	Fuel
Ireland	1955	1999	1958	1978		...	British	Manufactures
Israel	1957	1959	1958	1979		...	British	Manufactures
Italy	1958	1963	1968	1981		...	French	Manufactures
Jamaica	1962	1975	1962	N.R.	X	1962	French	Services
Japan	1953	N.R.	N.R.	2000		...	German	Manufactures
Jordan	1968	1963	1958	1998	X	...	French	Services
Kenya	1964	N.R.	1964	1979	X	1963	French	Diversified
Korea, Republic of	N.R.	1998	N.R.	1999	X	...	German	Manufactures
Lesotho	1966	1998	N.R.	N.R.	X	1966	Socialist	Services
Madagascar	1998	1961	N.R.	2000	X	1960	French	Primary
Malawi	1965	1965	1999	1997	X	1964	French	Primary
Malaysia	1961	N.R.	N.R.	1997	X	1957	British	Diversified
Mali	1964	1964	1962	N.R.	X	1960	British	Primary
Mauritania	N.R.	1963	1997	N.R.	X	1960	French	Primary
Mauritius	1969	N.R.	1969	1990	X	1968	French	Diversified
Mexico	N.R.	1961	1959	N.R.	X	...	French	Diversified
Morocco	1957	1963	1966	2000	X	1956	Socialist	Diversified

Table 2. Ratification of ILO Core Conventions (continued)

Country	Convention C98[c] (1951)	C111[b] (1960)	C105[c] (1959)	C138[d] (1976)	Developing[e]	Independence	Legal origin	Exports[f]
Mozambique	1996	1977	1977	N.R.	X	1975	French	Diversified
Myanmar	N.R.	N.R.	N.R.	N.R.	X	...	Socialist	Primary
Nepal	1996	1974	N.R.	1997	X	...	British	Services
Netherlands	1993	1973	1959	1976		...	French	Diversified
New Zealand	N.R.	1983	1968	N.R.		...	British	Primary
Nicaragua	1967	1967	1967	1981	X	...	French	Primary
Niger	1962	1962	1962	1978	X	1960	French	Primary
Nigeria	1960	N.R.	1960	N.R.	X	1960	French	Fuel
Norway	1955	1959	1958	1980		...	Scandinavian	Diversified
Pakistan	1952	1961	1960	N.R.	X	...	British	Diversified
Panama	1966	1966	1966	2000	X	...	French	Services
Papua New Guinea	1976	2000	1976	2000	X	1975	French	Primary
Paraguay	1966	1967	1968	N.R.	X	...	French	Primary
Peru	1964	1970	1960	N.R.	X	...	French	Primary
Philippines	1953	1960	1960	1998	X	...	French	Diversified
Portugal	1964	1959	1959	1978		...	French	Diversified
Qatar	N.R.	1976	N.R.	N.R.		1971	French	Fuel
Rwanda	N.R.	1981	1962	N.R.	X	1962	Socialist	Primary
Saudi Arabia	1988	1978	1978	1995	X	...	British	Fuel
Senegal	N.R.	1967	1961	N.R.	X	1960	British	Diversified
Sierra Leone	1961	1966	1961	N.R.	X	1961	French	Diversified
Singapore	1965	N.R.	N.R.	N.R.		1965	British	Manufactures
Somalia	N.R.	1961	1961	N.R.	X	1960	British	Primary
South Africa	1996	1997	1997	2000	X	...	British	Diversified
Spain	1977	1967	1967	1977		...	French	Diversified
Sri Lanka	1972	1998	N.R.	2000	X	...	British	Diversified

Table 2. Ratification of ILO Core Conventions (continued)

	Convention							
Country	*C98*[a] *(1951)*	*C111*[b] *(1960)*	*C105*[c] *(1959)*	*C138*[d] *(1976)*	*Developing*[e]	*Independence*	*Legal origin*	*Exports*[f]
Swaziland	1978	1981	1979	N.R.	X	1968	French	Primary
Sweden	1950	1962	1958	1990		...	Scandinavian	Manufactures
Switzerland	1999	1961	1958	1999		...	German	Manufactures
Tanzania	1962	N.R.	1962	1998	X	1964	French	Primary
Thailand	N.R.	N.R.	1969	N.R.	X	...	British	Diversified
Togo	1983	1983	1999	1984	X	1960	British	Primary
Trinidad & Tobago	1963	1970	1963	N.R.	X	1962	British	Fuel
Turkey	1952	1967	1961	1998	X	...	French	Diversified
United kingdom	1950	1999	1957	2000		...	British	Services
United States	N.R.	N.R.	1991	N.R.		...	British	Diversified
Uganda	1963	N.R.	1963	N.R.	X	1962	Socialist	Primary
United Arab Emirates	N.R.	N.R.	1997	N.R.		1971	British	Fuel
Uruguay	1954	1989	1968	1977	X	...	French	Diversified
Venezuela	1968	1971	1964	1987	X	...	French	Fuel
Zambia	1996	1979	1965	1976	X	1964	Socialist	Primary
Zimbabwe	1998	1999	1998	2000	X	1980	British	Primary

Source: ILO (2001); Easterly and Sewadeh (2001); CIA (2001); World Bank (1995).

a. Right to Organize and Collective Bargaining Convention.

b. Discrimination Convention.

c. Abolition of Forced Labor Convention.

d. Minimum Age Convention.

e. Low or middle income countries as defined by the World Bank.

f. Major export category: Major exports are those that account for 50 percent or more of total exports of goods and services from one category, in the period 1988–92. The categories are nonfuel primary (SITC 0, 1, 2, 4 plus 68), fuels (SITC 3), manufactures (SITC 5 to 9, less 68), and services (factor and nonfactor service receipts plus workers' remittance). If no single category accounts for more than 50 percent or more of total exports, the economy is classified as diversified.

N.R.: Not ratified as of March 2001.

Figure 1. Frequency Distributions of Ratification by Year of Ratification, 1950–2001

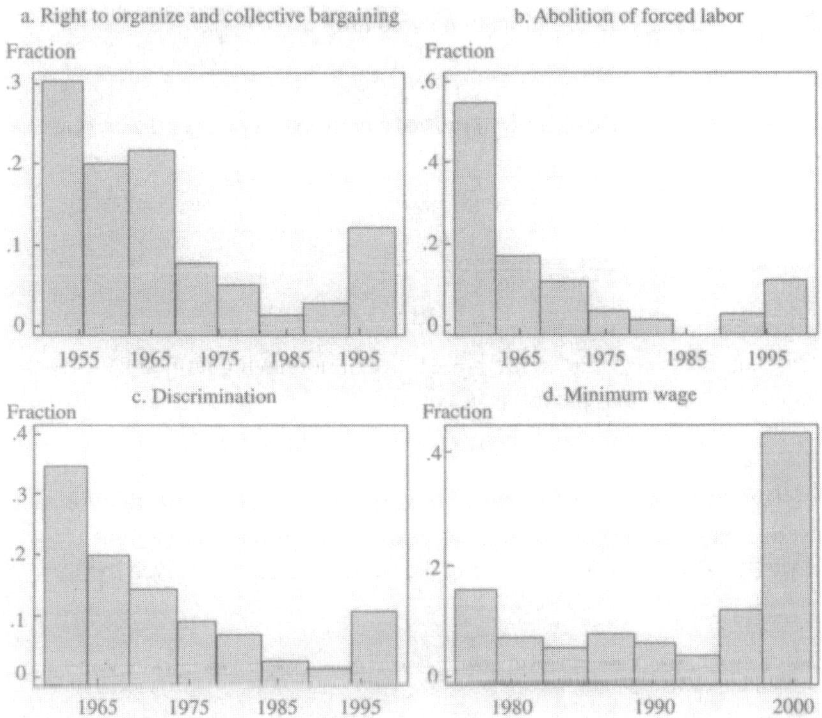

Source: Authors' calculations using data from ILO (2000).

member nations to observe internationally recognized core labor standards, and declared the ILO as the "competent body to set and deal with these standards."[13] The break in the frequency of ratification dates would seem to be particularly acute for C138, the minimum age convention. Between 1997 and 2001, forty-six countries ratified this convention, as compared to the fifty-nine countries that ratified it in all its previous twenty years of existence. Our econometric analysis in the Empirical Framework and Results section of this paper is restricted to the years 1950 to 1992 because of data limitations, but future analyses will have to carefully consider and allow for this late surge in ratifications.

For a typical convention, let t_i denote the effective years between promulgation of a convention by the ILO and its ratification by country i. If τ_0 is the year of promulgation, and T_i the year of independence of country i, define,

13. WTO (1996) Section 4.

$$\tau_{i0} \equiv \max\{\tau_0, T_i\}.$$

Then, if τ_i is the year of ratification by country i,

$$t_i = \tau_i - \tau_{i0}$$

Let the probability that country i ratifies a convention no later than t_i years be given by:

$$F(t_i),$$

with an associated density function

$$f(t_i).$$

The "survival rate," that is, the probability of not having ratified the convention when time t_i has passed, is of course

$$S(t_i) = 1 - F(t_i).$$

Figure 2 summarizes information on time elapsed to ratification for each of the four conventions, in the form of estimates of the survival function 1 – $F(t)$. The Kaplan-Meier estimate of the survival function is given by:

$$\prod_{s=1}^{t}\left(1 - \frac{d_s}{n_s}\right)$$

where d_t is the number of countries that ratify the convention between t and t + 1 years after τ_{i0} and n_t is the number of countries that have not yet ratified the convention at time t.[14] The survival curves estimated for each convention, that is, the probability that ratification does not take place after t years have elapsed, are plotted in figure 2 for developing and developed countries separately.

The figures show that developing countries were by and large late adopters of C98 (Right to Organize), C105 (Abolition of Forced Labor), and C138 (Minimum Age), but the survival probabilities for developed and developing countries appear to be similar for C111 (Discrimination). Moreover the different conventions took very different lengths of time to get ratified. The time elapsed for the survival probability for developing countries to fall to a half is about three years for C105, while it had not fallen to half after twenty years for C138. For C98 and C111 it was around ten years. This variation across country groupings and across conventions suggests that ratification is not sim-

14. Neumann (1999).

Figure 2. Summary Information on Time Elapsed to Ratification

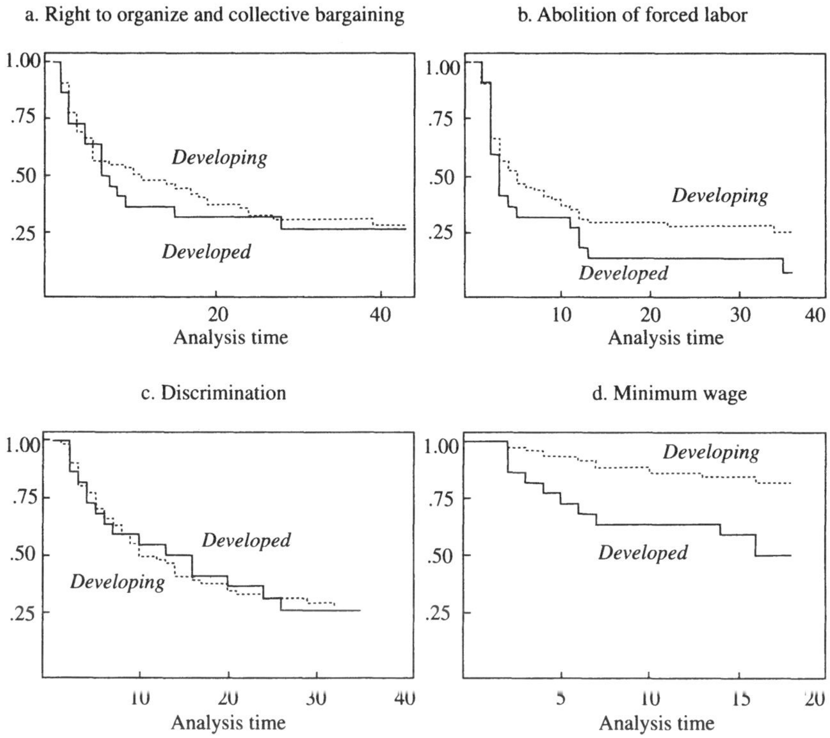

Source: Authors' calculations using data from ILO (2000).

ply a random occurrence, unrelated to underlying socioeconomic determinants. The next section begins the detailed task of understanding the ratification decision.

The Decision to Ratify

How are we to think about the determinants of the adoption or otherwise of international labor standards? One way to approach this is in two steps. First, imagine a world in which there are no international labor standards. Then we can model a country's optimal choice of standards as reflecting different costs and benefits of adopting the given standard. Second, superimpose on this a system and mechanism of international labor standards. The country decides whether or not to adopt them and enforce them depending on the costs and benefits of adoption and compliance. What we observe, namely the ratification of ILO conventions, then has these two components intricately entwined.

Let

$$W = U(s), \tag{1}$$

be the welfare of a country that implements domestic standard s when there is no international standards regime. Now suppose an international labor standards regime comes into being, requiring as standard $\hat{s}$. Should the country sign on? We suppose that when there is an international regime, the welfare of a country which does not ratify is given by:

$$W'(s,\hat{s}) = U(s) - V'(s,\hat{s}), \tag{2}$$

where $V'(\cdot)$ is a cost function dependent on s and $\hat{s}$. We suppose that $V'(\cdot)$ is positive for $\hat{s} > s$, and zero otherwise—in other words, there are no costs to deviating from the international standard in the upward direction.

Now consider what happens when a country ratifies the international standard. We suppose that there is a fixed gain of B at signing. This can be thought of in a number of different ways, including for poorer countries access to technical assistance and other support which signing-on makes possible. Moreover B could also be negative if, for example, the domestic political economy views signing as "caving in" to international demands or as unnecessarily restricting room for future maneuver. However, signing-on also intensifies the costs of deviating from the international standard, so that welfare after signing-on is

$$W''(s,\hat{s}) = U(s) + B - V''(s,\hat{s}), \tag{3}$$

with V'' also having the property that it is positive for $\hat{s} > s$ and zero otherwise, and furthermore $V'' > V'$ for all $(s, \hat{s})$.

The country's problem can now be characterized as follows. First of all, choose s to maximize equations (2) and (3). Then compare the maximized values of W' and W'' to decide on ratification. It will turn out that the value of s which maximizes equation (1) will also be relevant to this decision, so, in obvious notation, let $\tilde{s}$, $\tilde{s}'$, and $\tilde{s}''$ be the values of s which maximize equations (1), (2), and (3), respectively, and let $\tilde{W}$, $\tilde{W}'$, and $\tilde{W}''$ be the corresponding maximized values of welfare in the three regimes. Then clearly the choice of ratification depends on

$$\begin{aligned}\Delta W &= \tilde{W}'' - \tilde{W}' \\ &= B + \left[U(\tilde{s}'') - U(\tilde{s}')\right] + \left[V''(\tilde{s}'',\hat{s}) - V'(\tilde{s}',\hat{s})\right]\end{aligned} \tag{4}$$

To get a sharper insight into the determinants of the ratification decision, consider the following highly specific functional forms:

$$U(s) = \beta s - \tfrac{1}{2}s^2, \tag{5}$$

$$V'(s,\hat{s}) = \begin{cases} \tfrac{1}{2}\theta'(\hat{s}-s)^2 & \text{if } s < \hat{s} \\ 0 & \text{if } s \geq \hat{s} \end{cases}, \tag{6}$$

$$V''(s,\hat{s}) = \begin{cases} \tfrac{1}{2}\theta''(\hat{s}-s)^2 & \text{if } s < \hat{s} \\ 0 & \text{if } s \geq \hat{s} \end{cases}, \tag{7}$$

where β is positive and represents the country-specific marginal gains from implementing domestic standard s, and θ' and θ'' parameterize respectively the marginal costs of deviating from the international standard $\hat{s}$ depending on whether or not the country has ratified the standard.

With these functional forms, equation (5) implies that

$$\tilde{s} = \beta, \tag{8}$$

and thus β gives the optimal standard in the absence of an international standards regime. We refer to this as the "natural" domestic standard. Restricting attention first to the case where $\beta < \hat{s}$ we get

$$\tilde{s}' = \frac{\beta + \theta'\hat{s}}{1+\theta'}, \tag{9}$$

$$\tilde{s}'' = \frac{\beta + \theta''\hat{s}}{1+\theta''}. \tag{10}$$

It is straightforward to verify that $\tilde{s}'$ and $\tilde{s}'' > \tilde{s}$ whenever the marginal costs of deviating from the international standard θ' and θ'' are strictly positive. In addition, $\tilde{s}' < \hat{s}$ and $\tilde{s}'' < \hat{s}$ so long as θ' and θ'' are finite. If we further simplify θ' and θ'' to

$$\theta' = \bar{\theta} - \delta;\ \delta < \bar{\theta}, \tag{11}$$

$$\theta'' = \bar{\theta} + \delta, \tag{12}$$

it follows that

$$\tilde{s}'' - \tilde{s}' = \left(\frac{2\delta}{\left(1+\bar{\theta}\right)^2 - \delta^2} \right) \left(\hat{s} - \tilde{s}\right), \tag{13}$$

and the welfare of a country that ratifies the international standard changes by

$$\Delta W = B - \frac{\delta}{\left(1+\bar{\theta}\right)^2 - \delta^2} \left(\hat{s} - \tilde{s}\right)^2 \tag{14}$$

Finally when $\beta \geq \hat{s}$ we get

$$\tilde{s}' = \tilde{s}'' = \beta; \ \Delta W = B. \tag{15}$$

From equation (14), the ratification decision is seen to depend not only upon the "natural standard" for a country, $\tilde{s}$, but also the relative marginal costs of not enforcing the international standard, as captured in δ. The higher the natural standard in a country, the more likely the country is to ratify. The greater the relative cost of not enforcing when a country does ratify, the less likely the country is to ratify. Equations (13), (14), and (15) together also tell us that provided $\delta \neq 0$, the standard in a ratifying country is no lower than the standard in a nonratifying country.

In the empirical context, if we think of B as being an unobservable term not systematically related to labor standards, equations (13), (14), and (15) can help us to draw inferences from the econometric analysis of ratification. In particular if we find no systematic determinants of ratification, it follows that $\tilde{s} > \hat{s}$ or $\delta = 0$. If $\hat{s} > \tilde{s}$, which seems a reasonable assumption for many countries, then an implication of the allegation that deviation from international standards is almost totally costless is that we should not find systematic determinants of ratification. On the other hand if we do find systematic determinants of ratification in the data, this implies both that $\delta \neq 0$ and that $\hat{s} > \tilde{s}$. In this case, using equations (13) and (14), it also implies that actual standards with ratification are higher than actual standards without, which of course is the implicit assumption in the empirical literature on labor standards and performance, and it justifies the use of ratification as a measure of labor standards.

The key issue is then whether we can in fact find systematic determinants of ratification in terms of systematic determinants of $\tilde{s}$ (the "natural" standard) and δ (the costs of deviating from an international standard). Taking $\hat{s}$ first, the existing theoretical literature can be interpreted as providing at least five explanations for the choice of particular labor standards by a given country: (i) a by-product of the type of industrial and labor relations adopted in the development process; (ii) a consequence of greater openness to trade; (iii) a response to domestic political influences; (iv) a strategic response to labor standards set in peer countries; and (v) a legacy of a country's legal origin.

Taking the rapid growth of the East Asian newly industrialized economies and the subsequent improvement in labor standards in these countries as a backdrop, Fields distinguishes between direct and indirect promotion of labor standards.[15] Direct promotion involves aggressive programs aimed at regulating labor standards in the workplace. Indirect measures put emphasis on growth, and improvements in employment opportunities, wage, income, and other labor standards follow as by-products of the growth process. Indeed many newly industrialized economies underwent periods of wage repression policies, wherein restrictions on union activities, strikes and collective bargaining in the name of export-oriented industrialization were employed.[16] In this view, then, an increase in per capita income (or labor productivity) increases the likelihood of stronger labor standards in that country.

Rodrik argues that opening to trade makes standards more costly to maintain.[17] In particular the producer cost of high standards can be passed on to consumers via higher prices in closed economies, but the entire burden of the costs of high standards may be borne by producers if prices are determined competitively in the world market. In contrast Bagwell and Staiger show that import competition need not be an enemy of high labor standards.[18] If openness to trade reduces the social costs of raising labor standards in import competing sectors, opening up an economy to trade can in fact enhance governments' incentive to adopt higher labor standards.

Brown discusses the role of a well-functioning democracy in government regulation of labor standards.[19] In particular, if high labor standards also have the effect of improving worker-employer relations, the policy choice in democratic societies will likely be a revelation of these benefits of high labor

15. Fields (1990).

16. Fields and Wan (1989). Also see Kuruvilla (1996), which documents the link between industrial growth and policies on labor standards in Singapore, Malaysia, the Philippines, and India, and finds that export-oriented policies were implemented alongside repression on labor rights.

17. Rodrik (1996).

18. Bagwell and Staiger (2000).

19. Brown (2000).

standards. Political rights thus emerge as an important determinant. Cassella considers two democratic trading economies, where the median voter is decisive in the choice of labor standards.[20] If free trade leads to factor price equalization, and if the median voter in one country is a skilled worker, there may be a greater preference for higher standards than for an increase in employment opportunities there, compared to the case where the median voter in the other country is an unskilled worker. The skill composition of the work force, which we measure here in terms of schooling, thus emerges as another possible explanation for differing labor standards across countries.

Portes offers a different perspective on the globalization and labor standards linkage.[21] Rather than reflecting workers' needs, labor standards in developing countries are influenced by ideas, values, and institutional forms imported from abroad. But the segmentation of the work force into those that are protected and those that are not is a key factor underlying the emergence and growth of the informal sector. For example, Sabot documents the development strategy of Tanzania in the early 1960s, and argues that massive rural-urban migration was symptomatic of import substituting development policies in the post-independence period, favoring high wages and high standards in the unionized urban formal sector.[22] Thus "urban bias," which might be measured ceteris paribus by the degree of urbanization, could also play a role in determining labor standards in a country.

In the theoretical literature, labor standards in a given country have also been examined as a strategic response to labor standards set in peer countries. In particular Chau and Kanbur examine the possibility of a race to the bottom in labor standards in the context of export competition among developing economies.[23] It is shown that whether labor standards are strategic complements or substitutes depends critically on the nature of the import demand curves. Strategic complementarity here is defined as whether the adoption of high labor standards in one country raises the net benefits of raising standards in another country. Basu and Chau and Basu, Chau, and Grote examine the possibility of a race to the top in the context of social and green labeling.[24] More specifically in the context of ILO conventions, the practice of ratifying contingent on the ratification decision of countries that are considered as trade

20. Cassella (1996).
21. Portes (1990).
22. Sabot (1990).
23. Chau and Kanbur (2001).
24. Basu and Chau (2001) and Basu, Chau and Grote (2000).

rivals, and the possibility of a race to the bottom in ratification in particular, are discussed in International Labour Office and Stone.[25] These studies which emphasize strategic interaction suggest that peer effects will be in play—the adoption of a standard in one country may be influenced, for example, by how many countries in its competitor group have also adopted that standard.

Finally, since the ratification of international labor standards is after all a government undertaking to uphold the rights of labor, one may also expect institutional determinants such as legal origins to have a significant bearing on the desire to improve labor standards. In particular countries with socialist laws may be characterized by the predominance of the state's intent to control the ownership and allocation of resources, rather than to protect property and individual freedom. Civil law countries are also characterized by the intent to build institutions to further the power of the state, although to a lesser degree as compared to the socialist tradition. Common law countries, in contrast, put emphasis on the private rights of individuals, and as such, the power of the state to intervene in the marketplace may be expected to be limited.[26] Dividing the legal origins of countries into British common law, French civil law, German civil law, Scandinavian civil law and socialist law, La Porta and others find that government performance in terms of public goods provision, bureaucratic efficiency, protection of property rights, and the degree of market intervention vary significantly across countries with different legal origins.[27] At one end of the spectrum, socialist countries are found to have less efficient and highly interventionist governments. Meanwhile common law countries are found to be most market oriented. La Porta and others find that Scandinavian legal origin ranks highest in terms of the efficiency of the judicial system and the rule of law.[28] Thus institutional and legal factors may delay ratification via its impact on government efficiency, even when the underlying economic characteristics of the country in question would otherwise suggest a high propensity to adopt core labor standards.[29] In sum, legal origin can influence

25. International Labour Office (1931) and Stone (1996). For example, France's ratification of the Washington Conventions (night work of women, night work of children, and unemployment) were initially conditional on Czechoslovakia, Germany, the United Kingdom, Italy, Poland, and the United States also ratifying. Denmark, Finland, Norway, and Sweden, on the other hand, were engaged in the practice of jointly evaluating the conventions adopted by the International Labour Conference on an annual basis (International Labour Office, 1931, pp. 271–76).

26. David and Brierley (1978).

27. La Porta and others (1999).

28. La Porta and others (1998).

29. Charnovitz (1997), Weissbrodt (1982).

the natural labor standard (i) directly via the ideological bias it imposes on the relative importance of the state vis-à-vis the individual, and (ii) indirectly via its influence on the performance of government to protect the rights of individuals and government efficiency.

There is thus no single unifying theory of the determinants of domestic labor standards, and several diverse strands are present in the literature. A number of explanatory variables are suggested by this literature: per capita income and the level of development generally, the skill composition of the population, the degree of urbanization, political openness, openness to trade, labor standards in peer countries, and legal systems. These variables would determine, in theory, the labor standard that a country would choose to put in place—the $\tilde{s}$ of equation (8).

Let us now turn to the determination of δ. The key here is to think about how constraining the signing of a convention would be for a country, and for what sorts of countries these constraints would be lesser or greater. There is almost no detailed theorizing on this issue in the literature. However, we would a priori expect peer effects to be important. We have already identified peer effects as being important in determining the "natural" standard for a country. But the costs of deviation from a ratified convention are also plausibly subject to peer effects. Two opposing arguments come to mind. One says that the more countries that have signed on, the greater will be the peer groups' inflicted sanctions (economic or otherwise) costs for a country that has signed on when it deviates from the international standard, relative to if it had not signed on at all. In other words, the more countries that have signed on, the higher we would expect δ to be and hence peer effects would work to lower the likelihood of adoption of the international standard through this channel.

But there is a second argument. One may think of differences between θ' and θ'' in terms of the difference in the *expected* marginal cost of deviation. For any given cost of deviating from an international labor standard, the expected marginal cost of deviation depends on the probabilities of being discovered employing a standard $s \leq \hat{s}$. A natural assumption here would be that the probability of discovery is higher for countries that have ratified the convention. However, it can be argued that as more and more countries in a peer group sign on, the perceived likelihood that one among the entire pool of peer countries will be discovered violating the standard can reasonably be expected to be lower. We then have δ decreasing in the cumulative number of countries in the peer group.

The impact of peer effects on ratification is thus ambiguous in theory and open to empirical testing. However, one interesting issue is the identification of the peer group. For the determination of the "natural" domestic standard, as discussed earlier, the peer group consists of countries that are competitors in export markets or in the attraction of foreign investment. For the costs and benefits of signing *per se*, it is perhaps a broader community of nations that is relevant as the peer group. Moreover, this type of peer effect may be very different for rich and poor countries. It might be argued that richer countries can better bear the costs of ostracism from not signing. We might expect, then, this type of peer effect to be more pronounced among developing countries than among developed ones.

The intricacy of the causal relationships induced by the two-stage process described above should now be clear. The same variables are in principle involved in both stages, and the effects through $\tilde{s}$ and through δ may be difficult to disentangle. However, we can draw the following additional conclusions from the reasoning: (i) peer effects will be present in both stages—the empirical key may lie in defining reference groups which pick up on the first stage or second stage effects; (ii) noncompliance peer effects may be stronger for poorer countries than for richer countries; (iii) higher income will induce higher "natural" standards and will therefore increase the propensity to ratify high international standards, but this effect may be counteracted by the fact that the costs of noncompliance may be much lower for a rich country than for a poor country, so overall the income effect may be weak.

Our theoretical discussion of the incentives for ratifying an international labor standard concludes here. The theory has identified a number of variables as possible determinants of ratification. We now test the significance of these variables for our data set.

Empirical Framework and Results

In order to uncover the empirical determinants of the likelihood of ratification, we work with an empirical framework that allows us to analyze the data on ratification dates available from the ILOLEX database.[30] The interest here is to empirically ascertain the likelihood of ratification at a given point in time, and to discover in what ways economic, demographic, and political factors influence the time to ratification. We thus estimate a hazard model, with parameter estimates that can be interpreted as the change in the likelihood of ratification at a given point in time, given that ratification has not

30. ILOLEX (2001).

occurred in prior periods. We make use of a vector of time-varying explanatory variables $\mathbf{x}_{it}$ where t denotes the time after promulgation of the convention or country independence, whichever is later, and t runs from 0 till t_i, when the country ratifies the convention. Since only explanatory variables prior to t_i are to be used, the question of simultaneity does not arise. The vector $\mathbf{x}_{it}$ can be as comprehensive as theory requires and data allows. For example, in our case it includes information on how many other countries in country i's reference group have also ratified the convention.

The hazard rate at t—the probability of ratification when t years have passed, given that ratification has not taken place—is simply

$$h(t_i \mid \mathbf{x}_{it}) = \frac{f(t_i \mid \mathbf{x}_{it})}{1 - F(t_i \mid \mathbf{x}_{it})}.$$

We assume a model with proportional hazard, and specify in addition that each of the J time-varying covariates enters into the determinant of the hazard rate as follows:

$$h(t_i \mid \mathbf{x}_{it}) = \hat{h}(t_i) e^{\sum_{j=1}^{J} \beta_j x_{ijt}}, \qquad (16)$$

where $\hat{h}$ denotes the baseline hazard function.[31] The hazard ratio for a unit change in x_{ijt} is thus simply

$$e^{\beta_j} \geq (<) 1.$$

Parameter estimates of β_j of the Cox proportional hazard model are obtained by maximizing a partial log-likelihood function and have the virtue that the estimation procedure places no restrictions on the unknown functional form of the baseline hazard function.[32]

The variables required in the explanatory vector $\mathbf{x}_t$ are those suggested in the theoretical discussion. Our data set covers ninety-four countries. Real GDP per capita *rgdpch* is taken from the Penn World Table (Mark 5.6), and is available from 1950 through 1992. The variable *rgdpch* measures output per capita in relation to a common set of international prices based on a chain index (base 1985, in constant dollars). We take this to be a proxy for the average productivity of labor. Educational attainment (*educ*), measured by the ratio of total primary school enrollment to primary school age population, is obtained from Alesina and others for 1950 to 1982, and from the Global Development Network (GDN) Growth database of the World Bank for 1983 to 1992.[33] The

31. Cox (1972).
32. Kalbfleisch and Prentice (1980, chaps. 4 and 5); available at pwt.econ.upenn.edu.
33. Alesina and others (1996); Easterly and Sewadeh (2001).

extent of urbanization *urban* is also available from the World Bank database and from the World Urbanization Prospects.[34] The Polity IV database provides annual international ratings on political regimes, with scores ranging from ten (high democracy) to minus-ten (high autocracy).[35] Missing data points are assigned the polity score immediately prior to the missing point. For openness we use imports and exports as a share of GDP per capita from the Penn World Table. Legal origins (British common law, German civil law, French civil law, Scandinavian civil law, socialist law) are available from the GDN Growth database.

We consider three types of peer effects. We first classify countries into groups of countries based on their export orientation (exporters of manufactures, primary products, fuel, services, and diversified exporters).[36] A second classification divides countries into developed (*incdeveloping* = 0) and developing countries (*incdeveloping* = one), where developing countries refer to low, lower-middle and upper-middle level income countries as in Easterly and Sewadeh.[37] With these classifications, we can construct measures of peer effects in each case. Thus when t years have passed without ratification for a country, $cdev_t$ is the cumulative number of countries in the same development classification who have ratified the convention in the previous $t-1$ years. Similarly export grouping peer effects and regional grouping peer effects are captured by the cex_t and $creg_t$ variables respectively.

For each convention, we estimate the proportional hazard model first for the full sample of developed and developing countries. The results are reported in tables 3–6 for each of the four conventions. We present results for three specifications, each with the peer effects defined in one of the three ways discussed above. The variable t_i is included in all specifications with peer effects variables to control for the effect of the passage of time on ratification. The

34. United Nations (1995).

35. Marshall and Jaggers (2001).

36. Major exports are those that account for 50 percent or more of total exports of goods and services from one category, in the period 1988–92. The categories are: nonfuel primary (SITC 0,1,2,4, plus 68), fuels (SITC 3), manufactures (SITC 5 to 9, less 68), and services (factor and nonfactor service receipts plus workers' remittances). If no single category accounts for 50 percent or more of total exports, the economy is classified as diversified.

37. Easterly and Sewadeh (2001). These groupings are based on 1999 gross national income per capita. Gross national income per capita is $755 or less for low income countries; $756–$2,995 of lower middle income countries; $2,996–$9,265 for upper middle income countries; and $9,266 or more for high income countries. A final classification divides countries into seven geographic categories (East Asia and Pacific, South Asia, Sub-Saharan Africa, Middle East and Northern Africa, Latin America and Caribbean, Eastern Europe and Central Asia, Western Europe and North America.

results are reported in terms of the proportional impact on the hazard rate of a unit increase in the explanatory variable—in other words, the estimate of *exp* β. The last line of the table gives the probability at which the hypothesis that all coefficients are zero can be rejected.

From tables 3–6, four features stand out as being common to all conventions. First, the hypothesis that all coefficients are zero is rejected for all conventions. We have therefore found empirical determinants of the ratification decision. As argued in the previous section, this implies both that $\delta > 0$, and that $\hat{s} > \tilde{s}$. In other words for these conventions, on average, the international standards are higher than the "natural" domestic standard, and there are real differential costs to a country from ratifying and not meeting the international standards, compared to not meeting standards when it has not ratified the convention. Moreover, as established in the theory section, the combination of $\delta > 0$ and $\hat{s} > \tilde{s}$ also implies that actual standards with ratification are higher than actual standards without, a finding of some importance to those who would use ratification as a proxy for domestic standards.

Turning now to the detailed determinants of ratification, the second common feature across all four tables is that the time variable is significant—the probability of ratification increases with the lapse of time. More interestingly, the third common feature is that the legal system is a significant determinant of ratification probability, taking as given the British legal system as a baseline for comparison. For all four conventions, having a Scandinavian legal system increases the probability of ratification (with the exception of only one specification). A legal system with socialist origins, on the other hand, decreases the probability of ratification for all four conventions. The French-based legal system influences probability of ratification positively, but only for C111 and C138. German civil law countries are not significantly different from British common law countries in terms of the likelihood of ratification. It should be noted that these patterns for the influence of legal systems on ratification hold even for the third of our specifications, where regional peer effects are present—the legal system effects can thus be argued to be over and above regional effects.

The fourth common feature across tables 3–6 is the insignificance of the basic "standard" variables (with very few exceptions). Real per capita GDP, openness, education, political freedom, urbanization—none of these seem to affect the probability of ratification on average. On real per capita income, we identified conflicting forces in theory—as income increases, the natural standard might be higher, but the cost from not meeting ratified standards might

Table 3. Cox Regression: Right to Organize and Collective Bargaining (C98)

Hazard ratios	*I*	*II*	*III*
rgdpch	0.999805 ***	0.999761 ***	0.999739 ***
	(0.000088)	(0.000085)	(0.000088)
open	0.999030	0.997485	0.999603
	(0.004447)	(0.004556)	(0.004410)
educ	1.007877	1.009132 **	1.008863 **
	(0.005040)	(0.004094)	(0.004568)
polity	1.017024	1.013779	1.014576
	(0.022817)	(0.022931)	(0.021118)
urban	1.009698	1.018760 *	1.008839
	(0.010200)	(0.010862)	(0.010375)
leg_french	1.140852	0.993414	0.848690
	(0.438198)	(0.365642)	(0.307013)
leg_socialist	2.520E-15 ***	8.220E-16 ***	1.700E-16 ***
	3.830E-15	1.140E-15	2.330E-16
leg_german	0.831957	0.888777	0.678457
	(0.623241)	(0.631562)	(0.483051)
leg_scandinavian	3.050124 ***	4.328151 ***	2.584229 ***
	(1.345746)	(2.033472)	(1.166613)
cex98	1.139001 ***		
	(0.055333)		
cex98sq	0.995461 ***		
	(0.001821)		
cdev98		1.084722 ***	
		(0.021435)	
cdev98sq		0.999063 ***	
		(0.000235)	
creg98			1.269674 ***
			(0.069251)
creg98sq			0.990814 ***
			(0.002131)
time98	1.332484 ***	1.517792 ***	1.457735 ***
	(0.103551)	(0.152002)	(0.065225)
No. of observations	1,323	1,323	1,323
No. of ratifications	65	65	65
Log likelihood	-248.483	-244.112	-241.024
Wald chi^2	1133.800	1293.900	1099.850
Prob > chi^2	0.000	0.000	0.000

Robust standard errors (Lin and Wei 1989) in parentheses.

Source: Authors' calculations using data from ILO (2001); Penn World Table Mark 5.6; Alesina and others (1996); Easterly and Sewadeh (2001); Marshall and Jaggers (2001); United Nations (1995); World Bank (1995); CIA (2001).

Table 4. Cox Regression: Abolition of Forced Labor (C105)

Hazard ratios	*I*	*II*	*III*
rgdpch	1.000053	0.999986	1.000014
	(0.000065)	(0.000080)	(0.000056)
open	1.002509	1.001143	1.002562
	(0.003961)	(0.004259)	(0.004358)
educ	0.995340	1.001578	0.999879
	(0.005620)	(0.003863)	(0.004823)
polity	0.991591	0.992517	1.000496
	(0.021423)	(0.020705)	(0.020488)
urban	1.014142	1.014423	1.004497
	(0.009627)	(0.009197)	(0.009362)
leg_french	1.169846	0.969721	0.893537
	(0.379833)	(0.322358)	(0.296517)
leg_socialist	3.790E-15 ***	1.490E-15 ***	5.440E-16 ***
	5.680E-15	2.160E-15	7.340E-16
leg_german	0.869469	0.579092	0.541137
	(0.646604)	(0.474966)	(0.390753)
leg_scandinavian	2.544601 ***	2.971606 ***	1.761693 **
	(0.793382)	(1.014184)	(0.475612)
cex105	1.107186 *		
	(0.060443)		
cex105sq	0.997944		
	(0.001898)		
cdev105		1.080976 ***	
		(0.023346)	
cdev105sq		0.998986 ***	
		(0.000287)	
creg105			1.235882 ***
			(0.079700)
creg105sq			0.991132 ***
			(0.002923)
time105	1.179074 ***	1.113979 ***	1.104457 ***
	(0.033674)	(0.077178)	(0.019977)
No. of observations	930	930	930
No. of ratifications	72	72	72
Log likelihood	-276.569	-273.906	-273.456
Wald chi^2	1115.070	1171.550	1067.590
Prob > chi^2	0.000	0.000	0.000

Robust standard errors (Lin and Wei 1989) in parentheses.

Source: Authors' calculations using data from ILO (2001); Penn World Table Mark 5.6; Alesina and others (1996); Easterly and Sewadeh (2001); Marshall and Jaggers (2001); United Nations (1995); World Bank (1995); CIA (2001).

Table 5. Cox Regression: Discrimination (C111) Full Sample

Hazard ratios	*I*	*II*	*III*
rgdpch	1.000048	1.000041	1.000023
	(0.000059)	(0.000066)	(0.000058)
open	0.996141	0.995635	0.996800
	(0.004319)	(0.004237)	(0.004075)
educ	0.999006	1.001147	1.002047
	(0.006499)	(0.006458)	(0.006415)
polity	0.999968	1.000805	0.998167
	(0.022531)	(0.022760)	(0.022151)
urban	0.995891	0.997884	0.992012
	(0.010126)	(0.009847)	(0.010168)
leg_french	2.874382 ***	2.837655 ***	2.687574 ***
	(1.100526)	(1.101769)	-1.017041
leg_socialist	1.830E-18 ***	1.480E-14 ***	3.480E-16 ***
	1.750E-18	1.430E-14	3.600E-16
leg_german	2.211451	2.350498	2.116248
	(1.366444)	(1.565572)	(1.311469)
leg_scandinavian	5.539186 ***	7.266973 ***	5.698458 ***
	(2.885846)	(3.883530)	(3.170555)
cex111	1.006371		
	(0.073564)		
cex111sq	1.000457		
	(0.002520)		
cdev111		1.043943	
		(0.027676)	
cdev111sq		0.999517	
		(0.000333)	
creg111			1.030511
			(0.037574)
creg111sq			0.999028
			(0.000832)
time111	1.103181 **	1.773914 ***	2.321572 ***
	(0.048924)	(0.110068)	(0.160169)
No. of observations	1315	1315	1315
No. of ratifications	66	66	66
Log likelihood	-252.821	-251.616	-251.940
Wald chi^2	2336.170	2774.260	2348.200
Prob > chi^2	0.000	0.000	0.000

Robust standard errors (Lin and Wei 1989) in parentheses.

Source: Authors' calculations using data from ILO (2001); Penn World Table Mark 5.6; Alesina and others (1996); Easterly and Sewadeh (2001); Marshall and Jaggers (2001); United Nations (1995); World Bank (1995); CIA (2001).

Table 6. Cox Regression:Minimum Age Convention (C138)

Hazard ratios	*I*	*II*	*III*
rgdpch	1.000115 *	1.000010	1.000103
	(0.000065)	(0.000100)	(0.000065)
open	1.003750	1.001554	1.003493
	(0.003635)	(0.004193)	(0.003456)
educ	1.001357	1.000652	1.001235
	(0.008243)	(0.008583)	(0.008307)
polity	1.032394	1.017429	1.021559
	(0.036460)	(0.036474)	(0.033576)
urban	0.996745	1.002256	0.998631
	(0.016400)	(0.017245)	(0.016310)
leg_french	4.550206 **	3.776774 **	3.343452 ***
	(3.235685)	(2.553433)	(2.383641)
leg_socialist	2.310E-14 ***	1.110E-17 ***	4.940E-17 ***
	2.810E-14	1.310E-17	5.930E-17
leg_german	1.180980	0.913889	0.878491
	(1.536536)	(1.101271)	(1.161667)
leg_scandinavian	4.301139 *	3.420229 *	2.900743
	(3.419872)	(2.544211)	(2.467271)
cex138	1.143655		
	(0.266864)		
cex138sq	0.980741		
	(0.020406)		
cdev138		0.654979	
		(0.234070)	
cdev138sq		1.008501	
		(0.009538)	
creg138			1.244767
			(0.278420)
creg138sq			0.986094
			(0.018086)
time138	1.939607 ***	3.750306	1.925397 ***
	(0.108859)	(0.808554)	(0.105518)
No. of observations	1306	1306	1306
No. of ratifications	24	24	24
Log likelihood	-96.509	-96.255	-96.551
Wald chi^2	2893.130	2530.120	2992.000
Prob > chi^2	0.000	0.000	0.000

Robust standard errors (Lin and Wei 1989) in parentheses.

Source: Authors' calculations using data from ILO (2001); Penn World Table Mark 5.6; Alesina and others (1996); Easterly and Sewadeh (2001); Marshall and Jaggers (2001); United Nations (1995); World Bank (1995); CIA (2001).

be lower. The empirical results reflect this ambiguity. On the other variables, however, our empirical results suggest that some of the theories discussed in the previous section need to be reconsidered carefully.

Consider now the role of peer effects. We see a clear distinction between C98 and C105 on the one hand, and C111 and C138 on the other. In the latter case no peer effects are significant at all. For these conventions, all that matters for the probability of ratification is the legal system. For C98 and C105, peer effects are strongly significant and nonlinear—the likelihood of ratification increases with the number of countries in the reference group who have ratified, but at a decreasing rate. Notice that these effects are present even though the time variable has been introduced—this is not just a case of a spurious correlation brought about by "everybody ratifying eventually." The fact that peer effects matter for C98 and C105 is a confirmation of the hypothesis of *strategic complementarity* in labor standards, as discussed and developed in Chau and Kanbur.[38] However, why peer effects should be important for some conventions and not others is something that will bear a closer, more institutional, investigation.

We now turn to a closer look at two conventions, C98 and C105, in order to see if more can be said regarding whether our explanatory variables are indeed picking up the endogeneity of the natural labor standard $\tilde{s}$, or the relative costs of deviating from the international standard (δ). As a first pass, we explore this possibility by introducing a stage of development dummy (*incdeveloping*) into the estimation. One interpretation of this is that the stage of development dummy can be thought of as a rough guide as to whether a country's "natural" standard exceeds or lies below that of the international standard.

To recall, *incdeveloping* is equal to one (zero) for developing (developed) countries. We also introduce interaction terms that allow the sign and size of development and regional peer effects to take on different values respectively for developed and developing countries. Specifically, the explanatory variable $devcdev_k$ = *incdeveloping* x $cdev_k$ is equal to the development peer effect for developing countries, and zero for developed countries, and $devcdev_k sq$ denotes the corresponding interaction term with the nonlinear component of the development peer effect. The explanatory variable $ndevcdev_k$ = |1-*incdeveloping*| x $cdev_k$ is equal to the development peer effect for developed countries, and zero for developing countries. In a similar fashion, we denote $devcreg_k$ and *nde-*

38. Chau and Kanbur (2001).

$vcreg_k$ as the regional peer effect respectively for developed and developing countries, and $devcreg_k sq$ and $ndevcreg_k sq$ as the corresponding nonlinear terms. The objective of this exercise is to determine if there are systematic differences in the roles of development and regional peer effects between high and low income countries.

Tables 7 and 8 present the results for C98 and C105, respectively.[39] In table 7 the results for the first model—where only the stage of development dummy is introduced—suggest that developing countries are more likely to be late adopters of C98, although the estimated coefficient is insignificant at the 10 percent level. Consistent with the full sample analysis, real income per capita decreases the likelihood of early ratification. The rest of the economic explanatory variables are of the same sign as in the full sample estimation, but are insignificant. The results for legal origin variables likewise conform with the full sample estimation, with Scandinavian and socialist countries at the extremes in terms of the likelihood of early ratification. For this specification, the hypothesis that the estimated coefficients are jointly different from zero can be rejected at the 1 percent level.

Introducing peer effects into the analysis yields interesting differences, and in particular, both development and regional peer effects are shown to be positive and significant only for the group of developing countries, but not for developed countries. Additionally, real income per capita continues to negatively affect the likelihood of early ratification. Our measure of urban bias is positive and significant. Overall, the model with peer effects is significant at the 1 percent level.

Turning now to the Abolition of Forced Labor Convention in table 8, we find that in all three models, developing countries are more likely to be late adopters of C105, although the estimated coefficients are insignificant in all three cases. Controlling for stage of development also does not appear to improve the significance of the rest of the economic variables, nor does it diminish the importance of legal origins in determining the likelihood of early ratification. However, as is the case with C98, development and regional peer effects are in play. The estimated hazard ratio is greater than one and significant only for the group of developing countries, but not for developed countries. A hazard ratio that is less than one for the nonlinear term indicates that development peer effects raise the likelihood of early ratification, but at a decreasing rate.

39. We did the same analysis for the Discrimination and Minimum Age Conventions. In each case, we find no model specifications that yield parameter estimates that are jointly different from zero at 15 percent significance.

Table 7. Cox Regression: Right to Organize and Collective Bargaining (C98)

Hazard ratios	*I*	*II*	*III*
rgdpch	0.999782 **	0.999669 ***	0.999701 ***
	(0.000098)	(0.000103)	(0.000103)
open	0.999124	0.995877	0.999583
	(0.004339)	(0.004097)	(0.004611)
educ	1.007711	1.009364 **	1.009153 **
	(0.005080)	(0.004094)	(0.004704)
polity	1.017129	1.021325	1.016798
	(0.023128)	(0.025160)	(0.021557)
urban	1.008288	1.016210 *	1.006627
	(0.010033)	(0.009703)	(0.010501)
leg_french	1.158489	1.090064	0.858109
	(0.446729)	(0.403301)	(0.314329)
leg_socialist	2.810E-19 ***	4.250E-16 ***	1.580E-17 ***
	4.240E-19	6.570E-16	2.330E-17
leg_german	0.794829	0.740385	0.591997
	(0.568594)	(0.509425)	(0.419968)
leg_scandinavian	2.715532 ***	4.421451 ***	2.261950 *
	(1.219512)	(2.482845)	(1.068172)
inc_developing	0.745824	0.802274	0.612702
	(0.291105)	(0.582806)	(0.370194)
cex98	1.142112 ***	0.973542	1.026685
	(0.056395)	(0.056427)	(0.053631)
cex98sq	0.995371 ***	0.999499	0.998680
	(0.001845)	(0.001892)	(0.001824)
devcdev98		1.098928 ***	
		(0.025645)	
devcdev98sq		0.999081 ***	
		(0.000266)	
ndevcdev98		1.248424	
		(0.175533)	
ndevcdev98sq		0.9962253	
		(0.006165)	
devcreg98			1.266716 ***
			(0.079658)
devcreg98sq			0.991073 ***
			(0.002378)
ndevcreg98			1.191071
			(0.205721)
ndevcreg98sq			0.995728
			(0.012086)
time98	1.451454 ***	1.782031 ***	1.534007 ***
	(0.153000)	(0.094271)	(0.040721)
No. of observations	1323	1323	1323
No. of ratifications	65	65	65
Log Likelihood	-248.290	-241.324	-240.40134
Wald chi^2	1459.270	1754.940	2234.74
Prob > chi^2	0.000	0.000	0.000

Robust standard errors (Lin and Wei 1989) in parentheses.

Source: Authors' calculations using data from ILO (2001); Penn World Table Mark 5.6; Alesina and others (1996); Easterly and Sewadeh (2001); Marshall and Jaggers (2001); United Nations (1995); World Bank (1995); CIA (2001).

Table 8. Cox Regression:Abolition of Forced Labor (C105)

Hazard ratios	*I*	*II*	*III*
rgdpch	1.000043	0.999962	0.999989
	(0.000069)	(0.000101)	(0.000058)
open	1.002570	1.002236	1.002967
	(0.003944)	(0.004321)	(0.004059)
educ	0.995229	0.999802	0.997480
	(0.005703)	(0.004379)	(0.005526)
polity	0.991830	0.991124	0.989092
	(0.021481)	(0.022036)	(0.021267)
urban	1.013501	1.014299	1.011646
	(0.009727)	(0.009399)	(0.010092)
leg_french	1.177116	1.008091	0.917129
	(0.378602)	(0.328389)	(0.313320)
leg_socialist	3.630E-15 ***	2.770E-13 ***	1.370E-15 ***
	5.420E-15	(4.690E-13)	(2.090E-15)
leg_german	0.837971	0.720785	0.777968
	(0.618865)	(0.553160)	(0.566224)
leg_scandinavian	2.401866 ***	2.635517 ***	2.198110 ***
	(0.840632)	(1.079634)	0.850140
inc_developing	0.869839	0.652846	0.814786
	(0.303241)	(0.365545)	(0.394684)
cex105	1.107561 **	0.973157	1.047169
	(0.060200)	(0.081948)	(0.073591)
cex105sq	0.997933	1.001928	1.000020
	(0.001892)	(0.002628)	(0.002404)
devcdev105		1.095750 ***	
		(0.037660)	
devcdev105sq		0.998732 ***	
		(0.000424)	
ndevcdev105		1.177152	
		(0.135850)	
ndevcdev105sq		0.9943977	
		(0.005262)	
devcreg105			1.199455 ***
			(0.108106)
devcreg105sq			0.991621 ***
			(0.003831)
ndevcreg105			1.138974
			(0.221296)
ndevcreg105sq			0.996441
			(0.012603)
time105	1.748721 ***	1.795862 ***	1.287702 ***
	(0.292842)	(0.219649)	(0.127264)
No. of observations	930	930	930
No. of ratifications	72	72	72
Log likelihood	-276.524	-272.351	-270.943
Wald chi^2	1143.940	1376.870	1178.490
Prob > chi^2	0.000	0.000	0.000

This analysis suggests that the "ostracism" and other peer effects (as captured by δ in our model) may indeed be an important determinant of the observed ratification patterns for these two conventions. Ideally, of course, in order to explore the ratification decisions of countries with natural labor standards that exceed, or lie below that of the international standard, one would need information on actual labor standards prior to the adoption of the relevant labor convention by the ILO. Recall, however, from equations (8), (9), and (10), that $\tilde{s}'' \geq (<)\hat{s}$ if and only if $\tilde{s} \geq (<)\hat{s}$. This suggests that an alternative approach would be to divide countries into two groups: (i) those whose labor standards are consistent with the ILO conventions after ratification, and (ii) those whose labor standards continue to be lower than the international standard.

Interestingly, OECD provides a classification of countries based on the extent to which the first category of rights in table 1 are violated in the period 1989–99.[40] The country ranking is based on a four-point score, indicating increasing degrees of violation of the freedom of association and rights to organize, starting from a score of one indicating severe violations to a score of four, in which protection is deemed adequate. We apply this information to our framework for estimating the probability of ratification of C98. Based on the information in OECD, we construct interaction terms that allow the sign and size of development peer effects to take on different values for countries with these four levels of enforcement violations.[41] For example, the explanatory variable *en*1*cdev*98 = *en*1 x *cdev*98 where *en*1 is a dummy variable indicating a country with a score of one according to the OECD study.[42] Thus *en*1*cdev98* represents the development peer effect for countries for the severest level of violation. A dummy variable *endum* is introduced to the estimation control for other unobserved characteristics of countries that are selected into the OECD study.[43] (The fifth includes countries in our sample but whose enforcement record is not documented in OECD.[44] The dummy variable *endum* is equal to one for the first four groups of countries, and zero for the fifth.)

Table 9 summarizes our findings. The results are broadly consistent with our discussion on the distinction between developed and developing countries

40. OECD (2000).

41. OECD (2000).

42. OECD (2000).

43. There are thus five groups of countries. The first four correspond to the OECD (2000) compliance classification. The fifth includes countries in our sample but whose enforcement record is not documented in OECD (2000). The dummy variable *endum* is equal to one for the first four groups of countries, and zero for the fifth.

44. OECD (2000).

Table 9: Cox Regression: Rights to Organize and Collective Bargaining (C98)

Hazard ratios	*I*		*Hazard ratios*	*I*	
rgdpch	0.999824		en1cdev98	1.707917	***
	(0.000114)			(0.153322)	
open	0.997598		en1cdev98sq	0.990582	***
	(0.004768)			(0.069830)	
educ	1.010067	**	en2cdev98	1.087003	***
	(0.005192)			(0.028303)	
polity	1.027694		en2cdev98sq	0.999063	***
	(0.022082)			(0.000358)	
urban	1.014768		en3cdev98	1.046723	
	(0.010592)			(0.032957)	
leg_french	1.088870		en3cdev98sq	0.999395	
	(0.445914)			(0.000447)	
leg_socialist	3.660E-14	**	en4cdev98	1.029698	
	6.150E-14			(0.069830)	
leg_german	1.303191		en4cdev98sq	1.000004	
	(0.973683)			(0.000988)	
leg_scandinavian	5.233868	***	time98	1.522216	***
	(2.668160)			(0.140584)	
cex98	1.119705	**	No. of observations	1323	
	(0.059184)		No. of ratifications	65	
cex98sq	0.995877	**	Log likelihood	-239.467	
	(0.001824)		Wald chi^2	845.650	
endum	0.325568	***	Prob > chi^2	0.000	
	(0.136712)				

Robust standard errors (Lin and Wei 1989) in parentheses.

Source: Authors' calculations using data from ILO (2001); Penn World Table Mark 5.6; Alesina and others (1996); Easterly and Sewadeh (2001); Marshall and Jaggers (2001); United Nations (1995); World Bank (1995); OECD (2000); CIA (2001).

above. In particular, peer effects are positive and significant only for the first two groups of countries that are classified as not fully complying (one and two). Meanwhile, the estimated hazard ratios for the two groups of countries with the highest levels of compliance are not significant in the 10 percent level. In addition to these findings, education is positive and statistically significant, and likewise are legal origins of the Scandinavian civil variety. As is the case with all of the rest of our specifications, socialist countries are late adopters.

Summary and Conclusion

The starting point for this paper was the issue of using the ratification of ILO conventions as a labor standards variable explaining economic performance—a common practice in the empirical literature. The implicit assumption underlying this practice is of course that the ratification of ILO conventions provides information on domestic labor standards. We developed a framework in which the decision to ratify a convention is made simultaneously with the decision of how much to enforce it. The analysis suggested two key determinants of ratification—the factors determining the "natural" standard for a country, and those determining the costs of deviating from the international standard when the country did and did not ratify the convention. Following on from this, we reasoned that if we did find systematic determinants of ratification empirically, this would be evidence that (i) there were costs to violation when countries ratified, and that on average countries were violating standards they had signed on to, and (ii) that countries that ratified did have higher domestic standards than those that did not. This last point is clearly of some importance to the large and growing empirical literature on labor standards and economic performance that uses the readily available ratification data.

The theoretical discussion suggested several variables as determinants of ratification: per capita income, openness, education, urbanization, political rights, peer effects, and legal systems. The empirical analysis finds systematic determinants of ratification, thereby confirming, for these four conventions, that there are costs to violating ratified standards, and that ratification is indeed an indicator of higher domestic standards. There is therefore some justification for using ratification as a proxy for higher domestic standards.

However, many empirical studies go further than this—they add up the number of conventions ratified, implicitly assuming them to be perfect substitutes. But the empirical analysis shows varied patterns in the determinants for ratification, which suggests that these four conventions are not substitutes in a simple way. The legal system variables explain ratification in all specifications. The economic variables are not significant in all but a very few specifications. Peer effects are significant for two of the four conventions. The fact that standard economic variables are not significant determinants of ratification should lead us to reconsider carefully many of the current theories of the determinants of labor standards. The significance of peer effects supports the hypothesis of "strategic complementarity" in the adoption of labor standards, the theoretical implications of which have been investigated in Chau and Kanbur.[45] The linkage between origins of the legal system and ratification will bear further investigation—countries with legal origins which

45. Chau and Kanbur (2001).

are correlated with high government efficiency and rule of law turn out to be favorably selected into the pool of early ratifiers.

This paper has merely begun the analysis of the ratification of ILO conventions. The empirical investigation shows that the signing of these conventions is not random and meaningless. The evidence suggests that, on average, countries think about ratification, balance the costs and benefits, and, when they ratify, they have higher standards than when they do not. Further theoretical and empirical research is now needed to develop a deeper understanding of the detailed determinants of the ratification decision.

Comments and Discussion

Ann Harrison: Nancy Chau and Ravi Kanbur have written a very interesting paper exploring which countries adopt international labor standards and when the adoption occurs. This is an extremely important and current issue. While there is enormous interest in how globalization has affected the quality of our lives, there is simply not enough research on this question. Although much of the policy debate focuses on how globalization affects the labor force, the evidence in this area is slim. Chau and Kanbur's paper makes an important contribution by showing when countries are likely to adopt different types of international labor standards.

Chau and Kanbur's paper analyzes the determinants of the adoption of four kinds of ILO conventions: the right to organize, the abolition of forced labor, the elimination of discrimination, and the abolition of child labor. Somewhat surprisingly, the authors find that many factors do not matter, for example GDP per capita, openness to trade, education, political freedom, and urbanization. The factors that do matter include time (the probability of ratification increases over time), the type of legal system, and peer effects.

The results are provocative. Although standard measures of globalization, such as the share of trade in GDP, have no impact on the likelihood of adopting different labor standards, one measure does: whether similar countries have adopted the standard. To the extent that globalization implies that countries are more sensitive to what others do, this could imply a beneficial effect: countries are more likely to adopt labor standards when their neighbors do.

I have some suggestions for future revisions. One question of great policy interest is the relationship between openness to trade and measures of economic well-being. In particular many opponents of liberal trade policies have argued that trade leads to a "race to the bottom," as nations compete with each other by eroding labor standards and pay. The authors find no relationship between labor standards and trade. As their measure of openness to trade, the authors use the ratio of exports plus imports to GDP. The trade share is not, however, a policy measure. It is an outcome of trade policy and jointly determined with a number of other factors. Better measures of trade policy would include tariffs or quotas. The World Bank now publishes an average tariff measure that varies across countries and over time. It would also be interesting to see if there is any relationship between these other measures of globalization and the adoption of ILO conventions. Other interesting measures of globalization that could have effects on the adoption of labor standards would include capital flows or policies regarding the openness of the capital account. These types of data are compiled in the IMF's *International Financial Statistics* and its *Annual Report on Exchange Arrangements and Exchange Restrictions*.

The authors get the surprising result in some of their tables that higher GDP per capita is associated with a lower likelihood of adopting ILO conventions. This is puzzling. The authors may want to explore nonlinear effects of GDP per capita, and they might also try eliminating big data outliers, such as the United States. The United States has only adopted one out of the four conventions. The U.S. experience consequently implies that richer countries are less likely to adopt conventions, but it is probably a very unusual case.

The only robust determinant of adoption of ILO conventions, apart from legal status and time effects, are so-called peer effects. I worry that these peer effects may proxy for some omitted variables. It is unclear to me whether the authors allow for country-fixed effects, which could partially address this concern. I am also concerned that the coefficients on peer effects might reflect the fact that the time effect—which is significant and reflects the increasing likelihood of ratification over time—varies across different groups of countries. One possibility would be to introduce export status separately in the regression.

It is extremely interesting that legal systems are such critical determinants of the adoption of labor standards. The result that socialist countries are much more likely to adopt ILO conventions is a reassuring one. We would expect that socialist countries would be more committed to ensuring the rights of labor. The fact that the coefficient is significant and of the correct sign suggests the validity of the other results presented in the paper.

This paper stimulates a number of other questions along the same dimensions. For example, what is the relationship between adoption of international labor standards and actual enforcement of those standards? This would be a very interesting question to study. Chau and Kanbur assume that because there are some systemic determinants of adoption of standards, it must follow that these standards are in some way meaningful. I am not completely convinced. Since there is very little relationship between most of the independent variables in the sample and adoption of an ILO standard, one interpretation of the Chau and Kanbur paper is that lack of enforcement implies that adoption of ILO standards is somewhat random. I would like to see evidence showing that countries that agree to a minimum wage or agree to eliminate child labor are less likely than other countries to underpay or exploit children, but this would need to be proved after controlling for other factors. One possible data source would be the OECD data discussed in Chau and Kanbur's paper, which provides a classification of countries based on the extent to which they violate core ILO conventions. It would be interesting to see if violations of ILO conventions are less likely in countries that have ratified the conventions.

Future research should also extend the data to include the 1990s, when many countries joined the WTO. In addition individual events, such as the ILO campaign in May 1995 following the World Summit for Social Development, may have further affected the likelihood of ratification. Finally, can we trace the impact of different kinds of standards on labor market outcomes, including employment and wage levels, and inequality? The cross-country evidence presented here would be nicely supplemented with country-level studies examining the relationship between the adoption of labor standards and labor market outcomes.

Peter Morici: In this paper, the authors examine the determinants of the probability that countries will ratify ILO conventions in any given year.

They find for C98 (Right to Organize) and C105 (Abolition of Forced Labor) peer effects are significant among developing countries but not for developed countries. In addition their findings point to higher ratification among civil code countries and lowest ratification among socialist law countries. Economic variables, generally, are not found to be particularly important.

These findings are certainly reasonable, even if surprising for developed countries (that is, peer group pressure is not important) and for income level (higher per capita incomes reduce likelihood of ratification). However, these may be explained by certain characteristics of the ILO conventions and enforcement, and the relationship of the conventions to national legal systems.

There are two relevant characteristics of the ILO system. First, it is not at all clear that noncompliance imposes any real costs on large or important developing countries. For example, the 1996 OECD study cited by the authors found:

> In general, forced labour is of negligible importance in the OECD area. However, in several countries outside the OECD area, forced labour appears to be a prominent problem. In China, most prisoners are systematically required to work without pay. In India and Pakistan, bonded labor appears to be a prominent problem. Accordingly, many families and children are forced to work almost as slaves for certain individuals in order to pay off their debts. In Brazil, according to ILO experts, thousands of workers in rural sectors and mining are subject to forced labour conditions. It is dangerous for these workers to escape.[1]

India, Pakistan, and Brazil have ratified both forced both labor conventions—C29 (Forced Labor Convention) and C105.

Regarding freedom of association, the 2000 update to this study continued to place more than half of the nonindustrialized countries studied in the lowest two of four categories of compliance.[2]

Second, rather than merely establishing goals, ILO conventions tend to be quite specific about the means they require for ratifying countries. Generally speaking, the C87 (Freedom of Association) and C98 are based on European, not U.S. models of industrial labor relations, and European economies have ratified them. However, ratification of Conventions 87 and 98 would require wholesale changes in U.S. industrial labor relations law at both the federal and state levels. Some of the results might prove unappealing to unions, employers or both. For example:

> Under the National Labor Relations Act (NLRA), employees select by majority vote an exclusive bargaining unit. Compliance with Convention 87 would require U.S. law to permit employees to select minority or rival unions to represent them in grievances.
>
> In states with "right-to-work laws," unions may not negotiate security agreements providing for union shops. Convention 87 has been interpreted to include the right not to join a union, and U.S. ratification would essentially provide international approval for these laws.
>
> Several U.S. unions do not admit to membership persons who support or participate in the Communist Party, Ku Klux Klan or other fascist, totalitarian, or subversive organization. Convention 87 requires unions to admit all applicants.

1. OECD (1996, p. 47).
2. OECD (2000, p. 28).

> Both the NLRA and Convention 98 prohibit the discharge of employees for union activities outside of work. Adoption of Convention 98 would shift the burden of proof in favor of employees in National Labor Relations Board hearings.
>
> Generally, when the United States signs international commercial agreements, it agrees to obligations that are specific at the moment of ratification, and administering organizations such as the WTO are not permitted to create new obligations through supranational legislative procedures. Reflecting the legislative aspects of ILO deliberations, the requirements that Convention 87 and 98 would impose on U.S. labor law could change over time without U.S. assent.
>
> U.S. law is quite liberal in permitting unions to bring pressure on employers through boards of directors, shareholder suits and proxy fights. Convention 98 prohibits unions and employers from interfering in one another's affairs and could preclude such tactics.[3]

Among the major non-European common law countries, the United States, Canada, India, and New Zealand have all not ratified C98. Only Canada and Australia have ratified C87, and only Australia has ratified C98.

This leaves me with three sets of observations regarding the authors' findings.

First, developed countries have well-developed legal systems and regulatory frameworks that have effectively eradicated forced labor and protect workers' right to unionize. The changes necessary in their laws and regulations to accommodate the relevant ILO conventions may create formidable obstacles to their ratification. This may be the reason the authors found peer group pressure not to be particularly prominent for developed countries.

Second, the authors' GDP per capita findings may have been capturing this effect.

Third, in developing countries, violations of these two core rights, along with child labor, which is really a special case of forced labor, are prevalent. Once many developing countries have ratified these conventions, it may be easier to escape too much scrutiny by staying with the pack. Ratification seems to entail few costs.

General discussion: Edwin Truman asked whether the authors had looked at a model in which the costs of deviation in one standard depend on the costs of deviation in another, or the adoption of another. Kimberly Elliott emphasized the importance of being able to observe violations. The harder it is to

3. Morici (2001, pp. 31–32). This is only a short sampling of the conflicts between U.S. labor law and practices and the requirements of Conventions No. 87 and 98. For an exhaustive treatment, see Potter (1984).

observe and clearly identify a violation, the lower the cost of deviation. Kevin O'Rourke wondered about the exogeneity of the timing of ILO conventions. He also drew attention to the importance of institutional differences, such as legal regimes.

Daniel Tarullo pointed out that there is an extensive literature on the ILO, which has answered the questions that the authors and others raised about why developed countries have not ratified as quickly, or in the case of the United States, at all, a lot of international conventions. The reasons have a lot to do with the detail of ILO conventions. Some relate to civil versus common law. The fact is that the United States, the United Kingdom, and some others take the relationship between their international obligations and their domestic law seriously in the sense that international agreements become embedded in the political and institutional legal fabrics of the country, which in turn stands as an impediment to ratification. Second, he argued that one could not use the OECD measures as a measure of compliance with the ILO conventions. They maybe a reasonable measure of the effectiveness of the ILO in achieving certain outcomes. But compliance is dictated by the internal institutional requirements of the particular convention. And the ILO has a relatively weak enforcement system.

Susan Collins said that she found the peer effect variable very interesting, to the extent that it is not a time trend. She suggested that it might be interesting to look at the peer effect in a disaggregated way, by industry. The issues for countries that are major exporters of textiles and apparel, for example, are quite different from the issues faced by others. Dani Rodrik wondered on the time trend issue whether the simplest thing would be just to add a time variable to the hazard regressions, rather than doing complicated things.

Nancy Chau responded that peer effects continue to be important, even after they had added a time variable. The authors also had defined peer groups not just by development category, export orientation, and development category, but also by regions. With regard to openness, they trade as a share of GDP as an alternative measure of openness. Whether or not you are dependent upon international trade does not seem to be an important factor in terms of your ratification decision. She also clarified that "endum" is a dummy variable for countries that are somehow selected in the OECD study, rather than a dummy variable for enforcement per se. They wanted to control for unexplained heterogeneity in that regard, rather than trying to use that as an enforcement dummy.

Chau agreed with Morici regarding the inflexibility of ILO conventions. The question of why it takes developed countries a longer time to ratify an ILO convention had been on the authors' minds. So it was disappointing that they could not really find a positive coefficient on the GDP per capita variable.

References

Alesina, Alberto, Sule Özler, Nouriel Roubini, and Phillip Swagel. 1996. "Political Instability and Economic Growth." *Journal of Economic Growth* 1 (June): 189–211.

Bagwell, Kyle, and Robert W. Staiger. 2000. "The Simple Economics of Labor Standards and the GATT." In *Social Dimensions of U.S. Trade Policies*, edited by Alan V. Deardorff and Robert M. Stern, 195–231. University of Michigan Press.

Basu, Arnab K., and Nancy H. Chau. 2001. "Market Access, Rivalry, and Eco-Labeling Standards: Are Eco-Labels Non-Tariff Barriers in Disguise?" Mimeo (July), Department of Applied Economics and Management, Cornell University.

Basu, Arnab K., Nancy H. Chau, and Ulrike Grote. 2000. "Guaranteed Manufactured without Child Labor." Working Paper 2000–04. Department of Applied Economics and Management, Cornell University (September).

Brown, Drusilla K. 2000. "International Trade and Core Labour Standards: A Survey of the Recent Literature." Labour Market and Social Policy—Occasional Paper 43. Paris: Organization for Economic Cooperation and Development.

Cappuyns, Elisabeth. 1998. "Linking Labor Standards and Trade Sanctions: An Analysis of Their Current Relationship." *Columbia Journal of Transnational Law* 36: 659–86.

Cassella, Alessandra. 1996. "Free Trade and Evolving Standards." In *Fair Trade and Harmonization: Prerequisites for Free Trade? Volume 1: Economic Analysis*, edited by Jagdish Bhagwati and Robert E. Hudec, 119–56. MIT Press.

Central Intelligence Agency. 2001. *The World Factbook 2000*. Washington: Central Intelligence Agency (www.cia.gov/cia/download.html).

Charnovitz, Steve. 1997. "Trade, Employment, and Labor Standards: The OECD Study and Recent Developments in the Trade and Labor Standards Debate." *Temple International and Comparative Law Journal* 11: 131–63.

Charny, David. 2001. "Regulatory Competition and the Global Coordination of Labour Standards." In *Regulatory Competition and Economic Integration: Comparative Perspectives*, edited by Daniel C. Esty and Damien Geradin, 311–29. Oxford University Press.

Chau, Nancy H., and Ravi Kanbur. 2001. "The Race to the Bottom, From the Bottom." Working Paper 2687. Center for Economic Policy Research Discussion (February).

Cox, D. R. 1972. "Regression Models and Life-Tables." *Journal of the Royal Statistical Society*, Series B (Methodological) 34: 187–220.

David, René, and John E. C. Brierley. 1978. *Major Legal Systems in the World Today: An Introduction to the Comparative Study of Law,* 2d ed. New York: The Free Press.

Easterly, William and Mirvat Sewadeh. 2001. Global Development Network Growth Database (www.worldbank.org/research/growth/GDNdata.htm).

Elliott, Kimberly Ann. 2001. "The ILO and Enforcement of Core Labor Standards." *International Economics Policy Briefs*, No. 00–6. Washington: Institute for International Economics.

Fields, Gary S. 1990. "Labor Standards, Economic Development, and International Trade: Conceptualizing Labor Standards and Government's Role in Promoting Them." In *Labor Standards and Development in the Global Economy*, 19–34. U.S. Department of Labor, Bureau of International Labor Affairs.

Fields, Gary S., and Henry Wan Jr. 1989. "Wage-Setting Institutions and Economic Growth." *World Development* 17 (September): 1471–83.

International Labor Office. 1931. *The International Labour Organisation: The First Decade*. London: George Allen & Unwin Ltd.

———. 2000. *International Programme on the Elimination of Child Labour (IPEC) Highlights 2000*. Geneva: International Labor Organization (www.ilo.org/public/english/standards/ipec/publ/imprep99/report2000/draft7.htm).

International Labor Organization. 2001. *ILOLEX: The ILO's Database on International Labour Standards* (ilolex.ilo.ch:1567/public/english/50normes/infleg/iloeng/iloquery.htm).

Kalbfleisch, J. D., and R. L. Prentice. 1980. *The Statistical Analysis of Failure Time Data*. New York: John Wiley & Sons.

Kuruvilla, Sarosh 1996. "Linkages between Industrialization Strategies and Industrial Relations/Human Resource Policies: Singapore, Malaysia, the Philippines, and India." *Industrial and Labor Relations Review* 49 (July): 635–57.

La Porta, Rafael, Florencio Lopez-de-Silanes, Andrei Shleifer, and Robert W. Vishny 1998. "Law and Finance." *Journal of Political Economy* 106 (December). 1113–55.

———. 1999. "The Quality of Government." *Journal of Law, Economics, and Organization* 15 (April): 222–79.

Lin, D.Y., and L.J. Wei. 1989. "The Robust Inference for the Cox Proportional Hazards Model." *Journal of the American Statistical Association* 84 (December): 1074–78.

Mah, Jai S. 1997. "Core Labour Standards and Export Performance in Developing Countries." *World Economy* 20 (September): 773–85.

Marshall, Monty G., and Keith Jaggers. 2001. *Polity IV Project: Political Regime Characteristics and Transitions, 1800-1999* (www.bsos.umd.edu/cidcm/polity).

Morici, Peter, with Evan Schulz. 2001. *Labor Standards in the Global Trading System*. Washington: Economic Strategy Institute.

Neumann, George R. 1999. "Search Models and Duration Data." In *Handbook of Applied Econometrics Volume II: Microeconomics*, edited by M. Hashem Pesaran and Peter Schmidt, 300–51. Malden, Mass.: Blackwell Publishers.

Organization for Economic Cooperation and Development (OECD). 1996. *Trade, Employment, and Labour Standards: A Study of Core Workers' Rights and International Trade*. Paris: OECD.

———. 2000. *International Trade and Core Labour Standards*. Paris: OECD.

Palley, Thomas I. 1999. *The Economic Case for International Labor Standards: Theory and Some Evidence.* Washington: AFL-CIO.

Portes, Alejandro. 1990. "When More Can Be Less: Labor Standards, Development and the Informal Economy." In *Labor Standards and Development in the Global Economy*, 219–37. U.S. Department of Labor, Bureau of International Labor Affairs.

Potter, Edward E. 1984. *Freedom of Association, The Right to Organize, and Collective Bargaining – The Impact on U.S. Law and Practice of Ratification of ILO Conventions No. 87 & No. 98.* Washington: Labor Policy Association Inc.

Rama, Martin 1995. "Do Labor Market Policies and Institutions Matter? The Adjustment Experience in Latin America and the Caribbean." *Labour Special Issue:* s243–68.

Rodrik, Dani. 1996. "Labor Standards in International Trade: Do They Matter and What Do We Do about Them?" In *Emerging Agenda for Global Trade: High Stakes for Developing Countries*, edited by Robert Z. Lawrence, Dani Rodrik, and John Whalley, 35–79. Overseas Development Council Essay 20. Washington: Johns Hopkins University Press.

Sabot, Richard H. 1990. "Tanzania." In *Labor Standards and Development in the Global Economy*, 173–87. U.S. Department of Labor, Bureau of International Labor Affairs.

Srinivasan, T. N. 1998. *Developing Countries and the Multilateral Trading System: From the GATT to the Uruguay Round and the Future.* Boulder, Colo.: Westview Press.

Stone, Katherine van Wezel. 1996. "Labor in the Global Economy: Four Approaches to Transnational Labour Regulation." In *International Regulatory Competition and Coordination: Perspectives on Economic Regulation in Europe and the United States*, edited by William Bratton, Joseph McCahery, Sol Picciotto, and Colin Scott, 445–77. Oxford: Clarendon Press.

United Nations. 1995. *World Urbanization Prospects: The 1994 Revision. Estimates and Projections of Urban and Rural Populations and of Urban Agglomerations.* ST/ESA/SER.A150. United Nations.

Weissbrodt, David. 1982. "A New United Nations Mechanism for Encouraging the Ratification of Human Rights Treaties." *American Journal of International Law* 76 (April): 418–29.

World Bank. 1995. *World Development Report 1995: Workers in an Integrating World.* New York: Oxford University Press.

World Trade Organization. 1996. Singapore Ministerial Declaration Document 96–5316. Geneva: World Trade Organization (docsonline.wto.org/gen_browse).

THE
ECONOMIC
JOURNAL

The Economic Journal, **120** (*March*), 244–269. doi: 10.1111/j.1468-0297.2009.02298.x. © The Author(s). Journal compilation © Royal Economic Society 2009. Published by Blackwell Publishing, 9600 Garsington Road, Oxford OX4 2DQ, UK and 350 Main Street, Malden, MA 02148, USA.

TURNING A BLIND EYE: COSTLY ENFORCEMENT, CREDIBLE COMMITMENT AND MINIMUM WAGE LAWS*

Arnab K. Basu, Nancy H. Chau and Ravi Kanbur

In many countries, non-compliance with minimum wage legislation is widespread and authorities may be seen as having turned a blind eye to legislation they have themselves passed. We show that turning a blind eye can indeed be an equilibrium phenomenon with *ex post* credibility, in a model of minimum wage policy with imperfect competition, imperfect enforcement and imperfect commitment. Since credible enforcement requires costly *ex post* transfer of income from employers to workers, a government concerned only with efficiency but not with distribution is shown, paradoxically, to be unable to credibly elicit efficiency improvements via a minimum wage reform.

The comparative statics of a minimum wage have inspired a vast empirical literature and vigorous policy debates. The tradeoffs associated with a minimum wage hike are typically articulated in efficiency and equity terms, depending in particular on the competitiveness of the labour market.[1] Arguments based on a standard competitive model of the labour market imply sharp efficiency and equity tradeoffs, as employment is predicted to fall with a well-enforced and binding minimum wage.[2] In contrast, if the relevant frame is of the monopsonistic variety, predicted employment response runs in the opposite direction, so long as the minimum wage is not too high (Stigler, 1946). Consequently, both efficiency and equity improvements may be brought about at once provided the minimum wage is 'skillfully-set'[3] and perfectly enforced.

A standing assumption in both these archetypal settings is perfect enforcement, and by implication, full compliance with the minimum wage. This assumption is at odds with a growing body of empirical evidence however, which finds non-compliance with minimum wage legislation to be widespread. Specifically, the pioneering work of Ashenfelter and Smith (1979) found compliance rate in the US in 1973 to be around 65%.[4] Non-compliance is also found to prevail in an accumulating list of developing countries, including, for example, Brazil (Lemos, 2004, 2006), Costa Rica (Gindling and Terrell, 1995), Honduras (Gindling and Terrell, 2006), Indonesia (Harrison and Scorse, 2004), Mexico (Bell, 1997), Peru (Baanante, 2005), Trinidad and Tobago (Strobl and Walsh,

* We thank Gary Fields, Mick Keen, Russ Krelove, Jonathan Thomas, seminar participants at Edinburgh, the IMF, and Institute for the Study of Labor (IZA), members of the Cornell-SEWA-WIEGO Exposure and Dialogue Group, an Editor of this JOURNAL and two anonymous referees for helpful comments and stimulating discussions. The usual disclaimer applies.

[1] See for example Freeman (1996), Card and Krueger (1995), Bhaskar *et al.* (2002), Fields and Kanbur (2007), Neumark and Wascher (2007).

[2] Bhaskar *et al.* (2002) examine the usefulness and empirical relevance of the competitive, monopsonistic, oligopsonistic and monopolistically competitive frames. In the context of search theory of unemployment (Fershtman and Fishman, 1994; Mortensen and Pissarrides, 1994), a minimum wage has also been shown to be efficiency enhancing as equilibrium employment and equilibrium job retention rates rise with the legislated minimum wage.

[3] As Stigler (1946) notes, such an optimal minimum wage is endogenously determined, and should vary with occupation, among firms, and through time. As such, 'a national minimum wage, infrequently changed, is wholly unsuited to these diversities of conditions' (p. 361).

[4] There have also been exceptions. For example, Machin *et al.* (2003) observed little non-compliance with the national minimum wage of 1999 in the residential care homes industry in the UK.

2001), and a selection of Latin American countries (Maloney and Nunez, 2004).[5] Evidently, not only is it the case that compliant and non-compliant employers co-exist, there are also broad ranges of non-compliance, which come typically in the form of a spike at the official minimum, alongside a dispersion of subminimum wages in covered sectors.[6]

This emerging evidence underscores that the legislated wage floor and the intensity of enforcement are two indispensable arms of a minimum wage policy. Meanwhile, the same evidence also raises two issues that have so far evaded rigorous scrutiny. First, can a simple deviation from perfect to imperfect enforcement alone be sufficient to overturn the predicted impacts of a minimum wage hike when non-compliance is now a genuine possibility? Equally important, and backtracking one step, what are some of the reasons behind the pairing of lax enforcement but a high minimum wage, enough to provoke non-compliance to begin with? More formally, the first question deals with the comparative static properties of a minimum wage hike at a given but less than perfect level of enforcement. The second deals instead with the issue of endogenous enforcement and questions the underlying determinants of enforcement imperfection.

Answers to these questions contribute to the minimum wage policy debate in a number of ways. First, we study the full set of equilibrium labour market implications of an imperfectly enforced minimum wage hike in an imperfectly competitive labour market,[7] when labour supply is taken to respond endogenously to the extent of enforcement imperfection, given any minimum wage.[8] Whether employment response to a rise in minimum wage should be expected to be

(*i*) positive within the standard range, consistent with the familiar monopsonistic frame with perfect enforcement, or

(*ii*) negative, thus consistent with a competitive labour market response also with perfect enforcement, or

(*iii*) muted because precisely of enforcement imperfection,

are clearly key but nevertheless open questions.[9]

[5] Also see Saget (2001) for a survey of evidence in other developing countries.

[6] Kernel density plots and/or wage histograms of dispersed subminimum wage distributions and associated spikes at or about a binding minimum wage have been shown for many countries. See, for a few examples, Bell (1997) for Colombia, Maloney and Nunez (2004) for eight Latin American countries, Cardoso and Portugal (2002) for Portugal, Gindling and Terrell (2006) for Honduras, Strobl and Walsh (2001) for Trinidad and Tobago, Lemos (2004) for both the formal and informal sectors in Brazil.

[7] A theoretical literature modifies the effects of a minimum wage under different specifications of the enforcement and penalty regime based on a competitive labour market (Ashenfelter and Smith, 1979; Chang and Ehrlich, 1985; Grenier, 1982; Yaniv, 2001; Squire and Suthiwart-Narueput, 1997; Harrison and Leamer, 1997). This literature takes a single market determined subminimum wage as given, and does not address the issue of subminimum wage dispersion. Relatedly, Eckstein *et al.* (2006) examine a search model with exogenous exemptions to a minimum wage, but full compliance in the covered sector.

[8] Like our setting, Yaniv (1988) is an exception in the literature of minimum wage compliance in that it too departs from the competitive labour market assumption and examines the compliance behaviour of a monopsonistic firm with an imperfectly enforced minimum wage. But unlike our setting, labour supply is taken as exogenously given and, as such, it does not accommodate rational and endogenous labour supply response to any change in the likelihood of discovery or the possibility of subsequent wage settlement – the determinants of which are the central themes of this article. With a focus on compliance behaviour, Yaniv (1988) does not undertake a full-fledged comparison of the difference in employment comparative statics response that imperfect enforcement makes given *any* minimum wage, or an examination of the possible sources of enforcement endogeneity.

[9] See Neumark and Wascher (2007) for a survey of the recent empirical literature of minimum wage and employment in developed and developing countries.

Second, while there has been extensive discussion on the efficiency and equity tradeoffs associated with a perfectly enforced minimum wage (Freeman, 1996; Fields and Kanbur, 2007), a symmetric treatment of the tradeoffs associated with, and thus some of the underlying determinants of the enforcement of such a wage has not received equal attention. This is despite the fact that enforcement has been noted to differ widely between developed and developing countries (Neumark and Wascher, 2007). Within countries, enforcement is also known to differ across employers in different geographical locations (Ashenfelter and Smith, 1979) and in different industries (Weil, 2004). Further, the familiar distinction between covered and uncovered sectors (Maloney and Nunez, 2004; Gindling and Terrell, 2006) may also effectively be seen as a legislated distinction between sectors where there may be some enforcement, and others with no enforcement by design.

As a third contribution to the minimum wage debate, the combination of imperfect and endogenous enforcement can open up new ways to understand how the labour market responds, or fails to respond to minimum wage legislation, depending ultimately on whether the minimum wage is expected to be enforced *ex post*. The potential insights that this combination can yield was first pointed out by Ashenfelter and Smith (1979) in the context of the minimum wage provisions of the Fair Labour Standards Act in the US. Somewhat unexpectedly, the study finds that compliance rates were higher in the southern states of the US where wages were typically lower, while higher compliance rates also prevailed among employers of female workers compared to males. This counterintuitive finding can indeed be understood, as Ashenfelter and Smith (1979) reasoned, by recognising that government compliance efforts were either concentrated in handling reports of actual violations, or were otherwise devoted to the inspection of sectors where the potential for violation was the greatest. The result was a skewed enforcement resource allocation, with added weight put towards sectors where violations are in fact prevalent. With rational expectations, this anticipated bias should, in turn, be expected to influence equilibrium compliance and employment responses to a minimum wage.[10]

Based on these observations, in this article we develop an incentive compatible equilibrium model of a minimum wage policy, incorporating imperfect competition and imperfect enforcement of the minimum wage. We find this setting to yield results that are consistent with the stylised facts already noted. For the same minimum wage policy, there can be co-existence of compliant and non-compliant employers; a clustering/spike of employer types that uniformly comply; and a dispersion of firm-specific equilibrium subminimum wages.[11] With respect to our first question at the outset, having to do with how employment response to a minimum wage may change with an imperfect but fixed, as opposed to a perfect level of enforcement, we find that the

[10] Harrison and Scorse (2004) examines empirically the issue of endogenous minimum wage compliance in Indonesia. Taking the average of the observed dispersion of subminimum wages as a proxy for the market determined subminimum wage in the competitive frame, it is shown that foreign ownership and the corresponding emphasis on enforcement are associated with a firm-level employment increases subsequent to a minimum wage.

[11] With perfect competition in the standard sense, namely that of costless job search and wage-taking employers, there is by definition a market determined subminimum wage that employers then take as given, (Ashenfelter and Smith, 1979; Chang and Ehrlich, 1985; Grenier, 1982; Yaniv, 2001; Squire and Suthiwart-Narueput, 1997; Harrison and Leamer, 1997).

possibilities run the gamut from no change at all, to a class of cases where there is a sharp reversal in sign from positive to negative, and then further to cases where there is a muted response. We show that each of these cases can prevail within well-defined ranges of minimum wages and enforcement intensities. In addition, these minimum wage thresholds and enforcement intensities are themselves specific to the characteristics of the labour market in question, including demand and supply side parameters.

We then turn to our next question and consider the decision of a planner who is at liberty to choose a minimum wage and a level of enforcement[12] and who harbours a variable degree of concern for efficiency versus distribution. The concern for efficiency addresses underemployment in the face of an imperfectly competitive labour market, while the concern for distribution addresses earning shortfalls relative to the minimum wage on the part of workers attached to non-compliant employers, along with those who are unemployed. In view of the documentation of *ex post* complaints-driven enforcement resource allocation as in Ashenfelter and Smith (1979), we contrast the case of commitment, where both the minimum wage and enforcement levels are fixed *ex ante*, with the case of discretion, where the choice of enforcement intensities is determined *ex post*, depending in particular on whether there is in fact non-compliance with the minimum wage.

Interestingly, given our formulation of a social welfare function combining both efficiency and distributional concerns, we find that non-compliance can be a rational expectation equilibrium with *ex post* discretion but not with commitment. Commitment rules out non-compliance in our setting because if non-compliance is expected for any chosen level of enforcement, the minimum wage can always be adjusted downwards to alleviate the scale of any earnings shortfall. Meanwhile, full compliance cannot be a rational expectation equilibrium with discretion, because the *ex post* optimal level of costly enforcement will certainly be nil if there is literally nothing to enforce, which is of course the case when there is in fact full compliance.

Finally, we show that the endogenous level of enforcement subject to *ex post* credibility exhibits a number of interesting characteristics. First, credible enforcement is indeed need-based, in the sense that all else equal, enforcement will be higher when the incidence and severity of non-compliance is likely the greatest, due, for example, to low labour productivity. *Ex post* enforcement also rises with the minimum wage, provided that the planner espouses a sufficiently high degree of concern for distribution. Put simply, a government more concerned about the earnings shortfall relative to the minimum wage will have a higher *ex post* incentive to enforce. Finally, since *ex post* enforcement of a minimum wage is but a costly income transfer from a non-compliant employer to workers, a planner who cares only about efficiency, and who attaches no intrinsic value to the earning shortfalls of workers relative to the minimum wage, will be rendered least capable of enforcing a minimum wage in a rational expectation equilibrium. In this setting where a higher minimum wage can be used to raise employment and improve efficiency, we end with an intriging result: a planner who cares only about efficiency cannot credibly elicit efficiency-improving minimum wage reforms.

[12] As we show later, if the minimum wage is an exogenously imposed standard rather than optimally chosen, then it may come as no surprise at all that insufficient enforcement will be given to uphold the standard, and non-compliance naturally follows.

1. The Model

Consider an employer who draws labour input from a population of $\mathcal{L}$ heterogeneous workers and who possesses control over wages and employment within this population. The associated revenue is $R(\ell) = (a - b\ell/2)\ell$, where ℓ denotes the number of workers employed, and $a > 0$, and $b \geq 0$ are technological parameters respectively capturing labour productivity, and diminishing marginal product. The implied inverse labour demand schedule is therefore of the form

$$R_\ell(\ell) = a - b\ell \equiv w^d(\ell).$$

Workers differ according to a mobility cost of employment $t \in [0,T]$,[13] and are distributed uniformly along the $[0,T]$ interval. The utility of a worker with mobility cost t and employed at wage w is $u(t,w) = w - t$. The reservation utility of every worker is given by $\bar{u} \geq 0$.

Labour supply facing the employer, at given wage offer w, is accordingly made up of the sum of the individual labour supplies from workers with mobility cost not high enough to deter them from employment $u(t,w) \geq \bar{u}$, or $\ell^s(w) = (w - \bar{u})\mathcal{L}/T$. This implies an inverse labour supply schedule of the familiar form:

$$w^s(\ell) \equiv \bar{u} + \tau\ell, \quad \tau \equiv T/\mathcal{L}.$$

Two benchmarks can now be singled out, respectively the competitive outcome associated with a wage-taking employer and the monopsonistic outcome as in Stigler (1946).[14] So long as the reservation utility is not too high, $\bar{u} < a$, the competitive outcome is given by $\{w^*,\ell^*\}$:

$$\ell^* = \{\ell \mid w^d(\ell) = w^s(\ell)\} = \frac{a - \bar{u}}{b + \tau}, \quad w^* = w^d(\ell^*) = w^s(\ell^*) = \frac{\tau a + b\bar{u}}{b + \tau}, \tag{1}$$

where the marginal revenue product of labour coincides with the prevailing wage $w^d(\ell^*) = w^* = w^s(\ell^*)$. Thus, there is less than full employment ($\ell^* < \mathcal{L}$) if and only if mobility costs are large enough: $T > a - \bar{u} - b\mathcal{L}$. Henceforth, we focus on labour markets in which this mobility cost driven lack of full employment is a genuine concern, and assume that $\ell^* < \mathcal{L}$.

Now let $W(\ell) \equiv w^s(\ell)\ell$ denote total labour cost, and $W_\ell(\ell) = \partial W(\ell)/\partial\ell = \bar{u} + 2\tau\ell$ be the associated marginal labour cost. The monopsonistic labour market outcome $\{w^{do},w^{so},\ell^o\}$ is

$$\ell^o = \text{argmax}_\ell R(\ell) - W(\ell) = \frac{a - \bar{u}}{2\tau + b} \leq \ell^* \tag{2}$$

[13] t should be interpreted as any employment deterring transaction costs or barriers that drive a wedge between the supply price and a worker' reservation utility. These include: geographical distance; lack of information; the cost of correcting skill mismatch; or other worker-specific disutility of employment depending on the conditions of work.

[14] We note that the functional forms assumed here allow us to derive closed-form solutions, and are otherwise not necessary for our comparative statics findings. In particular, a revenue function $R(\ell)$ satisfying diminishing marginal product and any non-degenerate distribution on $[0,T]$ with positive density can alternatively be used without changing the qualitative findings.

$$w^{do} = w^d(\ell^o) = \frac{2\tau a + b\bar{u}}{2\tau + b} \geq w^*, w^{so} = w^s(\ell^o) = \frac{\tau a + (\tau + b)\bar{u}}{2\tau + b} \leq w^*, \text{ for } \tau \geq 0$$

with strict inequalities whenever $\tau > 0$. Thus, a strictly positive mobility cost and asymmetric bargaining power favouring the employer jointly implies that equilibrium marginal revenue product (w^{do}) strictly exceeds the corresponding equilibrium wage (w^{so}), as the employer takes advantage of per worker wage savings that come only with lower employment.[15] The result is a lower level of employment compared to the competitive benchmark $\ell^o < \ell^*$ and unemployed workers constitute a select group with some of the highest mobility costs.

2. Minimum Wage with Imperfect Enforcement

A minimum wage policy is the combination of a minimum wage $\bar{w}$ and an enforcement intensity based on a likelihood λ of inspection and discovery. The timing of the policy is:

- The government announces and commits to $\bar{w}$ and λ.[16]
- Employment and wage decisions are made $\{\ell^m(\bar{w}, \lambda), w^m(\bar{w}, \lambda)\}$.
- Employer inspections are carried out with likelihood λ. If the employer chooses not to comply, a penalty equaling the shortfall $\bar{w} - w^m(\bar{w}, \lambda)$, to be transferred to the worker, follows if inspection occurs. Otherwise, both the worker and the employer will be unaffected;
- Workers strictly prefer receiving the minimum wage directly from a compliant employer as wage payment up front, as opposed to receiving any shortfall as settlement *ex post*. The transaction cost expended in the process of wage settlement upon inspection is given by a fraction $1 - \sigma \in (0,1]$ of the settlement, $\bar{w} - w^m(\bar{w}, \lambda)$, forgone.[17]

For employers, imperfect enforcement implies three classes of options: over-compliance, exact compliance and non-compliance. Imperfect enforcement also implies that the income of workers attached to a non-complying employer now depends explicitly on enforcement and discovery. We consider each of these in turn.

2.1. *Imperfect Enforcement and Labour Supply*

Let $\bar{\ell} \equiv \ell^s(\bar{w}) = (\bar{w} - \bar{u})/\tau$ be the maximal labour supply corresponding to the minimum wage $\bar{w}$. Given λ, the expected utility of a worker facing a subminimum wage offer w is

$$\text{E}u(w, t, \bar{w}, \lambda) = (1 - \lambda)w + \lambda[w + \sigma(\bar{w} - w)] - t = (1 - \lambda\sigma)w + \lambda\sigma\bar{w} - t$$

where $w + \sigma(\bar{w} - w)$ and w are respectively labour income with and without inspection, while $\lambda\sigma$ denotes the transaction cost adjusted intensity of enforcement.

[15] With zero mobility cost, the monopsonistic and competitive labour market equilibria coincide, in which the single employer faces a take-it-or-leave-it offer of $\bar{u}$ from every worker.

[16] The question of whether such a commitment is credible is the subject of Section 4.

[17] As another useful interpretation, σ can also parameterise the effectiveness of the judicial system and government bureaucracy. See Flanagan (1989) for an empirical analysis of the role of substantial time lags, among other things, on employers' decision to comply with the US National Labor Relations Act.

The adjusted weight $\lambda\sigma$ is strictly less than λ itself whenever $\sigma < 1$ and depends jointly on the enforcement intensity and the cost wage settlement σ. Comparing $\mathrm{E}u(w, t, \bar{w}, \lambda)$ and the reservation utility $\bar{u}$, the corresponding enforcement adjusted labour supply and inverse labour supply ($\bar{\ell}^s$ and $\bar{w}^s$) schedules are:

$$\bar{\ell}^s(w, \bar{w}, \lambda) = \frac{(1-\lambda\sigma)w + \lambda\sigma\bar{w} - \bar{u}}{\tau} = \ell^s(w) + \frac{\lambda\sigma}{\tau}(\bar{w} - w) \geq \ell^s(w), \tag{3}$$

$$\bar{w}^s(\ell, \bar{w}, \lambda) = \frac{\bar{u} + \tau\ell - \lambda\sigma\bar{w}}{1 - \lambda\sigma} = w^s(\ell) + \frac{\lambda\sigma}{1-\lambda\sigma}[w^s(\ell) - \bar{w}] \leq w^s(\ell), \tag{4}$$

for a non-compliant employer with $w \leq \bar{w}$ for (3) and thus $\ell \leq \bar{\ell}$ for (4). In contrast, a compliant employer and his hired workers are unaffected by inspection. A worker's expected utility is thus $w - t$ as before. Meanwhile, labour supply $\bar{\ell}^s(w, \bar{w}, \lambda)$ reduces to $\ell^s(w)$, and $\bar{w}^s(w, \bar{w}, \ell)$ to $w^s(\ell) = \bar{u} + \tau\ell$ for a compliant employer.

From (3), enforcement adjusted labour supply exceeds the unregulated benchmark at constant contracted wage w, whenever there is a positive likelihood of income gains subsequent to employer inspection $\lambda\sigma > 0$. Also from (3), either an increase in $\bar{w}$, or an increase in λ further increases labour supply at given subminimum wage w. Thus, imperfect enforcement gives rise to shifts in the labour supply in response to changes in the minimum wage policy whenever there is non-compliance, to be accounted for in the employer's decision problem below.

2.2. *Imperfect Enforcement and Expected Labour Cost*

The expected profit of the employer is:

$$\max_{\ell} R(\ell) - (1-\lambda)\bar{w}^s(\ell, \bar{w}, \lambda)\ell - \lambda \max\{\bar{w}, \bar{w}^s(\ell, \bar{w}, \lambda)\}\ell \tag{5}$$

where the last expression $\max\{\bar{w}, \bar{w}^s(\ell, \bar{w}, \lambda)\}$ reflects the per worker wage cost conditional on inspection. For a non-compliant employer, $\max\{\bar{w}, \bar{w}^s(\ell, \bar{w}, \lambda)\} = \bar{w}^s(\ell, \bar{w}, \lambda) < \bar{w}$. Using (4), expected profit in (5) simplifies to

$$\max_{\ell} R(\ell) - (1-\psi)W(\ell) - \psi\bar{w}\ell \tag{6}$$

where ψ adjusts the weight given to the minimum wage as part of the expected labour cost per worker by accounting for (4). Further, ψ is less than λ itself, lies between zero and unity, and is monotonically increasing in λ:

$$\psi \equiv \frac{\lambda(1-\sigma)}{1-\lambda\sigma}.$$

In contrast, for an employer that over or exactly complies, expected profit is simply

$$\max_{\ell} R(\ell) - W(\ell). \tag{7}$$

Taken together, expected labour cost $\mathrm{E}\bar{W}(\ell, \bar{w}, \lambda) \equiv (1-\lambda)\bar{w}^s(\ell, \bar{w}, \lambda)\ell + \lambda \max\{\bar{w}, \bar{w}^s(\ell, \bar{w}, \lambda)\}$ and the corresponding expected marginal labour cost where the derivative exists, $\mathrm{E}\bar{W}_\ell(\ell, \bar{w}, \lambda)$, are given by

$$\mathrm{E}\bar{W}(\ell, \bar{w}, \lambda) = \begin{cases} (1-\psi)W(\ell) + \psi\bar{w}\ell & \text{if } \ell < \bar{\ell} \\ W(\ell) & \text{otherwise.} \end{cases} \quad (8)$$

$$\mathrm{E}\bar{W}_\ell(\ell, \bar{w}, \lambda) = \begin{cases} (1-\psi)W_\ell(\ell) + \psi\bar{w} & \text{if } \ell < \bar{\ell} \\ W_\ell(\ell) & \text{otherwise.} \end{cases} \quad (9)$$

Figure 1 illustrates. As shown, $\mathrm{E}\bar{W}_\ell(\cdot)$ is increasing and piecewise continuous in ℓ. Furthermore, for a non-complying employer with $\ell < \bar{\ell}$, $\mathrm{E}\bar{W}_\ell(\cdot)$ is a weighted average. As λ tends to 1 (and accordingly ψ to 1), $\mathrm{E}\bar{W}_\ell(\cdot)$ is perfectly elastic at $\bar{w}$ for $\ell \leq \bar{\ell}$, as in the perfect enforcement setting in Stigler (1946). In contrast, in the complete absence of enforcement so that $\psi = \lambda = 0$, the marginal labour cost schedule is independent of the minimum wage and coincides instead with the unregulated marginal labour cost. Finally, expected marginal labour cost is truncated exactly at $\bar{\ell}$ whenever $\lambda \in (0,1]$. Beyond $\bar{\ell}$, and thus for an employer that overcomplies, expected marginal hiring cost coincides with the no-intervention benchmark.

One of the key insights of Stigler (1946) is that a perfectly enforced, binding minimum wage in the appropriate range can encourage hiring by *lowering* the marginal labour cost of hiring. Equation (9) echoes and extends this insight to cases with imperfect enforcement. Consider therefore a binding minimum wage $\bar{w}$, henceforth taken to mean $\bar{w} \geq w^{so}$. Evaluating expected marginal labour cost at the no-intervention employment level, ℓ^o,

$$\mathrm{E}\bar{W}_\ell(\ell^o, \bar{w}, \lambda) = (1-\psi)w^{do} + \psi\bar{w}. \quad (10)$$

Stricter enforcement via an increase in λ, and thus ψ, *lowers* expected marginal cost at ℓ^o if and only if $\bar{w} < w^{do}$. Put differently, (10) shows that even in an environment of imperfect enforcement, in which the government turns a blind eye to the possibility of non-compliance with regular frequency $(1 - \lambda)$, raising enforcement continues to *lower* the expected marginal cost of hiring relative to the no intervention baseline in the range $\bar{w} \in [w^{so}, w^{do}]$. Outside the range, however, with $\bar{w}$ greater than the marginal revenue product of labour at $\ell^o(w^{do})$, $\mathrm{E}\bar{W}_\ell(\ell^o, \bar{w}, \lambda)$ is now strictly increasing in λ. These observations suggest that the comparative statics of a minimum wage policy $(\bar{w}, \lambda)$ will likely depend crucially on the size of the minimum wage relative to the thresholds w^{so} and w^{do}. We turn to these next.

2.3. *Labour Market Equilibrium and Minimum Wage Thresholds*

A labour market equilibrium $\{\ell^m(\bar{w}, \lambda), w^m(\bar{w}, \lambda)\}$ consistent with expected profit maximisation, expected utility decision making and a binding but imperfectly enforced minimum wage can be shown to exhibit a number of possible configurations, separated by three distinct minimum wage thresholds. Two of which have already been singled out: w^{so} and w^{do}. A third threshold $\bar{W}(\lambda)$ is endogenous and depends on enforcement. $\bar{W}(\lambda)$ divides labour market equilibria into those that are to the right, left, or exactly at the point where the expected marginal labour cost schedule truncates:[18]

[18] Since the $R_\ell(\bar{\ell}) - (1-\psi)(\bar{u} + 2\tau\bar{\ell}) - \psi\bar{w}$ is monotonically decreasing in $\bar{w}$, $\bar{W}(\lambda)$ is well defined and unique by standard arguments. In particular, with a binding minimum wage, $R_\ell(\bar{\ell}) \geq \mathrm{E}\bar{W}_\ell(\bar{\ell}, \bar{w}, \lambda)$ if and only if $a - b\bar{\ell} \geq (1-\psi)(\bar{u} + 2\tau\bar{\ell}) + \psi\bar{w}$. Rearranging terms and using $\bar{w} = \bar{u} + \tau\bar{\ell}$ yields $\bar{w} \leq w^* - \{[\tau(1-\psi)]/[\tau(2-\psi) + b]\}(w^* - \bar{u})$ as shown.

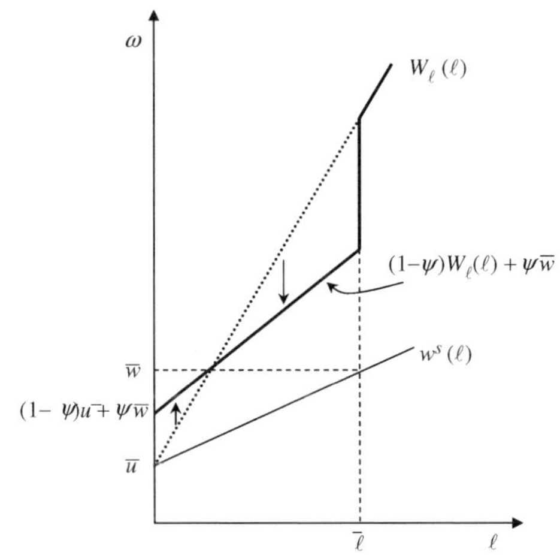

Fig. 1. *Expected Marginal Labour Cost with Imperfect Enforcement*

$$\begin{aligned}\bar{W}(\lambda) &\equiv \max\{\bar{w} \geq w^{so} | R_\ell(\bar{\ell}) - (1-\psi)(\bar{u} + 2\tau\bar{\ell}) - \psi\bar{w} \geq 0\} \\ &= w^* - \frac{\tau(1-\psi)}{\tau(2-\psi)+b}(w^* - \bar{u})(< w^* < w^{do}).\end{aligned} \tag{11}$$

Thus at given enforcement, expected marginal labour cost exceeds marginal value product, evaluated at the *maximal* labour supply available at the minimum wage, as soon as the minimum wage exceeds $\bar{W}(\lambda)$. As such, $\bar{W}(\lambda)$ puts an upper bound on the range of minimum wages, beyond which equilibrium employment will be scaled back to a level less than the available labour supply at the minimum wage. Using (1), (2) and (11), it is of interest to note that $\bar{W}(\lambda)$ lies between the unregulated wage w^{so} and the competitive wage w^*,[19] or

$$w^{so} \leq \bar{W}(\lambda) < w^* < w^{do}$$

whenever $\lambda < 1$. These are illustrated in Figure 2 for $\lambda \in (0,1)$. The corresponding labour market equilibria can be divided into:

Over-compliance: If $\bar{w} < w^{so}$, the minimum wage is non-binding, and there is equilibrium over-compliance. Thus, $\ell^m(\bar{w},\lambda) = \ell^o$, $\mathrm{E}u[w^m(\bar{w},\lambda), t] = w^{so} - t$, and $w^m(\bar{w},\lambda) = w^{so}$. Consequently, employment, expected utility, and the equilibrium wage are all independent of small changes in the minimum wage policy $(\bar{w},\lambda)$. In Figure 3*a*, inverse demand schedule $a_1 - b\ell$ is consistent with this regime.

Exact Compliance: Raise the minimum wage until $\bar{w} \in [w^{so}, \bar{W}(\lambda)]$. There is thus a binding minimum wage but the marginal revenue product of labour is greater than the expected marginal labour cost evaluated at $\bar{\ell}$, since $\bar{w}$ is less than the threshold $\bar{W}(\lambda)$.

[19] To see this, note that from (2) and (11) $\bar{W}(\lambda) - w^{so} = \tau(a-u)/\{(2\tau+b)[(2-\psi)\tau]+b\} > 0$. Meanwhile $\bar{W}(\lambda) \leq w^*$ by inspection of (11).

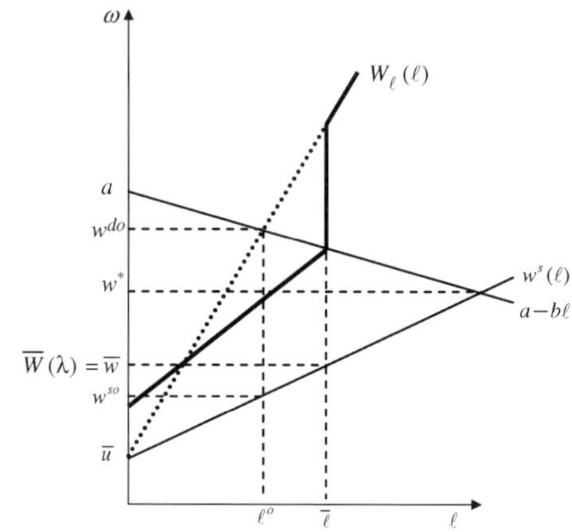

Fig. 2. *Minimum Wage Thresholds*

Labour market equilibrium is accordingly *supply-constrained* ($a_2 - b\ell$ in Figure 3*a*). Equilibrium employment and wages are determined based purely on supply side considerations, with:

$$\ell^m(\bar{w}, \lambda) = \frac{\bar{w} - \bar{u}}{\tau} = \bar{\ell}, \quad \mathrm{E}u[w^m(\bar{w}, \lambda), t] = \bar{w} - t, w^m(\bar{w}, \lambda) = \bar{w} \tag{12}$$

since $\bar{w}^s(\bar{\ell}, \bar{w}, \lambda) = \bar{w}$ from (5). The elasticities of equilibrium employment, expected utility, and equilibrium wage with respect to a rise in the minimum wage are all positive. In addition, since such an employer is already in strict compliance with the minimum wage legislation, a further increase in the intensity of enforcement has no further impact on equilibrium hiring or wage.

Non-compliance: As noted, for a minimum wage $\bar{w} > \bar{W}(\lambda)$, labour market equilibrium is *demand constrained* ($a_3 - b\ell$ and $a_4 - b\ell$ in Figure 3*b*).[20] Equilibrium employment is determined by the intersection of the marginal revenue product and the expected marginal labour cost: $\ell^m(\bar{w}, \lambda) = \{\ell \mid R_\ell(\ell) = (1 - \psi)(\bar{u} + 2\tau\ell + \psi\bar{w})\}$, while $\mathrm{E}u[w^m(\bar{w}, \lambda), t, \bar{w}, \lambda] = \bar{u} + \tau\ell^m(\bar{w}, \lambda) - t$. As long as there is positive employment, it follows from (2) and (9) that

$$\ell^m(\bar{w}, \lambda) = \ell^o + \frac{\psi}{2\tau(1 - \psi) + b}(w^{do} - \bar{w}) \tag{13}$$

[20] It can also be checked using (5) that whenever $\bar{w} > \bar{W}(\lambda)$, non-compliance strictly dominates compliance with employment rationing at $\tilde{\ell}$, where $w^d(\tilde{\ell}) = \bar{w}$. To see this, expected profit maximisation implies

$$\begin{aligned} R[\ell^m(\bar{w}, \lambda)] - \mathrm{E}\bar{W}[\ell^m(\bar{w}, \lambda), \bar{w}, \lambda] - [R(\tilde{\ell}) - \bar{w}\tilde{\ell}] &\geq R(\tilde{\ell}) - \mathrm{E}\bar{W}(\tilde{\ell}, \bar{w}, \lambda) - [R(\tilde{\ell}) - \bar{w}\tilde{\ell}] \\ &= (1 - \psi)\{\bar{w} - \bar{w}^s[\ell^m(\bar{w}, \lambda), \bar{w}, \lambda]\}\tilde{\ell} > 0. \end{aligned}$$

whenever $\tilde{\ell} < \bar{\ell}$ from (5).

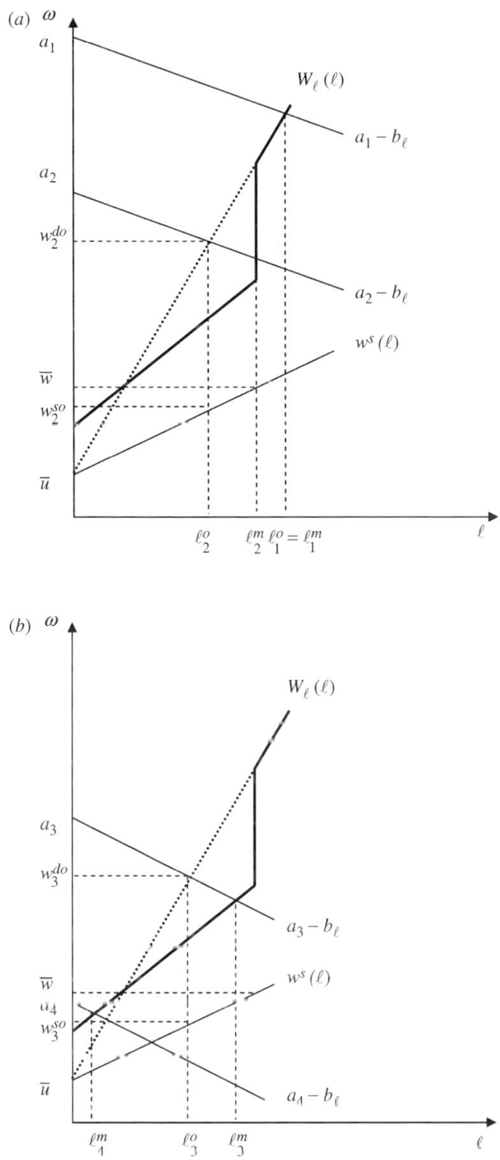

Fig. 3. (*a*) *Compliance* (*b*) *Non-compliance*

$$\mathrm{E}u[w^m(\bar{w},\lambda),t] = w^{so} - t + \frac{\tau\psi}{2\tau(1-\psi)+b}(w^{do} - \bar{w}). \tag{14}$$

Thus, employment and expected utility exceed (are less than) their no-intervention benchmarks whenever $\bar{w}$ is less than (greater than) w^{do}. Also, from (4), (11) and (13),

$$w^m(\bar{w},\lambda) = \bar{w} - \left[1 + \frac{\tau\psi}{2\tau(1-\psi)+b}\right]\frac{\bar{w} - \bar{W}(\lambda)}{1-\lambda\sigma} < \bar{w} \tag{15}$$

if and only if $\bar{w} > \bar{W}(\lambda)$ and $\lambda > 0$. Thus, equilibrium non-compliance, $w^m(\bar{w},\lambda) < \bar{w}$, is synonymous with a binding demand constraint. From (15), equilibrium subminimum wage depends on employer productivity and labour supply conditions, since $\bar{W}(\lambda) = w^* - (w^* - \bar{u})\tau(1-\psi)/[\tau(2-\psi)+b]$. In particular, a more productive employer (a), a smaller population of workers to draw from ($\mathcal{L}$) and a high mobility cost (T) are associated with a higher subminimum wage. Finally, since equilibrium employment is demand constrained in this range, (13)–(15) show that a further rise in the minimum wage decreases equilibrium employment, workers' expected utility and equilibrium wage at constant enforcement intensity. The preceding discussion suggests three sets of issues of particular empirical relevance, examined in greater detail below.

2.3.1. *Imperfect enforcement and comparative statics*

Figure 4 summarises and compares the relationship between equilibrium employment and the minimum wage for the case of perfect enforcement, $\lambda = 1$, and imperfect enforcement $\lambda' < 1$, based on (12)–(15). As shown, the predicted comparative statics responses of a minimum wage are highly sensitive to imperfect enforcement and accommodate cases ranging from

(*i*) no change,
(*ii*) a sign reversal and
(*iii*) a muted response,

depending systematically on the size of the minimum wage relative to the minimum wage thresholds already discussed.

For minimum wages less than the endogenously determined $\bar{W}(\lambda)$, there is either over or strict compliance despite imperfect enforcement. Equilibrium employment is accordingly independent of the intensity of enforcement, as in the perfect enforcement case. Next, for minimum wages in the range $(\bar{W}(\lambda), w^*]$, there is now non-compliance. Contrary to the case of perfect enforcement, a further rise in the minimum wage now decreases, rather than increases employment, even though the minimum wage is strictly less than the competitive baseline w^*. Finally, for minimum wages greater than the competitive wage w^*, employment continues to fall with respect to a rise in $\bar{w}$, albeit at a muted rate because of imperfect enforcement.

The same Figure also shows that at a given minimum wage, the relationship between enforcement and equilibrium employment is nuanced. In particular, for a binding minimum wage $\bar{w}$ in the range $[w^{so}, w^{do}]$, an increase in λ (from λ' to 1) leaves employment unchanged for a firm in strict compliance, raise employment for any other

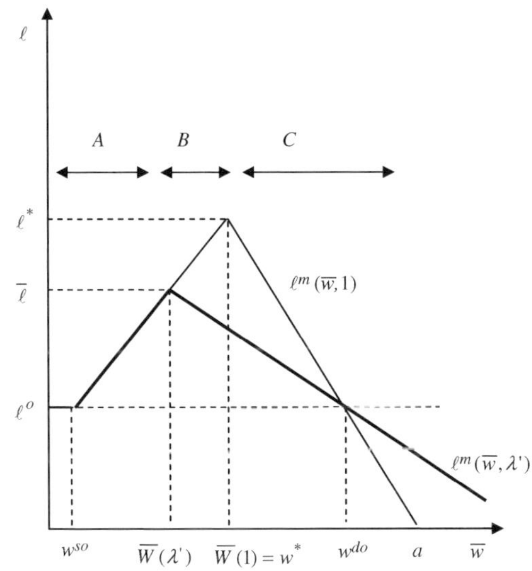

Fig. 4. *Employment and Minimum Wage With Imperfect Enforcement*
A: No Change; B: Sign Reversal; C: Muted Response

(newly compliant or non-compliant) firms. In Figure 3*b*, inverse demand $a_3 - b\ell$ is consistent with this regime. The intuition follows from (10), where the expected marginal labour cost at ℓ^o is shown to *decrease* with enforcement intensity in this range. Outside this range, with $\bar{w}$ higher than w^{do}, stricter enforcement can only decrease hiring by a non-compliant employer ($a_4 - b\ell$ in Figure 3*b*).

2.3.2. *Compliant clusters and wage dispersion*

It is worth reiterating that each of the minimum wage thresholds is endogenous, with w^{so}, $\bar{W}(\lambda)$ and w^{do} all positively associated with the productivity of labour a, the reservation utility $\bar{u}$, and supply side parameters, $T/\mathcal{L}$. Thus, the minimum wage thresholds can be re-expressed to give the combinations of labour demand *and* supply conditions consistent with over-compliance, strict compliance, and non-compliance, given the same minimum wage policy.

Figure 5 illustrates in $(a, b\mathcal{L}/T)$ space. Area A characterises the cluster of employers types and labour supply conditions consistent with exact compliance.[21] Any employer in this area responds uniformly to the same minimum wage policy by paying exactly the minimum wage. As labour productivity falls, or when the pool of available workers ($\mathcal{L}$) increases, for example, area B applies. Area B characterises the case of non-compliance

[21] From (11), strict compliance requires, $\bar{w} \in (w^{so}, \bar{W}(\lambda)] \Leftrightarrow a \in [\bar{w} + (1 - \psi + b/\tau)(\bar{w} - \bar{u}), \bar{w} + (1 + b/\tau)(\bar{w} - \bar{u}))$.

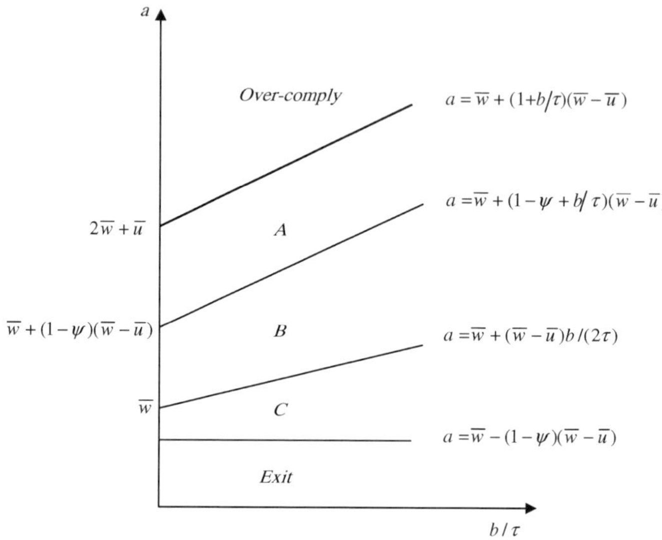

Fig. 5. *Labour Demand and Supply Determinants and Equilibrium Configurations*
A: Strict Compliance; B: Effective Enforcement; C: Ineffective Enforcement

with positive employment response to stricter enforcement.[22] Finally, area C corresponds to the case of non-compliance with negative employment response to stricter enforcement.[23] Both areas B and C admit a continuous range of subminimum wages depending systematically on combinations of a and τ via (15).

These observations are consistent with a number of well-known empirical findings already noted in the Introduction. The clustering of compliant employers as in Area A is consistent with the oft noted spike at the minimum wage along the wage distribution. Workers earning the minimum wage co-exist with other subminimum wage earners along a dispersed subminimum wage distribution, consistent with Areas B and C.

In addition, an increase in the minimum wage can now be seen to give rise to two distinct sets of effects on wages. A pure wage effect works through (12) and (15), indicating respectively a positive wage impact on those who exactly comply and a negative impact on those who do not. But the same rise in the minimum wage also embodies a composition effect, which now accommodates an endogenous switch from compliance to non-compliance. In Figure 5, such an increase in the minimum wage moves areas A, B and C upwards. The combined wage and composition effect of a

[22] This requires that $\bar{w} \in [\bar{W}(\lambda), w^{do}) \Leftrightarrow a \in (\bar{w} + b(\bar{w} - \bar{u})/2\tau, \bar{w} + (1 - \psi + b/\tau)(\bar{w} - \bar{u})]$.

[23] This final class requires $\bar{w} \in [w^{do}, [a - (1 - \psi)\bar{u}]/\psi]$, since a minimum wage greater than $[a - (1 - \psi)\bar{u}]/\psi$ induces zero employment upon rearranging (13).

minimum wage hike is thus ambiguous in general. Not surprisingly, then, co-movements of the legislated minimum and subminimum wage have also been observed in the empirical literature but these have so far come up with mixed findings on the direction of observed co-movements (Card and Krueger, 1995; Lemos, 2004; Baanante, 2005; Strobl and Walsh, 2001).

2.3.3. *Endogenous enforcement and turning a blind eye*

Implicit in our findings so far is that imperfect enforcement need not be associated with non-compliance. Indeed, the threshold $\bar{W}(\lambda)$ in (11) gives the largest minimum wage that can be applied without triggering non-compliance, for any $\lambda \in [0,1]$. Furthermore, $\bar{W}(\lambda)$ can be fine-tuned by adjusting λ. Routine differentiation with respect to λ gives an intuitive answer: the threshold $\bar{W}(\lambda)$ can be raised by increasing λ. As λ tends to 1, $\bar{W}(\lambda)$ approaches w^*, coinciding with the perfect enforcement case. But as λ approaches zero, $\bar{W}(\lambda)$ now tends to w^{so} implying in contrast that no employer will comply when a strictly binding minimum wage is not enforced.

Because of the monotonicity of $\bar{W}(\lambda)$ in λ, (11) can be used to retrieve the minimum enforcement intensity, $\Lambda^o(\bar{w})$, required to elicit compliance for any given minimum wage $\bar{w} \in (w^{so}, w^*)$:

$$\Lambda^o(\bar{w}) = \bar{W}^{-1}(\bar{w}), \text{ for } \bar{w} \in (w^{so}, w^*). \tag{16}$$

Naturally, this is the dual to (11), which seeks the maximum minimum wage that can be imposed without eliciting non-compliance, given λ.[24] Interestingly, the minimal level of enforcement also responds to the underlying productivity and supply conditions of the labour market. Using (11), $\Lambda^o(\bar{w})$ is strictly decreasing respectively in a and in $T/\mathcal{L}$. In other words, the level of enforcement required to elicit compliance relates systematically to whether non-compliance should be expected to begin with.

Of course, $\Lambda^o(\bar{w})$ also rises with a higher minimum wage $\bar{w}$. As such, (16) provides one possible endogenous link between the two components of a minimum wage policy, applicable whenever a minimum wage policy combines a legislated wage floor $\bar{w}$ and the minimal enforcement required to elicit the market payment of this wage, $\Lambda^o(\bar{w})$.

All these prompt two important questions: what is the nature of the comparative statics of a minimum wage with endogenous enforcement, represented by the pair $(\bar{w}, \Lambda^o(\bar{w}))$, when it is common knowledge that the government is committed to choosing enforcement systematically based on $\Lambda^o(\bar{w})$? Meanwhile, under what conditions will such a minimum wage policy $(\bar{w}, \Lambda^o(\bar{w}))$ be consistent with social welfare maximisation?

The first question points to an endogeneity problem, when enforcement is now dependent on the size of the minimum wage itself. To appreciate the potential scale of this problem, note from (12) that $\ell^m[\bar{w}, \Lambda^o(\bar{w})]$ for $\bar{w} \in (w^{so}, w^*)$ reduces to $\ell^s(\bar{w}) = (\bar{w} - \bar{u})/\tau$, and $w^m[\bar{w}, \Lambda^o(\bar{w})] = \bar{w}$. As such, the intricacies of the comparative statics of a minimum wage policy with imperfect (but fixed) enforcement are effectively cancelled out with this endogenous enforcement scheme. The predicted comparative

[24] For $\bar{w} > w^*$, full compliance will always require perfect enforcement.

statics of a minimum wage hike thus coincides with that of a world with perfect enforcement, even when imperfect enforcement is clearly still in play and $\Lambda^o(\bar{w})$ is strictly less than unity.

At the heart of the second question is the issue: why do governments turn a blind eye to the minimum wage law that they have themselves passed? A minimum wage policy like $(\bar{w}, \Lambda^o(\bar{w}))$ accordingly sets out a baseline, and turning a blind eye simply means a level of enforcement that is less than $\Lambda^o(\bar{w})$, given $\bar{w}$. In what follows, we examine the nature of the comparative statics of a minimum wage policy with an endogenous and social-welfare-maximising level of enforcement.

3. Minimum Wage and the Credibility of Enforcement

Starting with the announcement of a minimum wage $\bar{w}$, let λ be the *expected* intensity of enforcement, held by both employers and workers when employment contracts are made, as we have done up to now. Let p, in contrast, denote the actual intensity of enforcement carried out post contract negotiations. Thus, p also determines the fraction of contracted workers earning less than the minimum wage, who ultimately receive wage settlement net of transaction costs, $\sigma[\bar{w} - w^m(\bar{w}, \lambda)]$.

Consider therefore a social welfare function made up of three components, taking as given the expectation λ:

(*i*) the sum of the profit of the employer, the income net of mobility cost for all workers along the $[0, \ell^m T/\mathcal{L}]$ interval, and the reservation income equivalent $\bar{u}$ of the unemployed,[25]

(*ii*) a strictly increasing and strictly convex cost of employer inspection $C(p)\ell^m$, where $c \equiv C_p(0) \geq 0$, denotes the marginal cost of raising enforcement evaluated at $p = 0$,[26] and

(*iii*) a loss function which captures the government's distributional concern $D(\cdot)$, with respect to employer wage decisions that deviate from the legislated minimum.[27]

The first two components of the government's objective function capture efficiency concerns in the standard way. The third distributional concern component is captured by a loss function. With non-compliance, the loss function is

[25] This first component of the government welfare function is given by:

$$R(\ell^m) - [(1-p)w^m + p\bar{w}]\ell^m + \left\{\int_0^{\ell^m T/\mathcal{L}} [(1-p\sigma)w^m + p\sigma\bar{w} - t]\frac{\mathcal{L}}{T}\mathrm{d}t\right\} + \bar{u}(\mathcal{L} - \ell^m)$$
$$= R(\ell^m) - \left(\bar{u} + \frac{\tau\ell^m}{2}\right)\ell^m - p(1-\sigma)(\bar{w} - w^m)\ell^m + \bar{u}\mathcal{L},$$

where the expression $p(1-\sigma)(\bar{w} - \bar{w}^m)\ell^m$ denotes the transaction cost of enforcing the minimum wage policy when non-compliance is in place.

[26] We assume that the government finance enforcement activities through lump sum taxation. Any additional costs of the use of public funds incurred in the process are subsumed in the enforcement cost function $C(p)$.

[27] We suppress the arguments of equilibrium employment and wage $\ell^m(\bar{w}, \lambda)$ and $w^m(\bar{w}, \lambda)$ whenever there is no risk of confusion.

$$\gamma D(\bar{w},\lambda,p)=\gamma\left(\left\{\frac{\bar{w}-[w^m+\sigma(\bar{w}-w^m)]}{\bar{w}}\right\}p\ell^m+\left(\frac{\bar{w}-w^m}{\bar{w}}\right)\left(1-p\right)\ell^m.\right.$$
$$\left.+\left(\frac{\bar{w}-0}{\bar{w}}\right)\left(\mathcal{L}-\ell^m\right)\right)=\gamma\left[\frac{(\bar{w}-w^m)}{\bar{w}}(1-p\sigma)\ell^m+(\mathcal{L}-\ell^m)\right].$$

With full (exact or over) compliance, the loss function is just $\gamma D(\bar{w},\lambda,p)=\gamma(\mathcal{L}-\ell^m)$. Within the distributional realm, $D(\cdot)$ gives the number of workers receiving less than the minimum wage target, weighted by the corresponding proportional income shortfall. $D(\cdot)$ may also be interpreted as analogous to one of the Foster *et al.* (1984) measures of poverty, where the minimum wage serves as the government's definition of who is poor. The parameter $\gamma>0$ measures the government's concern for distribution relative to efficiency overall and represents the marginal social welfare cost of a small change in the poverty measure $D(\cdot)$. The social welfare function is thus:

$$\Omega(\bar{w},\lambda,p)=R(\ell^m)-\left(\bar{u}+\frac{\tau\ell^m}{2}\right)\ell^m-p(1-\sigma)(\bar{w}-w^m)\ell^m+\bar{u}\mathcal{L}-C(p)\ell^m-\gamma D(\bar{w},\lambda,p). \quad (17)$$

In what follows, we focus on minimum wages in the range $\bar{w}\in[w^{so},w^{do}]$ and do so for two reasons. First, and as has been discussed, $\bar{w}\geq w^{so}$ is required for the minimum wage to bind. Meanwhile, $\bar{w}>w^{do}$ always reduces employment relative to the unregulated benchmark and is thus inferior to no regulation at all both on efficiency grounds, and on equity grounds based on $\Omega(\cdot)$. Second, from (13)–(15), stricter enforcement of a minimum wage greater than w^{do} cannot improve social welfare since it raises enforcement costs but serves only to decrease employment, expected utility, and subminimum wages even further. As such, it will be not at all surprising that a government turns a blind eye to minimum wages greater than w^{do}.

3.1. *Commitment*

In this regime, the government simultaneously commits to a minimum wage and a corresponding level of enforcement to maximise the social welfare function $\Omega(\bar{w},\lambda,p)$. Let $(\bar{w}^c,\lambda^c)$ be such a minimum wage policy with *ex ante* commitment. Rational expectation in the case of commitment implies $p=\lambda^c$. We can thus denote social welfare as $\Omega^c(\bar{w}^c,\lambda^c)\equiv\Omega(\bar{w}^c,\lambda^c,\lambda^c)$.

We now show that social-welfare-maximising minimum wage policy with commitment $(\bar{w}^c,\lambda^c)$ exhibits two important characteristics: it must be the case that

(*i*) there is full compliance: $w^m(\bar{w}^c,\lambda^c)=\bar{w}^c$, and
(*ii*) the cost minimising level of enforcement is undertaken, $\lambda^c=\Lambda^o(\bar{w}^c)$ as in (16).

To see this, suppose in contrast that $(\bar{w}^c,\lambda')$ maximises the social welfare function but $\lambda'\neq\Lambda^o(\bar{w})$, and $\ell^m(\bar{w}^c,\lambda')=\ell'$ and $w^m(\bar{w}^c,\lambda')$ are the corresponding equilibrium employment and market wage. There are two possibilities:

(*i*) the hypothetical λ' is strictly greater than $\Lambda^o(\bar{w}^c)$ and
(*ii*) λ' is strictly less than $\Lambda^o(\bar{w}^c)$.

Suppose first that $\lambda' > \Lambda^o(\bar{w}^c)$. It follows by definition of $\Lambda^o(\bar{w}^c)$ that there is full compliance, with employment and wage respectively at:

$$\ell^m(\bar{w}^c, \lambda') = \ell^m[\bar{w}^c, \Lambda^o(\bar{w})], w^m(\bar{w}^c, \lambda') = w^m[\bar{w}^c, \Lambda^o(\bar{w})] = \bar{w}^c.$$

In other words, both employment and market wage are at their full compliance levels consistent with the minimum wage $\bar{w}^c$, but the cost of enforcement $C(\lambda')$ is strictly higher than $C[\Lambda^o(\bar{w}^c)]$. Thus, $\Omega^c(\bar{w}^c, \lambda') < \Omega^c[\bar{w}^c, \Lambda^o(\bar{w}^c)]$. Intuitively, therefore, there is no reason to raise enforcement beyond the minimal level $\Lambda^o(\bar{w}^c)$ required to guarantee full compliance.

Suppose instead that $\lambda' < \Lambda^o(\bar{w}^c)$ and enforcement is insufficient to guarantee full compliance. Equilibrium employment and the (subminimum) market wage are then:

$$\ell^m(\bar{w}^c, \lambda') < \ell^m[\bar{w}^c, \Lambda^o(\bar{w})], w^m(\bar{w}^c, \lambda') < \bar{w}^c$$

which follows since $\bar{w} < w^{do}$ and stricter enforcement increases employment from (13). Also from (13), a reduction in the minimum wage from $\bar{w}^c$ to $\bar{W}(\lambda')$ can thus raise employment and ensure full compliance at the same enforcement cost. It follows therefore that $\Omega^c(\bar{w}^c, \lambda') < \Omega^c[\bar{W}(\lambda'), \lambda']$ and $(\bar{w}^c, \lambda')$ is dominated by $(\bar{W}(\lambda'), \lambda')$. The intuition here is that if enforcement is too low to guarantee compliance, the minimum wage should be adjusted downwards since doing so can in fact raise employment. Thus, using (11) and $\ell^m(\bar{w}^c, \Lambda(\bar{w}^c)) = (\bar{w}^c - \bar{u})/\tau$, we have

PROPOSITION 1. *With ex ante commitment, if a minimum wage policy $(\bar{w}^c, \lambda^c)$ maximises the social welfare function $\Omega^c(\bar{w}, \lambda)$:*

1 *There is equilibrium compliance achieved at the lowest possible cost, with $\lambda^c = \Lambda^o(\bar{w}^c)$, and $w^m[\bar{w}^c, \Lambda(\bar{w}^c)] = \bar{w}^c$.*
2 *Given $\bar{w}^c, \Lambda^o(\bar{w}^c)$ is independent of γ.*
3 *Given $\bar{w}^c, \Lambda^o(\bar{w}^c)$ is higher in a labour market with lower productivity a, lower mobility cost T, or a larger available work force $\mathcal{L}$.*
4 *$\Lambda^o(\bar{w}^c) > 0$ is strictly increasing in $\bar{w}^c$. Equilibrium employment $\ell^m[\bar{w}^c, \Lambda^o(\bar{w}^c)]$ and expected workers' utility are both strictly increasing in $\bar{w}^c$.*

We have thus set out a benchmark and confirmed that there is little justification for governments to turn a blind eye to a minimum wage legislation that they themselves have passed in this setting, so long as they can commit *ex ante* and carry through *ex post* both parameters of the minimum wage law $(\bar{w}^c, \Lambda^o(\bar{w}^c))$. As shown, since endogenous enforcement is indeed given by the minimum enforcement required to guarantee compliance, $\Lambda^o(\bar{w}^c)$, demand conditions such as labour productivity and labour supply parameters such as T and $\mathcal{L}$ govern the size of $\Lambda^o(\bar{w}^c)$ but not the degree of government distributional concerns γ.

Finally, the last item of Proposition 1 highlights the comparative statics implications of the endogenous enforcement scheme $\Lambda^o(\bar{w}^c)$. Importantly, it suggests that the comparative statics of a minimum wage with a non-compliant employer are out of equilibrium phenomena in this case with commitment and occur only when starting with a minimum wage and/or an intensity of enforcement that are not optimally set.

With Proposition 1, the problem of the government can be simplified as essentially the choice of an optimal level of minimum wage, for full compliance implies that $\ell^m(\bar{w}^c, \lambda^c) = (\bar{w}^c - \bar{u})/\tau$. The maximisation problem of the government can therefore be rewritten via a change of variable (replacing $w^m(\bar{w}, \lambda)$ by $\bar{w}, \ell^m(\bar{w}, \lambda)$ by $\bar{\ell} = (\bar{w} - \bar{u})/\tau$ and λ by $\Lambda^o(\bar{w})$). We assume henceforth that the enforcement cost is sufficiently convex, so that the revised objective function

$$\Omega^c(\bar{w}, \lambda) = R(\bar{\ell}) - \left(\bar{u} - \gamma + \frac{\tau\bar{\ell}}{2}\right)\bar{\ell} + (\bar{u} - \gamma)\mathcal{L} - C[\Lambda^o(\bar{w})]\bar{\ell}$$

is strictly concave in $\bar{w}$. The first order condition for an interior optimum requires:

$$[w^d(\bar{\ell}) - w^s(\bar{\ell}) + \gamma]\eta^\ell = C[\Lambda^o(\bar{w})]\eta^\ell + C_p[\Lambda^o(\bar{w})]\Lambda^o_{\bar{w}}(\bar{w}), \tag{18}$$

where a subscript denotes partial derivative and η^ℓ denotes the elasticity of equilibrium employment $\bar{\ell}$ with respect to the minimum wage $\partial \ln \bar{\ell}/\partial \bar{w}$. The expression $[w^d(\bar{\ell}) - w^s(\bar{\ell}) + \gamma]\eta^\ell$ measures the efficiency and distributional gains from raising employment, to be balanced against the marginal cost of enforcement. Evaluating the first order condition above at $\bar{w} = w^{so}$, social welfare maximisation implies a strictly binding minimum wage if

$$w^{do} - w^{so} + \gamma > \frac{c(2\tau + b)}{\tau(1 - \sigma)} \Leftrightarrow \frac{(a - \bar{u})\tau}{2\tau + b} + \gamma > \frac{c(2\tau + b)}{\tau(1 - \sigma)}. \tag{19}$$

This follows since the degree of monopsonistic labour market distortion is given by $w^{do} - w^{so} = (a - \bar{u})\tau/(2\tau + b)$, while $\Lambda^o_{\bar{w}}(\bar{w})|_{\bar{w} = w^{so}} = (2\tau + b)\bar{\ell}/[\tau^2(1 - \sigma)]$ from (11) and (16), and also since $\bar{\ell} = (\bar{w} - \bar{u})/\tau$. Thus,

PROPOSITION 2. *With commitment, a binding minimum wage $\bar{w}^c > w^{so}$ and the associated endogenous enforcement $\Lambda^o(\bar{w}^c)$ improve social welfare beyond the no-intervention benchmark if labour productivity a and the degree of distributional concern γ are both sufficiently high relative to the cost of enforcement c so that inequality* (19) *holds.*

Put differently, a minimum wage legislation may no longer be welfare maximising in sectors where labour productivity is sufficiently low, since the costs required to enforce such a minimum wage outweigh benefits. Thus, even within the same country and hence arguably the same government objective function, the co-existence of covered and uncovered sectors (Proposition 2), and full compliance in covered sectors (Proposition 1) are consistent with social welfare maximisation with *ex ante* commitment.

3.2. *Credible Enforcement*

We turn now to the case where *ex ante* commitment is not feasible.[28] For any minimum wage announcement $\bar{w}$, enforcement credibility requires that p is determined *ex post* taken as given expectation λ, and hence $\ell^m(\bar{w}, \lambda)$:[29]

[28] The approach to time inconsistency problems adopted here has been applied in a variety of policy settings (Kydland and Prescott, 1977; Chau, 2001). Our contribution here lies in pointing out the importance of credibility in the minimum wage setting, particularly when perfect enforcement cannot be costlessly guaranteed.

[29] The second order condition of the maximisation problem in (20) is always satisfied.

$$p(\bar{w}, \lambda) = \text{argmax}_p \Omega(\bar{w}, \lambda, p). \tag{20}$$

A rational expectation equilibrium level of enforcement is thus given by the fixed point

$$\Lambda(\bar{w}) = \{\Lambda \mid p(\bar{w}, \Lambda) = \Lambda\}. \tag{21}$$

Turning a blind eye in a rational expectation equilibrium requires

$$\Lambda(\bar{w}) < \Lambda^o(\bar{w}), \text{ or } \bar{w} - w^m[\bar{w}, \Lambda(\bar{w})] > 0, \text{ for } \bar{w} \in [w^{so}, w^{do}].$$

We proceed first by taking as given the announcement of the minimum wage $\bar{w}$ and an expectation $\lambda \in [0,1)$. The *ex post* welfare implications of enforcement can be determined via

$$\frac{\partial \Omega(\bar{w}, \lambda, p)}{\partial p} = [\gamma\sigma - \bar{w}(1-\sigma)]\frac{(\bar{w} - w^m)\ell^m}{\bar{w}} - C_p(p)\ell^m.$$

It follows immediately that

PROPOSITION 3. *$p(\bar{w}, \lambda) = 0$ for any $\bar{w} \in [w^{so}, w^{do}]$ and $\lambda \in [0,1)$ if*

$$[\gamma\sigma - \bar{w}(1-\sigma)]\frac{\bar{w} - w^m(\bar{w}, \lambda)}{\bar{w}} < c. \tag{22}$$

Thus, there will be no enforcement of the minimum wage *ex post*, or $p(\bar{w}, \lambda) = 0$, if any one of the following holds:

(*i*) the cost of enforcement is too high,
(*ii*) the government harbours only efficiency concerns ($\gamma = 0$);
(*iii*) the labour market exhibits full compliance to begin with, or $\bar{w} \leq w^m(\bar{w}, \lambda)$, since there is literally nothing to enforce given full compliance; and
(*iv*) a transaction cost $1 - \sigma$ that is sufficiently large, even when $\gamma > 0$ and non-compliance is known to exist, $\bar{w} - w^m > 0$.

The latter applies since the transfer of wage settlement is costly whenever $\sigma < 1$.

Thus, as much as there may be a desire to enforce the minimum wage on equity grounds, enforcement alone may be made ineffectual if the resulting income gain for workers, net of transaction costs, is too low. This is reflected in the difference $\gamma\sigma - \bar{w}(1 - \sigma)$.

Suppose instead that (22) is not satisfied. The *ex post* optimal and thus credible level of enforcement $\lambda^D = \Lambda(\bar{w})$ implicitly solves $\Lambda(\bar{w}) = \{\Lambda \mid p(\bar{w}, \Lambda) = \Lambda\}$, or

$$[\gamma\sigma - \bar{w}(1-\sigma)]\frac{\bar{w} - w^m(\bar{w}, \Lambda)}{\bar{w}} - C_p(\Lambda) = 0. \tag{23}$$

Three issues of particular interest here are the uniqueness, slope and existence of the rational expectation equilibrium enforcement $\Lambda(\bar{w})$ for $\bar{w} \in [w^{so}, w^{do}]$. To this end, we continue to assume that the cost of enforcement $C(\Lambda)$ is sufficiently convex, while γ is large enough relative to the transaction cost of wage settlement $\bar{w}(1 - \sigma)$, such that the left-hand side of (23) is strictly decreasing in Λ and increasing in $\bar{w}$. Intuitively, these require that

(*i*) the marginal welfare gains from raising enforcement *ex post* in a rational expectation equilibrium is diminishing in λ^D and
(*ii*) the transaction cost of wage settlement is never high enough to offset the distributional gains from enforcing the minimum wage.

It follows then by standard arguments that $\Lambda(\bar{w})$, if it exists, is uniquely determined and strictly increasing in $\bar{w}$.

The credibility constraint (23) additionally implies that the range of credible minimum wage is bounded from below, since *ex post* incentives to enforce depend critically on the severity of violations, as measured by $\bar{w} - w^m(\bar{w}, \lambda^D)$. This new lower bound can be obtained by identifying the minimum wage consistent with $\lambda^D = 0$ in (23),

$$\hat{w} = \{\bar{w} \,|\, [\gamma\sigma - \bar{w}(1-\sigma)]\frac{\bar{w} - w^{so}}{\bar{w}} = c\} \tag{24}$$

so that there is no enforcement and thus $\lambda^D = 0$ exactly solves (23). It follows from (24) that as long as enforcement cost c is strictly positive, the new lower bound $\hat{w}$ is strictly greater than the monopsonistic wage w^{so}. Also from (24), this new lower bound $\hat{w}$ is decreasing in the degree of distributional concern γ. The range of feasible minimum wages that satisfies the credibility criterion but still capable of improving employment outcomes relative to no-intervention is thus $[\hat{w}, w^{do}]$ from (13). As a sufficient condition for existence, therefore, we assume henceforth that γ is large enough, so that $\hat{w} < w^{do}$ and the range $[\hat{w}, w^{do}]$ is accordingly non-empty.

With these observations in mind, (23) gives rise to a new set of comparative static responses to a minimum wage hike, in which it is expected that enforcement is too low to guarantee full compliance but the expected degree of imperfect enforcement systematically changes with the minimum wage itself:[30]

PROPOSITION 4. *A rational expectation equilibrium level of enforcement* $\Lambda(\bar{w})$ *that solves* (23) *has the following characteristics:*

1 *There is equilibrium non-compliance:* $\Lambda(\bar{w}) < \Lambda^o(\bar{w})$, and $w^m[\bar{w}, \Lambda(\bar{w})] < \bar{w}$.
2 *Given* $\bar{w}, \Lambda(\bar{w})$ *rises with* γ.
3 *Given* $\bar{w}, \Lambda(\bar{w})$ *is higher in a labour market with lower employer productivity* a, *lower mobility cost* T, *or a larger available work force* $\mathcal{L}$.
4 *If* γ *is sufficiently large,* $\Lambda(\bar{w})$ *is strictly increasing in* $\bar{w}$, *while equilibrium employment* $\ell^m[\bar{w}, \Lambda(\bar{w})]$ *and expected workers' utility are likewise strictly increasing in* $\bar{w}$.

Thus, turning a blind eye survives the credibility criterion laid out in (23), whereas full compliance does not.[31] Interestingly, a government that is only concerned with efficiency ($\gamma = 0$) and, hence, $p[\bar{w}, \Lambda(\bar{w})] = 0$, is guaranteed the *least* efficient (monopsonistic) labour market outcome ℓ^o, since the credible level of enforcement

[30] Since the left-hand side of (23) is strictly decreasing in Λ with $C(\Lambda)$ sufficiently convex, the Proposition follows by noting that the left hand side of (23) is increasing in γ and decreasing in a and $T/\mathcal{L}$ by (15). The last part of the Proposition follows from differentiating (13) using the implicit relationship defined in (23).

[31] Of course, another possibility that may give rise to equilibrium non-compliance may simply be because of a lack of full information concerning labour market conditions, including demand and supply side parameters. Proposition 4 shows that even in the absence of such information asymmetries, a case for imperfect enforcement induced equilibrium non-compliance can still be made.

rises with γ and is equal to zero for $\gamma = 0$. This is indeed striking – governments espousing only efficiency concerns cannot credibly implement efficiency-improving minimum wage reforms.

In addition, the *ex post* credible enforcement intensity is once again need-based, with $\Lambda(\bar{w})$ higher in labour markets where labour productivity is relatively low and where market wages are low driven by an excess supply of labour and a low mobility cost.

The last item illustrates the role of enforcement endogeneity on equilibrium employment via two sets of forces. From (13), an exogenous increase in the minimum wage negatively impacts employment whenever there is non-compliance. However, from (23), a re-definition of who is non-compliant relative to the new minimum wage increases the severity of the violation $\bar{w} - w^m(\bar{w}, \lambda)$ at constant λ. This raises the *ex post* incentive to enforce, as $\gamma\sigma - \bar{w}(1 - \sigma) > 0$, and runs contrary to the first round employment impact of a minimum wage increase since $\bar{w} \leq w^{do}$ and enforcement raises employment in this range from (13). As shown, the net outcome on employment will depend on the strength of the distributional concern parameter γ.

Finally, turning to the question of whether welfare maximisation involves a binding minimum wage policy even with non-compliance, note that the government's problem now involves maximising $\Omega[\bar{w}^D, \lambda^D, p(\bar{w}^D, \lambda^D)]$ by choice of an appropriate minimum wage $\bar{w}^D \in [\hat{w}, w^{do}]$, subject to $\lambda^D = \Lambda(\bar{w}^D)$. The first order condition requires that

$$
\begin{aligned}
[w^d(\ell^D) - w^s(\ell^D) + \gamma]\epsilon^\ell = C(\lambda^D)\epsilon^\ell + C_p(\lambda^D)\Lambda_{\bar{w}}(\bar{w}^D) - [\gamma\sigma - \bar{w}^D(1-\sigma)]\Lambda_{\bar{w}}(\bar{w}^D) \\
+ \frac{\bar{w}^D - w^m(\bar{w}^D, \lambda^D)}{\bar{w}^D}\{\gamma(1 - \lambda^D\sigma)\epsilon^\ell \\
+ [\gamma(1 - \lambda^D\sigma) + \lambda^D(1-\sigma)]\epsilon^w\}
\end{aligned}
\tag{25}
$$

where ℓ^D denotes employment $\ell^m[\bar{w}^D, \Lambda(\bar{w}^D)]$ and $\epsilon^\ell = \partial \ln \ell^D / \partial \bar{w}^D$ denotes the elasticity of ℓ^D with respect to the minimum wage. From Proposition 4, $\epsilon^\ell > 0$ provided that γ is sufficiently large. Meanwhile, $\epsilon^w = \partial \ln\{\bar{w}^D - w^m[\bar{w}^D, \Lambda(\bar{w}^D)]/\bar{w}^D\}/\partial \bar{w}^D$ denotes the elasticity of the proportional income shortfall with respect to the minimum wage. It can be readily confirmed from (23) that ϵ^w is also positive.

The choice of a welfare-maximising minimum wage thus involves equating the anticipated marginal benefits, $[w^d(\ell^D) - w^s(\ell^D) + \gamma]\epsilon^\ell$, with marginal costs. The latter is now made up of three parts. The first term $C(\lambda^D)\epsilon^\ell + C_p(\lambda^D)\Lambda_{\bar{w}}(\bar{w}^D)$ is analogous to the commitment case and expresses the marginal cost required to credibly enforce a rise in the minimum wage. The second term $[\gamma\sigma - \bar{w}^D(1 - \sigma)]$ denotes the *ex post* gains from enforcing the minimum wage, as has already been seen in (23). The final part expresses the efficiency and distributional losses associated with a rise in an *imperfectly* enforced minimum wage. Specifically, $\gamma(1 - \lambda^D\sigma)\epsilon^\ell$ and $\gamma(1 - \lambda^D\sigma)\epsilon^w$ respectively show the distributional losses associated with an increase in the number of subminimum wage earners and an increase in the proportional income shortfall as the minimum wage increases. Finally, the expression $\lambda^D(1 - \sigma)\epsilon^w$ represents efficiency losses via the transaction costs incurred by workers in the wage settlement process.

Making use of (23) and evaluating (25) at the lower bound $\bar{w}^D = \hat{w}$ in (24), or $\lambda^D = \Lambda(\hat{w}) = 0$, a social-welfare-maximising minimum wage policy involves $\bar{w}^D > \hat{w}$ if

$$w^{do} - w^{so} + \gamma > \frac{c\gamma}{\gamma\sigma - \hat{w}(1-\sigma)}\left(1 + \frac{\epsilon^w}{\epsilon^\ell}\right). \tag{26}$$

As before, since monopsonistic labour market distortion $w^{do} - w^{so} = \tau(a - \bar{u})/(2\tau + b)$ is strictly increasing in labour productivity, a, we have thus:

PROPOSITION 5. *With ex post discretion, a minimum wage $\bar{w}^D > \hat{w}$ and the associated ex post credible level of enforcement $\Lambda(\bar{w}^D)$ improves social welfare beyond the no-intervention benchmark if labour productivity a and distributional concern γ are both large enough so that* (26) *is satisfied.*

Thus, within the same country and given the same government objective function the co-existence of (relatively productive) covered and (relatively less productive) uncovered sectors (Proposition 5) along with less than full compliance in covered sectors (Propositions 3, 4), are consistent with social welfare maximisation with *ex post* discretion.[32]

4. Conclusion

There is now extensive evidence particularly from developing country labour markets that non-compliance with minimum wage legislations in covered sectors is pervasive. The stylised facts reviewed in this article include:

(*i*) co-existence of compliant and non-compliant employers,
(*ii*) a spike at the minimum wage,
(*iii*) a dispersion of subminimum wages and
(*iv*) co-movements of minimum and subminimum wages.

We have argued that all of these stylised facts can be consistent with a setting in which there is imperfect competition, imperfect enforcement, and imperfect commitment. But beyond this, our comparative static analysis further underscores additional insights that may be gained by taking seriously the issue of imperfect enforcement of a minimum wage. Indeed, a simple deviation from perfect to imperfect enforcement is shown to be sufficient for standard comparative static predictions to be overturned, with equilibrium employment now predicted to respond negatively to a minimum wage hike in an imperfectly competitive labour market, for cases when the standard Stigler model would yield a positive response to the same minimum wage hike when enforcement is perfect. The key message that can be drawn is that observed empirical relationship between minimum wage and employment can no longer serve as the litmus test of the competitiveness of a labour market when enforcement is imperfect.

We have also reviewed evidence that enforcement varies systematically across countries and across geographic regions, or industries within countries. This suggests a need for a theory of the endogenous determination of enforcement. Consistent with the

[32] In Basu *et al.* (2009), we point out that an employment guarantee scheme which directly generates employment through public funds can be an alternative but viable policy option for imperfectly competitive labour markets with or without the ability to commit, precisely in labour markets where labour productivity is sufficiently low.

pioneering study of Ashenfelter and Smith (1979), the endogenous enforcement we derive does indeed exhibit the characteristic that enforcement of any given minimum wage is higher in labour markets where non-compliance is likely to be prevalent, as would be the case where productivity is low or where the pool of available labour force, given labour demand, is large enough. The endogenous level of enforcement derived here is further shown to vary with the minimum wage itself. For a government that cares sufficiently about distribution, a rise in the minimum wage can signal a rise in enforcement. Indeed, equilibrium employment and expected workers' welfare can now rise with a minimum wage hike but for reasons that have to do with endogenous enforcement rather than with imperfect labour market competition *per se*.

Following on from the contribution to positive analysis, the article also analyses the behaviour of governments with and without the ability to commit *ex ante* to both the wage and enforcement dimensions of a minimum wage policy. Since *ex post* enforcement of a minimum wage is but a costly transfer of income from employers to workers, a government's concern for distribution is shown to interact in interesting ways with the problem of credible commitment on enforcement intensity. Simply put, a government that cares more about distribution will care more about violations of the minimum wage and can therefore signal a commitment to enforce. By the same token, a government that does not care at all about distribution cannot improve efficiency.

The basic setup that we work with should be seen as a beginning, with a number of useful extensions that await further exploration. These can be framed under four main categories. An obvious line of research is to consider the issue of enforcement and credibility with alternative specifications of distributional concerns. This can be accomplished in two ways. First, rather than a concern for those whose income fall below a specified threshold (in our case, the minimum wage), an alternative specification can also incorporate measures of income inequality, including possibly income disparity between employers and workers. Second, additional insights may also be obtained by introducing variable poverty aversion parameters associated with the proportional income shortfall (Foster *et al.* 1994). Regardless of how the distributional concern component of government objective is alternatively measured, however, our main conclusion that credible enforcement cannot come with a complete disregard for the intrinsic value of income transfer from employers to subminimum wage earners, will remain intact.

A second promising research agenda involves a re-examination of the different components of a minimum wage policy package, including particularly the role of fines and penalty in addition to the compensation of any income shortfall. These penalties may be officially sanctioned by legislation (Lott and Roberts, 1995), or more indirectly through the loss of goodwill upon discovery (Harrison and Scorse, 2004), for example. Of particular interest is whether a minimum wage policy package can be further fine-tuned to encourage compliance through the threat of fines and how the comparative statics of a minimum wage will depend on the credibility of such a threat.

In a variety of situations, the minimum wage can arguably be thought of as an exogenously imposed labour standard and the government is left with only the choice of an appropriate enforcement strategy. Such an exogenous minimum wage may correspond to an exogenous poverty line, a minimum labour standard imposed extra-nationally as a condition for exports, or a result of a political process, separate from the decision to allocate public funds to enforce the minimum wage, for example (Sobel, 1999). The issue of enforcement and credibility takes on a different type of significance here, particularly when the government may be held accountable not just to its own efficiency and equity concerns but also to the very set of forces that introduced the minimum wage as a labour standard to begin with.

Finally, the comparison between commitment and discretion highlighted here can potentially shed new light on a range of policies other than the minimum wage, where enforcement and compliance are central. Some examples include tax evasion and enforcement, as well as financial bailouts and *ex post* enforcement of bailout conditions.[33] In Basu *et al.* (2009), the distinction between commitment and discretion is further shown to be instrumental in understanding the labour market consequences of employment guarantee programmes, where the degree of distributional concern of the government is shown to directly impact the perceived credibility of the employment guarantee.

College of William and Mary
Cornell University
Cornell University

Submitted: 20 September 2005
Accepted: 17 December 2008

References

Anderlini, L., Felli, L. and Postlewaite, A. (2007). 'Courts of law and unforeseen contingencies', *Journal of Law, Economics and Organization*, vol. 23(3), pp. 662–84.

Ashenfelter, O. and Smith, R. S. (1979). 'Compliance with the minimum wage law', *Journal of Political Economy*, vol. 87(2), pp. 333–50.

Baanante, M. J. (2005). 'Minimum wage effects under endogenous compliance. evidence from Peru', available at http://www.grade.org.pe/download/docs/Minimum%20wages%20in%20Peru%20M.%20Jaramillo.pdf

Basu, A. K., Chau, N. H. and Kanbur, R. (2009). 'A theory of employment guarantee schemes: contestability, credibility and distributional concerns', *Journal of Public Economics*, vol. 93(3–4), pp. 482–97.

Bell, L. (1997). 'The impact of minimum wages in Mexico and Columbia', *Journal of Labor Economics*, vol. 15(3), pp. S102–35.

Bhaskar, V., Manning, A. and To, T. (2002). 'Oligopsony and monopolistic competition in labor markets', *Journal of Economic Perspectives*, vol. 16(2), pp. 155–74.

Card, D. and Krueger, A. B. (1995). *Myth and Measurement: The New Economics of the Minimum Wage*, Princeton: Princeton University Press.

Cardoso, A. R. and Portugal, P. (2002). 'Disentangling the minimum wage puzzle: an analysis of worker accessions and separations', IZA Discussion Paper No. 544.

Chang, Y-M. and Ehrlich, I. (1985). 'On the economics of compliance with the minimum wage law', *Journal of Political Economy*, vol. 93(1), pp. 84–91

Chau, N. H. (2001). 'Strategic amnesty and credible immigration reform', *Journal of Labor Economics*, vol. 19, pp. 604–34.

Eckstein, Z., Ge, S. and Petrongolo, B. (2006). 'Job and wage mobility in a search model with non-compliance (exemptions) with the minimum wage'. IZA Discussion Paper No. 2076.

Fershtman, C. and Fishman, A. (1994). 'The perverse effects of wage and price controls in search markets', *European Economic Review*, vol. 38, pp. 1099–112.

[33] Anderlini *et al.* (2007) examine another intriguing distinction between *ex ante* and *ex post* decision making of contract enforcing courts. In a setup that, unlike our setting, features asymmetric information between contracting partieis, it is shown that a court can improve the welfare of contracting parties by *voiding, ex post*, voluntary contracts that these same parties would like the court to enforce *ex ante*. In our context, the issue of minimum wage enforcement in the presence of information asymmetry (between workers and employers, or between employers and the government) is yet another promising avenue for future research.

Fields, G. and Kanbur, R. (2007). 'Minimum wage and poverty', *Journal of Economic Inequality*, vol. 5(2), pp. 135–47.

Flanagan, R. J. (1989). 'Compliance and enforcement decisions under the National Labor Relations Act', *Journal of Labor Economics*, vol. 7(3), pp. 257–80.

Foster, J., Greer, J. and Thorbecke, E. (1994). 'A class of decomposable poverty measures', *Econometrica*, vol. 52(3), pp. 761–66.

Freeman, R. (1996). 'The minimum wage as a redistributive tool', ECONOMIC JOURNAL, vol. 106, pp. 639–49.

Gindling, T. and Terrell, K. (1995). 'The nature of minimum wages and their effectiveness as a wage floor in Costa Rica, 1976-1991', *World Development*, vol. 23, 1439–58.

Gindling, T. and Terrell, K. (2006). 'Minimum wages, globalization and poverty in Honduras', IZA Discussion Paper No. 2497.

Grenier, G. (1982). 'On compliance with the minimum wage law', *Journal of Political Economy*, vol. 90(1), pp. 184–87.

Harrison, A. and Leamer, E. (1997). 'Labor markets in developing countries: an agenda for research', *Journal of Labor Economics*, vol. 15(S3), pp. S1–9.

Harrison, A. and Scorse, J. (2004). 'The impact of globalization on compliance with labor standards: a plant-level study', in (S. Collins and D. Rodrik eds.) *Brookings Trade Forum 2003*, pp. 83–94, Washington DC: Brookings Institution Press.

Kydland, F. and Prescott, E. (1977). 'Rules rather than discretion: the inconsistency of optimal plans', *Journal of Political Economy*, vol. 85, pp. 473–90.

Lemos, S. (2004). 'The effects of the minimum wage in the formal and informal sectors in Brazil', IZA Discussion Paper No. 1089.

Lemos, S. (2006). 'Minimum wage effects in a developing country', mimeo, University of Leicester.

Lott, J. R. and Roberts, R. D. (1995). 'The expected penalty for committing a crime: an analysis of minimum wage violations', *Journal of Human Resources*, vol. 30(2), pp. 397–408.

Machin, S., Manning, A. and Rahman, L. (2003). 'Where the minimum wage bites hard: introduction of minimum wages to a low wage sector', *Journal of the European Economic Association*, vol. 1(1), pp. 154–80.

Maloney, W. and Nunez, J. (2004). 'Measuring the impact of minimum wages: evidence from Latin America', in (J. Heckman and C. Pagès eds) *Law and Employment. Lessons from Latin America and the Carribean.* pp. 109–30, Cambridge, MA: NBER.

Mortensen, D. and Pissarides, C. (1994). 'Job creation and job destruction in the theory of unemployment', *Review of Economic Studies*, vol. 61(3), pp. 397–415.

Neumark, D. and Wascher, W. (2007). 'Minimum wages and employment', IZA Discussion Paper No. 2570.

Saget, C. (2001). 'Is the minimum wage an effective tool to promote decent work and reduce poverty? The experience of selected developing countries', Employment Paper No. 2001/13, Geneva: Employment Strategy Department, International Labour Office.

Sobel, R. S. (1999). 'Theory and evidence on the political economy of the minimum wage', *Journal of Political Economy*, vol. 107(4), pp. 761–85.

Squire, L. and Suthiwart-Narueput, S. (1997). 'The impact of labor market regulations', *World Bank Economic Review*, vol. 11(1), pp. 119–43.

Stigler, G. J. (1946). 'The economics of minimum wage legislation', *American Economic Review*, vol. 36(3), pp. 358–65.

Strobl, E. and Walsh, F. (2001). 'Minimum wage and compliance: the case of Trinidad and Tobago', *Economic Development and Cultural Change*, vol. 51(2), pp 427–50.

Weil, D. (2004). 'Compliance with the minimum wage: can government make a difference', mimeo, Boston University School of Management.

Yaniv, G. (1988). 'Enforcement and monopsonistic compliance with the minimum wage law', *Southern Economic Journal*, vol. 55(2), pp. 505–9.

Yaniv, G. (2001). 'Minimum wage noncompliance and the employment decision', *Journal of Labor Economics* vol. 19(3), pp. 596–603

Journal of Public Economics 93 (2009) 482–497

Contents lists available at ScienceDirect

Journal of Public Economics

journal homepage: www.elsevier.com/locate/econbase

A theory of employment guarantees: Contestability, credibility and distributional concerns[☆]

Arnab K. Basu[a,b,c], Nancy H. Chau[b,c,d,*], Ravi Kanbur[b,d,e]

[a] College of William and Mary, USA
[b] Institute for the Study of Labor, Germany
[c] Center for Development Research, University of Bonn, Germany
[d] Cornell University, USA
[e] CEPR, United Kingdom

ARTICLE INFO

Article history:
Received 27 August 2007
Revised 6 August 2008
Accepted 17 September 2008
Available online 8 October 2008

JEL classification:
I38
J21
K31
O12

Keywords:
Employment guarantees
Employment targeting
Credibility
Distributional concern

ABSTRACT

Both raw intuition and past experience suggest that the success of an employment guarantee scheme (EGS) in safeguarding the welfare of the poor depends both on the wage it promises, and the ease with which any worker can gain access. An EGS is thus at once a wage guarantee and a rationing device. We chart the positive and normative limits of such an EGS as an efficiency improving *and* poverty alleviating policy reform in a canonical labor market setting. At its core, an EGS provides an aggregate, not just EGS, employment target. Given the target, the EGS wage and access can be fine-tuned to deliver outcomes ranging from a contestable labor market to a simple universal unemployment benefit. The credibility of any such target, however, is shown to be triggered endogenously by a host of factors: the distributional concerns of the planner, private sector productivity, the prevalence of market power and the need for public works. Paradoxically, the outcome with a planner who cares only about efficiency can be *less* efficient than the outcome with a planner whose social welfare function also gives weight to poverty!

1. Introduction

Dating back as early as the 19th century, formal establishment of Employment Guarantee Schemes (EGS) has been a staple of relief policies in response to natural disasters and economic downturns worldwide. Contemporary schemes in many developed and developing countries have evolved to encompass a broad array of objectives: to provide income relief by generating employment; construct and maintain public infrastructure; ameliorate endemic poverty; improve workers' position to bargain in the private sector and to facilitate job search (Drèze and Sen, 1991; Lipton, 1996; von Braun, 1995).

The origins of EGS can be traced back to the 1817 Poor Employment Act and the 1834 Poor Law Amendment Act in Great Britain (Blaug, 1963, 1964), and the New Deal programs of the 1930s in the United States (Kesselman, 1978, Bernstein, 1970). Large scale poverty reduction remains the primary objective of more contemporary programs in the developing countries of Latin America (Chile 1987), Asia (India 1978, Pakistan 1992, Bangladesh 1983, Philippines 1990), and Africa (Botswana 1960, Kenya 1992).[1] One

☆ We thank Kaushik Basu, Gary Fields, Martin Ravallion, Abhijit Sen, K. Subbarao and Erik Thorbecke for stimulating discussions, seminar participants at Cornell and the Second IZA-World Bank Conference for their suggestions, as well as two anonymous referees and a Co-editor of this journal for insightful comments. Basu and Chau gratefully acknowledge research funding from the Alexander von Humboldt Foundation.

* Corresponding author. Department of Applied Economics and Management, Cornell University, Ithaca NY 14853, USA.
E-mail address: hyc3@cornell.edu (N.H. Chau).

[1] See Maharashtra Planning Department (1979), Drèze and Sen (1989), Lipton (1996), Keddeman (1998) and von Braun (1995).

doi:10.1016/j.jpubeco.2008.09.007

notable aspect of these programs, apart from their common stated objective of poverty reduction, lies in the specific limits they impose on reach and accessibility. For example, the Youth Employment Guarantee Act of 1991 in the Netherlands and Egypt's employment guarantee program respectively aim at guaranteeing employment to young persons and college graduates.[2] Still other programs impose limits on access in spatial terms. Tanzania's Special Public Works Programs (1978) was instituted within village limits, with employment guarantee limited only to residents (Teklu, 1995). The widely debated National Rural Employment Guarantee Act (NREGA) of India (2005) is one of the most recent attempts to provide statutory basis for a government guarantee of employment initially in 200 rural districts.

This wealth of government initiatives notwithstanding, conceptual understanding of the mechanics of Employment Guarantee Schemes (EGS) in general, and the difference that an official commitment has on the private labor market in particular, has been in short supply. In terms of mechanics, at the core of an EGS are three distinctive features, which clearly separate the workings of the program from other conventional policies that directly target the private labor market, such as a minimum wage, or a wage subsidy. These features include (i) an EGS wage, (ii) the ease of access to EGS employment, and (iii) the degree of contestability that such a scheme introduces into the private labor market. These have each been discussed, though yet to be articulated and analyzed as a unit. First and foremost, oft-noted has been the promise of EGS to alleviate poverty by delivering targeted transfers to the poor through workfare rather than welfare (Drèze and Sen, 1991; Lipton 1996; von Braun, 1995),[3] and an accompanying empirical literature establishes the size of such direct transfer benefits (Ravallion, 1991; Ravallion et al., 1993). The EGS wage, when viewed in this light, is arguably akin to direct transfers to the poor rooted in the principles of self-selection subject to financing constraints (Besley and Coate, 1992; Besley and Kanbur, 1993).

Second, while EGS has been touted as an employment oriented approach to anti-poverty policy-making, or invoked as a counter-cyclical labor market policy to economic downturns, such a *guarantee* alone has never implied universal elimination of unemployment. This suggests that another key metric by which the effectiveness of EGS can be gauged is the ease of access to such programs. Indeed, whereas a government may perfectly follow through with the letter of an employment guarantee legislation by paying a predetermined EGS wage, discretion with respect to the ease of access to EGS employment can nevertheless be viewed as an implicit employment rationing device, which goes against the original intention of the law.[4]

Lastly, employment guarantees have also been credited for their potential to induce positive labor market responses by improving the bargaining strength of workers (Drèze and Sen, 1991; Dev, 1995). The efficacy of an EGS accordingly also depends on the extent to which the introduction of such contestability matters. Naturally, this final dimension of an EGS becomes relevant particularly in an imperfectly competitive labor market, and should be expected to have no efficiency enhancing impact when a perfectly competitive framework is the relevant starting point. What is important to note is that in both rural and urban labor markets, there is evidence of market outcomes consistent with imperfect competition and market power (Bardhan and Rudra, 1981; Bardhan, 1979, 1984; Binswanger et al., 1984; Card and Krueger, 1995; Datt, 1997; Manning, 2005).

Once these three individual building blocks of an EGS are spelled out, the question of a need for an official commitment to employment guarantees acquires added meaning. The Indian National Rural Employment Guarantee Act of 2005 (NREGA), for example, provides that unless otherwise changed by the Central Government,

> "the minimum wage fixed by the State Government ... shall be considered as the [EGS] wage rate applicable to that area."

Further, the Act specifies 60 Indian rupees per day per person as the absolute minimum EGS wage in any State.[5] In terms of access, the Act further provides that

> "As far as possible, employment shall be provided within a radius of 5 kilometres of the village where the applicant resides at the time of applying"

leaving open to discretion therefore the ease of access facing workers who wish to participate. The Act contains additional terms that can similarly impact access. These include for example the provision of child care services for female workers, compensation for transportation and living expenses, minimal levels of work site safety regulations, and entitlement to medical treatment in case of injury.[6]

A legal employment guarantee can thus be seen as (i) a complete contract, which stipulates in full detail both the wage and access components of the act or (ii) an incomplete contract, in which one or more of these components are left open to discretion, and are impossible to fix a priori. Of particular interest, therefore, is how the effectiveness of an EGS in offsetting labor market imperfections and in alleviating poverty may be affected by this inability/impossibility of full commitment. There are thus two related sets of issues. The first concerns the labor market consequences of an EGS in which the EGS wage and access are juxtaposed. The second concerns questions of EGS policy formation and wage setting with and without commitment.

[2] See ILO (2006) for the Netherlands, Assaad (1997) for Egypt, and also Dar and Tzannatos (1999) for a number of OECD countries.

[3] Rural public works programs have been studied in a number of important contexts: (i) providing income insurance and impacting seasonal agrarian labor markets (Basu, 2007), (ii) building longer term capital assets (Basu, 1981), (iii) obviating the need for the dislocation of families in search of jobs and food (Drèze and Sen, 1991), and (iv) impacting the flow of rural-urban migration when EGS is location-specific (Ravallion, 1990).

[4] The reduction in EGS employment subsequent to the EGS wage hike in Maharashtra is one such case in point (Ravallion et al., 1993; Dev, 1995).

[5] See Subbarao (1997) for a tabulation of the EGS wages applied in various employment programs in developing countries such as Bangladesh, Pakistan, Philippines, Botswana and Chile.

[6] Indeed, Bhatty (2006) reports the success of the NREGA from an employment and registration standpoint in Dungarpur, Rajasthan, but simultaneously a lack of child care facilities at NREGA work sites. The report also notes the large scale involvement of female workers, and the cost of this neglect in terms of the condition of children.

To evaluate these issues, we introduce a formal model of an EGS in the context of a canonical model of the labor market in which a host of labor market structures, ranging from monopsonistic, oligopsonistic, and all the way to the perfectly competitive case, can be accommodated. As discussed, an EGS is characterized by the EGS wage, and the accessibility of EGS employment expressed in terms of a worker-specific cost of employment.[7] Analogously, private employment opportunities are also characterized by a market determined wage rate, and the associated worker-specific cost of employment. This setting captures a range of potential contributors to the equilibrium size of the pool of unemployed (including aggregate productivity slowdowns; sector- and worker-specific costs of employment, and oligopsonistic market power), and generates a number of key insights concerning both the positive and normative implications of an EGS.

In terms of positive implications, we find that an EGS is double-edged – it introduces contestability in labor hiring, while it raises the reservation wage. These two properties of an EGS can be fine-tuned by simultaneous choice of EGS wage and access, to generate a full range of outcomes including: (i) replication of the competitive level of private employment despite employer market power at no cost to the government, to (ii) expansion of aggregate employment beyond the competitive level but at a cost, as private employment are displaced.[8] In effect, an EGS can be seen as an *aggregate* (EGS plus private) employment target, to be set depending on the degree of distributional and/or efficiency concerns of the planner. Fine-tuning the EGS wage and access in turn provides an added degree of control, and allows the right mix of private and EGS employment to be designed into the scheme, given the target.

These observations shift the longstanding focus on the EGS from one which centers on poverty alleviation, to one which also emphasizes efficiency improvement in imperfectly competitive labor markets. This new focus will need to be qualified, however, as we move from what an EGS can accomplish in principle, to scenarios in which the credibility and time consistency (Kydland and Prescott, 1977) of the policy announcements may be in doubt. Two scenarios are taken up in turn, the first involves legislation that fully commits the planner to both the wage and access dimensions of an EGS, while the latter leaves the access dimension open to ex post discretion.[9] Consistent with many of the historical circumstances under which employment guarantees have been deployed, we find that the ex post credibility of any employment target set out by an EGS can be triggered by three sets of factors: (i) labor market triggers such as low labor productivity and oligopsonistic market power, (ii) cost triggers such as the revenue that can be generated from public works, and (iii) planners' preference triggers such as a high degree of distributional concern.

Accounting for issues with credibility, the task of setting the EGS wage at the "right" level is thus nontrivial, for a high enough EGS wage may lead employers and workers to the (rational) expectation that access will be limited ex post. We have three interesting sets of results. First, if none of the credibility triggers applies, the question of choosing an EGS wage clearly does not arise since equilibrium private and EGS employment are invariant to policy announcement. At the other extreme, if the credibility triggers are important enough to justify a higher than perfectly competitive level of aggregate employment, the EGS wage should be as close to the poverty line as possible, with access extended to meet the employment target. Doing so minimizes private employment displacement, and tilts the self-selection of EGS workers in favor of those who are otherwise left out of the labor market, due for example to high cost of employment.

Finally, for credibility triggers that justify intermediate levels of employment between the no government intervention and the perfectly competitive benchmarks, the EGS wage should be set just high enough as an announcement of contestability. Thus, we have an intriguing instance here where the effectiveness of the announcement of an EGS in giving rise to efficiency improvements now depends critically, among other things, on the distributional concern of the planner in question. In particular, the outcome for a planner who cares only about efficiency could be less efficient than the outcome for a planner who cares about poverty as well.

The rest of the paper is organized as follows. In Section 2, the basic model of the labor market is laid out. An EGS is introduced in Section 3, and its impact on private and public sector employment are discussed. Sections 4 and 5 are devoted to the workings of an EGS with or without commitment, depending on the types of objective that an EGS is expected to accomplish. Section 6 concludes.

2. The private labor market

There are $N=1, \ldots, \infty$ exogenously given number of identical employers and a population of heterogeneous workers with unit mass. For employers, the benefits and costs of labor hiring are characterized respectively by a marginal (and average) value product of labor, $a>0$, and the wage cost per worker, $w>0$.

---

[7] For example, this cost of employment may be due to distance, the disutility of work due to lack of child care facilities for female employment, the lack of information about job opportunities, skill mismatch and physical disabilities (Teklu and Asefa, 1999; Gaiha, 2000, 2005). The size of this cost is likely worker-specific, depending on a worker's residential location, gender, age, and physical ability. The design of an EGS can alleviate the cost of employment for at least some of these workers, by choice of location, provision of transportation subsidies, provision of child-care, and the employment of the unskilled for unskilled work. All of these are indeed stated goals of the 2005 Indian NREGA, for example.

[8] The 1834 Poor Law Amendment Act abolished government grants to supplement low wages, and embarked instead on the principle of "less eligibility" in Great Britain. This reflected, at least in part, the concern that workers who would otherwise find employment in the private sector chose to seek government assistance instead (Blaug, 1963, 1964), and the runaway budget consequence of the program.

[9] For example, the EGS wage hike in the State of Maharashtra in India may have instigated the need to ration EGS employment ex post (Dev, 1996; Ravallion et al., 1993; Gaiha, 1996). Incidences of EGS job rationing have also been noted for employment programs in Tanzania and Botswana (Subbarao, 1997; Teklu 1995).

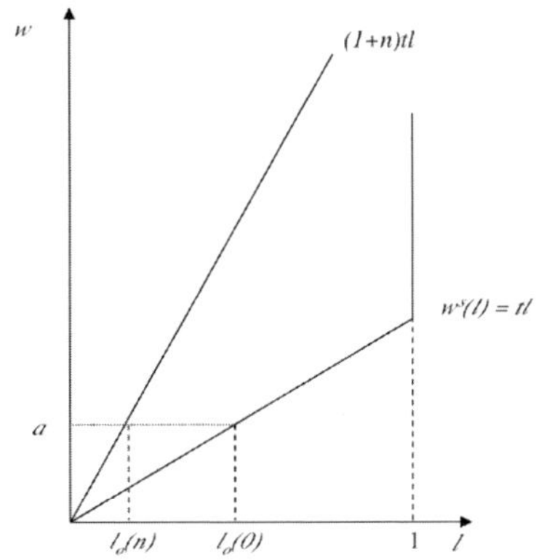

Fig. 1. The private labor market.

For workers, employment in the private labor market yields a wage benefit w, but at a cost. The cost of employment is heterogeneous among workers, given by $tx \geq 0$. This includes a worker-specific component x, and private sector-specific component t. The worker-specific component parameterizes heterogeneity among workers in terms of their individual access to the private labor market, expressed as a worker-specific the cost of employment.[10] We assume that the distribution of x among workers is uniform along the [0,1] range.[11]

The private sector cost of employment component, t, parameterizes any locational, informational, skill-related costs and disutilities, as well as any time away from home required to secure a job from one of the N employers.[12] Employment in the private labor market generates a worker-specific level of utility $u(x, w) = w - tx$. Every worker supplies inelastically one unit of labor unless otherwise deterred by the cost of employment. Normalizing the reservation utility of every worker at zero, the implied inverse private sector labor supply is given simply by: $w(\ell) \equiv t\ell$ for $\ell \leq 1$.

The N employers engage in non-cooperative competition for laborers: Each employer i maximizes profits $(a - t(\ell_i + \ell_{-i}))\ell_i$ by choice of the desired number of laborers, ℓ_i, taking as given the aggregate labor demand by the rest of the $N-1$ employers, ℓ_{-i}. Thus, $\ell \equiv \ell_i + \ell_{-i}$. In a symmetric Nash equilibrium $((N-1)\ell_i = \ell_{-i})$, the marginal value product of labor is equated with the perceived marginal labor cost schedule in the usual way:

$$a = (1+n)t\ell, \quad n = \frac{1}{N}.$$

Aggregate private labor market outcome is thus a wage and employment pair $\{w_o(n), \ell_o(n)\}$ (Fig. 1):

$$\ell_o(n) = \frac{a}{t(1+n)}, \quad w_o(n) = \frac{a}{1+n} < a \tag{1}$$

if $a/[t(1+n)] < 1$. Otherwise, $\ell_o(n) = 1$ and $w_o(n) = t$. As should be expected, these encompass a whole spectrum of labor market outcomes as special cases, ranging from monopsonistic:

$$\ell_o(1) = \frac{a}{2t}, \quad w_o(1) = \frac{a}{2} < a,$$

[10] Such heterogeneity can arise due to a wide variety of reasons, including differential disutility of work due for example to gender differences, the presence of children and the need for child care within the household, traveling and informational costs required for job search depending workers' residential location from village centers. The cost of employment x may also be interpreted as productivity difference if unit labor supply is measured in terms of efficiency labor units. Thus, workers with low x are also those who are relatively productive.

[11] See Mitra (2006) for example, for evidence of the role of the cost of employment on labor participation and job mobility in India, and more importantly, the heterogeneity of the cost of employment among workers. Teklu and Asefa (1999), and Gaiha (2000, 2005) provide evidence of the role of gender differences and the need for child care, physical capabilities, and workers' residential location in labor participation decision in Botswana, Kenya and India.

[12] In the sequel, this private sector cost of employment (t) will be contrasted with the cost of securing a public sector job made available via the EGS.

to perfectly competitive

$$\lim_{n \to 0} \ell_0(n) = \frac{a}{t} \equiv \ell_0(0), \quad \lim_{n \to 0} w_0(n) = a \equiv w_0(0),$$

if $a/t<1$, with the equilibrium wage given simply by the marginal value product.[13]

Note that if $a/t<1$, that is, if the productivity of labor a is low enough and/or the private sector cost of employment t is high enough, there will always be workers that are kept out of private sector employment ($\ell_0(n)<1$). Henceforth, these workers will be referred to as "the unemployed". The utility of all such workers is at the normalized level of zero — lower than any worker who has employment in the private sector. Meanwhile, the size of the unemployed population depends on three sets of factors: (i) labor productivity (a), (ii) the private sector cost of employment t, and (iii) the degree of imperfect competition in the labor market n.

3. Employment guarantees

A principle objective of an EGS is to provide relief to those who are otherwise deterred from joining the workforce because of employment costs on the supply side, or a lack of demand due either to low productivity or market power in equilibrium. Let ℓ_g be the number of such EGS workers. The revenue equivalent of the services provided on a per worker basis is denoted as a_g. The revenue parameter a_g can take on positive or negative values depending on whether the gross amount of services provided by the scheme exceeds or is less than the costs of administering the program. We assume that $a_g<a$, in order to rule out findings that by assumption call for the government to effectively nationalize the labor market.

For workers, EGS employment can be characterized by a wage and access pairing, w_g and $t_g \equiv t/(1+\tau_g)$. Both w_g and τ_g (and hence t_g) are policy variables. w_g gives the EGS wage per worker, and $1+\tau_g \equiv t/t_g>0$ denotes the relative ease of securing EGS as opposed to private employment.[14]

For EGS employment to offer relief for those workers who cannot otherwise find private employment, the EGS wage is assumed to be no less than an exogenously given income threshold $\bar{w}_g \geq 0$, that (weakly) exceeds the reservation utility at zero.[15] We assume that $w_0(n)>\bar{w}_g$, and accordingly either EGS or private employment is synonymous with achieving an income level above the exogenous threshold. The determination of $1+\tau_g>0$ should thus be thought of as part of the government's decision to provide job information to the pool of otherwise unemployed job seekers, to adjust the physical location of employment openings and/or the skill-requirements associated with EGS employment.[16] In each case, an increase in τ_g improves access and lowers the cost of employment $tx/(1+\tau_g)$.

3.1. Comparative statics

Let ℓ_e and w_e denote employment and wage in the private sector in the presence of an EGS with given w_g and τ_g. One way for an EGS to target workers who are otherwise excluded from the private labor market involves relaxing access to the EGS ($\tau_g>0$), though possibly at a lower wage.[17] The utility of private and EGS employment are respectively w_e-tx and $w_g-tx/(1+\tau_g)$. There are thus three groups of workers: those who are better off with (i) private employment, (ii) EGS employment, and (iii) remaining outside of the workforce despite an EGS. With $\tau_g>0$ and $w_g \leq w_e$, the first group is made up of workers with the lowest costs of employment, since

$$w_e - tx \geq w_g - \frac{tx}{1+\tau_g} \Longleftrightarrow x \leq \frac{(w_e - w_g)(1+\tau_g)}{t\tau_g} = \hat{\ell}_e.$$

[13] Note that this equilibrium outcome where all employers pay identical wages can also be achieved in an environment where firms compete for workers by choice of (i) a base pay, and (ii) a compensation for the cost of employment. All else equal, workers with low cost of employment tx will be favored, for the compensation required to induce these workers to prefer private employment is lower. With competition in base pay and compensation for employment costs, the base pay for workers with low xs will be bided upwards, for otherwise, incentive remains for employers to outbid another to gain the worker with lower x. In equilibrium, wage payment offers (base plus compensation for costs of employment) to all workers regardless of their worker-specific x must be the same. Together these give the wage payment w in our model, set in equilibrium at the minimal wage payment required to induce the marginal worker to prefer private employment. We thank a referee for encouraging us to think in these terms.

[14] We will refer to EGS employment interchangeably with public employment secured through the EGS, and private employment interchangeably with employment with one of the N private employers.

[15] The special case of $\bar{w}_g=0$ thus corresponds to a situation wherein an EGS in fact offers no income relief to any worker.

[16] For example, the Indian NREGA in 2005 addresses this question of access by emphasizing unskilled manual work, providing supplemental transportation compensation when employment is provided outside of a worker's village, free medical treatment to injured workers, child care in work sites, and work place safety requirements. The extent to which these measures offset the cost of employment naturally depends on a worker's skill level, gender, age, physical ability and propensity to injury. Correspondingly, we model efforts to ease access as a proportional reduction in the cost of employment. Doing so enables the EGS to better target those with higher employment of employment to begin with (high x).

[17] If one assumes, in contrast $\tau_g<0$, an EGS must offer a strictly higher wage than the N employers in order to generate positive employment. In addition, the EGS changes place with private employers by hiring workers with the lowest cost of employment, or equivalently those who are employed even in the absence of an EGS. These implications violate the stated aims of employment guarantee schemes, that direct competition with private employment is to be avoided.

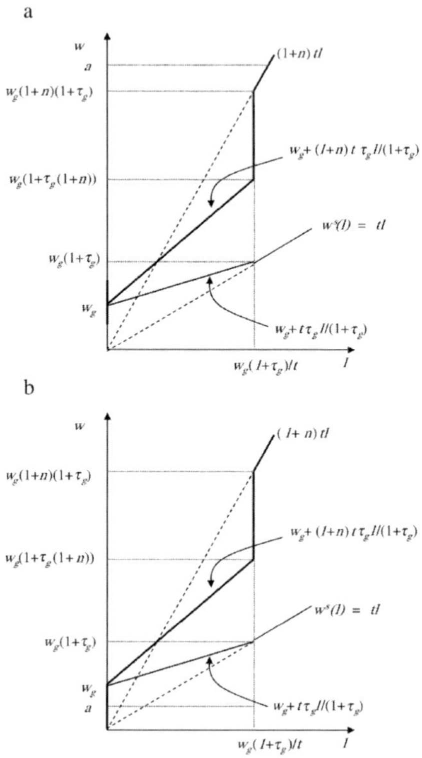

Fig. 2. Employment and wages with an EGS.

Workers in the third group are subject to the highest costs of employment, since

$$w_g - \frac{tx}{1+\tau_g} \le 0 \Longleftrightarrow x \ge \frac{w_g(1+\tau_g)}{t} = \hat{\ell}.$$

In between, the EGS attracts labor supply $\ell_g = \hat{\ell} - \hat{\ell}_e$ if and only if $\hat{\ell} \ge \hat{\ell}_e$, or equivalently $w_g(1+\tau_g) \ge w_e$. Otherwise, the EGS offers too little in terms of wage and access and aggregate labor supply facing the N employers is the same as if an EGS did not exist: $\ell_e(w_e, w_g, \tau_g) = w_e/t$, with $\ell_g(w_e, w_g, \tau_g) = 0$.[18] In sum, the associated (kinked) inverse labor supply schedule facing the N employers is of the form:

$$w_e(\ell, w_g, \tau_g) = max\left\{w_g + \frac{\tau_g t\ell}{1+\tau_g}, t\ell\right\}. \tag{2}$$

[18] This self-selection among workers into private employment, EGS employment and unemployment is consistent with empirical evidence to date. Teklu and Asefa (1999) and Gaiha (2000, 2005) demonstrate that workers who are least able to find work (e.g. those who are disabled, and those who live in very remote rural areas) fail to participate either in private or EGS employment. Meanwhile, although some [illegible] switched from private to EGS employment, the extent of displacement varies. See for example Bhatty (2006) for evidence of job switching from private to EGS employment subsequent to the NREGA, and Gaiha and Ima (2002) for evidence of reverse job switching from EGS to private employment subsequent to an expansion of private employment opportunities in the Amadnagar district of the Indian state of Maharashtra.

Now, since $\max\{w_g+\tau_g t\ell/(1+\tau_g),\, t\ell\}\geq t\ell$, the establishment of an EGS directly impacts labor supply by raising the minimal wage that the N employers must offer to secure positive employment. Effectively, the EGS raises the reservation wage of any worker contemplating private sector employment by exactly the amount of the EGS wage w_g.

Likewise, an increase in the ease of access to EGS employment, τ_g, also raises the private sector wage, w_e. Indeed, as $\tau_g\rightarrow\infty$, the EGS becomes a *true* universal guarantee of employment:

$$w_e(\ell, w_g, \tau_g) = max\{w_g + t\ell, t\ell\} = w_g + t\ell.$$

On the other hand, as $\tau_g\rightarrow 0$, accessing EGS employment is just as costly as accessing private employment,[19]

$$w_e(\ell, w_g, \tau_g) = max\{w_g, t\ell\}.$$

The N employers now effectively operate in a perfectly contestable labor market (Baumol, 1982), in which labor supply is perfectly elastic at the EGS wage w_g up until $\ell = \frac{w_g}{t}$.

With these two limiting cases in mind, the labor market implications of an EGS for intermediate values of τ_g should naturally be expected to be mixed, wherein the standard employment deterring effect of a reservation wage hike is interacted with the employment enhancing effect of contestability. The question remains as to which one of the two effects dominates, and for what range of parameter values?

Introducing Eq. (2) into the employers' profit maximizing problem, the intersection of the marginal labor cost $(\partial w(\ell_{-i}+\ell_i, w_g, \tau_g)\ell_i/\partial\ell_i)$ schedule and the marginal value product (a), evaluated at a symmetric equilibrium once again gives the equilibrium private employment and wage levels. This is shown in Fig. 2a and b. As should be apparent, if the EGS wage and access are jointly too low, $w_g(1+\tau_g)<a/(1+n)$, the EGS has no impact on private employment. At the opposite extreme, if $w_g>a$, the EGS completely displaces private employment. Other than these two cases, three possible types of nontrivial equilibrium labor market outcomes $\{\ell_e(n, w_g, \tau_g), w_e(n, w_g, \tau_g), \ell_g(n, w_g, \tau_g)\}$ can be identified relative to no government intervention scenario[20].

Proposition 1. *I. If $w_g[1+\tau_g(1+n)]<a\leq w_g(1+\tau_g)(1+n)$, the EGS raises private employment with no equilibrium EGS employment: $\ell_e = \frac{w_g(1+\tau_g)}{t} N\,\ell_o(n)$ and $\ell_g=0$ The private sector wage is simply $w_e=w_g(1+\tau_g)$.*

II. If $w_g(1+\tau_g)<a\leq w_g[1+\tau_g(1+n)]$, the EGS raises private employment and hires a positive number of EGS workers: $\ell_e = \frac{(a-w_g)(1+\tau_g)}{\tau_g t(1+n)} \geq \ell_o(n)$ and $\ell_g=w_g(1+\tau_g)/t-\ell_e>0$. The private sector wage is given by $w_e = \frac{a+nw_g}{1+n} \geq w_o(n)$.

III. If $w_g\leq a\leq w_g(1+\tau_g)$, the EGS now lowers private employment, and hires a positive number of EGS workers: $\ell_e = \frac{(a-w_g)(1+\tau_g)}{\tau_g t(1+n)} \leq \ell_o(n)$ and $\ell_g=w_g(1+\tau_g)/t-\ell_e>0$. The private sector wage continues to be $w_e = \frac{a+nw_g}{1+n} \geq w_o(n)$.

In all cases, w_e is higher than the EGS wage, and the no government intervention wage.

The private sector wage effect of an EGS should come as little surprise, since the introduction of an EGS effectively shifts the inverse labor supply schedule upwards. What may be somewhat unexpected, however, is that an EGS can either strictly increase (I and II), or decrease private sector employment (III). The increase in private sector employment should be attributed to contestability, wherein employers are in fact induced to pay a higher wage, and employ more workers than when an EGS does not exist. Here, the introduction of an EGS as an additional source of employment effectively erodes the market power embraced by each one of the N employers. With sufficiently high levels of wage and access (III), however, the reservation effect starts to dominate and employers respond by scaling back labor hiring.

While seemingly straightforward, these three employment regimes embody a wide array useful observations. Our discussion in what follows touches upon three sets of comparative statics results, with respect to the EGS wage, access to the EGS, and market power exhibited by employers in the private sector.

3.2. Non-monotonicity, the EGS wage and access

Our first observation concerns non-monotonicity. At given EGS access $(\tau_g>0)$ and market power $(n>0)$, private employment first rises and eventually falls with successively higher levels of w_g. This is shown in Fig. 3, in which schedule L_1^e traces the non-monotonic private labor market employment response to the EGS wage, starting from the no government intervention baseline $\ell_0(n) = \frac{a}{[(1+n)t]}$, given $\tau_g>0$ and $n>0$. These correspond to a starting phase (I) in which higher levels of w_g promotes contestability and raises $\ell_e = \frac{w_g(1+\tau_g)}{t}$, followed by two subsequent phases (II and III) in which further increases in the EGS wage trigger the reservation wage effect, causing $\ell_e = \frac{(a-w_g)(1+\tau_g)}{\tau_g t(1+n)}$ to bend downwards.

Taking instead the EGS wage and market power as given, a similar non-monotonic relationship between private sector and EGS employment subsequent to improvements in access to the latter – in which private employment first rises (I) and then falls (II and III) with access – can be shown using Proposition 1.

---

[19] As an alternative interpretation, suppose that the cost of employment includes an additive component as well: $T+tx$ in the private sector, and T_g+t_gx for EGS employment, with T and T_g positive. These imply that the ease of access to an EGS through T_g applies uniformly to all potential workers. A reduction in T_g is thus observationally equivalent to an increase in EGS pay w_g, with $\tau_g=0$ and $t=t_g$ set at unity. In equilibrium, the EGS loses its ability to selectively target workers, for all employed workers will be hired by the EGS $(w_g-T_g>w_e-T)$, or otherwise none at all will be. We thank an anonymous referee for pointing this out to us.

[20] The arguments of ℓ_e, ℓ_g and w_e are dropped whenever there is no risk of confusion in what follows.

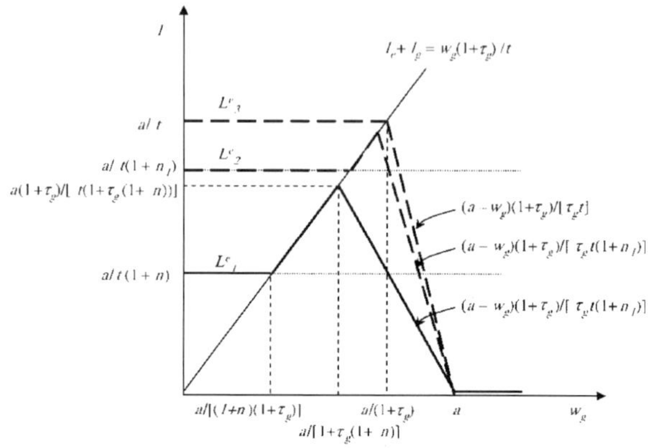

Fig. 3. Private employment and the EGS wage.

3.3. Local and global employment effects

With non-monotonicity, a simple demonstration that the marginal impact of an increase in w_g is a reduction in EGS employment, as is the case with types II and III outcomes, provides insufficient proof that the EGS has unambiguously lowered private employment relative to no government intervention. In Fig. 4, where $\tau_g>0$ and $n>0$ are once again exogenously given, the private employment outcome labeled $\bar{\ell}_e$ can be achieved either by (i) exploiting the contestability effect of an EGS, by setting the EGS wage at $w_{g_1} = \frac{t\bar{\ell}_e}{(1+\tau_g)}$, or (ii) by raising the wage even further so that the reservation wage effect is triggered with $\hat{w}_{g_2} = a - \frac{t\tau_g\bar{\ell}_e(1+n)}{(1+\tau_g)}$. In both cases, the same private employment level which exceeds the no government intervention level, $\ell_0(n)$, is achieved. However, in (ii) a local increase in w_g always reduces private employment.

3.4. Market power

If the labor market is perfectly competitive to begin with, it can be easily verified that the range of productivity levels in which the EGS raises total employment with no EGS employment collapses to a single point, $w_g(1+\tau_g)$. The range in which an EGS raises total employment by raising both private and EGS employment likewise collapses to the same point $w_g(1+\tau_g)$. As should be

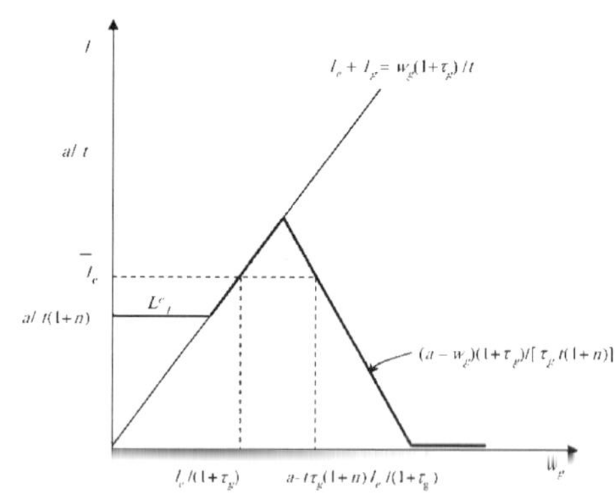

Fig. 4. Local and global effects of an EGS.

expected, where there is no pre-existing labor market distortion to begin with, the introduction of an EGS at most leaves unchanged, when $a \geq w_g(1+\tau_g)$, or otherwise strictly decreases private employment. Moving away from competitive markets, non-monotonicity is inevitable. Fig. 3 demonstrates. As shown, L_1^c, L_2^c and L_3^c constitute a family of private employment schedules with successively decreasing values of n, or equivalently successively more competitive labor market structure.

4. The desirability of an EGS

Given the wide array of possibilities in which an EGS can be adapted to impact private and EGS employment, the nature of an optimally designed EGS will naturally depend on the ultimate end that such a scheme is expected to achieve.[21] With employment determined jointly by the extent of market power, private sector productivity and the cost of employment, an EGS may be used as a means to target (i) private sector employment in order to offset market power, or (ii) private and EGS employment combined in order to lift workers out of poverty. Furthermore, an EGS may also be deployed to maximize a social welfare function in which a planner's concern for (iii) market efficiency and (iv) income distribution are accounted for. We will examine each of these possibilities in turn.

To fulfill any of one of these objectives, we assume that a lump sum tax on employers $T(w_g, \tau_g)$ is raised in order to finance the EGS. The budget requirements of an employment guarantee involves two types of government expenditures. The first involves the wage cost of the scheme, or simply, $w_g\ell_g(n, w_g, \tau_g)$. The second source of expenditure covers the cost required to reduce the cost of employment for each worker, τ_g. Thus,

$$B_e(w_g, \tau_g) = w_g\ell_g(n, w_g, \tau_g) + \int_{\ell_e}^{\ell_g+\ell_e}\left(t - \frac{t}{1+\tau_g}\right)x dx. \tag{3}$$

There are a variety of other modeling options here, but as a benchmark, we assume that the government does not enjoy any particular advantage, as compared to workers, in managing the cost of employment.[22] The reduction in the total cost of employment due to a reduction in t_g, and the budgetary requirement for doing so will henceforth taken to be one for one.[23] Government budget balance requires that

$$T(w_g, \tau_g) = B_e(w_g, \tau_g).$$

4.1. Private employment targeting

Consider here a planner with an aim to maximize private employment $\ell_e(n, w_g, \tau_g)$, for any given budget $B_e(w_g, \tau_g) \leq \bar{B}(\geq 0)$. Equivalently, the problem of the planner is simply:

$$\max_{w_g,\tau_g} \ell_e(n, w_g, \tau_g), \quad \text{s.t.} \quad B_e(w_g, \tau_g) \leq \bar{B}, w_g \geq \bar{w}_g.$$

An optimal EGS in this context is in fact straightforward. As shown in Fig. 3, for every $\tau_g \geq 0$, and $n > 0$, a maximal level of private employment can be reached through

$$\max_{w_g} \ell_e(n, w_g, \tau_g) = \frac{a(1+\tau_g)}{t(1+\tau_g(1+n))} \tag{4}$$

by setting $w_g = a/(1+\tau_g(1+n))$. Now,

$$\max_{\tau_g} \frac{a(1+\tau_g)}{t(1+\tau_g(1+n))} = \frac{a}{t} = \ell_o(0)$$

by setting $\tau_g = 0$. As such, the promise to guarantee employment alone can replicate the competitive labor market outcome. This is accomplished by an EGS wage and access pairing: $w_g = a$ and $\tau_g = 0$. Here, the EGS elicits the labor market outcome in a perfectly contestable market, in which the government behaves as an otherwise identical employer of *last resort* ($\tau_g = 0$), ready to pay the competitively determined wage a on demand. In equilibrium, this is accomplished at no cost to the government $B_e(w_g, \tau_g) = 0$.

Two points deserve attention here. First, if the labor market is perfectly competitive to begin with, an EGS can of course never raise private employment beyond the no government intervention level (Section 3.4). Second, irrespective of the degree of market

---

[21] There is a host of other possible labor market policies that may be used to offset the combination of reasons why unemployment prevail in the labor market we consider. In a companion paper, (Basu et al., 2007a), we take up the issue of minimum wage laws when enforcement is costly and commitment to reform and enforcement may not be credible. In footnote 26, we briefly discuss the findings of this minimum wage setup, and highlight the important differences that a lack of commitment makes. Other examples policy reforms include a wage subsidy, or a tax-cum-transfer scheme with unemployment insurance for example. It is well known that the effectiveness of these policies depends importantly on the credibility of the policy commitment (e.g. Boadway et al., 2003). A full ranking analysis of each of these policies and combinations thereof is devoted to future work.

[22] For an alternative way of incorporating the budget requirement of reducing the cost of employment, see the working paper Basu et al. (2007b).

[23] An alternative and equivalent assumption here is that the government provides a transportation cost subsidy to each worker that is equal to $\frac{\tau_g t x}{(1+\tau_g)}$.

power, an EGS can never raise private employment beyond the competitive level, for doing so would require employers to pay a wage higher than the productivity of labor, an impossibility if employers are to make non-negative profits.

4.2. Aggregate employment targeting

As opposed to maximizing private employment by choice of an appropriate EGS wage and access pairing, another question is how w_g and τ_g might be chosen to achieve an exogenous aggregate employment (EGS plus private employment) target, $\bar{\ell}$, with as much of it achieved via private employment as possible. In other words, the problem of the planner is simply:

$$\max_{w_g,\tau_g} \ell_e(n, w_g, \tau_g), \quad \text{s.t.} \quad \ell_e(n, w_g, \tau_g) + \ell_g(n, w_g, \tau_g) = \bar{\ell}, w_g \geq \bar{w}_g. \tag{5}$$

There are two cases to consider. Suppose first that $\ell_o(n) < \bar{\ell} \leq \ell_o(0)$. Such an employment target can be viewed as primarily efficiency-improving, aimed at delivering a labor market outcome closer to the perfectly competitive level $\ell_o(0)$. By adjusting w_g and τ_g, there exists in fact a continuous schedule of w_g and τ_g pairings that solves the maximization problem above.[24] An obvious choice, which once again invokes contestability, involves setting $\tau_g = 0$ and $w_g = t\bar{\ell}$. Here, the planner similarly behaves as an otherwise identical employer ($\tau_g = 0$), and commits to pay a wage $w_g = t\bar{\ell}$ just enough to expand total employment to $\bar{\ell}$ along the labor supply schedule. This is of course a special case of Proposition 1(I), in which there is no equilibrium EGS employment, and the target $\bar{\ell}$ is fulfilled completely by it expanding private employment over and above the no government intervention level.[25]

The more interesting case involves an *aggregate* employment target higher than the competitive level $\bar{\ell} > \ell_o(0)$. To this end, note that for at least $\bar{\ell}$ number of workers to be hired in the aggregate, it must be the case that $w_g - \frac{t\bar{\ell}}{1+\tau_g} \geq 0 \Longleftrightarrow w_g(1+\tau_g) - t\bar{\ell} \geq 0$. Denote

$$\bar{w} \equiv w_g(1+\tau_g) \equiv t\bar{\ell} \tag{6}$$

as the wage equivalent of the EGS aggregate employment target. Intuitively, this is the wage that an EGS must offer in order for $\bar{\ell}$ workers to be employed jointly by the private sector and the EGS, if access were to remain at the level of the private sector $\tau_g = 0$. With this definition, an EGS that generates more than the competitive level of employment in the aggregate must also provide a wage equivalent $w_g(1+\tau_g) = \bar{w}$ that exceeds the competitive wage, since

$$t\bar{\ell} > t\ell_o(0) \Longleftrightarrow \bar{w} > t\frac{a}{t} = a$$

As may be expected, an EGS wage equivalent that outstrips the competitive wage (a) can adversely impact private employment. More precisely, apply the definition of the employment target $\bar{\ell} = w_g(1+\tau_g)/t$ to Proposition 1, we have

Proposition 2. *I. If $\ell_o(n) \leq \bar{\ell} < \ell_o(0)/(1+n\tau_g/(1+\tau_g))$, the EGS raises private employment with no equilibrium EGS employment: $\ell_e = \bar{\ell} > \ell_o(n)$ and $\ell_g = 0$. The private sector wage is simply the EGS wage equivalent $w_e = \bar{w}$.*

II. If $\ell_o(0)/(1+n\tau_g/(1+\tau_g)) \leq \bar{\ell} < \ell_o(0)$, the EGS raises private employment and hires a positive number of EGS workers: $\ell_e = \frac{(a-w_g)\bar{\ell}}{(t\bar{\ell}-w_g)(1+n)} \geq \ell_o(n)$ and $\ell_g = \bar{\ell} - \ell_e > 0$. The private sector wage is given by $w_e = \frac{a+nw_g}{1+n} \geq w_o(n)$.

III. If $\ell_o(0) \leq \bar{\ell} < \ell_o(0)(1+\tau_g)$, the EGS now lowers private employment, and hires a positive number of EGS workers: $\ell_e = \frac{(a-w_g)\bar{\ell}}{(t\bar{\ell}-w_g)(1+n)} \leq \ell_o(n)$ and $\ell_g = \bar{\ell} - \ell_e > 0$. The private sector wage continues to be $w_e = \frac{a+nw_g}{1+n} \geq w_o(n)$.

This provides an exact demarcation, and shows that the reservation wage (private employment reducing) effect of an EGS takes on a dominating role whenever the EGS aggregate employment target exceeds the competitive employment level (III). Interestingly, Proposition 2 shows that such an EGS necessarily leads to a reduction in private sector employment. Thus, the double-edged EGS in fact comes with a built-in constraint — an EGS that raises total employment beyond the competitive level can never simultaneously raise private employment beyond the no government intervention level.

Also by virtue of Proposition 2(III), observe that given $\ell_o(0) < \bar{\ell}$, EGS employment $\bar{\ell} - \ell_e$ strictly rises with the EGS wage. In other words, in order to minimize EGS employment (displacement of private employment) given the target $\bar{\ell}$, w_g should be set as low as possible. Implicitly, this requires that access τ_g be accordingly relaxed in order to sustain the same aggregate employment target, $\bar{\ell} = w_g(1+\tau_g)$. In sum, the EGS wage and access pairing $\{w_g^*(n, \bar{\ell}), \tau_g^*(n, \bar{\ell})\}$ that minimizes private employment displacement depends critically on the size of the employment target $\bar{\ell}$:

Proposition 3. *For aggregate employment targets satisfying $\ell_o(n) < \bar{\ell} \leq \ell_o(0)$, private employment can be maximized to match $\bar{\ell}$ exactly with $w_g^*(n, \bar{\ell}) = t\bar{\ell}$, and $1+\tau_g^*(n, \bar{\ell}) = 1$. The associated EGS employment is equal to zero.*

For aggregate employment targets satisfying $\bar{\ell} > \ell_o(0)$, $w_g^*(n, \bar{\ell}) = \bar{w}_g$, and $1+\tau_g^*(n, \bar{\ell}) = t\bar{\ell}/\bar{w}_g$. The associated private employment is no greater than the no government intervention level.

24 In particular, any w_g and τ_g pair that satisfies $w_g(1+\tau_g)$ [illegible] will suffice. The aggregate employment target is met in this case completely by expanding private employment ($w_g(1+\tau_g) = t\ell_e(n, w_g, \tau_g) = t\bar{\ell}$).

25 To see this, note that with $\tau_g = 0$ and $w_g = t\bar{\ell}$, the relevant range of Type I employment can be simplified as $t\bar{\ell} < a \leq t\bar{\ell}(1+n)$. By definition of $\ell_o(n)$ and $\ell_o(0)$, this corresponds exactly with the feasible range of aggregate employment target $\ell_o(n) < \bar{\ell} \leq \ell_o(0)$ under consideration here.

There is thus a tight link between the ultimate objective of the EGS employment target and the EGS wage depending on whether the objective is to improve efficiency ($\ell_o(n)<\bar{\ell}\leq\ell_o(0)$), or to combat poverty left unchecked by market forces ($\bar{\ell}>\ell_o(0)$). Interestingly, the relationship between such an EGS wage and the employment target is discontinuous – to be set sufficiently high to elicit contestability if efficiency improvement is the only objective of the EGS, or as low as possible if unemployment associated with perfect competition is deemed too high. In both cases, access is adjusted accordingly to meet the target. What remains to be determined, therefore, is the important question of the optimal choice of employment target.

5. Efficiency, distributional concerns and credibility

We now turn to a more general social welfare function, $\Omega(w_g, \tau_g)$, made up of three parts. The first part comprises of the sum of the (i) profits of the N employers ($(a-w_e)\ell_e$), (ii) revenue generated from the EGS ($a_g\ell_g$) and (iii) utility of all workers $\left(\int_0^{\ell_e}(w_e-tx)dx+\int_{\ell_e}^{\ell_e+\ell_g}\left(w_g-\frac{tx}{(1+\tau_g)}\right)dx\right)$. The second part is a lump sum tax $T(w_g, \tau_g)$, raised in order to finance the EGS (Section 4). The third part introduces distributional concerns. We adopt a very simple formulation – the government cares about the number of workers whose income is below the exogenously given poverty line w_p. Thus, the EGS income threshold $\bar{w}_g$ is now set at the poverty line w_p. The weight given to this concern relative to efficiency is γ. The social welfare function is thus:

$$\Omega(w_g,\tau_g)=(a-w_e)\ell_e+a_g\ell_g+\int_0^{\ell_e}(w_e-tx)dx+\int_{\ell_e}^{\ell_e+\ell_g}\left(w_g-\frac{tx}{1+\tau_g}\right)dx-T(w_g,\tau_g)-\gamma H$$

where H is simply the poverty head count ratio (Foster et al., 1984) or the percentage of workers below a poverty line, w_p. Thus, $H=1-\ell_e-\ell_g$. Making use of the government budget constraint, the social welfare function above simplifies to

$$\Omega(w_g,\tau_g)=\left[(a-a_g)\ell_e\right]+\left[a_g+\gamma-\frac{t\bar{\ell}}{2}\right]\bar{\ell}-\gamma.$$

The first term in square brackets spells out the welfare cost associated with the displacement of private employment, as $a>a_g$. The second term in square brackets shows the average net welfare gains associated with expanding employment in the economy. Here, the revenue equivalent of EGS employment a_g, the distributional concern of the government, γ, and the cost of employment of each employed workers jointly determine the extent of this potential gain in welfare. A change of variables yields $\Omega(w_g, \tau_g)$ in terms solely of the employment target $\bar{\ell}$ and w_g:

$$\Omega\left(w_g, t\bar{\ell}/w_g-1\right)=\left[(a-a_g)\ell_e\left(n, w_g, \frac{t\bar{\ell}}{w_g}-1\right)\right]+\left[a_g+\gamma-\frac{t\bar{\ell}}{2}\right]\bar{\ell}-\gamma$$

Evidently, the task of social welfare maximization reduces down to simply the choice of an employment target $\bar{\ell}$, and simultaneously an EGS wage that maximizes private employment, conditional on the target – an exercise that has already been examined in Section 4. What the planner's problem here additionally illuminates, as should be evident, is the question of how high the employment target should be.

5.1. Committing to a complete contract

To establish a benchmark for subsequent comparison, consider an employment guarantee legislation in which a planner commits to a wage and access pairing, w_g^c and τ_g^c, to maximize the social welfare function $\Omega(w_g, \tau_g)$. Denote $\bar{\ell}^c=w_g^c(1+\tau_g^c)/t$ as the associated employment target. There are two sets of considerations. First, regardless of the degree of distributional concern, our discussion in Section 4.1 suggests that an EGS can be gainfully used to target private employment at no cost to the government. Meanwhile, employment beyond the competitive level may be justified if is sufficiently large. We have thus:

Proposition 4. *For a planner that exercises commitment to both w_g and τ_g, and a social welfare function augmented with distributional concern, there exists a critical level γ^c, with*

$$\gamma^c>(a-a_g)\left(1+\frac{w_p}{(a-w_p)(1+n)}\right)>a-a_g\Longleftrightarrow a_g+\gamma^c>a$$

such that if and only if $\gamma\leq\gamma^c$, the aggregate employment target is set at the competitive level $\ell_o(0)(=a/t)$, with no equilibrium EGS employment: $\bar{\ell}^c=\ell_o(0)$, $w_g^c=a$; and $1+\tau_g^c=1$. Otherwise, with $\gamma>\gamma^c$, employment target $\bar{\ell}^c$ exceeds the perfectly competitively baseline, and implicitly solves:

$$\bar{\ell}^c=\frac{a_g+\gamma}{t}-\frac{(a-a_g)(a-w_p)w_p}{t(t\bar{\ell}^c-w_p)^2(1+n)}>\ell_o(0).$$

In addition, $w_g^c=w_p$, and $1+\tau_g^c=t(\bar{\ell}^c/w_p)$. There is strictly positive EGS employment, and private employment is strictly less than the no government intervention baseline $\ell_o(n)$.

Proof. See the Appendix.

Accordingly, a strictly social welfare improving EGS can always be found so long as the labor market is imperfectly competitive. Indeed, even if the revenue derived from generating EGS employment is strictly negative ($a_g<0$), the proposition still calls for the government to invoke to the fullest extent possible the contestability component of the EGS.

The proposition also shows that productive EGS employment and distributional concern go hand in hand in determining the welfare maximizing wage and accessibility of EGS employment. In order to justify strictly positive EGS employment in equilibrium, it must be the case that $a_g+\gamma$ strictly exceeds the productivity of private employment a. However, in order to accommodate such a high aggregate employment target, displacement of private employment is inevitable (Proposition 2).

Importantly, Proposition 4 shows that the optimal EGS wage is invariant across a wide variety of parameter values of a_g and market power. In particular, so long as $\gamma\leq\gamma^c$, the optimal EGS wage is to be set high enough to elicit contestability in the labor market $w_g^c=a$. Meanwhile, for $\gamma>\gamma^c$, with aggregate employment target accordingly set beyond the competitive level, private employment displacement is minimized by choice of an EGS wage at the poverty line, while access is relaxed to accommodate the desired number of workers.

These findings are provocative particularly since they imply that whenever employers enjoy market power, an EGS can be an extremely cost effective way of raising employment, regardless of the productivity of private and EGS employment, and even if the planner is concerned only with efficiency. One may thus infer that even in labor markets of the highly skilled, government provision of EGS can have an important role to play. This may seem counter-intuitive at least at first sight, for such an inference runs contrary to the historical circumstances under which an EGS has been invoked in times of massive unemployment and adverse productivity shocks. In what follows, we contrast what a complete employment guarantee contract can do in principle as established above, with what an incomplete contract can hope to accomplish more realistically. We do so by relaxing the assumption that the contract pins down both w_g and τ_g ex ante, and by examining a set of credibility triggers that ultimately justifies the use of an EGS.

5.2. Discretion and incomplete contracts

We assume that from announcement to execution of the EGS, the following sequence of events unfolds:

- the government announces a wage w_g^d to be paid to workers employed under the EGS,
- employers and workers form expectations $E\bar{\ell}$ about the ex post EGS aggregate employment target of the planner, and the corresponding ease of access to the EGS, $E\tau_g$,
- conditional on $E\bar{\ell}$ and $E\tau_g$ private employment contracts are signed for $E\ell_e=\ell_e(n, w_g^d, E\tau_g)$ number of workers,
- having observed $E\ell_e$, the government adjusts the ex post target $\bar{\ell}^d$ and access τ_g^d. By doing so, the government implicitly rations/encourages access to EGS employment, available to any worker at wage w_g^d.

We assume in addition that workers and employers harbor rational expectations. A key difference with the case of commitment is that access to the EGS is not written into law, and is thus subject to discretion ex post. In contrast to the case with commitment, the government in this case is faced with the task of setting an EGS wage $w_g^d\geq\bar{w}_g$, with the full knowledge that private employers and workers can take this wage as a signal of the ex-post accessibility of the EGS.

Beginning with the final stage of the sequence. Let private employment $E\ell_e$ conditional on expectation $E\tau_g$ be given. An ex post social welfare maximizing aggregate employment target $\bar{\ell}^d$ can be achieved by relaxing access τ_g^d $(w_g^d, \bar{\ell}^d)$ to ensure that the marginal worker $x=\bar{\ell}^d$ is just indifferent between employment as an EGS worker, and not working at all:

$$w_g^d-\frac{t\,\bar{\ell}^d}{1+\tau_g^d\left(w_g^d,\bar{\ell}^d\right)}=0,\quad\text{or}\quad 1+\tau_g^d\left(w_g^d,\bar{\ell}d\right)=\frac{t\bar{\ell}^d}{w_g^d},\tag{7}$$

given the announced EGS wage. Note that τ_g^d is to be distinguished from $E\tau_g$ in that the former is the accessibility of EGS employment, to be chosen by the government conditional on the expectation $E\tau_g$, and the announced EGS wage w_g^d. Put another way, ex post discretionary limits on access (decreases in τ_g^d) works as a rationing device, and puts checks on total employment $\bar{\ell}^d$. The corresponding level of EGS employment is thus $\ell_g^d=\max\{\bar{\ell}^d-E\ell_e, 0\}$. We are now in a position to examine the planner's ex post problem, in which an ex post employment target $\bar{\ell}^d$ is chosen to maximize the social welfare function (7), taking $E\ell_e$ as given:

$$\max_{\bar{\ell}^d}(a-a_g)E\ell_e+\left(a_g+\gamma-\frac{t\,\bar{\ell}^d}{2}\right)\bar{\ell}^d-\gamma,\tag{8}$$

Since $E\ell_e$ is given ex-ante, ex post social welfare maximization no longer needs to internalize any private sector employment impact of the EGS, hence:

Proposition 5. *Given any $w_g^d\geq w_p$ and $E\ell_e\geq 0$, ex post maximization of the social welfare function augmented with distribution concern implies an aggregate employment target and an EGS employment level:*

$$\bar{\ell}^d=\frac{a_g+\gamma}{t},\ \ell_g^d=\max\left\{\frac{a_g+\gamma}{t}-E\ell_e,0\right\},$$

where actual EGS employment is increasing in $a_g+\gamma$ *and decreasing in* $E\ell_e$. *The implied ex post welfare maximizing access to EGS employment* $\tau_g^d(w_g^d, \bar{\ell}^d)$ *is strictly decreasing in* w_g^d, *with*

$$1+\tau_g^d\left(w_g^d, \bar{\ell}^d\right)=\frac{a_g+\gamma}{w_g^d}. \tag{9}$$

Intuitively, once employment contracts are signed and total private employment given, the government weighs the marginal benefits $a_g+\gamma$ of EGS employment relative to the marginal cost $t\bar{\ell}^d$. Ex post accessibility is thus increasing in the productivity of EGS employment (a_g) adjusted in such a way that reflects the distributional concern of the planner γ. Meanwhile, since the pool of available EGS workers $(w_g^d(1+\tau_g^d)/t-E\ell_e)$ rises with the EGS wage w_g^d, ex post accessibility is inversely related to the wage w_g^d set forth ex-ante.

As shown in section Proposition 2, an EGS produces non-trivial labor market consequences only if the aggregate employment target $\bar{\ell}^d$ is greater than the no government intervention level, $\ell_o(n)=\frac{a}{(1+n)t}$. We now know from Proposition 5 that this requires in effect

$$a_g+\gamma>\frac{a}{1+n}. \tag{10}$$

Thus, three sets of factors are simultaneously in play. These *credibility triggers* include: labor market triggers such as low labor productivity and oligopsonistic market power (a and n); cost triggers such as the revenue (costs) that can be generated from public works (a_g), and finally, planner's preference triggers subsumed under the term (γ). With discretion, the ex post optimal aggregate employment target $(a_g+\gamma)/t$ can indeed be greater than the competitive employment level a/t, whenever $a_g+\gamma>a$.

At the other extreme, if $a_g+\gamma$ is lower than $a/(1+n)$, the aggregate employment target that applies in a rational expectation equilibrium is so low that an EGS completely loses its ability to impact both private and EGS employment levels ex post. A special case is a planner who cares only about efficiency ($\gamma=0$). Since $a_g<a$, such a planner will of course never target employment beyond the competitive level. Meanwhile, if in addition $a_g<a/(1+n)$, any EGS policy announcement aimed at enhancing labor market efficiency will be deemed to lack credibility.

5.3. Getting the wage right

Our next task concerns the government's choice of a wage level w_g^d, which maximizes government welfare in the face of rational expectations. The answer, as it turns out, is surprisingly simple. Since the ex-post optimal aggregate employment target $\bar{\ell}^d$ is given by $(a_g+\gamma)/t$, employers and workers rationally expect that

$$E\bar{\ell}=\frac{a_g+\gamma}{t}=\bar{\ell}^d,\quad 1+E\tau_g=1+\tau_g^d\left(w_g^d,\bar{\ell}^d\right)=\frac{t\bar{\ell}^d}{w_g^d}. \tag{11}$$

Making use of Eq. (7) again, the planner's ex-ante problem is

$$\max_{w_g^d}\left[(a-a_g)\ell_e\left(n,w_g^d,\tau_g^d,\left(w_g^d,\bar{\ell}^d\right)\right)\right]+\left[a_g+\gamma-\frac{t\bar{\ell}^d}{2}\right]\bar{\ell}^d-\gamma, w_g^d\geq w_p.$$

Equivalently, the task involves once again the maximization of private employment ℓ_e, given the ex-post optimal aggregate employment target $\bar{\ell}^d=(a_g+\gamma)/t$, and the rational expectations of employers and workers in Eq. (11). By direct application of Propositions 2 and 3, we have

Proposition 6. *With ex post discretion on access, and a social welfare function augmented with a concern for distribution, there are three cases:*

I. *If* $a_g+\gamma<\frac{a}{(1+n)}$, *the optimal EGS wage is indeterminate, as the ex post optimal employment target is strictly less than the no government intervention level. The announcement of any* w_g^d *invokes a corresponding adjustment in expectations, which then jointly implies private employment at the no government intervention level* $\ell_o(n)=a/[t(1+n)]$. *In equilibrium,* $\ell_g=0$.
II. *If* $a_g+\gamma>a$, *the ex post optimal employment target exceeds the perfectly competitive level,* $\bar{\ell}^d=\frac{a_g+\gamma}{t}>\ell_o(0)=a/t$. *To minimize private sector employment displacement/EGS employment, the optimal EGS wage should be set at the poverty line. In equilibrium, access is adjusted to accommodate* $\ell_g>0$ *and* $\ell_e<\ell_o(n)$:
III. *If* $a_g+\gamma\in\left[\frac{a}{(1+n)},a\right)$, *the ex post optimal employment target lies between the no government intervention and the perfectly competitive employment levels. The announcement of an EGS wage* $w_g^d=a_g+\gamma$ *maximizes social welfare, by invoking the rational expectation* $1+E\tau_g=1$, *and an ex post aggregate employment target* $\frac{(a_g+\gamma)}{t}$ *greater than* $\ell_o(n)=\frac{a}{[t(1+n)]}$. *In equilibrium,* $\ell_g=0$.

Fig. 5 summarizes these results in $(a, a_g+\gamma)$ space, and emphasizes the intricate balance between the (i) welfare maximizing EGS wage, (ii) private and public sector labor productivity,[26] (iii) the degree of imperfect competition in the labor market, and (iv) weight attached to distributional concern.

[26] In a companion paper (Basu et al., 2007a), we examine the issue of a credible minimum wage. It is shown that one of the conditions for a credible minimum wage policy requires that private labor productivity be sufficiently high. This is in sharp contrast to a credible EGS shown here, where the credibility of the EGS requires that private labor productivity be sufficiently low. These two forms of labor market policies can thus be seen as complementing each other depending on whether the relevant labor market is characterized by relatively high, or low labor productivity.

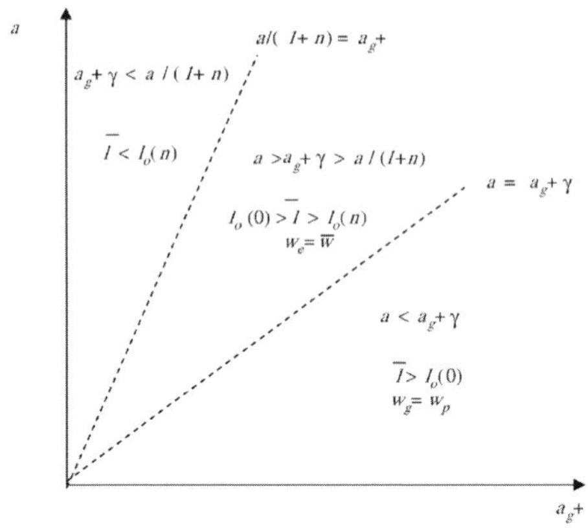

Fig. 5. Contestability, credibility and distributional concern.

First, for sufficiently high levels of private sector productivity relative to $a_g+\gamma$, $a_g+\gamma<\frac{a}{(1+n)}$, the announcement of any EGS wage inevitably lacks credibility. In a rational expectation equilibrium, private employment and wage levels are unaffected, and the universal applicability of an EGS in raising private employment levels as shown in Proposition 5 no longer applies. Comparing an EGS with commitment (Proposition 4) and an EGS with discretion (Proposition 6), the cost of policy discretion here comes in the form of an inability to elicit efficiency improving labor market reforms. In particular, the credibility of an EGS to improve efficiency is now questionable in labor markets with high private sector productivity (if the inequality $a_g+\gamma>a/(1+n)$ is violated).

At the other extreme, for planners exhibiting relatively high levels of distributional concern, with $a_g+\gamma>a$, the EGS hires a strictly positive number of workers. Even here, however, policy discretion comes at a cost, in the form of an inability to design a wage and access combination ex ante that displaces the least amount of private sector employment. Specifically, for γ in the range $(a-a_g, \gamma^c)$, an EGS with commitment can only be justified on the grounds of efficiency improvement (Proposition 4), and should never lead to displacement of private employment. With ex-post discretion, however, the same planner sets the EGS wage at the poverty line, implying strictly positive displacement of private employment (Proposition 6).

For credibility triggers that justify intermediate levels of aggregate employment targeting between the no government intervention and the perfectly competitive baselines, an EGS works purely as an announcement of contestability. Thus, we have an intriguing instance here where the effectiveness of the announcement of EGS in effecting efficiency enhancing change in the labor market now depends critically on the distributional concern of the planner in question. Of course, the relevance of this announcement effect depends on whether the labor market is imperfectly competitive to begin with (equivalently, if the range $[a/(1+n), a]$ is nonempty).

6. Concluding remarks and extensions

This paper has taken the first step towards understanding the labor market implications of an EGS. An EGS features a wage guarantee and a rationing device. The distinction between the two allows us to highlight an EGS as a policy capable of targeting aggregate employment, where the individual wage and access components can be adjusted so as to allow for an appropriate mix of private and EGS employment to be designed into the target. Aggregate employment targeting made possible by an EGS can potentially serve two distinct types of purposes: to enhance efficiency in labor markets plagued by employer market power, and to alleviate poverty by employing workers otherwise left out of the labor market.

We paid particular attention to the timing of the policy, distinguishing between the case where there is full commitment of wage and access, and where the ex-post credibility of an EGS may be in doubt. It is shown that the credibility of an EGS is triggered by private productivity downturns, excessive market power, and a concern for distribution by the planner. Ironically, therefore, planners who care only about efficiency are shown to lack credibility when an EGS is used to implement efficiency enhancing labor market reforms.

There remains a host of other important issues that warrants future research. To name two such examples, we have so far assumed a neutral scenario wherein the government enjoys no particular advantage over workers in managing the cost of employment. But in a variety of useful contexts (e.g. child care provision, job training and skill upgrading), the government may well be in a better position to overcome the costs associated with employment. Alternatively, the planner is assumed to care about the poverty head-count ratio. The exact manner in which a distributionally sensitive loss functions may be expected to impact the labor market implications of an EGS is an important question that warrants further attention.

Appendix A

Proof of Proposition 4. We begin with two observations: the government objective function (i) is piece-wise continuously differentiable in $\bar{\ell}$ and (ii) exhibits a discrete jump exactly at $\bar{\ell} = \ell_o(0) = a/t$, the competitive baseline. To complete the proof, we show that for an employment target greater than the competitive baseline to be a global maximum, the poverty aversion parameter must be sufficiently larger than γ^c as displayed in the Proposition.

For (i), we note from Proposition 2 that three cases can be identified. For $\bar{\ell} < \ell_o(n)$, the no government intervention baseline, an EGS has no impact on welfare as private employment is unaffected and no worker opts for EGS employment. Thus,

$$\Omega(w_g, \tau_g)\big|_{1+\tau_g = t\bar{\ell}/w_g} = \bar{\Omega}_o = (a + \gamma - a/2(1+n))a/(t(1+n))$$

For $\bar{\ell} \in [\ell_o(n), \ell_o(0)]$, $\ell_e(n, w_g, (t\bar{\ell}/w_g) - 1) \leq \ell_e(n, w_g^*(\bar{\ell}), \tau_g^*(\bar{\ell})) = \bar{\ell}$. It follows that for $\bar{\ell} \leq \ell_o(0)$,

$$\begin{aligned}\Omega(w_g, \tau_g)\big|_{1+\tau_g = t\bar{\ell}/w_g} &= \left[(a - a_g)\ell_e\left(n, w_g, t\bar{\ell}/w_g - 1\right)\right] + \left[a_g + \gamma - \frac{t\bar{\ell}}{2}\right]\bar{\ell} - \gamma \\ &\leq \Omega\left(w_g^*(n, \bar{\ell}), \tau_g^*(n, \bar{\ell})\right) = \left(a + \gamma - \frac{t\bar{\ell}}{2}\right)\bar{\ell} - \gamma \equiv \bar{\Omega}_1(\bar{\ell}). \end{aligned} \tag{12}$$

Thus, government welfare is increasing (strictly increasing) in $\bar{\ell}$ for $\bar{\ell} < a/t$, and $\gamma \geq (>) 0$. In addition, $\max_{\bar{\ell}} \bar{\Omega}_1(\bar{\ell}) = (a/2 + \gamma)a/t - \gamma$ by setting the employment target $\bar{\ell}_1^c = a/t$ at the competitive level. For $\bar{\ell} > \ell_o(0)$, $w_g^*(\bar{\ell}) = w_p$. Thus, $\ell_e(n, w_g, t\bar{\ell}) \leq \ell_e(n, w_g^*(\bar{\ell}), \tau_g^*(\bar{\ell})) = (a - w_p)(\bar{\ell}) = [(t\bar{\ell} - w_p)(1+n)] < \bar{\ell}$. It follows that,

$$\begin{aligned}\Omega(w_g, \tau_g)\big|_{1+\tau_g = t\bar{\ell}/w_g} &\leq \Omega(w_p, \tau_g)\big|_{1+\tau_g = t\bar{\ell}/w_p} \\ &= \frac{(a - a_g)(a - w_p)\bar{\ell}}{(t\bar{\ell} - w_p)(1+n)} + \left(a_g + \gamma - \frac{t\bar{\ell}}{2}\right)\bar{\ell} - \gamma \equiv \bar{\Omega}_2(\bar{\ell}).\end{aligned} \tag{13}$$

It can be readily verified that $\bar{\Omega}_2(\bar{\ell})$ is strictly concave in $\bar{\ell}$ for $\bar{\ell} > a/t$. Part (ii) of our argument now follows straightforwardly, since

$$\bar{\Omega}_2(\ell_o(0)) = \left(\frac{a - a_g}{1+n} + a_g + \gamma - \frac{a}{2}\right)\frac{a}{t} - \gamma < \bar{\Omega}_1(\ell_o(0)) = \left(\frac{a}{2} + \gamma\right)\frac{a}{t} - \gamma. \tag{14}$$

Thus, the solution to $\operatorname{argmax}_{\bar{\ell}} \bar{\Omega}_2(\bar{\ell}) = \bar{\ell}_2^c(\gamma)$ characterizes a local maximum. In particular, $\bar{\ell}_2^c(\gamma)$ is a corner solution, at the competitive baseline $\ell_o(0)$ if and only if $\frac{\partial \bar{\Omega}_2(\bar{\ell})}{\partial \bar{\ell}}\Big|_{\bar{\ell} = \ell_o(0)} \leq 0$, or

$$\gamma \leq \hat{\gamma} \equiv (a - a_g)\left(1 + \frac{w_p}{(a - w_p)(1+n)}\right).$$

For $\gamma > \hat{\gamma}$, $\bar{\ell}_2^c(\gamma)$ implicitly solves $\frac{\partial \bar{\Omega}_2(\bar{\ell})}{\partial \bar{\ell}} = 0$, or

$$\bar{\ell}_2^c = \frac{a_g + \gamma}{t} - \frac{(a - a_g)(a - w_p)w_p}{t(t\bar{\ell}^c - w_p)^2(1+n)} > \ell_o(0). \tag{15}$$

Since the right hand side of (15) is strictly increasing in γ, the locally maximum employment target $\bar{\ell}_2^c(\gamma)$ is likewise strictly increasing in γ, whenever $\gamma > \gamma$.

Finally, to confirm that $\bar{\ell}_2^c$ characterizes a global maximum, we require in addition that

$$\bar{\Omega}_1\left(\bar{\ell}_1^c\right) = \bar{\Omega}_1(\ell_o(0)) \leq \bar{\Omega}_2\left(\bar{\ell}_2^c\right)$$

To this end, note from (12) and (13) that

$$\bar{\Omega}_1\left(\bar{\ell}_1^c\right) > \bar{\Omega}_2\left(\bar{\ell}_1^c\right)$$

for any $\gamma \geq 0$ and hence, for any $\gamma \geq \hat{\gamma}$. In addition, by the envelope theorem,

$$\frac{\partial\left[\bar{\Omega}_1\left(\bar{\ell}_1^c\right) - \bar{\Omega}_2\left(\bar{\ell}_1^c\right)\right]}{\partial \gamma} = \bar{\ell}_1^c - \bar{\ell}_2^c = \ell_o(0) - \ell_2^c < 0,$$

and thus the difference $\bar{\Omega}_1(\bar{\ell}_1^c, \gamma) - \bar{\Omega}_2(\bar{\ell}_1^c, \gamma)$ is monotonically decreasing in γ. By the intermediate value theorem, there exists $\gamma^c > \hat{\gamma}$ such that $\bar{\Omega}_1(\bar{\ell}_1^c) - \bar{\Omega}_2(\bar{\ell}_1^c) < 0$ whenever $\gamma > \gamma^c$. The global maximum of the government maximization problem $\bar{\ell}^c = \bar{\ell}_2^c > \ell_o(0)$. Otherwise, $\bar{\ell}^c$ is set at the competitive baseline, $\bar{\ell}_1^c$.

References

Assaad, Ragui, 1997. The effects of public sector hiring and compensation policies on the Egyptian labor market. World Bank Economic Review 11 (1), 85–118.
Bardhan, Pranab, 1979. Labor supply functions in a poor agrarian economy. American Economic Review 69, 73–83.
Bardhan, Pranab, 1984. Land, Labor, and Rural Poverty: Essays in Development Economics. Oxford Univ. Press, Delhi.
Bardhan, P.K., Rudra, A., 1981. Terms and conditions of labour contracts in agriculture: results of a survey in West Bengal 1979. Oxford Bulletin of Economics and Statistics 43, 1 February.
Basu, Arnab K. 2007. "Impact of rural employment guarantee schemes on seasonal labor markets: optimum compensation and workers' welfare," College of William and Mary, mimeo.
Basu, Kaushik. 1981. "Food for work programmes: beyond roads that get washed away." Economic and Political Weekly, January 3–10.
Basu, Arnab K., Chau, Nancy H., Kanbur, Ravi, 2007a. Turning a blind eye: costly enforcement, credible commitment and minimum wage laws. IZA Discussion Paper, vol. 2998.
Basu, Arnab K., Chau, Nancy H., Kanbur, Ravi, 2007b. A theory of employment guarantees: contestability, credibility and distributional concerns. IZA Discussion Paper, vol. 3002.
Baumol, William J., 1982. Contestable markets: an uprising in the theory of industry structure. American Economic Review 72 (1), 1–15.
Bernstein, Irving, 1970. Turbulent Years: A History of the American Worker, 1933–1941. Houghton Mifflin, Boston.
Besley, Timothy, Coate, Stephen, 1992. Workfare vs. welfare: incentive arguments for work requirements in poverty alleviation programs. American Economic Review 82 (2), 249–261.
Besley, Timothy, Kanbur, Ravi, 1993. Principles of targeting. In: Lipton, Michael, van de Gaag, Jacques (Eds.), Including the Poor: Proceedings of a Symposium Organized by the World Bank and the International Food Policy Research Institute. The World Bank, Washington D.C., pp. 67–90.
Bhatty, Kiran. 2006. "Employment guarantee and child rights," Economic and Political Weekly, May, 1965–1967.
Blaug, Mark., 1963. The myth of the old poor law and the making of the new. Journal of Economic History 23, 151–184.
Blaug, Mark, 1964. The poor law report re-examined. Journal of Economic History 24, 229–245.
Binswanger, Hans P., Doherty, V.S., Balaramaiah, T., Bhende, M.J., Kshirsagar, K.G., Rao, V.B., Raju, P.S.S., 1984. Common features and contrasts in labor relations in the semiarid tropics of India. In: Binswanger, Hans, Rosenzweig, Mark (Eds.), Contractual Arrangements, Employments, and Wages in Rural Labor Markets in Asia. Yale University Press, New Haven, pp. 143–168.
Boadway, Robin, Cuff, Katherin, Marceauc, Nicolas, 2003. Redistribution and employment policies with endogenous unemployment. Journal of Public Economics 87, 2407–2430.
Card, David, Krueger, Alan B., 1995. Myth and Measurement: The New Economics of the Minimum Wage. Princeton University Press, Princeton.
Dar, Amit, Tzannatos, Zafris, 1999. Active labor market programs: a review of the evidence from evaluations. Social Protection Discussion Paper Series, vol. 9901. The World Bank, Washington D.C.
Datt, Gaurav, 1997. Bargaining Power, Wages and Employment: An Analysis of Agricultural Labor Markets in India. Sage Publications, London.
Dev, Mahendra, 1995. India's (Maharashtra) employment guarantee scheme: lessons from long experience. In: von Braun, Joachim (Ed.), Employment for Poverty Reduction and Food Security. International Food Policy Research Institute, Washington DC, pp. 108–143.
Drèze, Jean, Sen, Amartya, 1991. Strategies of entitlement protection. Hunger and Public Action, pp. 104–121.
Foster, James, Greer, Joel, Thorbecke, Erik, 1984. A class of decomposable poverty measures. Econometrica 52 (3), 761–766.
Gaiha, Raghav, 2005. Does the employment guarantee scheme benefit the rural poor in India? Some recent evidence. Asian Survey 45 (6), 949–969.
Gaiha, Raghav, 2000. On the targeting of the employment guarantee scheme in the Indian state of Maharastra. Economics of Planning 33, 203–219.
Gaiha, Raghav, 1996. How dependent are the rural poor on the employment guarantee scheme in India? Journal of Development Studies 32, 669–694.
Gaiha, Raghav, Ima, Katsushi, 2002. Rural public works and poverty alleviation the case of the employment guarantee scheme in Maharashtra. International Review of Applied Economics 16 (2), 131–151.
International Labour Organization (ILO). 2006. "International Labour Standards Department: Database of National Labour, Social Security and related Human Rights Legislation", ILO-Geneva. http://www.ilo.org/dyn/natlex.
Keddeman, Willem, 1998. Of nets and assets: effects and impacts of employment-intensive programmes — a review of ILO experience. Development Policy Department. International Labour Office, Geneva.
Kesselman, Jonathan R., 1978. Work relief programs in the Great Depression. In: Palmer, J.L. (Ed.), Creating Jobs: Public Employment Programs and Wage Subsidies. Brookings Institution, Washington, D.C.
Kydland, Finn, Prescott, Edward, 1977. Rules rather than discretion: the inconsistency of optimal plans. Journal of Political Economy 85, 473–490.
Lipton, Michael, 1996. Success in anti-poverty. Issues in Development Discussion Paper, vol. 8. International Labour Office, Geneva.
Maharashtra Planning Department, 1979. The Employment Guarantee Act No. XX of 1978. Maharashtra Planning Department, Bombay.
Manning, Alan, 2005. Monopsony in Motion: Imperfect Competition in Labor Markets. Princeton University Press, Princeton.
Mitra, Arun. 2006. "Labour market mobility of low income households," Economic and Political Weekly, May 2123 –2130.
Ravallion, Martin, 1990. Market responses to anti-hunger policies: effects on wages prices and employment. In: Drèze, J., Sen, A. (Eds.), The Political Economy of Hunger. Clarendon Press, Oxford.
Ravallion, Martin, 1991. Reaching the rural poor through EGS employment: arguments, lessons, and evidence from South Asia. World Bank Research Observer 6 (1), 153–176.
Ravallion, Martin, Datt, Guarav, Chaudhuri, S., 1993. Does Maharashtra's employment guarantee scheme guarantee employment? Effects of the 1988 wage increase. Economic Development and Cultural Change 41 (2), 251–275.
Subbarao, K., 1997. Public works as an anti-poverty program: an overview of cross-country experience. American Journal of Agricultural Economics 79 (2), 678–683.
Teklu, Tesfaye, 1995. Labour-intensive public works: the experience of Botswana and Tanzania. In: von Braun, J. (Ed.), Employment for Poverty Reduction and Food Security. International Food Policy Research Institute, Washington D.C.
Teklu, Tesfaye, Asefa, Sisay, 1999. Who participates in labor-intensive public works in sub-Saharan Africa? Evidence from rural Botswana and Kenya. World Development 27 (2), 431–438.
von Braun, Joachim, 1995. Employment for Poverty Reduction and Food Security. International Food Policy Research Institute, Washington DC.

CHAPTER 1

TAX EVASION, MINIMUM WAGE NONCOMPLIANCE, AND INFORMALITY

Arnab K. Basu, Nancy H. Chau and Zahra Siddique

ABSTRACT

We study the impact of tax and minimum wage reforms on the incidence of informality. To gauge the incidence of informality, we use measures of the extent of tax evasion, the extent of minimum wage noncompliance, and the size of the informal workforce. Our approach allows us to examine (i) the distinction between determinants of firm-level reported wage distribution and actual wage distribution, (ii) the complementarity of tax and minimum wage enforcement, (iii) the impact that a minimum wage reform has on tax and minimum wage compliance, and (iv) the impact that a tax policy reform has on tax and minimum wage compliance. We conclude with the design of optimal minimum wage and tax policies (even in the complete absence of minimum wage enforcement). We do so based on two objectives derived from popular concerns associated with an unchecked expansion of informality: tax revenue maximization, and poverty alleviation among workers.

Informal Employment in Emerging and Transition Economies
Research in Labor Economics, Volume 34, 1–53

ISSN: 0147-9121/doi:10.1108/S0147-9121(2012)0000034004

Keywords: Tax evasion; minimum wage reform; flat tax reform; poverty; informality

JEL classification: J3; J6; O17

INTRODUCTION

What determines the incidence of informality? The answer clearly depends on how one defines informality. Within the development literature there are two different perspectives on how one defines informality, each focusing on causality going from government regulations to informality as a market response (Perry et al., 2007; Schneider & Enste, 2000).

The first perspective takes informality as an involuntary state of employment in a segmented labor market. Good jobs in the formal sector, characterized by regulated wages and benefits, are in high demand but short supply (Chandra & Khan 1993; Fields, 1975; Harris & Todaro, 1970). Rooted in the labor market implications of informality, therefore, informality (according to this perspective) refers to

> workers, particularly the old and young, who would prefer a job with standard labor protections, but are unable to get one. (Perry et al., 2007, p. 21)

Associated with this perspective are measures of informality based on labor standards compliance. Such measures aim at capturing the coverage of workers by mandated labor protections such as the minimum wage (Saavedra & Chong, 1999). Table 1 provides some examples of such informality measures as: (i) the share of workers not covered by social security contributions (based on 2007 and 2008 EU-SILC), (ii) the share of workers not covered by an employment contract (based on the European Social Survey, 2008) and (iii) the share of workers not covered by social protection (OECD, 2009). From Table 1, there is substantial variation across countries in the degree of informality, irrespective of the specific measure used. If one focuses on measure (iii), which gives the share of workers not covered by social protection, then informality characterizes close to or more than 50% of workers in nearly all the countries for which this measure is available.

A second perspective takes informality as a voluntary firm-level response to evade taxes and other costly regulations (de Paula & Scheinkman, 2010; De Soto, 1989; Djankov, La Porta, Lopez-de-Silanes, & Shleifer, 2002;

Table 1. Informality, Labor Standards Compliance.

Country	Alternative Measures of Informality				
	I. Share of workers not covered by social security contributions		II. Share of workers without an employment contract	III. Noncoverage by social protection	
	2007	2008	2006	1995–1999	2000–2007
Algeria				42.7	41.3
Argentina				53.3	–
Austria	35.4	34.5	10		
Belgium	38.8	36.2	7		
Bolivia				63.5	–
Brazil				60	51.1
Chad				95.2	–
Chile				35.8	–
Colombia				38.4	–
Costa Rica				44.3	–
Czech Republic	40.8	40.4	2		
Denmark			12		
Dominican Republic				47.6	–
Ecuador				53.5	–
Egypt, Arab Rep.				55.2	45.9
El Salvador				56.6	–
Estonia	34.6	33.9	5		
Finland	23.0	23.5	1		
France	51.9	–	8		
Germany			4		
Greece	37.7	37.3	39		
Guinea				86.7	–
Haiti				92.6	–
Honduras				58.2	–
Hungary	40.6	42.4	4		
Iceland	13.4	13.3	26		
India				83.4	–
Indonesia				77.9	
Ireland	39.8	40.3	39		
Israel			38		
Italy	40.0	39.3			
Iran				–	48.8
Kenya				71.6	–
Kyrgyz Republic					44.4
Lebanon				–	51.8
Luxembourg	34.6	32.6	6		

Table 1. *(Continued)*

Country	Alternative Measures of Informality				
	I. Share of workers not covered by social security contributions		II. Share of workers without an employment contract	III. Noncoverage by social protection	
	2007	2008	2006	1995–1999	2000–2007
Mali				94.1	81.8
Mexico				59.4	50.1
Moldova				–	21.5
Morocco				44.8	67.1
Netherlands	17.7	21.6	9		
Norway	12.2	13.2	11		
Pakistan				64.6	–
Panama				37.6	49.4
Paraguay				65.5	–
Peru				–	67.9
Philippines				72	–
Poland	65.3	57.0	6		
Portugal	35.1	38.5	15		
Romania				5.4	22
Russian Federation			7	–	8.6
Slovak Republic	39.1	38.5	3		
Slovenia	24.7	25.2	11		
South Africa				–	50.6
Spain	41.5	41.4	10		
Sweden	22.7	22.0	2		
Switzerland			5		
Syrian Arab Republic				42.9	30.7
Thailand				51.5	–
Turkey			44	30.9	33.2
Tunisia				47.1	35
United Kingdom			22		
Venezuela, R.B.				46.9	49.4
West Bank and Gaza				–	43.4
Yemen, Rep.				–	51.1

Note: Measure (I) is based on EU-SILC 2007 and 2008, reproduced from Schneider (2011), measure (II) is based on the European Social Survey 2008, reproduced from Schneider (2011), and measure (III) is taken from OECD (2009) tabulations from national labor force surveys where informality is defined as noncoverage by social protection.

Friedman, Johnson, Kaufmann, & Zoido-Lobatón, 2000; Loayza, Servén, & Oviedo, 2005; Schneider, 2005), when weak or nonexistent enforcement of taxes and other costly regulations make informal operations more lucrative than formal regulated operations. Rooted in the public finance implications of informality, therefore, informality (according to this perspective) refers to

> firms and individuals avoiding taxation or other mandated regulations because everybody else does, and because enforcement is weak and uneven. (Perry et al., 2007, p. 22)

Associated with this perspective are measures of informality based on tax compliance. Such measures may result from tax audits that define the magnitude of the informal economy as the difference between the income declared in tax returns and the income actually found after an audit (World Bank, 2011). Table 2 provides examples of such informality measures, including measures that capture different shades of informality even among formally registered firms: (i) the percentage of firms expressing that a typical firm reports less than 100% of sales for tax purposes, (ii) the percentage of firms competing against unregistered or informal firms, (iii) the percentage of firms formally registered when they started operations in the country and (iv) the average number of years firms operated without formal registration. From Table 2, there is (as in Table 1) substantial variation across countries in the degree of informality, irrespective of the specific measure used. For example, if one focuses on measure (i), then Liberia ranks particularly high with respondents putting the percentage of firms which report too few sales to escape taxes as more than 97% while for Jordan this fraction is just 13%. Moreover, measure (ii) shows a higher degree of informality for each country than does measure (iii).

These two distinct perspectives on informality have also inspired a large subsequent literature on theoretical modeling, as well as empirical policy analyses. In terms of theoretical modeling, the seminal work of Fields (1975) and related subsequent studies address formal and informal labor market consequences of formal sector wage regulations. Early studies are in the tradition of dualistic labor market models (Doeringer & Piore, 1971, Fei & Ranis, 1964, Harris & Todaro, 1970; Stiglitz, 1974), while recent studies relax assumptions on competitive labor markets (Basu, Chau, & Kanbur, 2010), and contractual commitments (Basu, Chau, & Kanbur, 2011). Models of tax evasion incorporating both an above- and an under-ground sector (Jung, Snow, & Trandel, 1994; Kesselman, 1989) have also been developed. These models extend the traditional tax evasion frameworks of Allingham and Sandmo (1972) and Yitzhaki (1974) to a multisector setting and provide an analytical basis for

Table 2. Informality, Enterprise Surveys.

Country (Year)	Alternative Measures of Informality			
	I. % of firms which report too few sales	II. % of firms competing with unregistered/ informal firms	III. % of firms registered when starting operations	IV. Number of years firm operated without registration
Afghanistan (2008)	–	45.88	88.01	1.8
Albania (2007)	–	52.56	89.35	0.26
Algeria (2007)	–	66.84	98.32	0.04
Angola (2010)	–	41.25	62.65	1.12
Argentina (2010)	–	68.2	92.35	0.87
Armenia (2009)	–	44.57	96.23	0.14
Azerbaijan (2009)	–	40.71	85.12	4.73
Bangladesh (2007)	–	46.62	–	–
Belarus (2008)	–	50.43	98.48	2.9
Benin (2009)	–	77.25	87.93	0.55
Bhutan (2009)	–	19.92	99.05	0.08
Bolivia (2010)	–	80.51	72.43	4.25
Bosnia and Herzegovina (2009)	–	46.48	98.6	0.16
Botswana (2010)	–	54.64	93.94	0.16
Brazil (2009)	–	55.02	95.78	0.48
Bulgaria (2009)	–	54.11	98.48	0.08
Burkina Faso (2009)	26.45	74.95	77.74	1.01
Burundi (2006)	42.73	60.3	–	–
Cambodia (2007)	78.11	–	87.45	0.69
Cameroon (2009)	70.38	90.11	82.06	0.63
Cape Verde (2009)	–	44.54	81.25	1.96
Chad (2009)	–	89.8	77.13	1.23
Chile (2010)	–	55.84	96.05	0.2
China (2003)	49.45	–	–	–
Colombia (2010)	–	70.93	94.27	0.47
Congo, Dem. Rep. (2010)	–	89.96	61.86	1.87
Congo, Rep. (2009)	90.02	69.65	84.28	0.27
Costa Rica (2010)	–	70.36	80.84	1.04
Côte d'Ivoire (2009)	68.06	73.6	56.37	0.48
Croatia (2007)	–	31.66	98.07	0.03
Czech Republic (2009)	–	42.87	98.04	0.08
Dominican Republic (2005)	73.63			
Ecuador (2010)	–	65.72	85.1	0.65
Egypt, Arab Rep. (2008)	30	46.68	–	–

Table 2. *(Continued)*

Country (Year)	Alternative Measures of Informality			
	I. % of firms which report too few sales	II. % of firms competing with unregistered/ informal firms	III. % of firms registered when starting operations	IV. Number of years firm operated without registration
El Salvador (2010)	–	65.24	75.67	1.1
Eritrea (2009)	–	28.16	100	0
Estonia (2009)	–	26.32	97.39	0.06
Ethiopia (2006)	51.6	–	–	–
Fiji (2009)	–	39.6	93.48	1.15
Gabon (2009)	64.83	75.96	63.73	0.73
Gambia, the (2006)	88.05	60.34	–	–
Georgia (2008)	–	52.23	99.55	0.42
Germany (2005)	–	–	–	–
Ghana (2007)	59.2	69.13	66.44	2.17
Greece (2005)	53.19	–	–	–
Guatemala (2010)	–	69.84	89.98	0.59
Guinea (2006)	95.37	62.8	–	–
Guinea-Bissau (2006)	68.19	53.7	–	–
Guyana, CR (2004)	74.36	–	–	–
Honduras (2010)	–	63.17	81.29	0.86
Hungary (2009)	–	49	100	0
India (2006)	59.24	–	–	–
Indonesia (2009)	–	65.09	29.1	2.43
Ireland (2005)	28.78	–	–	–
Jamaica (2005)	28.77	–	–	–
Jordan (2006)	12.95	–	–	–
Kazakhstan (2009)	–	36.89	97.37	0.04
Kenya (2007)	60.54	–	–	–
Korea, Rep. (2005)	43.65	–	–	–
Kosovo (2009)	–	64.07	89.23	0.23
Kyrgyz Republic (2009)	–	67.46	95.94	4.3
Lao PDR (2009)	–	12.82	93.53	0.17
Latvia (2009)	–	41.67	98.49	0.12
Lebanon (2009)	34.08		97.63	0.28
Lesotho (2009)	–	59.6	86.8	0.63
Liberia (2009)	97.32	66.21	73.81	0.63
Lithuania (2009)	–	50.11	97.1	0.25
Macedonia, FYR (2009)	–	73.89	99.24	0.01
Madagascar (2009)	35.61	62.29	97.45	0.09
Malawi (2009)	–	77.84	78.58	0.57

Table 2. (*Continued*)

Country (Year)	Alternative Measures of Informality			
	I. % of firms which report too few sales	II. % of firms competing with unregistered/ informal firms	III. % of firms registered when starting operations	IV. Number of years firm operated without registration
Malaysia (2007)	–	–	52.97	0
Mali (2010)	–	75.38	79.22	0.51
Mauritania (2006)	82.5	65.16	–	–
Mauritius (2009)	36.25	50.95	84.17	1.54
Mexico (2006)	57.65	69.67	94.08	0.1
Micronesia, Fed. Sts. (2009)	–	41.11	96.87	0.16
Moldova (2009)	–	46.46	97.86	0.11
Mongolia (2009)	–	43.04	90.11	2.49
Montenegro (2009)	–	27.26	95.47	0.21
Morocco (2007)	–	47.68	86.02	0.21
Mozambique (2007)	73.1	75.45	85.86	0.6
Namibia (2006)	45.48	33.09	–	–
Nepal (2009)	–	49.37	93.96	0.33
Nicaragua (2010)	–	62.61	74.03	2.02
Niger (2009)	–	85.98	90.51	0.54
Nigeria (2007)	68	60.07	–	–
Oman (2003)	42.46	–	–	–
Pakistan (2007)	7.57	12.45	–	–
Panama (2010)	–	51.4	99.74	0.01
Paraguay (2010)	–	75.28	98.71	0.25
Peru (2010)	–	68.59	82.63	0.73
Philippines (2009)	–	37.52	97.53	0.53
Poland (2009)	–	32.73	99.25	0.02
Portugal (2005)	37.25	–	–	–
Romania (2009)	–	35.14	98.71	0.11
Russian Federation (2009)	–	32.23	94.68	0.77
Rwanda (2006)	28.9	47.07	–	–
Samoa (2009)	–	63.56	88.36	0.58
Senegal (2007)	21.63	74.11	78.86	0.95
Serbia (2009)	–	53.62	95.02	0.19
Sierra Leone (2009)	81.92	80.34	89.22	0.86
Slovak Republic (2009)	–	40.34	100	0
Slovenia (2009)		27.11	99.05	0.01
South Africa (2007)	40.3	45.32	91.03	0.26
Spain (2005)	18.33	–	–	–
Sri Lanka (2004)	41.97	–	–	–

Table 2. (*Continued*)

Country (Year)	Alternative Measures of Informality			
	I. % of firms which report too few sales	II. % of firms competing with unregistered/ informal firms	III. % of firms registered when starting operations	IV. Number of years firm operated without registration
Swaziland (2006)	74.57	39.72	–	–
Syrian Arab Republic (2009)	57.06	52.57	–	–
Tajikistan (2008)	–	35.31	92.74	6.78
Tanzania (2006)	71.03	66.85	–	–
Thailand (2006)	–	–	–	–
Timor-Leste (2009)	–	66.4	91.79	0.67
Togo (2009)	–	80.49	75.82	1.15
Tonga (2009)	–	86.77	93.54	0.25
Turkey (2008)	–	52.36	94.05	0.42
Uganda (2006)	74.49	73.11	–	–
Ukraine (2008)	–	48.48	95.76	0.92
Uruguay (2010)	–	67.66	94.61	0.64
Uzbekistan (2008)	–	39.17	100	4.09
Vanuatu (2009)	–	39.91	88.06	1.26
Venezuela, R.B. (2010)	–	29.76	95.61	0.13
Vietnam (2009)	–	55.56	87.46	1.38
West Bank and Gaza (2006)	25.68	–	–	–
Yemen, Rep. (2010)	82.33	37.16	81.69	0.82
Zambia (2007)	–	73.84	96.18	0.23

Notes: The four measures give the degree of informality among businesses in 125 countries. The table is reproduced from results based on surveys of more than 120,000 firms by the World Bank (Enterprise Surveys, http://www.enterprisesurveys.org, methodology available from https://www.enterprisesurveys.org/Methodology/).

Measure (I) is constructed from the percentage of firms expressing that a typical firm reports less than 100 percent of sales for tax purposes, measure (II) is constructed from the percentage of firms competing against unregistered or informal firms (Question: Does this establishment compete against unregistered or informal firms?), measure (III) is constructed from the percentage of firms formally registered when they started operations in the country (Question: Was this establishment formally registered when it began operations?) and measure (IV) is constructed from the average number of years firms operated without formal registration, computed only for the firms not formally registered when starting operations (Question: In what year did this establishment begin operations? Question: Was this establishment formally registered when it began operations? Question: In what year was this establishment formally registered?).

ongoing debates concerning the role of tax policy reforms on tax evasion among formal firms, as well as the underground informal economy.

In terms of empirical policy analysis, there has been a recent surge in empirical research generating the following set of intriguing insights about how the informal economy operates in response to labor and tax regulations:

- minimum wage noncompliance is widespread among formal sector employers, as well as informal sector employers (Ashenfelter & Smith, 1979; Gindling & Terrell, 1995, 2006; Lemos, 2004, 2006; Maloney & Nunez, 2004);
- tax evasion is widespread among formal sector firms, as well as informal sector firms (Cobham, 2005; Cowell, 1990; Feige, 1989; Fuest & Riedel, 2009; Tanzi, 1980, 1999);
- subminimum wages and informal employment can exhibit a diverse set of responses to minimum wage hikes (Baanante, 2004; Card & Krueger, 1995; Lemos, 2004; Strobl & Walsh, 2001);
- tax policy reforms can have a significant impact on the incidence of informality in an economy (Gabrieli, Galvao, & Montes-Rojas, 2011; Jonasson, 2011; Koettl, 2011; Slonimczyk, 2011).

Given the above, the point of departure of this chapter from existing literature is to provide a theoretical framework better equipped at capturing the realities that (i) both formal and informal firms may fail to comply with labor and tax regulations, while (ii) labor and tax regulations jointly determine the differing shades of informal firm like behavior through minimum wage noncompliance and tax evasion.

We posit a framework wherein formal establishments are subject to three sets of costs not borne by informal firms. With respect to wage regulation, formal establishments are expected to pay workers at least a minimum wage. With respect to tax regulations, formal establishments are obliged to pay authorities a tax on profits earned, and to withhold taxes on wage income to be transferred directly to authorities. With respect to the cost of entry, formal firms incur a cost of registration. In contrast, informal establishments and informal workers are free from both the state mandated regulation on wages and the need to pay taxes on profits or wages while operating in an environment where entry and exit is cost-free.

Firms must choose between operating in the formal or the informal sector, while workers seek wage protection in the formal sector (subject to wage income tax) using the informal wage as a reservation wage. Within this context, we examine three items of interest: (i) tax evasion via the misreporting of wage cost by formal firms, (ii) minimum wage noncompliance via the underpayment of the state mandated minimum wage among formal firms, and (iii) the incidence of informality as establishments choose to operate either in the formal or the informal sector.

In doing so, the contributions of this chapter are the following. First, and to the best of our knowledge, this is the first attempt at examining minimum wage noncompliance by simultaneously scrutinizing the endogenous determinants of the reported wage cost of a formal employer and the actual take-home wage of a formal employee, in a setting where tax and minimum wage enforcement are both imperfect. A clear distinction between the two can offer important insights into empirical studies of wage distributions based either on firm-reported data on wage costs, or on labor force surveys from which records of actual take-home wage can be ascertained. In particular, it is by now well known that empirical studies of wage distributions in developing countries exhibit spikes at or around the minimum wage, despite lax enforcement. Our analysis provides the rationale for researchers to go one step deeper, to distinguish between reported wage distribution and actual wage distribution. For example, is the spike purely a reflection of a lip-service reporting of firm-level wage cost? Or is the true take-home wage distribution of formal employee also marked by a spike at or around the minimum wage despite lax enforcement?

Second, the proposed model allows for a side-by-side comparison of tax compliance among formal employers, minimum wage compliance among formal employers, and the incidence of informality where neither tax regulations nor minimum wage regulations are fully respected. This is of particular importance for, in practice, tax enforcement in the formal sector is carried out via tax audits and random checks by tax authorities (Andreoni, Erard, & Feinstein, 1998), while minimum wage enforcement in the formal sector is carried out independently by labor inspectors (Weil, 2004). An understanding of how tax enforcement directly impacts tax evasion, alters minimum wage noncompliance, and changes the overall incidence of informality is clearly key to effective formation of tax and wage enforcement policies.[1]

Third, our model provides a setting in which the potential direct and cross-cutting impacts of wage and tax policies on various measures of informality can be better understood. For example, how does a minimum wage hike impact the extent of tax evasion by formal firms, and the number of firms that completely do away with the obligation to pay taxes as they exit the formal sector? In this regard, we present a list of testable hypotheses that complement a series of papers dedicated to understanding minimum wage noncompliance (Ashenfelter & Smith, 1979; Basu et al., 2010) without the additional complication of tax evasion. Next, how does a tax reform impact the extent of minimum wage compliance by formal firms, and the number of firms that completely evade the obligation to pay a minimum wage by exiting to the informal sector? In this latter regard, we provide results that will substantially extend those of an earlier literature on tax evasion, for example, in which one or both of the following are absent: the minimum wage mandate, and the existence of an informal sector where tax obligations and minimum wage protection do not apply (Tonin, 2011; Yaniv, 1988, 1990).

The model we posit allows us to identify six distinctive potential regimes of labor market equilibria and as many potential sets of comparative statics responses of labor market outcomes with respect to changes in minimum wage and tax policies, depending on the pairing of minimum wage and worker productivity, as well as the nature of the tax and minimum wage policies. These embody combinations of cases where in equilibrium (i) reported employer wage payment to government tax authorities exactly comply with, or exceed the official minimum wage, coupled with (ii) actual employer wage payment to workers that does not comply, complies exactly, or over-complies with the minimum wage law. In this chapter, we make a complete characterization of the six classes of labor market equilibria and the corresponding comparative statics responses.

To pick one case in point, for minimum wages that are sufficiently high relative to worker productivity, strictly positive but imperfect tax enforcement, and no minimum wage enforcement, all employers report the exact payment of the minimum wage as required by law, but in truth evade taxes as the reported wage cost is an over-statement of wage that workers take home. Since tax evasion (or wage understatement) is synonymous with minimum wage noncompliance (or paying less than the reported minimum wage) here, the gap between the minimum wage and the actual wage is determined only by the strength of tax enforcement in place. Consequently, at constant tax enforcement, raising the minimum wage raises the reported wage as well as the actual wage dollar-for-dollar even in the complete absence of directly minimum wage enforcement, leaving the gap between the two constant. This suggests intriguingly that even when there is no minimum wage enforcement, the observed reported wage distribution exhibits a spike at the minimum wage, while the actual wage payment also exhibits a spike at a wage relative to the official minimum wage determined by the strength of tax enforcement that is in place.

Making use of the rich array of possible equilibrium outcomes and comparative statics responses characterized here, we draw three broad set of conclusions illustrating the direct and cross-cutting effects of four policy instruments – the tax rate on profit, the tax rate on personal income, the minimum wage, and the strength of tax enforcement – respectively on informal employment, tax evasion, and minimum wage compliance. Specifically, we find that across all regimes of interest, and regardless of the size of the minimum wage relative to labor productivity, informal sector employment is weakly increasing in the four policy instruments. These follow directly from the weakly decreasing relationships between formal sector profit and respectively the two tax rates, the minimum wage, and the strength of tax enforcement, and the resulting weakly negative impact these policies have on job creation in the formal sector.

Contrasting the uniformity in the direction of informal employment response to the four policies, we find that the effectiveness of the four policies in combatting tax evasion differ sharply, depending critically on the height of the minimum wage relative to worker productivity. Suppose that the minimum wage is sufficiently low that in fact employers report a wage cost that exceeds the official minimum wage. Tax evasion here purely reflects employers' incentive to take full advantage of the gap between the profit tax and the personal income tax, adjusted for the strength of tax enforcement, to maximize posttax profits by under-reporting wage cost. Thus, raising the profit tax stimulates tax evasion, while raising the personal income tax, or the strength of tax enforcement discourages it. However, if the minimum wage is sufficiently high, we find that profit-maximizing employers no longer report over-compliance with the minimum wage, but rather they maximize profits by reporting the exact payment of the minimum wage. The distance between this reported wage and the actual take-home wage – the extent of tax evasion – naturally depends only on the strength of the tax enforcement in place. Thus, in sharp contrast to the case with low minimum wages, tax evasion here is fully independent of the two tax rates, and strictly decreasing in the strength of tax enforcement.

The effectiveness of the four policies in combatting minimum wage noncompliance is likewise critically dependent on the height of the minimum wage. With a sufficiently high minimum wage, as discussed the reported wage coincides with the minimum wage. As such, tax evasion becomes synonymous with minimum wage noncompliance. Since tax evasion depends only on the strength of tax enforcement in this case as discussed above, the same is true of minimum wage noncompliance. If, however, the minimum wage is sufficiently low, employers report over-compliance with the minimum wage. This severs the direct link between tax evasion and minimum wage noncompliance. Indeed, while tax evasion depends critically on the profit tax rate and the strength of tax enforcement, minimum wage compliance is wholly independent of these considerations.

The model concludes with a formulation of two sets of optimal wage and tax policies, respectively with the stated objective of poverty minimization, and tax revenue maximization, taking as given the strength of minimum wage and tax enforcement. These two objectives echo popular concerns regarding the consequences of runaway expansion of the informal sector. We show that the existence of a poverty alleviating minimum wage depends critically, among other things, on the strength of the tax enforcement regime, when minimum wage enforcement is lax. Meanwhile, we show that a flat tax reform can be justified, requiring the harmonization of the tax on profits and tax on wage income, on the grounds of tax revenue maximization, so long as corresponding adjustments in the minimum wage can be made as well.

The plan of this chapter is as follows: In the second section, the decision problem of a formal sector employer with respect to what wage to report to tax authorities, what actual wage to pay workers, and whether or not to exit to the informal sector will be established. In the third section, the implied determinants of equilibrium tax evasion, minimum wage noncompliance, and incidence of informality will be examined. In the fourth section, we provide an analysis of the optimal policy for poverty alleviation for a given poverty line, and finally in the fifth section, we provide an analysis of the optimal policy for tax revenue maximization. The sixth section concludes with suggestions for a number of directions for future research.

THE MODEL

Workers

We consider a labor market with a large pool of workers ($\bar{N}$). Each worker is distinguished by his skill level, $a \geq 0$, and the subset of skill type a workers is given exogenously by $N(a)$. Two states of employment are available: informal sector employment and formal sector employment. The informal sector is a free-entry sector: any worker that desires a job can find one there, and any worker that desires to exit the sector can do so at will.[2] By contrast, we denote the endogenous likelihood that a skill type a worker receives a formal sector job offer as $\alpha(a)$.

Formal sector workers are obligated to pay personal income tax, but informal sector workers are not. The corresponding formal and informal sector take home earnings, net of any personal income tax withheld by employers in the formal sector $t_f(a)$, will be denoted as $\omega_f(a) - t_f(a)$ and $\omega_i(a)$ respectively. Conditional on receiving a formal sector job offer, a skill type a worker compares $\omega_f(a) - t_f(a)$ with the reservation benchmark $\omega_i(a)$, and selects the best of the two. Otherwise, without a formal job offer, the worker earns $\omega_i(a)$ in the informal sector.

Formal Employers

Let there be an endogenous $M(a)$ number of employers in search of skill type a workers in the formal sector. A match between an employer and a skill type a worker in the formal sector generates net output a.[3] Formal employers are furthermore subject to a minimum wage legislation and a tax on profits, unlike informal sector employers who are free from these obligations. For any formal sector employer with a contracted worker, expected profit is given by the value of net output a net of wage cost $\omega_f(a)$, adjusted for any required tax withholdings of labor earnings $t_f(a)$, applicable taxes $T(a)$ on wages and profits, and expected penalties associated with the discovery of tax evasion $Ep(a)$, if any:

$$\pi_f(a) = a - [\omega_f(a) - t_f(a)] - T(a) - Ep(a) \tag{1}$$

Matching in the Formal Sector

The meeting of formal sector job seekers and formal sector employers is characterized by the presence of match friction in the formal labor market. Specifically, let $\Phi(M(a), N(a)) = \theta M(a)^{\beta} N(a)^{1-\beta}, \beta \in [0, 1]$ denote a matching technology that gives the number of matches between employers and workers, given $M(a)$ number of formal employers with a job offer no worse than an informal job, and $N(a)$ number of formal sector job seekers. As stated, $\Phi(\cdot)$ is increasing in both arguments, and homogeneous of degree one in $(M(a), N(a))$. The associated likelihood that an individual worker seeking employment is matched with a formal sector offer is

$$\alpha(a) = \frac{\Phi(M(a), N(a))}{N(a)} \tag{2}$$

while the likelihood that an employer seeking a worker is matched with one is

$$\alpha_e(a) = \frac{\Phi(M(a), N(a))}{M(a)} \tag{3}$$

Becoming a Formal Employer

Denote the cost associated with registering a formal sector firm plus any additional cost required to raise start-up capital, for example, as c_f. Expected formal sector profit is thus:

$$E\pi_f(a) = \alpha_e(a)\pi_f(a) - c_f \tag{4}$$

We now turn to employers in the informal sector. Many studies have argued that without formal registration, and without the ability to raise the start-up capital that a formally registered firm is able to, a productivity gap exists between formal and informal firms (Amaral & Quintin, 2006; Djankov, Lieberman, Mukherjee, & Nenova, 2003; Loayza, 1996; Straub 2005). We follow this line of argument and take the productivity of a worker in the informal sector to be only a fraction $w_i < 1$ of his full productivity.

With perfect competition and free-entry on both the supply and demand sides of the informal labor market, expected profits in the informal sector $E\pi_i(a)$ are driven to zero,

$$E\pi_i(a) = 0 \tag{5}$$

while the informal wage is given by the marginal value of product of laborers there, $\omega_i(a) = w_i a$.

Armed with Eqs. (1), (4), and (5), an employer makes a decision between operating in the formal and the informal sector by comparing $E\pi_f(a)$ and $E\pi_i(a)$. In equilibrium, employers are indifferent between the two sectors whenever

$$E\pi_f(a) = E\pi_i(a) \Leftrightarrow \alpha_e(a)\pi_f(a) - c_f = 0$$

By definition of the likelihood of a match with a worker $\alpha_e(a)$ in Eq. (3), and the likelihood of formal job arrival facing workers $\alpha(a)$ in Eq. (2),

$$\alpha_e(a) = \frac{c_f}{\pi_f(a)}, \quad \text{and} \quad \alpha(a) = \theta^{1/(1-\beta)}\left(\frac{\pi_f(a)}{c_f}\right)^{\beta/(1-\beta)} \tag{6}$$

It follows from Eq. (6) that in order to ascertain the likelihood of equilibrium formal sector employment, $\alpha(a)$, or that of equilibrium informal sector employment, $1-\alpha(a)$, information about after-tax profits of employers of skill type a workers, $\pi_f(a)$, is paramount. We turn to a detailed analysis of $\pi_f(a)$ now.

Tax Evasion, Minimum Wage, and Expected Formal Profits

The decision problem of a formal employer is twofold: choose a wage $r(a)$ to be reported to tax authorities based on which the formal employer's tax liability will be assessed, and an actual wage $\omega_f(a)$ to be paid to workers that need not be equal to $r(a)$. Whenever $r(a) > \omega_f(a)$, we say that there is over-reporting of wage cost. Otherwise, if $r(a) < \omega_f(a)$, we say that wage cost is under-reported.[4]

Let $\tau_\omega < 1$ denote the personal income tax rate. Formal employers are required to withhold taxes on labor income and transfer them directly to tax authorities. Thus, an employer's choice of reported wage cost $r(a)$ will have a direct bearing on the amount of tax withholdings from labor income, for tax withholding is given simply by the personal income tax rate multiplied by the reported wage $r(a)$:

$$t_f(a) = \tau_\omega r(a) \tag{7}$$

To ensure that formal sector employment is viable, in that the post tax income of a formal sector worker can exceed that of an informal sector worker, we work with parameter values such that $a(1-\tau_\omega)$ exceeds $w_i a$, or $1-\tau_\omega-w_i>0$, requiring effectively that the post tax net output that each formal worker can generate exceeds the informal sector counterpart.

Denote $\tau_\pi < 1$ as the profit tax rate. For a formal employer, the total amount of taxes due to tax authorities, calculated based on reported wage cost $r(a)$, is given by τ_π times pretax reported profit ($\min\{0, a-r(a)\}$), plus personal income taxes withheld ($\tau_\omega r(a)$):

$$T(a) - \tau_\pi \min\{0, a - r(a)\} + \tau_\omega r(a) \tag{8}$$

where $\tau_\pi \min\{0, a-r(a)\} \geq 0$ indicates a tax policy that does not provide subsidies to employers who reportedly earn negative pretax profits.

Henceforth, let $\phi(a)$ denote the likelihood of a tax audit. With probability $1-\phi(a)$, the formal employer is not audited, and profit is simply given by net output a, net of wage cost adjusted for personal income taxes withheld $(\omega_f(a) - \tau_\omega r(a))$, and net of profit tax due to authorities calculated based on reported wage cost $(\tau_\pi \min\{0, a - r(a)\} + \tau_\omega r(a))$:

$$a - \omega_f(a) - \tau_\pi \min\{0, a - r(a)\}$$

As may be expected, given the true wage cost $\omega_f(a)$, formal employer profit rises with the reported wage $r(a)$ since $r(a)$ is inversely related to a formal employer's calculated tax liability $\tau_\pi \min\{0, a - r(a)\}$.

With probability $\phi(a)$, the formal employer is audited. This leads to the discovery of the extent of misreported profits, if any. Let $p(a)$ denote the penalty associated with the discovery of misreported profits equaling $|[a - \omega_f(a)] - [a - r(a)]| = |r(a) - \omega_f(a)|$, and of misreported wage cost, also equal to $|r(a) - \omega_f(a)|$. Total penalty to be imposed on a tax-evading employer, if discovered, will given by $\bar{p}$ multiplied by the extent of misreporting:

$$p(a) = \bar{p}|r(a) - \omega_f(a)|$$

$\bar{p}$ parameterizes the severity of the penalty associated with each dollar of misreported wages and profits $|r(a) - \omega_f(a)|$. Throughout we will assume that $\bar{p} \geq 1$, so employers must at least pay back to tax authorities that amount which is misreported when discovered. In the event of a tax audit, therefore, formal employer profit must now account for the penalty cost $p(a)$, and is given by:

$$\begin{aligned} &a - \omega_f(a) - \tau_\pi \min\{0, a - r(a)\} - p(a) \\ &= a - \omega_f(a) - \tau_\pi \min\{0, a - r(a)\} - \bar{p}|r(a) - \omega_f(a)| \end{aligned}$$

We assume in what follows that the likelihood of a tax audit $\phi(a)$ is determined by the likelihood that a tax filing is red-flagged. We also assume that the criteria chosen by tax authorities to red-flag a tax filing are relevant, in the sense that the likelihood assigned to red-flag a tax filing rises with the extent of actual tax misreporting, $|(r(a) - \omega_f(a))|$. These are plausible assumptions. For example, the Internal Revenue Service in the United States formulates and implements a "discriminant function" on each tax return. The results inform the construction of a "DIF score", which is used to determine the likelihood of tax audit. According to Andreoni et al. (1998), over half of the tax audit selections in the United States are based at least in part on this score, and average tax assessments based on selections from the DIF score and other special examination initiatives are systematically higher than tax assessments generated by random audits.[5] In view of these evidence, we assume henceforth that the likelihood of a tax audit is increasing in the extent of tax misreporting, and specifically,

$$\phi(a) \equiv \bar{\phi}|r(a) - \omega_f(a)|$$

$\bar{\phi}$ parameterizes the frequency of tax audits, for given misreporting of true tax liability $|r(a) - \omega_f(a)|$.[6] It follows that expected formal employer profit is:

$$\begin{aligned} \pi_f(a) &= (1 - \phi(a))[a - \omega_f(a) - \tau_\pi \min\{0, a - r(a)\}] \\ &\quad + \phi(a)[a - \omega_f(a) - \tau_\pi \min\{0, a - r(a)\} - \bar{p}(r(a) - \omega_f(a))] \qquad (9) \\ &= a - [\omega_f(a) + \tau_\pi \min\{0, a - r(a)\}] - \bar{\phi}\bar{p}(r(a) - \omega_f(a))^2 \end{aligned}$$

where the sum $\omega_f(a) + \tau_\pi \min\{0, a - r(a)\}$ gives the sum of wage cost net of taxes withheld and applicable taxes to be transferred to tax authorities

$[\omega_f(a) - \tau_\omega r(a)] + [\tau_\pi \min\{0, a - r(a)\} + \tau_\omega r(a)]$ as shown in Eq. (1), and the expected penalty $Ep(a)$ in Eq. (1) is given by $\phi\bar{p}(r(a) - \omega_f(a))^2$.

We are now in a position to formally examine the decision problem of a formal employer. In choosing $\omega_f(a)$ and $r(a)$ to maximize profits $\pi_f(a)$, we note that any formal employer faces two types of constraints.

Participation Constraint

The first constraint that formal employers must take note of accounts for workers' option to seek employment in the informal sector at any time. Thus, to attract workers, a formal job offer must be no worse than an informal job offer. Equivalently, the take-home wage of a formal sector worker accounting appropriately for taxes withheld must be no less than the informal sector wage $\omega_i(a) = w_i a$ from Eq. (5). Furthermore, since taxes withheld is given by the tax rate τ_ω times reported wage cost, the participation constraint is:

$$\omega_f(a) - t_f(a) \geq w_i a, \Leftrightarrow \omega_f(a) - \tau_\omega(a) r(a) \geq w_i a \tag{10}$$

Minimum Wage Constraint

The second constraint that formal employers must also take note of accounts for the minimum wage legislation. In our context where actual and reported wages can differ, the minimum wage constraint requires that the employer must *report* at least the minimum wage as their per worker wage cost:

$$r(a) \geq \bar{w} \tag{11}$$

A failure to do so is tantamount to a willful disregard of the minimum wage legislation, and is taken to trigger an immediate audit and fines, large enough to obligate compliance with the reporting constraint.[7] Beyond this requirement that constrains employers' reporting of wage cost, we focus in this chapter on a government that completely turns a blind eye to the possibility of minimum wage noncompliance, among employers that reportedly pay the minimum wage. We do so to scrutinize the potential link between the frequency of tax audits and minimum wage compliance even in the complete absence of minimum wage enforcement, and also to account for the reality that minimum wage enforcement is far less than perfect in both developed and developing countries (Ashenfelter & Smith, 1979; Basu, Chau, & Kanbur, 2010).[8]

A number of observations are in order before we proceed any further. First, an employer's choice of $\omega_f(a)$ and $r(a)$ determines first and foremost the extent of tax evasion per worker employed as given by the difference:

$$|r(a) - \omega_f(a)|$$

A priori, it is not clear at all whether tax evasion should come in the form of over-reporting or under-reporting of wages. For one thing, we know from the definition of $\pi_f(a)$ in Eq. (9) that every dollar increase in reported wage cost raises employer profits by τ_π for given $\omega_f(a)$. But meanwhile, raising $r(a)$ decreases the take-home income of formal sector workers. If the participation constraint in Eq. (10) binds, every dollar increase in reported wage cost $r(a)$ would require a corresponding increase in actual wage cost by at least τ_ω dollars. These suggest that two sets of considerations should be expected to be in play in the employer's decision problem: (i) whether the participation constraint binds and (ii) whether a tax gap exists between the profit τ_π and the personal income tax rates τ_ω.

Second, an employer's choice of $\omega_f(a)$ and $r(a)$ also determines the extent of minimum wage noncompliance. We gauge this noncompliance by evaluating the difference between the post tax wage income of a minimum wage worker, $\bar{w}(1 - \tau_\omega)$, and the actual wage income of the same worker net of taxes withheld and calculated based on the reported wage, $\omega_f(a) - \tau_\omega r(a)$:

$$\bar{w}(1 - \tau_\omega) - [\omega_f(a) - \tau_\omega r(a)] \tag{12}$$

If strictly positive, Eq. (12) gives the extent of minimum wage noncompliance. If strictly negative, there is over-compliance with the minimum wage legislation. Finally, if Eq. (12) is equal to zero, formal sector workers receive exactly the minimum wage net of any government mandated personal income tax evaluated based on the minimum wage as their take-home earning. There are three open questions here, each requiring an in-depth analysis: (i) Are there systematic differences between reported wages $r(a)$ and actual take-home wages $\omega_f(a) - \tau_\omega r(a)$ across workers of differing skill levels? In other words, how should reported minimum wage compliance be expected to compare with actual minimum wage compliance? (ii) How does the extent of minimum wage noncompliance respond to a hike in the minimum wage when minimum wage enforcement is lax, but tax audit is carried out in regular frequency? (iii) What is the nature, if any, of the cross-cutting influence that changes in the tax rates may have on minimum wage noncompliance, or that changes in the minimum wage may have on the extent of tax evasion?

As a third observation, note that *economy-wide* tax evasion and minimum wage compliance depend not just on what formal sector employers do, but on the incidence of informal sector employment as well, since informal employers do not pay taxes, nor do they comply with the minimum wage law. From Eq. (6), the incidence of informality, as measured by the fraction of informal sector workers among skill type a workers, is:

$$1 - \alpha(a) = 1 - \theta^{1/(1-\beta)} \left(\frac{\pi_f(a)}{c_f} \right)^{\beta/(1-\beta)} \tag{13}$$

Thus, in order to ascertain the effectiveness of a minimum wage policy $\bar{w}$ in raising labor earnings beyond $w_i a$, and the effectiveness of the tax policy $\{\tau_\pi, \tau_\omega, \bar{\phi}\bar{p}\}$ in collecting tax revenue, the possibility that any policy shock can lead to a potential exodus of formal sector employers to the informal sector must be accounted for.

With these three considerations in mind, the ensuing analysis will focus on the role of four policy measures $(\bar{w}, \tau_\pi, \tau_\omega, \bar{\phi}\bar{p})$ on (i) tax evasion, (ii) minimum wage noncompliance, and (iii) incidence of informality as defined above. Later on in Section 4, the optimal choice of minimum wage and tax policies to fulfill two distinctive goals: to maximize tax revenue and to minimize the incidence of poverty, will be formally defined and examined.

TAX EVASION, MINIMUM WAGE NONCOMPLIANCE, AND INCIDENCE OF INFORMALITY

We undertake here an analysis of tax evasion, minimum wage noncompliance, and the corresponding incidence of informality for the case where the minimum wage is less than the net output per worker in the formal sector: $a > \bar{w}$. The complementary case of $a < \bar{w}$ would of course trivially generate a complete exodus of formal sector employers to the informal sector if the minimum wage law is enforced. It can be demonstrated that the qualitative findings in what follows remain unchanged even in the imperfect enforcement case, and the proof is available upon request.

From Eq. (9), the decision problem of the employer is:

$$\max_{\omega_f, r} a - \omega_f - \tau_\pi \min\{a - r, 0\} - \bar{\phi}p(r - \omega_f)^2 \tag{14}$$

subject to the participation constraint $\omega_f \geq w_i a + \tau_\omega r$, and the minimum wage constraint $r \geq \bar{w}$. Denote the solutions to Eq. (14) with an asterisk, there are six possible regimes to consider: with strictly positive reported profits $a - r^*(a) > 0$, (I) only the participation constraint is strictly binding, (II) only the minimum wage constraint is strictly binding and (III) both constraints are binding.[9] The remaining three possible cases apply when reported profit $a - r^*(a)$ is non-positive, with (IV) only the participation constraint is strictly binding, (V) only the minimum wage constraint is strictly binding and (VI) both constraints are binding.

Positive Reported Profits

We begin with the case of positive reported profits, and consider each of the three regimes (I)–(III) alluded to above.

Binding Participation Constraint

For an employer who reports positive pretax profit, $\max\{a - r, 0\} = a - r$, and as such from Eq. (14) his decision problem is:

$$\max_{\omega_f, r} a - \omega_f - \tau_\pi(a - r) - \bar{\phi}\bar{p}(r - \omega_f)^2$$

Maximizing the above subject to a binding participation constraint, $\omega_f - \tau_\omega r = w_i a$ the profit-maximizing choices of a formal employer are:[10]

$$r^*(a) = \frac{w_i a + \delta}{1 - \tau_\omega}, \quad \omega_f^*(a) = \frac{w_i a + \delta\tau_\omega}{1 - \tau_\omega}, \quad \omega_f^*(a) - r^*(a)\tau_\omega = w_i a \qquad (15)$$

where $\delta \equiv (\tau_\pi - \tau_\omega)/[2\bar{\phi}\bar{p}(1 - \tau_\omega)]$. Intuitively, with the participation constraint strictly binding, formal sector workers take home their reservation wage $\omega_f^*(a) - \tau_\omega r^*(a) = w_i a$, and any increase in formal sector income tax $\tau_\omega r^*(a)$ must be compensated by a corresponding increase in pretax wage $\omega_f^*(a)$. In addition, from Eq. (15), the formal employer over-reports wage cost $r^*(a) > \omega_f^*(a)$, or equivalently $\delta > 0$, if and only if the profit tax rate τ_π exceeds the personal income tax τ_ω, and under-reports wage cost $r^*(a) < \omega_f^*(a)$ otherwise when τ_π is less than τ_ω.

Table 3 displays separately the profit tax rates and the lowest personal income tax rates in 120 countries (PricewaterhouseCoopers, 2011; World Bank, 2011).[11] We take the lowest personal income tax rate as the relevant income class for minimum wage workers. As shown, in an overwhelming majority of these countries where tax data is available, the profit tax rate strictly exceeds the corresponding personal income tax rate. In view of this evidence, we will henceforth maintain the assumption that $\tau_\pi > \tau_\omega$, with the implication that formal employers will tend to

Table 3. Taxation.

Country	I. Tax Rate on Profit, τ_π	II. Tax Rate on Personal Income, τ_ω
Albania	40.6	0
Angola	53.2	0
Antigua and Bermuda	41.5	0
Argentina	108.2	9
Armenia	40.7	10
Australia	47.9	0
Austria	55.5	0
Azerbaijan	40.9	14
Belarus	80.4	12
Belgium	57	25
Bolivia	80	13
Bosnia and Herzegovina	23	10
Botswana	19.5	0
Brazil	69	0
Bulgaria	29	10
Cambodia	22.5	0
Cameroon	49.1	11
Canada	29.2	15
Chile	25	0
China	63.5	5
Colombia	78.7	0
Congo, Dem. Rep.	339.7	3
Congo, Rep.	65.5	1
Costa Rica	55	0
Croatia	32.5	12
Cyprus	23.2	0
Czech Republic	48.8	15
Denmark	29.2	37
Dominican Republic	40.7	0
Ecuador	35.3	0
Egypt, Arab Rep.	42.6	0
El Salvador	35	0
Equatorial Guinea	59.5	0
Estonia	49.6	21
Fiji	39.3	0
Finland	44.6	6.5
France	65.8	0
Gabon	43.5	0
Georgia	15.3	20
Germany	48.2	0
Ghana	32.7	0
Greece	47.2	0
Guatemala	40.9	15

Table 3. *(Continued)*

Country	I. Tax Rate on Profit, τ_π	II. Tax Rate on Personal Income, τ_ω
Honduras	48.3	0
Hong Kong SAR, China	24.1	2
Hungary	53.3	16
India	63.3	0
Indonesia	37.3	5
Iraq	28.4	3
Israel	31.7	10
Italy	68.6	23
Jamaica	50.1	0
Japan	48.6	5
Jordan	31.2	7
Kazakhstan	29.6	10
Kenya	49.7	10
Korea, Rep.	29.8	6
Kyrgyz Republic	57.2	10
Lao PDR	33.7	0
Latvia	38.5	25
Lebanon	30.2	2
Lithuania	38.7	0
Luxembourg	21.1	0
Macedonia, FYR	10.6	10
Madagascar	37.7	0
Malawi	25.1	0
Malaysia	33.7	0
Mauritius	24.1	15
Mexico	50.5	1.92
Moldova	30.9	7
Mongolia	23	10
Montenegro	26.6	9
Morocco	41.7	0
Mozambique	34.3	10
Namibia	9.6	0
Netherlands	40.5	33
New Zealand	34.3	10.5
Nicaragua	63.2	0
Nigeria	32.2	5
Norway	41.6	0
Oman	21.6	0
Pakistan	31.6	0.75
Panama	50.1	0
Papua New Guinea	42.3	22
Paraguay	35	8
Peru	40.2	0

Table 3. *(Continued)*

Country	I. Tax Rate on Profit, τ_π	II. Tax Rate on Personal Income, τ_ω
Philippines	45.8	5
Poland	42.3	18
Portugal	43.3	11.5
Puerto Rico	67.7	0
Romania	44.9	16
Russian Federation	46.5	13
Saudi Arabia	14.5	0
Senegal	46	0
Serbia	34	10
Singapore	25.4	0
Slovak Republic	48.7	19
Slovenia	35.4	16
South Africa	30.5	18
Spain	56.5	24
Sri Lanka	64.7	4
St. Kitts and Nevis	52.7	0
Swaziland	36.8	20
Sweden	54.6	31
Switzerland	30.1	0
Syrian Arab Republic	42.9	5
Tajikistan	86	8
Tanzania	45.2	0
Thailand	37.4	0
Turkey	44.5	15
Uganda	35.7	0
Ukraine	55.5	15
United Arab Emirates	14.1	0
United Kingdom	37.3	20
United States	46.8	10
Uruguay	42	0
Uzbekistan	95.6	10
Venezuela, RB	52.6	6
Vietnam	33.1	5
Zimbabwe	40.3	3

Notes. Tax rate on profit, τ_π, measures the amount of taxes and mandatory contributions payable by businesses after accounting for allowable deductions and exemptions as a share of commercial profits. Taxes withheld (such as personal income tax) or collected and remitted to tax authorities (such as value added taxes, sales taxes or goods and service taxes) are excluded. This variable is taken from the World Bank, Doing Business project (http://www.doingbusiness.org/), 2010 figures.

Tax rate on personal income, τ_ω, is the lowest tax on personal income taken from PricewaterhouseCoopers International Limited (PwCIL), Worldwide Tax Summaries, current estimates (August 2011).

over-report wage costs. Thus, $|r^*(a) - \omega_f^*(a)| = r^*(a) - \omega_f^*(a)$. This finding is intuitive, and consistent with Yaniv (1990) which analyzes the case without a minimum wage and without an informal sector. In particular, since the profit tax rate exceeds the personal income tax rate, under-reporting profits confers greater tax savings to the employer than under-reporting wage cost, when the post tax take-home income of formal workers cannot fall below the reservation level $w_i a$.

Tax evasion, in this case, depends critically on the tax gap $\tau_\pi - \tau_\omega$, in particular, from Eq. (15)

$$r^*(a) - \omega_f^*(a) = \delta = \frac{\tau_\pi - \tau_\omega}{2\bar{\phi}\bar{p}(1 - \tau_\omega)}$$

the larger the tax gap, the larger will be the equilibrium tax evasion. Furthermore, the frequency of tax auditing as parameterized by $\bar{\phi}$, and the penalty associated with discovered tax evasion $\bar{p}$, both mitigate against employer incentives to evade taxes. Small changes in the minimum wage do not alter the tax evasion calculation based purely on the tax gap and tax enforcement, and have thus no impact on equilibrium tax evasion.

From Eq. (15), minimum wage noncompliance is given by:

$$\bar{w}(1 - \tau_\omega) - (\omega_f^* - r^*(a)\tau_\omega) = \bar{w}(1 - \tau_\omega) - w_i a$$

Clearly, formal employers of sufficiently high skilled workers, with $a > \bar{w}(1 - \tau_\omega)/w_i$, over-comply with the minimum wage legislation for otherwise an informal sector job will be more attractive to workers. All other employers offer workers just enough to make a formal job attractive, though not enough to comply with the minimum wage mandate. For those that do not comply with the minimum wage legislation, since workers take home exactly their reservation income $w_i a$ in the presence of a binding participation constraint, the extent of minimum wage noncompliance is exactly equal to the difference between the government mandated take-home wage $\bar{w}(1 - \tau_\omega)$ and the reservation wage $w_i a$. It follows therefore that an increase in the government mandated minimum post tax take-home wage $\bar{w}(1 - \tau_\omega)$ stimulates minimum wage noncompliance. Meanwhile, small changes in the profit tax τ_π have no impact on this minimum wage policy induced mandate to increase wages by $\bar{w}(1 - \tau_\omega) - w_i a$, and thus have no impact on minimum wage noncompliance.

Now, substituting Eq. (15) into Eq. (13), and using Eq. (6), the incidence of informality $1 - \alpha^*(a)$ is given by:

$$1 - \theta^{1/(1-\beta)}\left(\left[\frac{1-\tau_\pi}{1-\tau_\omega}(a(1-\tau_\omega - w_i)) + \bar{\phi}\bar{p}\delta^2\right]/c_f\right)^{\beta/(1-\beta)} \tag{16}$$

Routine differentiation reveals that $1 - \alpha^*(a)$ is increasing in both tax rates, and in the frequency and penalty associated with tax audits $\bar{\phi}$ and $\bar{p}$ if and only if the employer misreports the true wage cost, or if and only if $\tau_\pi \neq \tau_\omega$. Again since workers are paid their reservation wage, formal employer profits are in fact independent of the minimum wage $\bar{w}$. This is true for employers of highly skilled workers $a > \bar{w}(1-\tau_\omega)/w_i$ who over-comply with the minimum wage law, as well as those who do not comply $(a < \bar{w}(1-\tau_\omega)/w_i)$.

We now check the conditions under which our starting premises are true: that (i) the participation constraint is the only binding constraint, and that (ii) reported pretax profit $a - r^*(a)$ is strictly positive. From Eq. (15), the participation constraint is the only binding constraint if and only if formal employers report a wage greater than the minimum wage $r^*(a) > \bar{w}$. From Eq. (15), this occurs if and only if the minimum wage is sufficiently small relative to the productivity of the workers:

$$r^*(a) = \frac{w_i a + \delta}{1-\tau_\omega} > \bar{w} \Leftrightarrow \bar{w} < \frac{w_i a + \delta}{1-\tau_\omega} \tag{17}$$

This is illustrated in Fig. 1(a). To the right of the 45 degree line are all combinations of a and $\bar{w}$ such that worker productivity exceeds the minimum wage. The upward sloping schedule labeled PC furthermore divides all $(a, \bar{w})$ combinations into two groups. For those $(a, \bar{w})$ that lie below the PC schedule, the inequality in Eq. (17) holds, and as such, the participation constraint is the only binding constraint. Otherwise, for all other combinations that lie above the PC schedule, the inequality in Eq. (17) is violated as $\bar{w}$ is high enough now so that the minimum wage constraint starts to bind.

Furthermore, and also from Eq. (15), reported pretax profit is strictly positive if and only if $a > r^*(a)$, or equivalently, when worker productivity is sufficiently high:

$$r^*(a) = \frac{w_i a + \delta}{1-\tau_\omega} < a \Leftrightarrow a > \frac{\delta}{1-\tau_\omega - w_i} \tag{18}$$

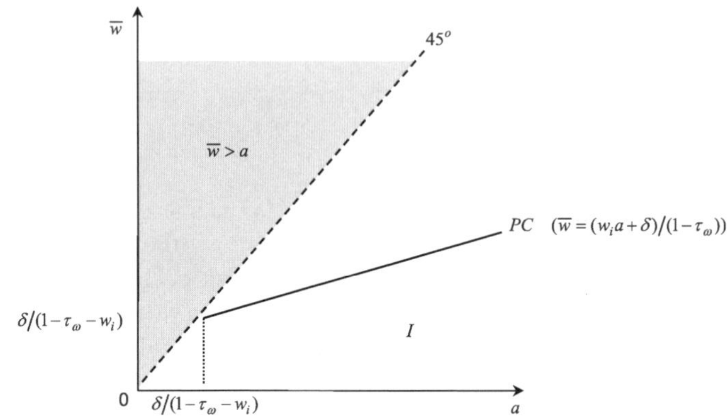

Fig. 1a. Binding Participation Constraint.

In Fig. 1(a), for all employer–worker matches involving $a \geq \delta/(1 - \tau_\omega - w_i)$, and all $(a, \bar{w})$ to the right of the upward sloping schedule labeled PC, formal employers maximize profits by reporting positive profits, and by reporting a wage cost that strictly exceeds the minimum wage $\bar{w}$. To the left of $a = \delta/1 - \tau_\omega - w_i$, worker productivity is too small and formal employer maximize profits by reporting non-positive profits. We will return to this case in the sequel.

Summarizing, with high output per worker, $a > \delta/(1 - \tau_\omega - w_i)$, formal employers report positive profits (from Eq. (18)). As long as there is a tax gap between profit and personal tax income $\tau_\pi \geq \tau_\omega$, over-reporting of wage cost occurs (from Eq. (15)). The extent of this misreporting depends importantly on the size of the tax gap, the frequency of tax audits and the associated penalty. For some employers in this range, particularly those with sufficiently high skilled workers, this over-reporting of wage cost occurs as they over-comply with the minimum wage legislation, and pay each worker more than what the minimum wage legislation mandates. Other employers in the range continue to over-report wage cost, but do not comply with the minimum wage legislation. Even accounting for wage over-reporting, however, in this range with relatively high worker productivity and relatively low minimum wage ($\bar{w} < (w_i a + \delta)/(1 - \tau_\omega)$), the participation constraint is binding, meaning that the post tax take-home earnings of formal sector workers is equal to the reservation wage $w_i a$ (from Eq. (17)). It follows, therefore, that in the absence of minimum wage enforcement, the minimum wage is ineffective in the sense that the income well-being of workers in this range is in fact fully invariant to the minimum wage, as well as the two tax rates τ_π and τ_ω.

Binding Minimum Wage Constraint

Now, let us consider the case in which the minimum wage constraint is the only binding constraint. Here, formal employers report paying the lowest wage mandated by the minimum wage legislation at $r = \bar{w}$, while at the same time offer contracted workers a post tax take-home wage that strictly exceeds their reservation wage $\omega_f - \tau_\omega r > w_i a$, consistent with a participation constraint that is not binding.

With this combination of r and ω_f, expected formal employer profit, when only the minimum wage constraint binds, is

$$\max_{\omega_f, r} a - \omega_f - \tau_\pi(a - r) - \bar{\phi}\bar{p}(r - \omega_f)^2, \quad \text{s.t.} \quad r = \bar{w}$$
$$= \max_{\omega_f}(1 - \tau_\pi)a + \tau_\pi \bar{w} - [\omega_f + \bar{\phi}\bar{p}(\bar{w} - \omega_f)^2]$$

The solution to the employer's decision problem when only the minimum wage constraint is binding is thus:[12]

$$r^*(a) = \bar{w}, \quad \omega_f^*(a) = \bar{w} - \frac{1}{2\bar{\phi}\bar{p}}, \quad \omega_f^*(a) - r^*(a)\tau_\omega = \bar{w}(1 - \tau_\omega) - \frac{1}{2\bar{\phi}\bar{p}} \tag{19}$$

As shown in Eq. (19), formal employers in this regime reports the minimum mandated wage $\bar{w}$ as the wage cost per worker. The actual pretax take-home wage $\omega_f^*(a)$ is strictly less than the reported wage $\omega_f^*(a) = \bar{w} - 1/(2\bar{\phi}\bar{p}) < \bar{w}$. The associated tax evasion is:

$$r^*(a) - \omega_f^*(a) = \frac{1}{2\bar{\phi}\bar{p}}$$

Clearly, the higher the frequency of tax auditing $\bar{\phi}$ and the more severe the penalty $\bar{p}$, the smaller will be the extent of tax evasion. Interestingly, while workers are paid strictly less than the minimum wage, their take-home subminimum wage co-moves with the mandated minimum dollar-for-dollar. Consequently, equilibrium tax evasion, or equivalently the difference between $r^*(a)$ and $\omega_f^*(a)$, is strictly invariant to $\bar{w}$. Furthermore, since small changes in the two tax rates (τ_π and τ_ω) bear no impact on the severity/frequency of the penalty associated with wage under-reporting, these changes have no impact on the extent of tax evasion either.

Turning now to minimum wage noncompliance, the difference between the mandated post tax wage and the actual post tax wage is:

$$w(1 - \tau_\omega) - (\omega_f^*(a) - r^*(a)\tau_\omega) = \frac{1}{2\bar{\phi}\bar{p}} > 0$$

Thus, minimum wage noncompliance is synonymous with tax evasion, in that both are exactly equal to $1/(2\bar{\phi}\bar{p})>0$. This implies that employers in this regime do not comply with the minimum wage legislation, and the post-tax income of formal workers is less than what the minimum wage mandate would require. Perhaps more importantly, since the extent of wage over-reporting depends on the strength of tax enforcement $\bar{\phi}\bar{p}$ alone, the extent of minimum wage noncompliance is independent of the size of the minimum wage, but strictly decreasing in $\bar{\phi}\bar{p}$.

Substituting Eq. (19) into Eq. (9), and using Eq. (6), the incidence of informality $1-\alpha^*(a)$ is:

$$1-\theta^{1/(1-\beta)}([(1-\tau_\pi)(a-\bar{w})+1/(4\bar{\phi}\bar{p})]/c_f)^{\beta/(1-\beta)}$$

Any policy measure that decreases formal employer profits will increase the incidence of informality. Routine differentiation reveals that these policies include increases in the minimum wage, increases in the profit tax rate τ_ω, and a strengthening of the tax enforcement regime $\bar{\phi}\bar{p}$. Note in particular that since the participation constraint is not binding here, small changes in the personal income tax τ_ω do not impact formal employers' ability to attract workers at constant $\omega_f^*(a)$, and the incidence of informality is thus in fact independent of τ_ω.

Let us now verify the starting premises in this regime: (i) the minimum wage constraint is the only binding constraint and (ii) reported pretax profit $a-r^*(a)$ is strictly positive. From Eq. (19), the minimum wage constraint is the only binding constraint if and only if $\omega_f^*(a)-r^*(a)\tau_\omega>w_i a$, or if the minimum wage is sufficiently high relative to the productivity of the workers:

$$\bar{w}>\frac{w_i a+1/(2\bar{\phi}\bar{p})}{1-\tau_\omega} \tag{20}$$

From Eq. (19), reported pretax profit is in fact always strictly positive in this regime upon substituting Eq. (19) into Eq. (14),

$$\pi_f^*(a)=(1-\tau_\pi)(a-\bar{w})+1/(4\bar{\phi}\bar{p})>0 \tag{21}$$

whenever worker productivity exceeds the minimum wage. This automatically rules out Regime V discussed at the beginning of this section, where the minimum wage is the only binding constraint in the presence of non-positive reported profit.

Fig. 1(b) illustrates. As before in Fig. 1(a), to the right of the 45 degree line are all combinations of a and $\bar{w}$ such that worker productivity exceeds the minimum wage. The upward sloping schedule labeled MW divides all

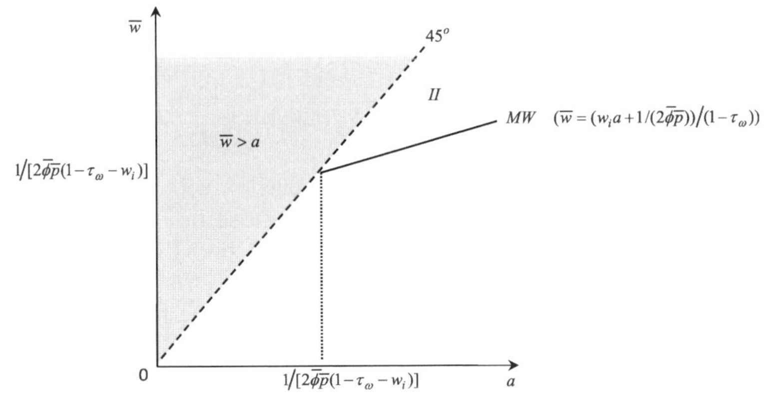

Fig. 1b. Binding Minimum Wage Constraint.

$(a, \bar{w})$ combinations into two groups. For minimum wage sufficiently high and above the MW schedule, the inequality in Eq. (20) is satisfied and hence the minimum wage constraint is the only binding constraint. Otherwise, for relatively low minimum wage and below the MW schedule, the inequality in Eq. (20) is violated and the participation constraint begins to bind. Using Eq. (21), all employer–worker matches $(a, \bar{w})$ that lie above the MW schedule report positive profits.

Summarizing, in sharp contrast to the earlier regime where the participation constraint is the only binding constraint when the minimum wage is low relative to the productivity of workers, the minimum wage constraint is the only binding constraint when the minimum wage is sufficiently high relative to the productivity of workers $\bar{w} > (w_i a + 1/(2\bar{\phi}\bar{p}))/(1 - \tau_\omega)$ (from Eq. (20)). Also unlike the previous regime where tax evasion depends critically on the tax policy induced tax gap $\tau_\pi - \tau_\omega$, while minimum wage noncompliance depends on the minimum wage policy mandated wage hike $\bar{w}(1 - \tau_\omega) - w_i a$, minimum wage noncompliance is in fact synonymous with tax evasion here in that they are both given by the same expression that depends only on the strength of the tax enforcement in place $1/(2\bar{\phi}\bar{p})$ (from Eq. (19)).

Thus, the stricter the tax enforcement regime, the higher will be the actual wage that formal employers voluntarily pay, and tax enforcement becomes a means to discourage tax evasion, as well as a means to encourage minimum wage compliance. Indeed, for all employer worker matches in this regime where the participation constraint is not binding, the formal sector wage accounting appropriately for the tax on wage income, $\bar{w}\tau_\omega$, or $\bar{w}(1 - \tau_\omega) - 1/(2\bar{\phi}\bar{p})$, strictly exceeds the reservation wage $w_i a$. Since the formal take-home wage $\omega_f^*(a)$ improves with tax enforcement $\bar{\phi}\bar{p}$, the formal–informal pay gap

$$\omega_f^*(a) - r^*(a)\tau_\omega - w_i a = \bar{w}(1 - \tau_\omega) - \frac{1}{2\bar{\phi}\bar{p}} - w_i a$$

is thus strictly increasing in the strength of tax enforcement as well. This is an important observation, to be developed further in the section to follows: even in the complete absence of minimum wage enforcement, both the reported and the actual post tax take-home wage of formal sector worker strictly increases with a sufficiently high minimum wage satisfying Eq. (20). The hike in take-home wages from the reservation level $w_i a$ in Eq. (5) to $\bar{w}(1 - \tau_\omega) - 1/(2\bar{\phi}\bar{p})$ in Eq. (19) is subject to the implicit discipline of the system of tax enforcement and audit in place $\bar{\phi}\bar{p}$. The stricter the enforcement against tax evasion, the steeper will be the hike in workers' take-home wage relative to the reservation level.

BINDING PARTICIPATION AND MINIMUM WAGE CONSTRAINT

Unlike in regimes I and II where the minimum wage is respectively sufficiently low, and sufficiently high for minimum wage in the intermediate range, $\bar{w} \in ((w_i a + \delta)/(1 - \tau_\omega), (w_i a + 1/(2\bar{\phi}\bar{p}))/(1 - \tau_\omega))$, both the participation and the minimum wage constraints are binding. The two binding constraints jointly and uniquely determine the reported and take-home wages in this regime:[13]

$$r^*(a) = \bar{w}, \quad \omega_f^*(a) = w_i a + \bar{w}\tau_\omega, \quad \omega_f^*(a) - r^*(a)\tau_\omega = w_i a \tag{22}$$

With a binding participation constraint, formal workers receive an after-tax pay that is equal to their reservation wage $w_i a$. With a binding minimum wage constraint, employers report a wage cost that is equal to the minimum wage. Jointly, these imply that formal employers compensate workers simply by paying the reservation wage $w_i a$, and top off with an additional amount that compensates workers for the personal income tax that a formal sector worker owes tax authorities $\bar{w}\tau_\omega$, evaluated at the reported wage cost $\bar{w}$.

The associated equilibrium tax evasion in this regime is

$$r^*(a) - \omega_f^* = \bar{w}(1 - \tau_\omega) - w_i a > 0$$

where the inequality follows since $\bar{w} \in ((w_i a + \delta)/(1 - \tau_\omega), (w_i a + 1/(2\bar{\phi}\bar{p}))/(1 - \tau_\omega))$. Thus, employers in this regime also over-report wage costs.

In addition, with both constraints binding, equilibrium tax evasion is simply given by the minimum wage policy mandated wage hike $\bar{w}(1-\tau_\omega) - w_i a$. Importantly, tax evasion is now fully independent of the frequency of tax audit $\bar{\phi}$ or the penalty $\bar{p}$. Small changes in the profit tax τ_π have surprisingly no local impact on tax evasion either. Effectively, in this range, the minimum wage is high enough so that reporting any wage higher than $\bar{w}$ invites too high an increase in expected penalty. Meanwhile, worker productivity is also high enough in this range, so that simply paying workers a wage that minimizes wage plus expected penalty costs, as in regime II above, is not sufficient to guarantee participation. Consequently, equilibrium tax evasion reflects these considerations as employers report exactly the minimum wage, while setting the true wage cost at a level that makes a formal job no worse than an informal job.

In terms of minimum wage noncompliance, we note that minimum wage noncompliance is once again synonymous with tax evasion:

$$\bar{w}(1-\tau_\omega) - [\omega_f^*(a) - r^*(a)\tau_\omega] = \bar{w}(1-\tau_\omega) - w_i a > 0$$

though the extent of minimum wage noncompliance is now independent of the strength of tax enforcement, unlike regime II. Taken together, both equilibrium tax evasion and equilibrium minimum noncompliance strictly increases with the mandated post tax income $\bar{w}(1-\tau_\omega)$. However, minimum wage noncompliance can be expected to decrease with work productivity a, and thus the reservation wage $w_i a$.

Now, the incidence of informality $1-\alpha^*(a)$ is:

$$1 - \theta^{1/(1-\beta)}\left(\pi_f^*(a)/c_f\right)^{\beta/(1-\beta)}$$

where

$$\pi_f^*(a) = (1-\tau_\pi)(a-\bar{w}) + \frac{1}{4\bar{\phi}\bar{p}} - \bar{\phi}\bar{p}\left(\frac{1}{2\bar{\phi}\bar{p}} - [\bar{w}(1-\tau_\omega) - w_i a]\right)^2 > 0 \quad (23)$$

It is straightforward to verify that $\pi_f^*(a)$ is strictly decreasing in all three policies τ_π, τ_ω, and w in this range. Consequently, the incidence of informality is accordingly strictly increasing whenever either one of the two tax rates, or when the minimum wage rises.

To close this section, let us check that reported pretax profit $a - r^*(a)$ is strictly positive in this regime as well. From Eq. (23) above, $\pi_f^*(a)$ is always strictly positive. This automatically rules out Regime VI, where both constraints are binding in the presence of non-positive reported profit.

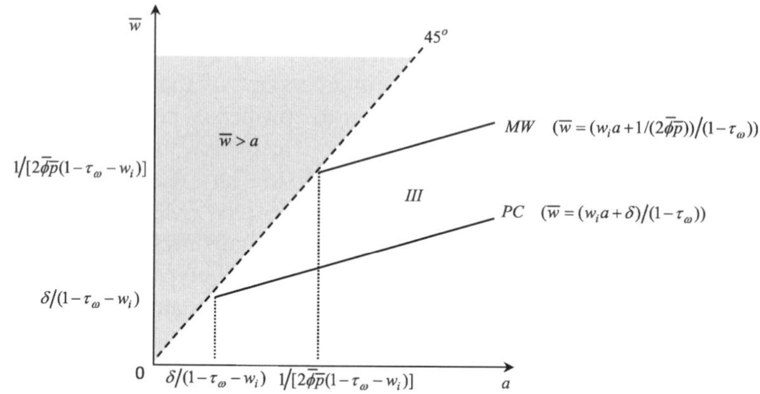

Fig. 1c. Binding Participation and Minimum Wage Constraints.

Fig. 1(c) illustrates the $(a, \bar{w})$ combinations that come under this regime. As shown, all $(a, \bar{w})$ combinations to the right of the 45 degree line, and in between the PC and MW schedules belong this regime.

To summarize, for intermediate levels of the minimum wage, both the participation constraint and the minimum wage constraint are binding. While employers continue to under-report wage cost from Eq. (22), the reported wage cost is bounded below by $\bar{w}$ here, and workers' post tax take-home wage is bounded below by the reservation wage. Consequently, tax evasion and minimum wage noncompliance are once again synonymous, though this value is now equal to the extent to which the government mandated post tax wage $\bar{w}(1-\tau_\omega)$ exceeds workers' reservation wage $w_i a$. In sharp contrast to regime II, where employers also report the minimum wage as the wage cost, the strength of tax policy enforcement no longer play a role in determining employers' compliance to tax and minimum wage laws (from Eq. (22)). Similarly, the profit tax rate has no impact on equilibrium tax evasion or minimum wage noncompliance (also from Eq. (22)).

Zero Reported Profits

Since regimes V and VI have both been ruled out in the preceding paragraphs, a final regime to consider here involves regime IV. This has been shown to be a real possibility in equilibrium for the case where the participation constraint is the only binding constraint, and specifically when worker productivity is lower than a threshold:

$$a < \frac{\delta}{1 - \tau_\omega - w_i}$$

as shown in Eq. (18).

Binding Participation Constraint

When reported profit is non-positive $r \geq a$, and when the participation constraint is the only binding constraint, formal employers' decision problem is as follows:

$$\max_{\omega_f, r} a - \omega_f - \bar{\phi}\bar{p}(r - \omega_f)^2, \quad \text{s.t. } r \geq a, \ \omega_f - r\tau_\omega = w_i a$$

$$= \max_{r} a - w_i a - r\tau_\omega - \bar{\phi}\bar{p}(r(1 - \tau_\omega) - w_i a)^2, \quad \text{s.t. } r \geq a$$

As shown, expected profit is strictly decreasing in r. Intuitively, since formal employers are no longer subject to profit tax upon reporting non-positive profit, further raising the reported wage cost r will only raise the expected penalty associated with the misreporting of profit $\bar{\phi}\bar{p}(r(1 - \tau_\omega) - w_i a)^2$, with otherwise no further beneficial impact on profits. The solutions to the employer's problem in this case involves setting[14]

$$r^*(a) = a, \quad \omega_f^*(a) = a(w_i + \tau_\omega), \quad \omega_f^*(a) - r^*(a)\tau_\omega = w_i a \tag{24}$$

The associated tax evasion is given simply by

$$r^*(a) - \omega_f^*(a) = a(1 - \tau_\omega - w_i)$$

Since formal employers report zero profits $r^*(a) = a$, and make job offers by compensating workers for the reservation wage $w_i a$ and any applicable personal income tax $\tau_\omega r^*(a) = \tau_\omega a$, the extent of tax evasion is independent of the strength of tax enforcement, or the size of the minimum wage.

Meanwhile, the extent of minimum wage noncompliance is given by:

$$\bar{w}(1 - \tau_\omega) - (\omega_f^* - r^*(a)\tau_\omega) = \bar{w}(1 - \tau_\omega) - w_i a$$

Based on reasoning that should by now be familiar, since the participation constraint is binding, employers make job offers that are just attractive enough to compensate workers for their forgone reservation earning $w_i a$. It follows that the extent of minimum wage noncompliance is given by the government mandated post tax take-home wage $\bar{w}(1-\tau_\omega)$ and the reservation wage itself. Thus, the strength of tax enforcement does not have any local impacts on minimum wage noncompliance.

Finally, the incidence of informality $1-\alpha^*(a)$ is given by:

$$1-\theta^{1/(1-\beta)}(\pi_f^*(a)/c_f)^{\beta/(1-\beta)}$$

where

$$\pi_f^*(a)=\frac{1}{4\bar{p}\bar{\phi}}-\bar{p}\bar{\phi}\left(\frac{1}{2\bar{p}\bar{\phi}}-a(1-\tau_\omega-w_i)\right)^2 \tag{25}$$

At zero reported profit, actual profit $\pi_f^*(a)$ and thus the incidence of informality, $1-\alpha^*(a)$, are both independent of the profit tax τ_π. However, increase in the personal income tax raises actual wage cost ω_f^*, and decreases formal sector profits. Thus, the incidence of informality is strictly increasing in the personal income tax rate. Strengthening tax enforcement similarly lowers formal sector profit, and increases the incidence of informality.

Synthesizing our findings up to this point, Tables 4 and 5 display the tax evasion and minimum wage noncompliance responses to the four policy measures τ_π, τ_ω, $\bar{w}$, and $\bar{\phi}\bar{p}$. A number of features are particularly striking. First, with the lone exception of the case where the personal income tax on minimum wage workers is greater than the profit tax rate, which we have demonstrated in Table 3 to be the exception rather than the rule empirically, we find that employers over-report wage costs. From the perspective of tax authorities, this over-reporting of wages manifests itself as tax evasion. From the perspective of labor inspectors, this over-reporting of wages gives rise to minimum wage noncompliance. However, tax evasion and minimum

Table 4. The Determinants of Tax Evasion $|r^*(a)-\omega_f^*(a)|$ in the Four Regimes, Assuming $\tau_\pi>\tau_\omega$.

	I $\delta=(\tau_\pi-\tau_\omega)/(2\bar{\phi}\bar{p}(1-\tau_\omega))$	II $1/(2\bar{\phi}\bar{p})$	III $\bar{w}(1-\tau_\omega)-w_i a$	IV $a(1-\tau_\omega-w_i)$
τ_π	+	0	0	0
τ_ω	–	0	–	–
$\bar{w}$	0	0	+	0
$\bar{\phi}\bar{p}$	–	–	0	0

Table 5. The Determinants of Minimum Wage Noncompliance $\bar{w}(1-\tau_\omega) - [\omega_f^*(a) - \tau_\omega r^*(a)]$ in the Four Regimes.

	I $\bar{w}(1-\tau_\omega) - w_i a$	II $1/(2\bar{\phi}\bar{p})$	III $\bar{w}(1-\tau_\omega) - w_i a$	IV $\bar{w}(1-\tau_\omega) - w_i a$
τ_π	0	0	0	0
τ_ω	–	0	–	–
$\bar{w}$	+	0	+	0
$\bar{\phi}\bar{p}$	0	–	0	0

wage noncompliance made possible by less than perfect enforcement raises expected formal employer profits. This puts checks on the incidence of informality, in which employers pay no taxes at all, and the minimum wage legislation is neither respect nor enforced.

Second, in both regimes II and III where the minimum wage is sufficiently high, or at an intermediate range, we find that tax evasion and minimum wage noncompliance are synonymous. Thus while the four policies have regime-specific impacts depending on which of two constraints are binding and whether reported profit is positive, the effects of four policies on tax evasion, and on minimum wage noncompliance are identical. In other words, there are well-defined regimes of interest in which policies targeted toward mitigating tax evasion and minimum wage compliance can be complementary to each other.

Third, it is clear from Tables 4 and 5 that a minimum wage hike can encourage tax evasion (regime III), while raising the personal income tax can tame minimum wage noncompliance (regimes I, III, and IV). Similarly, strengthening tax enforcement can discourage tax evasion (regimes I and II) and mitigate against minimum wage noncompliance (regime II). Thus, there are indeed cross-cutting impacts that a minimum wage policy can have on tax evasion, and that tax policies can have on minimum wage compliance.

This apparent plethora of possible comparative statics responses suggests that the devil is in the details, and furthermore, that the nuanced responsiveness of tax evasion and minimum wage noncompliance to policy changes is likely to depend on the precise specification of the penalty scheme, the tax auditing technology, in addition to the height of the minimum wage, the two taxes, as well as the strength of the tax enforcement regime. All of this make for a very fruitful agenda for future research, and particularly on the design of an optimal penalty scheme. This said, our analysis so far summarized in Tables 4 and 5 suggest a number of generalizations, and testable hypotheses:

Proposition 1. *For all $a \geq \delta/(1-\tau_\omega - w_i)$, and minimum wage $\bar{w}<a$, the extent of tax evasion $r^* - \omega_f^*$ is*

- *weakly increasing in the profit tax rate τ_π;*
- *weakly decreasing in the personal income tax rate τ_ω;*
- *weakly increasing in the minimum wage $\bar{w}$;* and
- *weakly decreasing in the strength of tax enforcement $\bar{\phi}\bar{p}$.*

The extent of minimum wage noncompliance is

- *independent of the profit tax rate τ_π;*
- *weakly decreasing in the personal income tax rate τ_ω;*
- *weakly increasing in the minimum wage $\bar{w}$;* and
- *weakly decreasing in the strength of tax enforcement $\bar{\phi}\bar{p}$.*

Table 6 summarizes responsiveness of the incidence of informality with respect to the four policy measures. Contrary to Proposition 1, the effectiveness of the four policies is more uniform:

Proposition 2. *For all minimum wage $\bar{w}<a$, the incidence of informality is weakly increasing in the profit tax rate τ_π, τ_ω, and the minimum wage $\bar{w}$, and strictly increasing in the strength of tax enforcement $\bar{\phi}\bar{p}$.*

These results embody important policy implications, and some of these may not be apparent at first sight. Consider, for example, the consequences of a flat tax reform, which equates τ_ω and τ_π.[15] Starting from an equilibrium with $\tau_\omega<\tau_\pi$, a flat tax reform can be accomplished either by raising τ_ω, or by decreasing τ_π. While our analysis of regime I suggest that closing the gap $\tau_\pi - \tau_\omega$ decreases individual formal sector employer's incentives to evade taxes, Proposition 2 suggests that the overall tax consequences of a flat tax

Table 6. The Determinants of the Incidence of Informality $1-\alpha^*(a)$ in the Four Regimes.

	I	II	III	IV
τ_π	+	+	+	0
τ_ω	+	0	+	+
$\bar{w}$	0	+	+	0
$\bar{\phi}\bar{p}$	+	+	+	+

reform, accounting for the incidence of informality, will likely depend critically on whether the proposed flat tax requires an increase in τ_ω – which is expected to entice employers to turn to the informal sector, or a reduction in τ_π – which will have the exact opposite impact.

OPTIMAL POLICIES FOR POVERTY ALLEVIATION

A key departure of this model from the existing literature is in its unique ability to identify and distinguish between two wage distributions that prevail among workers of differing skills. First, the reported wage distribution pertains to the wage distribution that can be ascertained from firm-level tax records for example. Second, the actual wage distribution pertains to the true take-home income of working individuals that may be ascertained from household/labor force surveys for example.

Our objective in this section is to evaluate the effectiveness of policies in alleviating poverty, evaluated based on the actual, rather than the reported post tax take-home wage of individual workers. To do so, we first combine Figs. 1(a)–1(c) to yield Fig. 2, which summarizes in one diagram the juxtaposition of the four regimes (I–IV) examined so far. To recall,

- in regime I, the reported wage exceeds the minimum wage, formal worker are paid their reservation income post tax, and employers report positive profits;

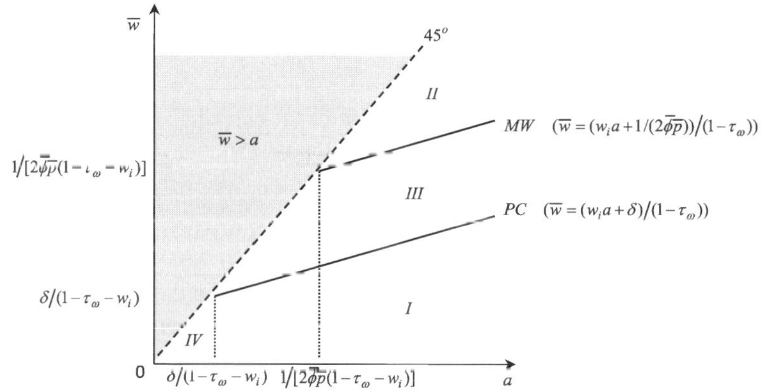

Fig. 2. The Four Regimes.

- in regime II, the reported wage is equal to the minimum wage, formal workers are paid strictly higher than their reservation income post tax, and employers report positive profits;
- in regime III, the reported wage is equal to the minimum wage, formal workers are paid their reservation income post tax, and employers report positive profits;
- in regime IV, the reported wage exceeds the minimum wage, formal workers are paid their reservation income post tax, and employers report zero profit.

We begin with a preliminary result, which can be verified simply by inspection of Fig.2:

Proposition 3. *I. For all $a > \bar{w}$ and tax enforcement sufficiently strict ($\bar{\phi}\bar{p}$ sufficiently large) such that*

$$a > \frac{1}{2\bar{\phi}\bar{p}(1 - \tau_{\omega} - w_i)}$$

the post tax take-home earnings of formal sector workers strictly exceed their reservation benchmark $w_i a$ if and only if the minimum wage exceeds the threshold:

$$\bar{w} \geq \frac{w_i a + 1/(2\bar{\phi}\bar{p})}{1 - \tau_{\omega} - w_i}$$

The stricter the tax enforcement regime, and thus the higher $\bar{\phi}\bar{p}$ is, the lower this threshold will be.

II. For all $a > \bar{w}$ and tax enforcement sufficiently lax, however, with

$$a < \frac{1}{2\bar{\phi}\bar{p}(1 - \tau_{\omega} - w_i)}$$

there does not exist a minimum wage $\bar{w} < a$ that can raise the actual post tax income of formal sector workers beyond the reservation benchmark $w_i a$.

When tax enforcement is strict enough, the threshold minimum wage is given simply by the MW schedule in Fig. 2, which separates $(a, \bar{w})$ in regime II from that of I, III, and IV. As noted earlier in our discussion of the employer's decision problem in regime II, what is particularly notable here is that a minimum wage is shown to raise the income of formal sector workers even though an official minimum wage enforcement mechanism is nonexistent. Rather, enforcement against tax evasion serves as the implicit discipline device, and prevents formal employers from over-stating their wage cost by too much, or equivalently, enforcement against tax evasion effectively discourages formal employers from paying workers too low a wage relative to the reported minimum wage $\bar{w}$.

Now, the vertical dotted line at $1/(2\bar{\phi}\bar{p}(1-\tau_\omega-w_i))$ in Fig. 2 divides the range of possible workers' skill levels into two regions separated by a critical skill level $\bar{a}=1/(2\bar{\phi}\bar{p}(1-\tau_\omega-w_i))$. To the right of $\bar{a}$ and hence for workers with relatively high skills given the tax enforcement regime, a minimum wage which raises the post tax take-home earnings of formal sector workers beyond $w_i a$ can always be found for region II is nonempty for $a \geq 1/(2\bar{\phi}\bar{p}(1-\tau_\omega-w_i))$. However, to the left of $\bar{a}$ and hence for workers with sufficiently low skills given the tax enforcement regime, there does not exist a minimum wage, however high or low, that raises the post tax take-home income of formal sector workers beyond the reservation level, since the set of $(a,\bar{w})$ in region II with $a<\bar{a}$ is empty. Strengthening tax enforcement through an increase in $\bar{\phi}\bar{p}$ shifts this critical skill level $\bar{a}$ to the left, accommodating more formal workers whose income can be raised beyond $w_i a$ via an appropriately set minimum wage.

In what follows, we examine the choice of a minimum wage and tax policy package $\{\bar{w},\tau_\pi,\tau_\omega\}$ for each skill level that minimizes poverty among workers of a given skill level a, taking as given the strength of the tax enforcement measures $\bar{\phi}\bar{p}$ in place. To this end, let $z>0$ denote the poverty line. Consider all skill levels such that the benchmark reservation income is less than the poverty line $w_i a<z$, or

$$a>z/w_i \equiv a_z$$

In the absence of poverty intervention through a minimum wage for example, all workers with $a<a_z$ are poor, while those with $a \geq a_z$ are not. We consider the policy problem:

$$\min_{\bar{w},\tau_\pi,\tau_\omega} 1-\alpha^*(a), \quad \text{s.t.} \quad \omega_f^*(a)-r^*(a)\tau_\omega \geq z$$

for $a<a_z$. The objective of the policy maker is thus to minimize the incidence of informality, while at the same time guaranteeing formal sector workers an income level no less than the poverty line. Since $a<a_z$, all informal workers are by definition poor. Stated differently, the objective of the policy maker is to minimize the poverty head count, when formal sector workers are guaranteed an income level no less than the poverty line.

From Proposition 3, we know that in order to strictly raise the income of formal sector workers above the reservation level $w_i a$, what is required is a minimum wage that is sufficiently high, as well as a tax enforcement mechanism in place that is sufficiently strict, so that regime II applies. There are thus two distinctive possibilities:

1. if tax enforcement is sufficiently lax such that

$$a_z \leq \frac{1}{2\bar{\phi}\bar{p}(1-\tau_\omega - w_i)}$$

it follows from Proposition 3 that there does not exist a minimum wage $\bar{w} < a$ that can lift any worker with $a < a_z$ out of poverty since regime II is empty;

2. if tax enforcement is strict enough so that

$$a_z > \frac{1}{2\bar{\phi}\bar{p}(1-\tau_\omega - w_i)}$$

there are thus two types of workers who will live under the poverty line in the absence of policy intervention. Those with relatively low skills $a < 1/(2\bar{\phi}\bar{p}(1-\tau_\omega - w_i))$ for whom regime II is empty, and those with relatively high skills $a \in [(1/(2\bar{\phi}\bar{p}(1-\tau_\omega - w_i))), a_z]$, for whom regime II is nonempty. For the former group of lower skill workers, a minimum wage that lifts workers out of poverty continues to be nonexistent.

Suppose therefore that $a_z > 1/(2\bar{\phi}\bar{p}(1-\tau_\omega - w_i))$. Let us consider the group of workers with relatively high skills, $a > [(1/2\bar{\phi}\bar{p}(1-\tau_\omega - w_i)), a_z]$, who would otherwise be living under the poverty line in the absence of policy intervention. From Proposition 3, any minimum wage $\bar{w} < a$ but greater than the threshold demarcated by the MW schedule in Fig. 2, $(w_i a + 1/(2\bar{\phi}\bar{p}))/(1-\tau_\omega - w_i)$, raises the post tax take-home income of formal sector workers beyond $w_i a$. From Eq. (19), the corresponding post-tax take-home wage is given by the government mandated post tax take-home wage $\bar{w}(1-\tau_\omega)$, net of the extent of wage under-reporting, $1/(2\bar{\phi}\bar{p})$ in this regime, or $\omega_f^*(a) - r^*(a)\tau_\omega = \bar{w}(1-\tau_\omega) - 1/(2\bar{p}\bar{\phi})$. The higher the minimum wage, the higher will be the take-home wage of formal sector workers in this regime. It follows that if the post tax take-home wage is to exceed the poverty line, the minimum wage will need to be sufficiently high, since

$$\omega_f^*(a) - r^*(a)\tau_\omega > z \Leftrightarrow \bar{w} > \frac{z + 1/(2\bar{\phi}\bar{p})}{1-\tau_\omega} = \bar{w}(z) \tag{26}$$

Eq. (26) above shows that the smallest minimum wage $\bar{w}(z)$ that lifts formal sector workers out of poverty is decreasing in the strength of the tax enforcement regime, and increasing in the personal income tax. Such a wage is feasible, in the sense that it does not exceed the net output a of a worker if and only if

$$\bar{w}(z) = \frac{z + 1/(2\bar{\phi}\bar{p})}{1 - \tau_\omega} < a$$

It follows that for all workers in the range $a < \bar{w}(z)$, a minimum wage $\bar{w} < a$ that lifts workers out of poverty does not exist. Otherwise, for workers in the range $a \in [\bar{w}(z), a_z]$, setting $\bar{w} = \bar{w}(z)$ puts formal sector workers exactly at the poverty line.

Now, turning to the minimization of poverty head count, which requires minimizing the incidence of informality subject to Eq. (26) above, recall from Eqs. (6) and (21) that the incidence of informality in regime II is given by:

$$1 - \theta^{1/(1-\beta)}\left([(1 - \tau_\pi)(a - \bar{w}) + 1/(4\bar{\phi}\bar{p})]/c_f\right)^{\beta/(1-\beta)}$$

Clearly, the higher the minimum wage, the higher will be the incidence of informality implying that the constraint in Eq. (25) must be strictly binding. Substituting $\bar{w}(z)$ into the equation above, it is straightforward to see that the incidence of informality is furthermore strictly increasing in τ_π as well as τ_ω. We have thus:

Proposition 4. *I. If tax enforcement is sufficiently lax, so that $a_z \le 1/(2\bar{\phi}\bar{p}(1 - \tau_\omega - w_i))$, there does not exist a poverty alleviating minimum wage for all $a < a_z$.*

II. If tax enforcement is sufficiently strict, so that $a_z > 1/(2\bar{\phi}\bar{p}(1 - \tau_\omega - w_i))$, a poverty alleviating minimum wage does not exist for low skilled workers with $a < \bar{w}(z) \equiv (z + 1/(2\bar{\phi}\bar{p}))/(1 - \tau_\omega)$. For higher skilled workers, with $a \in [\bar{w}(z), a_z]$, setting

$$\bar{w} = z + \frac{1}{2\bar{p}\bar{\phi}}, \quad \tau_\pi = 0, \quad \tau_\omega = 0$$

minimizes the poverty head count.

To verify the final item noted in Proposition 4, suppose that the minimum wage is set below $z + (1/2\bar{p}\bar{\phi})$ as indicated in the proposition. It follows from Eq. (26) that formal sector workers live below the poverty line. Since all informal sector workers live below the poverty line as well for $a < a_z$, a minimum wage policy $\bar{w}$ that stipulates $\bar{w} < z + (1/2\bar{p}\bar{\phi})$ is completely ineffective in alleviating poverty.

Now suppose instead that the minimum wage is set above or equal to $z + (1/2\bar{p}\phi)$. It follows from Eq. (26) that all formal sector workers live at or above the poverty line, but all informal sector workers remain poor. To minimize the incidence of poverty, the policy maker should set $\bar{w}$ exactly at $\bar{w}(z)$ and $\tau_\pi = \tau_\omega = 0$, since the incidence of informality decreases with $\bar{w}$, τ_π, and τ_ω.

Importantly, Proposition 3 demonstrates that a poverty minimizing minimum wage is set at the poverty line z, plus an additional expression that depends only on the strength of tax enforcement $\phi\bar{p}$. This remarkably simple formula is independent of the productivity of the worker, or the informal sector wage. What Proposition 3 also points out is that this such an optimal minimum wage can be effective even when the minimum wage itself is not enforced, but that a sufficiently strict tax enforcement regime is in place.

OPTIMAL POLICIES FOR TAX COMPLIANCE

We focus now on evaluating the policy package $\{\bar{w}, \tau_\pi, \tau_\omega\}$ that maximizes total expected government revenue, including all tax revenue on profits and wage earnings, as well as any applicable fines and penalties collected, taking once again as given the strength of the tax enforcement regime in place.

Since informal employers and workers do not pay taxes, total government tax revenue $G(a)$ is given simply by the sum of per employer tax on formal profits $\tau_\pi \min\{0, a - r^*(a)\}$, tax on wage earnings $\tau_\omega r^*(a)$, and the expected fines and penalties collected: $\phi\bar{p}(r^*(a) - \omega_f^*(a))^2$, multiplied by the total number of formal sector employers, $\alpha^*(a)N(a)$. From Eq. (14), and by definition of $\pi_f^*(a)$,

$$
\begin{aligned}
G(a) &= N(a)\theta^{1/(1-\beta)}\left(\frac{\pi_f^*(a)}{c_f}\right)^{\beta/(1-\beta)}\left(\tau_\pi \min\{0, a - r^*(a)\} + \tau_\omega r^*(a) + \phi\bar{p}(r^*(a) - \omega_f^*(a))^2\right) \\
&= N(a)\theta^{1/(1-\beta)}\left(\frac{\pi_f^*(a)}{c_f}\right)^{\beta/(1-\beta)}\left(a - \omega_f^*(a) + \tau_\omega r^*(a) - \pi_f^*(a)\right) \qquad (27)
\end{aligned}
$$

Intuitively, the true pretax profit $(a - \omega_f^*(a) + \tau_\omega r^*(a))$ net of the post tax post-penalty profit per employer $\pi_f^*(a)$ gives the total tax take per employer.

Using the results in section "Positive Reported Profits," government revenue can be evaluated at $(a, \bar{w})$ combinations consistent with regimes I–IV. Suppose to begin with that the minimum wage is sufficiently high, as in regime II, so that the participation constraint is not binding. From Eq. (19), the post tax take-home wage of a formally employed worker is

$\omega_f^*(a) - \tau_\omega r^*(a) = \bar{w}(1-\tau_\omega) - 1/(2\bar{p}\bar{\phi})$, while formal sector expected profit $\pi_f^*(a)$ as displayed in Eq. (21), has been shown to be strictly decreasing in the minimum wage $\bar{w}$. Substituting these expressions into Eq. (27) above, we obtain:

$$G(a) = N(a)\theta^{1/(1-\beta)}\left(\frac{\pi_f^*(a)}{c_f}\right)^{\beta/(1-\beta)}\left(a\tau_\pi - \bar{w}(\tau_\pi - \tau_\omega) + \frac{1}{4\bar{p}\bar{\phi}}\right)$$

It follows by inspection that since $\tau_\pi \geq \tau_\omega$, total government revenue $G(a)$ is strictly decreasing in $\bar{w}$ for all $(a, \bar{w})$ combinations in regime II. Put differently, any tax, and minimum wage policy combinations that put an employer in the interior of regime II can be ruled out from the set of government revenue maximizing policy. This is in sharp contrast to the set of poverty alleviating tax policies, which we have just shown to necessarily put employers in regime II (Proposition 4).

Next, consider instead relatively low minimum wages such that regimes I, III, or IV apply, wherein the participation constraint is strictly binding, or, $\omega_f^*(a) - \tau_\omega r^*(a) = w_i a$, and formal sector expected profits $\pi_f^*(a)$ are displayed in Eqs. (16), (23), and (25) respectively for regimes I, III, and IV. Thus:

$$G(a) = N(a)\theta^{1/(1-\beta)}\left(\frac{\pi_f^*(a)}{c_f}\right)^{\beta/(1-\beta)}\left(a(1-w_i) - \pi_f^*(a)\right)$$

Observe that changes in formal employer profits impact government revenue in two distinctive, and opposite directions. First, raising $\pi_f^*(a)$ decreases the incidence of informality through $\alpha^*(a) = \theta^{1/(1-\beta)}(\pi_f^*(a)/c_f)^{\beta/(1-\beta)}$. Second, and going in opposite direction, a higher $\pi_f^*(a)$ necessarily requires lowering the government revenue per employer $a(1-w_i) - \pi_f^*(a)$. On balance, total government revenue is maximized by choice of $\pi_f^*(a)$ satisfying:t

$$\pi_f^*(a) = \beta a(1-w_i)$$

so that profit per formal employer is a fraction β of the profit per formal employer in the absence of any taxes or minimum wage $a(1-w_i)$. One way to exactly achieve this level of profit is summarized in the following proposition:

Proposition 5. *A flat tax reform at minimal minimum wage protection maximizes government revenue $G(a)$. This is accomplished by setting*

$$\bar{w} = 0, \quad \tau_\pi = \tau_\omega = (1-\beta)(1-w_i)$$

A zero minimum wage (regime I, or IV) reflects the government's desire to raise revenue, rather than to alleviate poverty. Next, by removing the tax gap, and thus by setting $\delta = 0$, regime IV (where $a < \delta/(1 - \tau_\omega - w_i) = 0$) vanishes, and as such all formal employers of workers with $a > 0$ report positive profits. With regime I remaining, setting $\delta = 0$ also removes any incentives on the part of formal employers to evade taxes evaluated at $\bar{w} = 0$ since $r^*(a) - \omega_f^*(a) = \delta$ from Eq. (15) for regime I.

To balance the role of the uniform tax rate $\tau_\pi = \tau_\omega$ on tax revenue per formal employer, and the incidence of informality, the optimal tax rate is set at $(1 - \beta)(1 - w_i)$ with two considerations in mind.[16] First, the higher the elasticity of employer entry on job creation $\beta = d \log \Phi(a)/d \log M(a)$, the lower the tax rate will be. Meanwhile, the higher the productivity of informal sector workers relative to formal sector workers w_i, the lower the tax rate should be.

CONCLUSION

In this chapter, we study the impacts of tax and minimum wage reforms on the incidence of informality, as measured by the extent of minimum wage noncompliance, the extent of tax evasion, and the size of the informal workforce. These measures are based on two distinctive perspectives on informality, associated with labor standard compliance, and tax compliance. The model we propose offers a list of empirically relevant observations and testable hypotheses, featuring (i) the endogenous distinction between firm-level reported wage distribution and actual wage distribution, (ii) the complementarity of tax enforcement on minimum wage enforcement, (iii) the impact that minimum wage reform has on tax and minimum wage compliance, and (iv) the impact that tax policy reform has on tax and minimum wage compliance.

The chapter concludes with a look at the design of optimal minimum wage and tax policies, given the objectives of tax revenue minimization, and poverty alleviation among workers. For example, we provide conditions under which a tax reform is consistent with the objective of tax revenue minimization. At the same time, we also offer an optimal minimum wage and tax policy formula consistent with the objective of poverty alleviation. In each case, we highlight the role of the strength of the tax enforcement regime on the optimal tax and minimum wage policy formula.

This chapter is a first attempt at analyzing the role of minimum wage and tax policy reforms jointly on minimum wage and tax compliance.

Many possible routes for future research remain. For example, while we highlight the role of tax enforcement in this chapter, ample opportunities for extension of the basic framework by introducing a combination of tax and minimum wage enforcement remain. In addition, in the tradition of the theory of tax enforcement, the risk attitudes of the employers naturally matter. The introduction of risk aversion, for example, into our basic model is a promising avenue for future work. Finally, in our optimal policy formulation, we have taken the strength of tax enforcement and minimum wage enforcement as given. An extension of the model to allow for endogenous tax and minimum wage enforcement regimes will also be of real interest in efforts to better understand the various nuances of tax and minimum wage policies on informality.

NOTES

1. The literature on the determinants, duration, and separation probability of formal employment, informal employment, and unemployment is a much better researched topic. On the duration, separation probabilities, and entry probabilities of formal and informal employment in Brazil, Argentina, and Mexico, see Bosch and Maloney (2010). Almeida and Carneiro (2011) study the impact of labor standards enforcement on mandated benefits on formal employment, informal employment, and unemployment in Brazil. Chong, Galdo, and Saavedra (2008) consider the role of labor legislations and worker productivity on the incidence of informality in Peru. Fugazza and Jacques (2004) theoretically examine the role of unemployment benefits, minimum wage, taxation, and audits on labor allocation in a matching model. In a search theoretic setup, Albrecht, Navarro, and Vroman (2009) examine the role of labor market policy on the incidence of informality and the distribution of wages across formal sector workers.
2. Though informal employment is modeled as wage employment here, the results of the our analysis will remain unchanged if informal self-employment is considered instead, when each self-employed informal sector worker receives a skill-specific take-home income of $\omega_i(a)$.
3. Net output a is taken to account for any other costs of production, associated with capital use for example, per worker hired.
4. We focus here exclusively on the possibility of tax evasion based on the misreporting of costs, and assume that revenue a is verifiable upon audit. Other methods of tax evasion clearly exist. For example, in a setting where a firm employs multiple workers, under-reporting the number of workers is another interesting possibility. We thank a referee for pointing this out, and leave the issue for future research.
5. In Danziger (2010) which studies the issue of minimum wage noncompliance, the probability of detection is taken to be strictly increasing in the number of workers hired, and independent of the extent of the minimum wage violation. In our setup

where each employer hires one worker, the question of the endogeneity of inspection likelihood does not arise. As another alternative, $\phi(a)$ is a constant with random auditing. It can be easily verified that regardless of worker productivity, a corner solution applies – no employer ever evade taxes, or all employers evade taxes to the maximum extent possible. We thank two anonymous referees for pointing out these possibilities.

6. Given this assumption on $\phi(a)$, we will check in what follows that upon substituting for the equilibrium employer choice of tax evasion $|r^*(a) - \omega_f^*(a)|$, where an asterisk denotes equilibrium values, the implied equilibrium likelihood of a tax audit $\phi(a) = \bar{\phi}|r^*(a) - \omega_f^*(a)|$ is a fraction in the [0,1] interval.

7. Of course, reporting the payment of the minimum wage does not guarantee the actual payment of such a wage. Ashenfelter and Smith (1979), for example, touch on the strategy of issuing a bonafide paycheck. Employers issue a pay check for the amount requirement by the minimum wage, and in exchange, extract some value of the paycheck from workers. By contrast, Saget (2008) points out that there are countries in which payment of the minimum is optional rather than compulsory. This is the case in Indonesia for example where the minimum wage legislation lays out clearly exceptions that can be made for employers who are not able to pay the minimum wage. In our chapter, we focus our analysis the case where the payment of the minimum wage is compulsory by law, and nonpayment of the minimum wage is illegal. We thank an anonymous referee for pointing this out.

8. A full account of a formal employer's decision problem in the presence of tax and minimum wage enforcement would require a full-length analysis that is beyond the scope of the current study. We leave this for future research.

9. It is straightforward to verify that for any (ω_f, r) pair such that neither of the two constraints bind, $(\omega_f > w_i a + \tau_\omega r)$ and $r > \bar{w}$, an alternative pairing (ω'_f, r') can be found along a binding participation constraint that raises expected profit, $a - \omega_f - \tau_\pi(a - r) - \bar{\phi}\bar{p}(r - \omega_f)^2 < a - \omega_f - \tau_\pi(a - r') - \bar{\phi}\bar{p}(r' - \omega'_f)^2$. A formal proof is relegated to the appendix.

10. In this, as well as in all of the subsequent maximization problems, it is straightforward to verify that the second order conditions are satisfied. In addition, from Eq. (15), the implied equilibrium likelihood of a tax audit $\phi^*(a) = \bar{\phi}(r^*(a) - \omega_f^*(a)) = 1/(2\bar{p})$ in regime I is in the interior of the [0,1] interval since the penalty parameter $\bar{p}$ is assumed to take on values greater than or equal to unity.

11. World Bank (2011) data is from 2010 survey (latest data available for 2011) and PricewaterhouseCoopers (2011) is also the latest available (accessed 2011).

12. The associated equilibrium likelihood of tax audit $\phi^*(a) = \bar{\phi}|r^*(a) - \omega_f^*(a)| = 1/(2\bar{p})$ continues to lie in the interior of the [0,1] interval for $\bar{p} \geq 1$.

13. The associated equilibrium likelihood of tax audit $\phi^*(a) = \bar{\phi}|r^*(a) - \omega_f^*(a)| = \bar{\phi}[\bar{w}(1 - \tau_\omega) - w_i a] \in ((\tau_\pi - \tau_\omega)/(2\bar{p}(1 - \tau_\omega)), 1/(2\bar{p}))$ lies in the interior of the [0,1] interval for $\bar{w} \in ((w_i a + \delta)/(1 - \tau_\omega), (w_i a + 1/(2\phi\bar{p}))/(1 - \tau_\omega))$ in this regime, and $\bar{p} \geq 1$.

14. The associated equilibrium likelihood of tax audit $\phi^*(a) = \bar{\phi}|r^*(a) - \omega_f^*(a)| = \bar{\phi}a(1 - \tau_\omega - w_i) \in ((\tau_\pi - \tau_\omega)/(2\bar{p}(1 - \tau_\omega)), 1/(2\bar{p}))$ lies in the interior of the [0,1] interval for $\bar{w} \in ((w_i a + \delta)/(1 - \tau_\omega), (w_i a + 1/(2\phi\bar{p}))/(1 - \tau_\omega))$ in this regime, and $\bar{p} \geq 1$.

15. We follow convention and refer a flat tax reform to a policy of constant marginal tax rate.

16. It can also be verified that evaluated at this optimal tax rate $(1-\beta)(1-w_i)$, the post tax net output of a formal sector worker exceeds that of an informal sector worker, consistent with our assumption that $1-\tau_\omega-w_i>0$ throughout this chapter.

ACKNOWLEDGMENT

We are grateful to Hartmut Lehmann for encouraging us to write this chapter.

REFERENCES

Albrecht, J., Navarro, L., & Vronman, S. (2009). The effects of labor market policies in an economy with an informal sector. *Economic Journal*, *119*, 1105–1129.

Almeida, R. K., & Carneiro, P. (2011). *Enforcement of labor regulation and informality*. IZA Discussion Paper No. 5902. IZA, Bonn.

Allingham, M. G., & Sandmo, A. (1972). Income tax evasion: A theoretical analysis. *Journal of Public Economics*, *1*(3–4), 323–338.

Amaral, P. S., & Quintin, E. (2006). A competitive model of the informal sector. *Journal of Monetary Economics*, *53*(7), 1541–1553.

Andreoni, J., Erard, B., & Feinstein, J. (1998). Tax compliance. *Journal of Economic Literature*, *36*(2), 818–860.

Ashenfelter, O., & Smith, R. S. (1979). Compliance with the minimum wage law. *Journal of Political Economy*, *87*(2), 333–350.

Baanante, M. J. (2004). Minimum wage effects under endogenous compliance: Evidence from Peru. *Económica*, *50*(1–2), 85–123.

Basu, A. K., Chau, N. H., & Kanbur, R. (2010). Turning a blind eye. Costly enforcement, credible commitment and minimum wage laws. *Economic Journal*, *120*, 244–269.

Basu, A. K., Chau, N. H., & Kanbur, R. (2011). *Contractual dualism, market power and informality*. CEPR Discussion Paper No. 8485. CEPR, London.

Bosch, M., & Maloney, W. F. (2010). Comparative analysis of labor market dynamics using markov processes: An application to informality. *Labour Economics*, *17*(4), 621–631.

Card, D., & Krueger, A. B. (1995). *Myth and measurement: The new economics of the minimum wage*. Princeton, NJ: Princeton University Press.

Chandra, V., & Khan, M. A. (1993). Foreign investment in the presence of an informal sector. *Economica*, *60*, 79–103.

Chong, A., Galdo, J., & Saavedra, J. (2008). Informality and productivity in the labor market in Peru. *Journal of Economic Policy Reform*, *11*(4), 229–245.

Cobham, A. (2005). *Tax evasion, tax avoidance, and development finance*. Working Paper No. 129. Queen Elisabeth House. University of Oxford, Oxford, UK.

Cowell, F. (1990). *Cheating the government: The economics of evasion*. Cambridge, MA: MIT Press.

Danziger, L. (2010). Endogenous monopsony and the perverse effect of the minimum wage in small firms. *Labour Economics*, *17*, 224–229.

De Paula, A., & Scheinkman, J. (2010). Value added taxes, China effects and informality. *American Economic Journal: Macroeconomics*, *2*, 195–221.

de Soto, H. (1989). *The other path*. New York, NY: Basic Books.

Djankov, S., La Porta, R., Lopez-de-Silanes, F., & Shleifer, A. (2002). The regulation of entry. *Quarterly Journal of Economics*, *117*(1), 1–37.

Djankov, S., Lieberman, I., Mukherjee, J., & Nenova, T. (2003). Going informal: Benefits and costs. In B. Belev (Ed.), *The informal economy in the EU accession countries: Size, scope, trends and challenges to the process of EU enlargement* (pp. 63–80). Sofia: CSD.

Doeringer, P. B., & Piore, M. J. (1971). *Internal labor markets and manpower analysis*. Lexington, MA: Heath.

Fei, J. C. H., & Ranis, G. (1964). *Development of the labor surplus economy*. Homewood, IL: Irwin.

Feige, E. L. (1989). *The underground economies: Tax evasion and information distortion*. Cambridge: Cambridge University Press.

Fields, G. (1975). Rural urban migration, urban unemployment and underemployment, and job search activity in LDCs. *Journal of Development Economics*, *2*(2), 165–187.

Friedman, E., Johnson, S., Kaufmann, D., & Zoido-Lobatón, P. (2000). Dodging the grabbing hand: The determinants of unofficial activity in 69 countries. *Journal of Public Economics*, *76*, 459–493.

Fuest, C., & Riedel, N. (2009). *Tax evasion, tax avoidance and tax expenditures in developing countries: A review of the literature*. Report prepared for the UK Department for International Development. Oxford University Center for Business Taxation, Oxford, UK.

Fugazza, M., & Jacques, J.-F. (2004). Labor market institutions, taxation and the underground economy. *Journal of Public Economics*, *88*(1–2), 395–418.

Gabrieli, T., Galvao Jr., A. F., & Montes-Rojas, G. V. (2011). Who benefits from reducing the cost of formality? Quantile regression discontinuity analysis. Paper presented at the IZA/World Bank Workshop: Institutions and informal employment in emerging and transition economics, IZA, Bonn.

Gindling, T., & Terrell, K. (1995). The nature of minimum wages and their effectiveness as a wage floor in costa rica, 1976–1991. *World Development*, *23*, 1439–1458.

Gindling, T., & Terrell, K. (2006). *Minimum wages, globalization and poverty in Honduras*. IZA Discussion Paper No. 2497. IZA, Bonn.

Harris, J. E., & Todaro, M. P. (1970). Migration, unemployment and development: A two sectors analysis. *American Economic Review*, *60*, 126–142.

Jonasson, E. (2011). Government effectiveness and regional variation in informal employment. Paper presented at the IZA/World Bank Workshop: Institutions and informal employment in emerging and transition economics, IZA, Bonn.

Jung, Y. H., Snow, A., & Trandel, G. A. (1994). Tax evasion and the size of the underground economy. *Journal of Public Economics*, *54*, 391–402.

Kesselman, J. R. (1989). Income tax evasion: An intersectoral analysis. *Journal of Public Economics*, *38*(2), 137–182.

Koettl, J. (2011). Does formal work pay? Paper presented at the IZA/World Bank Workshop: Institutions and informal employment in emerging and transition economics, IZA, Bonn.

Lemos, S. (2004). *The effects of the minimum wage in the formal and informal sectors in Brazil*. IZA Discussion Paper No. 1089. IZA, Bonn.

Lemos, S. (2006). *Minimum wage effects in a developing country*. Mimeo, University of Leicester, Leicester.

Loayza, N. (1996). The economics of the informal sector: A simple model and some empirical evidence from Latin America. *Carnegie-Rochester Conference Series on Public Policy*, *45*, 129–162.

Loayza, N., Servén, L., & Oviedo, A. M. (2005). *The impact of regulation on growth and informality: Cross-country evidence*. World Bank Policy Research Working Paper WPS 3623. Washington, DC.

Maloney, W., & Nunez, J. (2004). Measuring the impact of minimum wages: Evidence from Latin America. In J. Heckman & C. Pagès (Eds.), *Law and employment. Lessons from Latin America and the Caribbean*. Cambridge, MA: NBER.

OECD. (2009). *Is informal normal? Towards more and better jobs*. Paris: OECD.

Perry, G., Maloney, W., Arias, O., Pajnzylber, P., Mason, A., & Saavera-Chanduvi, J. (2007). *Informality: Exit and exclusion*. Washington, DC: The World Bank.

PricewaterhouseCoopers. (2011). *Worldwide tax summaries*. Retrieved from http://www.pwc.com/gx/en/worldwide-tax-summaries/index.jhtml. Accessed in August 2011.

Saavedra, J., & Chong, A. (1999). Structural reforms, institutions and earnings: Evidence from the formal and informal sectors in Urban Peru. *Journal of Development Studies*, *35*(4), 95–116.

Saget, C. (2008). Fixing minimum wage levels in developing countries: Common failures and remedies. *International Labour Review*, *147*(1), 25–42.

Schneider, F. (2005). Shadow economies around the world: What do we really know? *European Journal of Political Economy*, *21*(3), 598–642.

Schneider, F. (2011). *The shadow economy and shadow economy labor force: What do we (not) know?* IZA Discussion Paper No. 5769. IZA, Bonn.

Schneider, F., & Enste, D. (2000). Shadow economies: Size, causes, and consequences. *Journal of Economic Literature*, *38*(1), 77–114.

Slonimczyk, F. (2011). The Effect of taxation and informal employment: Evidence from the Russian flat tax reform. Paper presented at the IZA/World Bank Workshop: Institutions and informal employment in emerging and transition economics. IZA, Bonn.

Stiglitz, J. E. (1974). Alternative theories of wage determination and unemployment in LDC"s: The labor turnover model. *Quarterly Journal of Economics*, *88*(2), 194–227.

Straub, S. (2005). Informal sector: The credit market channel. *Journal of Development Economics*, *78*(2), 299–321.

Strobl, E., & Walsh, F. (2001). Minimum wage and compliance: The case of trinidad and tobago. *Economic Development and Cultural Change*, *51*(2), 427–450.

Tanzi, V. (1980). Underground economy and tax evasion in the United States: Estimates and implications. *Banca Nazionale del Lavoro Quarterly Review*, *32*, 427–453.

Tanzi, V. (1999). Uses and abuses of estimates of the underground economy. *Economic Journal*, *109*, F338–F347.

Tonin, M. (2011). *Minimum wage and tax evasion: Theory and evidence*. IZA Discussion Paper No. 5660. IZA, Bonn.

Weil, D. (2004). *Compliance with the minimum wage: Can government make a difference*. Working Paper HR 05. Harvard Center for Textile and Apparel Research. Harvard University, Cambridge, MA.

World Bank. (2010). *Doing business project*. Retrieved from http://www.doingbusiness.org/

World Bank. (2011). *Enterprise surveys*. Retrieved from https://www.enterprisesurveys.org/

Yaniv, G. (1988). Withholding and non-withheld tax evasion. *Journal of Public Economics*, *35*, 183–204.

Yaniv, G. (1990). Tax evasion under differential taxation. *Journal of Public Economics*, *43*, 327–337.

Yitzhaki, S. (1974). A note on 'income tax evasion: A theoretical analysis'. *Journal of Public Economics*, *3*(2), 201–202.

APPENDIX

In this appendix, we verify that for any (ω_f, r) pair such that neither of the two constraints bind, $\omega_f > w_i a + \tau_\omega r$ and $r > \bar{w}$, an alternative pairing (ω'_f, r') satisfying the a binding participation can be found that raises expected profit, $a - \omega_f - \tau_\pi(a - r) - \bar{\phi}\bar{p}(r - \omega_f)^2 < a - \omega_f - \tau_\pi(a - r') - \bar{\phi}\bar{p}(r' - \omega'_f)^2$.

To see this, note that by adding and subtracting $(\tau_\pi - \tau_\omega)(r - \omega_f)/(1 - \tau_\omega)$ and rearranging terms,

$$\begin{aligned}
a - \omega_f - \tau_\pi(a - r) - \bar{\phi}\bar{p}(r - \omega_f)^2 &= \frac{1 - \tau_\pi}{1 - \tau_\omega}(a(1 - \tau_o) - \omega_f + r\tau_\omega) \\
&\quad + \bar{\phi}\bar{p}\left(\frac{\tau_\pi - \tau_\omega}{2\bar{\phi}\bar{p}(1 - \tau_\omega)}\right)^2 \\
&\quad - \bar{\phi}\bar{p}\left(\frac{\tau_\pi - \tau_\omega}{2\bar{\phi}\bar{p}(1 - \tau_\omega)} - (r - \omega_f)\right)^2 \\
&\leq \frac{1 - \tau_\pi}{1 - \tau_\omega}(a(1 - \tau_\omega) - \omega_f + r\tau_\omega) \\
&< \frac{1 - \tau_\pi}{1 - \tau_\omega}(a(1 - \tau_\omega - w_i)) \\
&= a - \omega'_f - \tau_\pi(a - r) - \bar{\phi}\bar{p}(r' - \omega'_f)^2
\end{aligned}$$

where $\omega'_f = w_i a + r'\tau_\omega$ from (I), $r' = (w_i a + \delta)/(1 - \tau_\omega)$, and $\delta = (\tau_\pi - \tau_\omega)/(2\bar{\phi}\bar{p}(1 - \tau_\omega))$.